Sacheverell Sitwell

Other books by Sarah Bradford

The Englishman's Wine, The Story of Port, 1969, reprinted as a
Christie's Wine Publication, 1978, 1983
Portugal and Madeira, 1969
Portugal, 1973
Cesare Borgia, 1976
Disraeli, 1982
Princess Grace, 1984
King George VI, 1989

Splendours and Miseries

A Life of Sacheverell Sitwell

SARAH BRADFORD

FARRAR STRAUS GIROUX
NEW YORK

IN MEMORY OF

Ronnie and Marietta Tree

Library of Congress catalog card number: 93–71240

Contents

List of Illustrations

Weekend at Denham, July 1930: Cecil Beaton, Georgia, Tom Mosley, Sachie, Cimmie Mosley and the Mosley children (*Cecil Beaton photograph, courtesy of Sotheby's London*)

Lady Bridget Parsons in the mid-1930s: drawing by William Acton (*collection of the Earl of Rosse*)

Pearl Argyle, c. 1933: Sachie's favourite photograph (*collection of Francis Sitwell*)

Sachie and Georges Duthuit at Eisenstadt, September 1932 (*collection of Francis Sitwell*)

The Sitwells at Renishaw, August 1930, by Cecil Beaton (*Cecil Beaton photograph, by courtesy of Sotheby's London*)

Montegufoni as it was in 1909 when Sir George wrote of it: 'The air of forlorn grandeur is very attractive and this I hope to keep. . . .' (*collection of Sir Reresby Sitwell, Bt*)

The Sitwell trio: Osbert, Edith and Sachie (*photograph by Maurice Beck, collection of Sir Reresby Sitwell, Bt*)

'We are hopeless Gramophonists': Osbert and Sachie at Carlyle Square, 1933 (*from a magazine photograph in the collection of Francis Sitwell*)

'Beautiful Adonis' – a youthful David Horner (*reproduced by permission of the Provost and Fellows of Eton College*)

Christabel McLaren, later Lady Aberconway: portrait by James McEvoy (*collection of Francis Sitwell*)

Georgia and Beaton on the Lido, Venice, September 1933 (*collection of Francis Sitwell*)

Sachie and Gertrude with an unidentified group of Roumanians in a Roumanian orchard, September 1937 (*collection of Mrs Bernard Stevenson*)

Family group: Georgia, Francis and Reresby in the gardens at Connaught Square, c. 1937 (*collection of Francis Sitwell*)

Monsieur Rivain, 'Baba' Metcalfe and Sachie, Rabat, Morocco, February 1939 (*collection of Lady Alexandra Metcalfe*)

The unwilling warrior: Sachie in Home Guard uniform during the Second World War (*collection of Francis Sitwell*)

Moira Shearer as The Aristocrat in Massine's *Mlle Angot*, 1947 (*photograph by Vivienne, courtesy of Mrs Ludovic Kennedy*)

Georgia and 'the Cop', Captain R.H.D. Bolton, on the Cam, April 1942 (*collection of Francis Sitwell*)

Reresby and Penelope Sitwell in their first London flat, 1952 (*collection of Francis Sitwell*)

Susanna and Francis Sitwell with their eldest son, George, at his christening, June 1967 (*collection of Francis Sitwell*)

Sir Sacheverell Sitwell in old age: the octogenarian poet among the orange trees and scented geraniums in his conservatory at Weston (*collection of Francis Sitwell*)

Text Permissions

Acknowledgements

I am deeply grateful to Sacheverell Sitwell's family for the kindness and encouragement which they have shown me during the writing of this book, and particularly to Reresby and Francis Sitwell who have generously made available to me the unpublished private family papers in their possession which have been supremely important sources of information on Sachie's life. They have also kindly provided me with many of the photographs and drawings used as illustrations in the book and given me guidance on the captions.

The generous help of the Hélène Heroys Foundation has made my research for this book in American libraries possible. No one could write a book on any of the Sitwells without a visit to the Humanities Research Center at Austin, Texas, or to the other major Sitwell Collections in American archives. The Foundation's generosity has, therefore, been a key element in the making of this book.

I owe a debt of gratitude to the following who have kindly helped me recreate Sachie's life, either by taking the time to recall their memories of him, by lending me photographs, papers and documents, or by giving guidance on archives and potential sources of information: Sir Valentine Abdy, Bt; Lord Aberconway; Sir Harold Acton; Mark Amory; Nicolas Barker; Sir Alfred Beit, Bt, and Lady Beit; Miss M.J. Belfitt; Alan Bell; Richard Buckle; Viscountess Camrose; Mrs Paul Channon; the late Peter Coats; Lady Cooke; Jilly Cooper; Teresa Cuthbertson; Dr H.G. Damant; Lady d'Avigdor Goldsmid; Peter Davison; Dr Alberto Lecerda; Dame Ninette de Valois; Jessica Douglas-Home; Pamela, Lady Egremont; Valerie Eliot; Duncan Fallowell; James Fergusson; Alastair Forbes; Sir Brinsley Ford; Sir Edward Ford; Lord Gladwyn; Adrian Goodman; Celia Goodman; Victoria Glendinning; John Gross; The Rt Hon. the Earl of Gowrie; Lady Selina Hastings; Alexandra Hayward; Christian, Lady Hesketh; Derek Hill; Susan Hill; Alastair Hinton; Anthony Hobson; Hermione Hobson; M. V. Hodson; Biddy Hubbard; Barry Humphries; Bruce Hunter; Virginia Hussey; Gervase Jackson-Stops; Zita James; Elizabeth Jenkins; Julie Kavanagh; Moira Kenedy; Daniel J. Leab; James Lees-Milne; Mark Le Fanu; Patrick Leigh Fermor; Professor Peter Levi; Dr Guy Lewis; The Hon. Lady Lindsay of Dowhill; Maude Lloyd; Candida Lycett-Green; Frank Magro; Henry Markham; C.W. McCann O.B.E.; Lady Alexandra Metcalfe; Leonard Miall; Glenys Miles; Viscount Norwich; Derek Parker; John Pearson; Anthony Powell and Lady Violet Powell;

Alan Pryce-Jones; David Pryce-Jones; Philip Purser; Roland Pym; Sir Peter Quennell; Michael Raeburn; Claude Reymond; Charles Ritchie; Neil Ritchie; The Earl of Rosse; Anthony Rota; Perdita Schaffner; Barbara Scott; Lady George Scott; Lady Sitwell; Susanna Sitwell; William Sitwell; The Earl of Snowdon; Sir Hugo Southern; Kenneth Snowman; Stephen Spender; Alannah Harper Statlender; Bernard Stevenson; Gertrude Stevenson; Henry Swanzy; Lady Thomas of Swinnerton; Hugo Vickers; Alison Waley; Lady Walton; Auberon Waugh; and Peter Williams.

I am also grateful to the following for their invaluable help in the relevant libraries and archives: Dr Vincent Giroud, Curator of Modern Books and Manuscripts, and Patricia Willis, curator of English Literature, the Beinecke Rare Book and Manuscript Library, Yale University; Francis Mattson, Berg Collection, New York Public Library; Dr Howard B. Gotlieb, Director, and Karen Mix, Archivist, Special Collections, Mugar Memorial Library, Boston University; Mark Jones, Director, BBC Sound Archives; Dr C.J. Wright and Dr Anne Summers, Curators in the Department of Manuscripts, the British Library; C.D.W. Sheppard, Sub-Librarian, the Brotherton Collection; Dr Robert J. Bertholf, Curator, the Poetry/Rare Books Collection, University of New York at Buffalo; Dr P.N.R. Zutshi, Keeper of Manuscripts and University Archives, Cambridge University Library; Amanda Savile, St John's College, Cambridge; Dr James Tyler, Assistant Rare Books Librarian, and Lucy B. Burgess, Senior Special Collections Assistant, Department of Rare Books, Cornell University; Dr Margaret O'Sullivan, Assistant Director (Archives), Derbyshire Record Office; Michael Meredith, Librarian, Eton School Library; Paul Quarrie, Librarian, Eton College Library; Thomas F. Staley, Director, Catherine Henderson, Research Librarian, and the staff of the Harry Ransom Humanities Research Center, University of Texas at Austin; Jennie Rathbun, the Houghton Library, Harvard University; Jacqueline Cox, Modern Archivist, King's College Library, Cambridge; Douglas Matthews, Librarian, and the staff of the London Library; Brenda Weedon, Archivist, and the staff of the Paleography Room, University of London Library; John Burgass, Librarian, Merton College Library, Oxford; Michael Bott, University of Reading; Charles Seton, Librarian, *Spectator*; Times Newspapers Limited; Sidney F. Huttner, Curator, Department of Special Collections, the McFarlin Library, University of Tulsa; Tina Oswald, Manuscripts Librarian, Holland Library, Washington State University at Pullman, the staff of the Theatre Museum, London.

Lastly, I should like to acknowledge the expert help of my editor, Linda Osband, and of my picture researcher, Lynda Marshall, both of whom have given unstintingly of their time and enthusiasm; and the encouragement of my agent, Gillon Aitken, and of my publisher, Christopher Sinclair-Stevenson. Douglas Matthews has contributed his usual, expert index. The unselfish support of my husband, William Ward, has made my work possible.

Physical Landscapes –
Scarborough and Renishaw

1897–1900

'My journeys have . . . brought me to many different parts of the
world [but] I could as well say that each and every one of them
has started and had its end upon the Scarborough sands. It was
there, scrambling upon the rocks, that I first began to think, and
hear and see.'

Sacheverell Sitwell, *For Want of the Golden City*

For Sachie Sitwell, the twin madeleines of childhood were the spiced
scent of wallflowers under a hot sun and the susurration of a shell held
close to his ear, instant reminders of Scarborough, the elegant spa town
on the North Yorkshire coast where he was born. Scarborough provided
his first aesthetic experience and the beginnings of his sensory perceptions
of a world beyond the confines of his family. 'This Northern sea-coast,
North Sea town', he was to write of it, 'has a physical beauty denied to
other watering-places.'[1]

Like Susan Hill, another Scarborough-born writer, he found himself
dreaming of the town long after he had left it. It is, as he said, a place 'with
bones' and a clearly defined physical landscape, dramatically sited on the
dark limestone cliffs of a huge bay and crescent beach facing the North
Sea. To the north, the battlements of a twelfth-century Norman castle
crown a steep headland sheltering the fishing harbour; several miles to the
south flat-topped cliffs, the seaward end of the Yorkshire wolds, bound
the horizon. The bay is divided into two distinct social spheres by the bulk
of the Grand Hotel jutting out midway along the beach. To the north of
the hotel, along the foreshore, is the popular resort with amusement
arcades and, in Sachie's day, vaudeville theatres; to the south, the bow-
fronted terraced houses of genteel Scarborough, where he was born,

overlook the Spa, an elaborate Edwardian building which would not be out of place in Monte Carlo.

The Grand Hotel itself, an elaborate mid-nineteenth-century affair of mansard windows, domes, cupolas and caryatids, grand staircase and palm court, inspired by the Paris of the Second Empire, held a particular fascination for Sachie. Not only did it offer evidence of a glamorous world beyond the isolated North Yorkshire town, but, more significant to his poetic imagination, he believed that his hero, Rimbaud, had stayed there with Verlaine and that it had been the inspiration for the hotel in the poem 'Promenade' in *Les Illuminations*. 'It was a landmark in my childhood,' he wrote, 'being as prominent in any memory of Scarborough as is Vesuvius in any view of the town and bay of Naples; and indeed it is wonderful and extraordinary to think that Rimbaud, so unexpectedly, should have had this same image fixed on his retina and changed to poetry.'[2]

In the summer months when the town was crowded with 'trippers', the beach was a stage for pierrot and Punch and Judy shows performing to the background music of a twelve-piece orchestra playing in a filigree-iron bandstand in front of the Spa. It was here that Sachie first heard, and was enchanted by, Tchaikovsky's *Casse Noisette*. In winter the 'trippers' vanished and the town changed, reduced to its permanent residents, who included Yorkshire county families taking refuge from the extreme cold of their country seats, rich local industrialists like the Rowntrees, and retired military men and widows, some of whom were hanging onto their 'gentility' by the skin of their teeth. The weather was often ferocious in mid-winter – 'north-east winds cutting you in half, and scudding grey skies, and enormous seas with waves a hundred feet high roaring over the rocks and rearing up high into the air, to crash, white and seething, on to the foreshore road, and the Marine Drive'.[3] From December to the end of March there would be snowstorms, the flakes driving in horizontally from the North Sea.

> In the month of November, in the noise of timber,
> I was born in November by the stormy sea

Sachie wrote in 'Upon an Image by Dante'. He was born on 15 November 1897, a few hundred yards from the beach in an area so dominated by his relations that it could be called a family enclave. The Crescent, a sweep of five-storeyed Georgian-style terraced houses in local limestone streaked by weather and coal smoke, had been built sixty years earlier by a local speculator with more taste than grasp on reality. Only the western crescent, of which Sachie's birthplace, No. 5 Belvoir Terrace, known as Belvoir House, formed part, had been built. The east side overlooking the sea had been sold for the construction of four sizable houses, all but one of which at the time of his birth were or had been occupied by members of his family. The centreground comprised a private garden and croquet lawn with high iron railings designed to keep out stray dogs, cats and non-residents. The Crescent area was exclusive, the preserve of its rich and aristocratic residents. Sachie's parents and grandparents, the Sitwells and the Londesboroughs, were leading members of this clan.

Sitwells had been prominent visitors to Scarborough since 1736, driving up from their ancestral home in Derbyshire in their own carriages painted a smart yellow picked out in black (a two-day journey with the intermediate night spent at York) to take the waters at the 'Spaw'. After the early death in 1862 of Sachie's paternal grandfather, Sir Reresby Sitwell, at the age of forty-one his widow spent part of every year at Scarborough, where in 1867 she built a handsome house in golden-coloured limestone, with the classical seaside lodging-house name of Sunnyside. Some years later she bought Wood End, the house on the central Valley in which Sachie was to spend much of his childhood.

Louisa Lucy, Lady Sitwell, born Hely-Hutchinson, whom Sachie would know as 'Grannie Sittie', was fanatically religious. She and her unmarried daughter Florence (Sachie's sister, Edith, unkindly dubbed them 'Lambeth Palace Lounge Lizards' on account of their fondness for the clergy) devoted a great deal of their time to prayer and good works, maintaining the King's Cliff Hospital and a Home for Fallen Women in a large, bright-red brick house at the top of a somewhat dingy cul-de-sac known as Sitwell Street. An atmosphere of Christian piety prevailed in Lady Sitwell's various households, which featured a retinue of attendant curates, elderly servants and ancient dogs. The treat of the day would be a visit from 'the dear Bishop', Dr Blunt, vicar of Scarborough for more than forty years (also suffragan Bishop of Hull and paternal grandfather of Wilfrid and Anthony Blunt). 'My grandmother', Sachie wrote, 'was a lady of much character, but of pious proclivities as powerful and tyrannical as any form of drug addiction', which, in his Aunt Florence, 'reached to pathetic and serio-comic limits'. On one occasion he remembered kneeling beside her in the library window at Wood End, looking into the conservatory, as she prayed for him for indulging in the sin of playing with matches and setting fire to the hearthrug in his bedroom.[4] Perhaps not surprisingly, he was extremely anti-religious from an early age and grew up to be a pagan.

One of the few things he did inherit from his Sitwell grandmother was her love of flowers and tropical plants. At Hay Brow, her house just outside Scarborough, his memories were of tea-scented roses hanging down into the windows, of a garden with mimosa growing in the open air on the banks of a lake, and of glades of bamboo and tropical vegetation, while her conservatory at Wood End was a mass of orchids and palms. He also inherited from her the family fear of colds. Like many women of her age and class, Lady Sitwell was prone to invalidism and hypochondria, which in her son, Sir George, to whom she often referred as 'the dear invalid', became practically a mania. Perhaps because his father's early death was attributed to his habit of stalking and shooting all day without food and being careless of coughs and colds in pursuit of his sport, Sir George and his children were pathologically afraid of colds. Osbert, Edith and Sachie's letters are full of references to them, each manifestation of which would be attributed to some particular offender – 'Osbert Lancaster's cold', 'Christabel's *dreadful* cold', etc. Osbert even contributed an appendix on 'The History of the Cold' to one of his volumes of autobiography.

Lady Sitwell was, however, beneath her gentle Christian demeanour, both shrewd and tough, with a strong instinct for domination. 'Her habitual expression of sweetness, sympathy and resignation . . . masked an iron will and disguised with a semblance of calm the fires of her temperament,' Sachie wrote; 'she was, and must be, the dominant ruler in her house, and an absolute ruler.' She was also an acute business-woman, and it was largely due to her management of his affairs during his long minority that Sachie's father was a rich man.

Sir George Reresby Sitwell, the fourth baronet, was head of an old family in the neighbouring county of Derbyshire and owner of a 400-year-old mansion, Renishaw Hall, happily situated above working coal seams which had restored the family fortunes. Aged thirty-seven at the time of Sachie's birth, he was a tall, thin, pale, serious-minded man with a high-bridged nose, light-blue eyes, fine fair hair and a darker golden moustache, which curled upwards in the manner of the German emperor. He possessed a strong sense of his own importance and place in society developed by the unusual circumstance of his having been the only son and head of the family since the age of two. Aged only four the infant snob had replied to the question 'Who are you?': 'I am George Sitwell, baronet. I am four years old and the youngest baronet in England.'

Sir George was clever; he had an original mind and considerable forensic and financial ability. At Eton and Christ Church, Oxford, he had done well academically despite spending much of his time on sport. At Oxford he 'rode a great deal, hunted a little, rowed, played cricket and tennis, took lessons in boxing, and went through the gymnasium course'. In spite of his piety and his own blood relationship to the Archbishop of Canterbury, he was a resolute unbeliever and achieved fame in 1880 by unmasking a flesh-and-blood medium masquerading as a spirit at the headquarters of the Spiritualist Society in London. As a young man he travelled abroad during university vacations, even going as far as Moscow, where, as Westminster's youngest MP, he was invited to attend the Tsar's coronation. He was a scholar and a man of taste and considerable artistic capability, which expressed itself in building and landscape gardening. His love of art, sightseeing and travel, and of Italy in particular, was to have an enormous influence on Sachie. However, for all his talent, Sir George was not a happy man. Cold, shy, suspicious and solitary by temperament, increasingly selfish, spoiled and eccentric in his behaviour, he found it impossible to establish normal relationships, a failing which was to have a crucial bearing on his future family.

In 1897 Sir George was a distinguished figure in Scarborough society, having twice represented the borough as Conservative MP from 1885–1886 and from 1892–1895. A reporter on the *Scarborough Magazine* described him thus:

> He has lived amongst us all his life, is bound up with our institutions, has played a prominent part socially and politically amongst us for at least a dozen years, has many friends and a few enemies . . . and is, without doubt, one of the most important figures in a town of some importance.

The anonymous reporter was impressed by the 'quiet good taste' of Sir George's Belvoir Terrace house, with its principal rooms hung with wallpapers in the recently fashionable 'silk brocade' design, most of them 'specially designed' or 'struck in flock for the first time'.[5] He remarked upon the large and handsome curtains, the absence of unnecessary ornament, the 'Georgian' white panelling in the drawing room and vestibule, and the enormous 'old Dutch landscapes' lining the billiards room. Sir George, he wrote, was not only interested in politics, architecture, landscape gardening, newspaper managing, history and science, but was also a member of the Statistical Society and one of the earliest supporters of the 'Arts and Crafts' exhibitions, a captain in the Yeomanry, a county and borough magistrate, a printer and publisher, and a railway director.

Sir George's ambitions as Conservative candidate for the borough were supported at some expense and annoyance to himself by his position as backer of the local Conservative newspaper, *The Scarborough Post*, 'an evening newspaper and weekly review', which carried on a bitter and vociferous war against its rival organ, the Liberal *Mercury*. As the *Post*'s historian remarked, there were drawbacks in having Sir George as a proprietor. He was not an easy man to work for and, consequently, there was a high turnover in editors at the offices in Huntriss Row. The third to depart under his proprietorship fled leaving a note: 'When I came down to the office this morning, I found that I had three alternatives before me, exposure, flight or suicide: I chose the second.'[6] Sir George's election campaigns were accompanied by vigorous mud-slinging from the opposing *Mercury*, notably after his first victory in 1885, when the Conservatives were accused of securing his return by bribing tradesmen, and his supporters were denounced as bankrupts, 'drunken swearing blackguards' and 'fallen women'. '. . . is it not time that clergymen and religious people reconsider their position, when they find that their allies in their political work include the publicans and brothel-keepers of the town and those who support them?' the paper enquired. Sir George lasted only a year as MP before being defeated by a local businessman, Joshua Rowntree, of the great Quaker chocolate manufacturing family of York. However, next time he managed to hold the seat for three years before being unseated by the Liberal, Mr Compton Rickett, by only twenty-four votes. In 1900 he unsuccessfully challenged Compton Rickett for the last time. He did not stand again and, in 1906, for undisclosed reasons, became a Liberal himself. He had not enjoyed the rough and tumble of local newspaper business, admitting that the *Post* had been 'the greatest difficulty with which he had had to contend', and after the failure of his last parliamentary candidacy in 1900 he divested himself of management of the troublesome newspaper.

He was a man with a supreme passion for the history of his family (Sachie had been christened Sacheverell after a family related to the Sitwells by marriage, whose name was supposed to derive from the Norman French, '*Saut de Chevreuil*', i.e. Stag's Leap). Sir George's aim was to bring glory to the Sitwell name. Few of his ancestors had been particularly distinguished beyond showing a singular capacity for survival and a tenacity in holding on to and increasing their landholdings in the same area of Derbyshire for almost 500 years. Such prosaic achievements were not enough for Sir George, who intended to advance his family to greatness through selective breeding. He had an almost mystical belief in his role as the procreator of a splendid dynasty, telling his eldest son, Osbert: 'It's quite evident, if you read the family letters, that we've been working up towards something for a long time, for well over a century.'[7] In the event, the future of the dynasty was decided by the shape of a nose. Travelling to the family seat of a prominent Yorkshire peer to inspect his daughter, who appeared to be a suitable candidate, Sir George was met at the station by his prospective bride driving a dogcart. To his horror he noticed immediately that she possessed an unsuitably pronounced aquiline nose; when the lady deposited him at the door of her home and drove round to the stableyard, Sir George, without further ado, picked up his bag and bolted down the drive.

Sir George's next choice, the Hon. Ida Denison, daughter of the second Lord Londesborough, was a seventeen-year-old beauty with a perfect, straight Grecian nose, which he considered ideal. She had other dynastic qualifications designed to appeal to a romantic snob like Sir George, including royal connections on both sides. Her paternal grandfather, Lord Albert Conyngham, was reputed to be the son of George IV by his mistress, the Marchioness of Conyngham,[8] while her mother, formerly Lady Edith Somerset, daughter of the seventh Duke of Beaufort, could trace her descent from the Plantagenet kings of England through Katharine Swynford, mistress of John of Gaunt. All this appealed intensely to Sir George as it was also to do to his children, particularly Edith, who made the most of their Plantagenet blood. However, there were wild cards in the pack as far as Lady Ida's bloodlines were concerned. Lady Conyngham's father, Joseph Denison, was a self-made man and not at all aristocratic. There was also potential for disaster which Sir George, in his haste to improve his quarterings, seems to have overlooked: Lord Albert, who had been left the Denison fortune by his mother's brother and who then gratefully took the name Denison and in 1858 was created first Baron Londesborough, was notably extravagant. The resultant débâcle was to traumatise the next generation of Sitwells.

Sir George and the Hon. Ida Denison were married at the most fashionable London church, St George's, Hanover Square, on 23 November 1886. When the couple arrived in Scarborough for the first time as newly-weds in January 1887, the horses were taken out of the carriage shafts at the Bar Gate and their place taken by a team of lifeboatmen, the whole occasion being formally recorded in oils by a local artist, a tribute to the position their families enjoyed in the town. In local terms, Sir George was marrying 'the girl next door'. Her father, William Henry Forester Denison, was a 'swell' on the London social scene, a rich, extravagant, sporting magnate with an estate in Yorkshire and a house in Berkeley Square. In Scarborough he owned Londesborough Lodge, a fan-shaped summer pavilion on the seaward side of the Crescent, where he entertained the Prince and Princess of Wales as his house guests, with unfortunate results on one occasion in 1871 when the heir to the throne went down with typhoid fever while staying there. Where his father, the former Lord Albert Conyngham, had imitated his royal father by collecting furniture, paintings and *objets d'art*, the second Lord Londesborough spent the Denison windfall on thoroughbred horses, actresses and the stage. In Scarborough he was a generous patron of local causes and the principal supporter of the Scarborough Cricket Festival, to which he brought his own team of Gentlemen Players whom he entertained at his own expense, and of the local regattas, on one occasion contributing the entire cost. A keen sailor and oarsman, he was popular among the fishing community whom he helped financially in times of disaster and gave an annual dinner to the crews of the local lifeboats. Londesborough was a handsome man with a fresh complexion, aquiline nose (which does not seem to have put Sir George off marrying his daughter), dark brown eyes and hair, but his looks were marred by a shooting accident in 1884 which cost him his right eye. He died in 1900, when Sachie was not quite three years old, of psittacosis, the rare disease transmitted by parrots. Despite being the cause of his grandfather's death, parrots were to have an exotic significance for Sachie, recurring frequently in his poetry and prose.

Londesborough's widow, 'Grannie Lonnie', seems to have played little part in her grandson's life. Edith described her as 'a fantastic, wave-like Chinoiserie, a Laideronette, Princesse de Pagodes. Beaked like a harpy she had queer-roofed, Byzantine eyes, and these characteristics I have inherited from her. . . . [She] lived in luxury like a gilded and irascible wasp in a fine ripe nectarine.'⁹ There could have been no greater contrast than that between the pious, thrifty household of Grannie Sittie and the luxurious, hedonistic atmosphere surrounding the Londesboroughs.

Sachie's mother, Lady Ida as she became in 1887 when her father was elevated as first Earl of Londesborough, resembled her father in temperament. Beautiful, charming, empty-headed, ill-educated, pleasure-loving and easily bored, she had been brought up in a circle of Philistine relations which her children later described as 'the Golden Horde' – men whose lives concentrated on sport and women whose lives were bounded by gossip and frocks – in which any intellectual pursuit was regarded as odd or funny. Her brother, Francis, second Earl of

Londesborough, a larger-than-life figure whom Sachie later compared to the Bourbon kings of Naples, was a magnifico like his father, a giant of a man with luxuriant sidewhiskers and moustache, melancholy blue eyes and a gift for invective. He had a passion for the circus (among his best friends at Scarborough was a clown named Whimsical Walker) and for musical machines: revolving, self-banging drums and self-smiting cymbals, self-sawing violins and self-blowing trombones. He had his own red fire engine, on which he would tear off into the night, abandoning his dinner guests, to attend some fire in the vicinity. Until he was eight Sachie would occasionally be taken to spend Christmases at Blankney with 'the Golden Horde', in an atmosphere of Edwardian hothouse luxury where the women spent their time changing their clothes in the intervals between the vast and interminable meals, while the men slaughtered everything that moved in the surrounding countryside. The Sitwells, despite their sporting ancestors, did not get on with hunting men. Sachie was to live all his life in the country, but his view of fox-hunting remained that of Oscar Wilde: 'the unspeakable in pursuit of the uneatable'.

The omens were not propitious for the mingling of the Sitwell and Denison blood. According to Sachie, his mother had only met his father twice at luncheon before their marriage; within a few days of the wedding she ran home to her parents, but was firmly sent back to her husband. This was perhaps not surprising; sex did not rank high on the long list of Sir George's interests. According to family tradition, Edith, Osbert and Sachie were conceived with a ritual deliberation. Sir George would prepare himself for his act of dynastic responsibility by immersing himself in suitable books and works of art. He would then announce, 'Ida, I am ready!' and the procreation of another Sitwell genius would take place.

Sachie was the baby of the family, ten years younger than Edith, who was born on 7 September 1887, and five years younger than Osbert, born on 6 December 1892. Edith was rejected by her parents from birth, first because as a girl she was not the longed-for male heir to the Sitwell baronetcy, and second because even as a girl she failed in her duty to be beautiful and winning. 'I was unpopular with my parents from the moment of my birth,' she was to write in old age, '. . . my mother hated me throughout my childhood.' Although, according to Sachie, his sister was much given to exaggerating and fantasising the extent of her unhappiness in childhood, she certainly felt herself rejected and her account of the cruelty of her treatment, including the imprisonment of her body in an iron cage, an orthopaedic device designed to strengthen her spine and ankles which she called 'the Bastille', was nearer to the truth than he liked to think. She was a formidable child with a strong sense of her own destiny. When asked, aged four, what she was going to be when she was grown up, she replied, 'A genius.' 'Little E', as she was known, complained to her grandmother about her nursemaid Martha, showing a precocious gift for economy of phrase. Martha, she said, 'does nothing to amuse, and everything to displease me'. She had a passion for fairy tales, a fascination for words and a great ability in memorising them. She was to be Sachie's poetic muse and his passionate advocate throughout his writing career, but in the early part of his life he saw little of her:

> I cannot be certain of my first memory of you.
> It was perhaps when you were fourteen years old
> In your not happy – more than unhappy childhood,
> With every chance loaded against your becoming what you
>   wished to be:
>
> Already, even then, you were determined
> Though drawn aside later into music
> Till you were ready for it;
>
> On the fourth floor, high in air,
> How can I forget you opening the door
> Like a statue from Chartres Cathedral,
> Tall and thin . . .[10]

Despite the inequality of her parents' treatment of her compared with her brothers, Edith grew up singularly free from sibling or professional rivalry as far as her brothers were concerned, bestowing on them both a protective, even anxious, love.

Osbert, the longed-for heir, was his mother's favourite and the focus of his father's dynastic expectations, a burden which he often found hard to bear. As he grew up, his appearance tended to the Hanoverian: solid, jowly, with the heavy, hooked nose of the Londesboroughs. Edith and Sachie, with their long, thin noses, high, arched eyes and cheekbones, were Plantagenets; neither of them would have been out of place as effigies on a medieval tomb. In character Osbert was the most complicated and least generous of the trio, troubled by his homosexuality and obsessed with his father, whose dominance over him he would seek to exorcise by turning him into a figure of fun. In turn he would dominate his sister and brother, whose natures were kinder and more affectionate than his own.

Sachie suffered neither the pain of rejection nor the pressure of family expectation: 'perhaps being the youngest child I had the best of the love and affection of both my parents,' he wrote more than half a century later. Although in his autobiographical writings he liked to depict his childhood as unhappy, it is unlikely that this is an entirely accurate picture. Despite his dark-tinged reminiscences, he was, by his father's account at least, a sunny-natured, appealing child, who was embarrassingly wont to invite strangers in off the street to lunch with his parents.

Sachie's first memory of Scarborough was of hearing the bells toll for the death of Queen Victoria on 22 January 1901; he remained fascinated all his life by the nineteenth century into which he had – just – been born. His first public appearance in the town was again connected with royalty when, aged five and a half, he presented Queen Victoria's youngest daughter, Princess Henry of Battenberg, with a bouquet of pink orchids, lily of the valley and fern on her arrival at Scarborough railway station to open the new town hall. On another royal occasion, the seven-year-old Sachie spilled his lemonade into Queen Alexandra's black silk ear-trumpet. 'She was delighted,' he remembered, 'she laughed and laughed and laughed . . .'[11]

In 1902 Sir George and Lady Ida moved with their family into Wood End, 'Grannie Sittie's' house at the end of the Crescent, which remained their Scarborough home until the 1920s. Built in 1837 on the sides of the steep cleft called the Valley which ran down to the sea, dividing the Crescent from the South Cliff, Wood End was a handsome, comfortable house with well-proportioned rooms. A triple drawing room ran the length of the south front, the west end opening on to the conservatory which at night was lit with Chinese lanterns. Sir George's description of it, a resonant list of bird species, might have come from one of Sachie's own books:

> . . . this conservatory was filled with exotic birds flying at large amongst the creepers and flowering trees: red tailed *Cordons-bleus*, Indigo Birds splashed with green, Nutmeg and Zelva Finches, Wax-Bills of cinnamon with rosy beaks, Budgerigars like little green paroquets [*sic*], deep crimson and scarlet, Cardinal Birds, Blue Robins of all shades from dark to light, Japanese Rice Birds, Pekin Nightingales, with the mellow russet tints of autumn leaves. These birds sang early and late throughout the year, the Selva Finches making a gentle pleasant trumpeting sound, the song of the Blue Robin being something like that of a thrush, of the Cardinal Bird like a blackbird, of the Pekin Nightingale like the sweet singer whose name it bears. . . .

The Whydah birds, blue-black with silvery breasts, orange throats and long, leaf-shaped tails, were attracted by music and, when there was dancing in the drawing room, would sometimes fly in to flutter over the heads of the dancers.[12]

On the opposite side of the conservatory from the drawing room, a mullioned window gave on to the library extension, built by Sir George as a miniature copy of the room at Renishaw, with Carolean ceiling and stone fireplace. Above the main bedroom floor the children and servants occupied the attics, where the sloping ceilings with their square, mansard windows seemed like the cabins of a sea-going ship. Sachie remembered sleeping in eight different rooms at Wood End, but particularly in the attic room, where he would lie at night listening to the sound of the sea beating relentlessly on the nearby shore, driven by the equinoctial gales which flattened the trees in the Valley below the house.

Servants played an important part in Sachie's life; in the Sitwell family, relationships with their 'retainers' were much closer than was usual at the time. When Evelyn Waugh stayed at Renishaw in 1930, he was amazed by the familiarity with which the servants treated their employers. Figures like Henry Moat, Sir George's butler-valet, Mrs Powell, the motherly housekeeper to Sachie and Osbert at Carlyle Square, and later Gertrude and Bernard Stevenson at Sachie's home, Weston Hall, were an intrinsic part of the family comedy. The dominant figure at Scarborough and Renishaw in Sachie's youth was Henry Moat, whose relationship with his employer had more than an element of Don Quixote and Sancho Panza, although Moat was a more substantial figure in every way than Cervantes's squire.

'Henry', as they called him, loomed large in the lives of Osbert and Sachie when they were children. A huge Yorkshireman, well over six feet tall, and with the high complexion characteristic of his native county, Henry came from a long line of fishermen and whalers who had occupied the same house in Captain Cook's home port of Whitby for more than 250 years. He had joined the Sitwells in 1893, the year in which they first moved into Belvoir House, and remained with them on and off for forty-two years, his absences being caused by his giving notice to Sir George, usually because of some eccentric new idea of the baronet's. 'Henry,' Sir George told his butler one day, 'I've a new idea – knife-handles should always be made of condensed milk!' 'Yes, Sir George,' replied the disgusted Henry wearily, 'but what if the cat gets at them?' As Osbert wrote in *Left Hand, Right Hand!*:

Sometimes Henry would ask to come back sometimes my father would invite him to return but . . . back he always came in the end. He and my father [were] mutually critical and at the same time appreciative. My father always referred to Henry as 'the Great man', and Henry, for his part, mixed with feelings of the utmost disrespect, cherished towards him as well, sentiments approaching veneration. He realised his quality, both mental and physical, and that he was an uncommon, if difficult, character.[13]

Henry's earthy and irreverent common sense was an important counter-point to the dotty atmosphere engendered by Sir George and Lady Ida. In the pantry at Scarborough and at Renishaw Sachie and Osbert liked to listen to him imitating some guest whom they particularly disliked, or telling stories of the sea, or singing in his handsome, bass bellow. Henry was conscious of his role as imparter of worldly wisdom to Sir George's sons of a kind which they would certainly not learn from their father. Whether or not this included sex, Osbert, perhaps from a certain understandable reticence, does not report; Henry was always getting Lady Ida's maids pregnant and later was equally successful with the women at the Sitwells' Tuscan castle, Montegufoni. From retirement in Scarborough in 1938, he wrote to Osbert after reading a cutting about the latter's famous entry in *Who's Who* ('Educated during holidays from Eton'):

> Well, Sir, I make bold to claim some of that, because whether you were at Scarboro', Renishaw or abroad, if you or Master Sachie wanted to know anything about things on the earth, the sea under the earth or in the air above you generally came to me, even when you had a tutor, and often the tutors came too.[14]

The things that Sachie learned from his first tutor, Major A.B. Brockwell, one of the pillars of his childhood, had equally little to do with formal education. In his first autobiographical fantasy *All Summer in a Day*, Sachie describes 'Brockie' as 'the earliest and most permanent' of the personalities in his memory. Major Brockwell featured in the writing of all three children: as the eponymous 'Colonel Fantock' in Edith's poem about her childhood; as Fantock again, 'A Military Ghost', in *All Summer in a Day*; and, disparagingly, as 'Major Viburne' in Osbert's *Tales My Father Taught Me*. 'Brockie' first entered Sachie's life in the high summer of 1906 as his tutor for the summer holidays. According to Osbert, who regarded him, as he did many people, as a figure of fun, he was previously employed by Sir George to polish up his knowledge of grammar for the writing of his master work, *On the Making of Gardens*. It was typical of Sir George, Osbert wrote, that he should have employed for this task a man whose knowledge of syntax was far inferior to his own. During Sachie's absences at school the Major was occasionally employed as a factotum at Renishaw.

> This paladin was disinterred from time to time and chartered by my
> father to oversee the household, muddle the accounts and misorder the
> food [Osbert wrote]. Major Viburne posed as a warrior and a gourmet,
> but in both instances his experience was limited. During the days of
> which I am speaking, for example, he was confined, by his own
> digestion, to a diet of dry biscuits, and he certainly never got nearer than
> Scarborough to any front line in the whole course of his long life. . . .[15]

Sachie, however, loved him; when he left home for school at the end of the holidays, he always feared the possibility that he might lose 'Colonel Fantock – one of my few friends'.

Sachie recorded the Major's gallant struggles with poverty and old age with sympathy. 'Brockie' was completely bald, but his white mustachios 'curled gravely downward at their ends', his clothes were 'a little worn, a little too tidily frayed', and he sported yellow boots of an almost primrose hue, which the expert Moat reckoned must have been worn for at least ten years in order to achieve that particular tone. At Renishaw Sachie watched him punctiliously dressing for dinner in an old dinner suit carefully preserved in layers of tissue paper:

> . . . in his own case, this evening suit that he tended so carefully was the
> symbol of life, and if he were forced to give it up, then all the pretension
> on his part that made living endurable on such straitened means would
> break down, and he would be as dead as anything, save the actual touch
> of death, could make him.

'With Colonel Fantock', Sachie observed, 'it was decidedly a life of outside appearance . . . and a great part of the game consisted in hiding behind your own façade.'[16] The Major lived with his second wife and youngest daughter in a neat, yellow-brick house in Scarborough with a carefully tended garden. Dependent for his living on teaching a class of young children there during term-time, his subsistence was precariously balanced. Sachie imagined that, none the less, he was happy,

> for he had imprisoned his ambitions within such confined limits that the
> direst poverty could hardly have reduced them further: some pipe tobacco

and two or three whiskies-and-sodas daily being his ordinary and unvarying demand, while he had two other needs that came in rotation with the seasons, a little coal in winter and a few hours of sun in summer; the price of the one, and the niggardliness of the other, formed, indeed, his two grumbles against life, and if only these could have been assured to him, he would not have minded his bare table or cold bed.[17]

For Sachie, the Major's principal role was as interpreter of Scarborough. As they sat among the wallflower beds on the cliff-top looking out over the bay, or walked on their daily 'constitutional' over the sand and slippery rocks at low tide, the old man illuminated for him the teeming social life which went on behind the long lines of lace-curtained, stuccoed houses. There was hardly a person whom he did not know, nor a house he had not been into either as a friend or as a canvasser; he had political ambitions, was a popular speaker and had even edited the *Post*. Sachie questioned him about the 'Gentlemen's Club', a bow-fronted structure painted an alarming red, strategically situated on St Nicholas's Cliff and equipped with a telescope through which the members could observe the bathers emerging from the women's bathing machines on the beach below, or perhaps some intimate drama through the windows of the Grand Hotel opposite. The Major was the moving spirit of amateur theatricals and the organiser of public balls for charity; he also knew all the endless intrigues of the doctors, who, with their rival teams of nurses and patients and their own nursing homes, 'wielded the same sort of power in this seaside town that the priests possess in some provincial capital of Italy or Spain'. Sachie also heard of the intense rivalries of the bridge-playing ladies of independent means who formed the largest contingent of native social life at Scarborough. Their protagonists featured in two of his early poems, 'Mrs H. . . . or a Lady from Babel' and 'Week-ends', and in Osbert's first and favourite novel about Scarborough, *Before the Bombardment*.

Major Brockwell satisfied Sachie's passionate interest in the past and in historical connections:

I would travel down his memory, that long corridor, going into one room after another that led off it, following this continuous thread of connection in all its ramifications. In this way he was a true teacher, not overloading my own mind, but allowing me to travel about in his experience, where I could find an answer to every question I wanted to ask. He could tell me anything between 1840 and the summer before last . . . and he would start off with the earliest historical fact . . . that had made itself known to him as something worth remembering, and this was his story: that he used to see some withered, wizened objects stuck, like coco-nuts, on the masts that adorned the Temple Arch, and these were, so he told me, and I have never had the courage to find out if he was wrong, the heads of 'traitors' executed after the 1745 rebellion.[18]

The one person, however, who most embodied for Sachie the mystique of the past, was Miss Emily Lloyd, the 'Miss Morgan' of *All Summer in a Day*. Miss Lloyd was tiny, well under five foot, white-faced and white-haired, with delicate features set off by a silk stock or scarf, which she always wore round her neck. Her past was wreathed in mystery and, indeed, her own fantasy. She and the Major disliked each other, each suspecting the other of being a liar. All that was definitely known of her was that Lady Sitwell had met her in the 1870s while she was working in a pottery studio in the South of France. There had been a vague, abortive project of going into business in England; Miss Lloyd had come to Scarborough and become almost a part of the Sitwell family. No one knew her age (she always said that she had been born during the Crimean War, although Sachie suspected that she had been born a generation earlier) nor her parentage, although she had a 'cousin' who was in reality her brother, a well-known actor, and an 'uncle' who owned trading ships. She was English on her father's side, Belgian on her mother's; a miniature of a woman and child beside her fireplace was claimed by Miss Lloyd to be either her mother and herself or the Duchess of Kent and Queen Victoria, 'according to her caprice for realism or grandeur'. From her uncle's yacht in the Golden Horn she had taught china painting to the Sultan's harem and narrowly escaped being included in his seraglio; she had been Gounod's favourite pupil at the piano and accompanied the maestro to Rossini's Sunday evening parties. For Sachie, Miss Lloyd 'managed to live in a kind of double mist of romance which consisted first of the mystery of her origins and history, and second of the aura of improbable legend that she distilled around her. . . .'

In the memories of the Sitwell children it was always tea-time at Miss Lloyd's enchanting house a stone's throw from the Crescent. She had decorated the drawing room herself, embroidering the walls and curtains with roses on a cream background beneath a frieze of blue silk ribbons entwined with roses hand-painted by her; she had also painted the furniture in a brilliant imitation of marquetry and the plates and vases on tables and the mantelpiece. The bow window was lined with elaborate window boxes, a shelf of tit-bits for the birds, and three miniature greenhouses filled with cacti. Tea was mixed with Green or Orange Pekoe out of a tortoiseshell box. There would be plates of two or three different kinds of bread, home-made marrow jam, chocolate biscuits and tea-cakes with a sandwich filling of a liquid yet crunchy toffee. On a table in a corner stood a cage containing a mynah bird, which could imitate perfectly the voices of every member of the Sitwell family. Miss Lloyd's house and her teas appealed to Sachie's appreciation of craftsmanship and his greed for gourmet treats. She was part of his family and, like the Major, a bridge to the behind-the-scenes life of Scarborough. In the summer she would stay with them at Renishaw, where she once set up her own darkroom; at Christmas she would spend a few days with them in London, producing tickets given to her by her 'cousin' for the Drury Lane pantomime. For Sachie, she held the lure of the familiar and yet the infinitely strange, a world of gaslight and Victorian murders, of the Parisian boulevards and even beyond, 'in some indefinable antiquity of her own which was certainly not later in date than the reign of Louis Philippe'.[19]

'All acting and impersonation', Sachie wrote, 'is in essence a form of sacred magic; and the theatre its sanctuary or temple.' The pierrot shows on Scarborough sands which he watched with Major Brockwell were his initiation into these mysteries. There would be two or even three companies performing in their booths laid on trestles on the wet sand at low tide. Sachie and the Major would either stand in front of them entranced or, better still, look down on them from the Esplanade above, 'when there was the extraordinary sensation of hearing them all competing with each other, but not being able to catch the music of their songs . . . in that marvellous amphitheatre of the bay . . . such was the natural theatre of my holidays from school.'[20] There was a sense of the transitory, even the unreal, about them; in winter they might never have existed at all, and even in summer their season was short – ten days at Easter and the first week in August. They could not perform on the sands at high tide, and on wet days would retreat into the beachside theatres, the Olympia and the Arcadia, along the popular Foreshore below the Grand Hotel.

Catlin's company of pierrots on Scarborough sands were the distant descendants of the sixteenth-century, Italian *commedia dell'arte*, which still flourished in the Drury Lane pantomimes before the First World War. At Scarborough Sachie remembered the 'Captain', the male lead in yachting cap, blue blazer and white trousers, and the 'juvenile lead', the harlequin of the company, with powdered pierrot's face, who sang in a cracked voice: 'Have you another little girl at home like Mary? Another little peach on the family tree?' At Drury Lane, when aged six or seven, he saw the famous, tragic Cockney comedian, Dan Leno. This first experience of the world of illusion, of spangles and greasepaint, rough and tumble, jokes, cruelty and beauty, was the beginning of a lifelong passion for the performing arts (and of star-struck, romantic feelings for the artists, ballerinas in particular), extending even to televised bouts of all-in wrestling. The figures of the *commedia dell'arte* remained fixed in his mind and, in particular, Harlequin, the daring master of wit and illusion, masked and clad in diamond-patterned tights, with whom he particularly identified. It was as Harlequin that he would appear painted by Gino Severini in the frescoes at Montegufoni; and his second book of poems was entitled *The Hundred and One Harlequins*.

'There was also', Sachie wrote of the pierrot company, 'a male member of the troupe who took female roles and was, clearly, a pronounced case of transvestism. I think I realized this, then, but without its implications.' The Major, naturally, did not explain this, but they were told that he was a rich man who paid to be allowed to perform and who had a collection of dresses and a large motor-car. Tall and dark, with a heavily shadowed chin, he appeared to sing a song in one sketch wearing a green evening dress and smoking a cigarette in a long holder. Later Sachie and the Major recognised him in his expensive open car with the cracked-voice harlequin and another companion, looking extraordinary among the Scarborough crowds and, by the slight extravagances of their behaviour, clearly enjoying it. Nor was this the only intimation of an alternative life: there were rumours of a foreign nobleman who had a big yacht lying out in the bay and who was fleeced to the extent of nearly £500 by an equivocal singer-comedian at the Aquarium. 'This experience of the seaside pierrots, though so slight and transitory, was equivalent to a full-scale immersion or baptism into the magic and mystery of the theatre,' Sachie wrote, 'and with intimations of other things besides. . . .'[21] It was, in many ways, his introduction to life.

Sachie's earliest memory was, however, not of Scarborough, but of Renishaw Hall and of his rocking-horse standing in a top-floor passage outside the nursery. A photograph shows him, a curly-haired child in skirts aged between two and three, on that same rocking-horse on a summer's day outside the southern front. Renishaw occupies an over-powering place in Sitwell mythology, its brooding presence rather like that of Manderley in Daphne du Maurier's *Rebecca*. Just as the sensations he absorbed at Scarborough affected his future interests and view of life, so the great house and the surrounding Derbyshire countryside had a great influence upon him as a writer and a poet:

> So back to the Derbyshire hill country
> and that rail-ridden though still green valley,
> Below the magical, most magical Bolsover
> which was to me the school of poetry:–
> Woods where I first perceived what a wood should be . . .[22]

Renishaw was a dark and rather forbidding house. 'I was very fond of it and rather frightened of it,' he wrote. 'There was something of the extinct monster about it.' This was especially true at night; there was no electricity and the endless succession of high rooms and winding passages were lit by oil lamps and candles. He remembered 'shuddering nights' lying awake as the old house creaked around him and the flame of the nightlight flickered casting shadows into the corners of the room, conjuring up apprehensions of the several ghosts who haunted Renishaw. Sachie remained frightened of the dark and intrigued by ghosts, poltergeists and manifestations of the supernatural all his life.

At Renishaw it was not difficult to sense the continuing presence of people who had lived in the house over the 300 years since it had been built. For Sachie, the past was always present to be stepped into at will; it was there behind a curtain to be experienced and brought to life by the exercise of his imagination. At Renishaw there were constant reminders of the reality of the past: the rocking-horse on which he was photographed had appeared in a watercolour of the Sitwell children painted by Octavius Oakley in 1826; and on the night-nursery window someone had scratched on the glass with a diamond: 'Charme des yeux at Renishaw 1825', a message which inspired one of his best-known poems, 'On a Name Scratched upon a Window':

> Deep do the letters bite that spell the name.
> Though the last strokes waver as the hand grows weak
> Holding firm the diamond lest it slip and fall.
> Did fruit like a lodestone hang outside the window,
> Or were the shining fences of the rain pitched there?
> When it rains –
> Like the spider's web linking leaf to leaf,
> The name glitters out and links the lines of rain;
> When the sun burns free –
> The letters like a pattern of frost stay on the glass.

Here, where he traced it, will the name still live
Dwelling like a mote in the eye of all who see it
As though he had fixed it in the very eye of time
Till time breaks, shattered, as a sheet of glass.

Everywhere at Renishaw there were indications or representations of members of the family who had lived there since George Sitwell built himself a manor house on the site and moved there with his bride in 1625, defending it for the King in the Civil War twenty years later. His house, with its low-patterned plaster ceilings and great stone fireplaces, still survives as the heart of Renishaw. It had been built with the profits of the ironworks which the enterprising George Sitwell had founded at Eckington nearby. By the late 1600s the Sitwells were the principal makers of iron nails in the world and one-tenth of the entire output of the iron trade in England passed through their hands.

In the dining room a brilliant painting by John Singleton Copley portrayed the first generation of Sitwells who were not really Sitwells. They were the children of Sitwell Hurt, whose father, Francis Hurt, inherited Renishaw from his maternal uncle, William Sitwell, a bachelor and the last male heir of the family in 1776. Francis Hurt changed his name to Sitwell, thus making his young son Sitwell Sitwell. (Evelyn Waugh suggested that in view of Osbert's extreme touchiness, he should revert to the old family name and call himself Hurt Hurt.) These Hurt Sitwells showed an extravagant streak in contrast to their prudent predecessors. Inheriting a fortune from a cousin as well as land, they became horse-racing, cock-fighting, fox-hunting Tory squires. Sporting pictures multiplied on the walls of Renishaw and the old house was embellished to suit their social ambitions, with a high-ceilinged dining room, a huge drawing room and a ballroom built by Sitwell Sitwell in 1808 for the sole purpose of giving a ball in honour of the Prince Regent. The appreciative Prince rewarded him with a baronetcy, but the sporting Sitwells soon came to grief. Sachie's great-grandfather, Sir George Sitwell, lost most of his fortune; in 1847 auction sales cleared the house of all but the heirlooms, and Renishaw stood empty until the exploitation of the coal seams under the land in the 1870s enabled Lady Sitwell to reopen it.

Despite its interior elegance Renishaw was somewhat forbidding in appearance, its long, battlemented façades overlaid with the grime of the nearby collieries. Coal dust blackened the trees and grass; coal wagons rattled along the railway in the valley below the house and colliery flares lit up the night. But just as iron had helped his seventeenth-century namesake build the first house of Renishaw, coal now provided Sir George with the means to exercise his passion for landscape gardening and decoration. On the south-facing side of the house he created an Italianate garden with terraced lawns, evergreen hedges and baroque statues within sight of the colliery stacks, and a lake in the valley. The result was a curiously successful contrast between the classical sophistication of the gardens and the rustic Derbyshire woods and valleys, enhancing the position of the house on the ridge and giving it presence and grandeur.

Certain objects at Renishaw had a special significance for Sachie. His emotions, sensations and imagination worked through, or were triggered by, a particular piece of music or work of art. Among them was the Copley portrait. His descriptions of his childhood at Renishaw have a melancholy tinge: 'a dreary long waste before the eyes . . . the real and authentic dark tunnel'. 'No one', he wrote, 'can ever have hoped more fervently than I did for the traditional lighter spot to appear among these shadows and draw one towards it out of the long vaults and passages.' The Copley portrait of the Sitwell children playing happily in a room flooded with morning light seemed to him 'like a beacon of hope', almost the only visible proof in the gloomy house where time stood still in an ocean of nothingness, of a safe and assured reality. '. . . although one suspected the possibilities of happiness, there seemed to be but little proof that such a condition had ever, or ever could, exist.' To him, the Copley painting carried a kind of authority that all would be well, 'as though one's great-great-grandfather had been able to speak out of the picture and tell one that everything was all right and that one could go on hoping'.[23]

The aesthete in him made him dismiss the family portraits and Italian madonnas on the staircase as unable 'to satisfy any really deep feeling', a deficiency entirely compensated for by the five fabulous panels of Brussels tapestry, which hung in the drawing room and ballroom and which exerted an extraordinary fascination on the three children. These tapestries influenced Sachie more perhaps than any other single work of art. They had a lasting effect upon his imagination, even his way of looking at things and of expressing his emotions as he did so, and they very probably inspired his passion for the baroque. This is how he was to describe them in *All Summer in a Day*:

They portrayed five triumphs, of such abstract qualities as justice and commerce; but it was a world of Indian suavity and opulence, and Indian in the poetic sense, for it was the East before artists had learned

the difference between India, China, and the El Dorados of America, and
so it contained subtle exaggerations on what the designer considered as the
mean level of this trebly-distilled land of beauty. There were elephants and
black slaves, bell-hung pagodas and clipped hornbeams; in the background
were clouds tacking like fleets of sailing ships, and, lower down, terraces
with pots of orange-trees upon their balustrades, and continual fountain
jets that gave a cool note to the hot summer portrayed in every other symbol
. . . it is one of the laws of this paradise that only the scaffolding, the bare
bones, the actual fact of being alive, are unchanging and permanent: leaves,
clouds and water showing as much change as they are capable of, so that
there is hardly any monotony except the heart-beat, and all externals are
mobile and differing in their phases.[24]

The Arcadian woods and gardens in Renishaw, even the melancholy of
long, rainy afternoons spent there, were a source of poetic inspiration
which Sachie tapped over and over again in poems like 'Derbyshire
Bluebells' ('The wood is one blue flame of love'), 'The Lime Avenue' ('It
rained/Upon the tall windows/In the tall old house,/In the morning and
in the evening./. . . In midst of it/We walked in the wet garden,/Under
the wet limes;/And so the long morning/Wept itself away.'), or 'The
Eckington Woods' ('These showers among green reeds, like rolling
drums were hushed,/And we were back in the faunal silence that no word
can break,/Waist deep in bracken . . .'). His empathy with the countryside
and his ability to reproduce elegiac images of it were one of the strengths
of his poetry; its beginnings lay in his Derbyshire roots.

Psychologically, however, the house seems to have had an oppressive
effect upon him. An anguished sense of transience is a repeated theme
running through his childhood memories and throughout his life; it was
particularly strong at Renishaw. When he was there he had 'the feeling
that something awful would happen and one would have to leave it'. The
collapse of Sitwell fortunes and the near-loss of the house just over fifty
years before was a grim reminder, constantly impressed upon the children
by Sir George, of the abyss which careless extravagance could open up. It
was a story which was to come true in his own lifetime when he, too, would
lose Renishaw. The sense of transience and loss was emphasised by the
fleeting nature of their occupation of the house. Sachie spent three times
as much of his childhood at Scarborough as he did at Renishaw, which
was only opened up for August and the first part of September, so that,
particularly when he began to go to boarding-school, there would be a
constant sense of things about to end, of the moment when the great
unwieldy house would be shut up with its ancestral ghosts.

D.H. Lawrence wrote of the three Sitwells that their childhood was as isolated as if they had been brought up on a desert island. This feeling of isolation comes through strongly in Sachie's descriptions of his youth at Renishaw. He wrote of the misty Derbyshire mornings, when the moisture whitened the blades of coal-blackened grass and the colliery chimneys were bulky shapes looming out of an icy marsh: 'Everything in this atmosphere, in fact the whole of this misty glass-like bell of space, was waiting for something to happen, for some noise to crack the stillness. But it never came, and sometimes this sense of waiting, and this end-of-the-world feeling, peculiar to the district, would last many days. . . .' The miners and their children, the only human beings he would encounter outside the park, seemed like creatures from another world; he appears to have taken no interest in their lives nor even to have regarded them as fellow human creatures with whom he could communicate. 'Soon, like smuts in the air, they had drifted away with their curious hob-nailed, lumbering walk,' he wrote after meeting miners returning home when he was out blackberrying with his brother and sister.

The miners' children, encountered later that morning round the blackberry brambles, seemed no less remote:

> They were of a very flaxen, long-headed, Danish type, and their hands
> and faces were of an indescribable blackness which accentuated the
> pallor of their skin . . . in spite of this extreme of blackness and
> whiteness, when a little way from you they faded away altogether into
> the background of green-black fields, green-black trees, and black stone
> walls. . . .

The three Sitwells were able to pick the highest blackberries on the bush, watched in silent astonishment by the smaller miners' children.

> A moment or two later they had disappeared from view, though their
> voices could still be heard out of the shrill, sharp briars; however, the
> wood had soon built up its dark screen again and they were out of the
> world altogether, underneath the earth, perhaps, like mushrooms before
> the summer nights' warm rain. . . .

Only the ruins of Bolsover Castle and the windowed magnificence of Hardwick Hall comforted him as evidence that 'any people who had known painters or musicians had ever lived, however long ago, so near to us'.[25]

This feeling, which they experienced at Renishaw, of being isolated, apart from the world and of a different race from the (to them) invisible human beings outside the park, bound the clever, eccentric trio even closer together. 'We all have the remote air of a legend,' Edith was to write, projecting their image as they liked to see themselves in 1925 when the Sitwell cult was at its height. The most expert publicist of the three, she created in 'Colonel Fantock' a mythical portrait of three superior Plantagenet beings stalking through the grounds of their ancestral home as if in a medieval tapestry. With its romantic snobbishness and undoubted beauty it fascinated followers of the Sitwells. Equally it would provide rich comic material for enemies like Wyndham Lewis when he turned against them in *The Apes of God.*

> All day within the sweet and ancient gardens
> He, Fantock, had my childish self for audience –
> Whose body flat and strange, whose pale straight hair
> Made me appear as though I had been drowned –
> (We all have the remote air of a legend)
> And Dagobert [Osbert] my brother, whose large strength
> Great body and grave beauty still reflect
> The Angevin dead kings from whom we spring;
> And sweet as the tender winds that stir in thickets when the
>   earliest flower-bells sing
> Upon the boughs, was his just character;
> And Peregrine [Sachie] the youngest with a naive
> Shy grace like a fawn's whose slant eyes seemed
> The warm green light beneath eternal boughs.
> His hair was like the fronds of feathers, life
> In him was changing ever, springing fresh
> As the dark songs of birds . . . the furry warmth
> And purring sound of fires was in his voice
> Which never failed to warm and comfort me.[26]

The cold, hard light of reality was never to have much appeal for the Sitwells. Each of them, including Sir George, saw the world through their own eyes, coloured by their own imagination and fantasy, the Sitwell family itself being their most enduring myth.

2

Family Portrait

1900 – 1915

'The dark clouds . . . were massing on her horizon . . . the
sordid litigation would begin which, while I was still at school
. . . did permanent injury to my nerves and made it so hard for
me to face up to certain sides of life. . . .'

Sacheverell Sitwell, *Splendours and Miseries*

In the spring of 1900 Sachie, a fair, curly-haired child of two and a half,
sat, clad in a silk dress, on the floor of John Singer Sargent's studio in Tite
Street, while the painter whistled in his 'peculiar and elaborate' way or
repeatedly intoned a limerick to keep his attention:

> There was a Young Lady of Spain
> Who often was sick in a train,
> Not once and again,
> But again and again,
> And again and again and again.

As long as Sargent kept this up, the future poet and *aficionado* of the
performing arts remained, according to his brother, rooted to the right
spot, before fidgeting uncontrollably and being replaced by an identically
dressed wax doll.

Sachie and the doll were playing a minor part in an elaborate *mise en
scène* orchestrated by Sir George, in which an idealised version of the
Sitwell family would be immortalised in the public eye and for the benefit
of descendants. The painting was intended, after going on display at the
Royal Academy, where it was admired by, among others, the young Serge
Diaghilev, to be hung at Renishaw as a companion to the Copley portrait.
Sargent himself had exclaimed on seeing the Copley, 'I can never equal
that!', and his Sitwell portrait entirely lacked its predecessor's freshness

and spontaneity. The Sargent painting, polished and elegant though it was, exuded an Edwardian hothouse glamour in which hereditary possessions, sporting instincts and feminine luxuriousness were heavily hinted at.

The picture was a fake in almost every way as the Londesborough clan, headed by the formidable Countess, always eager to put down the Baronet's pretensions, was quick to point out. Sir George was depicted in riding boots while Lady Ida, incongruously, wore an evening dress and a large afternoon hat. 'Why riding things and an evening dress?' they demanded. 'Why an evening dress and a hat?' And, reinforcing their most cherished prejudices, 'Why not go to an *ordinary* painter? Why go to an American?' Mercilessly they picked away at Sir George's scene-setting – his riding boots (although he now never rode) intended as a reference to his sporting ancestry, and Lady Ida, the picture of a dutiful and gracious wife, arranging flowers in a silver bowl. This she never would have done (the flowers in the house would have been arranged by the head gardener), nor would she have had any idea of how to do it, having been brought up to be professionally helpless as the badge of her high breeding. The painting was posed against a background of Sitwell heirlooms: one of the huge panels of Brussels tapestry from the ballroom at Renishaw, and a commode designed by Robert Adam and made by Chippendale and Haig for the marriage of Francis Hurt Sitwell in 1776. As the elegant projection of an image the painting was a triumph; as the representation of a real family – the dominant father, his hand resting protectively but affectionately on his daughter's shoulder, the beautiful, submissive wife absorbed in her domestic task, the happy children playing on the floor – it was a fantasy.

Family relationships were not at all what they seemed. Edith later described herself during the sittings as 'white with fury and contempt, and indignant that my father held me in what he thought was a tender paternal embrace'.[1] She had been made to feel yet again how sadly she fell below her father's chocolate-box ideal of female beauty. Her nose was developing a distinctly aquiline appearance as Sir George did not fail to point out distastefully to Sargent. (The artist, who sympathised with Edith, retaliated by making Sir George's distinctly crooked.) Her lank, greenish-blonde hair failed to fulfil his dictum that 'all hair should be inclined to curl, and so soften the lines of the face'; he therefore ordered it to be unbecomingly frizzed up for the occasion. Edith, in Sir George's eyes, represented dynastic failure. His heir, Osbert, dressed in the inevitable sailor suit which was the upper-class child's uniform of the day, had a challenging, even arrogant look in his eye when he posed for photographers, but, as yet, that look had not been turned upon his parent. Sachie already showed that he had an enquiring mind; the idea of death, in which he was to have such an abiding interest, first took hold of him in that year, 1900, when his Londesborough grandfather died of psittacosis in April. Sent down out of the way with Edith and Osbert to their Sitwell grandmother at Gosden, he anxiously asked where the long-dead Grandfather Sitwell might be – 'Gone puff-puff? Gone sail?'

Sir George's principal problem was to be with his wife, whose Plantagenet blood had seemed such a prized addition to the Sitwell lineage. Unfortunately for Sir George, however, both Ida's appearance and her personality came from her new, exuberant Denison blood rather than the older Somerset line. As Osbert wrote:

> My mother's acuteness of the senses was much stronger than my
> father's. Her love of pleasure, her sensual delight in driving through
> summer woods at night, catching their scent and feeling their cool air,
> had much of a child's and perhaps of an artist's feeling in them, as, too,
> had her swiftly seizing on the peculiarities of people and places and her
> vivid gift of instantaneous mimicry, keen and acute imitations which she
> could do once but never again. The kindness and cruelty in her seemed
> without reason or basis. She was so impulsive. Her love of flowers,
> especially if they were strong-scented, was overwhelming: the rooms,
> summer and winter, were crowded with lilies and tuberoses and
> stephanotis, and, from the time I can first remember her, she always
> wore at her waist gardenias or tuberoses, with sweet geranium leaf, so
> that I associate her with their scent.[2]

At Renishaw and Wood End, the window boxes of her bedroom would be full of sweet geraniums, sometimes the variety named after her mother, Lady Londesborough. Even in her love of flowers she differed sharply from her husband, whose ideal was the Italian Renaissance garden of architectural lines, lawns, statues and hedges of unrelieved green purity. At Renishaw, as a tease, she had the gardener erect a particularly vulgar structure covered with ostentatious suburban roses. Sir George, to whom anything more colourful than the ethereal pale blue of 'love in the mist' was anathema, was shocked to the core by 'that extraordinary thing' and ordered it to be taken down instantly. When Osbert also became an insurgent against his father, he adopted the same line, walking past Sir George's study window at Renishaw bearing a peculiarly loud form of rhododendron as if intent on planting it.

Sachie adored his mother. One of his earliest memories, of himself on the rocking-horse, was also of her presence. 'My mother, then thirty years old, stood very near to me, behind the rocking-horse, which I was riding. It is a memory of nothing in particular. But of the awakening of affection. Of the first warmth of love. Of the safety and comfort of that emotion. . . .' She was

> Tall and thin, and dark, and beautiful, with straight Grecian nose, small mouth, dark brown eyes, and little shell-like ear, set close to her head. With a little head, also, and a straight, thin neck that was exquisite in its pose upon her shoulders. She had a wonderful way of carrying herself, and, thereby, an extraordinary distinction. There was always something tragic in her appearance, which I felt as a child in spite of her gaiety and powers of mimicry which so amused me. . . . Her character, when I first remember her, was a compound of natural high spirits and a sort of palace bred or aristocratic helplessness, as of one who was made with her brothers and sisters to wear gloves, indoors, in order that they should have white hands, was scarcely allowed to put foot to the ground, and could not add up.

Later, with hindsight, he was to add, 'She very decidedly could not subtract.' Perhaps because of her childish nature, her humour and her human understanding, he remained absolutely devoted to her until he was at the edge of adolescence, she on the threshold of middle age. 'We were, then, companions, and intellectually of an age. That, of course, was a reason for our peculiar affection,' he wrote.[3]

Looking back across a gulf of memory towards an age of innocence, Sachie did not mention, as Osbert did, the more curious side of his mother's character, what he called her 'strange temperament, her kindness, indulgence, and furious, sudden rages'. Nor did he mention the thick loop of old rope twisted in a knot round the head of the bed as a talisman. One day, after repeated questioning by Osbert, Lady Ida enlightened him: 'It's a bit of hangman's rope, darling. Nothing's so lucky! It cost eight pounds – they're very difficult to get now.'[4]

Sachie grew up against the background of the developing drama of his parents' marriage, which culminated in the traumatic spring of 1915. 'As a result of all this,' he later recalled, 'both of them, my father and my mother, were the wrecks of each other and of themselves.'[5] Sir George and his wife had not one interest or characteristic in common. Where she was gregarious and pleasure-loving, he was austere and solitary. Where his humour was heavy-handed and ironic, hers was witty and quick. He spoke as though he had a mouthful of dust, she with the clipped accents of the Edwardian smart set. She lay late in bed every morning in a bedroom heavy with the scent of discarded gardenias and tuberoses, reading French novels, newspapers and letters scattered about the bed, or playing patience on a flat-folding, leather card-tray. She was addicted to cards, playing bridge endlessly every afternoon. He would be shut up in his study smelling of the strong Egyptian cigarettes of which he smoked twenty or thirty a day, reading scientific journals and indulging his multifarious intellectual interests by keeping his notebooks up to date. In one, entitled 'The Wisdom of Life', he entered the aphorism: 'Never open a letter from a correspondent known to be troublesome until after luncheon.' In another he corrected the date of 'Hugh Fitz Osborne, called Blundus' from 1084 to 1086, and in his garden notebook he added that the Byzantines used to gild the trunks of cypress trees, before reading over an account he had written of 'Domestic Manners in Sheffield in the year 1250'. He might be working on a family pedigree, the origin of part-singing or decorative motifs in leaden jewellery of the Middle Ages, keeping his accounts (the household bills were always too high in his opinion), writing a speech or ordering new improvements to be made at Renishaw.

He had literary ambitions; while aged sixteen and still at Eton he had published, anonymously, a slim volume of satires and parodies. At twenty-five he had co-authored a serious work of county history, *The Feudal History of Derbyshire*, and at twenty-nine a book with the portentous title, '*The Barons of Pulford in the Twelfth Century and their descendants the Reresbys of Thrybergh and Ashover, the Ormesbys of South Ormesby and the Pulfords of Pulford Castle*, being an historical account of the lost baronies of Pulford and Dodleston in Cheshire, of seven Knights' Fees in Lincolnshire attached to them, and of many Manors, Townships and Families in both Counties, by Sir George R. Sitwell, Bt, FSA, FSS'. Based on notes taken in the Public Record Office by a Mr Greenstreet, 'the most accurate and learned of record agents,' and on charters culled in the British Museum by Sir George himself or 'by an expert, whose work I have corrected', this exceedingly dull work was, not surprisingly, published by Sir George himself on his own press at Scarborough. In 1894, the year in which he allowed himself to be interviewed by the Scarborough journalist, he published, again on his own press, a biography of his ancestor by marriage, William Sacheverell, and in 1900 and 1901 two more books based on the letters of the Sacheverells.

'Ginger [the later family nickname for Sir George] writes like a

nineteen-eighties don,' Arthur Waley commented unkindly. Sachie's
literary style was never academic, but none the less there were unconscious
traces of his father in his tendency to write with a total disregard for his
readers, his occasionally stilted phraseology, and his fondness for reeling off
long lists of names of plants and birds. Sir George had a powerful influence
on his children despite their lifelong battles with him. Edith was as much a
poseur as her father when it came to her appearance; the huge rings and, in
later life, medieval-looking hats were subtle references to her Plantagenet
blood. Osbert's five-volume autobiography, *Left Hand, Right Hand!*, was an
act of ancestor worship equal to any of his father's productions. Sachie also
owed a good deal to his father. Sir George introduced him to Italy and was a
pioneer traveller in the towns which inspired *Southern Baroque Art*; his
passion for medieval artefacts was echoed by Sachie in *The Gothick North*.
Sachie inherited from his mother many of his more attractive traits: his sense
of humour, love of laughter and gift of mimicry, together with the strong dash
of her feckless extravagance and self-indulgence and her responsiveness to
sensual pleasures. As a connoisseur and a pathfinder in the field of taste,
however, he owed more than a little to his father.

After his last parliamentary defeat in 1900, Sir George seems to have
suffered from an increasing sense of ineffectualness, which manifested
itself in domestic tyranny exercised through his hold upon the financial
resources of the household. At Christmas 1902, the year of his fortieth
birthday, he had a nervous breakdown. (Osbert's first intimation of this
was to hear the governess remark to the tutor at Wood End 'how
extraordinary it was to have a nervous breakdown just because you could
not get your own way in everything'.) The Scarborough doctor recommended 'a change'. Sir George interpreted this as a prolonged journey
abroad. He went to Italy, a step which was to change not only his but his
children's lives, and to lead to the writing of his masterpiece, *On the
Making of Gardens*, which he published seven years later in 1909, and to
the acquisition that same year of Montegufoni, his castle in Tuscany.

A clue to the cause of Sir George's 'breakdown' came in his
conversation with the Scarborough reporter eight years earlier. At Eton,
he told the reporter 'with a smile', he had swotted in the hottest summer
weather reading for the history prize, sitting up for nights on end with his
feet in a basin of cold water and a wet towel round his head. When the
results were announced, he discovered that he had failed to win the
history prize but had gained instead the school divinity prize, for which
he had never intended to compete. 'Looking back', he said, 'this seems
characteristic of many things I have done since then.'

Chief among those things was no doubt his marriage, entered into as deliberately as he had swotted for the history prize. The results were just as unexpected and unwelcome. His prize, the Earl's daughter, would not conform to his prearranged plan and was to bring shame and disaster on the house; his children, though brilliant, were extravagant and rebellious, ultimately inimical towards him. His wife mocked the title of which he was so proud – unusually, for an author, it always appeared on the title page of his books: 'A baronet', she was fond of saying, 'is the lowest form of life'; as for his obsessive economies, she would add, 'my father would spend a million without even noticing'. Her family, accustomed, although they were not the slightest bit interested in art, to the magnificent objects accumulated by Lord Albert Conyngham or to the ancestral treasures of the Somersets at Badminton, liked to put down Sir George's pretensions as a connoisseur. When he invited his mother-in-law to admire some painted hangings he had recently bought in Italy, telling her, 'I paid the owner forty pounds for these!', he received, instead of a compliment on his artistic perception and bargaining powers, the comment, 'How pleased he [the shop-owner] must have been!'

In the earlier years of their marriage, before Lady Ida's disgrace poisoned family relations, Sir George loved his wife. His letters to her written in 1904 from abroad were pathetic instances both of his affection and his ineffective, earnest attempts to mould her into an ideal wife and mother. 'My darling little heart,' he wrote on 7 February from Taormina, ostensibly charmed to hear that she proposed to bring her Londes-borough sister-in-law with her as companion, but clearly apprehensive that 'Gracie', wife of the millionaire Francis, would want to travel too extravagantly: 'I trust she is so simple & sensible she won't expect us to travel differently from what we usually do. Of course we shall have a separate table, but I mean she will not expect us to have a separate dining & sitting room or to reserve railway carriages. . . .' Anticipating that Ida and Grace would leave him out of their conversations and would be unwilling to accompany him on rigorous sightseeing expeditions, he wrote asking her to bring Edith also: 'I should like to take Edith too, as then I should have a companion when you two were together & could take her for walks if you prefer to sit out in the garden. I think also it would be so good for E.'[6] Miss Rootham (Edith's new governess and lifelong friend) could join them in Venice and Sachie could be sent to their cousins, the Reynell Packs. Ida was 'very naughty' not telling him that she had been to a ball and taken part in the tableau: 'Do be very careful of yourself.' Meanwhile, a bill from Dore & Cie, an expensive Sloane Street florist, showed Lady Ida, in the absence of her careful husband, giving free rein to her passion for exotic flowers. In the month of February she spent £16 15s 8d (her annual allowance from her family was £500) on her favourite tuberoses (six dozen on one day alone), gardenias, carnations, especially the fashionable pink malmaisons, lilies, including two bunches of the new Japanese auratums for 12s, lilies of the valley, huge bunches of lilacs with their foliage and, on one occasion, an orange blossom tree for 12s 6d.

From the baths at Bad Nauheim where he was accompanied by Edith and Helen Rootham, Sir George wrote on 21 May 1904 to Lady Ida, who was spending three weeks at Aix: 'I am so glad you are only to be away for three weeks. I love having you with me.' Four months later, again from Bad Nauheim where he was now staying on his own, he wrote a highly characteristic letter to 'My darling little pet': 'I was so pleased with your dear letter this morning. I am so glad you are really being kind to E. The child is very fond of you, & will soon be going away.' This was wishful thinking on his part. Lady Ida was rarely kind to Edith, whose intelligence and independence intimidated her, while Edith's feelings for her mother could by no stretch of the imagination be described as 'very fond'. But Sir George, when away from them, still clung to the 'happy family' image, writing of the six-year-old Sachie rather as if he existed purely for the benefit of his parents: 'I am glad Sachie is having a success again at the cricket [Sachie's cricketing success must have been short-lived, as he dreaded and detested games throughout his school career]. I hope he is still as lively & amusing as he was last year.' He still hoped to teach his wife his own careful habits. 'I inclose a cheque for £5,' he wrote. 'I see you haven't really been keeping an account day by day, and now you are less busy I hope you will. You should put down the sums tidily £1-0-0, 0-5-0; 0-0-10 one under the other with lines between as I have put them, & then it is easy to follow.'

His correspondence, as Sachie was to learn to his exasperation, followed a set pattern detailing financial instructions, recent bargains in art and antiques (he had a passion for collecting, from whole painted rooms to walking-sticks and particularly elaborate antique beds, fancying himself as driving a hard bargain, although Osbert claimed that he was regularly cheated by the dealers), and, above all, health bulletins. From the time of his 'breakdown' Sir George, although tireless in pursuit of his principal interests – sightseeing and antique hunting – had become a dedicated hypochondriac. 'I wish so much I could have been with you,' he wrote referring to his wife's provincial pleasures, a bazaar and amateur theatricals at Scarborough, '[but Dr] Schott seems so pleased about my heart I suppose it really must be mending, and if I can only keep this year free from worries or little irritations of any kind my nervous system may recover. If not this year, I think never. If you will be as kind and dear to me as you were all the time we were together at Wood End, it will do wonders.'

That year Sachie was to make his first trip abroad, to San Remo. Writing from Milan on 26 October 1904, his father seemed none too sure of his precise age: 'Sachie is, I think, under 7 and can go for a half ticket. . . .' The letter was full of interminable instructions in what Lady Ida called her husband's 'hall-porterish' mode. She should leave Scarborough on Saturday morning and, when in London, order plenty of cold chicken for the journey from the Army & Navy Stores, enough for the hours between Calais and Paris; but from Paris to Genoa there would be a restaurant car: 'Cold eggs in aspic are nice there & cold cutlets.' Sir George, eccentric in his eating habits as in everything else, practically lived on breast of chicken; servants in houses where he stayed used to complain that they were forced to live on chicken legs as a result. Henry Moat once told Osbert: 'You ask me what's the use of Sir George. . . . He keeps the chickens down. If it weren't for him the world would be overrun with them.'

The sojourn at San Remo was a success, at least as far as wifely and even maternal behaviour was concerned:

> I was so sorry to go from San Remo, you were so dear to me except a
> little on two days; indeed you almost always are now. I was so much
> pleased to see that you really think of what is best for Osbert and Sachie
> and are firm about it: this is important for their health and character,
> and no one can do so much for them as you can if you will really try to
> be a wise mother to them both.

Sir George's next letter to her harps again on motherhood and includes some slighting references to the defects of the Londesborough's upbringing, which could only have infuriated his wife, who idolised her family:

> You must find it hard to be firm with Osbert & Sachie, but they will love
> you the better for it when they grow up, and will not be able to say that
> you have ruined their lives as Arthur Pack thought his mother had done
> & I think Francis [Ida's brother] to some extent feels about your
> Mother. I know you have a great deal of good in you which would have
> come out more strongly if you had had a better bringing up yourself, and

it makes me so happy when I realise that you are thinking of duty and of
what is best for the children, and not merely upon pleasure. The great thing
is to be firm without being unduly severe, but you should not allow Osbert
to be disrespectful to you or to his tutor. I think he is very good on the
whole, but a little discipline is needed, it is a great thing, as Peveril
Turnbull [his agent] once remarked to me, that he is 'serious'.

The letters make pathetic reading. Lady Ida, left alone during her
husband's long peregrinations, paid not the least attention to his careful
instructions. She lost money at cards and was battened on by a
sycophantic group of friends to whom she was extravagantly generous,
giving them dresses or even jewellery if they happened to admire it. A
letter of 4 January 1906, written by Sir George from Wood End, marks
the first appearance of the 'cloud no bigger than a man's hand' on
the Sitwells' horizon, Lady Ida's debts. Gracie Londesborough had
apparently been making mischief, implying that Sir George was mean and
kept his wife on too tight a financial string. At this stage, Sir George was
still fond and indulgent:

> If she had been wiser & you had asked me prettily [he wrote], the debts
> would have been arranged about before now. You may ask me about
> them the day before the boys go back to school
>   Please don't worry, my darling, or make yourself miserable.
> Everything will come right in time, if you wish it to be a happy life for us
> both. If you would think out how you could gain influence with me, you
> would find how much you might have.
>   I inclose a cheque for £10 on account: please let your maid have a
> pound or two. You didn't tell me what the money was for that I
> telegraphed to you. Do let me have letters, as I want them badly....

Sachie tended to paint a gloomy picture of his childhood, which was
certainly exaggerated. Before his parents' relationship deteriorated, there
is no reason to believe that his life was particularly sad. There were treats
at Christmas and frequent trips abroad. In 1905 they had spent Christmas
in Monte Carlo, and on Christmas Day he had had his first ride in a
motor-car and paid his first visit to the theatre to see *The Nutcracker Suite*.
Tchaikovsky's music and that particular ballet were to have a special
significance for him after he had seen it for the first time in the jewel-box
theatre, all mirrors, gilding and plush, in the casino building at Monte
Carlo. The family seem to have spent regular periods at San Remo.
Writing in 1985, when both he and Sachie were in their late eighties, A.

'Buster' Closson, the son of a Cincinnati store-owning magnate, looked back over seventy-five years of friendship since their first meeting there:

> I remember clearly the first days at the Villa Trollope (1907) when we played with soldiers – fighting the Revolutionary Wars. I couldn't let you win historically so you evened things up by giving me a good pummelling. I suppose that is where I got the name Buster – being short and feisty and you tall and handsome. . . .[7]

Sachie is often represented as rather an effete figure; in fact, he had a fierce temper and, when angry, would sometimes physically attack people, even his friends.

In his earlier years before he went to Eton and the clouds began to gather over his family, the sadness he felt was chiefly at parting from them and going to school, which suggests that he was certainly not unhappy when at home. 'There were too many sad partings, personal sadnesses even at sunsets, difficulties with playing games which I was so bad at, and that I thought might hamper and cripple my life when "grown up", long stretches of being bored, bored, bored, while time flew by without one knowing it. . . .'[8] The 'sad partings' came at an early age: in September 1905, aged not quite eight, he was despatched to Mr Pinckhoff's boarding establishment at Folkestone. Years later, when he happened to hear Dvořák's *Songs My Mother Taught Me*, he would remember not only the luxuries of Christmases with his mother's family at Blankney, their country house near Lincoln, but also the poignant times of luncheons with his mother in a Folkestone hotel. 'I was loved by her, and it has never happened to me again in life that every mouthful I ate, and every moment that I breathed, were indescribable pain and ecstasy, both together, from the strength of my affections.'[9] There were

> agonies of separation when I went back to school, made worse in the certainty that she would be miserable without me, for I have no doubt at all that she often thought of me, and am sure that in the first week or two of term, when I cried secretly, she was crying too. . . . I am thinking of 1906–7–8–9.

In 1908 Sachie followed Osbert (removed from his previous preparatory school, Ludgrove, after a furious exchange of letters between Sir George and the headmaster) to St David's, Reigate. Again his principal memory of St David's was of the 'appalling disappointment' he suffered in the summer of 1908, when he had hoped to escape from school in the middle of term because of an epidemic. His mother had come down to arrange this plan, dressed in a black-and-white checked dress, but it failed and he was kept at Reigate 'through all the hated afternoons of "nets" and cricket that I might have spent with her'. Sachie could never understand the obsession of the English for any form of game played with a ball and liked to quote H. G. Wells saying that visitors landing in England from some other planet must think that certain small spherical objects were inimical to the human race, 'as whenever and wherever seen they were immediately hit, or kicked, or, in sign of their dangerous proclivities, picked up, and as quick as possible hurled back again'.[10] He thought most of the masters unpleasant and the surroundings dreary, 'as uninspiring a background as can be found even in Surrey, perhaps the tritest part of the whole world'.

There were occasional periods of relief from the general tedium: walks on the chalk hills behind the house, along the Pilgrims' Road, which had been Chaucer's pilgrims' route to Canterbury – 'even the most disagreeable of school comrades took a turn for the better in this environment' – and reading bound volumes of the *Illustrated London News* dating back to the 1840s in the school library (his favourite passages included the visit of Louis Philippe to Eton and Queen Victoria's return visit to the Château d'Eu). His only other pleasant memory was of the art teacher, an impoverished, middle-aged spinster named Miss Corder, and her brother, also a painter. 'She was the first artist I had ever met, or even seen, and she sprang for this reason into an instant importance.' Miss Corder's classes on Friday evening, the prelude to the week-end, gave him the sensation of art as a treat and an introduction to a pleasurable experience. He was already making judgements on the type of art which appealed to him, rejecting Miss Corder's preference for J. S. Cotman's drawings of northern France: 'I associated these drawings with the sad and forlorn kind of travel quite at variance with the blue skies and sunny architecture that I had discovered for myself. . . .'[11]

Sachie was always fascinated by other people's lives. Once he asked Miss Corder why she always walked the three miles from her home in the neighbouring town and never took a cab. Her answer, that the school only paid her £80 a year and, therefore, she could not afford to spend half of it on cabs, illuminated for him the life she must lead, so completely remote from his own experience that it seemed both dreary and yet almost exotic. His depiction (written from memory twenty years later) of the artistic spinster in her suburban lodging was as sympathetic as his portrait of old Major Brockwell. 'Brockie' wrote regularly to Sachie while he was at school and at Renishaw, sending him postcards for his collection and retailing news of his cherished chicken farm at Thornton-le-Dale, where he hoped to be able to retire from the wearisome routine of teaching. 'We have 16 hens and 50 chickens,' he reported proudly on 6 July 1907, but a year later Sachie was writing to Osbert: 'Badger's [i.e. Brockie's] chicken farm does not seem to be getting on very well, I'm afraid.'

In September 1908, just before Sachie left for his first term at St David's, Edwin Lutyens's acute eye had been turned on the Sitwell family at Renishaw: 'Sir George, a young and old, old-fashioned man like a character in a Disraeli novel'; Lady Ida, very graceful with 'the remains of great beauty'; Edith, 'a tall daughter more like her father than he is to himself . . .'; and Sachie, 'a son, evidently with character, as he cannot go to sleep without everyone in the house including housemaids and guests attending his bedside'.[12] Lady Ida was miserable because Sir George was about to change his politics and stand as a Liberal (later she described him as 'a socialist'). Sir George, Lutyens said, 'had got the hump' because 'What [he] wants is recognition i.e. a peerage! His reason for change is vindictiveness only. . . .'

Disappointed by the Conservative Party in his hopes of a peerage, Sir George still believed that he might gain recognition in another field. In May 1909 John Murray published his *On the Making of Gardens*, with its subtitle 'being a study of old Italian gardens, of the nature of beauty, and the principles involved in garden design'. It was the first book by Sir George to be published by a general publisher and he had high hopes of its being a financial success, explaining to Osbert that he expected it to provide for Sachie in the wake of 'Lloyd George's destructive Budget'. 'The greater part of [this essay]', Sir George wrote in a preface which produced a wry smile in his family, 'was written during a period of broken health, when slowly recovering from the effects of over-work.' He had, he said, visited over 200 Italian gardens. Osbert has left a memorable portrait of him as he did this:

> . . . a tall, distinguished-looking Englishman with a high-bridged nose, and with fine, fair hair and a slightly darker golden moustache . . . wearing a grey suit and a wide-brimmed hat, a striped linen shirt with a stiff-winged collar and starched cuffs fastened by large carbuncle links; probably he would be sitting on a circular air cushion shaped like a lifebuoy, so well known a seat-mark in the daily life of the Reading Room of the British Museum . . . beside him – for he took care to sit in the shade – a sun-umbrella lined with green. Not far off . . . from the thick blackness of an ilex grove would peer a ponderous figure, watchful

but with an eye for those who passed, as well as for the safety of the
rectangular, varnished wicker box in his custody, which each day contained
a cold chicken. . . .[13]

The book was an attack on the Capability Brown school of landscaping,
which had brought 'featureless lawns to the windows of the house' and a
'dreadful eruption' of mongrel garden architecture, classical temples,
Gothic chapels, Chinese pagodas, Egyptian pyramids, and inscriptions
in Greek or black letter. Sir George also berated Edwardian taste: 'the
mown grass and rather undecided gravel path, and the scentless roses and
the rich and startling masses of horticulturists' flowers and the unhappy
blotches of subtropical foliage'. His purpose was to influence the newly
discovered art of garden design: 'If the world is to make great gardens
again, we must both discover and apply in the changed circumstances
of modern life the principles which guided the garden-makers of the
Renaissance . . . Alberti, Michelozzo, Bramante, Vignola, Raphael and
Michelangelo.' In essence it was a rhapsodic essay on the great Italian
gardens like Villa d'Este at Tivoli, Villa Lante and the Giusti garden at
Verona, with their 'indescribable' haunting beauty, their air of neglect,
desolation and solitude, and their green alleys, fern-fringed dripping
fountains, fluteless fauns and headless nymphs. The purpose of the
garden, Sir George wrote, was to relate the house to the landscape, to
create a mood of 'garden magic'. The designer should use sculpture,
water and huge romantic effects: a cascade of climbing roses, never
'stunted, unnatural' and charmless ranks of rose-beds.

On the Making of Gardens deserved more success than it achieved,
although it was hardly likely ever to be a best-seller since Sir George's
vision necessarily required a great deal of space for its fulfilment. After
his death there were two further editions and an American edition under
Osbert's auspices, one of them illustrated by John Piper. In 1909,
however, his lack of success and appreciation had a definite effect upon
him. He had hoped, he told Osbert, that his *Essay* would rank with
Bacon's *On Gardens*, but instead, as Osbert wrote, many of his wife's
friends, 'violently opposed to books in general, now regarded him as a
traitor who had placed himself on the wrong side of the fence'. He reacted
to this second disappointment by drawing into himself even more than
before, becoming increasingly eccentric, self-regarding and solitary in his
habits. He ate alone, avoiding the company of his wife's chattering friends
and his children since they upset his gastric juices. Above all, he began to
turn his back on England and its inconvenient realities.

In the autumn of 1909, halfway between Florence and Volterra, his motor-car broke down in front of two antique stone lions. Beyond them a path vanished uphill through the olive trees. It led, he was told, to a castle which happened to be for sale. Its name was Montegufoni, the hill of the screech owls; it was vast, medieval and had once belonged to the Acciauoli family, Dukes of Athens, who had been, like the Sitwells, originally in the iron and steel trade and whose crest, like the Sitwells', was a lion rampant. The castle was in a dreadful state and occupied by peasant squatters. Sir George described it as 'a rookery of poor families who lived by agriculture and straw plaiting, there being 297 inhabitants of the castle all told'. There were no drains, but Sir George was enchanted by the indefinable air of ancient grandeur. He had found his future role, living, as he had always envisaged himself, as lord of a medieval castle with endless scope for restoration and infinite bargaining in antique shops. He bought it for £4,000, registering it in Osbert's name. He did this, subconsciously perhaps, to give substance to the fiction that, rather than indulging in a monumental piece of extravagance (for it was obvious that Montegufoni would need thousands of pounds spent on it to make it even reasonably habitable), he was actually adding to the Sitwell patrimony.

In 1909 Sir George took Sachie and Osbert to Venice, which from now on became Sachie's favourite city. It was a momentous experience for both brothers; from then on travel became a habit and Italy their second country. Sachie recalled sitting with Osbert at an ogival window on the stairs of the Hotel Daniele watching the SS *San Marco* leave for Dalmatia and wondering 'if we would ever reach such places when grown up'.

At about this time, he had an experience which impressed him deeply, so much so that he remembered it some sixty years later:

> When I was about ten years old I was taken by my father to see [Villa] Marlia, then lived in by the Count of Capua, son of a renegade Napolitan Bourbon prince who was supposed to have betrayed the last king, Francesco II, to Victor Emmanuel, and was recompensed by being given Marlia. . . .
>
>   The gardener asked if we would like to see the old Conte . . . and I was lifted up by the gardener to look over the wall into the summer house, where I saw the old gentleman with a long white beard *playing with a rocking-horse*. He was insane and supposed to be a throwback to primitive mankind – much studied by specialist doctors, as he used to run away into the woods and try to shave his beard with a sharp stone or flint. . . .[14]

The child peering over the wall into the garden of a beautiful Italian villa to watch a mad, old aristocrat playing with a rocking-horse symbolised Sachie the spectator, fascinated by the beautiful and the strange. The episode of the Count of Capua had a sequel, which gave it a symmetry particularly appealing to Sachie. The mad Count's father had married an Irish girl. Years later, exploring an extraordinary neglected Irish country house in County Cork with Bendor Westminster, Sachie recognised a portrait on the wall as the Count of Capua. The owner of the house, living like Sleeping Beauty behind a dense forest of rhododendrons, with a hip bath in his bedroom and an umbrella over his bed to catch the rain, was the cousin of the mad, old man of Marlia.

On his visit to Venice in 1909 Sachie fell ill and was treated by the doctor who had looked after Baron Corvo; as a result, he missed the beginning of the summer term at St David's. En route back to England with his mother, they spent a day in Paris, where the precocious aesthete was again, or so he said, made ill with the excitement of the whirling traffic, the vivid green of the trees along the boulevards, and 'what I thought of to be the wilful ugliness of the lakes and islands in the Bois'. On this journey with his mother through the spring countryside he became aware of the end of childhood and was seized with an overpowering sense of loss:

> Upon the journey from Dover to London the lambs were playing in the fields; and again, all the way from King's Cross to Yorkshire, in a never ending ecstasy of the green meadows; but which saddened me because I knew, already, that it was a sort of childish happiness that passes, or is changed. It became unbearable in the endless flat green fields, midway upon the journey. A few days later, 25 May, it was my mother's fortieth birthday. . . .

He knew that it was the end of youth for them both and was conscious of a great unhappiness, 'because of her coming birthday . . . an occasion of terrible significance. . . . It would all change and I knew it. The dark clouds were even then massing upon her horizon. . . .'[15]

'My objects of affection were, then, my mother and my brother,' he wrote, looking back on his childhood. As Lady Ida gradually retreated behind a curtain of misery and alcohol, and his father took refuge in increasing eccentricity, his relationship with Osbert became the most important in his life. Despite the five years' difference in age, the two brothers werre passionately fond of each other. Sachie recalled partings from Osbert with the same sharp pain as separations from his mother. In a poem written towards the end of his life, he still remembered them:

> And in one of the agonies of childhood,
> It would be in the second or third week of September,
> going our hateful different ways to school
> For we were never at school together;
> In our misery at the separation,
> For twelve weeks is a long time for a child,
> We buried something, I forget what, under the mulberry tree
> In token of our love for each other,
> It could have been a pair of cuff-links,
> which I suppose must still be there:–
> To this day it upsets me and I do not like to think of
>   it . . .[16]

Osbert would come down to Reigate to see Sachie when he could. Sachie remembered 'the appalling and insufferable sadness of the sunsetting at the level crossing' in the middle of Reigate when he was accompanying Osbert to the station. 'I felt then, that I simply could not stand the future of so many years at school and the tearful, dreadful separations.'

Osbert, too, was unhappy. By 1910 his relationship with his father was in the opening stages of their lifelong guerrilla war against each other. Sir George by now regarded his son and heir as a dynastic failure. He had intended to bring glory to the Sitwell name with a new generation, who would become shining examples of success in public life – governors-general, viceroys even. All his hopes and dreams had been concentrated upon Osbert, but by 1910 the omens were not promising. Osbert had been both a social and academic failure at Eton, thus slipping up on the first stepping-stone. Moreover, Sir George, although capable of singular fits of extravagance himself in pursuit of his own interests, was ever on the watch for manifestations of the spendthrift Denison blood in his wife and children, and at seventeen Osbert was already displaying unmistakable signs of it. In a misguided attempt to stiffen his heir's backbone, Sir George sent him to a dreary army crammer, the Army College, Heath End, at Farnham in Surrey, where, Osbert told Sachie, his fellow inmates were 'rather awful youths with their cigarette-smoking, and snapping and re-pocketing of cigarette cases, and talk of their immature attempts at love-making'.[17]

Sachie and Osbert were allies in the financial war against their father, with Osbert using Sachie to extract money from his parents. 'I paid a lot of my debts with that money,' he wrote to Sachie at home, probably in August 1910, in a letter marked 'Private' with the instructions: 'Don't show this letter or leave it about. Tear it up at once!' 'Do you think you could get 10/– for me. It doesn't matter if you can't. I do so love getting your letters.' On another occasion Sir George was too mean to give Osbert the train fare to go and see Sachie from London. 'My darling Sachie,' Osbert wrote, 'Father won't let me come to see you but is dragging me off to Renishaw. The train for Reigate is 3/8, and "really we can't go on spending at this pace". On Saturday I go [to] Army College, and will try to see you the following Saturday – It is so hard never seeing you. . . .'[18] Their close relationship was all the more remarkable in that Sachie was then twelve – at an age when 'Brockie' could write to him on his arrival at Renishaw from St David's in August 1910: 'I expect you have been on the lake . . . had a fight with pirates on the island etc. How are the B.B.B. etc. etc. & what is the password?' – whereas within six months Osbert would be elected to the Marlborough, which was, as his mother proudly emphasised to Sachie, 'the smartest club in London.'

The rest of the family suffered as Sir George tried to keep Osbert under constraint, and at all costs out of London, the source of temptation. As Edith complained to Sachie from Wood End in November 1910, 'I do wish Osbert wouldn't write Mother cross letters. . . . I am so terrified of Father turning round, and saying we are not to go up to London at all. And after all, he *is* extravagant. . . . And we are all being punished for it more than he is, for I at any rate will have to be here for 2 months!'[19] Edith's fears were soon confirmed, as Lady Ida wrote to Sachie on 9 November: 'I fear we do not go to London till after Xmas – your Father says Osbert is so extravagant in London!'[20] Osbert was particularly unpopular at that juncture. On his and Sir George's return from an inspection of Montegufoni in October, it was discovered that he had not passed his army exam. The pressure was now on Sachie to excel. His father wrote him a typical letter on 5 November:

> Your half-term report is as always very good for conduct, but it is not satisfactory as far as school is concerned. Do try and do your best in the second half of the term & give your full attention to the work. It seems that both in classics & mathematics when confronted with a difficulty you act like the British army in the South African war; you do not wait to consider how to outflank the enemy but make a frontal attack at once without the slightest consideration. You should stop and think: it would be better to be slow than do the wrong thing quickly.

'My darling little man,' Lady Ida wrote the same day. 'I am sure you will work hard, Father was a bit worried and wrote, we are both devoted to you. . . .' 'Father', she added, 'went off to Renishaw yesterday for two nights. He was very fussy and more Hall porterish than ever. . . .'[21]

This was hardly a respectful way to refer to Sir George, although any one who had received a letter from him with its detailed itineraries and instructions could not deny that it was a fair one. Sachie was being drawn into the burgeoning war between his parents, which would result in the final destruction of their relationship. Within two years the situation had so deteriorated that he could write to Osbert in 1912 about his parents as 'these 2 basilisks Father & Mother. Collectively & in practice I hate them. . . .'[22] Osbert, already engaged in financial and unfilial skirmishing with his father, was Lady Ida's principal confidant and, to Sachie's increasing horror, was dragged by her into the sordid tale of her debts. His mother's letters to him were still short scrawls of passionate affection, such as this, written on 27 January 1911, on the evening Sachie returned to St David's:

> My darling little man, I have just got home. I miss you so much my precious, you'll take care of yourself won't you my darling. Let me know how you get on & how you are in your room if you are not happy you are to be sure & say & I will see about it. Bless you, my darling, I do love you so much.[23]

But in her next letter references to her lack of money began: 'I had a line from Osbert who wants me to buy him some things for his gramophone but am *too* poor.' Yet in the same breath she mentions one of her daily bridge sessions, no doubt a contributory factor to her poverty. She was putting pressure continually on Osbert, writing to him from Venice on 17 June 1911: 'Darling you will try & see what can be done won't you. You don't know what I feel like I never sleep. If Father finds out about these Bills there would be such a row & I really can't face it.'

Despite her loving letters, Sachie was certainly not in the forefront of Lady Ida's mind, preoccupied as she was in concealing the extent of her indebtedness from her husband, or dragged in his wake on his incessant continental peregrinations. As Henry Moat wrote humorously to Sachie on 20 November 1910 from London hoping that Sachie had enjoyed a huge birthday cake he had been sent, 'Well, Sir George and Lady Ida Sitwell are in the best of good health. I think you know them they live at Wood End Scarborough. I believe you met this year. . . .'[24]

Nor was Sachie so close to Edith at this time in their lives as he later became after the family disaster in 1915 bound the trio together. Edith had been educated at home by governesses, first Miss King-Church, who left in 1902 to marry one of Osbert's tutors, and then Helen Rootham, who was, perhaps, the strongest influence on her in adolescence. Helen was a gifted musician and encouraged Edith to develop her love of music. Visitors to Renishaw at that time remembered Edith as always at the piano, when streams of Debussy or Brahms (a composer Sachie disliked) would float out of the ballroom windows. Edith apparently also, briefly, learned to play the harp. (Sir George, on being congratulated on some literary success she had achieved, would only remark, 'Such a pity that Edith gave up the harp.') She was not yet writing poetry, although she was living on a diet of Shakespeare, Swinburne, Keats, Shelley and Yeats, whom she used to read aloud to Sachie in the nursery. Helen Rootham widened her experience, introducing her to the French symbolists, Baudelaire, Rimbaud and Verlaine, all of whom were to influence Sachie in his turn. Sachie remembered Edith as

> A tall thin young woman in a pelisse of green sheepskin and a wide-brimmed hat, who walks between the hedges upon the smoother grass. She has long, thin hands and jet black rings and bracelets. She has sloping shoulders, and picks her way among the falling twigs. And from her shadow the wood leads on into poetry. . . .[25]

The time for poetry had not come yet, for either of them.

So Sachie often felt lonely and bored, immured at school or sent to his Sitwell grandmother's house at Bournemouth to be entertained by his Aunt Florence and Lady Sitwell's attendant spirit, the tomato-faced Sister Edith Woods, whom he particularly disliked. To his dismay, in June 1911 he was forbidden to go home to Wood End for the Coronation *exeat* and instead had to spend the week with his grandmother. The reason may have been the death of 'Aunt Puss', his great-aunt, Lady Hanmer, at Scarborough in May. 'Do you know whether we shall get Weston or not?' Sachie wrote to Osbert, his first mention of the Hely-Hutchinson manor in Northamptonshire which was to be his home for the rest of his life. It may also have been because of his Eton entrance exam at the end of June. 'It was so boring at Bournemouth,' he wrote to Osbert. 'It poured with rain, nearly the whole time. . . . Auntie Floss and Sister Edith the only people there. . . . Auntie Floss did nothing but dust books and line drawers. . . .'[26]

Sachie left St David's in July 1911. For all his complaints to Osbert of 'boredom', his time there had been relatively successful. As usual, he had charmed everybody, even the school matron, Dora Green, who wrote from Great Yarmouth thanking him for the inkstand he had sent her as a farewell present: 'I shall miss my Captain in the B dormitory very much next term, he kept very good order!' He had made friends with Ralph McMicking, G.R. 'Giffy' Gunter and Tommy Fox-Pitt, who wrote to him from his home at Anglesey an extremely illiterate letter in execrable writing describing the excitements of the miners' strike, when he had accompanied his father, who was a special constable, to a picket and been hit on the knee by a broken bottle. Fox-Pitt, however, was clearly a Liberal:

> I don't know why you are annoyed with Lloyd George who settled the strikes and delivered you and the rest of the nation from the tiranny [*sic*] of the Peers. I suppose you think the strikers are very wicked well the conservatives who yelled traiter [*sic*] at Asquith were as bad if not worse. My stories of the strike is [*sic*] just as true as yours.[27]

Perhaps to spite his father, now a Liberal, or perhaps under the influence of Major Brockwell, a pillar of the Conservatives, Sachie was a Tory. He liked helping 'Brockie' write his speeches – 'Brockie' was at this time in demand and boasted that he earned £500 a year from public speaking – and he joined the junior branch of the Imperial Maritime League, a jingoistic organisation advocating increased armaments for the Royal Navy. A year later, he was apparently a member of the Junior Unionist Association Governing Committee. Eton and Futurism, however, were to turn him in the opposite direction.

In September 1911 Sachie, aged not quite fourteen, went to Eton as a pupil in A.A. Somerville's house. Osbert's view of his own time at Eton can hardly have prejudiced him in its favour. 'I liked Eton', Osbert later wrote, 'except in the following respects: for work and games, for boys and masters.' Sachie's housemaster, Mr Annesley Ashworth Somerville, was an Anglo-Irishman with a passion for sport; Sachie later described him to Osbert as 'the second stupidest man in the world after Father'. The house was primarily dedicated to winning at games; in 1912, the year following Sachie's arrival, A.A. Somerville's won the House cups in cricket, football and fives. Sachie's reaction, faced with the prospect of returning to Eton for his second half, was predictable and predictably exaggerated: '. . . how awful to have to return . . . to people the very sight of whom I hate, & to surroundings which have nothing beautiful in them.'[28]

It hardly helped that in his first half at Eton not one of his family came down to see him. Sir George was engrossed in writing *The Pilgrim*, a dissertation on the Middle Ages which took as its starting-point the departure of an ancestor, Walter de Boys, on pilgrimage to the Holy Land in 1301. Lady Ida had already begun the saga of debts and involvement with fraudsters and moneylenders which was to darken the family horizon over the next four years. By the summer of 1911 her debts amounted to some £2,000, which she had no means of repaying. Not daring to approach Sir George again (he had already paid a considerable number of her debts), she appealed for help to Osbert, who thought that he had found the answer when a young army friend of his named Martin introduced him to Julian Osgood Field, whom he described as a financial wizard, a gentleman and a literary figure who was accustomed to assisting people of good family with their money problems.

Field was a bizarre character perfectly suited to the tragi-comic Sitwell ambience; he was one of nature's oddities, a white Anglo-Saxon Protestant black sheep. Born of a prominent New York family (his father had been Assistant Secretary of the US Treasury), he had been educated in the American anglophile upper-class tradition at Harrow and at Merton College, Oxford. His literary acquaintances ranged from Jowett to Swinburne; in Paris, where he moved in the 1870s and 1880s, they included Proust, Victor Hugo and Maupassant. Field had written a book of sketches of Parisian society under the significant title *Aut Diabolus aut nihil* and, under the pseudonym 'XL', a volume of Russian sketches and the ghosted memoirs of the Duke of Hamilton. Osbert later described Field, in his sixties when he visited Renishaw for the first time, with a jaundiced pen: 'his stunted, stooping paunchy body . . . carried a heavy head . . . with a beak like that of an octopus, which spiritually he so much resembled, and a small imperial and moustache that were dyed, as was his hair, a total and unnatural black'. Initially, however, Osbert was fascinated by Field and his exotic past; what he did not know was that on 22 July 1901 Field had been convicted of forgery at the Central Criminal Court and sentenced to three months' imprisonment, or that he was an undischarged bankrupt. When Osbert met him, he was living in apparently comfortable circumstances at the Grosvenor Hotel, but, like some shady character in a Dickens novel, he actually earned a precarious living by swindling the gullible rich.

Field proposed that Lady Ida should make use of an eccentric but rich woman of his acquaintance named Dobbs; in return for Lady Ida's good offices in Society, Miss Dobbs would be willing to lend £6,000 at five per cent interest. This loan could be repaid by Lady Ida taking out life insurance. Lady Ida was impressed, but said that she did not need £6,000 since her debts were only £2,000. Field airily replied that it was always a good idea to have something in hand and to borrow more than one strictly needed while it was possible. He would handle the whole transaction for Lady Ida, paying off her debts for her while deducting a certain amount for incidentals, his own expenses and those of his agent, a Mr Herbert, who was arranging everything with Miss Dobbs. Of course, Lady Ida would not get quite all of the £6,000. Miss Dobbs would 'back' a bill – i.e. guarantee a loan over a period, say six months, so as to give him time to find a moneylender who would 'discount' the bill, paying in cash a certain sum on the strength of it. This would be less than the £6,000 and Lady Ida would have time then to arrange her life insurance so that repayment would be met. Lady Ida, desperate and financially illiterate, swallowed Field's plan, hook, line and sinker.

It was not long before Field hauled his catch to the surface for the first time. Early in 1912 the two bills for £3,000 each backed by Miss Dobbs (who was under the impression that she had only backed one bill for £3,000) were discounted by a moneylender named Owles for £4,800. The money was paid to Field, who passed on £1,000 immediately to Herbert; only £200 of it seems to have reached Lady Ida. When she complained, Field blackmailed her by telling her that if she was not satisfied she should tell her husband what had happened. When she replied that she would do anything but that, Field told her that the only way of avoiding this and paying for her life insurance would be by borrowing more. For someone in her social position, this should be easy: all she had to do was to find someone rich to back a further bill and he, Field, would do the rest. He suggested that she could find many such persons – rich, ambitious women who would be ready to pay something for the privilege of being promoted socially by the Earl of Londesborough's sister. Osbert, by now a member of the ultra-fashionable Marlborough Club and an officer in a smart cavalry regiment, should be able to find rich young fellows who would be willing to guarantee a bill for Lady Ida, a bill which would produce immediate ready money.

Somehow, however, these willing, socially ambitious women did not prove easy to find, as Lady Ida explained to Field in a series of letters which were to make unedifying reading in court three years later: 'Oh dear! Have just had a letter from Lady – saying she does not see her way to signing the paper. . . . Is it not possible to get hold of this woman you told me about? Of course, I will do everything in my power to get her into the society she requires. . . .' 'It seems impossible to make the woman understand that our transaction is absolutely sound and straight,' she wrote on another occasion. 'So do try to get me a man as a second backer.'²⁹ The truth was that, despite her grand relations, Lady Ida, mainly due to her husband's solitary character and reluctance to spend money on social events, was very far from being a leader of Society, a fact that was perfectly obvious to her targets. Young men were more gullible, or soft-hearted. Osbert's friend Martin came forward for a small sum and Lady Ida had hopes of other brother officers of Osbert's, as she wrote in a disgraceful letter to Field: 'My boy, quite hopes, if he joins the 11th Hussars, there must be some boy he can get hold of.' A young Yorkshire cricketer named Wilson was persuaded to sign a further bill for £4,000 for a down payment of £300 and Lady Ida's promise to persuade her brother, Londesborough, to propose him for the Marlborough Club. But Lady Ida had been unable to arrange for the life insurance she needed to pay off the £6,000 she now owed to Owles, who was pressing for repayment, as were the other moneylenders who were demanding the money they had paid out in short-term loans on bills backed by Martin and Wilson. By the end of July 1912 Field had arranged a two-month extension of the Dobbs loan, but Wilson was compelled to mortgage his reversion for £4,000 to meet his guarantee, while the moneylenders threatened Martin that they would tell his colonel of his debt. Both Martin and Lady Ida appealed to Osbert for help. In August Herbert wrote to Lady Ida, Sir George and Londesborough threatening to expose Ida's conduct at her own charity ball at Scarborough and was bought off with £600.

Pressure from and worry about his mother, coupled with his absolute detestation of his regiment, precipitated a breakdown in Osbert. At the end of August 1912 he fled Aldershot and turned up in Italy, where his father, who had, after all, forced Osbert against his will into the army and who was perhaps aware of the other worries besieging him, was, for once, sympathetic. It was then agreed that Osbert should leave the 11th Hussars and join the Brigade of Guards. In Florence Lady Ida, not for the first time, was reduced to borrowing money off the servants – from 'that spiteful maid, who has a very bitter tongue about me,' and the considerable sum of £125 from Henry Moat, whom she ungratefully described as 'the brute, I want to get out of his clutches'. Returning to England that autumn, however, there was no respite. The first of a series of legal actions by moneylenders over the Dobbs's bills took place, while at the same time one of young Wilson's trustees furiously demanded the £4,000.

Osbert was by now seriously worried at the trouble which his mother's irresponsibility threatened for his friend Martin, as is evident from a letter which Lady Ida wrote him from Wood End on 24 November 1912:

> Darling I beg of you to stick by me darling, am miserable –
> You know I would never let any of your friends in. I am telling Field that he has to pay what ever is due to Mr Martin *at once* – I am sorry if it has worried you. I enclose Mr Field's letter. Don't worry as I promise faithfully that Mr Martin shall *not* [three underlinings] be made a Bankrupt over me, am sending part of your letter to Mr Field to let him see *how* important it is – The money is *there* so I insist on clearing Mr Martin for your sake.
> Your very sad mother . . .[30]

At home that Christmas, Sachie was well aware of the true horrors of the family situation, reporting to Osbert from Wood End on Boxing Day. His mother had, apparently, been seriously ill: 'She has had clots of blood, & congestion of the brain, & very nearly became off her head.' In her misery Lady Ida took refuge in alcohol. 'Every day after dinner Mother goes to get her medicine, and you know what that means. Before she undresses she has a glass of hot Whiskey. In fact things are worse than usual. . . . Father tells me that Mother is liable *not* to 6000£, but to 11000£. . . .'[31] On New Year's Eve 1912 he wrote another wryly gloomy bulletin, wishing Osbert a happy new year: 'Certainly a worse [one] than 1912 would be almost impossible.'

Sachie had no one to keep him company beyond Miss Lloyd and 'Brockie'. His mother preferred her sycophantic female friends, one of whom, 'Minx' Armytage, habitually referred to her as 'the Adorable' and to being 'bird-happy' with her at Renishaw. He told Osbert:

> Minx comes today for one night so Mother is sending Miss Lloyd, Brockie, & I to the pantomime 'Dick Whittington' at the Hippodrome. Mother of course has done this so as to have a night alone with Minx. She was so anxious to altogether get rid of me, that she did not want us to dine here even although I had already asked Miss Lloyd to dine here. She told me to ask Miss Lloyd to let us dine at her house. Brockie as you know is not very friendly with Miss Lloyd. You can imagine what it will be like.

His mother accused him of being 'brutal' to Minx and even deputed the family doctor, Dr Salter, on the pretext of taking him for a drive in his motor-car, to give him a 'long lecture about filial affection, & obedience'. 'However,' he added, 'I am satisfied to think, that I told him exactly what I thought of him in a few well-chosen words.' None the less, he still had a residual affection for her: 'In spite of these fearful things, I still find that I can't help being a little fond of Mother.' His father, having told Sachie the extent of his mother's liability, added that, 'if she paid back £250 a year, half her income, it would take her 44 years to clear her debts, by which time she would be 87. The moneylenders were charging her 300%, but if the case came into court, they cannot by law charge her more than 5%.'[32]

Sachie was alone among the siblings in having to bear the brunt of Christmas holidays with his tortured family at Scarborough. Edith rarely features in his correspondence at this time. Although she had not yet officially left home, she spent as much time as she could escaping from her parents, usually in the company of Helen Rootham. 'I wonder where Edith is . . .', Sachie wrote. He did not much care for Miss Rootham, whom Osbert and he referred to as 'Helen of Troy', finding her too intense and, as he told Osbert, 'so fearfully depressing that she nearly kills one. Her conversation was centred on the white slaves, the Inquisition . . . so cheerful & elevating. . . .' In the new year of 1913 Edith seems to have begun her bid for freedom, as Sachie wrote to Osbert in a pathetic lament from Eton on 20 February 1913:

> As Edith has, I do sincerely hope, escaped from home for good, I shall be left from now till I am 19, or so alone with *them* [triple underlining] during the holidays. Neither of them are really fond of me & neither is Edith. I am hated here, & consequently you are the only person who could be fond of me. . . . I wish you could realise that I love you much more than you have ever imagined, & although I am growing up shall continue to do so. . . Think of me, when you can, at night. I am very lonely & unhappy.[33]

Sachie had not, apparently, been told by Edith of the publication of her first poem, 'Drowned Suns', in the *Daily Mirror* that month, nor did he see a copy until March when Osbert sent him one. 'I thought Edith's poem quite lovely in rhythm, & feeling, but it was rather a come down to publish it in the "Daily Mirror" wasn't it. Is she going to publish any more?'[34] In August, however, Edith was again at Renishaw with Sachie and his tutor, Mr Pearce, son of one of the Scarborough band of doctors. 'Things are in the most miserable position here,' Sachie wrote to Osbert on the 22nd; 'Heaven knows what will happen to us all.' He and Edith were to remain there until early September, when they would be sent down to Bournemouth to stay with the dreaded Sister Edith. He was miserable and missing Osbert. 'I do so love you,' he wrote, 'just as much as I ever did. . . . Think of me tonight.'[35]

Sachie's hope that the new year of 1913 would be better than 1912 proved a vain one. There was to be no respite from the nightmare, which now spread to enmesh Lady Ida's *grande dame* sister-in-law, Gracie Londesborough. A letter of Lady Ida's to Osbert that holidays, dated 14 January 1913, gives some idea of the atmosphere at Wood End: 'My darling boy . . . I feel very depressed darling & I wish I was dead. Father never leaves my affairs alone for one moment, last week he told me I ought to be serving my time.' She was still pressing Osbert to do her dirty work, writing to him on 12 February:

> Would you be a darling & go and see Warborough. Tell him he is to make Sir Henry pay the enclosed bill – I cannot keep the poor woman waiting. Father knows all about it as some time ago I asked him to advance the money, but *she is* [underlined twice] in a bad way. I won't write to the brutes as I don't want any dealings with them. I wish I could hear what the executors of Owles [who had just died] mean to do? It is awful hanging on like this. Dobbs says Herbert got money out of her under false pretences but all the time I believe is living with him. . . .[36]

Sir George's tactics in the face of this were to keep his wife's chequebook locked up and herself out of the country, not necessarily accompanied by himself. In June she was in exile at the Villa d'Este. 'Your father with his loving heart keeps me out here all alone,' she complained to Osbert, while Sir George remained at Renishaw with Edith and Miss Rootham, whom she greatly disliked. Sachie described them as being 'at daggers drawn' the previous holidays. Edith was, in fact, contemplating escape to London with Helen Rootham, a determination which seems to have brought on paroxysms of fury in her mother, which she poured out to Osbert: '[Your father] has Miss Rootham & Edith who I hate. I do hope you will persuade him that I never want to see Edith again, Miss Rootham was detestable since when I was ill not a word, she is the only person I know who never did. I know you like her but I hope some day you will find out what a deceitful liar she is.'[37] A month later she was imploring Osbert to persuade Sir George to send her money and, on 1 August, to get Coutts Bank to hand over her money to Warborough, as Sir George refused to let her have her chequebook. Apparently he succeeded, but his mother remained terrified that Sir George would find out, writing three days later: 'Thank you for all you have done – I hope Coutts won't give me away about the cheque. . . . I hope I haven't been a dreadful nuisance, will you try to get Warborough to get Coutts not to give an account!'

The autumn of 1913 was overshadowed by the case brought by Owles's executors, 'Owles v. Dobbs and another', in which Lady Ida and Miss Dobbs were co-defendants before Mr Justice Horridge. The case which had been brought in July had been put off until Lady Ida could appear. In October judgement was entered for the plaintiff for £6,000 plus costs, but stayed pending appeal; the judge, however, sympathised with Miss Dobbs, upon whom, he said, a 'horrible fraud' had been perpetrated. 'His Lordship', *The Times* reported, 'commented severely on the conduct of Lady Ida Sitwell in writing a letter containing lies in order that it might be shown to Miss Dobbs to induce her to accept the bills, and he expressed the hope that she would do something in order to pay Miss Dobbs who had been swindled.'[38] Lady Ida's family shuddered at the resultant publicity. 'The case was very bad', Edith wrote to Osbert from London on 20 October, '& the Judge very severe. The *Daily Mail* had, in large headlines, "Lady Ida Sitwell. Horrible fraud on a woman." '[39]

All this was bad enough, but Lady Ida's troubles were far from over. She was now being threatened by the trustees of the unfortunate young Wilson. On 25 October she wrote to Osbert:

> You have it seems to me poor darling to have to do all the dirty work. I want you to put to the Trustee[s] how serious it is about the Wilson boy that comes off soon, truly that would be worse than Dobbs, it means ruination of the wretched boy's career if it is public property which it must be if it comes into Court – . I had a charming letter from Willie Worsley [trustee of the Sitwell estate] which I will show you on your return, he is most anxious about this boy & writes strongly to say something ought to be done. You see if we can get hold of this brute [presumably Field] afterwards naturally the money must go back to Father. I should never *dare* show my face in Yorkshire if we fight – *do make* Father see it.

She followed this up with an even more desperate letter:

> I am so perfectly miserable I truly & honestly think the only thing to do is to do away with myself, after all I have brought enough shame on you & this would not be as bad, I cannot face the Wilson trial. . . . It is no use Father coming home he would only poor darling get on my nerves –you see on the Tuesday he would not talk to me at lunch & cheer me up as I was so done up I lost my head in the box – I have nothing to live

for but absolute misery. Darling could you get him to send Briar [her maid]
her money if we go to Wood End and she has to pay ready money for her
food. . . .

She was also trying to involve the Londesboroughs, whose social
position made them extremely wary of the possibility of scandal. Her
sister-in-law had apparently obliged:

Gracie has promised if more money is wanted it shall be there *Monday*,
they do *not* want publicity. For God's sake tell it to your Father.
Something must be done he is all for paying [the] £200 that I got [from
Field] & that is all . . . it truly means more publicity I am down to the
world & I much fear you will have to leave the regiment, it is nothing to
your Father as he knows nobody & he is a socialist & does not care what
people think. . . .[40]

At Eton Sachie was frantic with anxiety about his brother. Worried that
Osbert might respond to their mother's appeal, he wrote:

Just a line to say above all things *NEVER PAY* [triple underlining]. This
is most important. If you once pay, you will always have to, & they will
always be coming down on you! I am sure you won't have to leave the
Grenadiers, & if you do I shall become a strike leader, Larkin No. 2.
Poor Mother is dreadfully bad, but you must not pay. Colonel
Chandos-Pole has written to your Colonel about you. How awful things
are. . . .
    I expect you sympathise with Father. I do. In spite of his faults. And
yet I am sorry for Mother. . . . What will happen to us all?[41]

However, Aunt Gracie was doing all she could to help avert a public
scandal, which she feared could both damage Osbert's career in the
Guards and result in Sachie being removed from Eton. As she wrote to
Osbert from Blankney:

You know how fond I am of you & anything that may hurt your career
now, just when you are getting on so well & are so much liked in the
Regiment, would make me perfectly miserable also Sachie's future
career! I think by hook or by crook *you* [double underlining] must find
the £2000 . . . to stop the Wilson boy's case from coming on. I suppose
[you] need your Father's *signature* [double underlining] only in case of
your death & you *could* easily borrow from the bank, at 4 per cent. . . .
I know your Father gives you a good allowance, but perhaps he is so

fond of you two boys he would help. I hold no brief for your Mother as you know, but I do know this, that in the box she incriminates *herself* in the most awful manner, & absolutely if *this* [double underlining] case comes out they *assure* me you must leave the Regiment & Sachie ought to leave Eton or they will ask your Father to remove him. I am writing one line to him. Your Father I know it is *hard* for him but something must be done for your sake & if no one else will you *must* [double underlining] raise the money yourself.[42]

Sir George's tactless self-righteousness, however, put paid to any chance of his brother-in-law coming to the rescue, as Lady Ida discovered while staying at Blankney towards the end of November. As she wrote to Osbert on the 25th:

I am perfectly miserable & feel so ill again at Father doing all this worrying, they tried to keep it from me but I was sitting at lunch when your Father rang up. He makes Gracie positively ill the letters he writes. She has done all she can it is out of her *pocket* & it is rather hard to try to make her pay more, owing to his telegram to Francis he [Londesborough] won't listen or do anything – I believe he was quite prepared to have helped before. I never slept. . . . Your Father is slowly killing me by inches the way he goes on – I am so bad tonight I can hardly move all power in my legs goes the minute I am the least bit worried. I am dreadfully sorry for you it must be quite dreadful . . . do let me know what he is doing if he does not look out he will put Francis's back up and then we are done. Do *implore* him not to write these quite impossible letters. . . .[43]

Gracie Londesborough also put Osbert in the picture:

Everything looks very black. I have tried my best to get help to pay off this claim but it is useless. The boy's trustees will advance £500 & Francis won't help. It was too unfortunate that telegram [from Sir George] to him beginning 'No it is you that is disgraced not me' or words to that effect. Crushed what I had been working for *completely*. I heard through my sister that Co[lonel] Cotton who was staying with Lord Methuen said that if this trial comes on & the letters read that Ida wrote to young Wilson, (in all ignorance) you will have to leave the regiment. The letter is so fearfully incriminating. . . . Osbert it *must* be stopped somehow. . . .[44]

Immured fearfully and resentfully at Wood End, having been forced to leave Blankney by the imminent arrival of a shooting party, Lady Ida continued to rail at her absent husband, snapping even at Osbert. 'I do hope Father won't let this case be public,' she wrote incoherently on 30 November. 'I shall really be done for it will be dreadful being all alone. I have not written to Father for days so that we can't quarrel if I don't write; but there is one thing certain he doesn't care for me or what happens to me. . . .'[45]

Sir George, however, did come forward and, in mid-December 1913, the Wilson affair was settled without Lady Ida being dragged into court. 'Dearest Osbert,' Gracie wrote, 'I was so glad to hear from your Father after all this it was a great joy to think it was settled without any reference to Mother & I am glad Father is at Woodend [*sic*]. . . . I am glad too Mr Wilson's stumped up *1000* [underlined twice] I could not pay any more *I* [underlined twice] don't know where this £1000! is coming from to repay the person I borrowed from – '[46]

Home again for another drearily claustrophobic Christmas at Wood End, Sachie kept in touch daily with Osbert. On 23 December he wrote:

> Lord! how impossible our parents are. It really is a unique experience to live for months at a time in the world of pantomime, like I am doing at present. Father has just been telling me for the last 20 minutes his system of taking the soap out of his eyes when washing, a process apparently which he proudly announced took him '20 years to discover'. . . . Mother does not seem at all to realise what she has done, & thinks that poor Father has behaved shockingly. She wants Father to pay the whole thing. He has already payed 1750£ direct expenses, not counting lawyers, doctors, nurses etc. etc. So it really is rather hard on him. She really is hopeless, & so unstable to poor unfortunate me – *What I have done*, I must confess, I really cannot quite see.[47]

He had no money for Christmas presents and had not succeeded in extracting any from Sir George by Christmas Eve, when, under the heading 'Wood End, Siberia', he addressed another wry lament to Osbert, on duty as the King's Guard at St James's Palace:

> This letter written on the eve of the most boring day of the year can hardly fail to be infected by the same complaint, but when you read it remember I am writing it in the wilds of the North Riding surrounded by lunatics & octogenarians. . . . Mother is, at present, carrying on an indiscriminate quarrel with everybody of her acquaintance, which is hardly likely to improve her popularity.[48]

'I do pity you so,' Osbert replied from the Marlborough Club on the 26th. 'What Scarborough must be like! Especially in combination with our family.' He sent Sachie some Shaw to cheer him up: 'In all Shaw's books there is a sincere feeling of revolt & disgust at the present system of "Government by Grey Hairs",' adding a postscript reference to Sachie's world of 'pantomime': 'The Family may still make some money as I see the Harlequinade has been revived at Drury Lane. . . .'[49]

The family pantomime was destined to run and run until its humiliating conclusion just over a year later. In addition to dealing with his wife's creditors, Sir George had been conducting a fierce battle with Osbert over the latter's own indebtedness. In July 1914 he ended this phase of hostilities with a cruel coup. Osbert was to leave his regiment, the Grenadier Guards, and his fashionable London life to do penance in the Town Clerk's office in Scarborough. He arrived home at Renishaw on 20 July 1914 to find the whole family there and his father sporting the red beard which led to his nickname 'Ginger'. (A London cabman, after a furious altercation with Sir George over the fare, told him: 'I'll get even with you, Ginger, when the war's over!')

Everything seemed the same, Osbert recalled, 'But with a strange uneasy difference' in the last days before the outbreak of war.[50] The weather was very hot and the scent of the huge lilies, a speciality of the Belgian gardener, Ernest de Taeye, floated in through the windows, combining with stocks, clove carnations, tobacco plants and box with the faint underlying acrid smell of coal smoke. Lady Ida, ill from the strain of her worries, lay in bed, while Helen Rootham played Debussy in the ballroom and Edith, shut away from the trivialities of everyday life, copied passages from Baudelaire into her notebooks. Sachie talked to 'Brockie' in the garden. Aunt Florence hovered in the background like a fading Fra Angelico. Only Henry Moat was away on one of his periodic absences, his place taken by Robins. The feeling of tension increased. Sachie, 'a tall figure, broad-shouldered, thin, with an unusual grace', implored Osbert to telephone London to find out if there would be war. On 3 August Osbert left for London to report to the reserve battalion of the Grenadiers. Sachie, agonised by his departure, lay awake listening for the sound of his train passing southbound down the valley below the house.

From Renishaw that August he sent reports to Osbert of their father's exasperating behaviour. 'Father now makes me walk about & carry a book on my head for 20 minutes a day – It is too aggravating for words, & makes me feel I am a complete lunatic – But it is just like him, isn't it,' he wrote on the 18th. They had played a game of consequences in the ballroom the previous evening when 'the following sentence appeared, "The fish-faced negress Edith Sitwell met the flat-footed Sister Edith in the Chamber of Horrors" – you can imagine what a dreadful lull in the conversation ensued. Father came out as "pig-faced & obstinate & pompous!" '[51] On 26 August he reported gloomily: 'Edith goes away on Friday for good & all. It *will* be awful here, won't it. . . .' The war was used as an excuse by Sir George for stringent and irritating economies: only cheap notepaper was to be used, and the groom who drove the pony cart was dismissed so that they had to walk everywhere.[52] The Baronet observed with gloomy satisfaction that his brother-in-law, the Earl, was financially pressed: ' "your uncle" has now to housekeep on £100 monthly – i.e. the same as we have. They have now I believe as much a year as they had a month. I believe it is all owing to the Bank Rate. I suppose "your uncle" must have borrowed just before the war. . . .' Mother, too, was being 'so tiresome' that they had constant rows. Aunt Florence's Christian attempts at peace-making did not help: 'Aunt Floss said to me this morning, "I do hope you will not be cross to your Mother, as even Jews & Moslems do not curse their mothers & fathers!!" But after all, I could not prevent my parentage & I certainly do not curse them half as much as they deserve.'[53]

Lady Ida's temper was, as usual, connected with 'the case'. Her liabilities in various quarters now amounted to some £12,000 in return for advances of £8,350, of which £7,775 had gone into Field's pocket. It had been decided that she should sue Field for the return of the money and expose him for the swindler he was. 'It is really too awful, there is never any peace from it,' Sachie had written to Osbert from Eton in June; 'there has been a case now every half I have been here except my first two. I do hope this one will not be particularly awful. . . .'[54] The same question was foremost in Edith's mind when she wrote to Osbert describing life with her mother as 'the case' entered a new phase:

> She is drunk all the time now, & I think has really come to imagine that she has done the right things & covered herself with glory. She says only middle-class people look down on her! I wish you would tell me what really has happened about Aunt Gracie & Sir George Lewis [one of London's most successful Society solicitors, accustomed to handling 'delicate' cases for celebrity clients such as Lily Langtry at the time of her involvement with the Prince of Wales], as Mother is more than incoherent with 'emotion' & whisky. Oh, it's been a *lovely* summer. . . .[55]

'Mother's temper is awful today,' Sachie wrote on 9 September. 'She is very X about Sir George Lewis & Aunt Gracie, so I give you a word of warning about it. Really what will happen in this case, I don't know. Father says unless it comes on she will be arrested, yet why & for what reasons? Mother thinks she is conferring benefits on us, with these perennial cases of hers! She is really not an unmixed blessing.'[56] Osbert was not, therefore, surprised to receive a stormy letter from his mother, railing against his father and appealing, as usual, to him for help:

> Sir George Lewis has written to me tonight saying he is going to throw up the case. Your Father holds to the thing that Gracie told Sir George Lewis she did *not* want the case in July, it rests *all on that*. Perhaps when you see him (your Father) on Monday you may be able to do something but I think it very serious that your Father should do all this damage from petty jealousy & runs the risk of my being arrested any moment if Owles's [executors] realize we do not fight. I will have *no* [double underlining] other lawyer. It is sad the damage that is done by just making a joke, & when one realizes that Father is always down on Francis & Gracie it would be better not to tell him.[57]

Sachie, from Renishaw on the eve of his departure via London for Eton, kept Osbert posted on the domestic front:

> There were awful scenes yesterday as Sir George Lewis wrote & said he would not go on with the case, because of Father's insolent letters. . . . Of course it is playing into Field's hands, but at the same time Father says Lewis declares Mother will be arrested now whatever happens & so perhaps we are well out of the case, as there is now no room for it in the papers owing to the war, which was the whole point of having the case at all. . . .[58]

Osbert, however, seems to have succeeded in calming down Sir George Lewis and 'the case', which was intended to clear Lady Ida's name, came on in November. Sachie, having returned to Eton, described his life as 'hell'; he was miserable, both on his mother's behalf and on Osbert's, and he hated Eton, which was 'just like a life in prison surrounded by people, whose intelligence is that of a child of 4, & whose character & bearing is that of the most hardened criminal'.[59] He felt lonely and isolated. 'Do write to me, please, & do please come down & see me. . . . I do so miss telephoning you at nights. . . .'[60] The worst nightmare, however, was the thought of the possibility of Osbert being killed. On Sunday, 20 September, Sachie wrote him a letter of passionate devotion:

My poor angel how sad your having to go on Tuesday or Wednesday. . . . I do wish I could come up & see you before you go. Perhaps if you, or Father, wrote to Mr Somerville, he might let me come up. I think you really must make an effort to come through alright, as you don't know & can't recognise, what it would mean to Edith & I if you didn't. I am already 90 years older than I ought to be, & you are the *only* person who makes me realise I am not, & keeps me sane. I am sure if anything happened to you I should go mad, & slowly decay. I wish I had a little religion and faith to carry me through this terrible time, but fear I have not. However I am sure, my angel, if you will only take care of yourself you will be allright. And even if this is not so, you must not think it at all final, as I am quite sure part of you will go on living in me. We have been such friends & I am sure we could not be seperated [*sic*]. You see you are really the only friend I have ever had, or ever am likely to have, we used at one time to think we should end like the 2 old brothers in Nicholas Nickleby. . . . Think of me at eleven o'clock at night when I go to sleep.

In November Lady Ida appeared in the King's Bench Division for her long-awaited action against Field. As it turned out, the actual trial was nothing like the ordeal which the family had feared. It was a brief one-day hearing. Her counsel made a brisk, efficient speech alleging fraud and breach of duty against Field in that he had misappropriated £7,775 borrowed in Lady Ida's name. Field appeared but, to what must have been her Ladyship's profound relief, made no attempt to contest his guilt. The jury gave their verdict against him and judgement was given in Lady Ida's favour for her lost £7,775 and the costs of the action. As was claimed at the time, Lady Ida's honour had been vindicated and Field exposed for the fraud he was, but it was not hard to see why he had not defended himself. As an undischarged bankrupt, his own debts were enormous and there was not the faintest chance of Lady Ida or Sir George ever recovering the money they had been awarded by the court. Moreover, Owles's executors had still not recovered the money owing to them and, as long as they were not paid, there would be no end to 'the case'.

While the doom of the Sitwells was thus being prepared, an event occurred which symbolically marked the end of Sachie's childhood. On 16 December 1914, almost exactly a month after his seventeenth birthday, three German warships loomed out of the North Sea and bombarded Scarborough. Although the physical damage was real enough, the psychological effect was far greater. It was the end of an era for Scarborough, as Osbert recognised when he wrote a nostalgic novel

about the town ten years later with the title *Before the Bombardment*. Sir
George and Lady Ida were living in their by now accustomed state of cold
misery at Wood End when the bombardment took place. According to
local tradition, Sir George took refuge on the island in the ornamental
lake, fearing imminent invasion by the Germans, but by Osbert's account
he retired to the cellar, subsequently issuing instructions to Osbert, then
at the front, on how to avoid being shelled – 'retire to the undercroft'. Late
in December Sachie was in a nursing home with influenza, mistakenly
diagnosed as German measles; 'Brockie' wrote to him there on New
Year's Eve 1914, lamenting the dire effects of the bombardment and 'the
loss of life & loss of employment inflicted on many people who were
deprived of employment, myself among that number. None of the schools
will reopen after the holidays in Scarborough & what I am going to do I do
not know. Two hundred families have fled from the South Cliff [the smart
residential quarter] alone. . . .'[61] Sachie's housemaster, A.A. Somerville,
sent him his best wishes for the new year with a form for the Eton Officers
Training Corps for Sir George to sign on his behalf. 'May this year end
more happily than last year!' the letter concluded.

It was a pious hope. The spring of 1915 was to bring the most traumatic
experience of Sachie's life as 'the case' moved inexorably to its final
dénouement. Since Miss Dobbs the previous summer had successfully
appealed against the original judgement holding her responsible, the
solicitors for the Owles estate turned to Sir George for the repayment
of their late client's £6,000 loan plus interest. If they did not obtain
satisfaction, they threatened to prosecute everyone involved: Field,
Herbert, his 'agent' and Lady Ida. Since Lady Ida had already secured
judgement against Field, they now had no alternative but to allege a more
serious charge than non-payment of a loan, that of conspiring to cheat and
defraud Miss Dobbs when Field and Lady Ida had originally persuaded her
to guarantee the bill. Sir George's obstinate self-righteousness almost as
much as Lady Ida's fecklessness brought on disaster. Lady Ida, backed
by the Londesboroughs, who were sophisticated enough to see what the
outcome must otherwise inevitably be, had been trying frantically to get him
to settle with the Owles estate. He adamantly refused to do so as a matter of
principle. His view was that Field had been judged a criminal in a court of
law; it was he who had obtained the money from the moneylender and,
therefore, he who ought to repay it. This was patently absurd since it was
obvious that Field could not do so. The inevitable result was that on Friday,
15 January 1915, at Marlborough Street Police Court, Lady Ida, Field and
Herbert were prosecuted for conspiracy to defraud Miss Dobbs.

Initially the Sitwells, perhaps buoyed up by the success of the Field case, did not seem to realise the possibility of the consequences. In mid-January 1915 Osbert's letters to Sachie from the front were full of pessimism about the war – 'I can't tell you how I hate the War. Nothing but dead animals. . . . I think [it] will end in about November 1988 or 9 . . .' – and requests for fresh fruit and Bar-le-Duc jam. Only on 22 January, the day of a further hearing at the Police Court, did Osbert mention 'Mother's case' and ask how long it would be going on.[62] 'I think the case against your mother has practically broken down,' Sir George wrote optimistically to Sachie at Eton on the 23rd. Sachie, after having received this blinkered letter from his father, was, however, well aware of his mother's anguish and wrote her a supportive letter, to which she replied on 26 January with a torn and incoherent missive:

> My darling little man, Your letter has touched me so much. You must know by now how much I love you & if I am (which I fear is often) the least bit irritable – it is (text torn off) my darling I *am so* [double underlining] miserable. . . . I do hope Osbert is not very unhappy about the case. I saw Lewis who says he is not to worry. Darling I have stupidly torn the paper so please forgive it all like this. My best love darling & I love you just as much as I ever did.[63]

If Sir George Lewis did tell Lady Ida that there was nothing to worry about, his confidence was certainly misplaced. After a week's adjournment, Field gave evidence on 12 February about lending Lady Ida money in 1911 to pay both hers and Osbert's debts; the magistrate committed the defendants for trial at the Central Criminal Court.

Sachie came up from Eton to comfort his mother in the week before the trial opened on Monday, 8 March. 'I was miserable at your going [back to Eton] it was the greatest comfort having you with me,' she wrote in a distracted note on 4 March. Osbert returned from France for the trial, which he still seems to have taken lightly, writing to Sachie on the eve of its opening: 'On [Monday] Mama will give her farewell performance at the Old Bailey. Father is going to give evidence, & probably me. . . .' Indeed, the case initially had its comic aspects centring on the ludicrous figure of Miss Dobbs, with the prosecuting lawyers and even the presiding judge playing music-hall turns. Miss Frances Bennett Dobbs, of Northside, Streatham Common, told the court that she had her work cut out to defend herself against 'the plunder gang' that followed her, not only Herbert, who had proposed marriage to her, but also a previous fiancé, a clergyman who had deceived her. When asked by counsel to identify 'the plunder gang', she replied: 'They are connected with the Church . . . the clergy of the Church of England are my enemies. . . .'[64] No one, however, was much interested in the plight of the rich Miss Dobbs; *The Times* headlines reporting the case regularly made the point – 'Lady Ida Sitwell's Bills'. Things became deeply embarrassing for the Sitwells on Thursday, 11 March, when some of the letters Lady Ida had written to Field were read out in court. One of them referred to her efforts to get rich women to back her bills:

> it really seems impossible to make women understand that our transactions are absolutely sound and straight doesn't it? So do try and get me a man as a second backer. Of course I can push the ladies into good society if they would only have faith, but somehow they don't seem to believe my word. I never would have believed what funk sticks women can be. . . .

The worst possible impression was made by one which read: 'I find Glass is only 20. My boy [Osbert] thinks if he were with him for a few days he could get hold of him and he quite hopes if he joins the 11th Hussars there must be some boy he can get hold of. . . .'[65]

Osbert was appalled and humiliated. 'My dearest Sach,' he wrote, 'I am sick of life. What do you think of the way I have been treated? I return, to my relief, to the trenches on Sunday. . . .'[66] Edith, frantic at the thought of how upset Sachie would be by the newspaper reports, wrote the following day:

> My darling Sachie, I know how painful all this is for you, but try not to worry too much about it, my poor old darling. – A notice will be put in the paper after the case is over, that Osbert *never* did any of these foul things. I saw Osbert today, and he was quite calm, though naturally *awfully* upset, as I am, and as you must be. She is a *monster*. There is no other word for it. It is very sordid. My poor darling, I feel for you *very much*; anything of this sort is so dreadful for anyone young like you; it is horrible that anyone young should have to hear what you have to hear.
>
> Osbert is well again, and goes back to the front, I am afraid on Sunday. . . .[67]

But Osbert did not go back to the front that Sunday. On Saturday, 13 March, Mr Justice Darling pronounced sentence. Field got three years, Herbert was acquitted with a warning and Lady Ida was condemned to three months in Holloway. 'Lady Ida Sitwell Sentenced', *The Times* headline read, 'Judge's Severe Censure'. Mr Justice Darling was hard on Lady Ida, charging her with 'cruel and heartless treatment' of Miss Dobbs; 'you must have known with your knowledge of the world and education and knowledge of affairs that what you were doing was a dishonest thing,' he told her, adding that he would have liked to have passed a more severe sentence and was only prevented from doing so by consideration for her state of health.

At Eton Sachie learned of his mother's imprisonment from the *Sunday Express* and was overcome by horror, shame and pity. 'What is going to happen to poor Mother now. It is really too dreadful,' he wrote to Osbert. 'Please write to me. . . . I do hope everybody will not see it. Do come down tomorrow.'[68] Osbert, however, fled to Renishaw with his father and did not write to Sachie until Monday, leaving him in anguish for the week-end:

> My darling . . . I didn't write to you before, as I was making frantic efforts to get you here for the week I'm here. But I think it's really wiser of you not to come.
>
> The whole affair is the most awful tragedy. There is nothing to be said about it. The sentence ends on June 2nd or possibly a fortnight before.
>
> I am here alone with Father. Return to fight on Sunday, or even Sat. . . . I am broken hearted. . . .'[69]

Sachie was frantic for news of his family; he felt totally abandoned. Edith and Helen Rootham were horrified on receiving a miserable letter from him to hear that he had been left at Eton to suffer the consequences of the newspaper headlines. On Tuesday, 16 March, three days after the sentence, Helen wrote to him:

> I am distressed beyond all words to find that you are still at Eton . . . your Father wrote to Mr Somerville on Saturday asking him to let you go to him, and I thought you were joining him and Osbert. I am miserable at the thought that you have had these three dreadful days at Eton. . . . Edith and I dined with your Father and Osbert on Saturday. I have never seen anything so sad, but at the same time so wholly worthy of admiration as Osbert's conduct. In his great distress for your poor mother, I really believe he entirely forgot the awful wrong she had done him. . . .'[70]

Sachie did get leave from Eton, but he was back there by 28 March when Helen wrote to him reporting on his mother's state of mind in prison, where, apparently, she behaved exactly as she did at home: 'she is quite contented and happy, and just lies quietly in bed surrounded by flowers'. Another visitor described her as continuing her mannerism of taking out a lace handkerchief and flourishing it as she talked, completely oblivious to the fact that the handkerchief was now rough cotton with 'HM Prison' stamped on it.

Sachie spent the Easter holidays with his father, Aunt Florence and Sister Edith at Bournemouth, from which dreary exile he wrote piteously to Osbert on 25 April: 'My holidays are a perfect Hell now. Mother in Holloway, you at the front and with Father alone at Renishaw.'[71] His mother was released on 18 May before the date to which she had been sentenced, 2 June. Sachie wrote her a loyal letter from Eton on 19 May: 'Darling Mother . . . I want you to know that in my estimation you are completely and entirely innocent. Even if I thought you guilty your magnificent courage and bravery would take it away. I am sure you know what *I* think. . . .'[71]

Sachie – and Osbert – blamed their father, now known as 'the bloody Baronet', for their mother's imprisonment and so, it seems from Lady Ida's reply, did she. 'Thank you very much for your dear letter,' she wrote in a brief, self-absorbed note from Renishaw on the 20th. 'I was so glad to get it. I am very miserable. I don't think Father realizes what I have gone through he is trying to make out he wants me to be happy but he has money absolutely on the brain but doesn't mind putting my money into his pocket.'[73] 'The case' had been the last straw in the marital relationship; both parties now felt irremediably aggrieved by the behaviour of the other. Lady Ida was, in effect, a broken woman, tainted by scandal, her wings now financially clipped for ever. Sir George withdrew finally into his shell. From Renishaw in June, Osbert reported:

> We are having a charming time here. Father has not spoken to Mother or me for two days. I have never known him so trying before. The Trouble is as follows:
> Father complained to us yesterday about the cost of feeding Mother's spaniel [provided by Major Brockwell to cheer her up on her homecoming] 'really I can't afford it.' We both giggled. So Father said 'Oh! But I assure you. They're [*sic*] the dog-biscuits and etc.' So I asked him if dog-biscuits had gone up since the war. 'Really what an idiotic fool you are! What an idiot the boy is!! etc.' I then left the room with dignity, telling him he was the idiot. He then came upstairs, and said he would not have meanness imputed to him '[after] all I've done'.
> He hasn't spoken since. . . .[74]

For Sachie, Osbert and Edith, the family pantomime would have to run as a comic turn from now on. The situation at the heart of the comedy was black, but the public would not be allowed to see it; it would be all glitter, illusion, buffoonery and bravado like the *commedia dell'arte*. Their parents' eccentric personalities and odd relationship, the cause of the disgrace, would be turned into 'a source of innocent merriment'. As 'the Gingers' Sir George and Lady Ida were to be presented as a music-hall turn for the amusement of their children's friends. The family disgrace of 1915 not only united them against their parents – and especially their father – but also welded them into what Osbert called 'a closed corporation' against the possible slights of a hostile world. The character of their trio would be consequently aggressive and slightly paranoid. It would also be directed against the middle-class attitudes which had condemned their mother; they would be defiantly aristocratic, resolutely anti-bourgeois. Becoming writers, they would shock 'the Golden Horde'. 'That moment of a terrible time in our family history', Sachie wrote, 'was to tie the three of us together . . . in our determination to live, and leave a mark of some kind . . . it was to precipitate us into action, into taking pen in hand.'[75]

3

The Education of an Aesthete

1915–1918

'What an exciting world it was
When the three of us were young together:–
Even in trouble for being young
and having talent:–'

Sacheverell Sitwell, 'The Octogenarian'

The shock of his mother's imprisonment had a traumatic effect upon Sachie at the age of seventeen. Psychologically it led to a flight from reality; for the rest of his life he would be unable to face up to unpleasant facts. Paradoxically, it also heightened his interest in death and the macabre, her disgrace seeming to him confirmation of the existence of a dark abyss beneath the thin skin of normal human life.

Sachie had become aware of the ease with which human beings slip into a situation from which there is no escape. 'They have been caught in a trap; and their efforts to extricate themselves only involve them still further in damnation,' he was to write twenty years later in the semi-autobiographical 'entertainment of the imagination', *Dance of the Quick and the Dead*. His mother's sentence inspired a terrible chapter headed 'Purgatorio' describing the suffering of prisoners in the nineteenth century under the Hood-Beak or the Silent System. Hieronymus Bosch's paintings of Hell would be another source of inspiration.

The dark side of life, murder and the supernatural fascinated him. It had begun with Miss Lloyd's recounting of the Waterloo Bridge murder in his childhood at Scarborough; while still at St David's in 1910 he had been gripped by the mysterious death of an actor in an empty flat, and later by the fate of a man named Matterig, who committed suicide on Brighton beach, stabbing himself after cutting his left hand off, finger by finger, with his right. Just after leaving Eton he heard from Oscar Wilde's friend, Robbie Ross, about the nineteenth-century poisoner, Madeleine Smith, and remained almost in love with her. Years later, when a distinguished professor visited him hoping to interview him about French literature, he found him only interested in the Yorkshire Ripper – 'What would he have been like to his wife at breakfast after a night of murder?' His interest in crime was partly a congenital fear of boredom and the humdrum; he enjoyed the sensation of the extraordinary. 'I like things to be excessive,' he told an interviewer. 'Either very beautiful or very macabre.' Talking about crime, he told him how, in his view, beauty was often 'closely interwoven with the tortured and the violent'.[1] He had been frightened as a small child at Renishaw by his first intimations of mortality, a bony hand found sticking out of a slag heap, the charred remains of an old actress burned to death in her caravan on Eckington Common; they were to be recurrent images.

At Eton, art and literature were his refuge during 'the case' years of 1912–1915; his aesthetic predilections were already beginning to develop. He was indulging them, ordering objects far beyond his means and, increasingly, failing to pay his bills. As early as 1911 he made his first order from the celebrated ballet bookseller, C.W. Beaumont, to whose shop in the Charing Cross Road Osbert had introduced him, spending his entire monthly allowance – 10s – on a biography of Karsavina as a result of the huge success of Diaghilev's Ballets Russes in London during the Coronation celebrations that year. Osbert took him to hear Chaliapin and, in March 1913, to see Nijinsky and Karsavina in *Spectre de la Rose*; the Ballets Russes had a profound effect upon him as it had upon all art-lovers of his generation. Subsequently Osbert had bought him Leon Bakst's *The Decorative Art* for the then staggering sum of four guineas, and Sachie had become an avid collector of anything to do with the Russian ballet, spending more than his pocket money on old programmes and periodicals like the expensive (it cost 10s a month) *Gazette du Bon Ton*, with its hand-coloured plates of costumes by Bakst.

From the outset of 1915, at the height of his misery over his mother, he embarked on an orgy of collecting. His papers include correspondence with enamel studios and suppliers of arts and crafts, with Douglas Cockerell at W.H. Smith's bindery, and with monks and nuns at various abbeys where illumination had been revived; there are also catalogues and bills for De Morgan pottery, Royal Lancastrian lustred pottery, Gaudier-Breszka cats from the Omega workshops and Japanese prints and paintings. *The Annals of Chinese and Japanese Art* were among his aesthetic bibles. He was fascinated by the decorative arts of Japan, an interest which flowered decades later in one of his best travel books,

The Bridge of the Brocade Sash. In May 1915 he commissioned a painting from the Japanese dealer, Ken Hoshino, for 14s 6d, and enquired about another, possibly a screen, from Yamanaka & Co. of Bond Street, who estimated that it would cost him about 5s per square foot. His expenditure on ballet books and special issues that year was, considering his income, prodigious; by 13 November his debt to C.W. Beaumont, 'long overdue', was 18s 6d. Pointers to future interests were a copy of *Royal Palaces of Spain* from The Times Book Club for 5s 4d, and a subscription to *The Gypsy*, a new quarterly published by the Pomegranate Press. His correspondents included one Thomas B. Mosher, Publisher, of Portland, Maine, who offered him some volumes of *The Bibelot* to complete his set and who later, in response to a request from Sachie, sent him a photograph, adding with some surprise, 'I am very pleased to do this although I fear you may possibly be disappointed as I am no longer young and truth compels me to say not particularly attractive. . . .'[2]

Sachie was already interested in the modern movement in art. A note in his hand, dated '24.VIII.1915' on the back of a letter from The Times Book Club informing him that *L'Art de Notre Temps* had ceased publication for the time being, reads: '1. Blast – Vortex. 2. Gaudier-Bresyka [*sic*]. 3. Horace Brodzky. 4. Henri Matisse.' He corresponded with F.T. Marinetti, the leader of the Futurists, whose manifesto advocated the destruction of museums and libraries as embodiments of the deadweight of the past and that artists should, like Baudelaire, draw their inspiration from '*l'Heroisme de la vie moderne*': crowds, factories, automobiles and aeroplanes. Marinetti rejected the status quo and anything founded on 'wisdom' and 'reason': 'Let us leave Wisdom behind like a horrible mine,' he exhorted. 'Let us throw ourselves to be devoured by the Unknown, not because we are desperate, but simply to enrich the bottomless reservoirs of the Absurd!'[3]

Such iconoclastic bombast exactly fitted Sachie's view of his parents' world and the bourgeois certainties which had plunged the younger generation into war. At Eton the obituary notices in the *Eton College Chronicle* were a regular feature; now they were not of elderly masters or Old Etonians gathered to their fathers in the fullness of time but of young men whom Sachie had known, many of them still in their teens. They would soon include some of his closest friends. At a House Debating Society meeting on 25 September 1915 he opposed the idea that sending married men to the front was shameful: 'Surely it is still more shameful that young unmarried men should go . . . [their] extinction would mean the absence of a younger generation.' In Serbia old men over fifty were sent to the front on every possible occasion; Sachie suggested that Britain should follow the Serbian example. 'It is too often forgotten that old age is a quantity, and not necessarily a quality,' he argued. '. . . I should like to see the "Old Age Pensions" given to the young, and free education given to the old.'[4]

In 1914 he had found an English translation of Flaubert's *Salammbô* in the Post Office at Eckington during his summer leave. It was, he later wrote, a discovery which 'has probably had more effect upon my life of the imagination than any other single fact except those accidents of birth which gave me my sister and brother'.[5] He paid tribute to Flaubert's influence upon him in a late poem, whose title is the opening sentence of *Salammbô*, 'C'était à Mégarra, faubourg de Carthage', recalling the images of the North African sunlight striking the carapaces of the tortoises on the shore and the Carthaginians' query as to who could be this race of men who crucified lions? 'All of which created an instant, if brutal antiquity . . . and gave me the first delight I had ever experienced from the written word.' It was a sensation he never forgot and would constantly try to recreate:

> But Flaubert was a master,
> the supreme master in prose . . .
> And he could light up the mind as no one else
> Making me determine to extend and widen however little
> the boundaries of feeling and of apprehension
> . . . And to try for the hand of a professional
> in describing music, painting, architecture and
> many lesser things . . .[6]

Sachie believed that everything he subsequently wrote in prose had its roots in his first reading of Flaubert's extraordinary historical novel. Its 'undisciplined lyricism', as Cyril Connolly called it, combined with the scenes of torture and mutilation ('violence and beauty'), greatly appealed to him. It was an unfortunate influence. *Salammbô*, although greatly admired in the nineteenth century, is nowadays almost unreadable for its subject matter and over-ornate style.

He sent copies of Flaubert's novels to Osbert and spread the gospel of French literature among his friends at Eton. One of them, Cecil Sprigge, later wrote to him from a convalescent home for officers in Dieppe that Flaubert's *La Tentation de St Antoine* and *Trois Contes*, and Balzac's *Le Curé de Tours* had roused him from 'the intellectual and spiritual torpor with which I had drugged myself on Dickens, Thackeray and the Eneid'.[7]

Despite his complaints to Osbert in 1914 that Eton was like a prison and its inmates no better than convicts, Sachie had found a circle of congenial friends by the time of his mother's imprisonment. Most of them, like himself, had been unpopular when they had at first arrived at the muscular, games-orientated school. Ivor Spencer-Churchill, son of the Duke of Marlborough and Consuelo Vanderbilt, recalled how he and Sachie had both been so disliked in their respective Houses that no one would 'mess' with them and they had had to eat alone; by the time Sachie was sixteen, both were members of an inter-House clique of like-minded friends and, in September 1915, Sachie was unanimously elected to the 'Library' (i.e. becoming a prefect), which indicated a certain amount of popularity.

He was an attractive boy: tall and willowy, with faun-like charm, a head rather like the fashionable Pan, with reddish gold curls, small ears set close to his head and green eyes, which quickly lit with amusement, crinkling as his mouth curved upwards. He was good company despite the intense gloom of his letters to Osbert, his inherited hypochondria and talk of 'nerves'. His sense of the ridiculous was enhanced by the illogical traditions and Byzantine hierarchy of public school. Some years later he told Anthony Powell one of his favourite incidents when, during a service in chapel, a boy threw a lighted firework into the aisle. Instantly, to a background of bangs and sparks, the Lower Master rose majestically to pronounce anathema: 'The boy who has done this thing has disgraced himself as an Etonian, as a gentleman, as a Christian, and as a man.' Sachie's comment was: 'The Lower Master's descending order of values was so good.'[8]

Sachie had begun his Eton life in the top classics division, but he later specialised in history, choosing as his tutor one of the most brilliant young masters, C.H.K. Marten, later Provost of Eton and employed by King George VI to teach history to the future Queen Elizabeth II. He worked hard enough to come second in the competition for the Rosebery history prize in December 1915, but on the whole his school work came second best to his other interests. He and his friends at Eton were interested in poetry, modern art, the Russian ballet, French literature and music – their craze was listening to the gramophone in the room above the school tuck shop – and Sachie was already beginning to run up debts with the Bond Street music shop, Chappell's, for gramophone records. Most of them were members of the Essay Society, where they read papers on the Post-Impressionists (Sachie) or the 'Times of Louis XV' (Ivor Spencer-Churchill). Sachie's friends included Yvo Charteris, son of Lady Wemyss, one of the Souls; Victor Cunard, cousin of the fascinating

Nancy; and Victor Perowne, whose poems were published to favourable reviews in April 1915.

Ivor Spencer-Churchill was the school 'siren', lusted after by many. Homosexuality was a part of the ethos of Sachie's circle, the natural accompaniment of 'decadent' aesthetic attitudes. There is no evidence that Sachie was ever homosexual, although many of his friends at Eton were. 'It's distinctly up to you', Cecil Sprigge wrote to him from France in March 1916, 'to write and read an Essay entitled "The Development of Greek Ethics" ending up with an eulogy of homosexualism and a plea for its recognition in the modern state. Would the Essay Society survive it? . . . ' Many of Sachie's aesthetic friends were in the Officers Training Corps, where their activities were not necessarily warlike, as Leonard Bower had written at the end of August, reporting the goings-on at the OTC camp: 'Johnny Barnard and A. Bishop behaved too disgracefully on the last night at Camp. They & the Pink Ribbon Brigade went to the latrine & never went to bed but ———. Everyone was beginning to get affected by that mania. . . .'9

The 'mania' proved to be the downfall of Sprigge, who had been hoping to contribute to the first number of Edith's poetry review, *Wheels*, but who wrote to Sachie on 12 September 1916 telling him that he must withdraw as he was about to be involved in a 'painful *cause célèbre*', which would entail his retirement from his regiment and 'disappearance from polite society'. 'I am paying the penalty for "seeing red" on one unfortunate occasion. How Victor P[erowne] and C[unard, both homosexual] will enjoy having another scandal to discuss. . . . Believe me,' Sprigge continued, 'you are one of the very few whose friendship I hate to be obliged to forego. . . . I hope you will think of me in charity, & excuse in your heart the vulgarity of my being discovered in an over-literal discipleship of Plato.' Cecil's father, Sir Samuel Squire Sprigge, editor of the *Lancet* and Chairman of the Society of Authors, a doctor and a nephew by marriage of Robbie Ross, should have been understanding; instead, he sent Cecil to a private 'nervous hospital'. Sachie, however, wrote him an immediate, loyal letter on 15 September, to which he replied:

> I cannot say how touched & moved I was by your letter. Your attitude is most generous & quite undeserved. . . . To people like you who are prepared to overlook (I hope not to condone) the perversity and inconsistency of the action which brought me to my downfall, I shall owe a debt of my gratitude which (as Oscar Wilde says) I shall be glad never to be able to repay.10

The late summer of 1915 was a turning-point in Sachie's life. At the beginning of the summer holidays, in the last week of July, he booked a room for himself for two nights at the Complete Angler by the Thames at Marlow to be near Osbert, whose regiment was encamped there. For two days the brothers talked about their future as they walked among the hanging beechwoods on the hills above the river or sat in the hotel garden in the high summer heat listening to the sound of the water rushing over the weir. 'How well I remember on both mornings wondering if I would be able to write poetry when I was older,' Sachie wrote of that moment when he resolved to become a poet.[11] On both nights he and Osbert travelled to dine in the epicentre of London artistic Bohemian life, the Eiffel Tower, whose steamy windows overlooked the street where a barrel-organ played, a sound which ever after recalled for Sachie, with the tumbling of the weir water, the moments of decision. The restaurant in Percy Street off the Tottenham Court Road was run by its Austrian proprietor named Stulik on Robin Hood lines: he allowed his needier clients an almost unlimited degree of credit while over-charging the rich. It had a genuine artistic ambience: its walls were covered with paintings by Stulik's clients, many of whom were extremely talented, and Wyndham Lewis and his assistant, William Roberts, had created a Vorticist Room on an upper floor.

It was Sachie's first introduction to High Bohemia. That evening as he sat at a table with Osbert and Yvo Charteris, he met Nancy Cunard and Iris Tree but was too shy to speak to them; they were both poets, both young and beautiful. There was a strong contingent of artists: Dora Carrington, with her bobbed pale yellow hair and her 'distinctive but classless appearance'; Walter Sickert, whom both Osbert and Sachie knew well as the lover of their aunt, Mrs Swinton; Nina Hamnett, who was to give Sachie a letter of introduction to Modigliani; Wyndham Lewis, soon to become a friend; and Augustus John, whom Sachie described as having 'a kind of aura and a beard-blown . . . blue-eyed Gypsy arrogance which was peculiar to him'.[12]

Those two idyllic days and magical nights in August 1915 were brought brusquely and inevitably to an end by a telegram from 'the bloody Baronet' summoning him to Renishaw. But for Sachie, the die was cast. 'A climacteric evening when much was decided. . . . A strange, strange moment,' he later recalled, 'and the first poems I wrote were written in that same month of August when I returned home.'[13]

Sachie was haunted in that late summer of 1915 by what he called 'that feeling of imminence; of everyone leaving school, and going into the

Army, or being in it already and in likelihood of being, at best, wounded, or else killed'.[14] At that time the life expectation of a young officer at the front was rumoured to be about six weeks. Eton seemed an irrelevance when Osbert and his friends were either in or about to go to France. 'I suppose you are longing to get away from Eton. Lord, how I hated the place the last year or two!' his cousin, Peter Lycett Green, wrote from the 3rd Battalion the Grenadier Guards attached to the British Expeditionary Force. That autumn he was severely wounded and had to have a leg amputated. 'I can quite understand it is pretty bloody at Eton now,' E. Wyndham 'Bimbo' Tennant wrote from Osbert's mess in France. 'It isn't really bad out here, & I'm rather enjoying it. It would be quite a bearable existence were it not for the tragedies that come so suddenly & make one so miserable.'[15] He, too, was a young poet, one of Sachie's many friends who died in the war.

The tragedy for Sachie was the death of Yvo Charteris, killed by a stray bullet at the age of nineteen on 17 October 1915. They had not seen each other since the night at the Eiffel Tower in August. Sachie had insisted that he accompany Osbert to stay at Renishaw that month, sending him a telegram, 'I shall never speak to you again if you don't come', but Yvo was ill in London at his mother's home in Cadogan Square and left for France in September. The misery was made worse by false reports of his death a week before. On 6 October Edith had written Sachie a letter of condolence about Yvo: 'He was such a great friend of yours; & he was devoted to you. . . . He said to me "I love Sachie".' She hastily followed it up three days later: 'It is all a muddle about Mr Charteris. He isn't (or wasn't dead). . . .' But just over a week later she heard the bad news before Sachie did: 'My darling, Yvo was killed yesterday. It is too awful. How curious that rumour of his death a week ago was! . . . he felt no pain, was shot in the chest and died instantly.'[16] Sachie attributed his death to the malevolence of an older officer, as he told Susan Hill: '[He] was sent out on an entirely useless wirecutting operation because, I think, his horrible commanding officer disliked him.'[17]

The war against the older generation had already begun on the Sitwell home front. Ginger was being particularly difficult in 1915–1916, no doubt as a result of 'the case', as Osbert wrote to Sachie from France: 'Father, *Gott strafe* him, is being bloody. He has nearly got me turned out of the Guards Club . . . by giving me no money so that I can't pay my subscription.'[18] When Sachie pleaded with Edith to support him at Renishaw during the Easter holidays, she told him she dared not:

I realise that Ginger is in the sort of state that it would be most dangerous for me to go down alone. I don't see how I would ever get away again.

My darling, it *isn't* a lack of love for you. Only I *have* to think of the future, when you get away for good. It would be fatal if I once let them get a grip on me again. . . .

For heaven's sake, burn this as soon as read.

I shall let you have books, so as to try and make the time as little awful for you as possible. Would you like Baudelaire's 'Fleurs de [*sic*] Mal?'[19]

By June, Sir George was on the verge of another nervous breakdown, or so he seems to have thought. Osbert was at Wood End with them, having sprained both ankles falling out of a taxi in London. Sir George, he reported to Sachie, had travelled from Renishaw to Scarborough in a special invalid's carriage with a bed in it costing £7 10s, and insisted that he must have one for his return. 'I asked Ginger what was the matter with him . . . & he replied "The nerves of my BRAIN are affected" in which sentiment I agreed heartily. . . .'[20] At Wood End, Sir George spent the day resting with his head out of the window: ' "Oh, I am alarmed. . . . But I find this treatment helps me. It rests the spine, I get fresh air, & it interests the passers-by. But I am alarmed!" '[21]

Between Renishaw and Wood End, Osbert and his mother, with Sachie's approval, got their own back on Sir George by annoying his favourite servants, the Justins. 'Father says Osbert and I have got rid of the Justins,' Lady Ida wrote to Sachie from Wood End on 8 July; and, at the end of the month: 'Isn't it splendid about the Justins – he says he is leaving as Father is the only one he can get on with. . . .'[22] Lady Ida inadvertently left a letter of Sachie's lying around; reading it, Sir George found that he, too, was part of the conspiracy to get rid of the Justins, as he wrote furiously on 31 July to Osbert, now in London at the Curzon Hotel:

Your Mother put on my table here an old letter from Sachie, which I thought she intended me to read, which has the following:

'How wonderful you have been over the Justins. Really it is a triumph for us. I am so pleased.'

I hope there will be no more pretence that the getting rid of my servants when I was ill wasn't done on purpose.[23]

Sir George's weapon against his children was money, a potent one as far as Osbert and Sachie were concerned, less so for Edith, to whose well-being he barely contributed. He had always hated spending money, except on things which pleased him. A pathetic letter from his man-servant, Robins, to Osbert in 1913 begged Osbert to send him money towards his suit: 'I would not ask you only I do not like asking Sir George as he is not in the best of tempers, and I would very much like to pay for it before Xmas. . . .'[24] History does not relate whether Osbert was able to oblige as he was constantly in debt; piles of contemporary bills for luxuries like Asprey cuff-links and hired Daimler motor-cars testify to his expensive tastes. The war had made Sir George's economies more obsessive, even reaching a point, according to Osbert, when he offered to pay Sachie's Eton fees in sacks of potatoes. To get their own back, his children teased and ridiculed him. On one occasion he remarked, stroking his silky beard: 'It's a pity you children haven't got a little of this sort of thing.' Later at luncheon, the three young Sitwells appeared wearing beards designed by Edith 'made out of the hideous, lightly tasselled fringe of an orange-coloured rug . . . fastened over the ears with two loops of tape, and had bells attached to them, which, with the movement of the jaws when eating, gave out a melodious alpine tinkle'.[25] Sir George's riposte was to give no indication whatsoever that he had noticed anything unusual.

With Osbert in the army and Sachie at Eton, Edith had been the first of the three to 'take pen in hand' with the publication of her poem 'Drowned Suns' in March 1913, followed by her first volume of poetry, significantly entitled *The Mother and Other Poems*, in October 1915. It was principally her influence which had determined that the Sitwells should make their mark as poets. 'Perhaps, in my own case,' Sachie wrote, 'I was as much of a pupil of my sister as any one poet has been of another.'[26] After her death he wrote in tribute to her inspiration:

> That was my first beginning,
> And you prompted it,
> My sister;
> Were ever such hands as yours for poetry?
>
> To live as a young man in your flowering shade
> Was wonderful indeed,
> You could read a poem, and inspire one to poetry
> By the inflections in your voice,
> So that one went out, and the street musician
> Was a starving genius,
> The barrel-organ with tongue of metal,

Turning, churning in the rain,
Became all London in a hot sun,
Burning.[27]

Edith made the dingy flat she shared with Helen Rootham, four flights up in a mansion block in an unfashionable part of London, Moscow Road, Bayswater, into an intellectual 'salon' by sheer force of personality. Aesthetes and poets who climbed the stairs for mugs of murky tea and iced buns did so because they either admired Edith or were curious about her; there were no material compensations. Brian Howard, who first visited Edith there as a precocious seventeen-year-old poet up from Eton in 1922, was disdainful about her surroundings. Moscow Road was 'an uninviting Bayswater slum', while Pembridge Mansions 'looked like an inexpensive and dirty hospital' with 'a nasty green door'. As he wrote to Harold Acton:

I do not care for the people she usually has around her – to Saturday teas, for example, at all. They are common little nobodies. Also I don't like her teas – *as teas* at all . . . I got *one penny bun, and three-quarters of a cup of rancid tea in a dirty cottage mug*. Also I don't like her apartments, or, rather, room. It is small, dark, and I suspect, dirty. The only interesting things in the room are an etching by (Augustus) John, and her library, which is most entertaining. The remainder seems to consist of one lustre ball and a quantity of bad draperies. Miss Helen Rootham, whom she lives with, is one of those terrifyingly forceful women. . . .[28]

In 1915 when Edith was unknown, her 'teas' at Pembridge Mansions were attended by friends of Sachie and Osbert – Yvo Charteris, Victor Perowne and 'Bimbo' Tennant – Etonians and Guards officers, mixing oddly with the 'common little nobodies'. Poetry was the attraction. Sachie's contacts, through Eton and through Edith, were already carrying him towards the heady mixture of intellect, art and Society of the immediate post-war years of which he, Osbert and Edith were to be the icons. A typical letter from Victor Cunard to Sachie that year read: 'I plead guilty to not going to Edith's on Friday but Nancy [Cunard] carried me off to Chelsea. . . . I met Guevara [known to the Sitwells as 'Chile', a bisexual who painted Edith and was the first of her 'impossible' loves] Nancy's lover, he looks more than ordinary & dull, however I am prepared to believe he is a genius. . . .'[29]

The Sitwells' campaign against the old and the Philistine, promoting the cause of youth, free verse and modern art, was launched in 1916. On

11 May Osbert's war poem, 'Babel', was printed in *The Times*, under the auspices of Edith's mentor, Richard Jennings. In June Edith and Osbert published their first joint volume of poetry, *Twentieth Century Harlequinade*. Sachie's debut was to come in December with the publication of *Wheels*.

Wheels, which Edith characteristically described to Sachie as 'the Ultimatum', was the brainchild of Nancy Cunard, who wrote the title poem. The energy behind it was Edith's, who seized on the idea as the perfect launching-pad for a Sitwell-fired literary movement; she acted as editor and persuaded her publisher, Basil Blackwell, to produce it. It was presented as a counterblast to Edward Marsh's *Anthology of Georgian Poetry* and a challenge to the poetry establishment headed by the genial J.C. Squire, editor of the *London Mercury*. As an anthology of younger poets, its purpose was to promote modernism and free verse against the banal rhyming, scanning and 'simple' sentiments of the 'Georgians', described by Brian Howard as 'Varsity *naïveté*'. A further aim was to express disgust with the war and the domination of the old, who had been only too willing to sacrifice the young for their own survival.

The cover showed a nurse wheeling a baby in a perambulator. 'None of the contributors can be quite so young as that,' the *New Statesman* remarked sarcastically. Rebellion against their parents was a unifying link. 'One need only to be unable to get on with one's father to have all the glorious dead on one's side . . .', as Brian Howard, a contributor to the 1921 'Cycle', wrote. The frontispiece depicted a wheel whose spokes bore the names of the three Sitwells, Nancy Cunard, Iris Tree, Victor Perowne, E.W. Tennant, Arnold James and Helen Rootham. Sachie's contribution, a twenty-line poem 'Li Tai Pé Drinks and Drowns', was a short polished exercise in free verse influenced by translations from the Chinese. It displayed an ivory tower-like lack of concern about the war which was at variance with most of the other contributors, including Osbert, whose 'The End' was a war poem featuring monster snail-like creatures leaving slime upon the mud and 'an evil lichen that proclaims world doom,/Like blood dried brown upon a dead man's face'. His 'Twentieth Century Harlequinade' drove home the message of the sins of the old against the young, conjuring up sinister images of the *commedia dell'arte*, with aged pantaloons destroying ordinary human lives with their war.

Wheels was a squib rather than a salvo, but it created a sensation out of proportion to its slim size. The poetry establishment rightly interpreted it as an attack on their ideals. The *Times Literary Supplement* dubbed the young poets as 'on the whole, dour and morose, seeing nothing bright in the present and no bright hopes in the future'. With two exceptions, E.W. Tennant and Victor Perowne, whose poems harked back to a more accepted style, the reviewer accused them of being poseurs lacking in true poetic feeling. 'All this studied and determined melancholy is . . . broken in upon by Mr E. Wyndham Tennant with the rippling charm of "Home Thoughts". . . . He and Mr Victor Perowne are certainly the truest poets in the old sense – seekers after a simple fragrant beauty. . . .'[30] Osbert fought back in a characteristically pugnacious preface to the second edition in March 1917, entitled 'In Bad Taste', in which he attacked the 'platitudinous multitude' of critics and their 'favourite axiom: "That age is but a virtue, youth a sin" – This line is gloomy and this view is false. Life is a thing of joy and platitudes. Oh! to be simple now that Spring is here!'

Sachie was still at Eton when 'Li Tai Pé' was published in *Wheels*. However, 15 November 1916 was his nineteenth birthday, when he could be called up for the services. His family had been campaigning to keep him out of the army for as long as possible. Dr Salter was consulted and wrote a suitably pessimistic certificate as to his fitness:

> I hereby certify that I have attended professionally Mr Sacheverell
> Sitwell since childhood; that at the age of ten, he contracted four fevers
> in one year – measles, german measles, 3rd disease, and chickenpox;
> that he had never gained his full strength permanently since that age,
> and has been left with a weak heart for which he has had treatment . . .
> ever since; that the condition of his heart is that of tachycardia, it is
> dilated and the apex beat is in the nipple line; that in consequence of his
> weakness he is quite unable to run more than a few yards, he suffers
> from shortness of breath on any exertion more than the ordinary, and
> this is combined with a very tall growth of his frame; that in my opinion
> he is totally unfit for any form of active service.

As usual, however, the family – Lady Ida and 'Brockie' in particular – made a muddle of it. In September 1915 Sachie had had to go before an Army Board to pronounce on his fitness. 'If he is accepted [for the army],' Dr Salter had advised Lady Ida on 14 September after a consultation with Sachie, 'the excuse must be given that he is to go back to school until he is nineteen, and in the meantime move heaven and earth for a Commission.'[31] This advice was taken to heart by Lady Ida with unexpected results; Sachie was apparently pronounced fit to apply for a commission in the Grenadiers and was consequently passed as fit for service by a Special Board. As Sir George wrote crossly to Sachie on 1 October, 'You now see the result of fussing and bringing your mother into this. Of course it was the statement that you were likely to get a commission in the Guards that passed you. They would never have passed you as a private, but you may have to serve as one.'[32] 'Brockie' discovered that if Sachie were to join the OTC at Eton, he would probably be left in England at least for some time, and could not be called up in any case until after his nineteenth birthday. Sachie himself appeared to feel that if he was going to be bored and uncomfortable in the OTC, he might be better off in Osbert's regiment. Alarmed at the prospect of their ewe lamb going to the slaughter, Helen Rootham wrote on 5 October on behalf of Osbert and Edith: 'We all three feel that it would be a good thing if you entered the OTC. I think the fact that you might be bored is a very slight disadvantage compared with the other things. . . .' Osbert preferred not to be the means of getting him into the Grenadiers if that would mean him almost immediately being sent to France. 'As Major Scobell says you can get in, you obviously can, and there is no point in having a short training with a regiment which is on active service, when you can have a longer training and stay in England a bit.'[33]

Boredom, however, was the one thing which Sachie dreaded. He left Eton at the end of the Michaelmas Half, 1916, just before Christmas, and early in 1917 joined the 5th Reserve Battalion, the Grenadier Guards, stationed at Chelsea Barracks in London. This comfortable billet was no doubt the result of string-pulling by his brother. Osbert, now a captain, had been stationed there since the latter part of 1916 after contracting blood-poisoning in April, as a result of which he had been sent home. Sachie was even less suited than Osbert to military life, making, as he later described himself in relation to the Home Guard in the Second World War, a 'dreary and incompetent' soldier. He had no leadership qualities and lacked the mental toughness which enabled Osbert to cope with military arrogance. While disliking horses he equally never understood mechanics and never learned to drive. On the whole, however, his fellow officers were tolerant of his failings. As he wrote later:

My military incapacity must have been infuriating. On one occasion, on a manœuvre, the Commanding Officer told me to take his bicycle and ride off with it to deliver a message. I had never been taught to ride a bicycle, nor had I even handled one, so that I had to walk away wheeling this unfamiliar object, but even that piece of futility and ignorance brought down no wrath upon me.

Within a few months he had caught jaundice and lay an invalid at the Curzon Hotel, a Sitwell favourite, spoiled by Lady Sackville with presents of asparagus and Malmaison carnations. At the end of May he went to Renishaw to convalesce, returning to duty on 21 June. He seems to have spent a good deal of his time writing poetry in preparation for the 'Second Cycle' of *Wheels*, which appeared on 4 December 1917.

This time six of his poems were included: 'Tahiti', 'Barrel Organs', 'Trumpets', 'Song: The Feathered Hat', 'The Nightingale' and the long 'Soliloquy and Speech from "The Major of Murcia" '. 'Tahiti' contained some strong imagery and inner rhythms, which showed precocious talent for a twenty-year-old poet:

> Lanterns are lit – great stairs of light
> Shake in the water;
> All dank and wet I seem to climb,
> Swaying on soundless gold – go silently
> Above the land, unto the distant moon,
> Alone and ringing clear as a bell.

'The Nightingale', later retitled 'The Moon', a short poem of considerable beauty, owed a good deal to Keats. Sachie's shorter poems showed Edith's influence in their musical rhythms; Constant Lambert set two of them, 'The Moon' and, later, 'The Rio Grande', successfully to music. 'Barrel Organs' evoked Scarborough's fishing quarter in winter, glimpses of life behind the frosted glass doors of saloons, shop signs creaking in the wind, a drunkard reeling to his 'dreary starving home'. In poems like 'Trumpets' Sachie's intoxication with words and his facility for using them often carried him away into meaningless and repetitious sounds. The obscurity of which so many people complained was already there, but equally it was clear that he was an unusual and gifted poet. The *Times Literary Supplement* condescended with a few grudging lines: 'Mr Sacheverell Sitwell certainly gives us in "Tahiti" and "Barrel Organs" a taste of the luridly spectacular. . . . His "Soliloquy and Speech from 'The Mayor of Murcia' " we should appreciate more if it had a note of explanation. . . .' Sachie's fellow contributors were Edith and Osbert, Aldous Huxley, Arnold James, Iris Tree, Sherard Vines, E.W. Tennant and Helen Rootham. The *TLS* reviewer's highest but still unenthusiastic praise was for Helen Rootham, who 'had a clearer notion than any of her companions of the possibilities of poetry'.

Edith's and Osbert's talents for publicity had succeeded in attracting a good deal of attention for *Wheels*, although it was not, in literary terms, a heavyweight production. Despite all the trumpeting about 'modernism' and 'free verse', neither T.S. Eliot nor Ezra Pound was tempted to join the band. Edith had, however, succeeded in luring Aldous Huxley into her fold. Huxley was then overrated as a poet, although not – significantly – by Edith herself. As a member of the intellectual *haute bourgeoisie*, which was the backbone of Bloomsbury, he wrote condescendingly to his brother Julian about *Wheels* and the Sitwells:

> I am also contributing to the well-known Society Anthology, *Wheels*, in company with illustrious young persons like Miss Nancy Cunard, Miss Iris Tree and the kindred spirits who figure in the gossip page of the *Daily Mirror*. This year, containing as it does, selections from me and Mr Sherard Vines, it should be quite a bright production. The folk who run it are a family called Sitwell, alias Shufflebottom, one sister and two brothers, Edith, Osbert and Sacheverell – isnt [*sic*] that superb – each of them larger and whiter than the other. I like Edith, but Ozzy and Sachy are still rather too large to swallow. Their great object is to REBEL, which sounds quite charming; only one finds that the steps they are prepared to take, the lengths they will go are so small as to be hardly perceptible to the naked eye. But they are so earnest and humble [not qualities usually associated with the Sitwells] . . . these dear solid people who have suddenly discovered intellect and begin to get drunk on it . . . it is a charming type.[34]

Six months later Huxley had become a regular contributor, telling Julian: 'I rather like the notion of *Wheels* with its toreador attitude to the bloody-bloodies of this world.'

Eliot, later a friend of the trio, writing to Pound on 31 October 1917, called them 'Shitwell' (as, of course, did Pound): 'I have been invited to contribute to a reading of POETS: big wigs, OSWALD [*sic*] and EDITH SHITWELL, Graves . . . Nichols and OTHERS.'[35] He did not mention Sachie, who, as a practically unpublished poet still in his teens, was fortunate to be invited to perform at such a celebrity occasion. Probably he owed it, as he did so much, to Edith's insistence that he should be included. The timing helped: the reading was to be held at Lady Colefax's house on 12 December, shortly after the publication of *Wheels*. Huxley, describing the evening to his brother, was patronising about everyone there, himself and Eliot excepted, although he did graciously admit to enjoying dinner at the Sitwells afterwards, 'the best part of the whole affair':

I spent a strange day yesterday . . . being a performing poet for the sake of charity or something before a large expensive audience of the *BEST PEOPLE*. [Edmund] Gosse in the chair – the bloodiest little old man I have ever seen – dear Robbie Ross stage-managing, Bob Nichols thrusting himself to the fore as the leader of us young bards (*bards* was the sort of thing Gosse called us) – then myself, Viola [?Iris] Tree . . . and troops of Shufflebottoms, alias Sitwells bringing up the rear: last and best, Eliot. But oh – what a performance: Eliot and I were the only people who had any dignity: Bob Nichols raved and screamed and hooted and moaned his filthy war poems like a Lyceum Villain who hasn't learnt how to act . . . the Shufflebottoms were respectable but terribly nervous. . . .[36]

After that meeting at Lady Colefax's house Eliot and his wife, Vivien, became extremely friendly with the Sitwells. They regularly took tea together at a café near Marble Arch, an occasion which Eliot, not being English, seemed to regard as somewhat exotic; both the Eliots attended Edith's Pembridge Mansions tea parties. Eliot had published *Prufrock and Other Observations* in the summer of 1917; Sachie was influenced by him as he was by Jules Laforgue, the Symbolist, to whose work Eliot may well have introduced him. Eliot thought highly enough of Sachie as a poet to print a recent poem of his, 'Psittachus eois imit ratrix ales ab indis', in *The Egoist* in May 1918. When he wrote this poem Sachie must have been thinking of his Londesborough grandmother, or even his Beaufort great-grandmother, who used to drive out accompanied by a parrot which she was too old and blind to see was stuffed. He was always at his best when exploring the sensations of his memory:

> His voice, and vivid colours
> Of his breast and wings,
> Are immemoriably old;
> Old dowagers in crimped satin
> Boxed in their rooms
> Like specimens beneath a glass,
> Inviolate – and never changing,
> Their memory of emotions dead;
> The ardour of their summers
> Sprayed like camphor
> On their silken parasols
> Intissued in a cupboard.

Sachie was in distinguished company in *The Egoist*, with an article by

Ezra Pound and a poem by William Carlos Williams in the same issue; on the page opposite 'Psittachus' an advertisement announced the imminent publication by The Egoist Ltd of Wyndham Lewis's novel, *Tarr*. Eliot had a high opinion of Sachie's talent, writing to Mrs Jack Gardner in November that he had 'unusual poetic merit';[37] and when Sachie published his first solo volume of poetry, *The People's Palace*, on 15 June 1918, Eliot reviewed it favourably in *The Egoist*. 'We have attributed more to Mr Sitwell than to any poet of his generation,' he wrote. 'We require of him only ten years of toil.' It was high praise and a considerable achievement for a young man of twenty.

The title, *The People's Palace*, was taken from the Scarborough underground entertainment halls which had so fascinated him as a child. It was published by Blackwell as No. XXII of their 'Adventurers All' publications, described as 'A series of young poets unknown to fame', which had previously included Aldous Huxley's *The Burning Wheel*. Several of the poems in *The People's Palace* had already been printed in *Wheels*; most of them had been written in the spring of 1918 and almost all of them were still considered good enough nearly twenty years later by Sachie and Edith to be included in his *Collected Poems* (1936). Edith was not, however, always a wise judge; in an overly-eulogistic preface to the collected edition she held up one of his poems, 'Outskirts', as an example of Sachie's 'humanity':

> And here disposed upon the grass, I see
> Confetti-thick the amorous couples –
> What thoughts, what scenes, evoke evaporate
> In leaden minds like theirs
> Can I create them? . . .

The answer to this rhetorical question would seem to be clearly a negative. Sachie was not an interpreter of the human scene; his poetry, except on the subject of death, did not provide a universal meaning. He was a poet of images, rhythm, solipsistic sensation. Aldous Huxley hailed him as '*le Rimbaud de nos jours*'; Robert Nichols, admittedly a Sitwell partisan, called his work 'the most "advanced" poetry we have had so far'. To be 'advanced' was, however, in the eyes of the 'bloody-bloodies', dangerous and subversive; to be 'difficult' and out of the ordinary invited their censure. *The World*, a middlebrow gossip paper, was scornful: ' "The People's Palace" purports to be a collection of verse by Sacheverell Sitwell. Its sheer inanity is beyond description. The audacity of wasting precious paper, to say nothing of printing ink, on such unadulterated drivel take [*sic*] one's breath away.'[38]

By early 1918 Osbert and Sachie were established in a rented house in Chelsea, 5 Swan Walk, where they had already begun to create their own particular ambience of art, wit and style, which was to be the model for the aesthetes of the 1920s. The house overlooked the Chelsea Physic Garden and an old mulberry tree near the river. The two brothers, according to Sachie, 'lived extravagantly and had huge weekly bills . . . we knew all the painters and poets'. They led a rather grand Chelsea Bohemian existence; the same people who haunted the Café Royal and the Eiffel Tower were entertained at Swan Walk, when there would be drunken charades. On one occasion the subject of the charade was, as Sachie told Wyndham Lewis, 'The return of Lord Kitchener [drowned in 1916] from the "Hampshire" . . . "Chile" Guevara wrestled with [P.G] Konody and Augustus John and "the Icelander" [Haraldut Hamar, a young playwright usually known as 'Iceland'] were notably drunk.'[39] Among the poets whom Sachie met briefly was Wilfred Owen, introduced by Robbie Ross and Siegfried Sassoon. Owen came to Swan Walk for raspberries and cream in July 1918 before returning to France, where he was killed four months later. Then there was Arthur Waley, the eccentric, highly intelligent poet and translator of Chinese and Japanese verse, whose greatest work was the six-volume translation of the enormous tenth-century Japanese novel, *The Tale of Genji* (1925–1933), one of the most successful books of the inter-war period. Waley was a man of great intellect and erudition, an aesthete who was at the same time an ascetic, respected and loved by London intellectuals from T.S. Eliot to Bloomsbury. He and his equally eccentric companion, the wayward and rich Beryl de Zoete, a pioneer in anthropological studies, became great friends, admirers and encouragers of Sachie. There was also Walter Sickert, the poet W.H. Davies, author of *The Autobiography of a Super-Tramp*, Nina Hamnett, Aldous Huxley, Lytton Strachey and the Eliots.

Wyndham Lewis, whose Vorticist manifesto *Blast* Sachie had admired while still at Eton, was already a friend. Edith sat to him for a portrait and Sachie tried to get him commissions. In July Sachie wrote inviting him to a dinner party with Lytton Strachey – 'it ought to be vaguely amusing'; a week later he wrote reminding him about the dinner and asking him for two of his drawings – 'the Bacchic Festival . . . or the green Bacchus – or both – if you can spare them'. He also sent Lewis a copy of the recently published *The People's Palace*. By August Lewis's two drawings were framed, looking 'very beautiful, and very provocative evidently, from the feelings of the stupider who see them'.[40]

In August Sachie had to give up his intoxicating *vie de bohème* at Swan

Walk for the prosaic military surroundings of the Guards' Camp at Tadworth in Surrey. He was 'terribly depressed' and missing Osbert; 'all I can think of is living in Chelsea once more,' he wrote on arrival at Tadworth. 'Meanwhile, as for myself, I am sure I shall never be able to write again. . . .' To make things worse, an officer whom they both particularly disliked was in command at Tadworth and would be again at Aldershot. Sachie was also facing another medical board.

> I am not saying this like Mother [he wrote to Osbert], but really if I am meddled & muddled much more, I shall really become a maniac. I have never known anything to touch it for horror. Now the awful golf-tennis-cricket-ping-pong side comes in – and the mere anticipation strangles one . . . one is only 20 or 25 once – and one does not forgive these years being spoilt – especially in an Art like ours where hardly anyone can do much after they are 30 or 35. As it is they have driven all the *joy* [underlined twice] out of it, as far as you and I are concerned. As for me, if life or inclination is left, I shall be 22 before I get another chance, I'm sure.

Rebellious resentment against the hidebound establishment who had condemned him to take part in this war burst out:

> How I welcome the Russian assassinations. Oh! for a regime – a reign of terror – when all these pasteboard dummies may feel the pinpricks. It's the only way out of it now, I'm afraid.
>
>   However, I absolutely refuse to give in, or to submit – I am going to stick to my last gun – I'll get back one day. If there is a 'question-time' after the war, my turtle voice will reecho through the wilderness.[41]

Later that month he was moved to a training battalion at Albuhera Barracks, Aldershot. Most of the recruits were boys of eighteen and nineteen, many of them miners from his own part of the world, South Yorkshire and Derbyshire. He watched a farewell parade when several hundred of them left for France. Nearly fifty years later he wrote:

> I well remember the band playing 'The British Grenadiers' and the Commanding Officer saying in a broken voice that few of them would be living in a few weeks' time. . . . The awfulness of those concluding months of the War, and the apparent hopelessness of the outlook, had the effect of driving one in upon oneself and making one hold, more than ever, to what one loved and valued. Somehow or other I contrived to write poetry at Aldershot, but my mental and spiritual recreation was

in the news that Diaghilev and his company were about to return to London. . . . It was an augury of Peace and at that time there seemed to be no other.'[42]

'I became ever more futile in military life,' he wrote. Taking part in military manœuvres on the dreary silver-birch studded heath of Aldershot Plain, he could only concentrate on thoughts of Gabriele d'Annunzio, the Italian Romantic poet whom he then thought the greatest living writer, and of the Ballets Russes.

The return to London of Diaghilev's company in September 1918 after five years' absence was the sensation of the season. The first night of the revived Ballets Russes took place at the Coliseum, on 5 September, with scenery by Bakst and with Lydia Lopokova and Léonide Massine as the principal dancers. The company had lost some of its brilliance and glitter during the difficult war years since Nijinsky and Diaghilev had parted, but Sachie spent every night he could in the following weeks at the Coliseum. The great experience, however, for him was getting to know Diaghilev, even though 'owing to a surfeit of excitement' he could remember nothing of their actual meeting when he was introduced to him and shook his hand. Over the coming weeks they were to see a good deal of each other; the impresario was puzzled by Sachie's regular abrupt departures from supper parties to catch the last train back to Aldershot. 'Who is this Aldershot?' he asked Sachie one night. 'Is she your mistress?' He spoke in French, the only words he was ever heard to say in English being 'More chocolate pudding, please.'

Within weeks the war was over. On 11 November 1918, Armistice night, Diaghilev and Massine dined with Osbert at Swan Walk; among the other guests were Ethel Sands and Lalla Vandervelde, organiser of the famous poetry reading at Lady Colefax's the previous year. Sachie was not among them, having been kept down at Aldershot on duty, but he did arrive later in London by train to join Osbert and his guests at the great Armistice night party at Montague Shearman's apartment in the Adelphi. Outside, in the Strand and Trafalgar Square, huge crowds surged singing and dancing; inside the elegant walls of the Adelphi, the scene was equally bacchanalian, the guest list a roll call of London's cultural life, as described by Osbert:

> The spacious Adam room covered with decoration as fine as a cobweb, was hung inappropriately with a few large pictures of the Paris school – by Matisse, for example – and by several of the Bloomsbury Group. Here, in these rooms, was gathered the elite of the intellectual and

artistic world. . . . Tonight the Bloomsbury Junta was in full session . . .
Lytton Strachey, [Dora] Carrington, Clive Bell, Roger Fry, Mark Gertler,
Lady Ottoline Morrell, D.H. Lawrence and his wife, Maynard Keynes,
Duncan Grant, Lydia Lopokova and David Garnett.

Nina Hamnett battled her way from a celebration at the Café Royal, and
Augustus John came in wearing uniform and accompanied by land-girls
in leggings and breeches. Everyone danced; even Lytton Strachey's
gangling figure was to be seen 'jiggling about', as Osbert put it, 'with an
amiable debility'.[43]

Almost everyone there was to be a part of Sachie's social life in the early
post-war years, but for him the most important and influential figure was
Diaghilev. For Sachie, the massive Russian impresario who stood there,
impeccable, impassive, watching the dancers with a distant expression on
his pale, fleshy, sensuous face, represented everything which he found
most exciting in the future and in the past. Diaghilev had a presence, a
poise, which recalled Oscar Wilde. Indeed, he resembled Wilde in many
ways, in his aestheticism and his sensuality, both in food and sex;
Diaghilev's homosexuality was a part of his creativeness. He was the idol
of the modernist movement in French high culture, which Sachie himself
was to promote, of Proust and Cocteau, Picasso and Satie. He has been
described as the leader of the great trailblazers of the twentieth century.
Sachie, like everyone else in Diaghilev's world, sensed that the
bourgeoisie were everywhere in retreat, destroyed by their responsibility
for the war. 'I look forward to our Massacre of the Innocents when it [the
war] is over!' he had written to Wyndham Lewis. That night, a young man
who had been a guest at the Shearman party tried to set fire to Nelson's
column, a gesture against the Great British Past. Like Wilde and
Diaghilev, Sachie believed in the overriding importance of art. It seemed
to him that in its civilising influence lay the only hope for the future, which
he saw as dominated by the young, the spirit of the 1920s.

4

Looking for the Gods of Light

1919–1924

'Now the message is
   to enjoy ourselves,
And look for such there be,
   dead or alive, the Gods of Light –'

Sacheverell Sitwell, 'Looking for the Gods of Light'

On the frescoed walls of Montegufoni a twenty-three-year-old Sachie is portrayed as a harlequin, his long, slim legs encased in the diamond-patterned costume of the *commedia dell'arte* hero, his face concealed behind the traditional mask. Harlequin and the other figures of the *commedia*, Pierrot, the sad clown, with his white face, shaven head, conical cap, ruff and baggy white suit, Columbine, the heart-breaker, and Punchinello, the ruffian, were the icons of the modern movement. They appeared repeatedly in Picasso's paintings of the period, in those of Douanier Rousseau and Cocteau, as the theme of an important series of poems by Laforgue, who influenced Eliot, and in Diaghilev's ballet, *Petrouchka*. Sachie identified with Harlequin, the elusive figure darting in and out of the scene, light, witty, fantastic, apart from the crowd and yet at times of it. At other moments, when he felt buffeted by the world, he saw himself as Pierrot, the sad clown of Watteau's poignant portrait, *Le Grand Gilles*.

In the spring of 1919 he was Harlequin, ranging the world in search of novelty, beauty and enjoyment; his message, the modern movement in the arts. 'By now', he told a biographer, 'I had become terribly ambitious to do everything possible for and about the arts. As well as writing poetry I had ideas of becoming a sort of artistic impresario, mounting exhibitions, commissioning books and paintings, organising concerts and discovering geniuses.'[1] Having escaped from the army early in January, he went to Oxford as an undergraduate at Balliol, but found the immediate post-war university dull and depressing. Oxford was in the doldrums; the brilliant undergraduate life imagined by Max Beerbohm in *Zuleika Dobson* had vanished in the Flanders mud. The age of the aesthetes, followers of the Sitwells, personified by Harold Acton, Brian Howard and their friends, had not yet begun. Sachie found the climate abominable, the food worse, and his fellow undergraduates, mostly serious ex-servicemen intent upon their degrees, completely lacking in interest. Fortunately for him, Siegfried Sassoon, whom he had known since 1917, was living in rooms at Oxford and had intellectual friends like Raymond Mortimer down to stay.

It was through Sassoon that Sachie 'discovered' William Walton, then not quite seventeen, who was to become one of his closest friends and a Sitwell protégé for the next sixteen years. Walton, born on 29 March 1902, was five years younger than Sachie. He, too, was a North Country man, having been born in Oldham in Lancashire, but from a very different background, a small terraced cottage with the classic working-class outside lavatory. Both his parents were singers. His father had been one of the first students at the Royal Manchester College of Music in 1893, but was subsequently forced to earn his living as a worker in the local Platt's Ironworks; his mother came from a respectable family of furniture makers and upholsterers. Walton had not got on with his father, a martinet of violent temper who would rap him publicly over the knuckles whenever he made a mistake singing in the local choir, but his life had changed dramatically when, at the age of nine, he won a place as probationer chorister at Christ Church, Oxford. He began to compose at the age of eleven; in 1916 he heard Sir Thomas Beecham conduct *Le Coq d'Or*, an experience which turned him definitively in the direction of modern music. With the war the Walton family's precarious finances had reached rock bottom; William's father threatened to take him away from Christ Church, but the Dean, Dr Strong, the first of Walton's patrons, put up the £8 annual fee so that he could stay on in the choir school and become an undergraduate in October 1918.

When Sassoon took Sachie to see Walton, he was struck by the young composer's 'very clever-shaped head, rather like the great John Wesley'. Walton was small, thin, pale and frail-looking and seemed shy and reserved; he also appeared to be half-starved. Sachie used to ask him out to luncheon despite the food shortage and what he described as 'the fearful nastiness' of what was available. Walton's fragile appearance was deceptive; he was mentally robust and physically tough and would prove perfectly equal to life with the Sitwells, which, according to Peter Quennell, was 'like being ushered into a cage at the zoo, full of furious but friendly animals'. A friend described him as 'a little North Country womaniser', who would enjoy roistering Bohemian evenings with his friend and fellow Sitwell protégé, Constant Lambert, in circumstances which sometimes shocked the Sitwells.

Osbert, invited to tea with Sassoon and Sachie by Walton in his rooms at Christ Church, discerned above Walton's bird-like profile 'the so-called bar or mound of Michelangelo that phrenologists claim to be the distinguishing mark of the artist – and especially of the musician'. Walton had a long, thin nose reminiscent of a snipe's beak, very like Edith's, leading people to believe that he was an illegitimate Sitwell, a myth fostered by Constant Lambert, who spread the rumour that Walton was the son of Sir George by the lesbian composer, Dame Ethel Smyth. This initial audition, however, was an awkward occasion. Walton was very shy and when he sat down at the piano to play the slow movement from his Piano Quartet, it was obvious that, in Lady Walton's words, 'William couldn't play the piano . . . so it was very much on trust that Osbert accepted Sachie's view that William had great talent.'[2]

In that first term Sachie discovered, or rather rediscovered, another 'genius', Ronald Firbank, later an aesthetic cult figure but then in February 1919 living a reclusive life in rooms opposite Magdalen. Firbank, author of *Valmouth* and *Prancing Nigger*, was more like an exotic bird than a human being. Tall, thin and fine-featured, with fluttering hands, he was extremely shy and allegedly suffered an affliction of the throat, which prevented him from eating although not from consuming quantities of champagne. When invited to a dinner specially given for him, he refused to eat more than one green pea; he was so nervous and shy that, on an early visit to the Eiffel Tower, he had taken fright at the sight of the head-waiter and hidden under the tablecloth. The Sitwells had been admirers of Firbank since 1915, when Edith had read a passage from *Vainglory* quoted by a critic as being absolutely unintelligible; the 1890s' whiff of a green carnation about his prose and his persona particularly appealed to them. He had been living in Oxford for two years, a refugee from the khaki-clad, war-mad world with which he was totally out of sympathy. '*That awful persecution*' was his phrase for the war, persecution presumably of the Germans, whom, he said, he always found 'most polite'. When the War Office, after innumerable medical examinations, had finally pronounced him unfit for military service, then blundered and sent him his call-up papers, he had threatened to sue it for libel. For two years he had spoken to no one except the charwoman who cleaned his rooms and the guard of the train on which he travelled to London, but he received Osbert and Sachie with a blazing fire and a profusion of orchids and peaches.

Later that month, Sachie, Osbert and Sassoon gave a dinner for Firbank at the Golden Cross Inn, Oxford – a party of poets which included Wilfred Childe, Thomas Earp, Frank Prewitt and Gabriel Atkin (with whom Sassoon had recently started an affair). Firbank refused to attend the dinner – since he was not going to eat anything – but arrived with the dessert to read a chapter of his unfinished novel, *Valmouth*. 'You have no idea', he said to Osbert, 'how difficult it is to keep up one's interest, when writing of a heroine who is over a hundred and twenty years of age . . . .' Osbert later published the chapter in *Art and Letters*, the magazine of which he was co-editor. Firbank became a feature of the Sitwells' life in London and in Florence, where he lived in a villa in Fiesole, delighting them with precious remarks like the one on this postcard: 'Tomorrow I go to Haiti. They say the President is a *Perfect Dear!*'³

The end of the war reopened the possibilities of travel in Europe and beyond; through the 1920s the Sitwells were the trailblazers, making it fashionable to travel in search of the beautiful and the obscure. In March 1919 Sachie left Oxford to join Osbert in Biarritz for a trip to Spain. He spent a few days in Paris seeing the latest modern paintings and meeting, as he reported to Wyndham Lewis, Georges Braque, Amedeo Modigliani and Jacques Lipchitz. Nina Hamnett had given him a letter of introduction to Modigliani, whom he visited in his studio on the top floor of a dark, old, rickety building. The painter's two rooms were bare, without gas or electric light and with only an old coke stove for heating and cooking. He was desperately poor and his paintings were, Sachie told T.S. Eliot, 'very cheap'. Sachie bought two full-length oil paintings for £4 each and several drawings for £1 apiece, some of which were later ruined by being used as wrapping for his shoes at the hotel he subsequently stayed in at Biarritz. Later, after Modigliani's death, his dealer and friend, Leopold Zborowski, offered Sachie the entire contents of his studio, 'twelve large nudes, sixty to eighty paintings, and many sculptures and drawings for a hundred pounds'. Sachie could not afford it, nor could he persuade his father to lend him the money.⁴

His visit to Paris had given him the idea of mounting an exhibition of modern French art in London that year and a showing in Paris for Wyndham Lewis and his circle. From Biarritz en route for Spain he wrote suggesting this to Lewis: 'Let me know your ideas, and I will at once get to work and arrange matters – an exhibition in London, and one in Paris – a *vorticist* . . . .'⁵ When Sachie returned to Paris for three days at the beginning of April, it was already too late to organise the Lewis show as the 'season' ended with the month of June, but he arranged that Zborowski should come to London in secret at the end of May and stay at Swan Walk to arrange the London exhibition for which he was to act as agent. 'Nobody in London knows of the plan', he told Lewis, 'or of Z's existence. Let us keep it involved in mystery! This is important!!'[6] He had the idea of increasing the impact of the exhibition with a concert of modern European music to coincide with it and wrote to Dorothy Sayers from Madrid on 27 March asking her advice and help as 'a musical luminary of Oxford':

> I believe the Philharmonic Quartette [sic] could be produced, and also a first-rate singer in the shape of Helen Rootham. . . . The Philharmonic one hopes would perform a quartet by van Dieren, of whom it is time people heard – songs by Delius – van Dieren – Stravinsky – Schoenberg – and piano solos by Béla Bartók – Laszlo – Kodály (the young Hungarian musicians) and Prokofiev or Stravinsky etc. . . .[7]

Nothing came of this scheme; there were so many delays over the French exhibition that it finally opened in August, a most inconvenient date.

From Biarritz Sachie had also written to Eliot about his Paris experiences including,

> A new show by Juan Gris, who is frightfully good I think. Evidently, Juan Gris and a man called Lipchitz are the best after Picasso. They seem to have shoved Cubes and their futures overboard, and now it is a medley of playing cards, shepherd's crooks, printed music. . . .

He had also been given 'armfuls of poetry by new people', none of it remotely interesting as they 'all go in for too many typographical puns and it becomes dreary having to turn your book around as you read'. He had spent the previous Saturday in London with Eliot, who had evidently shown him his latest poem, not yet published, 'Burbank with a Baedeker: Bleistein with a Cigar'. Sachie had been 'overwhelmed' by it, liking it best of anything of Eliot's so far. He had also been shown another poem which he referred to as being about the ' "hillsmen" of Hampstead'. One line had particularly thrilled him: 'They discuss the evening papers, and other bird-news'. 'It excited me so much because it hits the exact keynote of what I want to do in "Bird-Actors",' he wrote. 'Just the effect of people fidgetting [sic] and chattering in crowds like flights of birds – and all the aerial qualities in a well-conducted conversation. . . . I am going to try "Bird-Actors" tomorrow. When ready I should love to send it to you for your opinion. . . .'[8] He ended with a plea to Eliot to send him a copy of 'Baedeker-Bleistein', which he may have shown to Osbert, who later published it in the summer number of *Art and Letters*.

On 28 March Sachie and Osbert left Biarritz for Madrid and Toledo, where they were to spend three weeks. Seeing the paintings of El Greco for the first time was for Sachie one of the great aesthetic experiences of his life. El Greco was not then a fashionable painter; '. . . it was possible to go into any church [in Toledo] and not know what paintings by El Greco one might find.'[9] Sachie was particularly struck by *St Maurice and the Theban Legion*, which was then hanging in the Sala Capitular at the Escorial. Snow lay thick outside the grey-yellow granite walls and upon the blue slate roofs of the great monastery-palace, enhancing the impact of the painting, as Sachie was later to describe it in *Canons of Giant Art*. Fifty years on he could write of this and other El Grecos seen at Toledo, of their colour, drama, distortions and flashes of unearthly light, as if he were seeing them for the first time at the age of twenty-one.

Trinity term at Oxford began on 27 April. Sachie was still in Madrid at that date, writing to Dorothy Sayers with the feeble excuse that 'there had been difficulty in obtaining passports', but that he hoped to be back by 1 May. Osbert had developed jaundice and retired to Monte Carlo to convalesce and be cherished by his friend, the rich hostess, Mrs Ronald Greville. Sachie spent three days in Paris in further discussions about the projected exhibition and was back at Balliol by mid-May. Osbert was in debt and worried about approaching his father; Sachie responded by suggesting that he ask the shrewd Mrs Greville for advice and, in any case, 'you need not tell him how much it is'. He was confident: 'I think that evidently we shall all have to go for him concertedly. We can, after all, make things very unpleasant for him – we have a pull over him about the family having never in its glorious history produced anybody who wrote before – genius at last. . . .' Considering that Sir George was himself the author of various books and regarded writing as merely the 'hobby' of a gentleman, it was not a promising line of approach. Sachie was 'rather angry' because he could not get away from Oxford until Tuesday, when he would be in London: 'Little Walton is coming up for a day or two to hear Opera etc: he has never been to London before. . . .' Sachie had been seeing Sassoon and both were anxious that Osbert should write the libretto for an opera or ballet based on the story of Maria Marten and the Red Barn murder. Sachie outlined the action and Sassoon assured him that they could be quite certain of an American performance of it. There was no diminution of his affection for Osbert. 'I long to come out to Paris – &

Italy – We must cling together like the people in *Caprice* [a novel by Firbank],' he wrote. 'You know how much I love you, darling – I miss you terribly. . . .'[10]

Oxford's attractions, even in summer, could not compare with London, where the sensation of the season was the première at the Coliseum of Diaghilev's new ballet, *La Boutique Fantasque*, with a backcloth designed by André Derain. Sachie missed the first night on 5 June, but was there for the second performance. He left Oxford for good at the close of the Trinity term on 21 June. That month he was taken to see Picasso at work in a big studio near Leicester Square on his drop curtain for the next ballet, *Le Tricorne*. 'The canvas was lying on the floor and Picasso and his scene painter were sitting on it eating their luncheon,' Sachie remembered. 'Their bottle of wine stood upright just where the painted bottle and two glasses stand upon the tray [on the curtain].' Picasso also designed the costumes, Sachie's favourite being 'the glorious red and gold Torero-Harlequin in red and yellow with a cocked hat'. He considered Picasso's drop cloth (again featuring a harlequin) for the revival that autumn of the Satie–Cocteau ballet, *Parade*, to be possibly the painter's masterpiece. Sachie conceived an ambitious plan for Picasso to paint frescoes in the *gran sala* at Montegufoni. 'Negotiations were entered into . . . and in the autumn we saw Picasso in Paris and talked over the project,' Sachie wrote. 'There were to be painted balconies over the doors, with Italian musicians, and big painted landscapes in the style, I hoped, of Benozzo Gozzoli. . . .'[11]

At Swan Walk in the late summer of 1919 Sachie and Osbert concentrated on their exhibition of modern French painting, which was to be held at the Mansard Gallery in Heal's. It was a hectic, last-minute operation; the paintings arrived in London by mid-July, but, as Sachie told Arnold Bennett on 26 July, inviting him to preview them, there was a shortage of labour at the gallery and they had not yet been unpacked. The hanging of the pictures became a social occasion in the Bloomsbury–Sitwell circle. Sachie, Osbert and Zborowski, helped by Roger Fry, sponsor of the two great Post-Impressionist exhibitions of 1910 and 1912, supervised the hanging of the paintings; after dinner on the hot late July evenings, friends came in to watch from the Eiffel Tower and studios in Fitzroy Street nearby. The exhibition included works by Picasso, Modigliani, Vlaminck, Soutine, Suzanne Valadon, Léger, Utrillo, Derain and Dufy, and sculptures by Archipenko and Zadkine. Sachie and Osbert had asked Arnold Bennett to write the preface to the exhibition catalogue, hoping to avert criticism by obtaining the benediction of the man who was then a best-selling novelist of international reputation, the most highly paid journalist in London and its most influential literary critic. Bennett was enthusiastic: 'the first exhibition of its kind since the war, and the best of its kind since the celebrated exhibition at the Grafton Galleries many years ago'.

The general public, however, took it as an affront, despite, or perhaps because of, an appreciative review by Clive Bell in *The Nation*:

> Anyone who cares for art . . . will be thankful to those enterprising poets, the two Mr Sitwells, and to M. Zborowski for bringing over from Paris just what he wanted to see. We stay-at-homes have long been asking what the French painters have been about since the long summer of 1914, and, above all, whether any new ones have appeared. We are answered. Here is, not exactly a third Post-Impressionist exhibition, but one so rich and representative that any professed amateur who fails to return from the country and visit it may safely be reckoned a fraud.[12]

Bell's praise roused the Philistines to fury. 'I felt the whole show to be glorifying in prostitution,' a Scottish doctor thundered from the Reform Club. 'I am a Philistine, I admit, and an engineer by trade, with a strong dislike of having my leg pulled,' wrote another critic. 'Is Mr Clive Bell pulling our legs or is he not?'

At Polesden Lacey, Mrs Ronnie Greville's sumptuous country house near Dorking, Sachie and Osbert were ostracised by their fellow guests. Mrs Greville, illegitimate daughter of a Scottish brewer, had inherited a fortune and married into Edward VII's circle; her tastes were very much those of her set. The interior of the house, designed by the architects of the Ritz, resembled a luxury Edwardian hotel, embellished with French furniture and pieces of demolished Italian palazzi. Her guests tended to be as stuffy as the upholstery – ambassadors, senior politicians, old American money and royalty. Writers were normally not invited to cross her threshold, an exception being made in Osbert's case no doubt because he was the heir to a baronetcy and an ex-Guards officer. On his side Osbert waived his objection to Philistines when they were either, like Mrs Greville, very rich, or simply royal. Sachie came to dislike 'Mrs Ronnie', describing her as 'sheer hell'; Cecil Beaton went further, calling her 'a galumphing, greedy, snobbish old toad, who watered her chops at the sight of royalty'. Sachie, like Beaton, preferred her rival hostess, Lady Cunard, in whose drawing room all the most brilliant and amusing people were to be found.

Osbert revelled in confrontation with his fellow guests at Polesden as

much as he did firing off insolent answers to the rude missives in the
newspapers:

> Each evening, when Sacheverell and I returned to Polesden, no less
> tired out by the heat of the days than rendered uneasy by profitless
> argument in the Gallery, and by the ferocious attacks delivered on us in
> the evening papers, which we had just read, unsuspecting, in the train,
> we would find the bulk of the guests assembled to meet us, grouped
> either just outside the front door or on the stone steps of the loggia.
> This chorus of ambassadors, political peers, retired Speakers, ministers
> and their wives were ready for us . . . [associating] in their minds a
> political regime they disliked with certain works of art.
>> 'I think Bolshevism should be put down!'
>> 'I have no sympathy with Bolsheviks in politics or art!'
>> 'I don't hold with Bolshevism!'
>> 'Cézanne wanted shooting'
>> 'I should think Sargent was good enough for anyone.'[13]

An eminent example of upper-class reaction to non-academic art was
provided by King George V, who, on being shown round the National
Gallery by Kenneth Clark, threatened to attack a Cézanne with his cane.

The Sitwells became associated in the public mind with Bolshevism in
art; that their views appealed to the young made them seem even more
dangerous. *Wheels* had been their first salvo fired for the modern
movement against the Philistines; the exhibition of modern French art in
1919 was the second. *Façade*, when first performed in public in June 1923,
would be the third.

In the wake of the exhibition Sachie still hoped that he and Osbert
could own a gallery and that art-dealing might subsidise poetry. In
October he was in Venice with his parents, writing to Osbert at Wood End
and pleading with him to join him in Paris: 'Do please come to Paris. If
you do not all our plans are definitely skied, and the advantage from the
exhib. in August is gone beyond recall. . . . A week . . . is all we want – but
I can do nothing there by myself. Remember all our Future profession, so
called, because Poetry is amateurism apparently.' As might have been
foreseen, Sir George had not accepted Sachie's argument that literary
genius in the family required his financial support, nor was he prepared to
put up the money for any ventures in the art world. 'I am afraid this Italian
trip has been an unmitigated misfortune,' Sachie wrote. 'If I had been in
England, we could probably have got a gallery, and found another
house.'[14]

Even if the idea of a career in fine arts was blocked by Sir George's refusal to co-operate, the Sitwells were making public progress as poets. The appearance of each 'Cycle' of *Wheels* was now regarded as an event. *The Athenaeum* had devoted a full-page review, entitled 'The Post Georgians', to the 'Third Cycle', published in January 1919. *Wheels*, it declared, had 'assuredly made an impression from the start. It indicated that an hour had struck, a mode had passed, that a new fashion had arrived.' The reviewer had particular praise for Sachie: 'In Mr Sacheverell's best poems there has always been an insight, a unit of vision. . . . He is capable of something exceptional.' Sachie had contributed six poems, only one of which was new – 'Fables', combining classical imagery with, an unusual mode for him, rhyming couplets. The following month his latest poem, 'Extract from "The Bird-Actors" ', appeared in *Art and Letters*. Inspired by memories of a pierrot show, as an exercise in *vers libre* it resembled Edith's style but less wittily and less successfully. 'Church and Stage', elegant, empty and obscure, was considered good enough to be published in the first issue of *The Monthly Chapbook* in July 1919. *Wheels, 1919 (Fourth Cycle)* contained four poems by Sachie: 'Serenade (from "The Bird-Actors")', whose language had echoes of Edith's but some lovely lyrical passages; 'The Italian Air', a typical Sachie production, beautiful but obscure; 'Mrs H. . . . or a Lady from Babel', based on a Scarborough neighbour, light and skilful but in a vein better done by his sister; and 'Valse Estudiantina', a more successful piece woven round the experience of a young girl at a piano lesson in her suburban house while outside in the park crowds enjoy a summer evening:

> A wall of cactus guards the virgin sound –
> Dripping through the sword-edged leaves
> The wayward milking
> Of your mental stalactites
> On the strung bells of music,
> Arrest the moment,
> Petrifies the air.

He liked the 'wall of cactus' image so much that he repeated it elsewhere, an irritating habit derived from his belief that in poetry, as in music, phrases, like themes, could resurface in the same work.

Sachie's achievement was overshadowed in this issue of *Wheels* by the posthumous publication of seven new poems by Wilfred Owen, a considerable coup for Edith. The anthology also featured ten poems by

Edith in her best vein, including 'Clown's Houses', and Osbert's 'Corpse Day (July 19th 1919)', one of his most powerful war poems. Aldous Huxley, already described by Proust as a literary phenomenon, had contributed no less than seven poems. Sachie's individual voice was virtually drowned among these heavier guns.

The year 1919 had been very much Osbert's with the publication of his anti-war satirical verse in *The Winstonburg Line* and *Argonaut and Juggernaut*, which contained some of his most acute satires on the bourgeoisie: 'Church Parade' and 'At the House of Mrs Kinfoot', the latter an unkind depiction of Lady Colefax. Sachie's last poem of 1919, 'Week-ends', on a light-hearted social theme, was printed in the December issue of *Coterie*, one of the liveliest, new, avant-garde magazines to appear after the war, edited by Chaman Lall and an editorial committee including Eliot, Wyndham Lewis, Huxley, Richard Aldington, the critic Tommy Earp (with whom Sachie and Osbert were contemplating sharing a house that winter after leaving Swan Walk) and, later, Nina Hamnett.

'A March Past at the Pyramids', the most virtuoso and the longest of Sachie's poems so far, appeared in the winter issue of *Art and Letters*. It was also his most strongly autobiographical work, revealing him at the age of just twenty-two as ambitious, even arrogant and confident of success. The opening lines evoked Scarborough, with one of those indomitable women from the bow-fronted terraced houses on the cliff emerging to face the world:

> The door grates open. Two wild eyes look out,
> Reconnaissance. Until a readjustment
> Of feathers, clothes, and gloves
> Has made her ready for the street fighting.
>
> Make way, malicious children!
> Stand back, until she finishes the steps
> And moves along the molten asphalt. . .

Having followed her 'Past the regimental flowers/And close-cropped lawns,/As far as where the pathways merge their stiff geometry/Into a simplified horizon', Sachie left her to pursue his own path from Scarborough into what he evidently believed would be a glorious future. He described himself as having overcome an early obstacle, his lack of athleticism, by widening the scope of his knowledge and ambition:

> A natural clumsiness had always been
> my bar to progress
> until I conquered it by calculation . . .

Once, reflected in a river, he had watched a shower of meteors fall (the 'Leonids' he called them – 'netting the Leonids' was his metaphor for achieving his highest ambition). The potential stretched into infinity:

> I made a poor Narcissus
> When I pored into the river,
> But in its smooth black mirror
>
> I watched the meteor acrobats,
> Whose shining wings and fiery hair
> Illuminated the insensate air,
> And in the straight lines of their flight
> Among the archipelagoes
> That glitter like a golden rose,
>
> I saw the roads that never meet
> And on them those that never talk
> Although together on their walk . . .
> My knowledge can hang nets to catch
> The flaming sparks . . .
> The ideal pyramid will raise
> its pinnacle too proud for praise,
> that, like a diamond, writes a name
> across the skies, and gives me fame.
>
> And so, while smaller men may make
> the soft singing and the golden shake
> with which the ripe fields greet the sun,
> into the joys for which they run
> tired lives into a broken mould,
> and then renounce the joy and fold
> crippled limbs, rehearsing in their mind,
> sights to remember when quick eyes go blind:
> I can reach above the crowd
> without a mask, without a shroud,
> and watch them counting grains of sand
> to tell the height my buildings stand.

It was not a particularly good poem, but it was certainly a hubristic declaration of intent. To Sachie, everything seemed possible.

In November 1919, Sachie and Osbert moved into 2 Carlyle Square, the handsome, four-storeyed brick and stucco house off the King's Road, Chelsea, which was to provide the setting for their spectacular literary and social success during the 1920s. Mrs Powell, their housekeeper at Swan Walk, came with them and they also had a manservant named Spencer. The house was furnished in Osbert's eclectic, somewhat florid taste – Bristol blue glass, feather flowers and stuffed birds under domes, and other camp Victoriana – while the walls were crammed with modern drawings and paintings. Osbert rather pompously described this decor as 'a synthesis of Victorian objects and modern pictures and brocades which remained for a long time peculiarly my own'. Sir George's equally characteristic comment was: 'I find it inexcusable in Osbert to like blue glass.' The Sitwells' younger friends thought it 'amusing'. One room had pink walls contrasting with red lacquer woodwork, the drawing room was painted blue, pink and violet, and the long, narrow dining room was designed to look like an undersea grotto with dark green silk walls, a reflecting marble table-top, silvery Venetian shell chairs and golden dolphins.

Anthony Powell, later the Sitwells' editor at Duckworth, described them as living 'in fairly sumptuous style . . . although usually complaining of bankruptcy'. Significantly, on a table in the back half of the ground-floor sitting room, 'a kind of ante-room where pre-dinner drinks were likely to be served', stood a huge bowl 'filled with ever-replenished press-cuttings'. 'Food,' Powell commented, 'usually topped up with some specially bought delicacy, was simple but excellent; wine, flowing always in abundance, sometimes of exotic vintages, never less than first-rate.'[15] Arnold Bennett, a gourmet, recorded his approval of both the food and the literary company:

> Dined at Osbert Sitwell's. Good dinner. Fish before soup. Present W.H. Davies, Lytton Strachey, [Leonard] Woolf, [Robert] Nichols, S. Sassoon, Aldous Huxley, [Gabriel] Atkin (a very young caricaturist), W.J. Turner and Herbert Read (a very young poet) . . . Osbert is young [he added], [but] he is already a very good host.[16]

Bennett saw Osbert as the impresario of the family; the entertainments at Carlyle Square were an important part of the Sitwells' presentation of themselves as a group, distinct from Bloomsbury, who, with the exception of Lytton Strachey and Roger Fry, regarded them with a wary, condescending and slightly jealous eye. Like the 'Bloomsberries' they attracted young disciples; friends were rewarded, enemies excluded. Virginia Woolf attended one party at the Sitwells at which it was proposed to read aloud a sentence of banishment on Lady Ottoline Morrell, 'but this of course meant no more than that we withdrew to somebody's bedroom in great numbers and left Ottoline, got up to look precisely like the Spanish Armada in full Sail, in possession of the drawing room.'[7] Evenings at Carlyle Square were amusing, but not for the faint-hearted or those who had happened to offend the trio (an extremely frequent occurrence). Walton described the Sitwells as 'Holy Terrors, all of them'; Edith herself remarked: 'We are as cosy as a nest of tigers on the Ganges.'

There was a distinctly Wildean tinge about Osbert's entertainments in the early 1920s. As a poet, aesthete, homosexual and enemy of the bourgeoisie, Wilde was a hero to Osbert, who collected stories about him and cultivated his friends, particularly Robbie Ross. Ross had introduced Sachie and Osbert to Wilfred Owen and Siegfried Sassoon and often invited them to his bachelor apartments at Half Moon Street, where the cockney landlady, Mrs Nellie Burton, presided over a 'gentlemen only' establishment much as Rosa Lewis did over the rowdily heterosexual Cavendish Hotel in Jermyn Street. Ada Leverson, Oscar Wilde's 'Sphinx', was another connection. She was fifty-seven and Osbert twenty-eight when they met at the house of her sister, Violet Schiff, but she conceived what Peter Quennell called a 'crepuscular passion' for him which embraced his entire family, except Sir George. Sphinx, who had once accompanied Wilde and 'Bosie' to first nights and after-theatre suppers, her golden hair piled high on her head and wearing the most extravagant Paris frocks, had by now lost her figure and her money. She wore voluminous, dark, tent-like dresses surmounted by large, mushroom-shaped hats over what Quennell described as 'a golden Gorgonian wig'. She was also extremely deaf, although still capable of the wit which had amused Wilde. 'I hear your father's changed belfries,' she remarked to Osbert on hearing that the Baronet had moved from his usual London hotel to Batt's in Dover Street. From 1918 to her death in 1935 Sphinx was an inevitable part of the Sitwell entourage either at Renishaw, where she was deputed to bore Sir George so that he would go to bed even earlier than his accustomed ten o'clock, or accompanying Osbert, Sachie and Walton on their journeys abroad every winter and introducing them to the world of Oscar Wilde – to Reginald Turner in Florence and Max Beerbohm in Rapallo. By now a ridiculous and pathetic figure, she was cruelly but accurately caricatured by Wyndham Lewis in *The Apes of God* as 'Sib', supplying 'Lord Osmund [Osbert] with tit-bits of Gossip arranged with his favourite sauces, the old yellow sauces of the Naughty Nineties,' while he encouraged 'her devoted clowning, her decrepit somersaults'.

The Sitwells had taken care to cultivate the older generation of influential literary figures like Ross, Bennett and Gosse. Sydney Schiff, Sphinx's brother-in-law, who wrote novels under the pseudonym, Stephen Hudson, was a generous friend and patron, as he was of Wyndham Lewis and T.S. Eliot; Vivien Eliot described him as 'the Sitwells' Holy Ghost'. He backed Osbert financially in *Art and Letters* and was always particularly kind and encouraging to Sachie. The trio also had younger literary friends, Wyndham Lewis, Tom and Vivien Eliot, Aldous Huxley and his wife, Maria, whom he married in July 1919, Siegfried Sassoon, Arthur Waley and Richard Aldington. Aldington wrote in his memoirs that 'the two Sitwell brothers' were among the compensations left in London after Pound's 'cruel abandonment' of the city to the 'powers of intellectual darkness. . . . Osbert Sitwell attracted me by his wit and honesty and his brother by his passion for beautiful things and a sensitive taste which amount almost to genius.' The Sitwells arranged poetry readings for groups of friends; on one occasion Sachie was chairman of a meeting at which Aldington was the reader when, to everybody's consternation, he burst into tears and fled from the platform. When Aldington asked what had upset him, he replied: 'Oh, I suddenly caught sight of Lady Mond's face, and it looked so awful I couldn't go on.'[18] Lady Mond was the wife of Sir Alfred, capitalist *par excellence*, founder of ICI and a favourite target for the Sitwells and their friends. At another of these meetings Eliot was reading one of his poems which made a comic reference to Mond when Lady Mond got up and sailed indignantly out of the room.

Sachie continued to see a good deal of the Eliots over this period. In the summer of 1919 he had been sailing with them and Mary Hutchinson in Chichester Harbour when they got stuck on a sandbank, and he had accompanied them to the first night of *Le Tricorne* in July. That autumn Osbert, still in poor health from the jaundice he contracted in Spain and suffering, according to Edith, from a 'dilated heart', almost quarrelled with both Eliot and Schiff over a rumour that Eliot was to replace him as poetry editor of *Art and Letters*,[19] writing simultaneously to Schiff and to Eliot letters which Eliot described to Schiff as 'extraordinary'. In a subsequent letter Osbert confessed to Schiff that he was suffering from a touch of persecution mania (a family failing): 'It sometimes seems to "my diseased egotism" that almost everyone outside my own immediate friends, & my brothers & sister, are bent on the sole purpose of harassing me, & thus preventing me from writing at all. . . .'[20]

Eliot dismissed it as 'this absurd affair', feeling, as he told Schiff, a 'paternal responsibility' towards his younger friends. Despite a 'personal affection' for Osbert, he did not admire his poetry, suspecting him as he did other poets, Huxley in particular, of plagiarism. 'Heaven preserve me from being reviewed in the company of Osbert,' he told John Quinn. 'I may say that any of his poems which appear to have any affinity with mine were published *subsequent* to mine.'[21] He preferred Sachie's verse, which he occasionally published in the *Criterion*. Their friendship continued; in February 1920 Sachie and Osbert, with Aldous Huxley, dined with the Eliots and went on to a party at Lady Ottoline's, where a Japanese mimed a hara-kiri dance, disembowelling himself with a fan and uttering horrid cries.[22] On one occasion Vivien Eliot invited Sachie and Osbert round to help her set tea for her disapproving mother-in-law, and during her acute illness in 1923 they took part in one of Eliot's curious charades. Invited to dinner at Burleigh Mansions, they were told mysteriously to ask the porter for 'the Captain'; at dinner Eliot was wearing green face-powder, to accentuate, Osbert thought, his look of suffering and provoke sympathy.

Walton was now a permanent guest and adopted member of the family. When he was sent down from Oxford for failing his exams, he had asked Sachie what he should do to avoid being apprenticed as a cotton clerk in Oldham and Sachie had insisted that he come to them in London. He and Osbert were determined that Walton should not be turned into an academic musician and for the next ten years they paid him an annual sum which they could ill afford, supplemented by the generosity of Siegfried Sassoon and other friends of theirs, including Gerald Berners and Christabel McLaren. Although a rift later developed between Walton and the Sitwells, he never forgot what he owed them. 'If it hadn't been for them,' he said, 'I'd have ended up like Stanford [a professor at the Royal College of Music], or would have been a clerk in some Midlands bank with an interest in music. Life would have been a great deal duller.'[23]

Life was never dull with the Sitwells, whose circle of friends encompassed everyone who was clever, amusing or talented in London. An extraordinary diversity of people gathered at Carlyle Square or Pembridge Mansions. Sachie collected composers and musicians, among them Bernard van Dieren, the Parsi composer, Khaikosru Sorabji, Angus Morrison, Peter Warlock (Philip Heseltine), Violet Gordon Woodhouse and, above all, Gerald Berners and Constant Lambert. Lambert, Walton's boon companion, had literally turned up on the Sitwells' doorstep in Carlyle Square early in 1922, hoping for an entrance to their world. Since he was very young and extremely good-looking and Osbert susceptible, he was invited in, becoming a habitué of the Sitwell circle. At Renishaw in August he and Walton performed duets and 'musical skirmishes'.

Gerald Berners, multi-talented, eccentric and complex, became a close friend of Sachie's, collaborating with him on a ballet, *The Triumph of Neptune*, produced by Diaghilev in 1926. Berners had already made a name as a writer and painter before becoming a composer of modern music. He loved jokes, both musical and verbal. His early work included three funeral marches for a statesman, a canary and a rich aunt, while Osbert described staying with him in one of his various homes as like living a perpetual April Fool's Day. Edith called him an 'instance of *real* eccentricity . . . the result of a sheer sense of fun'. Like the Sitwells he had what she called 'a superb power of retort'. An acquaintance who had 'the impertinent habit' of saying 'I've been sticking up for you' repeated it once too often. Berners replied: 'And I've been sticking up for you. Someone said you aren't fit to live with pigs, and I said that you are.' On another occasion when Edith and Sachie were lunching with him, his 'stately, gloomy, immense butler', Marshall, entered the dining room bearing a huge placard:

> 'The gentleman outside says would you be good enough to sign this, my Lord.'
> Gerald inspected the placard and wriggled nervously. 'It wouldn't be any use, Marshall,' he exclaimed. 'He won't know who I am – probably has never heard of me.'
> It transpired that the placard was 'An appeal to God that we May Have Peace in Our Time'.[24]

Berners, having succeeded his uncle as fourteenth Baron Berners in 1918 at the age of thirty-five, had instantly determined to divest himself of all the ancestral possessions which did not appeal to him aesthetically, including several 'vast, draughty, machicolated mansions', keeping instead an exquisite eighteenth-century country house, Faringdon, a house in Belgravia and an apartment in Rome. From then on he devoted himself to music, the arts, and amusing himself and his friends.

Sachie's closest male friend, Dick Wyndham, was, like Berners, another rebellious Englishman who was completely uninterested in ancestors and ancestral possessions. He abandoned the family house, Clouds, a favourite meeting-place of the Edwardian 'Souls', built by the Arts and Crafts architect, Philip Webb, for the Wyndhams, and sold their collection of Pre-Raphaelite pictures, to buy a Sussex millhouse, Tickerage, and devoted himself to painting and travelling.

In the spring of 1920 the Sitwells took Walton to Italy; it was the first time that he had ever been out of England. They stayed, as was to become their habit for months during the winter, in an ancient, white-walled Capuchin convent converted into a hotel among vines and orange groves on a precipitous slope overlooking the Bay of Naples at Amalfi. Here the Sitwells installed themselves to work in individual vaulted cells with stunning views of the bay, emerging to walk along the hills to Ravello for lunch, or, in the evening, to meet for White Lady cocktails before dinner.

Sachie found the huge vistas, the mountains, cliffs, rocks and the wide horizon of the bay infinitely inspiring. An air of classical antiquity hung over the place, as if the days of Tiberius had been only yesterday. 'Such was the scenery of my ambition for several of the most impressionable years of life,' he wrote later; 'I found far more in it than would ever have reached me among the spires of Oxford or the cafés of Montparnasse.'[25] Years later he wrote 'Tangerine', a poem evoking the winters at Amalfi when he was working on *Southern Baroque Art*:

> When shops are lit,
>   sleet falls in the Midlands
> And it is cold without and in,
> I am back at the white columns of the Cappucini
> with the long stairway leading down to the sea,
> Listening to the Sicilienne!
> On a December afternoon with the frost beginning
>   with the zampognari coming,
> And frost upon the tangerines,
> Hearing the bagpipes of the shepherds
>   come up from Calabria for the novena,
> Music, as of goatskins with the hair on,
>   filled with wind,
> Listen! how it skirls from its own entrails,
>   and how the drone goes on,
> Rough hairy music, but it is the Sicilienne!
>
> I connect it in my memory
>   with frost upon the black-green leaves,
> And lit lanterns of the tangerines...

His poems were becoming longer and more ambitious, mysterious and incomprehensible in 'Laughing Lions will come', and in his best lyrical vein in 'Et in Arcadia Omnes (from "The Bird-Actors")', both of which appeared in *Wheels, 1920 (Fifth Cycle)* in October 1920. When 'Et in Arcadia Omnes' was issued two years later in a collection with the title *The Hundred and One Harlequins*, the *Times Literary Supplement* critic found echoes of Blake in its opening lines:

> The stars, but prophets call them sons of God,
> Lay in the fresh field and the cool wind trod,
> Striding across the bodies where they slept,
> And woke them to the glory that they kept
> All day in bondage until darkness came,
> When movement flowed as water, gold as flame.

Arnold Bennett wrote that the poems, despite being 'damnably difficult', seemed to him 'a wonderful portent' with 'a very considerable amount of new beauty . . . a Sitwellian beauty . . . [which convinces] that the Sitwells live in a world of perceptions and sensations of their own. . . .'[26]

Sachie was back with Osbert in southern Italy that winter. In September they had found themselves 'marooned' with the Gingers in a hotel at Baveno on Lake Maggiore, always Sir George's first stopping-place on his Italian travels. As the rain came down in sheets, driving the drenched white peacocks into the potting-sheds, and dripping from the lemon trees in their water-darkened terracotta pots, Sachie and Osbert determined to escape to the sun. Sir George attempted to detain them with offers of books from his travelling library, but as the floods rose above the hotel steps they fled, leaving by boat from beside the concierge's desk. 'All of October and November we were in Naples,' Sachie wrote. 'I can never forget the excitement of discovering for myself the two long narrow streets that traverse the old town with all their palaces and churches. . . . I had found the theme or subject I was looking for . . . it was an inspiration, a transmission almost . . . a transfusion of poetical germs and ideas that no one of my temperament is ever likely to forget.' He was particularly struck by the monumental palace of the Bourbon kings of the Two Sicilies at Caserta, 'the theatrical, if Neronic splendour of the marbled atrium above the grand stair, a "realisation" of a stage design of the Bibiena school. . . .'[27] The Bourbon kings, execrated by British liberals, represented precisely the kind of 'over-the top', *ancien régime* personalities to appeal to the Sitwells. Extravagant, eccentric, at fits and starts extremely cruel or conversely simple and kind, King 'Bomba' (Ferdinand II) of Naples seemed to them rather like their Uncle Francis Londesborough.

Sachie had hero-worshipped d'Annunzio since first hearing Edith read his poetry at Renishaw, admiring him as the author of *Il Fuoco* and *La Città morta*, 'the greatest living poet of the day'. D'Annunzio fitted all his ideas of a romantic poet. At fifteen he had tried to imitate Shelley, attempting to drown himself in the Bay of Castellamare; subsequently he had become as celebrated as a lover as he was a poet. In the autumn of 1920 he had recently installed himself at the head of a republic of the arts in Fiume, whose constitution included a clause defining music as 'a religious and social institution' of the state. Sachie was irresistibly attracted by the idea of meeting d'Annunzio. He also hoped to get him to write the introduction for an edition of Rabelais in French and English with drawings by Picasso, 'a project', he wrote later, 'for which I had already asked Picasso to make the drawings'.

He and Osbert travelled to Fiume from Naples with a certain amount of difficulty, including Osbert's being mistakenly identified from the passport signature as Lord Curzon. Impeccably dressed as was their wont, they found themselves surrounded by the army of the 'Regency of the Cornaro', a motley collection of Italian Romantics, Futurists and mercenaries, with beards, shaven heads or six-inch tufts of hair, cloaks, feathers and black ties; there were even two white-haired veterans in Garibaldian uniform. The poet himself was less colourful and romantic in appearance than his followers, being completely bald and disconcertingly equipped with a glass eye. He was clearly overwrought and embarked on an 'absurd' conversation about sport, the last subject the Sitwells wished to discuss, talking of English greyhounds 'running wild over the moors of Devonshire'. They were disappointed, although sympathetic when he talked of his fifteen lonely months in this outpost surrounded by soldiers and peasants with the relentless pressure of the Italian Government 'trying to bore me out'.[28] Perhaps Sachie felt that it was not the moment to talk of illustrated editions; within six weeks d'Annunzio had been forced out of Fiume under threat of bombardment by the Italian fleet.

Soon after the Fiume adventure, Sir George signalled his refusal to occupy a niche in the history of European art by commissioning the Picasso frescoes. Sachie's 'rage and disappointment' at the frustration of his scheme brought on, or so he later wrote, a serious illness. 'I think it was these excitements and their attendant frustrations that in some curious way curdled my blood and made me ill.' En route back to London from Fiume in December, the Sitwells stopped at the Hotel Lotti in Paris, where Sachie had a presentiment of illness, taking the form of 'an unknowing and unreasoning dread of what was to come. I remember, even, wishing that I could be in pain in order to have some tangible and definite reason for my nervous dreads.' Immediately on reaching Scarborough, he began to write furiously, the first pages of *Southern Baroque Art*. 'I can remember dipping my pen into the inkpot and having no other wish than to describe the feeling of a hot early morning at Naples.'[29] He completed five or six pages before being seized by violent pains and a high temperature. The immediate cause appeared to be an abscess in the groin, the result of straining himself as he jumped from one rock-pool to another on the beach. He woke in the middle of the night and crawled to Osbert's room with the sensation that he was dying. He nearly did die of blood-poisoning in those pre-antibiotic days. He spent almost three months in bed, the poisoning followed by a nervous breakdown when he was unable to read and could not bear to talk. While lying in bed he grew to six foot six; a tailor came and measured him in bed for new clothes, but he shrunk two and a quarter inches back to his normal height again, so that when he got up the cuffs of his new suits hung down to his fingertips. On 18 February 1921 he wrote to Eliot inviting him and Vivien to stay at Wood End. Vivien had been ill again and he could sympathise. 'Today is my first day up after 9 weeks in bed with blood-poisoning & nervous breakdown – not a nice combination,' he wrote. '. . . On about 15th March we go abroad – very likely for months to come.'[30]

Sachie and Osbert, accompanied by Walton, made a leisurely progress south, staying at Rapallo and meeting Max Beerbohm, before going on to Florence, where they found their friends the Huxleys staying at the Villa Minnucci. They invited Aldous and Maria over to Montegufoni, where Huxley was deeply impressed by their eccentric parents and their 'Peacockian' setting, which he determined to use as the backdrop for a novel (*Those Barren Leaves*), describing it to his brother Julian as 'the most amazing place I have ever seen in my life'. Sir George and Lady Ida were to feature in *Crome Yellow*, which he wrote over the following two months, Lady Ida as 'Old Priscilla' Wimbush, who had once nearly gone bankrupt through extravagance and gambling, and Sir George as Henry Wimbush, described as having 'dotty archaeological passions, writing a book on family history and being a collector of antique beds'. The identification was unmistakable and the Sitwells were not pleased when *Crome Yellow* came out to immense acclaim in November 1921. Making fun of the Gingers was their own prerogative; when it was done by others, they resented it. They did, however, remain on social terms with Huxley until his lampooning of Osbert in *The Tillotson Banquet* in late 1922.

That spring, Sachie had one object in mind, an idea which had possessed him as he lay ill in Scarborough: to see Lecce, 'the Florence of Rococo Art' as it had been described by Gregorovius, the art historian he had read while at Eton. He had also read the pioneer work in English, Martin S. Briggs's *In the Heel of Italy* (1910), from his father's travel book collection. Sir George himself had been to Puglia some fifteen years earlier, meticulously counting eighty flea-bites on one arm between wrist and elbow after a night spent at Manfredonia on the Gargano peninsula. Sachie, accompanied by Osbert, made the pilgrimage to Lecce – the train journey from Salerno to Brindisi alone took twelve hours. Walking out of his hotel the next morning, he was immediately entranced by the façades of golden stone and the blinding whiteness of the walls. Lecce, he wrote in *Southern Baroque Revisited* (1967), 'was entirely theatrical. Every street was a stage set, elaborate balconies, windows framed as if they were baroque mirrors, stone balustrades and fanciful roundels with empty space behind where the painted backdrop would have had blue sky and clouds.' He even saw, on the whitewashed walls, graffiti which looked like Pulcinella, the rogue of the *commedia*, whose baggy white suit resembled the dress of the Apulian peasants.

Lecce seems to have effected a final cure. Back in London that summer, Sachie was writing poetry again, working on *Dr Donne and Gargantua, First Canto*, which he was to complete at Wood End that autumn. In August he was at Renishaw with the family and Siegfried Sassoon, who appears from the jaundiced remarks he made about his hosts and their surroundings in his diary to have been in an extremely bad mood: 'Blighted skies and blackened trees and landscape. Women in a gloomy room. What time is the next meal? Look at this! Look at that! . . . Disgruntled offspring of distrusted parents. . . . Harassed and skulking servants; furtive gardeners. Undoubtedly wicked influences. Crazy behaviour late at night.' There were charades on the 'Ginger' theme after Sir George had gone to bed with Edith dressed up in a suit of his clothes and Sassoon making 'hectic attempts' at heartiness enlivened by his champagne. Rich food and sweet vintage champagne seem to have made Sassoon increasingly dyspeptic. 'The Sitwells are parasitic on their possessions,' he wrote. 'They fasten on an old house with its charming pictures like lice in a cavalier's costume. . . . The trouble is they've all got too much taste.' He was disgusted by their incessant wrangling about money:

Osbert trying to snatch money from Ginger, etc. Why does O. let
himself be under G.'s thumb? A complete break would be more
dignified, surely? But O. is too fond of luxuries and prestige to sacrifice
a single square meal. So they go on with their skirmishings about 'pay
and allowances', and wait for someone to die off. . . .[31]

The roots of Sassoon's hostility lay in his dislike of situations which he
could not dominate and the strong current of his feelings towards Osbert.
'I can't hope to blot him out of my life and thoughts,' he had earlier
confided to his diary; '. . . my attitude towards O. is strongly sadistic . . .
my stab at his feelings . . . aroused in me acute sexual feelings.'[32] Sassoon
was boiling up for a break with the Sitwells, which was to come in
November with the publication in *Wheels* of a pseudonymous satire by
Osbert on Squire, in which he also ridiculed Robert Graves and W.J.
Turner, two of Sassoon's closest friends. '*I can't tell you what Siegfried has
been like,*' Edith wrote to Sachie in November, 'however he has been told
the truth by me. . . . *Do nothing, and know nothing*, certainly not till you
have seen me.'[33] Sachie, as usual, was caught up in Osbert's and Edith's
quarrels not of his making. Sassoon, although feeling neutral towards
Sachie, refused to speak to any of the Sitwells from November 1921 until
the summer of 1924.

Sachie was, however, still on the best possible terms with Wyndham
Lewis, to whom he wrote from Wood End in October asking him to
produce a design for *Dr Donne* and *Gargantua*:

> . . . a device, ornament, or drawing of some kind. Either as a
> frontispiece, or to cover the first page of the book. . . . Between
> ourselves I do not think the drawing need have *much* connection with
> the poem. Can it be a pen and ink with rather hard outline – If I might
> suggest a subject from the poem – Gargantua preaching – or Gargantua
> usurping the Almighty's position – something of that kind. You will
> notice that whenever God speaks, he does so in the rhythm of the
> charge at Balaklava.[34]

Sachie was delighted with the poem and went on to write five more cantos
on the same theme, a laboured contrast between the metaphysical
attitudes of Donne and the materialistic antics of Gargantua (a subject
clearly much in his mind since the failure of the Picasso edition).
Unfortunately, Sachie's intellectual equipment was not up to the
ambitious scheme and most people were to find it unintelligible. He had it
privately printed by the Favil Press for £6, sending Lewis 'the not too

magnificent sum of £5. I daresay this is not enough, but if you can do the drawing soon – we can discuss the matter on my return.' The book came out in December 1921 and was limited to 101 copies, fifty of which Sachie reserved for himself, sending two to Sydney Schiff. Despite strategic distribution, *Dr Donne* . . . received no major notices until the sympathetic Richard Aldington reviewed it almost a year later in the *New York Evening News, Literary Review*, with the rather desperate recommendation: 'this little privately printed book . . . will certainly become a bibliographical rarity'. Sachie wrote gratefully to Aldington of 'the extraordinary effect' his review had had upon sales of the book. 'I had previously only sold about twelve copies & those were entirely of the Blackmail to Friend character . . . all bought by friends who could hardly avoid doing so. But in the last three weeks I have had about twenty orders for it from the States – queer places like Chicago – Denver & so on.'35

Edith, as usual, greeted *Dr Donne* . . . with the extravagant praise she lavished on all Sachie's work: 'I am *convinced* . . . that whoever else lives or does not live for the future, *you* do. . . . People who don't recognise you as a great poet . . . are simply making fools of themselves. . . .'36 She never let a breath of criticism pass her lips as far as he was concerned, an attitude which had a baneful effect on him as a poet. It was counter-productive in every aspect. The literary public was irritated by the hyperbole of her praise; in her preface to his *Collected Poems* she was to claim, not for the first time, that as a poet Sachie was 'one of the greatest that our race has produced in the last hundred and fifty years'. Sachie himself was encouraged in his fatal penchant for self-indulgence, his intoxication with words and beautiful but empty phrases. His poetry had richness but it could become a surfeit. He would not discipline his natural talent or the flow of his imagination. He might have listened to Edith had she ever tried to offer critical advice. She was his muse, but all he heard from her were paeans of praise and flattering comparisons with Shelley and Keats.

Sachie's tastes and Edith's were, except in poetry, quite unalike. She had, he wrote, 'no visual sense, no visual curiosity'. She lived for poetry; '. . . if you took poetry away from Edith', Dylan Thomas said of her, 'she mightn't die but she'd be bloody sick.' She shared her brothers' taste for luxury when she could afford it (and often when she couldn't), but she did not share their passion for architecture, the decorative arts, even painting, although the great love of her life was a painter, Pavel Tchelitchew. She particularly did not share one of Sachie's central passions, the ballet, which she regarded as a frivolous distraction unworthy of the genius she considered him to be. For Sachie, however, the ballet, the music and, later on, the ballerinas were a recurrent source of inspiration.

On 2 November 1921 at the Alhambra Theatre Diaghilev presented his revival of Tchaikovsky's *La Belle au Bois Dormant (The Sleeping Beauty)* with, among others, Nijinsky's sister, Bronislava, Lydia Lopokova, Lydia Sokolova and Anton Dolin. Sachie described it as the most exciting first night he had ever seen in his life. It was the last great production by Bakst, whom he had admired so intensely; this evening he finally saw the master. Bakst had fallen into disgrace with Diaghilev before the opening night and attended it sitting in the stage box wearing a tweed suit instead of evening clothes as a defiant, alienated gesture. Sachie was ecstatic. 'The music was an enchantment from the first note,' he recalled. 'Being, even then, fanatical in my love for the Bibiena, the great first scene of Bakst was like an intoxicating revelation to a young man of twenty-three.' Not everyone shared his opinion; Lytton Strachey told Sachie in the interval 'that it made him feel sick, it was so degraded, especially the music'.[37]

For the past six months the Sitwells had been planning their next artistic statement, *Façade*. Edith had been writing a new series of poems in what she called 'transcendental technique', composing verses on the basis of jazz rhythms. It was Sachie's idea that Edith should recite them to music set by Walton. By the autumn of 1921, the project was far enough advanced for him to write from Scarborough to Wyndham Lewis for advice as to who should be commissioned to paint the curtain for the performance. 'We are debating in our minds about [Frank] Dobson, or Lipchitz. I think in many ways Dobson....'[38] Sachie had suggested the title, taken from a patronising comment someone had made about Edith: 'clever, but only a façade'. Through November and December 1921 Walton worked on the settings; one, the fanfare for 'Long Steel Grass', Sachie remembered first hearing played by an itinerant fortune-teller in Catania. As the performers were going to read the poems from behind the curtain (painted by Dobson) and Edith's voice could not be heard above the music, Sachie suggested that they use a Sengerphone; he and Walton travelled by bus to Hampstead to interview Herr Senger, a Swiss operatic baritone who had designed the instrument, made of *papier mâché*, and used it during a performance at Bayreuth.

Sachie later recalled the composition of *Façade* that summer at Pembridge Mansions in a long poem he wrote after Edith's death:

> So up to the 'fourth floor high in air'
> Where you my sister lived for eighteen years.

Writing some of your best and most individual poems
In a vein of fantasy that never slackened
Or abated;
Written quickly,
Even effortlessly it seemed,
To have the music fitted to them.

Let me hear the barrel-organ,
    that played on Saturday afternoons in Moscow Road.
It matters not how banal the tune:
Let it be 'When Irish eyes are smiling',
And I am back with you
On a blazing June evening in 1921 or 1922.'[39]

You could hear, he said, 'her happy laughter in her poems'; but when they were performed in public, most people missed the point. The uninitiated were puzzled and then enraged. '. . . it has now at last dawned on these people that *Façade* is a work for the most part of gaiety, although sometimes there is a veiled sadness,' Edith wrote later. 'The audience is meant to laugh.'[40]

The first private performance of *Façade* was given on 24 January 1922 in the pink, blue, white and violet drawing room at Carlyle Square, where the audience was enlivened by Mrs Powell's rum punch, a delicious concoction with the addition of green tea, sherry, China tea and fresh pineapple juice. Many of them were baffled by both the words and the music ('Long steel grass –/The white soldiers pass –/The light is braying like an ass.'). Virginia Woolf's friend, Violet Dickinson, reported that 'the Sitwells have been reciting what seemed to her sheer nonsense through megaphones';[41] but Mrs Robert Mathias, a great patron of Diaghilev and the ballet, was so enchanted with it that she insisted on a second performance on 7 February at her house in Montagu Square. It was well over a year before *Façade* was to be launched on an astounded public at the Aeolian Hall, off Bond Street.

The Sitwells were acquiring followers of the younger generation. In March one of Sachie's most recent poems, appropriately entitled 'Portrait of a Harlequin', was published in *The Eton Candle*, an anthology of verse by Etonians past and present produced by the precocious aesthetes, Brian Howard and Harold Acton, and suitably bound in Schiaparelli shocking pink with bright yellow endpapers. The sixteen-year-old Howard, whose disastrous life seemed then on the verge of great promise, wrote a perceptive essay on 'The New Poetry' praising Pound (then a very

esoteric taste), the Imagists, *Wheels* and the Sitwells, for their champion-
ship of free verse and their 'courageous introduction into England of the
purely modern in literary *decor* and subject'. Like Acton, Howard was an
admirer of the Sitwells even before he met them; although Edith had
published one of his poems under the pseudonym Charles Orange in
Wheels in 1921, he did not actually meet her until July 1922. 'I've got to
have my cubist posters – my dances – my visits to the Sitwells,' he wrote
to his mother; '. . . Let me smell green carnations while I am still of an
appropriate age.'[42] While particularly praising Edith as 'the leader of the
[*Wheels*] movement' and Osbert as 'one of the most interesting literary
personalities in England . . . a master of the flashing imagery and . . .
modernist irony', he found Sachie 'difficult for the reader of normal
culture to understand . . . a poet of the few'.[43] It was a damaging label
which was to hang round Sachie's neck as a poet and writer of prose for
the rest of his life. Acton, however, admired the Sitwells (and Eliot)
unreservedly, praising Edith's 'hardness and clarity', and Osbert's and
Sachie's 'qualities of vivid light and colour entirely lacking in the English
verse commended by contemporary critics':

> Their imagery was all the more bracing [he wrote] after the faded
> pastels of the Georgians, as effete a gang of poetasters as ever won
> praise from a misguided public. . . . Few shared my opinions at Eton or
> after at Oxford, where I did more than anyone else to celebrate the
> achievements of Eliot and the Sitwells. A later generation came round to
> my point of view.[44]

Sachie continued the Sitwell assault on the literary establishment with
the publication on 18 July 1922 of *The Hundred and One Harlequins*, the
first collection of his poetry to be produced by a general publisher, Grant
Richards. Sachie dedicated it to Sphinx and probably owed its publication
to her since Grant Richards had been in love with her. The dust-jacket
underlined the *commedia dell'arte* theme, featuring Gino Severini's
recently completed Montegufoni fresco portrait of Sachie as Harlequin,
as did the titles of the poems which included: 'One Hundred and One
Harlequins (Selections)' and 'Two Clowns' Psychology'. It received a
long individual review in the *Times Literary Supplement*, an indication of
how his standing had risen since he was merely mentioned, almost in
passing, as a member of the *Wheels* group. The review, headed 'The Wind
Bloweth where it Listeth', again made the point raised by Brian Howard:

The difficulty of his poetry – and it is often difficult as well as poetry – comes from the fact that, whether from instinct or design, he allows his unconscious to lead him where it will. Often he seems to compose by a kind of dream-process, trusting to association rather than to logic, and expecting the reader to follow, without explanatory help, the caprices of his fancy. . . . He lets words lead him on as if they were flowers on a walk; the word, found by accident, expands itself into a whole mass of associations. . . . The effect is often like that of music heard in a dream which is peculiarly vivid and satisfying to the dreamer, because he is dreaming. But it exacts of the reader an effort which he may not be ready to make. . . . The result is a curious mixture of pleasure and irritation. . . .[45]

It was a fair review, highlighting the virtues of Sachie's poetry as well as its drawbacks. His strong points were his technical virtuosity and mastery of internal rhythm and a very English lyrical quality; his faults being his remoteness, obscurity and lack of control over his imaginative processes, which made the thread of his writing, both poetry and prose, often difficult to follow. His avoidance of realism, contemporary issues or ostensible 'meaning' indicated that he would never be a popular poet in the twentieth century. Anthony Powell wrote of him: 'Sachie Sitwell's poetry, strongly influenced by the 17th century, remote in feeling, at times a trifle stiff, remains always unique to himself; the minutiae of aesthetic sensation, rather than the poet's relations to other people. . . . Often the lines describe some infinitely delicate state of physical consciousness. . . .'[46] Arnold Bennett saw *The Hundred and One Harlequins* as an important projection of Sitwell imagery, 'a wonderful portent' full of 'new beauty', despite being 'most damnably difficult'. '. . . more than any other Sitwell book or manifestation', he wrote, '*The Hundred and One Harlequins* persuades you to be convinced that the Sitwells live in a world of perceptions and sensations of their own. . . .' Sachie's poetry tended to feature oblique references and imagery whose meaning was clear only to himself, his brother and his sister. One such was perhaps the theme of a poem, 'Laughing Lions will come', from 'Zarathustra', a reference to Nietzsche's call for leaders: 'laughing lions . . . merry ones such as are built squarely in body and soul'. The Sitwell shield shows three lions; it might not be too fanciful to suggest that 'Laughing Lions' was a reference to the trio themselves.

Meanwhile, Sachie was completing *Southern Baroque Art*. He had apparently been discussing it with Huxley and regretted having done so. 'Aldous is really becoming rather too much of a good thing as regards

Plagiarism,' he wrote to Osbert. 'I am lunching with him on Tuesday, and shall warn him definitely off the course as regards Farinelli, Mexico etc: I really will not let [him] bag all my ideas.'[47] Sachie was enlarging his acquaintance with the baroque and rococo that year: in May he was in Italy; in September in southern Germany with Osbert, Edith and Walton. In Munich they came across Sassoon, much to his consternation; he had been travelling with his most recent lover, a placid German aristocrat, and Gerald Berners. Despite his self-imposed feud, he remained obsessed by the Sitwells, referring to them frequently in his diary whether they were present or not. In May he had reviewed *Façade* for the *Herald* with the heading 'Too Fantastic for Fat-Heads'. He noted in his diary:

> Edith's poetry is original and beautiful in its modes of fantastic
> plumage. . . . It is Osbert who angers me. . . . His neurotic spite and
> jealousy are ill-concealed by his 'social charm'. He seems incapable of
> serenity, or of tolerance towards his contemporaries. . . . How tiresome
> he can be with his everlasting chatter about his antiquarian father; and
> his disreputably-aristocratic mama; and his untidy financial difficulties.
> Perhaps I am severe on him, but he is always merciless towards
> everyone but himself and his brother and sister.[48]

In Munich he dined with his lover 'P' and Berners in an almost empty restaurant, only to find the Sitwells sitting there. After dinner the Sitwells marched out, Osbert and Sachie stopping to talk to Berners; they did not even glance at Sassoon, who sat there embarrassed and 'feeling rather sad' about the feud he had created, but also with some sense of relief when he thought how he might have been travelling with them and perhaps 'lugging' Gabriel [Atkin] about as well. 'What an irritable crowd we should be at the end of a week or two! . . . What a brilliant, disintegrating family they are!'

In October Sachie, Osbert and Walton were in Venice, as was Sassoon, still with 'P'. It was, of course, impossible to avoid meeting, crossing each other in the piazza or sitting outside Florian's. The Sitwells were in a large crowd there, which included Richard Wyndham, the American poet, Robert McAlmon, with his wife, Bryher, who, twenty years later, would become Sachie's patroness, Francis Meynell, Nancy Cunard and Wyndham Lewis, who were having an affair and staying together in Victor Cunard's palazzo. The Sitwells were still on excellent terms with Lewis. In October the previous year Edith had written to Sachie contrasting his behaviour favourably with that of Sassoon. 'Lewis has been so nice and has given me a drawing he did of me, sitting eyeless, beaked and superb, on what appears to be a ship on the waves. . . .'⁴⁹ While in Venice Lewis did a fine portrait head of Sachie, wearing, as Lewis liked to describe it, 'his habitual air of sedate alarm'. The Sitwells took him round Venice in a gondola and introduced him to Dick Wyndham (who later became his pupil and patron and would be satirised with the Sitwells in *The Apes of God*). They then went on with Walton to Naples and Sicily.

From Taormina, Sachie wrote to Gilbert Seldes, managing editor of the *Dial*, asking him if he would consider publishing *Southern Baroque Art* and sending him a sample chapter. 'I have spent two years in writing [it] and two publishers have refused it,' he told Seldes. 'It is a study of 18–17 Century Art – music etc. in Spain, Italy & Mexico. As it is written in an original and unusual manner I can find no one in England to consider it.'⁵⁰ He sent Seldes the chapter entitled 'The King and the Nightingale', the story of the great Neapolitan castrato singer, Farinelli, who cured King Philip V of Spain of melancholy by his singing, which he had feared Huxley might 'bag' from him. Osbert had apparently suggested trying Seldes, possibly because the *Dial* had recently published Eliot's *The Waste Land* in November 1922. The *Dial*, however, turned it dwn, saying that it was too long. By the end of February Sachie and Osbert were back at Carlyle Square, summoned to England because of the death of their ninety-five-year-old aunt, Mrs Frederica Thomas, on 1 January 1923, an event which eventually brought Sachie Weston, the manor house in Northamptonshire which would be his home from 1927 until his death. He was still, as he told Aldington, vainly trying to find a publisher for *Southern Baroque Art*;⁵¹ three months later, in May 1923, he had no alternative but to come to an agreement with Grant Richards (who had rejected it the previous October) by which he would pay Richards £50 to publish it.

Earlier in February he had written from 'Weston Manor' near Towcester in Northamptonshire, the first letter ever from his future home; he was there with Sir George, who was eagerly making an inventory of the contents. He was in correspondence with Harold Monro of the Poetry Bookshop over *Dr Donne and Gargantua, Canto the Second*, which, like the first canto, was being privately printed by the Favil Press.⁵² In June he wrote to Monro offering him 'twelve very short poems . . . the set of them are called "Hortus Conclusus" '.⁵³ Although he insisted on pursuing his Donne and Gargantua sequence, the 'Hortus Conclusus' poems, written on the theme of fruit and flowers and strongly influenced by the 'garden' poetry of the English seventeenth century, marked a new departure, one which he was to carry through until the end of his writing life. They were to appear in the next collection of his poetry, *The Thirteenth Caesar*, published in October 1924.

The sensational event of the summer of 1923 from the Sitwells' point of view, one which, perhaps more than any other, made them celebrities, was the first public performance of *Façade* at the Aeolian Hall on 12 June. Harold Acton was there with a party of young friends, which included Evelyn Waugh and Desmond Harmsworth. Acton had met Edith the previous December, when he too had climbed the four flights to her flat in Pembridge Mansions; he had already met Osbert and Sachie in Florence, where his family lived in the magnificent Renaissance Villa La Pietra. The Sitwell brothers, he wrote, reminded him of eighteenth-century Englishmen on the Grand Tour, 'robustly languid, noting everything of interest with alert, shrewd eyes. . . . They were ever on a leisurely chase after neglected beauties in the visual arts . . . [off] the beaten track, rediscovering forgotten painters and architects.'[54] Acton's cosmopolitan background (his mother was a rich American; his father, a member of a distinguished English expatriate family in Naples, was a connoisseur art dealer), his knowledge and taste in literature and works of art, made him the aesthetic leader of the Brideshead Generation at Oxford; he took Waugh and Harmsworth to the party at Carlyle Square after the performance and introduced them to the Sitwells.

The *Façade* stage was hung with Dobson's curtain, featuring two masks, one large half-pink, half-white one in the centre, and a smaller black one on the right, with Sengerphones protruding through their mouths. Osbert announced the poems through the smaller mask, followed by Edith reciting them through the largest to the accompaniment of a sextet conducted by Walton. The performance ended with 'Sir Beelzebub at the Hotel':

> Like Balaclava, the lava came down from the
> Roof, and the sea's blue wooden gendarmerie
> Took them in charge while Beelzebub roared for his rum
> . . . None of them come!

Accounts of the audience reaction differed. Acton merely said that some people 'tittered and made inappropriate remarks', but Walton, according to his wife, 'was very upset by the way the audience behaved, booing and hissing'. Edith and Osbert presented the hostility in more dramatic terms, Edith going so far as to say that she had had to stay behind the curtain for fear of being physically attacked by 'the inevitable old symbol of the enemy, poised, with raised umbrella, ready to smite me'.[55] Walton concluded later, probably correctly, that 'the three Sitwells were pleased with the uproar caused by the performance', telling his wife how embarrassed he had been at this and subsequent performances when there always 'seemed to be a row, egged on by Osbert'.[56]

'Drivel They Paid to Hear', one headline ran. The Sitwells were, of course, delighted when the old enemy, the Philistine, raised a hostile umbrella. They were less pleased when Noël Coward, who had been in the audience at the Aeolian Hall, ridiculed them in his hit revue, *London Calling*, that September. Coward, as much of a poseur in his way as the Sitwells, was at heart conventional and middle class and detested modern poetry and music. He was also a friend of C.K. Scott-Moncrieff, the translator of Proust, who was an old adversary of Osbert's. Coward's review featured 'the Swiss Family Whittlebot', the poetess Hernia and her brothers Gob and Sago, delivering verses which were a parody of Edith's. Edith was outraged, particularly as she was convinced that Maisie Gay, the actress who played Hernia, had presented her as a lesbian, an imputation to which she was always sensitive. Osbert accused Coward of 'spitting in the face of a lady' and the great Sitwell/Coward feud began.

From the time of the Aeolian Hall performance of *Façade* the Sitwells were headline material. Press reports, particularly in the popular papers which would not normally feature the arts, presented them as outrageous, exactly the image which they wanted to project. They incurred the hostility of Lord Beaverbrook, but retaliated by capturing the higher ground of the Society gossip columnists, including one of his own favourites, Tom Driberg. Satires on the Sitwells, caricatures of them and articles about them became staples of Fleet Street and the stage; they were what would now be called media stars. 'But why are they thought daring & clever?' Virginia Woolf queried somewhat plaintively. 'Why are they the laughing stocks of the music halls & the penny a liners?'[57]

The Sitwells made good copy: they were unconventional aristocrats; they were physically outstanding, all being six foot or more; and there were three of them. They were bold and, in the dandy tradition, invited trouble from the mob. They brought colour to a drab post-war world in which, according to Kenneth Clark, fantasy, richness and elaboration were completely excluded. 'Into this yard of virtuous fowls, laying their identical eggs, there strayed three golden pheasants – the Sitwells.' They could also be provokingly puerile, as their 1929 entries in *Who's Who* showed:

EDITH *Educ.*: privately; in early youth took an intense dislike to
simplicity, morris-dancing, a sense of humour, and every kind of sport
excepting reviewer-baiting, and has continued these distastes ever since.

OSBERT *Educ.*: during the holidays from Eton . . . deeply interested in
any manifestation of sport . . . played against Yorkshire Cricket Eleven
(left-handed) when 7 years old; was put down for M.C.C. on day of
birth by W.G. Grace, but has now abandoned all other athletic interests
in order to urge the adoption of new sports such as: Pelota, Kif-Kif, and
the Pengo (specially the latter); spent the winter of 1927–8 in the Sahara
studying same . . . *Recreations*: Sensitive Dentine, regretting the
Bourbons, Repartee, Tu Quoque.

SACHEVERELL *Educ.*: Left [Balliol] owing to continued success of
Gilbert & Sullivan season at Oxford . . . *Recreations*: model aeroplanes,
plats regionaux, improvisation, the bull-ring.

Beneath the silliness there was a seriousness of purpose. As Anthony
Powell wrote:

> The great thing about the Sitwells was that they believed, however
> idiosyncratically, that the arts were to be enjoyed; not doled out like
> medicine for the good of people's social or political health. Their
> phalanx impeded not only straight philistinism (never dormant in any
> society), but also a wholesale takeover by the pedantic, the doctrinaire,
> the 'committed'; assailants by whom the arts are also eternally
> menaced.[58]

For Evelyn Waugh, writing for his own post-1914 generation, the
Sitwells represented 'sheer enjoyment'. It was they, not the literary giants
like Hardy, or even the Bloomsberries, whom he and his friends wanted to
meet,

> for they radiated an aura of high spirits, elegance, impudence,
> unpredictability. . . . They declared war on dullness. The British
> *bourgeoisie* was no longer fair game. Their self-complacency had gone
> with their power during the war. The Sitwells attacked from within that
> still depressing section of the upper class that devoted itself solely to
> sport and politics.

Waugh had diagnosed the Sitwells' principal target absolutely correctly –
'the Golden Horde', who had made their Christmases hideous at
Blankney and who had disapproved of Lady Ida in her fall from grace. In
Waugh's view, the Sitwells succeeded, in that aim at least.

By 1939 English society had been revolutionised, lightened and brightened, very largely through the Sitwell influence. They taught the grandees to enjoy their possessions while they still had them. They made the bore recognised and abhorred as the prime social sinner.[59]

The Sitwells, Waugh said, scorned the conventions of the middle class who thought publicity vulgar. They revelled in their huge bowl of press cuttings: 'Popular newspapers with all their absurd vulgarity were just a part of the exciting contemporary world in which the Sitwells romped. They were weapons in the total war against dullness.' Arnold Bennett described the trio as exulting in a scrap: 'Battle is in the curve of their nostrils. They issue forth from their bright pavilions and demand trouble. And few spectacles are more touching than their gentle, quiet, surprised, ruthless demeanour when they get it. . . .'[60] Osbert, he said, was the impresario, 'presenting' the family; Edith the chief gladiator; and Sachie the interpreter of the harlequin beauty of the Sitwell world, 'extraordinarily, insultingly different from anybody else's'. There would be a price to be paid for all this, as the Sitwells fed on their own myth and the public perception of them. Sachie, at least, would feel stifled by it. 'The triune nature of the cartel', Anthony Powell wrote, ' – fatally effective at the time as a weapon of publicity – has not otherwise been advantageous to the Sitwells as writers. . . .'[61]

Southern Baroque Art, the work with which Sachie would always, to his considerable irritation, be identified, was finally published on 20 February 1924. Inspired by his experience of baroque architecture in southern Italy in 1920, 1921 and 1922, it was originally to have been called, rather more accurately, *Four Essays on Baroque Art*. Neither of these titles conveyed the kind of book it was, something which, in its reeling imagination and its displacement of time and space, could only have been written by Sachie. It was neither a formal architectural critique, nor even a travel book. It was most certainly not a guide book; the last essay, on Mexico, dealt with a country which Sachie had never seen and was not to visit for another thirty years. Sachie intended it to be an interpretation of the spirit of the baroque: 'My aim', he wrote in the preface, 'has been so thoroughly to soak myself in the emanations of the period, that I can produce, so far as my pen can aid me, the spirit and atmosphere of the time and place. . . .' Sachie's genius was precisely this capacity to shed every vestige of the twentieth century and to experience the past in a visual time machine. 'Nobody I have met has so vivid a sense of whole stretches of the past as Sachie,' Harold Acton wrote of him. 'He reconstructs them in flashes wherever he goes.'[62] Sachie believed, perhaps rightly, that the unique sensations he experienced through his own imagination were the message which he as an artist had to communicate. He never ceased to believe this, writing on through success and failure, appreciation and oblivion, tracing his own individual furrow.

He was in search of the new, the masters of baroque art, once famous but then ill-considered and obscure; artists like Churriguera, Solimena, San Felice, even Luca Giordano, whose work was hidden in the largely unvisited churches, palaces and villas of Apulia, Naples and Sicily, Spain, Portugal and, finally, Mexico. He chose them deliberately because they were unknown and, where they were known, unpopular. Bernini and Borromini were already appreciated by people like Huxley, who considered themselves very avant-garde to do so. 'I am an enthusiastic *post*-Raphaelite,' Huxley wrote to his brother after a visit to Rome in 1921. 'I feel sorry for people who come to Rome with the preconceived certitude of the badness of Bernini and the seventeenth century.'[63] Sachie had long passed that stage.

His conception of the spirit of the period came not only from his own but also other artists' visions. In the case of Naples and Sicily, it was Fragonard's etchings for the Abbé de Saint-Non's *Voyage pittoresque dans le royaume de Deux Siciles* and his enthusiasm for the works of Solimena, Pietro da Cortona and Tiepolo, which caught Sachie's imagination. When it came to Mexico, he found huge mounted albums of Sylvester Baxter's *Spanish Colonial Architecture* in the library of the Victoria and Albert Museum: 'I was able on this evidence to concoct my account of the glittering convents of Santa Clara and Santa Rosa di Viterbo at Queretaro,' he wrote. 'My poetical diet had fitted me for such expeditions, preparing and intoxicating my imagination with my descriptions of Farinelli's singing, and steeping myself in the Spanish atmosphere upon the strength of a visit to Madrid and Toledo in March 1919. . . .'[64] 'Intoxication' is a key word; driven by the highly coloured violence of his imagination, Sachie's prose at times reeled. In the untrodden Persian Gulf, rivers rolled pearls down to the coast, piling 'high in loose, crumbling mounds, ready to rattle down at the first sound of plundering feet', skeletons of whales lay bleaching their ribs, falling apart like the timbers of a wreck 'down to where the huge herds of waves are feeding at the far end of their fields, the crackling sands, over which the waters run, lie bare and unmarked by any footfall'.[65]

The first essay, 'The Serenade at Caserta', began as if Sachie were present in the dawn light at the church of San Domenico in Naples as

Solimena started work on his vast fresco, *The Expulsion of Heliodorus from the Temple*, painting a fabulous world reached by a flight of steps down to a waterside. The language Sachie used to describe the scene was as wild and fantastic as the fresco, throwing up all sorts of images: the painted mooring posts for Venetian gondolas, medieval tapestries, Stravinsky's firebird and the Derbyshire woods near Renishaw into which a circus tiger had once escaped:

> There were striped posts to fix the boats to, fiercely coloured as if to accustom wild animals to this new haunt by pretending to belong to the sun-slashed woods in which they wandered. Sometimes a man and woman would be drawn here by unicorns, sometimes a guest would alight from the air with one or two fire-like feathers still clinging to his clothes. . . .

Less than a third of 'The Serenade at Caserta' is devoted to actual description of the king's summer palace and the customary 'serenades' held there; the rest is a dizzy interchange of imagination and reality – the churches and palaces of Naples and Catania, the crazy 'wizard-world' of Prince Palagonia's villa at Bagheria near Palermo with its distorting mirrors and grotesque statues, the Certosas (Carthusian monasteries) of San Martino and Padula, the frescoes of Verrio, Domenico Tiepolo, Luca Giordano and Solimena, with a detour to the Esterhazy domains in Hungary, to Tsarskoë Selo for a concert by the Neapolitan composer Domenico Cimarosa in an amphitheatre of ice prepared for Catherine the Great, interspersed with a magpie collection of information – that the town of Monte Cassino, for instance, supplied the world with organ-grinders. 'Les Indes Galantes', the second chapter, taking as its contrepiece, El Greco's *St Maurice and the Soldiers of the Theban Legion*, ranges over the life and experience of the artist, the power and personality of his employer, Philip II, and his contemporary, Sultan Suleiman the Magnificent, Persia and the India of the Great Moghul. Part Three, 'The King and the Nightingale', was a springboard for discursions into Spanish and Portuguese architecture, and even the music of Franz Liszt. The fourth, 'Mexico', was a progression westwards from Spain to the New World and a tour of the 'glittering' convents and churches there; it ended with a vivid, horrific description of a bullfight, similarly a spectacle which Sachie had not yet seen.

To an England deprived of colour and aesthetic adventure by the war, Sachie's unfurling of a brilliant tapestry of southern heat and excess sounded like a trumpet-call. Cultural perception had been dominated for well over half a century by John Ruskin's *Seven Lamps of Architecture*, by Walter Pater and other authorities to whom the *cinquecento* was the great century and style of Italian art. As Kenneth Clark wrote:

> Baroque and rococo were still terms of abuse. In Southern Italy they were considered vulgar beyond words. Yet such was the sureness of Sacheverell Sitwell's eye, and the persuasive eloquence of his prose, that in a single volume the whole was changed. *Southern Baroque Art* created a revolution in the history of English taste. The change was not confined to architecture. The music of Scarlatti, the singing of Farinelli, the *Commedia dell'Arte*, all these were part of the Sitwellian revolution.[66]

Cyril Connolly called the book 'a milestone in the development of our modern sensibility'. John Piper, who read it when it first came out, described it as 'a most wonderful book', which 'showed a completely revolutionary approach to architecture', reversing everything he had previously been taught.[67] It appealed particularly to the Brideshead Generation, who, in Robert Byron's words, were 'besotted by architecture'. Sachie's book and his advocacy of the art and architecture of the seventeenth and early eighteenth centuries changed the way in which people looked at buildings, paintings and furniture, what they looked for and where they went on their travels. Peter Quennell, picking up *Southern Baroque Art* on a visit to Renishaw in the summer of 1925, was entranced by Sachie's style – 'his soaring poetic flights, his constant rush of ideas and his headlong flow of imagery. . . . I soon became an ardent follower of my new friend's prose style which . . . I did my best to imitate, with, alas, extremely poor results.'[68]

Southern Baroque Art was Sachie's first prose work, setting his style for the future. In his own mind it marked a crucial transition from seeing himself only as a poet. In October 1924 he sent his latest collection of verse, *The Thirteenth Caesar*, to Arthur Waley. Writing from the British Museum where he worked in the Print Room, Waley replied with a detailed critique of Sachie's poetry which is perhaps the best example of the effect which it had upon his contemporaries:

> Dear Sachey [*sic*]
>   It is very difficult to talk about poems when one likes them as much as I like yours; almost as difficult as if I did not like them at all. To begin with, I think poets are the greatest people on earth, and as I feel that you are certainly the best poet in England & perhaps (I do not know much

about other countries) the best living poet anywhere, it follows that I think you the most important human being existant [*?sic*], and I feel as diffident of talking to you about poetry as one would feel of talking to Alexander the Great about battles. Sometimes you remind me most of Campion. At other times you are a Blake whom one can understand without having to read tiresome books by Archie Russell or Yeats. The whole of Hortus Conclusus seems to me perfect. I like the four bands and Doctor Donne less. The end of the 'Comendador turns Burlador' I have already told you astounds me by its beauty; as also 'the name scratched on a Window'. The 'winter walk' seems to me monotonous in rhythm and leads up to the line 'to guard the golden apples when they come upon the tree', in which the rhythm which you have been skirting round crystallizes in a jingle. . . . I don't like much of 'Actor Rehearsing' and none of the 'Opening of the Tombs'. . . . In general I like your poetry best when it is purely lyrical & least when it deals with politics, history, ideas or the like. . . .[69]

The *Times Literary Supplement* reviewing *The Thirteenth Caesar* in a piece entitled 'Fantasy and Nature' confirmed Waley's judgement. Sachie's poetry, 'with its queer mixture of flow and intricateness', had an exciting quality: 'He writes . . . out of an inner fire for certain things; and these are repeatedly the things of nature. . . . He writes of it in a kind of ingenious ecstasy.' 'The Gardener's Song', from the section of poems, '*Hortus Conclusus*', reminded the reviewer of Andrew Marvell. He praised the romantic effects and 'dream-like' changes of measure in 'Bolsover Castle', a fantasy reconstruction of the masque given at Bolsover (now a ruin which was part of Sachie's Derbyshire landscape) for Charles I with a performance of Ben Jonson's *Love's Welcome* in a setting designed by Inigo Jones. 'Often as we read him', he concluded, 'we come upon a radiance and lightness that suggest a joy akin to Shelley's.'[70]

The year 1924 had been an *annus mirabilis* for Sachie. With the publication of *Southern Baroque Art* and *The Thirteenth Caesar* he was, at the age of not quite twenty-seven, already a celebrity. However, he was beginning to find his role as juvenile lead in the Sitwell comedy irksome and the atmosphere at Carlyle Square oppressive. Osbert was courtly and urbane; Alice B. Toklas, Gertrude Stein's companion, described him as being 'like the uncle of a king'. His manners, to those who had not offended him, were exquisite. 'He dominated a dinner-table with geniality, but essentially as a protagonist,' Anthony Powell wrote of him. 'Domination' was the key word with Osbert. He was the leader and the head of the trio; his Guards officer background had accustomed him to command. 'You never get used to not being saluted,' he once confessed to

Powell. Even Walton found the position of being inferior to Osbert sometimes hard to take, especially when ordered to do things in front of other people. Constant Lambert (after a newspaper story of a boy killing himself as a result of fagging at his public school) spread the rumour that Walton had committed suicide because of the fagging at Carlyle Square.[71]

Behind his imposing façade of wit, dandy and leader of fashion, Osbert was emotionally insecure with a great need for love and was enormously dependent on his relationship with Sachie. He had not yet openly admitted his homosexuality (although he did, apparently, once make a pass at Walton, who told him that 'that kind of thing was not my cup of tea'), nor had he found a partner. For Sachie the strain of being younger brother and, at the same time, emotional prop to Osbert had become increasingly hard to take. According to Walton, Sachie was 'always in love and desperately wanted to get married, probably to get away from Carlyle Square', where 'the atmosphere was often strained'. By the late summer of 1924 he had found his own solution.

5

Harlequin and Columbine

1924–1925

A Creole Winter have I found,
iced with flame, with hot fire bound,
safe in these branches can I hide
whose warm leaves lull the snow outside.

Sacheverell Sitwell, 'Song: A Creole Winter have I found'

Sachie's first intimations of sex were the sight of a gypsy woman suckling her baby when he was a schoolboy at Reigate – 'it appalled me . . . for I did not know human beings were animal' – and of a stallion with penis erect in a field near Renishaw. Then words and rhymes scrawled in pencil by young colliers on the paintwork of the bridge over the trout stream began to take on some meaning when he saw couples entwined among the bluebells in Eckington Woods. He seems to have remained unaware of women until the age of nineteen, when the young wife of a painter friend of theirs fainted in the middle of dinner. She was sitting next to him and he found himself holding her in his arms. 'The first time I had ever had this proximity with a young girl,' he wrote years later, 'it was an extraordinary revelation and experience of another kind or species of human being.'[1]

He was shy and incurably romantic. His passions tended to be visionary as well as physical, triggered by his imagination, usually identifying a woman with a work of art, an object seen or a favourite piece of music. He was particularly attracted by dancers, the first of whom he was to describe in his autobiographical *All Summer in a Day*. He was twenty when he fell in love from afar with Anita Elson, star of a revue called *The Whirligig* at the Palace Theatre. She was young, aged about eighteen or nineteen, green-eyed, long-legged and graceful. Sachie followed her one Sunday evening in Leeds, where she was appearing in pantomime at the Queen's Theatre, and stayed at the same hotel just to catch a glimpse of her, haunting the Palm Court to watch her and her companions lunch before a matinée. He found her fellow actors and especially her dancing partner 'unpleasant' and 'awful' in the flesh. 'At that table in the dining-room I now saw what, before, had seemed to me divinely inspired and animated statues come down, and standing in the shadow of their own pedestals with a harmless life bordering on bathos after what I had expected of them . . . thrown out of focus . . . by the violence of their bad jokes.'[2] It did not matter; in the theatre, the 'unpleasant young man' became a harlequin, while his Columbine, the object of Sachie's obsession, danced in a 'haze of beauty'. Afterwards, the four members of the troupe sat opposite him in the hall where he had been awaiting their arrival. They glanced at him, discussing him in low voices; he knew that if he had gone over to them, they would have welcomed him. He was too shy to do so; for an agonised instant he sat there picturing himself taking the dancer to Venice, playing Pygmalion to her Galatea – 'I should have been at great pains to explain antiquity to someone who had never seen anything old before except her grand-parents.' He imagined watching her reaction to the Tiepolo frescoes of Antony and Cleopatra in the Palazzo Labia, a work of art which had a particular significance for him in terms of love, passion and sensuality. Tiepolo's masterpiece, he wrote, presented 'a painted world as dead as was her sham of verandah and suburban house', but he 'found it easier to walk about in that world, which, if painted, has at any rate attained some kind of permanence, and I now felt the necessity of cutting myself adrift from this other realm of possibility. . . .'[3] Preferring the dream to the reality, he got up and walked, leaden-footed, from the room.

He was twenty-six in the summer of 1924 when he fell in love with a beautiful Canadian girl eight years younger than himself. For the first time his feelings for a woman were direct, both romantic and physical, uncomplicated by any artistic vision. Georgia Doble was dark-haired with a slightly olive-tinged skin and hazel-green eyes set wide apart in a round face (Sachie called it 'lunar' and nicknamed her 'Moon'). She was tall with a slim figure, fine legs and ankles, and perfect teeth. One of the singular things about her was a deep, husky voice, so much so that as she grew older, people would mistake her for a man when she answered the telephone. Her father's family came from Redruth in Cornwall; Sachie liked to believe the tradition that descent from an Armada sailor wrecked on the Cornish coast was responsible for the glowing dark looks of Georgia and her elder sister, Frances, a voluptuous, much-admired actress. Georgia was direct, down-to-earth, highly sexed, materialistic, ruthless and socially ambitious. A friend said of her in the 1950s: 'If you took Georgia to watch cricket at Lord's she would ask "Does Mr [Len]

Hutton entertain?" ' She was also loyal, warm, vital, energetic, amusing and an excellent hostess. Sachie had found the perfect complement to himself, a helpmate in a very real sense who would shelter him from the tedious or unpleasant aspects of life and enable him to be independent – in so far as he ever could be – of his family. Cyril Connolly was to write of Sachie and Georgia half a century later:

> One had only to encounter them for a moment to see how inevitably
> right it was that the sensitive poet with his omnivorous antennae for all
> that was strange or marvellous in the visual arts should depend on the
> glowing dark beauty of this practical and life-enhancing Canadian . . .
> for the devotion and constant companionship necessary to carry him
> through his aesthetic adventures.[4]

'My ravishing angel, and Mother, and nurse,' Sachie was to write to her, an accurate analysis of her role in his life.[5] Georgia saw herself as both muse and guardian to a genius. Both Osbert and Edith thought her intellectually ill-equipped to play the part and that her passion for smart society diverted Sachie from the company he ought to keep. This became increasingly true, although it is arguable how much harm it actually did him. If Edith saw her role as fostering the flame of genius in her brother and refusing to provide any critical appraisal of his work, Georgia did the same. The result was that Sachie received no criticism at all except from reviewers, often for the wrong reasons, and refused to accept it. At the age of eighteen, Georgia was star-struck by literary celebrity, seeing herself (or so she remembered) as 'very, very high-brow'. 'I had heard a lot about the three Sitwells and longed to meet them.' She delighted in playing Galatea to Sachie's Pygmalion. 'From the beginning', she wrote, 'it was fascinating for me to be in Sachie's company – I always wanted to learn and realised how little I knew. . . . I had read *Southern Baroque Art, One Hundred and One Harlequins* etc. and I marvelled. His personality and appearance were not disappointing.'[6]

Sachie was very tall, six foot three, thin, angular and long-legged. Osbert described him in a typically lengthy and convoluted passage as having a

> very handsome head, with hair curling at the sides . . . its cut and
> contours so Italian in essence but so northern in colour, translated so
> perfectly the strange power and intensity which have always been his,
> the generous warmth of his temperament, so genial and impulsive, the
> passion that burns in him . . . for people, for books, for learning, for

works of art, for old lamps that can be lit again at his fire – the wit,
distinguished and apt, which he despises in himself and does nothing to
cultivate, instead preferring the jokes of others which he so immensely
enjoys: the flash, deep as bright, of his anger, large as the scale of his mind
and frame, but never enduring, breaking down eventually into a smile,
though by no means an easy smile. . . .[7]

He had a distinctive manner of speaking, pronouncing 'th' as 'f'; one of
the first things Georgia noticed about him when they met at tea in Carlyle
Square was his curious pronunciation of 'a' as he leaned across the table
and offered her another 'saandwich'. He had already developed the
darting, leaping conversational style which friends like Cyril Connolly
and James Lees-Milne struggled to describe in memoirs of him and
which could only really be conveyed by being transcribed verbatim.
Connolly called it 'disconcerting, even intimidating', an obstacle course in
general knowledge.

Sachie first became aware of Georgia's existence at a dance on 4 April
1924 given at his house in Cadogan Square by Arnold Bennett, whom the
Dobles had met while staying with the Beaverbrooks at Cherkley. It seems
that he did not meet her that evening although Osbert told him that he
had been introduced to 'a beautiful young girl, eighteen years old, from
Canada' and encompassed what was, in his view, his own downfall by
inviting her to tea at Carlyle Square. Sachie's manner, according to
Georgia, was notably relaxed; after plying her with sandwiches in the
dining room, he 'strolled upstairs' after her into the drawing room and
asked if she would dine with him one night. The languid attitude
disguised the impact she had made; he felt his 'senses numbed. The past
and future . . . nothing but a haze . . . complete and total blindness . . . at
the first shock of contact with her.' He took her to *Stop Flirting* at the
Strand Theatre and then to supper at the Savoy Grill. Acting, he said
afterwards, on 'pure instinct', he determined to marry her. 'It was brave to
ask for everything, and for all of life, almost at the first meeting, but such
was the counsel of desperation,' he wrote sentimentally fourteen years
later. 'It was an appeal for help, for the holding out of hands, to which a
soul opened and a heart made reply.'[8]

It was only the beginning of their romance. It was another year, during
which Sachie played the role of star-crossed lover to the hilt, before they
became engaged. For most of the intervening period they were separated
as Georgia travelled Europe with her parents. Most of the letters they
wrote to each other during that time have survived to trace the ups and
downs of their relationship. They were both still in London when Sachie

wrote her his first letter on 8 July inviting her to lunch at Carlyle Square on the 18th. He did not, apparently, yet know how to spell her name, addressing her as 'Dear Miss Dobell'. Georgia, however, was going to Cornwall. 'Do write and say when you can come to lunch after Cornwall,' he wrote the next day, adding disingenuously, 'we both want to see you again very much'. Meanwhile, he and Osbert were ordered over to see the Gingers at Dieppe, pursued by hoax telegrams from Gerald Berners purporting to be from various enemies, the most recent of whom was Eleanor 'Baba' Brougham, the sharp-tongued literary daughter of Lord Brougham, threatening her imminent arrival. Baba was not the only annoyance to contend with; the brothers were given a tongue-lashing by the Baronet on the perennial subject of their extravagance. '. . . my father is seriously trying,' Osbert wrote to his confidante, Christabel McLaren, the future Lady Aberconway and a noted Society hostess, '& says that "sooner or later the bailiffs will be in possession" at Carlyle Square. I tried to reassure him by saying that I never went to sleep without looking under my bed for a bailiff, but that only made matters worse. . . .'9

Georgia was still 'Miss Doble' (but not 'Dobell') when Sachie wrote on the 24th, after her return from Cornwall, inviting her to join Osbert and himself for lunch with Richmond Temple at the Savoy. (Richmond Temple was an extremely successful public relations consultant and a director of the Savoy Hotel Company, so no doubt the lunch was at his expense.) By 1 August 'Miss Doble' had become 'My darling Babs . . . I love you much more than anyone else has or ever will. . .'; two days later he was telling her that he had never had such a happy week in his life and that they were born for each other.

Osbert, Edith and Sachie were down at Weston, without their parents, from the middle of the first week in August. Sachie had arranged for Edith to invite Georgia for the week-end. 'Do please come, and after that I shall be alright till the end of September,' he wrote on the 4th. 'I do really adore you and can't get you out of my mind.' 'Are you coming as a vampire, or as the innocent ewe-lamb?' he asked. 'I personally prefer you in the former role but think the latter more suitable for home consumption.' They were being inundated by local county callers, he warned, and had had to give out that they were in quarantine for measles. 'You will be a darling and come here, won't you,' he wrote anxiously the next day. 'You will be an inspiration for as long as I live. . . . It gives me such marvellous peace and calm to see you.' 'Dear Willie' [Walton]' and he would meet her at Brackley station.

Georgia spent three days at Weston, her future home, with Walton,

Arthur Waley and Gerald Berners as her fellow guests. It was apparently a success. She was welcomed by Edith telling her, 'I understand that my brother Sacheverell loves you and so I know I will love you too'; she was also, initially and on the surface at least, popular with Osbert. 'You were an angel,' Sachie wrote to her on the 12th at the Old Ship Hotel, Brighton, where she was staying en route for Italy. 'This afternoon Osbert again told me how frightfully he liked you. . . . Write and tell me you want me to go on with my work and not be unhappy, won't you! . . . I miss you frightfully and don't know how I'm to get along without seeing you. I am longing for September more than I can say.'

Georgia's letters for this period are patchy, Sachie at one point having burned all his favourites in a fit of anger against her. Those which survived his holocaust, however, were affectionate enough not to justify the anxious floods of questioning passion which he unleashed to her at the Hotel Miramonti, Cortina d'Ampezzo. He was aghast to hear from their mutual friend Richmond Temple, who had been at Weston, that Georgia would not be returning to London that autumn as he had hoped, but might even be going on from Italy to Canada. In a passionate letter he wrote:

> It is so sickening because I *know* I could have made you love me in the autumn. So far you have seen nothing of the interesting side of my character, and my sentimentality has overflowed from my fear of you escaping me. . . . Don't think for one moment that I shall 'get over this'. The agonizing thing to me is that you are not in love with me, because I know you would have been soon – you may be now, even, a little more than you imagine. I am, though I say it myself, about the cleverest young man of my age in the country, and I know you would like my companionship. . . .[10]

She seems to have warned him off raising the subject of marriage, for his next letter boasts of being restrained – 'not a sound of wedding bells'.

At Cortina, Georgia had obviously decided to give Sachie the bad news about the impossibility of her returning to London in September. She chose to interpret his references to not being able to see her because he planned to spend the winter and spring abroad with Osbert as a slight:

> My dear, dear Sachie [she wrote]. I had not intended telling you this [that she was not returning to London that autumn] as I thought it might depress you, but as you seem to have resigned yourself to not seeing me until April I might as well let you know the worst at once. Of

course I should have told you soon in any case, but as I am sure that with the progress of time you cannot help caring less, I had thought it better not to mention this at once. I am very selfish about things and cannot help feeling rather bitter because I do love you to love me & I am sure it will not last long. I am very devoted to you already & however selfish it may be, I cannot contemplate the inevitable reaction of your feelings with equanimity. . . . But you so suddenly liked me that it still appears a house built on insecure foundations [she taunted him], whereas my affection for you grows in a more steady and normal fashion.

She wouldn't hear of his suggested dash to Italy to see her as it would only distress both their families. Having provoked him, she settled back into her role of muse:

> Write often and remember to work and that every word that you write & publish I will read as Columbus discovered America, and as Keats Chapman's Homer, and though I cannot appreciate it with the value of the great minds who will truly praise, everything you write I will feel has been reached by a tiny breath of my affection for you & my ambitions for you & my confidance [*sic*].[11]

In the meantime she received his letter of the 17th, breathing anxiety and passion. 'You insatiable hysterical angel,' she replied. He must not fuss so; if she were with him she would tell him not to be such a silly child and give him a pat on the head:

> You are not giving your mind as you should to your work. . . . I think it very unkind of you. I won't believe you are the cleverest young man in the country if there is nothing to show for it in future. I will dismiss you as a worn-out infant phenomenon. . . . Your devoir is to write *for* the world and a little *to* me. . . .

Reassured, Sachie reported that he was working marvellously on the play which he was writing with Osbert, their first, and that it was going on pretty well.

Despite Osbert and the play, he rushed out to join her in Venice in September, arriving on the 18th for two romantic weeks of sightseeing and kisses in hooded gondolas. They had a final, tearful rendezvous (which they later always referred to as the 'Niobe' dinner) inside Florian's on a wet Sunday evening, when they discussed marriage and Sachie agreed to stay away for a trial six-month period to prove his devotion. Back in Carlyle Square in the first week in October he began to regret his own 'caution and reserve' in accepting such a condition, but comforted himself with the thought that it was 'really more valorous to retire for six long months like I am doing, in order to hope for a real victory at the end of it'.

> I think of you day and night [he wrote] – and shall never forget last
> Sunday night, when we went out in that hooded gondola, and my tears
> mixed with the brackish water of the canals. It is what the 'Daily
> Express' calls a 'landmark' in my life – like the night in the 'Strand
> Theatre' – which, as I told you, is another place I can never revisit –
> under any circumstances.[12]

Georgia, irritated by these poetical posturings, accused him of manufacturing situations to suit emotions which had little enough basis in reality. Describing his letter of the 4th as 'the most depressing missive', she added:

> I am so afraid that you are drrawing [a recurrent spelling mistake of hers
> which greatly irritated Sachie] on imaginary romance because you seem
> to want to complete each episode as though it were impossible for life to
> reproduce the happiness or emotion that you have already felt. You keep
> refusing to revisit the scenes of places where we have most enjoyed
> ourselves & I cannot help realizing that this must be because it is not my
> prresance [sic] or affection that you love but your isolated personal mood
> that has given you pleasure. . . . It seems so probable that you will
> change your mind about me during the next 6 months because
> possibilities of the future do not offer you the same joy as what has
> already happened & you cannot love an accomplished fact for as long as
> you can a dream that seeks fulfilment. . . .

She worried that his unhappiness might prevent him working: 'If only you were happy you would do such great things & that is so much more important than anything. If I am the cause of such gloom I must remove myself from your life.'[13]

Before receiving this rebuke, Sachie continued to bombard her with letters describing his wretchedness: 'I seem to have no energy or desire to go on being alive. . . .' 'What is going to become of me, I wonder . . . I know I shall never be happy again like I was with you.' 'I do adore you so much and am so dependant [sic] on you as much as if I was the infant at your breast,' he told her, writing in bed after midnight and sending her a poem – 'a very good one' about the *great night* we saw the Astaires together [at the Strand]'.[14] At the same time he did not forget his preceptorial duties, instructing her to see the Palazzo Pisani at Strà – 'lovely palace – Tiepolo ball room & garden' – and sending her Casanova's memoirs. By the 12th, Georgia's letter had arrived and his tone was, as a result, loving but more sensible. Plans to go to Spain had had to be cancelled as Osbert was in bed with gastric 'flu and Walton's father was dangerously ill. 'I'm afraid we shall have to content ourselves with Montecarlo instead – a very poor substitute.' Rumours about a romance concerning him were going round London. He and Osbert had met Michael Arlen in Piccadilly, who had said, with a significant glance, that he had heard Sachie had been in Venice, and 'several boring people' had tried to find out if he was engaged.

The Magnasco Society, which he and Osbert had founded for the promotion of seventeenth-century art, had held its first exhibition on 14 October. Publicised by Richmond Temple and riding on the wave created by *Southern Baroque Art*, it had, Sachie reported on the 23rd, been a great success and widely mentioned in the papers; 'they take over £5 a day in gate money'. Sachie was Honorary Secretary of the Society and wrote the foreword to the catalogue of its first exhibition; he had also written an article for *Apollo* on the preceding exhibition of seventeenth-century Italian painting at the Burlington Fine Arts Club earlier that year. The Society was very Sitwellian; the committee consisted largely of their friends, including Ivor Spencer-Churchill and Tancred Borenius, the Finnish art expert, with Lord Gerald Wellesley as President, and its events were marked by dinner parties in a private room at the Savoy under the auspices of Temple, a noted gourmet. Despite all this, however, its success was ephemeral. In 1926 Wellesley wrote to Sachie resigning the Presidency on the grounds that the Society had been a 'flop'; he was replaced by the Sitwells' connection by marriage, the Marquess of Carisbrooke, husband of their cousin, Irene Denison, but within a decade the Society had disappeared. Not everybody shared Sachie's passion for Magnasco's huge canvases representing 'the play of hermits, bandits, monks, and vagabonds, in the wreckage of a yet recent world'.

Meanwhile, Georgia and her parents moved on to Florence, causing Sachie frissons of excitement since the Gingers would also be there haunting the same hotel. 'You'll find my mother and father at the Anglo-American,' he warned. 'My mother is tall, dark, & thin, always with a black cocker spaniel, & my father has, as you knew, a red beard. Be careful with them, won't you?'[15] From then on his letters were full of nervous enquiries about his parents. Had she seen them yet? She must be 'awfully tactful' with them. 'Father and Mother are plaguing me to come out to

Florence, but I think I had better not, because they *are* so tiresome. You can imagine the torture of renunciation I am going through in consequence.'[16] He was even trying to disguise his handwriting on the envelopes of the letters he sent her in case his mother recognised it, thoroughly enjoying the conspiracy of concealment. As soon as she saw his parents, he instructed, she must write and tell him what she thought of them. His mother always sat at the same table near the door of the dining room, and his father, who was probably at Montegufoni, would frequently come to Florence for lunch promptly at 12.30.[17] On 31 October, the eve of his and Osbert's departure for Paris, then Avignon and Cap d'Ail, they lunched with Richmond Temple at the Savoy, making him feel very sentimental 'visiting the scene of my capture'.

At Avignon, he found a loving letter from Georgia which also detailed her hectic social life and many admirers: an Austrian baron called Sacha, who danced like a winged mercury and combined the characteristics of Casanova and Beau Brummel, a photographer, a Florentine *marchese*, an American 'automobile king' and a Russian. She had met Arthur Acton (father of Harold and William), who had asked her up to lunch at La Pietra and recommended that she meet the Sitwells and see Montegufoni: ' "I am sure Lady Ida would be delighted to show her house to such a charming young lady. You know her sons? One of them is engaged I hear." ' 'Sacha darling,' she reassured him, 'I love you so much more now because I realize that all this just bores me to death – these dancing men are too tiresome for words & all I want now is to have you for my very own. . . ."[18] 'I'm much nicer than Sacha, or the Marchese,' he replied from Avignon. 'Remember Osbert is a Marchese, too and I believe I am also, as it goes with Montegufoni, so that I suppose there is little reason to feel jealous. . . . I miss you frightfully.'[19] On his arrival in Nice he wrote:

> How I hate those brutes you are seeing in Florence and how I envy
> every second they can talk to you, while I have to keep away from you
> for a long six months. . . . I shall never cease to be sorry that I didn't try
> and make you run away when I was in Venice. . . . I think of you all
> night and day and long for you; and dream of you continually, and never
> want to see or hear of any other woman: in fact I hate the whole lot of
> them. . . .[20]

Georgia had by now identified Lady Ida among the guests and reported to Sachie on 1 November: 'She is at the moment drinking coffee with two young men who lunched with her' at the table next to the door, which was within a few feet of the Dobles but fortunately concealed from her parents by a large palm. 'Yes! It must be your mother they are talking of you and Osbert. . . .' Sachie was amused to hear about his mother's activities, identifying the two young men as Old Etonians called Lawford, who had been there with Osbert and himself: 'vaguely nice – but intensely silly & rather aggravating. They have modelled their voices and manner on Mrs Patrick Campbell.' 'Be very careful', he warned, 'because it is more than probable that she knows who you are, and is subjecting you to close & minute scrutiny.'[21] On 15 November, his twenty-seventh birthday, he arrived at the recently opened Eden Hotel at Cap d'Ail to find a telegram from Georgia: 'Don't forget that 27 is my lucky number.' Sachie wrote her a loving letter: 'I know I am behaving atrociously badly as I am much older than you and ought to know better than write these long stupid letters to you. But I can't help being in love with you, and what is more, won't!' To celebrate his birthday, he told her, they had dined at the Hotel de Paris in Monte Carlo and gone on to the casino, where they had found Cocteau.[22]

Within days, however, his happiness was shattered by the news that Georgia might be forced to accompany her father to Canada and the United States instead of returning for the London Season. He was terrified that he might never see her again. 'I shall have an awful night of it worse than 30 September in Venice,' he wailed. She *must* remember the 'Niobe' evening and not let him down; she *must* be in London that summer.[23] From Florence Georgia tried to calm him; she might not have to go, and if she did it would only be for April and May. 'Don't let the idea of the last month of "separation" taking place a thousand miles apart allow you to lose sight of the simplicity of our conclusions,' she begged him.[24] Three days later she was able to tell him that her mother had wheedled her father into going alone, leaving them behind. In Florence, however, the Gingers were already on her trail. One of her admirers had lunched with Lady Ida, who had begged him not to tell Sir George (who already knew) that Sachie had been in Venice – 'so apparantly [*sic*] both of them know without either of them knowing that the other does'. It was quite evident that Lady Ida was well aware of Georgia's identity as, sitting so near their table at meals, she stared a good deal and must have thought it very odd that Georgia had been avoiding her. To top it all, the malicious and indiscreet Violet Trefusis had told their friend Atholl Hay that Georgia was engaged to Sachie. Georgia was convinced that Sir George's servant was shadowing her – 'I am really suffering from an acute attack of persecution mania,' she wrote.[25] Rumours of Sachie's engagement had even reached Manchester, where, as Sachie retailed to Georgia, 'a low-down . . . paper says "one of the Sitwells . . . famous in song and story" is to marry a beautiful American girl. . . . I *also* am worried to death about my Mother. I should think that bloody fool Atholl Hay told her,' he added.[26] Georgia reproached him for sending such a 'neurasthenic letter' full of qualms about his own physical attractions or lack of them, and about Georgia's love and her possible admirers:

> I've put off my trip to Canada partly on your account. I write to you at least three times a week, & tell you I'm devoted to you & that you've more chance than anyone else & all you do is say you want to die & that life is not worth living. Unless you can be a little bit more cherrfull [*sic*] I'm going to give up the whole thing because I clearly see that this might lead to a life-time of reproaches. Darling Sachie why will you do it? Can't you love me any other way?[27]

At Cap d'Ail the pining poet was contrite. Osbert had been being very difficult with 'nerves', no doubt caused by irritation and anxiety about Sachie's obvious preoccupation with Georgia, but the arrival of Walton had lightened the atmosphere. None the less, they were bored and the imminent arrival of 'a ferocious Aunt of mine' (Lady Londesborough) was frightening them away to Rapallo.[28] Aunt Gracie might 'gab' to friends, who would inform on them to the Gingers, it being by now a cardinal rule that their parents should never know where they were. They even went to the lengths of having writing paper printed with the heading '*M.Y. Rover*', which would be posted from various places, giving the impression that they were at sea and, therefore, incommunicado. On 4 December Sachie, Osbert and Walton arrived at the Hotel Bristol, Rapallo. Sachie feared that it would be 'rather dull', although within twenty-four hours of their arrival they had already seen both Max Beerbohm and Ezra Pound. Their only diversion was 'a kind of wretched Casino . . . with a bad band', where 'two Brazilian negresses get up and dance a tango with their respective cut-throat husbands . . . really marvellously'. Otherwise there was Ezra Pound resplendent in 'a pale blue coat with triangular cornelian buttons, and white flannel trousers – complete with pince nez, and red beard and whiskers.'[29] It was not enough. 'I may go off my head here one day from boredom,' he told Georgia. To stave off the tedium he was working hard, writing plays, articles and poems. 'I have been thinking out poems about "it" today,' he wrote guardedly. 'In one of them the word "*Creole*" occurs.'[30] The love poem to which he referred was 'Song: A Creole Winter have I found'; the word 'Creole' implied Georgia's dark looks and

Canadian birth.* 'D'you mind about Creole?' Sachie wrote; 'You know my views.'[31]

The news that Georgia had actually met his mother at last and been invited to Montegufoni had him on tenterhooks. Georgia had herself taken the initiative and had asked one of her admirers to introduce her to Lady Ida. 'She has been charming to me & I have spoken to her about three times, I met her about five days ago. To-morrow she is taking us all out in the morning to see your villa.'[32] Lady Ida's intelligence network had been working overtime; although believing Osbert and Sachie to be in Sorrento, she was otherwise well informed. 'She knows you were in Venice, knew all the time who I was ... she knew I'd been at Weston, in Venice and lots of other things,' Georgia reported. She herself was trying to appear indifferent to disabuse Lady Ida of the impression caused by the rumours spread by Violet Trefusis, Atholl Hay and others. Sachie, she told him, must on no account come to Florence now, nor must they lunch together in Pisa as they had planned.

'It was an awful shock,' Sachie wrote, warning her to be careful with the Gingers. 'For Heaven's sake, don't say where we are. They think we are at Cap d'Ail. Also don't talk about Weston too much; or about poor little Willie, whom they hate.'[33] 'I am terrified of what mischief my parents might concoct with yours,' he wrote two days later. The rumours about their engagement made him nervous. 'Little Johnny R.[othenstein] gasses to everybody' and he himself would like to slit the gossiping Atholl Hay's throat from ear to ear. He was still panicking at the thought of the trouble Georgia might innocently cause with the Gingers: '... whatever you do do not divulge our address, because we never like them to know where we are. Do not be deceived by their being pleasant. They are false, treacherous & nasty, more especially him.'[34]

Dick Wyndham was due to arrive in his Hispano Suiza with a plan to motor to Parma and Mantua for a few nights. He duly appeared and, with Osbert, Sachie and Walton clinging on for dear life, drove at breakneck speed eastwards across Italy. 'We came here across the Apennines at about 100 mph,' Sachie wrote from Parma, 'and have been rushing wildly about ever since. . . . I sent you some horrid Parma violets yesterday.'[35] The following night they were in Bologna – 'after about 60mph through Modena and all kinds of other towns' – returning to Rapallo late on Christmas Eve, 'after being lost in cloud in the Apennines to a really terrifying degree'.

* The *Oxford Dictionary* defines 'creole' as a person 'born or naturalized in the West Indies and other parts of America, Mauritius etc. but of European descent'.

Meanwhile, Lady Ida had been entertaining Georgia, taking her to tea with the Actons at La Pietra, which Georgia thought 'rather like a lovely antiques shop'. She went with the three male Actons to dance at the Palazzo Davanzati, and on Sunday Lady Ida was to take her to tea at the Huxleys. 'Your mother thinks I ought to dance more often & hopes mine won't think she's a bad friend for me! She is so sweet & all for the younger generation,' she reported on 20 December. A week later Sir George arrived at the hotel '& talks Sicily to us occasionally'. 'How did you like Aldous?' Sachie enquired. 'He is so nice and so intelligent; and a perfect comic appearance.' Although he was working well, he was not enjoying Rapallo. 'Nothing but bores here . . . also rain, and disgusting food,' he wrote on the 28th, and on New Year's Eve: 'The Bores here are poisonous!' Among these he would certainly not have included Sphinx, who was there with them, although he might have indicated Mrs Driberg senior, staying in Rapallo with young Tom, later an admirer and friend of Sachie's.

In January 1925 the Dobles moved to Rome, joined by Georgia's sister, the beautiful and flirtatious Frances, known as 'Bunny'. Before leaving Florence, Georgia had become attached to Lady Ida, even feeling protective towards her. In Florence, as at Scarborough, Lady Ida had become a target for hangers-on. 'I really hated leaving your mother in Florence,' Georgia wrote. 'I think she is wretchedly imposed on by everyone. Her friends make me quite ill the way they give her advice over trifles & she is such a pathetic person. I loved her & I do think you ought to be kinder to her.' 'Mother is pathetic and nice but maddening,' her son replied.

There was the inevitable misunderstanding between Rome and Rapallo. Georgia, quarrelling with her father and with her nose out of joint at the flocks of her sister's admirers, asked Sachie to come to Rome. He was working hard and was reluctant to drop everything to please her, the boot for once being on the other foot. Osbert was correcting the proofs of his new book, *Discursions on Travel, Art and Life*, which would be published that spring with, as a graceful gesture, a dedication to Georgia. Would she like 'G.D.', 'to Georgia', 'to Georgia Doble' or what?, Sachie asked. It was eventually agreed that a discreet 'Georgia' would be the least incriminating. It would be difficult for him to come to Rome just yet, he told her on 15 January, because he and Osbert were in the middle of writing the play, *All at Sea*, which they had begun in London that autumn and were hoping to finish in two weeks' time. Sachie's refusal of her invitation to Rome – he had sent a cable saying that he couldn't abandon the play – enraged Georgia. She despatched a lofty letter withdrawing it in terms which so frightened Sachie that, dropping Osbert and the play, he sped panic-stricken to Rome. It was not a happy reunion; both of them were nervous and Sachie resented being told to calm his passion. They had a furious row at the Majestic Hotel where they were staying when Sachie described himself as being 'put in the dock' by Georgia.

On his return to Rapallo he took drastic action: 'I have just destroyed a diary I have kept since 1917, 40 letters from you (all except the two I want to keep, & [birthday] telegram) & 8 poems to you. So now we start again clear,' he informed her on 21 January. Georgia riposted in the same lofty tone, lecturing him about friendship. 'The treasures of your thought are invaluable', she wrote, apparently straight-faced as she compared Sachie's petulant destruction of his manuscripts with the demolition by French archers of Leonardo da Vinci's unique plaster cast for his equestrian statue of Ludovico Sforza, '& their loss is irreparable. It is as though Leonardo had himself aimed arrows at the Cavallo. . . .'[36] On the same day she also wrote a placating letter to Osbert, who was understandably annoyed by Sachie's precipitate dash to Rome and probably also by the effect it had had upon him. During Sachie's stay in Rome, she told Osbert, she had made her 'last, and I think successful, attempt at stopping his fussing, gaining his friendship, and I hope making him ultimately happier'. She added a threat, intended to be passed on to Sachie, that if he continued to fuss she would give up writing to him and avoid him in London.

Sachie, however, coming to his senses, realised that discretion was the better part of valour. He apologised for his 'erotic behaviour'. 'Niobe is dead,' he wrote; 'there'll be no more of *her*!' He sent Georgia a Severini drawing of himself as Harlequin, presumably a preliminary sketch for the Montegufoni fresco. He and Osbert had finished their comedy, which he thought 'awfully funny', he told her on 31 January, enclosing a cutting about himself from a Montreal newspaper. He was now engaged on a preface to an edition of William Beckford's works and writing *All Summer in a Day*, the first of his 'autobiographical fantasia', his own homage to Proust, an intensely personal and poetic prose form which he was to publish at intervals until the onset of old age. He had high hopes of it: 'Do you realize that prose book of mine is the same sort of thing as "Under the Hill" only better!' he told Georgia on 3 February. 'If fate is kind to me, and I can cultivate the desert in which I find myself now, I shall be famous when you are covered with wrinkles and crowsfeet.'

He appeared to have forgotten about Rome and the disastrous dinner he called his 'Waterloo Night' and was looking forward to London in April. He and Osbert were already planning their Renishaw house parties for the summer. By the 20th, he was bolder, though still adopting a jokey tone. 'I am as fond of you as I was on 16 June 1924,' he told her, appending her his lover's banner inscribed with dates of significant defeats and victories:

Carlyle Square 16 June 1924 [the tea party]
Savoy Hotel London
Café Royal
Strand Theatre
Weston
Hotel Regina, Café Florian, Doge's Palace, and various canals.
Hotel Majestic, Rome
Catacomb Restaurant
scene in the Dock at Hotel Majestic.

By the next day he was regretting his temerity – 'Forgive banner,' he pleaded. On the 24th they left for Genoa en route for Spain; 'the last few days at beastly Rapallo', he reported, 'were enlivened by Willie's conduct with the daughter of an English colonel. . . .'
    From Naples Georgia responded with encouragement, spelling out her role as guardian and muse:

Do work particularly hard so that you will be able to frivol a bit with me
in May. . . . How dreadfull [sic] it would be if your work had
deteriorated since 16 June 1924. If this should be so then I give up
because it becomes obvious that the mission in life which I seek to fulfill
[sic] . . . is unaccomplished – to inspire to the pinnacle, to impede the
ultimate disgrace.

To this she appended a sketch, presumably inspired by Sachie's poem, 'A March Past at the Pyramids', in which a matchstick Sachie ascends via the Muses a pyramid marked SUCCESS to be greeted by a figure marked significantly WISDOM while clouds of FAME and GLORY hover above. Beneath the pyramid of success lurks 'FOLLY', 'SELF-DECEPTION' and 'MEDIOCRITY'.[37]
    'I adored your symbolical drawing,' Sachie wrote from Valencia on 3 March, en route for Seville via Madrid. In Madrid he found in the Prado a Goya drawing of the Inquisition with the word 'Doble' on it, an odd

coincidence since he had addressed Georgia as 'Torquemada' in his last letter. More flatteringly he told her that she and Bunny looked like Goya beauties. 'It all seems to substantiate the evidence narrated by Mrs Dobson in Cornwall [that they were descended from Armada sailors] & I am going to erect a monument in Redruth to the memory of the good souls who lost their lives in the Armada,' she replied from Taormina.[38] 'Yes! I believe more and more in the Armada story,' Sachie wrote from Seville, where they were having 'a rapturous time of it . . . and hardly ever retire to bed before dawn. Were you fond of me I should be giving you qualms and alarums but luckily this is not so! (I mean the first part.) . . . Write to me soon, creature, for goodness sake'; he signed himself, 'from Sachie without any love this time'.[39]

With Osbert and Walton Sachie visited Cordoba, a disappointment apart from the wonderful mosque with its forest of Moorish pillars. Cadiz was

noisy and unbelievably smelly without any of that halo of romance with which one had associated it. We had some appalling adventures there, including a visit – unawares – to a female lunatic asylum where there is a church with some indifferent pictures by Murillo. I think it was the most awful experience I have ever been through and it haunts my dreams still.[40]

Although they had enjoyed seeing the great *rejoneador*, Canero, practising bullfighting on horseback in the country, Seville was beginning to pall as it filled up with crowds for the Easter Week feria, including 'awful Americans of the worst kind and, worse still [English] people from Gibraltar' on what was known as 'the fishing fleet' trawling for husbands through the garrisons of Empire. 'Apparently many young women who are considered by their parents as *not* likely to set the Thames on fire are "given a chance" at Gibraltar, and should that prove hopeless they then proceed to Malta, and finally India,' Sachie wrote on 30 March to Georgia, now back in London. 'You'll get this letter about the 4 April . . . the anniversary of my first hearing of your existence.' If she should go to Max Beerbohm's exhibition at the Leicester Galleries, he warned her, she would see 'a very rude drawing of me'.

On 2 April they were at Ronda, staying in an incongruous English hotel 'exactly like a Thames Valley villa' perched on the edge of a cliff with a 1,000-foot drop at the end of the garden. There was such a strong wind in the evening up the cliff face that if a handkerchief was dropped over the edge, it sailed up into the air like a kite. Childishly, they threw 'lots of lighted newspapers over, setting fire to the roof of the hotel.' Sachie was already excited at the prospect of going to Granada, where Edith, recovering from an operation the previous month, was to join them. Granada, seen for the first time, did not disappoint him: 'really marvellous. The Alhambra a dream of beauty. . . . Then there is the Albaicin, which is a hill entirely honeycombed with caves in which a whole gipsy town dwell; and the gipsies are most extraordinary to look at.'[41] The weather was divine, the flamenco superb and the fruit trees glowing with oranges, but Sachie was already thinking of London, where Georgia's parents had taken a flat in Curzon Street – 'nice and near my hairdresser, Trumper's, where I go every morning,' he told her.

The Sitwell party at Granada made an arresting sight: Gothic Edith, squirearchal Osbert and languid, elegant Sachie, all over six foot, with the diminutive, fragile Walton in tow. They were in force, having been joined by Dick Wyndham and Constant Lambert. Cyril Connolly, aged twenty-one and on vacation from Balliol, came across them at their hotel, the Washington Irving: 'They were really quite alarming – alarming rather than forbidding. All of them were wearing capes and black Andalusian hats and looked magnificent. . . . I'd never met them before but they *seemed* like the Sitwells . . . we immediately became great friends. I was totally bowled over by them.'[42] The chance meeting marked Connolly's literary and social allegiances and attitudes for the next decade. Over thirty years later he asked himself whether, 'if it had been my fate to have encountered High Bloomsbury in Almeria on their visit in 1923 rather than the Sitwells in 1925, I should have been purged of that trait of Oxford dandyism which brought down the epithet "cocktail critic" on me in Virginia Woolf's journals many years later.'[43]

High Bloomsbury, as it happened, was to be encountered in Toledo, where the Sitwell party found themselves, having motored from Madrid, on 22 April. Across the street crowded with spectators and the giant effigies of the Holy Week procession, they glimpsed the unlikely figure of Lytton Strachey, conspicuous in his wide-brimmed brown hat, towering limply above the lesser mortals and accompanied by his faithful Dora Carrington, who, as Osbert put it, 'with fair hair and plump, pale face, added a more practical, but still indubitably English-esthetic note to the scene'. When the crowds broke tumultuously behind the procession, the Sitwells and Strachey were swept apart from each other in life as they were in art.

In London Georgia was discovering what it meant to be linked romantically with a Sitwell; the effect was to make her, for the first time, unsure of herself. '*Do* come back soon, I miss you most frightfully,' she wrote. 'I shall be quite shy at meeting you after all the stories that have come back to me about us. Newspaper paragraphs, gossip etc. . . .'[44] By 16 April Sachie was in the dog-house. Due to the vagaries of the Spanish postal service she had, apparently, not heard from him for a fortnight, and the letter, when it did arrive, was insufficiently passionate and somewhat sarcastic in tone:

> I *am* sorry, my dear, to have involved you in all this unnecessary and needless gossip and scandal. . . . So far, you must admit, the man has paid this time more than the woman (How awful that sounds – as if I had lent you money or something!) Of course you know what I really mean when you think of various experiences I have had this winter.

The teasing tone of the letter was, Georgia found, extremely provoking. Sachie complained that he had been abroad so long that his remaining clothes would have to be combined into one patchwork suit. 'I suppose that means that I daren't see you for about a fortnight after my return till I have got hold of some new suits from the tailors. In spite of long absence I shall have lots to tell you when I see you. I see the Russian Ballet are coming over which will be rather amusing.' The ending was coolly superior, although Sachie no doubt intended it as a joke: 'Goodbye, my dear, and do write soon, with best love from Sacheverell.'[45]

'My dear Sacheverell,' Georgia replied furiously:

> Your last letter was brought to me five minutes ago, just before breakfast, which I cannot touch as a result. The pent-up rage of two weeks finds vent at last. I consider your silence unfeeling & your letter cruel but like all wise women I realize that to hold a man's affection [one] must not tax him with his short-comings. There is no news, which would interest you, for me to communicate, you have the newspapers & numerous letters from your many friends so I will not venture to bore you with personal trivialities.

She could not keep up the tone until the end; after all, she did not want to lose him, only keep, if she could, the situation under her control, although, as so often, her spelling slipped. She concluded: 'Semper fidelis, in spite of your brutality I look forward . . . [illegible] to seeing you & remain Your obediant [*sic*] servant, Georgia Doble.'[46]

'I wish you *were* "my obedient servant",' Sachie replied from Madrid, his withers unwrung. 'You wouldn't be in London if you were!' No doubt he thought it wiser not to point out her spelling mistakes at this juncture: 'I have only just got back from Toledo and found your letter waiting for me. You know perfectly well that the only thing I look forward to is seeing you again; and I adore [you] more than ever.' He seemed more concerned with the logistics and presentation of his return to London. They expected to be back on Sunday, 3 May; would she send a note to Carlyle Square saying when they could meet? 'Can you spare *the time* to lunch with me on the Monday? If so it had better be somewhere awful like that Spanish restaurant because my clothes are unpresentable until I can get some new ones. . . .'[47] The tailoring problem was easily solved; on 5 May, the day after they were reunited, Sachie reported from the Burlington Fine Arts Club in Savile Row, where he had been writing the preface to the catalogue of another exhibition of seventeenth-century painting, that he had been 'ordering double-breasted suits by the dozen', many of them in his favourite brown which Georgia detested.

The question of marriage, however, was a delicate one. Marriage to Georgia would mean the break-up of the Sitwell trio; more seriously, perhaps, the introduction of a third person into the symbiotic relationship between Sachie and Osbert. At the outset, at least, Osbert liked Georgia, or pretended that he did, but in his heart of hearts he was jealous of Sachie's love for her and desperate at the prospect of losing him. Subconsciously he never forgave Georgia for being the cause of Sachie's desertion and, years later, was to have his revenge.

Sachie loved Osbert and felt unhappy at the thought of his misery. 'My darling,' he wrote to Georgia on the evening of 25 June. 'I feel quite happy to be alive again after a talk I had this evening with darling Osbert! Everything seems much better.' Osbert was the principal, though not the only, obstacle. Edith, too, was unhappy, although she kept her doubts to herself. Georgia, who was perhaps not ultra-sensitive, always remained convinced that Edith had welcomed her, having told her from the outset, 'I know I am going to love you because you love Sachie.' This, however, was not quite the case. While on the surface Edith was always kind, friendly and affectionate, appreciating Georgia's devotion to Sachie, on a deeper, Sitwellian level she thought her not quite good enough either in brain or in blood for her genius of a brother. Perhaps no intruder into the sacred trio would have been considered good enough. And she worried deeply about the effect of Sachie's desertion upon Osbert, as she wrote to his great friend Christabel McLaren in the month before Sachie's wedding in reply to a letter of 'condolence' on the coming event:

It must make a difference, of course – these things always do. At the same time, it would really be too dreadful to contemplate if, at least part of our life – the part that really counts [i.e. the artistic side], were not left to us in its entirety. This has more than the personal importance. And that, *you* understand. . . . How nice Heaven will be – where there is neither marrying nor giving in marriage. . . . I've only had a short letter from Osbert. I do *hope* he is alright. I feel rather worried about it. . . .[48]

Sachie had already endured six months of trial waiting for Georgia; now that she had agreed to marry him, he had to stand up to both their families. Neither set of parents was particularly enamoured of the match. Sir George would have liked to have been able to boast of a higher lineage for his daughter-in-law than that of Miss Georgia Doble, younger daughter of a Canadian banker, or at least a very large fortune to compensate for the lack of it; Lady Ida, although she liked Georgia, no doubt thought the same. All the Sitwells, however, seem to have overestimated Arthur Doble's wealth. He was successful and comfortably off but by no means excessively rich. From the Doble point of view, the younger son of a baronet, although a celebrity in his own right, was no great catch for Georgia after two seasons trawling through Europe, and she was, after all, very young. Sachie, however, was determined and confident. '*You must have reliance on me*, and I really *am sure* everything will be alright. Anybody who objects is an old fogey. . . . I don't think there is *anything* to be afraid of.'[49] He was, nevertheless, in a highly nervous state and one evening had 'an awful fight with poor Willie outside our house'. He had the worst of it and got a black eye as a result. The *casus belli* was that Walton had promised to leave Sachie alone with Georgia, but had forgotten his promise and 'stayed on and on and would not leave.'[50]

By the end of June they were engaged. There was a good deal of press attention on 'one of the most interesting engagements of the summer'. Both of them posed for photographs, Sachie showing a poetic profile against the framework of a baroque armchair, Georgia smouldering with half-closed eyelids in pearls and silk chiffon. Sachie was described as having, with Osbert and Edith, 'invented the characteristic attitude to life, the style of imagery, and the distinctive taste which we have come to sum up as Sitwellism'. Georgia was invited to contribute to a symposium, 'How I would earn my living'. She plumped for being a manicurist, 'the only trade I can think of which is open exclusively to women. . . . Men are still our superiors, even at those trades which appear essentially feminine, such as cooking, hair-dressing, and dress-designing. . . .' On 26 July she left with her parents for Paris, pursued by ardent love notes from Sachie raving about the 'wonderful summer' they had enjoyed together and wishing he could come to Paris and take her to '*le Boeuf sur le Toit*', introduce her to Cocteau and Picasso, and show her off to all his friends. He was deluged with requests for her photograph from 'the *Sketch*, *Tatler*, etc.'. On the 31st he went up to Renishaw with Osbert and Edith; Georgia was destined for the beach resort of Les Sables d'Olonne in the Vendée – 'sounds dreary and rather awful,' Sachie commiserated.

Renishaw that August was far from dreary. The Sitwells had invited a large party of friends and followers. Arthur Waley, who had praised Sachie's latest collection of poems so highly, was there with Beryl de Zoete. Waley was Sachie's closest connection with Bloomsbury. 'Though not one of Bloomsbury's highest inner praesidium, he ranked as an authentic Bloomsbury of the next grade,' Anthony Powell wrote of him.[51] Slight and sallow, Waley had a disconcerting social manner:

> He spoke always in a high clipped tone, as if slightly offended, habitually refusing to make the smallest compromise in the way of momentarily lowering intellectual standards in the interests of trivial courtesies. Conversations would be interrupted by long unnerving pauses, while, through narrowed eyes, Waley allowed the pageant of vulgar life to sweep past him as he pursued some distant internal vision. When bored or irritated, his high voice became supersonic.

Peter Quennell, a great admirer of Waley's and much influenced by him, described him as 'a scholar-poet, with a fine, austere mask, the features of a sage or saintly hermit, for whom the world most of his contemporaries inhabited was an alien and mysterious place'.[52] Although well-off as a result of his descent from a rich City Jewish family, Waley lived ascetically in his Bloomsbury flat, conveniently situated near the British Museum Print Room. He lived separately from his mistress, Beryl de Zoete, also the descendant of a City family, although they read, wrote and played music together, Waley on the flute and Beryl usually dancing, a subject on which she was an expert. An outgoing, uninhibited personality, she would travel all over the world in pursuit of her subject, ethnic dancing, often sending back to Arthur 'some outlandish local genius' she had picked up on her travels, including once a Foreign Legion deserter. Edith found her enthusiasms, particularly for younger men, tedious, and her passion for dance demonstrations when well into middle age ridiculous. She was wont to call her 'Baby Beryl' and poke relentless fun at her in her letters. Waley, however, bore with her patiently and devotedly. He had a warm heart and, despite his reserved and alarming manner, an indomitable sense of fun. In private conversation he was an amusing talker and loved gossip. One of the Sitwells' favourite stories was of Sphinx saying to this formidable intellectual, 'I expect, Mr Waley, you often go to *The Mikado.*'

Sphinx herself was, of course, in attendance, duly boring Ginger early to bed. Peter Quennell observed her 'crepuscular passion' for Osbert with amazed sympathy. Osbert, he said, treated her with delicacy and was never unkind, except when she indulged in her awkward habit of getting up at seven or eight o'clock in the morning at Renishaw. 'Dressed in a long black velvet robe, her golden Gorgonian wig surmounted by a velvet picture-hat', she could be seen tiptoeing across the lawn beneath his windows, when he would despatch Moat's assistant with a message that Mrs Leverson must please go back to bed again.[53]

Quennell, 'that friend and disciple of Edith's' as Sachie, who then scarcely knew him, described him to Georgia, and whom Edith praised as 'the greatest young genius after Sachie', had had a precocious reputation as a poet by the time he had arrived at Balliol in the autumn of 1923. He looked the part with 'pale hair, attenuated features, abstract demeanour', but, as Anthony Powell recorded, this poetic languor concealed a businesslike attitude towards literature and a 'down-to-earth approach where the opposite sex was concerned',[54] unusual at Balliol at the time and one which was soon to get him sent down from Oxford. Invited to spend two weeks at Renishaw, Quennell was much struck by what he called 'that strange Peacockian household'. He was impressed by Sir George, whom he described as 'a tall, noble-looking, neatly bearded man' wearing a wide-brimmed grey hat, ceremonious, gravely courteous with the guests and seemingly 'more or less detached from the other members of his family', living a solitary, self-sufficient life. 'At fixed hours, he would walk round the lake or inspect his park and gardens; his conversation was a measured monologue, of which even his irreverent son Osbert could not completely break the thread.' The once-beautiful Lady Ida seemed to Quennell 'very old', her clipped upper-class cockney reinforcing her curious appearance; she was always dressed in a black toque and black silk dress, supporting herself on a cane. To the young poet she seemed more like the Widow Twankey than an Edwardian beauty. 'Ain't it amusin', Henry?' she would ask Moat, showing him at luncheon in Sir George's absence a caricature of Sir George in the costume of a scoutmaster, to which Moat replied with an unappreciative growl, '*Very* amusing, I am sure, milady.'[55]

Sir George, although keeping his wife at a distance both physically and mentally (in Florence she spent a good deal of her time in hotels rather than at Montegufoni), was still suspicious of her drinking habits. It was understood at Renishaw and the surrounding houses that when Lady Ida asked for a lemonade, the innocent drink would be strongly spiked with gin. Anthony Powell recorded that Sir George had (perhaps not surprisingly) a strong prejudice against drink, so that at Renishaw there was none of the vinous plenty to be found at Carlyle Square and a house party of twenty at dinner would be lucky to get more than a glass of cheap white Bordeaux each. After the ladies withdrew, the men would sit gloomily round draining the dregs of their coffee while Sir George, who did not consider the lack of port or liqueurs any reason for cutting short the traditional male after-dinner interlude, held forth on one of his favourite topics, such as Nottingham in the Middle Ages. Before dinner the Sitwell children's favourite guests would assemble secretly in Lady Ida's sitting room for a quick pre-prandial nip. On one occasion Sir George found Osbert and his mother there enjoying an afternoon bottle of Maraschino. Seeing the bottle, the Baronet started dramatically back as if aghast, '*Not* Maraschino!'[56]

Powell was less impressed by Sir George than were the others. There was, he felt, something 'wrong' (i.e. not quite genuine) about him. 'Badly wrong,' he added, 'and for me he always lacked the air of distinction possessed by his children and by his unhappy wife. The eccentricities were certainly genuine enough, not in the least assumed to make an impression; yet he was in some manner an actor dressed up to play a part; that part perhaps not a very pleasant one.' Moat's verdict on his employers given to Constant Lambert was, 'Sir George is the strangest old bugger you ever met, and as for poor old Ida, she doesn't know whether she's coming or going.'

Renishaw presented the perfect setting for the Sitwells and their extraordinary guests. At first sight, Powell wrote, it 'suggested something not much short of decay, an atmosphere melancholy, even sinister', modified by Sir George's Italianate terraces adorned by baroque statues. Sir George had planted trees to screen the pitheads and smoke-stacks from view, but had not entirely succeeded; after dark a host of fiery points of light winked or glowed among the branches. Sir George ignored them. Inside, the house was a mixture of ordinary country-house neglect (it had been three years since it was last inhabited by the family) and objects of extraordinary magnificence. At night, there was no electricity and the house was lit by lamps; in the bedrooms the enormous curtained Italian beds furnished by Sir George, crowned with tufts of faded, dusty feathers, looked forbiddingly sepulchral. One wing was left unused 'on account of the aggressive nature of its ghosts', Powell wrote. The ghosts, however, did not confine themselves to the wing reserved for them. Among them was a sad, damp little ghost of William Sacheverell, drowned as a boy in the mid-eighteenth century, an 'impertinent phantom' said to have slapped Sir George's face as he was coming down the stairs, while a postman claimed to have seen a bat-like horror 'hideously stuck' to an outer wall as he was bicycling up the drive.

The ghosts, having been left in peace for three years, resented the disturbance and made their presence felt. 'The Ghosts are on the warpath here,' Sachie wrote to Georgia. 'We have had some weird and extraordinary experiences lately.'[57] Raymond Mortimer arrived. Edith was not fond of him, sneering in a letter to Violet Schiff at his 'craving for originality, when coupled with such vanity . . . his dining-room papered with old newspapers and drawing-room painted by Duncan Grant.'[58] Recently he had committed some offence against the Sitwells, who never passed up a chance to take their revenge. The day of his arrival a raging thunderstorm turned Renishaw into a house of Gothic horror to equal Horace Walpole's Castle of Otranto, as Sachie reported to Georgia. 'We put Raymond Mortimer in a ghost room (of which there are three) selecting the most blood-curdling one for his punishment. . . . He was duly frightened.'[59] Peter Quennell was similarly assaulted. 'Still awfully rainy', Sachie reported on the 14th, 'and the ghosts are being very lively. Last night they raided poor little Quennell's room.' Walton was due to appear the next day and also suffered their attentions. 'The ghosts are being very active – after Willie at the moment – they played a harp in his bedroom and a number of other tricks last night.'[60]

Christabel McLaren arrived in response to a plea from Osbert to take the burden of entertaining off Edith, Lady Ida being now quite hopeless in that respect. 'You *must* come to Renishaw,' he wrote. 'Ginger . . . exhibits every known symptom of "working up for trouble". He sighs, moans, walks up and down, talks to himself sleeping and waking. Sachie is worried and my Mother cross.'[61] Christabel, the daughter of Sir Melville Macnaghten, a former head of Scotland Yard, was a Society beauty, bossy and with a famously affected manner, but she was intelligent, had literary leanings and was a generous patroness of writers, composers and artists like Walton and Rex Whistler. She was half in love with Osbert, while he had as strong a feeling for her as he could have for a woman. Ten years later he was to write to her of their relationship: 'Certainly you've been the most important & lovely happening in my life . . . my heart is always lifted when I see you . . . what a wonderful friendship it is and what warm and wonderful companionship you've given me.'[62] They were friends to the end of his life, a friendship which was to cause Sachie, Georgia and, to a lesser extent, Edith considerable trouble. Christabel, fanatical in her devotion to Osbert, was often a trouble-maker where his immediate family was concerned.

Sachie's letters showed no sign of the worry attributed to him by Osbert. He was working well, surrounded by 'holy relics' of Georgia: photographs and a black pearl earring. 'I am writing marvellous poetry here, inspired by the idea of you,' he told her. He had finished seventeen poems in ten days and was also writing a good deal of prose and trying to think up plots for plays. Best of all, his family were leaving him alone: 'Mother and Father and Osbert are all being so nice and not fussing me at all.' Osbert would be going to Venice for the first time without him on 5 September and then on for two or three weeks to Montegufoni. 'I am sure it is better he should go there alone just for once,' Sachie wrote. 'He will be quite alright, I think.'[63]

Sachie had no intention of accompanying him. He was looking forward to joining Georgia in Paris at the beginning of September, hoping to arrange the wedding as soon as her father arrived from Canada. It was all too much for him; emotional excitement and the strain of writing so much in so short a time provoked a minor breakdown and he was forced to postpone his journey to Paris for a few days. On 2 September from Carlyle Square, which he found 'deluged with pieces of awful old silver' as wedding presents, he wrote Georgia his last note before their marriage.

With the Sitwells, however, nothing was ever simple, even getting married. Edith at first thought that she was too poor to go to the wedding if it took place abroad. 'Darling boy & most lovely of poets,' she wrote to Sachie on 10 September, 'there is no possibility of going to the wedding, as I am in the worst financial crisis I've ever been in'. Coutts Bank having written that she was £68 overdrawn beyond her guarantee and demanding immediate repayment; she had agreed that the bank was to keep three-quarters of her dress allowance, 'so no railway journeys, no books, no new clothes & no taxis'.[64] Money, probably from Osbert, was somehow found, for Edith did attend the wedding. Osbert, in Venice with Adrian Stokes, a beautiful young art historian whom he had met at Rapallo the previous year, was miserable. He had arrived with a cold and felt very ill, while 'Adrian has piles & can hardly move'. Dick Wyndham and Raymond Mortimer were both there, which was some comfort, he wrote on 9 September to Sachie, who was now staying with his prospective in-laws at the Hôtel Impériale in Paris. There was, apparently, still no decision as to the date or even the place of the wedding. 'I do miss you so & look forward to seeing you,' Osbert wrote, giving his address as care of the British Embassy at Rome. 'I fear you must find out about your marriage. I *cannot* find out, & time is short. Write to the British Chaplain at Rome, why not? October 18th is a good day, I think.'[65]

By 14 September, things were still not settled. 'Dearest Sach,' Osbert wrote from Venice, where he still had a bad cold and missed his brother very much, 'I have written to Georgia fully about the ways of getting married. If possible I advise you to get the civil marriage done in Paris at once at the Consulate. And then have a religious one at Rome. In this case you should write at once to the Chaplain at Rome so that your date (Oct. 20th) shall not be booked up.'[66] Osbert was being driven from Venice by the imminent arrival of Ginger; he and Adrian were escaping to Brescia. Not surprisingly, therefore, there was a further muddle as Sachie's letter announcing the final date for the wedding pursued him round Italy, finally catching up with him at Montegufoni.

'Dearest, darling Sach,' Osbert wrote. 'Alas, when it [Sachie's letter] arrived, I had just arranged to go later, and had wired to you. It makes me very unhappy, as I don't want to let you down.' Some of the responsibility for the muddle was laid at Mr Doble's door; at first he had seemed disinclined to hurry from Canada, sending Sachie frantic at the thought that the wedding might have to be delayed until November. Now he was apparently digging in his toes over the marriage settlement.

' "Ginger" says you should not make a will in Georgia's favour unless she makes one in your favour at the same time,' Osbert advised. 'In any case you should not make a will but a new *settlement* – which takes ages. . . . Please explain this to Mr Doble. I am sure he will see that it is not the correct moment to worry you about it. It is absolute nonsense; and even "Ginger" admits it.' Osbert had had trouble in restraining Sir George from joining Sachie and Georgia on their honeymoon: ' "Ginger" is very aggravating, and wants to "be near you on your honeymoon, in case the boy needs me". I had to tell him not to interfere. Darling,' he continued, snatching at straws, 'I do hope you will be happy, and am sure you will be. But if you have *any* doubt, even now, say so. It would be better for everyone in the end.'[67]

Most people connected with the affair seemed to be more concerned about Osbert than anything else. Mrs Edith Powell, their housekeeper, wrote to 'Mr Sashie', having heard that the wedding was fixed for 9 October, that she felt 'very sorry for Mr Osbert', who was 'feeling hurt and sad at losing you' and that she too felt 'rather sad now it has come to the end'.[68] Christabel was roped in to support Osbert in Paris and even Lady Ida stirred herself to write inviting her to accompany him on to Montegufoni after the wedding: 'Osbert will be very sad and it will help to cheer him up.'

In the event, even the date of the wedding was altered to suit Osbert. The ceremony finally took place on 12 October. 'Poet's Marriage in Paris' was the headline above the *Daily Express* correspondent's report on the eve of the wedding. Sir George and Lady Ida Sitwell would not be present, having been 'unavoidably detained' in Florence, but Sir George had presented the bride with a pair of sixteenth-century emerald earrings and Lady Ida had given her 'a magnificent antique pendant of black pearls with rubies', a wedding present from her father. Osbert, Edith, Christabel and Walton were there on the Sitwell side, outnumbering the three Dobles, Bunny and her parents, at the short civil marriage at the British Consulate followed by a service at St George's Anglican Church. The chaplain who conducted it would not have been pleased to know that the bridegroom was fond of saying that he preferred theatres to churches. The Dobles lost a daughter in a very real sense, while the absent Sir George and Lady Ida, perhaps ungratefully, gained one. Chameleon-like, Georgia strained every nerve to become absorbed in the Sitwell ethos. In the words of a friend, she 'took on Sitwell lore with an extraordinary receptivity'. She not only married a Sitwell, but she became – in so far as anyone could – a Sitwell. Looking back in his long autobiographical fantasy, *For Want of the Golden City*, almost half a century later, Sachie recognised the effect his marriage had had upon his relationship with Osbert and Edith, but none the less did not regret it: 'Marrying . . . which lasting happiness of our own may have broken, or snapped, or strained the strings of family attachment. But it gave me my liberty, it made my own life, and let me work in peace.'[69]

6

Sitwelldom

1925–1929

'If only Sach could . . . emancipate himself a little [from] this syndicate existence of petty hopes and fears . . . this obsession which one can only call Sitwellism. . . .'

Georgia Sitwell, diary, September 1928

Sachie and Georgia spent a two-week honeymoon in the Low Countries before returning to Paris to catch a train south to join Osbert at Amalfi. They stopped off in Basel specifically so that Sachie could see El Greco's *Laocoon*, a painting which particularly fascinated him and about which he later wrote a long poem.

From London Walton had kept 'dearest Sachie' posted with home news, not all of it agreeable. One black Friday bailiffs from both the Army & Navy Stores (for the groceries) and Chappell's (gramophone records and hire of Walton's piano) had turned up waving bills and refusing to move unless they were paid. 'I know you'll be furious,' Walton wrote on 18 October, well aware that Sachie liked to defer paying bills for as long as possible; 'Wire brass. I am so contrite about it.' Having received a long letter from Georgia describing their happiness, he teased, 'I am overjoyed to hear of your angelic & sweet disposition. I always knew you had one, though I must say that up till now you have done your best to hide it. Let it be permanent, especially . . . for the next few months. It will make all the difference to Osbert.'' He was too busy to come out to join them at Amalfi until Boxing Day, but Peter Quennell, 'rather subdued' after being sent down from Oxford because of a liaison with a Mrs Chambers (heterosexuality being considered almost an offence at the Balliol of those days), would be there soon. 'Don't let the fell P[eter] cut me out in either of your affections,' he warned. 'He nearly did it once & might easily do it again. . . .' He also gave him the latest musical news of their circle; he had finished the overture, *Portsmouth Point*, and Sorabji, Constant Lambert and Philip Heseltine were coming to tea. Lambert had written a ballet which he hoped Diaghilev would take; Diaghilev would be 'off his chump' if he didn't, Walton told Sachie. 'I think it's marvellous. In fact he [Lambert] is the genius amongst a lot of talent.'[2] Later he had shown *Portsmouth Point* to Diaghilev, who had praised it as 'a most brilliant, fresh & exhilarating work' and intimated that he might use Walton's music for a ballet.[3]

Sachie and Georgia arrived at the Hotel dei Cappuccini at Amalfi on 1 November to join Osbert and Adrian Stokes and to resume the well-established Sitwellian routine. It was as if nothing had changed. Inevitably, Sphinx appeared and characteristically questioned Georgia point-blank as to how the marriage was faring. Georgia clearly felt a little out of her depth; furtively looking round to make sure the brothers were not within earshot, she whispered, 'I want to ask you four questions – quickly now. What is the difference between Romanticism & Classicism? Who is Harry Melville? What is behaviourism & is Julie Thompson received?'[4] Osbert, however, had no complaints – yet – to make about his new sister-in-law. At the end of November he reported to Christabel that, although it had rained for three weeks without stopping, Sachie and Georgia seemed 'amiable and happy'. The irruption of Peter Quennell destroyed the peaceful atmosphere.

As usual with the Sitwells, thunder lurked in the offing as the winter storms pursued each other across the Bay of Naples, blotting out the horizon and drenching the narrow ledge on which the hotel stood with incessant sheets of rain. The mountains behind were seldom visible, the sea below a muddy churning mass, and the streets of Amalfi beneath the castle that had once belonged to Webster's duchess had a peculiarly damp and dispiriting smell. According to Quennell, hints of tension, malaise and ennui began to creep into their daily life in the ancient former convent. Behind their cell doors Osbert was writing *Before the Bombardment*, Sachie was 'weaving the rich autobiographical tapestry of *All Summer in a Day*', and Adrian Stokes was beginning a book of art criticism. Penned in by the weather, the atmosphere grew electric at their daily meetings for White Ladies and conversation in Osbert's sitting room followed by luncheon or dinner. As Quennell recalled:

> Osbert's Hanoverian features now grew particularly autocratic, and he
> gave free rein to his love of teasing; Sachie's visionary remoteness
> increased; while Adrian's high-flown speeches and romantic attitudes
> grated on my irritable nerves. There were rows at dinner, often

provoked by me, when I heard a voice – I knew it could only be mine – making a remark I repented of even before I had completed it. I was not the sole cause of the general malaise; but I was unquestionably the chief offender. . . .[5]

Quennell's crime arose from his daring to make fun of Osbert's protective affection for Adrian Stokes, a striking-looking, somewhat affected young man who described the colour of his hair in his passport as 'old gold'. On one occasion when Osbert was fussing because Adrian had not yet returned from swimming, Quennell said airily, 'Oh, I expect he's drowned.' Osbert was not amused. When Quennell went in the New Year to stay with the novelist, Francis Brett Young, and his wife on Anacapri, he was declared *persona non grata* by a Sitwell kangaroo court and Georgia was deputed to write him a letter suggesting that, although they would be delighted to see him in London, he had better not rejoin them at Amalfi. Quennell told 'dearest Sachie' that he felt 'sick with surprise and distress' at receiving, after their perfectly affectionate parting, 'three quarters of a page of rather rude dismissal'. 'Perhaps its [*sic*] literary gaucherie on Georgia's part, after all. I am sorry to make a commotion, but you must put it down to extreme fondness for you. I can't believe that you can have seen and let pass such a piece. . . .'[6] He was later forgiven and remained a great friend of Sachie's, but, although it was the first row he had with them, it was to be by no means the last. 'With the Sitwells', he said, 'there were apt to be bad moments when you didn't know what you'd done, but you'd done something wrong.'[7]

Edith, snowed-up in London, wrote supportive letters. 'I can't get over Peter's behaviour to Adrian,' she told Georgia. 'It makes me so angry. . . .I feel – you have made me feel – as though you have always been in the family – as though you have grown there. . . .I do feel absolutely as though you were my own sister – How happy I am, how lucky I am, to have you, darling.'[8] She also skilfully made Georgia feel that they were on intimate terms. In her Christmas letter to Georgia that year, she gave her formal admission to the family, writing somewhat pathetically: 'I think life is really going to be happy with us four.' Georgia was to discover that life with the Sitwells, although never dull, was never merely 'happy'; her new in-laws of both generations were not 'happy' people. Edith left Georgia in no doubt as to how she viewed her principal role as Sachie's wife: 'Whenever people ask me "What is your sister-in-law like", I, having said what *I* feel about you, say "and apart from all that, she is a perfect wife for a great poet".'[9]

Ironically, this moment, which marked the beginning of the dissolution of the trio with Sachie's marriage, was also the high point of the Sitwells' literary celebration of their childhood and of frequent public appearances together. Edith, the most expert publicist of the three, drew a poetical portrait of herself and her brothers – 'Dagobert' and 'Peregrine' – at Renishaw in 'Colonel Fantock' published in *Troy Park* in March 1925 and in October, the month of Sachie's marriage, the three of them had published a joint book of poems, *Poor Young People*. In the spring of 1926 they were Gertrude Stein's sponsors when she visited England to address university literary societies at Oxford and Cambridge; both Edith and Osbert gave parties for her while Osbert soothed her stage fright, his 'pleasant kindly irresponsible agitated calm' reminding her of 'the uncle of a king'. At Oxford her host, Harold Acton, described her as accompanied by her 'tall bodyguard of Sitwells' and Alice B. Toklas, who 'looked like a gypsy and Bostonian.'[10] Stein was a controversial figure and the audience had come prepared to heckle, but Stein trounced them with her repartee, to Sachie's delight. On 29 June 1926 *Façade* was given another public performance, this time at the Chenil Galleries. Walton had reworked and extended the score with the help of Constant Lambert, who also took part in the reading, and this time it was a great success. Diaghilev was there and told Sachie that Walton's music, good as it was, had shades of Elgar in it, an opinion which would not have pleased the young composer.[11] Osbert had drawn on their mutual Scarborough background in *Triple Fugue* (1924) and his novel on the same theme, *Before the Bombardment*, published in October 1926. At the same time Sachie was writing, for simultaneous publication, his own Proustian evocation of the sensations of childhood, *All Summer in a Day*, on which he had been working almost from the moment he met Georgia. It was as if he subconsciously realised that marriage was the final end to childhood and wanted to recapture his memories and set them in amber before they disappeared for good. He had always been obsessed with the transience of people and experience. 'With regard, then, to one's private mythology, for in this way one might describe the arsenal of memory,' he wrote in the preface explaining why he had undertaken an autobiography while still in his twenties, 'those who know anything of interest had better say it; for such little flashes and flickers of light are one's own property and visible to no one else. They get further and further away and will soon be beyond recall.'

All Summer in a Day was not a conventional autobiography. It was an examination of a few moments in the past and of the sensations he had experienced then. The Sitwells' first biographer, R.L. Mégroz, wrote that the book established Sachie as a master of prose; in fact, it demonstrated that, although he could write prose, he was essentially a poet. *All Summer in a Day* is Proustian only in the sense that *À la recherche du temps perdu* must have been a subconscious influence. There are only two 'ghosts in his cupboard', as he puts it – 'Brockie' here again called 'Colonel Fantock' in 'A Military Ghost' and Miss Lloyd in 'Miss Morgan' – presented as the child saw them, the yellow boots of the one, conjured up by the hot jammy scent of wallflowers, the tea-cakes and jewel-like setting of the other. The book begins with a blackberrying expedition in early September at the time of Edith's birthday, when Sachie became suddenly aware of the existence and passage of time. 'Time had halted by my side for a second, and I became suddenly drenched and wet for evermore in the waters of memory. . . . I was filled . . . with this double-consciousness, both realising the moment and wondering how long I should be able to remember it. . . .'

The book revealed the extraordinary empathy with nature which fed his poetry. In one long passage the three children raided the walled orchard for red currants through the nets draped over them as protection from the birds. Pushing their fingers through the meshes, they reached for the brittle red clusters, which would often break leaving them with just one berry:

> . . . it had an acrid, bitter taste with the hard black seed in the middle, though the fruit itself was cold and sharp as a raindrop. The taste of it was precisely that of the rain when it falls upon a leaf and rolls itself into some little hollow of the webbed tracery where it can keep its form, and if you could eat it there, you would have, like the caterpillar, the whole flavour and the actual being of the tree principle, both the sharp light of the boughs which is like the green alternation you see from looking at the sun through closed eyelids, and also the wild, goatish limbs of the tree. . . .

'I can't tell you how much I enjoyed *All Summer in a Day*,' Raymond Mortimer wrote to him. 'I am still dizzy with it . . . from wandering down hallucinatory glades, drugged and as it were on a lead. . . . It seems to me an awfully important book which will go on being read as long as sensibility and the English language continues. . . . At times it reminds me strangely of Proust. . . .'[12] The *Times Literary Supplement* reviewer also found the book 'sufficiently remarkable'. 'Mr Sitwell's remote viewpoint has its value,' the reviewer conceded, 'for it is the image of a poet and certainly it is a way of bringing fantasy to bear upon the ordinary events of life. . . .'[13]

A month earlier, Sachie had published *Exalt the Eglantine*, a collection of poems inspired by a marquetry table at Hardwick Hall not far from Renishaw inlaid with the mysterious lines: 'The redolent smelle of eglantine/We stagges exalt to the Divine.' Playing cards and musical instruments also appeared on the table and consequently as titles for the poems. Sachie's poetic inspiration was, as always, triggered by a visual or aural experience. *Exalt the Eglantine* was received by Edith, to whom Sachie had sent it in January 1926, with her by now customary raptures. Describing the poems as 'heavenly' and a 'dream', she was astounded how, 'by the use of sound, you evoke the smell of woods, growing flowers, and growing fruits and leaves'.[14] She did not stint her praise: '. . . you are', she told him, 'one of the greatest poets England has ever produced!', and she pitied people who did not realise 'that we have living among us today a poet as great as Milton'. The Hardwick poems were 'so strange and wild-wood, and haunted, and they are like nothing on this earth excepting Hardwick'.[15] She was 'violently proud' of being his sister. 'What does anything matter when one comes of a family which can produce poetry like that?' The *Times Literary Supplement* greeted the poems cautiously. 'Mr Sitwell is a real poet,' the reviewer admitted, but went on to castigate him for being selfishly obscure. Comparing his poetry with the seventeenth-century metaphysical poets, like Marvell, the *TLS* complained that Sachie expected too much of his readers. Where Marvell compared cattle on a distant plain to pimples on a face, 'if Mr Sitwell were to do this he might well speak of pimples on a face and expect the reader to understand that he meant cattle on a plain'.[16]

The Sitwell style provoked choleric reactions in readers brought up on a diet of Kipling. Arthur Baumann, essayist and *Standard* contributor, wrote furiously to Humbert Wolfe condemning his favourable review in the *Observer* of *All Summer in a Day* and *Before the Bombardment* by 'those insupportable bores, the Sitwells'. 'Can't you see what bores they are?' he raged; '. . . both books are entirely composed of descriptions of asphalte [sic] walks etc of Scarborough, which I happen to know. In Sachi's [sic] book no one talks but himself and no one does anything. I can't remember having been so bored for ages. Do try, in prose at least, to cultivate a taste for people who speak and do things.'[17]

That summer and autumn of 1926 Sachie had taken an entirely new departure, working with Diaghilev and Gerald Berners on a ballet, *The Triumph of Neptune*, for which Berners was to compose the music and he was to write the book. The idea of the ballet and Sachie's collaboration had been Berners', first mooted that summer. As late as August 1926, however, the theme of the ballet had not been finally decided upon. From Venice, where he and Diaghilev had joined with the international smart set for a ball to be given by Catherine d'Erlanger and Lady Colebrooke at the Fenice, Berners wrote hastily to Sachie asking him to send 'as soon as possible, any ideas you have gathered. . . . Could you perhaps make out, as you suggested, a few alternative "libretti" and send them to me here?'[18] This was followed up by an urgent telegram summoning Sachie to join him and Diaghilev in Venice for discussions about the ballet; a compromise was later reached by which Sachie would meet the pair in Florence in September.

Leaving Georgia in Paris with her parents, Sachie travelled alone to Florence to work with Diaghilev, George Balanchine, Serge Lifar and Boris Kochno at the Palace Hotel on the further side of the Arno, where they were staying mainly because it had a large room at the top, known as the Sala Santa Caterina, in which they could work. 'Everything so far has gone well,' he reported to Georgia on 9 September. 'Diaghilev is charming. Berners rather less so.' Berners was being elusive; Sachie wrote no less than two letters on one day, 12 September, complaining about his behaviour. 'Berners is rather tiresome. He is too busy with Lady Cunard to think of anything else, and is really rather hopeless. Also, he is rather on the defensive. . . .' He was beginning to regret having gone to the trouble and expense of going to Florence. 'Everything gets more and more difficult here,' he wrote. 'Really Berners is too odd for words. . . .I have only seen him for about 5 minutes since I came here, and am left absolutely alone all day long.' Diaghilev, however, continued to be charming; Sachie showed him the garden of the Villa Gamberaia and took him to lunch at a deserted Montegufoni (Osbert and the Gingers being still at Renishaw).

When the theme of the ballet was finally agreed, it was to be a mixture of naïve Victorian pantomime, Jules Verne and modern satire, featuring, of course, a harlequin to be danced by Lifar. Sachie's idea was that the scenery should be based on the early Victorian styles of Pollock's Toy Theatre which he had always loved. He took Diaghilev to Pollock's shop and to the old theatrical costumier's named May's next to the Garrick Club to show him their splendid collection of spangled Hoxton prints and five cut-glass tunics as worn in the old pantomines. Diaghilev was entranced and bought the lot; later Sokolova had to dance in *The Triumph of Neptune* perspiring under the weight of one of these tunics. Sachie also suggested to Diaghilev the drawings of Robert Cruickshank as an inspiration for the costumes. Among his other helpful duties for the ballet was to buy contraceptives for the star, Alexandra Danilova, who was living with Balanchine at the time and afraid of getting pregnant.[19]

The Triumph of Neptune was performed by the Diaghilev Ballet at the Lyceum Theatre in London on 3 December 1926. Both Walton and Lambert had helped Berners with the score, with Walton doing the orchestration. Walton also conducted a 'symphonic interlude' featuring the new 'Suite from "*Façade*" ', expanded for a forty-strong orchestra. The excitement about the 'new Sitwell–Berners ballet' was tremendous and the theatre was crammed with a fashionable audience. Among them, although not yet fashionable himself, was the young Cecil Beaton, already a Sitwell worshipper from afar. His account of the evening filled several pages of his diary with gushing prose which perfectly reflected the period:

> Never was an audience more congenial – Every point received more than its worth of applause & laughter. What fun it was going to be – mimes of 70 years ago & the curtain & scenery copied exact from the little toy theatres of that date. . . .The tremendous audience screamed with laughter. Everything went with a swing . . . such fun all the changes of scenery & dresses . . . the exquisite beauty of the fairies in their white tulle & diamond tiaras quite took away one's breath. . . . I, quite led away by the ecstatic enthusiasm of the audience, was enraptured with every minute. . . . Lifar looked lovely with the most shapely legs & buttocks tightly encased in white. There was one moment when I was quite sick with delight . . . really quite exquisite. The Ballet ended triumphantly with a very elaborate transformation scene which was terribly amusing. . . . That the curtain should fall on all these ballet dancers, fairies, harlequins etc. bursting with laughter was quite perfect! . . . the enthusiasm was terrific – flowers by the hundred. Lifar covered with laurel wreaths & bouquets. Lord Berners . . . like a bad wax figure in a cheap clothes shop stood bowing and smiling – & the curtain, of course, came down on his bald pate . . . at last, Sascheverell [sic] Sitwell took a call – very shy & aristocratic-looking, pale & tall, with long, thin hands.

Edith was resplendent in 'Royal blue silk, embroidered all over in Vivid colours in flowers, butterflies and ribbons'. Osbert, on a literary tour of the United States, was not there to see his brother's triumph. The evening ended at the Eiffel Tower, where Beaton again saw Sachie, 'looking like a little boy smoking an enormous cigar'.[20]

Not everyone was as enthusiastic as Beaton. One critic wrote a very hostile review, calling it an 'orgie [*sic*] of Sitwellism', and Berners's music 'pseudo-polyphony' with 'some nasty slabs of sound'. Although the stalls were enthusiastic, he noted, 'the booing from the *profanum vulgus* was loud and persistent'. Most of the reports, however, were fawning; one concluded that had Osbert been present at the Lyceum Theatre that night, 'he would probably have realised that England was already "fit for Sitwells to live in!" '

Later that month Sachie and Georgia left for Rome, where they stayed at the Hotel Majestic, the scene of Sachie's 'Waterloo Night' the previous January; they then went dutifully on to join Osbert in Naples. They had now been married just over a year, a marriage which seemed to be a success in every way. 'My darling angel,' Sachie had written to Georgia from Florence in September, 'I do miss you so much and realize how much my whole life depends upon you. The last year has been the most wonderful I have ever been alive.' 'My darling Sach,' Georgia had written to him on the first anniversary of their marriage, 12 October 1926, from the same hotel in Paris which they had left one year ago on their honeymoon, 'I feel I must write to you before going to bed just to tell you how I miss you & how much I have thought of you all day.' From her viewpoint the first year of marriage had not presented quite the same vista of unalloyed bliss: '. . . to think we left here together just a year ago to-day. We have been through some trying times, one way and another since then, but to me it has been infinitely worth while. You know darling that *I'd go through anything* so long as you really love me & would put up with anything. . . .' The 'anything' with which she was prepared to put up almost certainly included her in-laws and the couple's perennially precarious financial situation.

Within a year of their marriage Georgia had fulfilled one of her principal duties; by October 1926 she was pregnant. Sir George was delighted at the prospect of a Sitwell heir, writing from Montegufoni with a note of unconscious pathos which would have evoked a wry smile in his own children:

I really cannot tell you, my dear Georgia, how much pleased I am. There is nothing in the world like the love of a child if one can get it, and modern parents do get it by being always kind and considerate, and by explaining why some things can't be allowed and others can; that is where women get more out of life than men, for many children are taught to be afraid of their fathers.[21]

Their first son was born on 15 April 1927 at their rented London house, 18 Tite Street. It was a difficult birth; afterwards Georgia was weak and the baby seemed to be starving and gained no weight. Sachie was proud – 'the child is extraordinary' – but still fussed dreadfully. The family were, of course, thrilled. Osbert wrote to 'Darling Darling Georgia, A million congratulations', adding, 'I hope the child will prosper and be a terror to his grandparents, though not to Mother, Father or Uncle.'[22] He hoped that his nephew might be named Osbert Reresby, advising Sachie that Sacheverell Reresby would be too much of a mouthful, advice which Sachie disregarded. The baby was to be christened Sacheverell Reresby, but would always be known by his second family name. Despite his pleasure over the baby, which he constantly referred to as 'it', Sachie felt trapped by his new status and wrote Osbert a melancholy letter, to which his brother responded with loyal injunctions to cheer up:

> You must not write in this strain . . . it really is not fair on yourself or other people. One can't have everything . . . a wife, son, and perfect liberty as though you were a bachelor . . . really you are to be envied not pitied.
>   You know I adore you: you must therefore know that I want to be with you as much as possible.
>   As for money, it will be alright sooner or later, unless there's a revolution. I will go into it with you. For if it is not enough with what you have earned, there must be something wrong somewhere.[23]

Sachie, essentially a child himself, was not cut out to be a father. He did not enjoy parental responsibility and was to show very little sense of it; his son would not be allowed to get in the way of his own enjoyment or interests, while Georgia would be expected (and willingly complied) to concentrate on his life rather than the child's. Although pleased at the birth of his son, he was apprehensive about the limit he might place on his own freedom and about the expense he would necessarily involve. The early weeks after Reresby's birth were not easy, as the doctors had insisted that Georgia go on feeding him, despite the baby's obvious hunger and failure to gain weight. 'Very exhausting for us both,' Sachie commented selfishly to Christabel McLaren. Reresby was christened in June at Lambeth Palace – 'a ceremony which I dread,' Sachie confessed to Christabel – and equipped with a black nurse, Mary Cole, who was always known as 'Nannah', a woman of strong personality of whom Georgia was rather afraid. Like most upper-class children of the period, Reresby was kept very much in the background; he was to see less of his parents even than most. As they travelled, Reresby would be left behind with Nannah, either at home or with his Sitwell grandparents at Montegufoni, or the Dobles in France.

Marriage had by no means disentangled Sachie from his family of either generation. Sir George had moved to Montegufoni the previous year, leaving Renishaw to Osbert, but, having arranged that Sachie and Georgia should live at Weston, he still kept a close watch on their finances, which remained largely under his control. He was by now, with some justification, deeply suspicious of his family's extravagance and general carelessness and self-indulgence about money. Initially he had hopes of Georgia, who, as the daughter of a successful banker, might have been expected to have a head for figures. However, he had no illusions about Sachie: 'Some people learn from experience,' he wrote to Georgia in March 1927; 'others, like Ida, never touch anything without its going wrong all through their lives. You are practical & belong to the former class, but I am not so sure of Sachie.'[24]

In the first year of his marriage bills and summonses for unpaid bills had rained down on Sachie, some of them for accounts dating back over five years. He either ignored them or, in the case of particularly unwelcome communications such as bank statements, left them unopened. In November 1926 Sir George had been moved to issue a stern rebuke after hearing that a bill from Dr Salter, the Scarborough doctor who had treated Sachie in 1920–1921, had neither been paid nor forwarded to him for payment.[25] Sachie's attitude towards money was essentially Micawberish – something would turn up; something always did, but at a price which he was to find too high. His income from the Weston estate and family investments, together with the relatively small amount he earned from writing, totalled around £1,000 a year; he never made any attempt to live within it despite angry showers of advice from Ginger. He counted on an eventual inheritance to save him in the long-term; the short-term could look after itself. Georgia was essentially practical but she too was extravagant, determined to keep up the material standards expected of their social position whether they could afford them or not. 'We are both martyrs to comfort,' she was to write, looking back on their life together.

As a handsome, young, celebrity couple, Sachie and Georgia were becoming more and more closely involved with the London Society world of the 'Bright Young Things' and endless parties described by Evelyn Waugh in *Vile Bodies*. Sachie's life was becoming perceptibly less literary as he gravitated, not unwillingly, under Georgia's influence, towards 'smart' society, even though, as Waugh pointed out, it was a far less Philistine society than it had been before the First World War. Largely due to the Sitwells and their followers it had become, for the first time, smart to be intelligent and knowledgeable about art.

Despite his social life, Sachie still managed to do a good deal of work. *All Summer in a Day* in October 1926 had been followed by *Dr Donne and Gargantua, Canto the Third* in December that year. On 2 June 1927 he published his next collection of poetry, *The Cyder Feast*. The dedication, dated the day of Reresby's birth, was to 'My Brother, Sister, and Little Son'; curiously Georgia was not included, perhaps because she was not a Sitwell by blood. The dust-jacket by Severini showed a punchinello picking apples, continuing the *commedia* theme with which Sachie was still obsessed. (He had written the preface to Cyril Beaumont's *The History of Harlequin*, dedicated to himself and Osbert, also published that year.) The twenty-five poems in the book, inspired by flowers, plants and fruit, had been written in February 1927 as a continuation of the sequence 'Hortus Conclusus', which he had begun with the twenty-five poems published in *The Thirteenth Caesar* and further poems in *Exalt the Eglantine*. They were intended to form part of a large volume of short lyrical pieces on a similar theme. Sachie wrote that he had already 'considerably over one hundred' short poems and hoped to publish the collection in two or three years' time in final form with between 150 and 200 poems. It was a project which he only finally completed in the last decades of his life.

The Cyder Feast included a poem recalling his Renishaw childhood, perhaps inspired by Edith's 'Colonel Fantock'. In 'The Renishaw Woods' the trio wander in the August heat, punctured by thundery rain:

These showers among green reeds, like rolling drums were hushed,
And we were back in the faunal silence that no word can break
Waist deep in bracken,
With two-edged swords of ferns set round,
In hoarse smell of wet mustiness . . .

The title poem, 'The Cyder Feast', and its companion, 'The Chamber Idyll', were inspired in a way characteristic of Sachie's muse by the wood-engravings of Edward Calvert. Three poems, 'The Farnese Hercules', 'The Laocoon' and 'The Hermes', under the title 'Canons of Giant Art, Three Torsos', were part of a new series stemming, as he explained, from his first sight of El Greco's *Laocoon* in the museum at Basel in the autumn of 1925:

> The Laocoon is one of the strangest and most personal pictures in the world and I determined to write a poem in its honour. I wondered, in the first place, how Greco had ever come to admire that group of sculpture which we can consider as the complete negation of the sculptor's principles, yet by some magical process he has produced a work of art out of that meaningless and ineffective virtuosity. I resolved to put my own powers to the test, and during the autumn of 1925, while in the south of Italy, I wrote these Three Torsos as a kind of school for my poetical emotions. I have a profound horror of certainly two out of these three pieces of sculpture, yet I hope the intense pleasure that I derived from this commission for three poems . . . may be communicated in however diminished degree to the reader.[26]

One short poem, 'VI. Apricot', could, perhaps, have been a reference to a pregnant Georgia and the possibility of other lovers:

> So love in lonely hours will heat,
> The heart in this dark room will beat,
> And though the fruit is big with stone,
> Sweet flesh to that dead sullen bone,
> This apricot is not my all;
> I will find others on the wall.

Perhaps significantly, 'Apricot' was never reprinted in any of his other collections. He may not have thought it good enough; he may also have thought it indiscreet.

In 1927 Sachie did have another 'apricot' in mind, Zita Jungman, daughter of Beatrice Guinness by her first husband, Nico Jungman, an amiable half-Dutch painter, and sister of Teresa, always known as 'Baby', whose admirers included Evelyn Waugh. Their mother's huge house in Great Cumberland Place was among the social centres of Sachie's and Georgia's world. Beatrice Guinness was a noted hostess, despite being universally known as 'Gloomy Beatrice' for her sepulchral voice and occasionally extremely glum remarks – 'I want a hat for a middle-aged woman whose husband hates her,' she once announced to an astonished milliner's assistant. Zita and Baby, with their cousins by marriage, Tanis and Meraud Guinness, and Eleanor Smith, Lord Birkenhead's daughter, were the epicentre of the 'ain't we got fun' brigade, Zita herself being credited with the invention of the Bright Young Things' Treasure Hunt.

Behind the 'screaming', which was the normal accompaniment of 'fun', Zita was sensitive, dreamy and inclined to take life seriously. Cecil Beaton described her as 'quite marvellously lovely – great squirrels' eyes, fair hair & nice soft throaty voice'. She was a 'perfect young lady', he added quaintly, with 'a completely different personality to anyone I know – thoroughly unflashy, & quiet, but very original'.[27]

Sachie's attention had been caught by Zita's looks at a party some years before when he had been struck by her resemblance to a page in Tiepolo's *Antony and Cleopatra*, the painting that had such sensual connotations for him. He had written a four-line poem to her, 'The Golden Bell', an acrostic on her name, which he had published for the first time in *The Thirteenth Caesar*, but he had not met her until the autumn of 1926 when he and Georgia began an independent social life of their own. On 25 November they were at a lavish party given by 'Gloomy Beatrice' for her daughters. Beaton was there too, revelling in the glamour of the house with its magnificent furniture, huge tubs stacked with lilies and enormous glass vases filled with pink and yellow roses, and of the guests, a mixture of actresses, aristocrats and royalty including Tallulah Bankhead, Ivor Novello, the Duchess of Rutland and the Infanta Beatriz of Spain. Earlier Beaton, who admired Sachie but still only knew him by sight, had confided to his diary his fears that Georgia, 'that silly social fool', was leading him astray into a life unsuitable for a poet. At a party given by Madge Garland of *Vogue*, he noted that Sachie, 'under his wife's influence, is becoming rather unsuitably social. She is evidently going to ruin him by making him a social favourite & he is so miles above her – or his silly brother.'[28]

Sachie did not get to know Zita or, indeed, Beaton until the following June, when he and Georgia resumed the summer social round after Reresby was weaned. On 18 June they went down to stay with Stephen Tennant at Wilsford, the house designed by Detmar Blow for Stephen's father, Lord Glenconner, in a setting of lawns shadowed by ilex trees and a river overhung with willows. Osbert was with them, and the other guests included Zita, Beaton, now almost inseparable from the outrageously camp Tennant, Rex Whistler, Rosamond Lehmann, who had recently published *Dusty Answer*, Eddie Sackville-West, Baba Brougham and the American writer, Elinor Wylie. Stephen Tennant, with his slender figure, marcelled blond hair highlit with gold dust and delicate profile, epitomised the androgynous looks fashionable in the 1920s. Tennant himself was feminine, his beautiful mother, Lady Grey, having indulged him by allowing him to dress as a girl in his teens, surprising her week-end guests. At Wilsford that week-end there were endless jokes and laughter, some of it at the expense of Elinor Wylie, whom Rosamond Lehmann later described as 'pathologically neurotic and self-centred'. Wylie had arrived with a trunkful of elaborate toilettes; one of the insider house-party jokes was to see how many times she could be persuaded to change and exactly how much flattery she could swallow. The jokes turned sour after a wild midnight dash to Stonehenge with Gerald Berners and the Colefaxes, when she was hoisted on to one of the stones by a party of feigning worshippers. Wylie, dressed in a silver-lamé evening gown, was so moved by the occasion that she recited some of her poems in a strong New Jersey accent. At the house later, to everyone's embarrassment, she burst into tears, said that everyone was laughing at her and demanded to be taken back to London.

Sachie enjoyed this school-bully baiting as much as any of them, telling Christabel, 'We had a deliciously amusing week-end with Stephen Tennant. I don't think I have ever laughed so much before. It was absolutely perfect.' One of the reasons for its perfection was the presence of Zita. Behind the scenes and beneath the surface at Wilsford a *commedia dell'arte* scene had been played, involving Zita as a rather confused Columbine between the Sitwell brothers. Zita was fascinated by Osbert, Sachie by Zita. 'I represented to him some sort of imaginary person he'd had inside his head,' she said. Zita, deeply admiring of Sachie as a writer, and with a penchant for serious, spiritual conversation, was irritated by his refusal to enter into one. 'He didn't want to talk about ethereal things although they were a tremendous part of him. He wanted to talk about more mundane things and what was going on – he was terribly interested and excited by social life – what everybody was doing, what they were like.'[29] His pleasure was visual, romantic and, at the same time, physical; the last thing he wanted was a spiritual entanglement. Zita, a strict Catholic, was a virginal type, uninterested in sex; Georgia later perspicaciously compared her with Edith. Part of Osbert's appeal for her was that there was no subconscious threat of sex in the background.

Sachie and Osbert were together again in Paris for the opening performance of *The Triumph of Neptune* on 27 June. The Parisians received this ultra-English production with incomprehension. 'It was *not* a success in France,' Sachie later told Diaghilev's biographer. Early in September they left Renishaw to travel to Germany in search of the baroque and rococo with Siegfried Sassoon, at Sassoon's expense and accompanied by his beloved Mrs Nellie Burton. Sassoon had been back on speaking terms with the Sitwells since May 1925, when he had come across Sachie with Georgia at the Savoy Grill and, partly to annoy Noël Coward, who was at a nearby table, and partly because he thought Sachie 'looked so charming', went over to their table and spoke to them. This holiday was perhaps inspired by the imminent publication of Sachie's *German Baroque Art*. The party travelled south through Germany from Berlin, going on to Vienna and Budapest, where Sachie particularly enjoyed the gypsy band at the Hotel Dunapalota and the El Grecos in the Herzog Collection. From Budapest, Sachie returned to Paris to join Georgia, writing from there on 29 September to Sassoon to thank him 'for the lovely holiday you gave Osbert and me. It was such a treat . . . to know you more than I have ever done before,' he added.[30]

Sachie saw Sassoon again in October at Wilsford, where they were staying with Osbert, Zita, Walton, Beaton, Christabel McLaren and Baby Jungman. The principal amusement was to be the production of a series of *tableaux* in eighteenth-century costumes after Lancret to be filmed *en fête champêtre* by Beaton. Sachie and Osbert, as usual, refused to dress up. They never made the slightest sartorial concessions to the country week-end, wearing the same kind of suits in which they would be seen in London topped with a soft brown felt hat. They were still less prepared to prance about in make-up and fancy dress like the others, although they enjoyed egging them on. Zita recorded the scene in her diary:

> The room was like a mad house, Cecil as usual had covered [himself]
> with brick red rouge all over and was now heavily blueing his eyes.
> Stephen, a pale, delicate pink was thickly piling great beads of black on
> his eyelashes with a matchstick. Osbert, in hat and thick scarf to keep
> out the draughts, was wandering delightedly in and out of the room,
> urging Stephen to longer lashes, Cecil to a healthier complexion, and
> Willie to madness. Georgia was spending a good deal of time on her lips
> and Sachie was poking at the cosmetics with anxious eyes and the safe
> feeling that he did not have to make up.[31]

In the midst of all this Sassoon turned up, rugged, middle-aged and shy, and even more out of place than Osbert and Sachie. 'It was very amusing, and they were painted up to the eyes, but I didn't like it,' he wrote in his diary. Behind the scenes the *commedia* was complex: while Sachie cherished his romantic dream of Zita, she was attracted to Osbert, but had a powerful rival in the form of Christabel. Walton pursued Baby in his customary lustful, uncomplicated way and Sassoon was falling passionately in love with Stephen.

After lunch the next day most of the house party drove over to visit Lytton Strachey at Ham Spray on the outskirts of Newbury, while Sachie and Zita went for a drive in her Fiat with Walton in the dickey as chaperon. At last Zita managed to have a serious conversation with Sachie:

> We talked insatiably . . . dragged out all our innermost thoughts, feelings, ideas – everything we had known and felt about each other and had never dared to allow to escape into our commonplace conversations. 'Please don't ever marry just anyone,' said Sachie, 'I just couldn't bear it.' He told me all about his own falling in love with Georgia . . . we drove on . . . talking, dreaming, roving over our own souls and imaginations.

When they rejoined the others she felt 'entirely different', 'as though I had at last opened the hidden room of treasure that I had despaired of ever finding a key for.'[32] Later Sachie sent her one of his books, probably *The Cyder Feast* but it could also have been *The Thirteenth Caesar* in which 'The Golden Bell' appeared. 'It was such a delicious experience, though, to get to know you at all', he wrote to her, 'that I felt it necessary to celebrate it however humbly. Life is very short and I have known you by sight for quite five years.'[33]

German Baroque Art was published early in November. It broke new ground as the first book in English on the baroque and rococo architecture of central Europe, challenging the generally held impression of Germany as a predominantly Gothic country and highlighting the architects and craftsmen who underpinned the age of Handel, Bach, Haydn and Mozart. The *Times Literary Supplement* acknowledged Sachie as the rediscoverer of the baroque: 'Mr Sitwell earns our gratitude as being among the first . . . who have of late taken arms against these prejudices of ours' exemplified by the Century dictionary definition of baroque as 'the presence of ugly and repellent qualities'. The book had been completed in May 1925 and was based on Sachie's observations on his travels in Germany and Austria in 1921–1922. The original intention had been to have it published by Grant Richards, under the title *Later Architecture of the Holy Roman Empire*, but it had been delayed by Richards's bankruptcy (among other things Sachie had loaned his publisher money which he could ill afford only to be repaid with a dud cheque). The rights had finally been transferred to Duckworth in February 1927 after protracted negotiations and acrimonious correspondence between the Sitwells and Richards. Unlike *Southern Baroque Art*, it was a factual handbook, so much so that Sachie felt moved to write almost apologetically in the preface, 'the plethora of facts and names has made these pages into little better than a catalogue'. The bibliography at the end and the illustrations, always carefully chosen by Sachie for his books, showed the wide extent of his knowledge and taste as a bibliophile. To the reviewer, however, the great merit of the book lay in its desciptions of such then less well-known places as the great Abbey of Melk, or Vierzehnheiligen, which lay off the beaten track. It covered the whole of Germany and Austria from the Rhine to Silesia and from the Danube to the North Sea, only rarely taking off in bursts of poetic prose as when Sachie described the rococo marvels of the Amalienburg Pavilion at the Nymphenburg Palace in Munich.

   German Baroque Art added to Sachie's reputation as a trailblazer; where he went, the aesthetes and the fashionable followed. On 30 November, when Rex Whistler's murals at the Tate Gallery were unveiled, *The Times* art critic's piece on the subject made clear allusions to Sachie's work: 'Emerging from a palace in Southern Baroque . . . the hunting party scour the world . . . to return at evening through a Claude-like park, having enjoyed All Summer in a Day in the course of their excursion. . . .'

   The Sitwells were much in the public eye that month. Osbert wrote the foreword to the catalogue for Beaton's first exhibition of photographs at the Cooling Galleries, while Beaton designed the scenery for Sachie's and Osbert's play, now entitled *First Class Passengers Only*, which opened at the Arts Theatre Club on Sunday, 27 November. The *Daily Herald* reported that at Beaton's show the

> crowd grew denser with the arrival of the Sitwells. 'Do you approve of cocktails at an art show?' I asked Mr Osbert Sitwell. 'Of course,' he replied, 'but more I mustn't say at the moment, for I am giving my views on cocktails in my play "First Class Passengers Only" which is being produced next week.'

For the Sitwell play Beaton designed stools covered with oilcloth which adhered to the performers; they were not the only things about the evening which were sticky. The play on which Osbert and Sachie had spent so much time working and reworking (they had changed the title no less than three times and were still uncertain which was the best) was, although witty in parts, a flop. Even such a kind-hearted critic as Edith Olivier, who went to the glittering first night with Stephen Tennant, admitted as much, writing in her diary:

Everyone we know and the whole house crowding into the foyer to chatter and talk. . .The first two acts very brilliant, and bright, and quick and witty. The end quite feeble and everyone depressed when it was over. Cecil and Zita joined us, and we went behind [the scenes] but between ourselves could only moan and think they themselves must feel shattered by the change of moods since after Act II when everyone was so delighted.

There was a slightly disagreeable aftermath; Sachie had asked them to go on to supper with Mrs Ronnie Greville, but Stephen had heard that Osbert, in an act of petty disloyalty, had said that he wanted neither Stephen nor Cecil (who were becoming notorious for their camp appearance and behaviour) to join them. Stephen, understandably offended, did not go. 'How bad the Sitwell play was!!!' he wrote, '. . . I am sick to death of everything to do with it having seen it three times (spiritual not intellectual loyalty).'[34]

Although the performance was not for the general public, the breadth of newspaper coverage was all that the Sitwells could have hoped for. The full title of the play was *First Class Passengers Only: A Social Tragedy* and the action took place on a transatlantic liner, the SS *Inania*, the social tragedy being a case of mistaken identity where a young Englishman is confused with a celebrity by a lion-hunting hostess, obviously Sybil Colefax, Osbert's 'Mrs Kinfoot'. In the middle of the play, the three Sitwells appeared on stage as guests at a cabaret party and proceeded to shout five poems through the inevitable megaphone. It purported to send up the silly social comedies popular in the 1920s, but, despite some witty dialogue, was not strong enough to carry it through. There was almost no plot and a weak discernible theme. The Sitwells had trodden unwarily in a field that was dominated by Noël Coward, and it was obvious that the play had been concocted as a vehicle for hurling grapeshot at the Sitwells' various *bêtes noires*. Osbert, wearing a tuberose in his buttonhole, fulfilled his role as the impresario, the 'C.B. Cochran' of the trio, giving interviews to a respectful press in his 'rich, deep voice':

The purpose of the play is first to amuse, but, as in all our work, there is an underlying message. . . . The moral of our Transatlantic piece is 'don't be silly'. There are other morals pointed, such as 'don't drink before dinner', 'don't climb socially' and 'don't substitute fads for faith'. Our model for playwriting [he added portentously] is Aristophanes.

He condescended to flatter: 'The Press is to-day the greatest human force. . . . To an artist, its criticisms are invaluable.'

Osbert should have taken his own moral to heart. *First Class Passengers Only* was a prime example of the privileged silliness with which the Sitwells liked to confront the public and which was to bring them into disfavour with a more seriously minded decade. Moreover, Osbert chose to put the whole thing on record by publishing the play under the title *All at Sea* with a long, pugnacious and intemperate preface, 'A Day in an Author's Life', which attacked long-standing enemies and more recent ones – the BBC, the actor-manager Archie de Beer, Robert Hale and Maisie Gay, with whom he had been involved in a futile dispute the previous year. Its bombastic tiresomeness and overkill typified the more unfortunate aspects of Osbert's and Edith's public reactions to criticism. In a generally hostile article, headed 'At the Theatre: A Theatrical Tragedy', the critic George Warrington asked why, given their individual talents, the Sitwells should obscure them by performances such as this. The reason, he wrote spitefully but not inaccurately, could be found in the preface, which spelled out 'Osbert Sitwell's superiority to anything and everybody in general'.

While Osbert, wounded at the play's failure, retired to Italy, Sachie and Georgia spent their first Christmas at Weston with six-month-old Reresby, the first son, as Georgia recorded, born to an owner of that house since 1773. Weston was a gabled, seventeenth-century manor house in a small, stone-built village remote from the world in the folding Northamptonshire countryside, over four miles from the nearest station at Helmdon. When it came to the Sitwells in 1923 after the death of Sir George's aunt, Mrs Thomas, the house was a time capsule in which treasures had accumulated over more than 200 years' unbroken ownership. Sir George had previously inherited the money and the contents, but not the house, on the death in 1911 of his other aunt, Lady Hanmer, who had retired to live out her old age in Scarborough, and, upon the death of Mrs Thomas, he hurried there, fearing that it might be sold by his cousin, Franco Thomas. Through the winter of 1923–1924 he had made several visits to Weston, sitting up at night listing the contents and writing a history of the house after 1790. He then bought it for Sachie. The original house, dating from 1690, had descended in the female line since 1714, when a rich Northamptonshire man, Sir John Blencowe, purchased a seven-year lease on it for his daughter, Susanna Jennens, and subsequently bought the freehold for her in 1721 as a Valentine's Day present. From then on the house was handed down by the female line of

Barnardistons, Wrightsons and Hebers to Colonel the Hon. Henry Hely-Hutchinson, Sachie's great-grandfather.

Nothing had been sold over the years. As a result, there was an accumulation of fascinating objects: the needlework bed hangings embroidered by the original owner, Susanna Jennens, with carpet to match; trunks of clothes dating from 1760 to 1785; portraits of Henrietta Maria by van Dyck and of Louise de Kéroualle by Lely, ancestors painted by Reynolds, Lawrence and Cosway, and some fine Ingres drawings. Tables were strewn with feminine trinkets of all ages from 1690 to 1910; among them was a walnut containing a pair of tiny kid gloves given to Colonel Hely-Hutchinson by Pauline Borghese.

Weston was the perfect setting for Sachie, whose sense of historical connection was so strong. It was also, having been lived in by elderly ladies for a good many years, dilapidated, much in need of redecoration and extremely cold. There was no central heating and the gardens were overgrown. There was land with the estate, but it was unlikely that Sachie would show any hidden talents as a farmer, while Georgia, born and brought up in Montreal, was essentially urban and completely unused to English country life. The Sitwells' social life centred on London and their equally sophisticated friends, yet they did not have the income to keep Weston and a London house simultaneously. Weston represented a huge change in the way they lived and, at first, it was an unwelcome one. Both of them constantly complained to their friends of being 'forced' to live at Weston by Ginger, upon whom they were heavily dependent. 'Ginger is being amiable and has agreed to a motor and some cows,' Sachie had written optimistically to Georgia from Budapest, but the 'amiability' never lasted long. Sir George was for ever interfering, twitching the financial strings from afar. No changes could be made to either house or garden without his agreement and every bill had to be minutely scrutinised and haggled over. A stream of unwanted and unwelcome advice rained down upon Georgia. Sir George argued every point, his attention to detail prodigious. It was entirely unnecessary to make the extensive alterations for nurseries that she had planned: 'When my sister and I were children at Renishaw we did not have nurseries that opened out of each other. We were carried from room to room. . . .' 'The damask curtains will come back in rags if cleaned and dyed, & may be beautiful for 100 years if left alone. . . .'[35] 'One is hardly mistress in one's house,' Georgia wrote exasperatedly in her diary.[36]

Both of them felt trapped at Weston, where they lightened their lives by inviting friends for week-ends and making frequent expeditions to

London for social and artistic events. Among their first guests were Stephen Tennant and Siegfried Sassoon. The New Year, 1928, opened sociably as usual. They went up to lunch with Walton at the Café Royal and, with Tennant, Beaton, Dick Wyndham and Rex Whistler, heard Ernest Ansermet conduct Walton's *Sinfonia Concertante* at the Queen's Hall; then they went on to the Savoy Grill for supper with the same party plus Walton and Beryl de Zoete, and afterwards to Tennant's house in Smith Square to change for the Chelsea Arts Ball. On 28 January Christabel, Gerald Berners, Walton and Zita were to come for the week-end (Zita failed to turn up having had a car accident). It poured with rain and Berners, dressed in a white coat, painted what he could see out of the top landing window of the kitchen garden; 'a dreary little picture,' Georgia commented ungratefully.

During 1928 strains developed in Sachie and Georgia's marriage, as Georgia found the pressures of what she called 'Sitwellism' (i.e. the Sitwell family) increasingly hard to bear. Sachie was torn between his new family and his loyalty to Osbert, who continued to write him letters of heartbreaking loneliness. Even the presence of Adrian Stokes on his Italian sojourns had not consoled Osbert for Sachie's absence. The trip to Germany and Austria with Sassoon in September 1927 had been an attempt to revive the old times together. At Christmas 1927 Osbert had written pathetic letters from Rapallo where he was staying, again with Adrian; he was sleepless, unable to work and suffering from 'epic depression': 'I do a good bit of solitary howling. It's some sort of nasty spiritual crisis combined with the first flush of old age. . . . Let me know when you are coming out,' he pleaded. 'Let us settle somewhere and work from the middle-end of Febr. . . .' Adrian could not stay on beyond the end of January and Osbert could not bear to be alone; either Walton or Sassoon or Dick Wyndham would do, but Sachie '*must* come out and join him': 'I feel really horribly depressed . . . I've attained a real depth of lowness of spirit which I've never touched before. . . .' One reason for his depression was the failure of *All at Sea*, upon which he had unaccountably pinned so much hope. 'Surely someone must have liked the play?' he asked Sachie plaintively. 'I wish you'd tell me how much harm [the play] has done. . . .'[37] The major reason was, however, as Sachie well knew, the void in his life left by Sachie's marriage.

Loyally, Sachie went to join him in their old haunt, San Remo, early in February, leaving Georgia to undergo treatment at a Paris clinic for the gynaecological problems she had suffered since Reresby's birth. Sachie and Osbert stayed at the same hotel as on previous visits, the West End, which Sachie described in a glum letter to Georgia as big, bare and resembling a sanatorium. San Remo had memories of his childhood; 'when I was last here it was before you were born,' he told her. Both brothers were deeply depressed by news of the illness of Mrs Powell, their beloved housekeeper at Carlyle Square, who had breast cancer. 'It is simply awful,' Sachie wrote. 'I can think of nothing else because I do love her so.' Misery about Mrs Powell was compounded by the news that Helen Rootham was suffering from the same disease, although as yet unaware of it, and would have to have an operation in Paris. 'Osbert and Edith have now got two dying people to look after with a vista of probably hopeless agony and mutilation and these two are . . . those who have done most . . . to make their lives possible and enable them to write,' he wrote sadly on 25 February.

Sachie 'says that the last month has been hellish', Georgia commented after hearing what an awful time he had had looking after Osbert, who 'spent nearly the whole of every day in tears about Mrs Powell, Edith etc.' She was fighting the great 'nursery war' with Ginger, whom she called 'beastly' and 'wicked'. Sachie was quite happy for her to remain in the front line:

> Write to Ginger and point out that it is the child's permanent nursery
> and that when we gave up the idea of a London house you understood,
> definitively, that he was going to make Weston possible for us to live in
> and it is a nursery where, eventually, one or even more (?Oh! Lord)
> additional children may have to be put.

Lady Ida was, although hardly a major force in this case, supporting them. She had visited Georgia at the clinic, where a ridiculous scene had taken place between her and Cecil Beaton, who 'blew in with a mass of flowers worthy of Lifar', as reported by Georgia to Sachie:

> Ida: What do you mean by taking a photograph of my daughter in a coffin?
> Cecil: It was not a coffin. She was *simply* on the floor.
> Ida: My niece Lady Carisbrooke tells me you wrote asking her to sit for you.
> Cecil (white with fury): I never write asking people to sit for me. I have quite enough work without *asking* anyone.
> Ida: How very odd, she told me so herself.
> Cecil: Perhaps she was bragging?
> Ida: Bragging? Bragging! What do you mean young man. My lovely

niece, what is there to brag of in your asking her to be photographed. Too extraordinary people nowadays. What *does* he *can* he mean Georgia?

Cecil: I must say she has always been very civil to me.

Ida: She doesn't know you.

This went on for what seemed like an eternity & in the end yr. mother asked him to Montegufoni with one of those lightning changes of front & Cecil ended up by gliding out of the room saying, 'I should be *delighted* to come *Lady Sitwell*!'[38]

Osbert was delighted to hear of this encounter, wickedly relishing Beaton's solecism. 'Cecil Beaton has been to see Georgia and created rather a powerful impression on my mother who was there by calling her "Lady Sitwell",' he reported to Christabel. 'Cecil . . . said to Georgia, "I'm famous now. I'm smart. And I don't want to be anything else in particular. . . ." '[39]

Among the letters Georgia received from friends while she was in the clinic was one from Zita which provoked a flurry of catty remarks in her diary. 'I would like Sachie to see the letter as it would be such an eye-opener but I can't bear to throw icy water on the young flame of his love,' she commented furiously in her diary. According to Walton in a letter of 11 February, Sachie was 'in constant communicaggers' with Zita. Georgia suspected this and, despite the loving letters which she constantly received from Sachie, was irritated by his passion for Zita, although too astute to show it. 'There are . . . such wonderful ideas in that head of yours Tine darling ['Tine' was short for 'Tiny', hers and Walton's pet name for Sachie], she wrote to him at San Remo on 21 February. '. . . I do love you so & I want you to be so happy & our lives together to be an exception to every rule & to be really wonderful because we love each other – if only you do love your own devoted Georgia.' She could not resist a playfully anxious postscript: '*Dare* I ask how your work is going. I do so long to know. When are you going to write a poem about me. I bet you've written one about Zita lately?!'

Sachie's plan was for Zita to join their imminent expedition to Morocco. They had evidently discussed the possibility before they left England. '. . . do write and urge her to come,' he had written to Georgia on 11 February, when they were thinking of going to Athens rather than Morroco, 'only we had better say nothing to Osbert at present as he is in the sort of mood when the idea of seeing anyone irritates him. I am sure it would be alright if she just turned up.' Early in March Sachie and Osbert left San Remo to join the American painter, Ethel Sands, at Marseilles for the tour of Morocco in her motor-car. From Paris, where Georgia had attended a tea party of distinguished lesbians given by Gertrude Stein (including the journalist, Janet Flanner, whom Georgia described as "the chief Paris-American lady lady-killer'), and Dolly Wilde, she reported that Stein had repeated over and over again that Sands had 'a genius for friendship'. Sachie was still clearly nervous about Osbert's reactions to Zita's arrival and sent Georgia a warning telegram on 19 March from Fez: 'Do bring Zita. She must not [mind] if we work.' 'Zita is coming, I wonder what it will lead to?' Georgia noted pensively in her diary on 20 March.

Georgia and Zita arrived by boat at Casablanca on 26 March to be met by an uncomfortably sunburned Sachie and Ethel Sands's cousin, an artist named Giles Franklin, who drove them to Marrakech. Georgia had by now warmed to Zita, after long heart-to-heart talks on the ship had revealed that the situation had not changed since Wilsford and that Zita's romantic ambitions were directed towards Osbert rather than Sachie. 'We have just had a long talk about Sachie,' Georgia recorded on 27 March. 'She is obviously fond of him in a nice way & pleased by his admiration. It was amusing to find out small details of there [*sic*] contact & compare the two different versions.' Both women had played a cat-and-mouse game. 'Of course she is disarmingly frank & pretends to have told me everything there is to tell but I know she is playing a game the whole time as usual. I on the other hand achieve the same effect by being absolutely truthful – no one every [*sic*] credits one with telling the truth so one is just as secretive in the end,' Georgia confided to her diary. Zita wrote in hers in terms that would seem to clear her of Georgia's suspicions, that she and Georgia had had 'delicious conversations' about the Sitwells' relationship:

> How he proposed to her, what she thought of him etc. . . . Then we
> passed on to exactly what had taken place between Sachie and me! How
> many letters he had written to me, what he said to me, and what he said
> to Georgia. . . . It all grows rather complicated because despite the
> atmosphere of joke now surrounding Sachie and myself, I am hardly
> likely to avoid a great deal of embarrassment later on! . . . I have got over
> continual blushing at the mention of Sachie's name, thank goodness, but
> still react to Osbert's. I have tried to explain my blushing complexes to
> Georgia but I doubt if I have said enough to cover it all.[40]

Sachie was in a curious situation; he coveted Zita and wanted to have an affair with her while she, as a strictly brought-up Catholic, could not contemplate an adulterous relationship with a married man. Zita was attracted to Osbert and encouraged by a story told her by Walton that the

previous summer Osbert had told him that he intended to marry her. She
was far too innocent to consider the possibility of Osbert's homosexuality,
seeing him as a delightful, witty and intellectual companion and a
comforting, authoritative presence. 'I was really fascinated by Osbert,' she
later recalled; 'one didn't think of him like that. Because the people who
were like that, like Cecil and Stephen, were so very exotic compared to
Osbert, who was . . . a stout Hanoverian.'[41] 'Even with Stephen one didn't
think it came to anything, – ' her sister added. Sachie no doubt found
Zita's evident fascination with Osbert galling and he was not finding
dealing with his brother easy.

Osbert was in a particularly difficult mood; he was miserable about Mrs
Powell, Edith's sufferings over Helen Rootham, the failure of the play and
the critical reception of the preface of which he had been so proud. He
had been, unrequitedly, in love with at least one man, John Becket, but he
had not yet found a companion to replace Sachie in his life. Georgia still
referred to him, as Sachie did, as 'darling Osbert' in her letters, but she
was to find him increasingly capricious and difficult on their Moroccan
journey. At Marrakech they found him 'very nervy' and there was
immediately a row about divided loyalties; Georgia and Zita broached the
subject of their going to Fez, Meknes and Rabat, which Osbert and
Sachie had already visited and to which Osbert refused to return. 'Osbert
& Sachie fussed about it in the usual way', while Georgia, normally tuned
to the Sitwell wavelength, remained calm under Zita's nonchalant
influence. 'Poor darling Osbert,' she commented, 'he has had a lot to put
up with this year & his nerves are very bad.' They dined with the Pasha, El
Glaoui, enjoying a delicious dinner of pigeons stuffed with rice, sultanas
and attar of roses, the general effect of oriental luxury being somewhat
spoiled for Osbert when he spotted the Pasha's Jewish secretary hiding
the large, good cigars behind cushions and getting out some small, bad
ones. The Pasha and his secretary's wife 'talked scandal during dinner'
when El Glaoui revealed that he loved dancing and that, when in London,
he wore a dinner jacket and did the Charleston. Afterwards they went to a
dreary 'dancing' café filled with French officers and 'oriental' women, but
Osbert spoiled the evening, complaining of a violent headache, 'brought
on', Georgia commented, 'by the temper which he had been working up
all day because he may have to be alone for 9 days at Alegeciras (where *he*
insists on going) if Sach comes with Zita & me to Fez'. He infuriated
Georgia by coming to their room last thing at night as they were going to
bed '& fussed & fussed':

Poor darling, he will go off his head & drive everyone half dotty if he does not try to pull himself together soon. He is naturally feeling unstrung now as he has been through a lot lately but his nerves have always been far worse than they would be if he would only make some effort to control himself & not be so self-willed & 'hipped'.[42]

Prompted by this exhibition, Georgia the next day gave Zita some advice on 'how to get Osbert':

I agree with Sachie, who is as fond of her as ever in a very sweet way, that for his own sake *& our own*, the only way out of the restless loneliness which afflicts Osbert is to find a permanent companion. I can't think of anyone more suitable than Zita from, I think, every point of view but so far things don't look promising. Sach & I cannot fill the gap & the responsibility & depression of seeing him unhappy is more & more depressing & becomes worse by the day.

A military ball presided over by the Pasha was an occasion for some risqué conversation with his secretary's coarse but voluptuous wife, arrayed in silver tissue and tulle, spangled with glass bugle-beads, huge turquoise earrings weighing down her ear-lobes and a salmon-pink velvet flower sprawling on her shoulder. Osbert had petulantly refused to go as they were still arguing over who should have Sachie's company. Osbert absolutely insisted on carrying out his plan of two weeks' sea-bathing and working at Algeciras with Sachie; Georgia and Zita had, therefore, to be content with going on to Fez by themselves. Zita seemed amused rather than otherwise by these Sitwellian displays of temperament, but Georgia feared that it might affect her long-term plans: 'Unfortunately she realizes how difficult poor darling O is & that he is not playing up to her at all. . . .'

On 3 April the two women left Marrakech; 'Sachie grumbled heartbreakingly about having to be bored at Algeciras instead of coming with us,' Georgia wrote. 'Started off feeling very sorry to leave poor sweet Sach who wanted to come so badly for so many different reasons. . . .' The journey gave Georgia and Zita further opportunity to explore each other's characters – 'dangerous but interesting,' Georgia commented. Zita declared that 'things of the mind' mattered much more to her than 'the things of the heart'. 'I wonder?!' Georgia wrote cynically, and 'if so if it is a trait really to be proud of? It is astonishing how feminine Zita's mind is though physically she is almost sexless. Edith is like this too . . . they have so much of the feminine in their minds that none is left to direct them physically.'

At Algeciras Sachie and Osbert found a party of smart English homosexuals, including Gavin Henderson, whom Georgia described as 'awful', 'tremendously pompous and full of swagger', travelling with Robert Byron, whom Sachie greatly liked. Osbert's attitude towards Zita when the women joined them remained 'relentlessly uncompromising'. 'I think she is rather discouraged by it,' Georgia reported. 'She has managed to get a cold, an unforgivable offence as far as Osbert is concerned. He is sure to catch it from her which is likely to be the finish of anything between them.' Zita, however, apparently remained hopeful, buoyed up by Walton's story, and Sachie, perhaps out of loyalty to Osbert, did not press his own suit. He and Zita went for a walk along the beach at Algeciras for a serious conversation. 'Do you know I was once very much in love with you about four years ago,' he told her.[43] The nerves of the quartet were by now slightly on edge as they travelled to Cordoba (where they arrived on 17 April), Guadeloupe, Toledo and Madrid. In Toledo Zita and Georgia had a passage of arms over tea, with Zita making some biting remarks, egged on by Osbert, 'enjoying, as he always does, anyone's discomfiture', Georgia commented in her journal. In Madrid they went to a bullfight with Ethel Sands, dined at Botins' on sucking-pig, and drove to the Escorial in a Bentley lent by a friend of Osbert's in the Madrid Embassy. Going round the Prado Sachie sulked – 'that grim *completely* silent mood – because Zita has been snubbing him lately'. They lunched at a country club with Kipling's daughter, Mrs Bambridge, and visited the Duke of Alba's palace. At Guadalajara Sachie and Osbert had a notable tiff; they were accustomed to needling each other 'rather amusingly' in public, but at times it could get out of hand. At Burgos on the way home, the party met 'Chile' Guevara, who seemed to Georgia 'terrifyingly vague and far away'; she was convinced that he was on drugs and had a 'great argument with Sachie on this point'. In Paris Sachie surprised Georgia with the confession that he had been encouraging Zita by telling her that Osbert was 'more than interested'. 'He has begun to doubt the wisdom of this statement,' Georgia noted, 'which is likely to do a good deal to upset everyone's plans, not least his own.' Sachie clearly saw Zita as the answer to Osbert's loneliness and his own responsibility for him, seemingly refusing to admit to himself that Osbert's homosexuality might be a barrier. He may still have had hopes of Osbert leading a 'normal' life, although, as the practical Georgia had pointed out, such a marriage could put paid to his hopes both romantic and, as Osbert's eventual heir, financial.

South Bay, Scarborough, 1868: watercolour by Paul Marney
showing, from left to right, the Spa, the Grand Hotel and Castle Hill

Pierrots performing on **South Sands, Scarborough**, c. 1900

The rocking-horse: Sachie, aged about two, with his mother,
Lady Ida Sitwell, in front of Renishaw, c. 1900

Left: Osbert, aged three; *right:* Sachie, aged about three.
Sir Reresby Sitwell: 'My father seemed to have been born
with a walking-stick in his hand.'

The Sitwell
family by John
Singer Sargent

Sachie as a
schoolboy,
c. 1911

Renishaw Hall by Richard Wyndham, c. 1930

Weston Hall by Rex Whistler, c. 1929. The figure in the foreground
is Sachie, seen in a rare role as gardener.

Sachie as a young poet, Venice, 1922:
drawing by Wyndham Lewis

Cartoon drawing of Osbert and
Sachie by Max Beerbohm, c. 1925

Left: Wedding photograph of Sachie and and Georgia, Paris, 12 October 1925

Right: Osbert, Max Meyerfeld, Siegfried Sassoon, Mrs Nellie Burton
and Sachie in the Zoological Gardens, Berlin, 8 September 1927

Façade: Osbert, Edith, Sachie, William Walton and unidentified friend holding a sengerphone outside the Chenil Galleries, June 1926

Weekend at Wilsford, June 1927: (*left to right*) Zita Jungman, William Walton, Cecil Beaton, Stephen Tennant, Georgia, Baby Jungman and Rex Whistler

Sachie, Georgia, Eddie Compton, Loelia and Bendor Westminister,
and Zita Jungman taken aboard the *Cutty Sark* in Barcelona harbour, March 1930

Weekend at Denham, July 1930: (*left to right*) Cecil Beaton, Georgia,
Tom Mosley, Sachie, Cimmie Mosley and the Mosley children

Pearl Argyle, c. 1933:
Sachie's favourite photograph

Lady Bridget Parsons in the mid-1930s:
drawing by William Acton

Sachie and Georges Duthuit at Eisenstadt,
September 1932

Sachie and Georgia were back in London on 3 May, plunging immediately into a hectic social round. Sachie found himself dragged in Georgia's wake into a new social ambience. Oswald 'Tom' Mosley and his wife, Lady Cynthia, always known as 'Cimmie', were very much a part of what later became known as the 'international jet set' centred on a handful of hostesses, mainly American and extremely rich, in the principal European cities. It was a world of fashion, 'fun', gossip, wit of a rather cruel kind and very little intellectual content. The Mosleys' son, Nicholas, has described his parents' circle as one in which 'personal relationships, even love, were matters of intrigue, conquest, possession, power; everyone was in the business of becoming one up on everyone else. Certainly there seems to have been little in it of music, literature, art. . . .'[44] Adultery was the accepted sport. Georgia flung herself into this new, smart, party life, taking to its customs and values with almost frantic enthusiasm. It seemed to her like a breath of fresh air and an escape from Sitwellism. Sachie sensed this and was unhappy about it; Georgia's relentless pursuit of pleasure was to be a source of tension over the years leading up the Second World War.

The Mosleys were a glamorous couple. Tom Mosley, later notorious as the leader of the English Fascists, was then Labour MP for Smethwick, at the height of his career and even spoken of as a future prime minister. His closest political colleagues were clever young men like John Strachey and Robert Boothby; in 1924 Beatrice Webb had called him 'the most brilliant man in the House of Commons . . . the perfect politician and the perfect gentleman'. However, acute instinct led her to qualify her opinion: 'So much perfection argues rottenness somewhere.' Mosley was an extra-ordinary orator capable of exerting real power over crowds, but as a politician he was essentially a maverick. In his private life he was hardly the perfect gentleman, being foully rude to servants and later to his doting wife, whom he constantly betrayed. He slept with all his wife's best friends, her sister and her stepmother. He was selfish and self-centred, driven by a desire to be the dominant male. He was the complete opposite of Sachie, which may have been part of his attraction for Georgia. Cimmie Mosley, the tall and beautiful daughter of Lord Curzon by his first wife, the American heiress, Mary Leiter, was also a socialist and later Labour MP for Stoke-on-Trent. She adored her husband, upon whom she was pathologically dependent and whose betrayals she tried to ignore. He was, she told him, her 'hero' and her 'baby boy'. Neither of them saw anything odd in attending Labour rallies and then dashing off to Venice or the South of France.

Sachie and Georgia were often with the Mosleys both in London and in the country, spending two week-ends in May and June at Savehay, their Elizabethan farmhouse near Denham in Buckinghamshire. Their circles of friends interlocked. Zita was a great friend of Cimmie's, as was Dick Wyndham, with whom Sachie had collaborated on A *Book of Towers*, published that year; Walton was a little in love with her. Beaton and Tennant were also there on both occasions. The others included Cimmie's eldest sister, Irene Ravensdale, Idina Erroll, chic wife of the Earl of Erroll, of whom Georgia, who was inclined to be prudish, wrote disapprovingly: '. . . she has been married 4 times and is reputed to have had lovers without number . . . a fair, heavily made-up face covered with blue-white powder, chic, empty, dissipated, hungry looking, spoilt & vicious, she has dyed hair & no chin. . . .' Everyone bathed but Sachie, who struggled with a punt and succeeded in breaking down one of the wooden bridges and dropping Cimmie's camera into the water, and Idina Erroll, who sauntered down at eleven o'clock in black-and-white chiffon. Dick Wyndham knocked himself out playing with a pogo stick, fracturing his jaw, and had to retreat to London leaving the others to dress up in the magnificent clothes which Cimmie's mother had worn as Vicereine of India. Even Sachie was persuaded to put on a frock, but looked so terrifyingly like his Aunt Gracie Londesborough that 'he gave himself the creeps' and went up after dinner to take it off. At dinner Mosley flirted with Georgia, whose reactions to him did not escape Zita. Driving back to London together in Zita's Fiat the next day, Zita asked her 'pointedly & shrewdly' what she thought about him. Georgia replied 'guardedly without committing myself one way or the other'. Sachie continued to see Zita for weekly lunches while Georgia lunched with Mosley. She took the Mosleys to the Theatre Arts Club for a series of poetry readings by the three Sitwells, and after the last session on 2 July the Mosleys joined the Sitwell quartet for supper at the Savoy. 'I felt very nervous as I know they would not all get on well together if they got onto certain subjects,' Georgia wrote, adding, '(I was right, Edith thought Tom *too* awful.)'

Sachie was becoming furiously jealous. There was yet another week-end at Denham on 6 July with Zita, Walton, Tennant, Wyndham, Jean Fleming and John Strachey as guests, at which the chief activity was making a film to an eventful script written by Tennant involving motor-car chases, seduction, abduction, attempted murder and an elaborate suicide by Beaton in the river. Sachie, Georgia and Mosley were uncomfortably cast together as three detectives. Georgia thought the week-end 'hilarious', Sachie quite otherwise. On 9 July he and Georgia dined at

Osbert's for the première of *Ode*, the Nabokov-Tchelitchew ballet. Late that night, Sachie made an angry scene when they discussed Georgia's plan of going to Antibes that summer to see the Mosleys. 'Frightful row with Sachie who is "*fou de jalousie de T*" ', Georgia reported laconically. On 11 July she lunched with Zita: 'I complained about life in general and almost gave myself away.' On the 12th Osbert and Edith gave a cocktail party for the opening of Tchelitchew's exhibition at the Claridge Gallery, after which there was a showing of the Denham film at Tennant's house and cold 'high tea' at Wyndham's; Georgia drove the Mosleys' car on to another party – without Sachie. The result was, 'such a scene I could not describe it as it is carved permanently on my mind', followed by another 'fearful scene' the next morning, a brief reconciliation, then more rows on the train going up to Renishaw when the pair of them quarrelled fiercely in front of Zita.

Zita was very much on Sachie's mind that day; in the intervals of rowing with Georgia, he was writing a love poem to her:

> Hear this,
>   my love,
>   my fair-haired prison,
> since my ghost is bound with yours,
> I was free once and we lived
> in a wood our wits contrived
> where masks of blossom ever hid
> the fruit, that sleepy underlid,
> so travesty to truth was close
> And you were all the mimes I chose.
>
> I'm still the prisoner of your locks
> In each mood your beauty mocks,
> here, more than all the wise can own,
> truth and beauty are both shown.
>
>   I
>
> My balm-giver, my golden tree,
> shake your curled hair ceaselessly,
> make the summer a soft wind,
> of fruit with blossoms hid behind,
> shut there, like the words we want
> to open our dumb covenant

II

this moment, some of Time's grey hairs
I held and caught him unawares,
he'll never break this spell of sun,
we are alone, and death's undone.

Z. . . , J. . . , now you've spoken
It is late, my life is broken,
Take one leaf of it, one day,
And mend me with your lips' delay.

I live and move, and yet I'm tied,
come cut my net and cure my pride.[45]

The poem was found among Sachie's uncatalogued papers at Weston. It was dated 13.7.28, the day he and Georgia had travelled to Renishaw with Zita. It was in an unopened envelope addressed to Gino Severini in Rome, clearly for transmission to Zita. He must have thought better of sending it to her and kept it. It was not the last time he wrote her a passionate declaration and then lacked the courage to send it.

Meanwhile at Renishaw the rows with Georgia continued; there were daily exasperated entries in her diary. Sachie, she wrote, was 'impossible', adding in French, as she always did on such occasions for fear the servants might read it, *'jamais je ne serai complètement réuni'*. 'Scenes all morning, reconciliation, scene at lunch, reconciliation,' was her diary entry for the day after their arrival. Sachie was thoroughly unhappy and angry about her plans to meet the Mosleys at Antibes; Georgia was determined to assert her independence, but she too was miserable, as she confided in her diary:

My own feelings too complicated, gloomy, discontented, cynical & contemptuous of myself to describe but so different to anything anyone imagines. *Je n'ose pas dire davantage mais je pense profondement.* What a nightmare it has been. I would not go through it again for anything in the world. We've had just as bad scenes but it has mattered less. This ruins everything & opens one's eyes to a vista of circumstances which in the past one has ignored but which one knows must be, in the future, a series of embittering burdens. Before I pretended that everything would come right. Now I know nothing ever will.

It is difficult to interpret exactly what she meant in this enigmatic passage. Clearly the marriage was going through considerable difficulties. Sachie was hot-tempered and jealous, in this case with good reason. Georgia was either already having an affair with Mosley or was contemplating it. She later confessed to a friend: 'Of course I went to bed with Tom. We all did and then felt bad about it afterwards.' Although the physical side of her marriage to Sachie seems to have been satisfactory enough up to a certain point and they went on sleeping together until he was in his seventies, Georgia was highly sexed and hungry for admiration. Beyond that there was her resentment at the strength of Sachie's bond with his family and his insistence that she should fall in with their plans. He was not in return prepared to be accommodating to her parents and Georgia frequently complained that he was unkind either to or about them. She was determined to fight her corner against 'Sitwellism':

> They expect one to stay for 4 weeks at Renishaw and 4 at Montegufoni without a break although the chief reason for [my] not wanting to is that they all grumble so! Such a typical Sitwellism . . . one must establish a precedent sometimes which allows one a little independence & peace.

At Renishaw that August the Sitwells were at their most Sitwellian. The Dobles, who had been renting Weston, arrived to stay bringing Reresby and Nannah. Georgia loved her parents dearly and was particularly close to her mother, but their presence at Renishaw grated on the Sitwells, increasing her tension. They were equally uncomfortable: 'Mother on her dignity, Daddy a bore,' Georgia wrote. Nannah was terrified of the ghosts and, like the Dobles, felt an outsider in the Renishaw household. 'What's for dinner, Henry?' she enquired of Moat. 'Cold, boiled, sliced missionary, Miss Cole,' he replied. The arrival of Arthur Waley and Beryl de Zoete failed to lighten the atmosphere. There were agonising moments when Lady Ida seemed on the point of insulting Beryl and after dinner she made 'one of her scenes and flounced out in a huff'. An American cousin, Evie Sitwell, and Anthony Powell, described dismissively by Georgia as 'a colourless young man with some humour who is employed by Duckworth's', arrived later, but the party was distinctly out of tune. According to Georgia, Evie seemed depressive, Edith depressed, Osbert morose and Sachie taciturn. 'It is almost more than I can bear,' she wrote, 'but nothing to what it will become by the time 3 weeks are up. . . .And this is only the 4th day! Ye Gods!' Sachie was being 'unreasonably violent about his loyalty to Osbert and the tiresomeness of his in-laws' when he was with Georgia, but otherwise spent a good deal of the time working on a new book, *The Gothick North*, the idea for which had come to him at Weston the previous winter. Sachie's trustee, Sir William Worsley, arrived with his bossy daughter Isabelle, who was thoroughly snubbed by Edith and insulted over the bridge table by Lady Ida. 'Ida too awful to Isabelle everyone embarrassed.' 'Everyone' now included Constant Lambert, Sphinx and Tancred Borenius, with whom Sachie had been carrying on an obscure feud on Walton's account. 'What times one does go through in this house,' Georgia groaned. 'It is always like living on the edge of a volcano.'

Sir Edwin Lutyens, who arrived for the night on 28 August, used exactly the same phrase. 'The great bare grey untidy house sinister ... Edith more extraordinary than ever and Osbert, as self-possessed as ever and growing more and more like his supposed great-grandfather, George IV ... Sachie is quick-tempered and with selfish Papa and unhappy dipsotic Lady Ida it was like being on a volcano,' he told his wife.[46] There was a violent eruption in the servants' quarters and a resultant atmosphere that could be cut with a knife. Sassoon arrived in the middle of dinner and was suspected by the Sitwells of having done it on purpose to annoy them. The servants' row continued unabated; Osbert, Sachie and Lady Ida went to remonstrate with them, Lady Ida letting her temper rip in the process and taking to the bottle as a result. The next day she and Edith remained in bed with nerves, Sachie had a cold, Osbert and Georgia complained of neuralgia and stiff necks.

There were bright episodes to punctuate the gloom. Harold Acton, Willie Walton, Gerald Berners, Rex Whistler and Edith Olivier arrived. Every evening after dinner Berners and Walton played violent impromptu duets on the piano in order to drive Sir George to bed. 'When they succeed,' Edith Olivier recorded, 'we sit round and Osbert tells many amusing and cruel stories about Lady Colefax and the other people he dislikes.' Edith Olivier thought the house 'lovely and haunted' and not just by the ghosts: 'Sir George is a shadowy man, exquisite and sinister and blade-like. Lady Ida seems to have had a stroke. The three young ones are *haunted* by them.' Edith, always on edge at Renishaw, burst into tears on reading to Olivier her new poem, 'Gold Coast Customs', ostensibly about Ashanti civilisation but, said Olivier, 'really a passionate, modest, macabre, poignant, agonising picture of *our* civilisation, terribly powerful and intensely felt'. 'Again there was this feeling of mystery and madness,' Olivier wrote. 'They say the house is haunted, but the ghosts are the living people.'[47]

By then Georgia had succeeded in escaping to Antibes, but not before she had been reduced to tears by Sir George who lay in wait for her in revenge for a tactless remark she had made about a political career being an extravagance; the result was a step-by-step account of his own political career. When Georgia attempted to wheedle him into paying the local antique dealer's bill for them, Sir George turned on her: 'He says we ought never to go to London, ever have anyone to stay, never go abroad, not have a motor car & only have one gardener three times a week.' Georgia cried with rage afterwards and Sachie, after hearing of the scene, tackled his father, 'but of course it made no difference either'.

By early September the whole caravan moved on to Montegufoni for the performance of *Façade* at the Siena festival. Sachie had visited Bruges with Wilfred Childe en route and then taken the train from Paris with Christabel. Zita and Georgia motored from the South of France, where the social scene had included the usual cast – the Mosleys, Boothby, John Strachey, Fulco di Verdura, Irene Ravensdale, the Casa Maurys, Sir Charles Mendl, Alice de Janzé, the Benjamin Guinnesses and their daughters Tanis and Meraud. Georgia had a surprise encounter with George Bernard Shaw, who was 'very amiable about Edith and "Sitwellism" in general'. At the Porta Rossa in Florence on 8 September Zita and Georgia found Sachie anxiously waiting. On the 9th they were at Montegufoni, the Gingers, Osbert and Edith having arrived that morning. 'My holiday is over,' Georgia confided gloomily to her diary, lapsing into French:

> *Je suis profondement troublée.* It has been great fun & I hope that it will make it easier to bear the burden of my in-laws, but I wonder. One could write for hours on the subject. I would like to have a complete record of my feelings tonight but anyone may read this so I must not risk the luxury of self-expression. . . .

She mused on Osbert and Zita and whether all hope of such a romance was over:

> Maybe she had better marry Mario [Panza] he adores her & at least is not English & can give her things that very few men who are not latin understand & that means a lot, such a lot, to most women, & I believe . . . even to Zita, she seems so beyond all that but she says she is just unawakened & I believe that's true.

From this passage it seems clear that Sachie was lacking in the Latin lover qualities that Georgia required; she was to find them soon in a Frenchman, Georges Duthuit.

The principal threat to any possibility of a Zita-Osbert romance was Christabel. Zita herself, who had been hesitating between Panza and Arthur James, had been reluctant to give up all hope of Osbert, but the intensity of his relationship with Christabel finally convinced her as she watched 'the attack of the indefatigable Christy and the final yielding of the flattered Osbert. It has been intensely amusing so much so that I gave up my game the first day and gave Christy the field to herself,' she wrote in her diary on 16 September. 'She has arrived panting at the goal and the two are to be found lolling in each other's arms spiritually if not entirely physically at any hour.' Both Georgia and Zita found Christabel 'too MADDENING'. 'Osbert & Christabel very thick,' Georgia wrote, 'she is making up to Ginger in a sickening way, more affected than ever. She is very sympathetic when you get her alone but her manner & mannerisms are really outrageous.' Georgia, as the Sitwell daughter-in-law, was irritated by Christabel's bossiness, her organising everyone even to the extent of asking Lady Ida, when they were in Siena, if she wanted to go to 'placey'. Ginger, annoyingly, was flattered by her girlish ways and consequently in a better humour than usual. Otherwise the Sitwellian atmosphere was much the same as it had been at Renishaw. 'Ginger and Lady Ida, both mad,' Zita wrote, 'but I think Ginger the madder. He has quarrelled with the butler of 50 years' standing [Henry Moat] who has packed but will remain.' Edith was depressed because she had not heard from her beloved Tchelitchew and once again cried when she read Zita 'Gold Coast Customs'. Sachie was edgy with Georgia and, when they were in Siena with Walton and Constant Lambert, made a 'maddening scene alleging that Willie's conversation at tea was revolting & that I [Georgia] joined in & encouraged him'.

All this took place against the backdrop of Montegufoni's feudal splendour and stunning Tuscan views, the streets of Siena crowded for the Palio (which had to be postponed once because of the pouring rain) and rehearsals for *Façade*, the first performance of which took place on 14 September with a curtain painted by Severini, to a mixture of enthusiastic cheers and loud boos. The afternoon was spoilt by a horrid scene after lunch when Lady Ida insisted on going home and would not go alone:

> Osbert made poor Edith go with her & miss the Palio. There was a hateful discussion & scene lasting about half an hour & then poor Edith was martyrised as usual. Ida is half mad we all know &

uncomprehendingly selfish & wilful but I cannot understand Osbert's insensitive selfishness.

Zita told Georgia she should not get so upset by these 'little Sitwell tragedies' as 'when Ida is in a temper or when Osbert & Sach quarrell [*sic*]'. 'I know this is only too true,' Georgia admitted 'but I can't help my feelings being involved. It is my life & I can't live it just on the surface without putting any heart into it & directly one puts one's heart in it it is bruised & beaten & trampled on & thrown back in one's face.'

Sachie's Sitwell ties were still too strong and Georgia felt diminished by them. She felt that he should pay more attention to her as an individual and themselves as a couple or rather, since the birth of Reresby, as a separate family entity. He was hurt by her affair with Mosley, which he suspected, and pained by her apparent love of the Mosley circle and the more frivolous aspects of the London scene. Georgia found the whole Sitwell atmosphere oppressive:

I feel so utterly shattered by it all, as usual, & appalled by the stretch of interminable Sitwellism which lies before me in the future. If only Sach could throw *some* of it off, emancipate himself a little & realize how much more his life with me & Reresby ought to mean than this syndicate existence of petty hopes and fears, chiefly fears, which is implicit with his present point of view. How much happier we would be if I meant even a little more to him than does this obsession which one can only call Sitwellism. Even his work means much less to him than it does. But he will never change & I'm afraid it's too late now.

She had to keep reminding herself that her original role in the marriage had been as helpmate to genius:

I have been thinking a lot & realizing that I must try not to lose sight, as I often do, of the objectives of my life. To know I have them & that they are worth while means a lot, but if I could feel that I really worked for them & came near achieving [them] there would be perhaps the greatest satisfaction one could have, anyway I am sure it ought to be one's ultimate aim. . . . It is difficult though, at times, not to be discouraged & feel that it is not worth very much – one's life & one's objectives. When S. seems, as he does now, *so* petty, it is difficult to be inspired to live for him. . . . I want to make him happy, if humanly possible, & the ideal is if I could do so & not at my own expense. How difficult it all is, how lonely, to be on such perfectly intimate terms with anyone & yet to be so completely out of touch, so absolutely without a contact & to know that

not only has this always been so but will get worse. He cannot understand
people at all. He sees them like pictures he has painted himself with no
resemblance to reality except in outline & sometimes without even that.
When he was first really desperately in love with me he did try at moments
to find out, to understand but now it is all accepted. . . .

As a Sitwell, Sachie was inured to scenes; he neither realised the depths of
Georgia's frustration nor took her rages against him very seriously; a few
pages after the heartfelt outburst quoted above, he wrote himself in her
diary: ' "Tine" is such a darling; I adore him more every day. Poor angel,
I'm afraid sometimes I'm rather cruel to him.'

Exasperated, Georgia wrote: 'He will let me go to Paris by motor with
Zita, partly of course to please her & get sympathy but he is jealous of us &
also ravingly jealous of Cimmie & Tom, not only him but her. I can't think
why.' Zita herself seems to have perceived none of these undercurrents.
'Sachie and Georgia and I make an amusing triangle,' she wrote in her
diary, contrasting their 'tact and diplomacy' with the more outrageous
behaviour around them. Sachie came to her room with a present for her
twenty-fifth birthday, a book (probably his collected poems for Humbert
Wolfe's *Augustan Books of Poetry No. 29*, to be published in November,
which included a reprint of the poem inspired by Zita, 'The Golden Bell').
None the less, for several days she had found him annoying and it was only
after a large party for the Siena festival, when everybody got drunk and
danced, that she found him ' "loveable" again and loving'.

Beyond the Sachie–Zita–Georgia triangle the atmosphere at
Montegufoni was stormy, its cause the non-arrival of Sassoon and
Tennant, who were enjoying an Italian idyll together and who had
promised to stay at Montegufoni for the *Façade* house party. Tennant's
valet and Nannie had arrived at Siena knowing nothing of their
whereabouts. Edith, who was already 'half off her head' because
Tchelitchew had not written to her, spent her time with Lady Ida planning
insulting things to say to the couple, whom she had christened 'the Old
Earl and Little Lord Fauntleroy', when they did arrive. She took their
non-arrival as a personal insult to herself on Sassoon's part. It may be that
she was a little in love with him at the same time as nursing her passion for
Tchetlitchew. She had a tendency in her virginal way to fall in love with
homosexuals, whom she referred to as 'herbaceous borders'[48] ('I think
they're rather *herbaceous*, don't you?' was her observation on a Venetian
poolside party). When by 15 September, the day after the performance of
Façade, nothing had still been heard of them, there were dark mutterings

on all sides. Georgia was in an agony of apprehension. 'It is unforgivably rude of them, of course,' she wrote, 'but I wish Osbert would put them off instead of letting them come to this house & then flaying them alive.' They finally appeared on the night of the 17th. Edith, having retired to bed 'angrier than ever', let it be known that she would receive Sassoon in audience at six the following evening, when she 'relented a little towards him' and the atmosphere grew more cheerful. Tennant, however, remained in permanent disgrace with Osbert, who declared that he never intended to see him again. Lady Ida, for once, was more restrained and there were less scenes than there had been at Renishaw, although 'quite enough to wear one out'.

Georgia left Montegufoni with Zita by car on 24 September to be joined by Sachie in Paris on the 29th. As the shores of England loomed, there were the by now inevitable scenes about the Mosleys, in-between reconciliations, orgies of mutual present buying at Charvet's, dining at the Ritz and dancing at the Grand Ecart, where Sachie adored the music. After Zita's departure and an expensive dinner at the Vert Gaillant, there was a 'frightful scene all evening because of and about the difference in our tastes. Tears. Reconciliation.' They dined with Edith, who retailed the difficulties she was having with Tchelitchew and Gertrude Stein. 'Each to her & with each other are or is tiresome. T.[chelitchew] accuses G.[ertrude] S.[tein] of having Virgil Thomson, whoever he is, as a lover, & G.S. says T is "carrying on" with Mrs Ford Maddox [*sic*] Ford. Edith is very cross with them all but very funny about them.'

Back in London at the beginning of October, the Mosleys were again occupying centre stage in Georgia's diaries. Tom had become Sir Oswald, having inherited his father's title in the meanwhile. Georgia had been surprised and amused by the socialist Mosleys' reaction to titles and hereditary possessions. When she remarked that being a baronet was rather a false position, neither one thing nor another, Cimmie was not amused, taking care to point out to her the exact rank of the Mosley baronetcy. 'So different a point of view', Georgia commented to herself, 'to what one feels ... a socialist should have.' Arriving for tea at the Mosleys' in London, she found Tom surrounded by family diamonds and talking about having them re-set and Cimmie wearing a tiara. 'As Queen of the Communists, I suppose,' was Georgia's reaction. Later that evening, after another row with Sachie about it, they went to the Savoy. 'Agonising evening as one felt Sach was hating it & feeling fearfully cross although he *actually danced* with Cim not once but three times. She is the only woman, except once at the Embassy with *me* years ago, that he has ever danced with. . . .' Later she wrote plaintively after yet another Mosley scene with Sachie: 'He hates them & all the people who may give one a good time & ask one to parties which are not purely intellectual.'

Sachie was working at Weston to finish his book, *The Gothick North*, and did not share his wife's frantic desire for social life. Going to London meant not only seeing people all day but probably having at least three evening engagements. But at Weston, while he was working, Georgia was bored, resentful and hankering for her London life. Rows escalated during a gloomy November to such a pitch that on the 15th, Sachie's birthday, Georgia, in bed with a cold and depressed, appealed to Osbert for help: 'Sachie's nerves are so bad again, he makes continual scenes about nothing or anything, scenes like that one at Naples which was one of the first . . . which you must remember only too well, as you were called up in the middle of the night to restore order!'

At her wits' end, she threatened Sachie that she would call in Osbert again, which had a temporarily calming effect, but Sachie soon convinced himself that she would not dare carry out her threat and the rows started again.[49] As Osbert, installed with Walton at Amalfi, had just written a soothing answer to Georgia's first appeal, a second one arrived, so he rewrote his letter, enclosing with it one of admonition to Sachie which Georgia had asked for:

My dearest Georgia,
   . . . I love you both so much, and am so sorry. Of course, it's country life in winter and servants that are impossible [despite complaining constantly of poverty, the Sitwells apparently employed no less than six servants at Weston, who, apart from the admirable Gertrude, their prop and stay throughout both their lives, seem to have been no more contented at Weston than Georgia was].
   . . . it is three years since you married: and three years, in a love affair, is one of the most critical times. . .
   Secondly, the really awful thing is that no really deep relationship, such as yours and Sachie's, ever leads to happiness, to everything else, higher and lower, but not that. Thirdly you are wrong in thinking that he has more to give than you have.
   Your love means everything to him, and that is why he acts as he does. And then, since all true love affairs run their own course, and have their own design, as much as plants or people, perhaps something else, another child, for example, is what Nature expects.
   All this I know does not make it any easier: but in spite of Sachie's *extreme nervous irritability*, what a brilliant success you've made of it.

. . . As for Sachie, if he is at all like me, it may be that he can't believe that people are fond of him unless they are continually telling him so – some sort of inferiority complex . . . if so, tell him as much as you can, how devoted you are, as I know you are, to him.[50]

Osbert, unsure whether this was a storm in a teacup, put it to Christabel, his adviser, to whom he forwarded both Georgia's letter and a résumé of his reply, 'Is her letter a prelude in any way to anything: or is it a real S.O.S. to me personally. . . .' He had been surprised by Sachie's gloomy response to his telegram of congratulations on his birthday – 'it seems so odd that anyone should still be pleased at my having been born' – but attributed this to his brother's 'constitutional melancholy'. His intervention, however, appeared to do the trick. 'They both seem delighted with my rather critical letter,' Osbert reported.[51] Georgia, however, remained dissatisfied; at twenty-three a domestic life at Weston was not enough. None the less, Sachie had been 'an angel' lately and she felt guilty, confiding to her diary: 'with him and darling Reresby one ought to be supremely happy'.

Sachie soon had another reason for unhappiness. On 19 December Zita became engaged to a suitor who had been pursuing her for some time. Arthur James, whom she described as 'blond, pink & sweet', was well-connected and rich, being the nephew of the Duke of Wellington and the owner of a Yorkshire estate. He was a conventional, upper-class young man and absolutely unintellectual, his conversation being confined largely to the Brigade of Guards, hunting, shooting and fishing. The Brigade of Guards was the only thing he shared in common with Osbert, whom undoubtedly Zita would have preferred as a husband. Sachie and Georgia were at the Mosleys for a dinner in honour of the newly engaged couple with Dick Wyndham, Baby and her admirer, Charles Brocklehurst. Everyone seemed pleased, Georgia noted, 'except Cimmie, myself and Sach who is shattered about it'. They spent a gloomy evening at the Savoy 'celebrating' and Georgia cried in the taxi on the way home, partly because she had had her case stolen but also for Zita, whom she suspected of 'making the old mistake of getting married for the sake of it'. Sachie was 'utterly miserable'; his Tiepolo page was marrying a member of 'the Golden Horde'.

On 29 January 1929 Zita, in ivory white satin with a huge train and a 'Russian crown' of orange blossom, married Arthur James at St James's, Spanish Place. Baby Jungman and Tanis Guinness were bridesmaids and all the usual set were there, including, of course,

Sachie and Georgia. Sachie had written a wedding poem for Zita, correcting the colour of her eyes which he had wrongly described as 'cold blue fire' – they were brown – in the original 'The Golden Bell'.

> But here my short sight, my half eyes,
> Did cheat me, did your flame disguise;
> So the cold blue fire I wrote
> I'll answer to a lion-note
> And then your tawny eyes will last
> In this truth by time held fast,
> While all the names there ever were
> Die for me and leave you here.[52]

It was a declaration of intent; Sachie was to continue his complicated relationship with Zita after her marriage to Arthur James.

Some of the problems between Sachie and Georgia had been caused by the strains of hard work and financial difficulties. He was finishing *The Gothick North* and had written another canto of *Dr Donne and Gargantua*, which he dedicated to Sassoon, who had recently been his customarily unappreciative self as a guest at Weston, telling Edith Olivier that 'it was all rather drunken and disreputable' and that he '*just had to keep squalor at bay* picking up cigarette ends and tidying things away'. The 'squalor' was probably due to 'servant trouble', a perennial problem at Weston at the time; it had been rumbling during November and escalated to crisis-point in December. The Sitwells' couple having been sacked for going to a dance without permission, their temporary replacement, George, Osbert's man from Carlyle Square, blotted his copybook three days before Christmas, when the newly married Peter Quennells came to stay, by being 'drunk and insulting before lunch' and had to be ordered out of the house. Sachie and Georgia fled to Dick Wyndham at Tickerage for New Year's Eve, with visits to Brighton for oysters and antiques, and dinner at the Mill with hare, Christmas pudding, champagne and old brandy. On the domestic side of the Sitwells' lives, however, there was hope for a better future. Gertrude Cooper, a young girl from Eckington, had arrived in July 1928 to act as Georgia's personal maid. Pretty, capable, intelligent and with a strong character of her own, it was not long before she and Georgia had the first of a lifelong series of rows. 'Will have to sack Gertrude,' Georgia noted in her diary; 'Sad but inevitable.' Gertrude was to remain with the Sitwells for sixty years.

Back at Weston early in January, Sachie wrote with affection and gratitude to Sassoon, who had generously come to his rescue with a loan to pay off the most pressing of his debts:

> I am dedicating it [*Dr Donne and Gargantua*] to you under the simple initials 'to S.S.' – which looks as if it is dedicated to myself, and will mean, I hope, nothing to anybody except you and me. I only wish I had something better, dear Siegfried. I am so fond of you and miss seeing you very much; and wish you could see the difference your generosity and goodness have made in me. Do make Stephen write to me![53]

Sassoon and Tennant were enjoying a last period of happy relationship in Sicily, where Sachie advised them to go and see Noto, 'a lovely baroque town'. Sachie and Georgia acquired two peacocks and a playful Springer spaniel puppy called Carlos. Harold Acton, Jean Fleming and Tancred Borenius came to stay; Robert Byron arrived with proofs of his new book, *Byzantine Civilisation*; and then Ginger, to inspect the green and gold decoration for the library.

The prospect of leaving Weston and its problems behind had a stimulating effect on Sachie and Georgia. On St Valentine's Day they felled a tree at Weston, Georgia inscribing her initials on it with the date 'to commemorate one of the happiest days of a very happy winter':

> The sun shone, the dogs romped, the peacocks strutted & we both felt gloriously well & happy & pleased with our home & also truly sorry to be leaving it in spite of the intense cold & the prospect of warm days abroad. . . .I shall always remember how happy my darling Sach and I were this afternoon.

This bliss did not last long; two days later, when Constant Lambert arrived to stay, the cold was extreme (it was the coldest February for forty years), the pipes froze and Georgia's hands were crippled with arthritis. Gertrude unmasked a thieving maid and Sachie gave the latest couple notice before they left on 19 February via London and Paris for their separate destinations, Georgia to her mother at St Jean de Luz, Sachie to Osbert and his entourage at Amalfi. In Paris Sachie dined with his father in an unexpectedly convivial evening, as Osbert later reported to Christabel:

> [Sachie] was expecting nothing to eat or drink as Ginger has for ages said that when in Paris he couldn't afford to eat more than 1 thing at each meal. However he gave Sachie an enormous meal & it developed

into what he calls 'an old-fashioned roarers'. They had a bottle of wine each
& masses of brandy afterward and Ginger became indistinct in speech, and
talked Einstein – always a suspicious, fourth-dimensional subject.[54].

At Amalfi, Osbert was surprised and somewhat suspicious to find, on
meeting Sachie off the train at Naples, that

> he had in some way become entangled in Zita's honeymoon tour! With
> the result that she and her husband are here till tomorrow. Georgia, I
> gather, has been very cross to Sachie about it. But he is contradictory in
> his statements.
>   a) Zita told me it was the result of complicated & prolonged
> planning.
>   b) Sachie told me he didn't know she was to be in Naples until he
> arrived there.
>   c) He told me 5 mins. later that Georgia was very cross with him
> about it. (How then, did she know, if he knew nothing about it?)
>   He is very irritable if one says anything about Zita.
>   What makes it a little irritating is . . . that I had a v. queer letter from
> Z. and under the circs. it would have been more tactful if she or Sachie
> had warned me.
>   Poor Arthur [James] isn't very inspiring, is he, really?[55]

Sachie was certainly lying to Osbert when he said that he had not
known Zita would be in Naples until he arrived there. Among his papers is
a telegram from Zita addressed to him at the Hôtel Impérial, Paris, dated
21 February 1929. It reads: 'Will be at Excelsior Naples Sunday. Shall
we dine.' He had almost certainly intended Zita to receive the love
poem he had written her in July as she passed through Rome on her
honeymoon, although he apparently got cold feet at the last moment and
did not send it.

None the less, Sachie's first letter to Georgia after the departure of Zita
and her husband breathed love and affection. 'I do miss you so much &
love you more than you can ever realize. I am so comforted by you & detest
the idea of your being such a long way away from me,' he wrote on 28
February. He confided to her his fears for Zita's marriage:

> I think Arthur J. shows awful signs both of meanness over money, &
> also of practically having none. I do hope it will all turn out alright for
> Zita, but really when you see him in cold blood, like we did here, he is
> very nearly quite impossible. He is so stupid & dense, & cannot take the

very slightest interest in anything of any description. How she will be able to put up with it, I can't imagine.

Money, or rather the lack of it, was a constant theme in Georgia's letters. The Dobles had offered to rent Weston again that summer (the previous year she had confided to her diary: 'I dread them going as they will find out how much we owe'), enabling them to rent a London house. She was extremely conciliatory and sensitive where 'Sitwellism' was concerned, even when it came to the location of the rented house: 'Don't let me push you into 80 Seymour Street if you don't like the idea, or if there is *any* danger of seeing less of darling Osbert or of irritating him. . . . I can't bear to be away from you longer . . . I miss you dreadfully,' she added.

Had she but known it, a new development in Osbert's life was to set them both free of the responsibility for 'darling Osbert' which had weighed on them since the day they married. It was also eventually to lead to further twists in the always complex Sitwell family saga. 'Life is not at all easy, and full of complications and dangers,' Sachie wrote, reporting with relief five days later, 'David Horner and John Becket are going away this afternoon.' If Osbert had been infatuated with John Becket, David Horner was to be the love of his life. By the time Georgia arrived at Amalfi on 28 March to a tremendous welcome by the hotel staff, who romantically put her in the room in which she and Sachie had spent their honeymoon just over three years earlier, their emancipation from 'Sitwellism' was about to begin.

7

The End of the Harlequinade

1929 – 1933

'A whole Gothic world had come to grief . . . there was no
armour glittering through the forest glades, no embroidered feet
on the green sward; the green and dappled unicorn had
fled. . . .'

Evelyn Waugh, *A Handful of Dust*

On 2 April 1929 Sachie, Osbert and Georgia left Amalfi for what was to
be the last united Sitwell Grand Tour. Sachie had been keeping a diary
since he had left Weston on 13 February, which, although no more than a
list of dates, places, sights and a few names, at least made it possible to
trace his movements. They were bound for Athens and Constantinople,
a tour which they had planned to make the previous year but had
abandoned in favour of Morocco.

After a train journey of almost eight hours, they arrived in Brindisi.
Sachie could not resist a day in Lecce to the south seeing 'all the old things
again' before embarking on the 5th on the SS *Tevere* for Piraeus with
Mussolini's youngest daughter on board. Reaching Athens on the
afternoon of the 6th, they went to the Hotel Grande Bretagne; then, after
tea, they visited the Acropolis, which Sachie insisted on returning to each
day of the four which they spent sightseeing in Athens itself. It was his first
visit to Greece and the reality of the classical landscape with which he had
been mentally familiar since his schooldays; he was looking for inspiration
for *Canons of Giant Art*, the Torso poems which he had begun with El
Greco's *Laocoon*. In the Athens Museum he found the two golden cups of
Vaphio, featuring men with Cretan wasp-waists bound tight with metal
belts hunting and taming wild bulls; they were to be the source of
'Pastoral'. 'Mycenae things' he noted for future reference.

Robert Byron had given him a letter of introduction to Alastair
Graham, Evelyn Waugh's ex-lover and old friend, who was then attached
to the British Embassy. (Two years previously, when Waugh had visited

Athens, he had found Graham living with an old Etonian contemporary of Sachie's, Leonard Bower, in a modern flat 'full of dreadful Dago youths . . . who sleep with the English colony for 25 drachmas a night'.)[1] Bower was not there, but Graham dined with them on 7 April, failing to impress Georgia, who described him as 'an utterly spineless very affected lady-like young man . . . not at all amusing and full of airs'. He boasted that his mother was the model for Lady Circumference in *Decline and Fall* and affected a favourite attitude of the Waugh circle that the Parthenon 'irritated' and 'annoyed' him. 'Such impertinence,' Georgia commented. Afterwards she and Sachie had a long talk with Osbert about 'impossible young men', when Osbert apparently agreed that Graham was 'typical of a great many one knows & as such what hope is there for England in the future? . . . another of these young monsters, Mark Ogilvie-Grant [a colleague of Graham's at the Athens Embassy], who draws so badly for Vogue, is going to Palermo to do sketches of . . . Fulco's [di Verdura] fancy-dress party. . . .' After more sightseeing and tea with the Ambassador, Sir Percy Loraine, they left by boat on 13 April, arriving the next day at Constantinople.

'April 15th Reresby's second birthday,' Sachie noted briefly in his diary after a visit to Santa Sofia, while Georgia wrote in hers that she hoped Reresby 'will learn to be really fond of me'. The intrepid Ethel Sands joined them on the 18th having travelled from Kenya, and after a week in Constantinople the party left for a three-day tour to the old Ottoman capital, Bursa, returning on 24 April to stay at the British Embassy with Sir George Clark. On the 26th Evelyn Waugh and his wife came off their ship to lunch at the Embassy. Sachie already knew Waugh through Harold Acton and had been instrumental, through his acquaintance with Beverley Baxter, in obtaining him his short-lived job on the *Daily Express*. According to Waugh's diaries, the three of them had dined together on 10 March 1927 when Sachie was 'extraordinarily nice' to Waugh and afterwards drove him to a party given by 'Layton the black man'. The Waughs had themselves invited the Sitwells to lunch on board, but the Ambassador asked them to the Embassy instead. Although Waugh, 'trying to impress his readers', had name-dropped in his subsequent travel book, *Labels*, that he had been to the Embassy and that 'Osbert and Sacheverell Sitwell were there, combining the gay enthusiasm for the subtleties of Turkish rococo with unfathomable erudition about Byzantine archaeology and the scandals of Ottoman diplomacy', he later confessed to Harold Acton that it had been 'a brief and rather uneasy luncheon party.'[2] The Ambassador evidently did not know Waugh by sight and, assuming that one of the women guests was Evelyn, attempted to draw her out on the subject of *Decline and Fall*. Neither, apparently, did Georgia, although she later became a confidante of Evelyn's; nor was she particularly impressed by the 'little Evelyns Waugh', as she called them: 'He is dapper and baby-faced like a drawing by Mabel Lucie Attwell . . . she has rather popping eyes but is pretty. Neither of them appear to have anything very amusing to say but they were painfully shy.'

Sachie and Georgia left Constantinople on 1 May by the Orient Express. The tour had been a great success for all three Sitwells, as Georgia noted in her diary: '. . . one of the happiest times of my life. Sach & Osbert have been angels too & equally happy I think.' Osbert was no longer lonely and already focusing on a future with David Horner; the problems which Sachie and especially Georgia would have with him in the future would be of a different nature. Sachie and Georgia stopped off in Budapest and Vienna, then spent three weeks in Paris. While in Paris they dined with Dolly Wilde and Clive Bell and his 'terrifying' bisexual girlfriend; at the *Boeuf sur le Toit* Cocteau came over and spoke to Sachie and with Clive Bell they met Matisse's daughter and her husband, Georges Duthuit, with whom Georgia was to have an intense romantic involvement. Bunny Doble arrived with her future husband, Sir Anthony Lindsay Hogg, whom Georgia and Sachie found 'a peaky, extremely callow young man . . . can't think what she sees in him'.

They arrived back in England on 26 May. Far-reaching changes had taken place since they had been away. The first Labour Government had been elected and women over twenty-one had won the right to vote. More importantly from Sachie's point of view, *The Visit of the Gypsies*, the first part of his three-volume *The Gothick North: A Study of Medieval Life, Art and Thought*, had come out on 24 April. *These Sad Ruins*, the second volume, was to be published in September and the final volume, *The Fair-Haired Victory*, the following January. 'This book is the best I have ever written,' Sachie had told Thomas Balston of Duckworth in a letter announcing that he was nearing completion of *The Gothick North* at the end of January 1929, 'and the only constructive book of criticism which has its own existence as a work of art, that there has been for ages. . . .' Ostensibly an examination of the achievements of Northern Europe – 'the fair-haired race' as expressed in the decorative arts and architecture of the medieval period – it was a most Sachiesque compendium of autobiography and interpretative art criticism mingled with comments on the state and future of contemporary civilisation. Despite the racist-sounding title of the third volume, *The Gothick North* barely touched on the subject. The triumph of the fair-haired races in art over the darker-skinned Mediterranean peoples (he included the Portuguese and the Catalans among the former) was no more than an excuse for his investigations into medieval artistic achievement. *The Gothick North* was poetry in prose descending in line from the fantasy of *Southern Baroque Art* rather than his last informative study of German baroque; its autobiographical elements harking back to *All Summer in a Day*.

For Sachie, the essence of medieval life was expressed not in the great cathedrals of Northern Europe (although he made an exception for Chartres and Beauvais), which he dismissed as 'lifeless as old steam engines lying about like waste machinery', but in the monasteries and their artistic productions, in illuminated manuscripts and embroidered vestments and tapestries, which he wrote about with an extraordinary vividness. Kenneth Clark thought his descriptions of particular tapestries in *The Visit of the Gypsies* amongst the best things he ever wrote. As a communicator of his own aesthetic sensations and a discoverer and interpreter of the fine and the unusual, he was unsurpassed. 'I am the Mercury or Harlequin of these pages, designed . . . to run into the world with the messages of my own feelings,' he wrote in *These Sad Ruins*.[3] *The Gothick North* exemplified all his faults and his virtues as a writer. Passages of reeling prose, which might have been written under the influence of some particularly powerful stimulant, were punctuated by penetrating shafts of great poetic beauty and a singing sense of the musical power of words. At times, however, his writing was careless and his grammar poor. His transitions from subject to subject were often clumsy and his comments on contemporary civilisation fatuous. After some soaring introductory pages on the doges of Venice, the dresses of the Second Empire, the swaggering feudalism of medieval Japan, the vestments of St Paul's Cathedral and the Great Wardrobe of Edward III, Miss Corder, Sachie's drawing mistress at St David's, Reigate, appeared suddenly with her brother to act as representative artists and to initiate a dialogue with the author.

In tiresomely artificial conversations with the Corders Sachie often appeared at his worst. Jealousy of their fellow writers was an unattractive characteristic of the Sitwells as a literary family. At Renishaw in August 1930 Evelyn Waugh would be taken aback by their vituperativeness about contemporary literary figures. Sachie gave rein to this with some ungenerous remarks about contemporary women writers, whose work was more widely read than his own. Justifying his particular prose form, the mixture of autobiography, fantasy, poetry and art interpretation which he had just invented, he pronounced: 'I have never believed that the only form of good prose is a novel. . . . They [novels] are all academy pictures now, and there is no good in a poet trying to enter the lists against the hundreds of young female geniuses who are declared every year.' Miss Corder is then made to interject: 'But "The Constant Nymph" and "Dusty Answer".' 'S.S.' then replies: 'Oh never mind! You'd hate to have to read them in three years' time. Let's leave our contemporaries alone; let their voices be heard now, since they'll never be heard of again. . . .'[4]

Sachie was an extremely solipsistic writer and liked to analyse his own sensual reactions in long, complicated, often obscure passages. Without warning he darted in *These Sad Ruins* from conducting a Platonic symposium with Miss Corder and her brother on the Neapolitan shore to London, where, after a visit to Berlin in September (probably the one he made with Sassoon and Osbert in 1927), he was pursuing a cool blonde. This was almost certainly Zita:

> . . . I saw the fair hair and heard the cold voice that had shaped and moulded my last few weeks. There was no doubt that Joaquina was cold – very cold – indeed chilly. Nothing pleasant or unpleasant had the slightest power to ruffle her, and she was able to pass, unscathed, through the most severe family storms and the most poignant stresses of affection. Nor could it be said exactly that she did not take her share in any of these troubles, for she certainly answered her mother with sufficient sharpness, and in my dealings with her I could not complain of her not being interested in our situation; but all the same she seemed to lead a life of her own with which she would allow no interference. What she meant this life to be, and what her aims were in trying to keep it separate from so many things out of which it was really composed, it was difficult to conjecture.

Further on, he presented Georgia and Zita as symbolising the two halves of beauty: '. . . as in the choosing between a milky skin and raven hair or a sunburnt and gypsy fairness, tawny as to its yellow and lion-like eyes. . . . These are the two alternatives to the soul. . . .' There followed an erotic episode which may or may not have been a fantasy. Feeling sexually frustrated on leaving Joaquina/Zita after an evening at the theatre, he stumbled by chance into the offices of an art editor where a Bohemian party was going on. There he met Miriam, a beautiful, shy, blonde twenty-year-old, and arranged to take her to dinner the following night. On purpose he took her to the same play that he had taken Zita to the previous night. 'It gave me a peculiar sense of delight to see the same thing again and to go over those stages of a longing and a gradual sinking into danger.' Later, in her rooms near Selfridge's, he made love to her. He could not bring himself to describe the sexual act directly; it took him nine pages of highly charged and fantastic prose to convey the experience.[5]

Sachie had finished *The Gothick North* on 13 February 1929, shortly after Zita's marriage and before he left to join Osbert in Amalfi. She was clearly very much in his thoughts; a passage in *These Sad Ruins* uses just the same language as the wedding poem he wrote for her, mentioning how he had mistaken her tawny eyes for blue. It was probably at this time, too, that he wrote the love poem which he never sent. Sexual frustration was near the surface in his relationship with Zita; he made repeated references to her 'cold and marble restraint' and, angrily, of her 'taking and asking for everything and giving nothing'. In the end he turned away from her, just as he did at the end of this chapter, 'Love Scene', because he found elsewhere the physical pleasure she would not provide.

The Gothick North received mixed reviews. The *Times Literary Supplement* was dismissive, accusing him of being both 'careless and limited' in his treatment of art history; 'everything in the book is made a prop for fantastic writing'. The *Spectator* was more friendly, mainly complaining about the decision to publish the book in three parts; the reviewer of the last volume (who may have been Peter Quennell) hailed it as a 'notable achievement . . . such stuff as dreams – and memories and an enduring literary reputation – are made of'. The Sitwells' biographer, R.L. Mégroz, pointed out that it should have been called not a study but a fantasia. Sachie thought that he had found a new prose form, using the dislocation of time and the juxtaposition of apparently unrelated images in the surrealist manner. He deployed words, as Edith did in her poetry, for their sounds or to convey sensation rather than sense. It was a form which suited him; he was incapable of rational or sustained argument, ill-equipped for realism. He belonged to the world of unicorns and harlequins and far-flung fantasies, baroque and rococo in its flights of fancy, 'Gothick' in its fascination with horror, the grotesque and the bizarre. His unique gifts were an unerring instinct for the beautiful and the unusual and an absolute confidence in the validity of his own aesthetic sensations. *The Gothick North* set the pattern of his literary future as he turned away from poetry to prose and his 'entertainments of the imagination'.

The year 1929 was a turning-point in many ways. For the first time since he could remember Sachie did not spend his August holiday with Osbert. Instead, he and Georgia remained at Weston, with occasional forays to stay with friends. Osbert was in Algeciras with David Horner with whom, unknown to Sachie, he had already been in love for at least a year. (In June 1928 he began a letter to David with one of his pet names for him, 'Dearest Dum-Dum'.) He had first met Horner at a London party in 1923, when he had been instantly struck by the twenty-three-year-old's looks. At Cambridge, a male admirer addressed Horner as 'Beauteous Adonis'; he was pale, willowy and elegant, with a finely drawn profile and blond curls. Osbert himself used the word 'orchidaceous' to describe him and he became known in the Sitwell family as 'Blossom'. His face had been his fortune; as the younger son of a younger son he had had little money of his own until left a considerable sum by his lover, Vicomte Bernard d'Hendecourt, an art dealer, who had had the tact to die in December 1928. He was well-connected; his father, John Stuart Horner, who owned a civil engineering business, was one of the Horners of Mells Park in Somerset. David's aunt, Frances Horner, was a noted hostess and a member of the 'Souls'; his cousin Katherine had married Raymond Asquith, son of the Prime Minister, and through him the Horners were connected with the Liberal aristocracy of Charterises, Wyndhams, Tennants and Asquiths. David had taste; he was a good gossip and maliciously amusing. He fitted perfectly into Osbert's world and filled the void of private loneliness left by Sachie's marriage. He was not, perhaps, an admirable character; Constant Lambert unkindly called him 'The Captain's Doll' from D.H. Lawrence's short story, and his influence on Osbert, as far as Edith and Sachie were concerned, was to be malevolent.

Horner's ally in Osbert's circle was Christabel, to whom he wrote affectedly from the Reina Cristina at Algeciras describing himself as 'the chosen darling of the gods' and his role vis-à-vis Osbert, who had contracted blood-poisoning from an infected mosquito bite on the hand, as 'nurse, scribe, bully, comforter in turn'.[6] Osbert, meanwhile, had been composing love poems to him, a new and unsuccessful departure from his usual satire; one of them began: 'You are my golden squirrel'.[7] The 'golden squirrel' was already making mischief, beginning the process of cutting Osbert off from the people closest to him. Walton was the first target.

On 25 August Walton had written to Osbert from Weston to tell him that he had fallen in love with Imma Doernberg. Imma, born Princess of Erbach Schonburg, now widow of Baron Hans-Karl von Doernberg, had royal blood, being first cousin through her parents to Princess Alice of Athlone and Princess (later Queen) Juliana of the Netherlands. Sachie and Georgia had met her in June 1929, when Walton had brought her down to the Daye House near Wilton where they were spending the week-end with Edith Olivier. By the end of August, when Edith Olivier came to stay at Weston, Walton and Imma were in love, to the point at which Walton, hitherto a relentless philanderer, wanted to marry her. He had always enjoyed an extraordinary success with women, despite his lack of physical – or financial – attributes. Edith Olivier had described him as looking like 'a pitiable little cad – a diseased one too, rather like a maggot'. On 25 August Walton had written to Osbert from Weston confessing, 'I am now fixed up with Imma for life', and telling him that they planned to spend the winter abroad ('subject to your august approval'), apparently in Osbert's company. 'It would make a great difference to my life & happiness, incidentally you won't find her a bore, in spite of what little D.[avid Horner] may say. . . .'[8] 'Little D.', ever jealous and mischievous where Osbert's close relationships were concerned, wrote complaining to Christabel: 'Willie seems determined to give trouble – Can he expect to riot around Europe in open sin?'[9]

For Sachie, the worst blow of the summer was Diaghilev's sudden death from diabetes at Venice on 19 August, aged only fifty-seven. Diaghilev had been the hero and inspiration of his youth and his death seemed to mark the end of an era for Sachie, both public and personal. Exactly a year later he began the preface to an exhibition of Lifar's picture collection and found himself overtaken by melancholy. 'Since then . . . it seems as if nothing more had happened. All the strings that he held in his hands, those small white hands that were in such contrast to his stature, dropped from him and the puppets never moved again. . . .' He had remained on close terms with Diaghilev, spending a good deal of time at the theatre with him over successive seasons, attending rehearsals and helping him choose music for the orchestra interludes. The great days of Diaghilev's ballets were over and the standard of dancing had declined, yet, although he was always short of finance, he had been as full of projects and as forward-looking as he had been in 1919. In recent years the popularity of his ballets had dwindled; Sachie and Georgia had remained loyal, attending regularly, sitting in the box given to them by Diaghilev's manager, Eric Wollheim, and trying, often in a half-empty theatre, to lead the applause.[10] Sachie had last seen Diaghilev at the end of the season at Covent Garden, looking ill; he had been planning to see him in Venice in September, where Tchelitchew was to work with him on a new ballet.

Sachie and Georgia left Weston early in September for Venice. Edith, who had planned to go there to see Tchelitchew, went with them, despite her disappointment that he had cancelled his visit because of Diaghilev's death. She shared a wagon-lit compartment with Zita, who was to accompany the Sitwells – without her husband. They stayed with the Courtaulds at the Palazzo Morosini until mid-September, then with Bertie Landsberg at the Villa Malcontenta. After a brief visit to Padua, they returned to Venice as guests of Sir Henry 'Chips' Channon. While staying with the Courtaulds Zita had attracted a new admirer, Prince Sapieha, who invited them to stay with his friends, the Potockis, at Lançut, their magnificent estate near Cracow. Sachie was fascinated; a Countess Potocka had been so much in love with his great-grandfather, Colonel Hely-Hutchinson, that she had wanted to leave him her estates in Poland, France and Belgium.

They travelled via Vienna to Cracow, where they spent two days visiting the cathedral and churches; the next day they went with Sapieha to Zakopane and the lake beyond. At Lançut, where they stayed for two nights, the Potockis lived in feudal splendour. The house was ruled by Countess Bedka Potocka, a vivacious, worldly widow with two sons, Alfred and Joseph. The Almanach de Gotha was the house bible; social life for the twenty guests staying at Lançut was ordered in strict conformity with their quarterings. Processions were formed according to precedence for church, for touring the gardens and greenhouses, or for going into whichever of the seven dining rooms happened to be chosen for the occasion. Footmen were stationed in shifts outside guests' rooms, sleeping there at night, summoned not by bells but by clapping hands to fetch ladies' maids or valets or to guide guests round the enormous house. From Lançut they travelled to Warsaw – 'no churches,' Sachie noted laconically – and spent a night in Berlin. Georgia went on to Paris to stay with her parents while Sachie returned, with Zita, via Utrecht to London, where he stayed in Gerald Berners's house in Halkin Street.

By mid-October they were back at Weston, where their first week-end guests were the Mosleys, Berners, Rex Whistler and Walton, a regular visitor now that he found Carlyle Square less congenial because of 'little D'. Apart from the Mosleys, the guests at Weston tended to be Sachie's friends rather than Georgia's. Zita, for once with her husband, was there for Sachie's birthday on 15 November. She had been married less than a year, but it was already clear that the Sitwells' reservations about Arthur James had been well founded. She was bored and unhappy in her marriage, craving the intellect and fun she had found in the Sitwells' circle and still spiritually dependent upon Sachie. Sachie was nervous and depressed, working on a book of short stories, a new medium for him. He accused Zita of being uninterested in his work, which she passionately denied. She, too, was feeling extraordinarily depressed by the monotony and isolation of her Yorkshire life, pleading with him in a letter to keep in touch.[11]

Sachie's answer was evidently a passionate one, for Zita replied on 29 November '. . . I felt [on reading it] as though the beautifully controlled stream of our careful past had suddenly broken its chains. . . .' Their relationship continued on the same pattern, with Sachie pressing, Zita retreating, but not so far as to risk losing him, occasionally teasing and holding out some faint hope of more than passion on paper.[12]

She was invited to stay, without her husband, for their first week-end party in 1930, with Harold Acton, Berners and Eleanor Smith. The Kenneth Clarks came down the following week-end, and Christopher Sykes and Tom Driberg were there for the first week-end in February, then Nancy and Peter Quennell. Edith stayed in mid-February, when she and Sachie spent an entire day correcting the proofs of her *Collected Poems*. The Weston visitors' book showed that they were the last guests to stay there for almost eight months. The Sitwells' financial position had not been helped by the Depression – 'business gloom', Sachie had entered in his diary that May. Various tradesmen were dunning them for payment to the extent of becoming threatening. The only solution seemed to be to go abroad to escape them and to leave Weston to spend a prolonged period at other people's expense.

Once again the noble Siegfried stepped in and saved the day with a loan. As Sachie wrote to him on 27 February 1930, the day before he left Weston:

> I wish there was any way of describing to you the difference in my life,
> now, to what it was a few weeks ago. Peace that passeth human
> understanding has descended upon me, thanks to you; though, as a
> matter of fact there are still a few turbulent, unruly voices about, but
> very far away. . . . My life was rapidly becoming impossible; so, as far as
> I am concerned, you have been instrumental in securing peace twice in
> ten years. . . .[13]

Sachie left Weston on 28 February to stay with Gerald Berners in London and to see the exhibition of Sir Philip Sassoon's art collection, which may have given him the germ of an idea for *British Narrative Pictures* which he wrote several years later. Georgia saw to it that they dined with the Mosleys the night before their departure for Barcelona on 1 March. They were to spend ten days with the Dobles in Mallorca before returning on 10 March to Barcelona to embark on the Duke of Westminster's yacht, invited by his new (third) Duchess, the former Loelia Ponsonby. 'The prospect terrifies and excites me,' Sachie told Sassoon. 'I believe it is the nearest one will ever get to Henry VIII. . . .' The comparison was an apt one, not only with reference to the ducal propensity for serial matrimony. Hugh Richard Arthur Grosvenor, second Duke of Westminster, was tall, blue-eyed (but never, like Henry, grossly fat), with fair, reddish hair. He had been heir apparent to the power and riches of his grandfather's Westminster title since the age of four and had inherited a huge slice of the most valuable London real estate, a great house in Cheshire which could accommodate sixty guests, numerous other properties in England, Scotland and France, and all the trappings of an Edwardian magnifico. He had been nicknamed 'Bendor' after his grandfather's racehorse which had won the Derby in the year of his birth; Coco Chanel had been his mistress and he owned two huge yachts – one a steam vessel, the 263-foot, 883.52-ton *Cutty Sark*, and the other a recently built 203.5-foot, 1178.74-ton, four-masted schooner, the *Flying Cloud*.

Bendor was, not surprisingly, extremely spoilt, having been able to do and have what he liked practically since childhood. With an overwhelming, boyish charm when he chose to exert it, he was generous, unpredictable, pathologically jealous, cruel when crossed or betrayed, acquisitive in the large sense of increasing his patrimony but equally given to the grand gesture in presents of jewellery to women, a sporting philistine, ignorant and prejudiced at one moment and a passionate sightseer the next. Despite his notorious liaisons, he was a prude where his wives were concerned; finding Loelia on a long train journey reading a book in which the word 'adultery' was mentioned, he threw it out of the window leaving her with nothing to read for the rest of the day. He was a phobic anti-Semite, owning a book called the *Jew's Who's Who* which purported to show the Jewish blood in the aristocratic English families, which he used to lock away with elaborate secrecy, yet Winston Churchill was one of his closest and most admired friends. He loathed and feared change, the young and London Society. While enjoying the company of Churchill, Birkenhead and Beaverbrook, he claimed to like what he termed 'Real People', who were in fact toadies or nonentities. 'The password into the Real Person Club', his wife remarked, 'was Obscurity.' He was as restless as any over-rich, under-employed man of innate perception and intelligence without intellectual resources can be. After their marriage, Loelia drew up for her parents' guidance two lists. One, headed 'To be run down', included 'White's Club, the Ritz Hotel, all performing animals except fleas, all modern art, Lady Cunard, Russia, Royalty in general but especially the King of Spain, Lord Londonderry, cocktail parties and Ramsay MacDonald'. The other list included subjects to be praised, such as Ponticum Rhododendrons (anathema to aficionados of the species including the Duke of York), South Africa (sternly anti-royalist), Circuses with Clowns, the Marx Brothers, Jorrocks, Mark Twain, and Beachcomber.[14]

Loelia was twenty years younger than Bendor, a former Bright Young Thing, credited with the invention of the 1920s' bottle party, and a great friend of Zita's. None of these credentials was calculated to appeal to Bendor; she was, moreover, the daughter of a courtier, a breed he particularly detested since he had been banned from Court after his first divorce. It was an unlikely match from the start; Loelia was intelligent and amusing, but found it difficult to fit in with the already set pattern of her husband's life. Brought up as a reserved and repressed upper-class girl, she was utterly unequipped to cope with the monster she had married. Instead of the freedom which she imagined a married woman enjoyed, she found she had exchanged the 'mild authority' of her parents for 'an almost insane tyranny'. 'My every action was watched and criticized, my words misinterpreted and derided, my plans sabotaged,' she later wrote. 'On the other hand, Benny's every passing whim had to be obeyed as if it were a divine command.' After five years, what Loelia described as 'my fairytale marriage' was to founder amid ferocious, bitter scenes. On one occasion Bendor seized a Cartier clock made of crystal with diamond hands, a wedding present to Loelia from one of her friends, and threw it against the wall, shattering it. Not content with that, half an hour later he returned, wastepaper-basket in hand, to scrape up the debris, saying that he was 'going to take jolly good care that I didn't save so much as a diamond hand'.[15]

Sachie and Bendor took to each other instantly. An unlikely friendship developed between them. Most of Loelia's contemporaries and relations were anathema to him. Sachie proved to be the exception despite being neither a sportsman nor a gambler, Bendor's two principal diversions. Bendor was the type of large-scale, extravagant, eccentric figure he had always admired, like Uncle Francis Londesborough or the Bourbons of Naples. Bendor, restless and easily bored, was fascinated and amused by Sachie, recognising in him a true original. It was a friendship which lasted, with a few hiccoughs at the time of Bendor's separation from Loelia, until his death. At Eaton, his vast nineteenth-century palace in Cheshire, he and Sachie would play silly duets together on the organ. They exchanged newspaper cuttings touching on private jokes or mutual pet hates. Bendor sent Sachie a cutting with a lyrical description of 'The Bats' Dormitory' by W.R. Calvert. 'Many die during the winter sleep. The feeble flame of life just flickers out in the little ruddy brown bodies. . . .' Beside this, he had pencilled, 'what a *comfort*'. Another reported the existence of a 'Hermits-Only' Club opened in Omaha, with membership limited to 'people who have lived apart from the world for 35 years or more in caves or shanties, and who are so resolved to live until they die'. The president, aged ninety-one, had been a recluse for eighty odd years, the vice-president for more than forty-five, and the secretary, 'Dynamite Pete' Everett, aged 'more than 70', since he was '18 or thereabouts'. 'My dear Sachie,' Bendor wrote, 'Could you communicate with Secretary of enclosed & make all necessary arrangements?'[16] For the next four years the Westminsters were an important part of Sachie's life, enabling him to travel on a scale and in a style which he could not otherwise have afforded. There would be cruises on the Westminster yacht or as Bendor's guests at the Hotel Lotti in Paris (where George Orwell as floor-waiter was once despatched on a desperate search for a mid-winter peach for the Duke), at Eaton, at Lochmore, his sporting estate in Scotland, Mimizan, his Dutch colonial hunting lodge in the forests of Les Landes, or at Saint-Saens, another, grander, hunting manoir which he owned in Normandy.

With Zita and another couple, Eddy and Sylvia Compton, as fellow guests, and using the *Cutty Sark* as their base, the ducal party visited Tarragona, the monasteries of Santa Cruz and Poblet, which Sachie had described in *The Gothick North*, Carcassonne and Aigues Mortes. All seemed set fair for Bendor and Loelia. 'The Duke is charming. He *adores* Loelia & she seems devoted to him,' Georgia noted on their return to Barcelona. Zita, however, did not find favour. 'Zita proved more callous etc. than I ever imagined,' Georgia wrote disapprovingly, but unspecifically, on 18 March, a comment inspired, perhaps, by jealousy. They left the yacht a week later for Venice to board the SS *Tevere*, the same boat in which they had sailed on their trip with Osbert the previous year. At Brindisi Osbert and David Horner joined them, Osbert, in the first flush of his romance with David, 'looking well and happy'.

Although David Horner's role in Osbert's life had taken the strain out of Sachie's and Georgia's relationship with him, at heart Sachie did not welcome the cause of his emancipation. He had not liked the vibrations which he had picked up at Amalfi while staying with Osbert in March 1929, when Horner and Becket had both arrived there. 'Life is far from easy and full of complications and dangers,' he had written to Georgia. Osbert's homosexuality was a source of pain to him; when John Pearson completed his biography of the Sitwells, *Façades* (published in 1978), Sachie wrote to his lawyers asking for a paragraph about Osbert and Adrian Stokes to be omitted, and objected strongly to Osbert's letters to Horner, and even more so the pathetic love poems which he wrote to him, being printed. He would have preferred to have the whole affair, publicly revealed for the first time in Pearson's book, omitted.[17] His own relationship with Osbert, once so passionate, was still deeply important to him and he suffered from a feeling that he was being excluded from his primary place in his brother's life, as, indeed, he was. Some six weeks earlier, in response to what had evidently been a hurt letter from Sachie, Osbert, who was at Amalfi with Horner, had tried to reassure him:

> I've just got your letter. . . . You know I adore you, more and more as
> the years go by; and I am so afraid that my not meeting you till the end
> of April may hurt you, but I'm sure you won't let it – but I promised to
> go with David to Rhodes, and he returns to England shortly after: and
> he has been very good staying on here so long – for we shall be together
> all May and end of April and in the summer. As for my writing, you
> know how I depend on you in every sort of way. . . . I was awfully
> depressed at your not writing to me for so long, so do write by return.
> I love you so much, my darling, and can't bear not knowing what you are
> doing. . . .[18]

The quartet spent three days in Athens, a week in Rhodes, another week in Cyprus, where they lunched at Government House in Nicosia with Sir Ronald and Lady Storrs, and then returned to Athens for a tour of mainland Greece. They were back in Athens on 13 April for just one night and left the next day for Mycenae. There had been a certain amount of grumbling about being 'slave-driven' by Sachie, of whom Osbert wrote to Christabel that he 'was a riot of plans for seeing all Greece in an unprecedentedly short time'. Sachie was an exhaustive and exhausting sightseer; a friend described his method as 'magnetic'. He would go into a room in a gallery making for one particular picture as if drawn by an invisible ray, absorb it and then shoot across the room to another target while everyone else was still contemplating the first. Then he would be off again, leaving them in his wake. He knew exactly what he wanted to see and never missed anything worthwhile in any room he passed through. 'Sightseeing with him demands great quickness on the uptake,' a friend wrote.

On 14 April they visited Mycenae and Agamemnon's tomb lashed by torrents of wind-driven rain; the next day they motored down to Mistra to see four monasteries, returning again to Mycenae, this time in brilliant sun. The Mycenaean tombs burned into Sachie's memory and were the source of inspiration for one of his best-known poems, 'Agamemnon's Tomb'. In Athens again on 21 April, they met Robert Byron, just arrived from India, who was to be their guide on this visit, and lunched with Leonard Bower. Byron took them to see three El Grecos, 'probably forgeries', in an as yet unopened part of the museum. They left Athens on the 25th, their eventual destination Montegufoni. At Assisi on the 28th, where Sachie, Osbert and Horner, having been joined by Gerald Berners, were spending a couple of days sightseeing, they heard that Mrs Powell had died. First Diaghilev, now Mrs Powell, two lynchpins of Sachie's past life with Osbert had gone.

The summer of 1930 was the occasion for two last great exhibitions of 'Sitwellism' rampant, with house parties at Montegufoni and Renishaw. Georgia arrived at Montegufoni on 27 April; on Sir George's orders, 'the boys' were to keep away from Montegufoni until further notice, as he had a tremendous plan afoot which involved Georgia's help. When they finally arrived on 1 May, they found the atmosphere in Osbert's words 'volcanic'. Ginger was mysterious and elated, Georgia harassed and bound to keep his secret, and Lady Ida 'in one of her rages' at being kept in the dark. 'Hysterical scene Ida & Ginger,' Georgia had noted tersely two days earlier; 'Sinister. Eccentric. Delirious.' Also staying in the house was the formidable Aunt Gracie Londesborough, now, in her nephew's words, 'an Amazonian wreck, a substantial ruin of the Edwardian age,' tall and imposing, with a slight limp which was the result of a hunting accident. There was no love lost between her and Sir George; there were old feuds over his behaviour at the time of Lady Ida's debts, and on his side he had never forgiven her for buying him a hideous 'Italian-style' stone bench at a Conservative fête, which she publicly declared was a present for her brother-in-law but afterwards sent him a bill for the considerable sum of £14. She was by now extremely vague. 'George,' she remarked one night, 'on my way home I'd like to stay at Monte Carlo – if only I knew where it was.' 'My father', Osbert wrote, 'always delighted at the thought of being able to stop anyone from doing something pleasurable . . . and as if he could detect some terrible danger lurking . . . replied: 'Oh, I shouldn't do anything as rash as that if I were you.'[19] She was now also, Osbert told Christabel, 'quite ga-ga and deaf. Neither she nor mother can hear or understand anything the other says.'

Sir George's dinner party, planned for the night of Sachie's arrival, included Gerald Berners and a party from Mrs Keppel's villa, L'Ombrellino, her daughters, Sonia Cubitt and Violet Trefusis, her brother-in-law, Lord Albemarle, whom Osbert unkindly described as 'always gaga and, on this occasion, blind too', his son, Lord Bury, and Sir John Aird. The local brass band played incessantly during and after dinner, alternating *The Fascist March* with *God Save the King*, while Ginger was seen to be in a high state of excitement all evening. It later turned out, Osbert wrote, that this was *the* evening of his life which he had been planning for two years. In the middle of dinner a servant came in to whisper in Sir George's ear; he stood up announcing that a ghost had been found and subsequently led the guests, one by one in order of precedence, to inspect it. Peering through a hole knocked in a wall into a hitherto unseen room, they saw a middle-aged man in cardinal's robes seated at a table furnished with a vellum-bound book and a skull, repeating in Italian with a noticeable cockney accent: 'Why don't you leave me in peace?' (He was, in fact, an Englishman named Procter.) The room in which he sat was elaborately furnished with Gothic cupboards of inlaid wood and an early table like an interior in a Carpaccio painting. The whole thing had been designed as an elaborate joke 'to amuse my friends' ('that phantom company', as Osbert unkindly remarked). It fell completely flat; the young were embarrassed, the old confused. 'We all felt we had gone mad & felt acutely anxious for poor "Ginger" & the real ga-gas, Aunt Gracie, Lord A. and Keppel [who] simply didn't know where they were or what it was about – naturally enough.'[20]

The remainder of the time was passed in the usual Tuscan round. The weather was bad, Berners painted Georgia's portrait all day, Aunt Gracie played 'her waltz' and *Home Sweet Home* on the piano, and there were visits from and to the local Anglo-Saxons, the Keppels, the Actons, the Florentine aristocracy whom Aunt Gracie amused with royal anecdotes, and exiled royalty in their villas on the hills above the city. They went to see the procession of Florentine footballers in their medieval costumes and to hear Toscanini conduct on 14 May. The next day Walton arrived with Imma Doernberg. Berners left, inviting Sachie and Georgia to stay with him in Rome, but they could not afford the fare; in any case, there was an additional reason keeping them at Montegufoni.

Georgia's entry for 12 May reads: 'Broke financial news to Ginger.' There were ferocious rows about money. Sir George, having been fortunate enough to enjoy full use of the revenues of Renishaw all his life, fought tenaciously to reduce his sons' expenditure while providing them with notable examples of his own extravagance. Nothing was too good for Montegufoni, the restoration of which had been the principal object of his life for the past twenty years. He had recently bought a painted room from a Venetian dealer for £1,450, while at the same time refusing to pay Edith's return fare from Montegufoni on the grounds of penury. Osbert now enraged him by announcing that he had taken out a £10,000 mortgage on his expectations as heir to Renishaw, while Sachie and Georgia had come to Montegufoni determined to force Ginger to make it possible for them to live at Weston. Osbert had told his father in no uncertain terms that he had saddled both his sons with houses they could not afford to live in, but Sir George remained adamant. He was, however, powerless to do anything about Osbert's plan, and while Osbert sat, in a state of relative contentment, writing besotted love letters to David Horner, Sachie and 'Juggins' (Osbert's unflattering nickname for Georgia) were having 'terrific rows with Ginger about money', 'not to mention screams and tears'.[21] 'He [Sir George] wants us to give up Weston,' Georgia wrote gloomily. As they left Montegufoni on 28 May, Sir George's heart apparently melted slightly. 'Ginger's cheque! What joy!' Georgia noted. Peace was temporarily restored, but it was only a lull in a bitter financial battle between Sachie and his father which was to rage over the next three years.

Sachie and Georgia travelled to Paris with Osbert and Horner, then on to London to their rented house, 80 Seymour Street. Their emotional lives were becoming as tangled as their financial affairs. Georgia was beginning an involvement with Georges Duthuit, whom she had seen on both days when in Paris, while Sachie's fascination with Zita continued. On 4 June they had a 'really serious row' about her, in the course of which Sachie, according to Georgia's diary, hit her extremely violently. Duthuit arrived from Paris; one night he, Georgia, Sachie and Zita, with Arthur Waley as an unexpected companion, went down to Maidenhead to dine and dance. At lunch at Zita's on 16 July, Sachie met the woman with whom he was to have a serious affair, Lady Bridget Parsons. It was their first meeting, but Sachie had already admired her from a distance. They met again at lunch at Zita's, and Sachie wrote her a list of things to see on her forthcoming trip to Germany. She spent the winter in America and he was not to see her again until the following year.

Sachie and Georgia motored up to Renishaw on 1 August for a six-week stay. A stream of guests arrived during the month including, for the first time, Evelyn Waugh, whom Sachie had seen frequently during the summer social season. He saw the Sitwells, according to Cyril Connolly, as 'exactly the sort of aristocrats he longed to be himself' and his eye lighted with glee upon Ginger, whose image so imprinted itself upon his memory that, staying at Renishaw twelve years later, he was able to recall for Osbert his first meeting with the Baronet, as he saw him one summer evening on the terrace in front of the house:

> Your father was wearing a long-tailed evening coat with a black waistcoat as though he had gone into mourning with the Court many years before, had taken a liking to the style and retained it in deference to some august and recent bereavement of his own. He seemed slightly estranged from the large party you and Sachie had invited and edged away to the extreme fringe of the group, where I was standing, and stood silently gazing out across the valley.
>
> I had noted with fascination during my stay how his beard would assume new shapes with his change of mood, like the supple felt hat of an impersonator. Sometimes he would appear as King Lear on Dover cliffs, sometimes as Edward Lear on Athos, sometimes as Mr Pooter at Margate. Tonight he was Robinson Crusoe. I think it was in his mind, then, that rather than being, as he was, a rare visitor at Renishaw, he lived there uninterruptedly all the year round and had in consequence lost touch with the wider life of fashion which was his birthright.
>
> In the valley at our feet, still half hidden in mist, lay farms, cottages, villas, the railway, the colliery and the densely teeming streets of the men who worked there. They lay in shadow; the heights beyond were golden.
>
> Your father had seldom addressed me directly during my visit. Now, since I was next to him, he turned and spoke in the wistful, nostalgic tones of a castaway, yet a castaway who was reconciled to his solitude. 'You see', he said, 'there is *no one* between us and the Locker-Lampsons.'[22]

Sir George and Lady Ida were staying at the Sitwell Arms, as Osbert was now the master of the house. Waugh admiringly noted down his seigneurial ways for future reference: 'Osbert['s] breakfast was large slices of pineapple and melon. No one else was allowed these. Osbert kept cigars and smoked them secretly. . . .'[23] The recreations of the house were bathing in the 'swimming pool' – the weather was extremely hot – visiting local houses and 'Osbert's Walk', which consisted of driving in the car a quarter of a mile to Eckington Woods, walking through them, which took about half an hour including struggling through bracken, the car meeting him on the other side and taking him home. Waugh had arrived with Robert Byron; at Renishaw he found Walton, who was to conduct one of his works locally, Harold Monro of the Poetry Bookshop, Gaspard Ponsonby, Loelia's brother, whom Waugh described as 'very mad and conceited' and in love with Georgia, Francis Birrell and Arthur Waley. Alastair Graham arrived, apparently at Waugh's invitation; Edith took against him. 'He will always be pretty silly,' Georgia commented, 'but he hardly deserves Edith's ferocious treatment.'

Waugh noted down his observations of the Sitwell family. Sachie 'liked talking about sex', Osbert was (inexplicably) 'very shy' and Edith 'totally ignorant'. She amazed him by claiming that, although Scarborough was very poor, she 'did not think the fishermen took drugs very much. She also said that port was made with methylated spirit; she knew this for a fact because her charwoman had told her'. The Sitwells and their 'very curious' servants lived on 'terms of feudal familiarity': 'E.g. a message brought by footman to assembled family that her ladyship wanted to see Miss Edith upstairs. "I can't go. I've been with her all day. Osbert, you go." "Sachie, you go." "Georgia, you go", etc. Footman: "Well, come on. One of you's got to go." ' There were the usual elaborate plots and secret jokes directed against Ginger. When Lady Ankaret Jackson, born a Howard, came to stay with her husband William, Ginger was unwise enough to enquire of Osbert: 'What are Lady Ankaret's interests? I should like to draw her out on her own topics.' 'Polar explorations,' Osbert replied, 'the embroidery of Church Vestments during the latter part of the thirteenth century, &, above all, Sassanian silver work.' 'Poor Ankaret was quite unprepared for the results of this conversation,' he told Christabel, 'tho' Sachie, who knew about it, led off saying to her at dinner, as soon as she'd sat down, "Don't you rather dread the blubber again this winter, Ankaret?" Which ought to have given her a clue of some sort. But for days & days she found herself a recognised authority on things about which she knew nothing. . . .'[24] Renishaw had a curious effect upon people. A later guest that summer, the usually reserved Arthur Waley, surprised and fascinated Sachie and Georgia with stories about his love life. 'Most unexpected. Very diverting,' Georgia commented.

Earlier guests had included the usual cast: Sphinx, Walton, Zita (briefly, with her husband), Christabel, Constant Lambert and Dick

Wyndham. Anthony Powell and Tom Balston came, as did Raymond Mortimer, Tom Driberg, Rex Whistler and Cecil Beaton. Beaton photographed incessantly: a 'conversation piece' of the entire family; exotic portraits of Edith and of Reresby's Nannah in fantastic clothes; and Georgia wearing a black evening dress, gloves and a flying helmet, accompanied by her borzoi, Feo, which she had imported secretly and hidden in the stables in the vain hope that Osbert would not know he was there. (Unfortunately, Feo reverted to his hunting ancestry and made himself deeply unpopular at Renishaw by coursing and killing the tenant farmer's sheep.) Edith, whom Beaton described as 'entirely beautiful, a most wonderful aesthetic object', was his favourite subject. He photographed her perched nervously on the top of a chest and, seated, playing a harp, against the background of one of the tapestries.

Beaton's 'conversation piece' family group taken at Renishaw that August 1930 was a classic of Sitwell iconography. It showed three generations of Sitwells posed in the drawing room against a background of one of the great Brussels tapestries. Lady Ida sat bolt upright on a massive gilt baroque throne, one of Sir George's Italian bargains, loftily described by Edith as 'brought to us from the palace of a Doge', with the three-year-old Reresby by her side. Sir George, a dignified, natty figure in wing collar and pepper-and-salt tweed, perched uncomfortably on the fender next to the throne. Sachie, lanky and boyish-looking, stood behind him wearing his habitual air (particularly when in the vicinity of his parents) of half-amused apprehension. Edith, a resplendent figure in a magnificent flowered-brocade dress, stood significantly apart from her parents, her left arm resting on the back of Osbert's chair. Osbert, now the real power in the house, was the only member of the family who looked comfortable, lounging, his elbow propped on a damask-covered table. Georgia sat curled on the floor at Lady Ida's feet, looking defensively poised as though straining to belong. The Beaton portrait cleverly distilled the Sitwell essence and the weird glamour which surrounded them. It was precisely as they saw themselves and as they liked to be seen. 'I simply can't *tell* you what excitement there is at Renishaw about the photographs,' Edith wrote afterwards to Cecil. '. . . We are all, including Mother, half off our heads with excitement . . . and are *longing* to have them published in papers. . . .'[25] When she began to write her memoirs, she chose the Beaton family group as her starting-point, writing of Beaton himself:

. . . that apparently light and airy young man . . . is in reality, one of the staunchest, loyalest, and best of our friends. His chivalry towards me has been one of the happy beauties in my life, for he has a curious wish and power to ennoble, to beautify, to clarify, to protect. . . .[26]

The Sitwells would need the protection and loyalty of their friends; they were to become positively an endangered species in the hostile intellectual climate of the 1930s. The first salvo of the decade had landed with a thud in June that year with the publication of Wyndham Lewis's enormous satire on his contemporaries, *The Apes of God*. Lewis had been writing it since the early 1920s, excerpts having appeared in the *Criterion* in 1924. Sachie called it a 'time-bomb' set to explode in the faces of literary London. Described as 'a cubist telephone book', it weighed five pounds, was three inches thick and illustrated with Lewis's own drawings. It comprised over 600 pages of venom, often tedious but sometimes well-directed. The subjects of its satire were the groups in London Society whom Lewis saw as dilettantes, who played at being artists but were in fact the enemies of genuine genius. The Sitwells were not the only targets of *The Apes of God*. Lewis's old Bloomsbury enemies, against whom he had originally allied himself with them, were denounced as a snobbish, exclusive, and self-regarding clique of poseurs. Some of his former friends and patrons, like Sydney Schiff and Dick Wyndham, also received their measure of abuse, but the Sitwells had the lion's share.

Edith got off relatively lightly. Sachie, 'languidly-youthful . . . gigantically Fauntleroy', was grudgingly admitted to be 'the more sympathetic' of the family. Georgia, whom Lewis had never met, was portrayed in an unpleasant passage as a 'a certain New Zealand jewess, Babs [the Doble family's pet name for Georgia] Kennson, [who] traps "Phoebus" [Sachie] with the magic of her Maori money-bags'. Osbert was the principal target. Lewis's unkind physical description of him and his relationship with Sphinx has already been quoted. His characterisation of Osbert was not entirely unfair. He accurately conveyed the claustrophobic, gossipy, sometimes malicious and bullying atmosphere of Osbert's soirées, with their toadies and clowns, and the elaborate mythologising of the servants like Mrs Powell and of Sir George as a private joke. He mocked their cult of youth, particularly their own, of which the satirising of Sir George was an important part in 'the abnormal perpetuation of their young-ness'. They were engaged in a permanent 'child-parent war-game', with Sir George as the 'wicked Giant' who tried to kill them during the 'big bad naughty World War'. They were a 'middle-aged youth movement . . . God's Peterpaniest family'. Lewis accused them of faking their ancestry (being descended from tradesmen, the ironmaster Sitwells) and their name (a reference to the name-change from Hurt to Sitwell), of being in fact not aristocrats but middle-class snobs. Most woundingly of all, he charged them with trading on their assumed aristocracy, of being 'the *showmen* of their Past'.

In the Bloomsberries' case, Lewis's general condemnation and subsequent attacks on Virginia Woolf in particular did little lasting damage. With the Sitwells, however, his caricatures of them as sham aristocratic amateurs trading on their social position set the tone for all the subsequent barrage which they would have to undergo. It was all the more damaging because there was a grain of truth in it, particularly where Osbert and Edith were concerned. No specific reason for Lewis's turning on the Sitwells has been given; they themselves seem to have been mystified by it. It may well have been a question of an unpaid bill or an imagined slight. The Sitwells retaliated by sending Lewis silly telegrams at intervals, but his attack upon them was more serious than they seem to have realised. *The Apes of God* provided ammunition for their critics to fire.

At Renishaw the house party began to break up at the end of August. Osbert left on the 31st, to Sachie's great unhappiness. Edith, too, was depressed. Their antennae, sensitive to the *zeitgeist*, registered the closing of an era in their mutual past and apprehension at the immediate future. Sachie and Georgia remained there until 15 September, with the occasional company of Gerald Berners and Arthur Waley, when they left for a tour of southern Germany and the Tyrol, joined by Dick Wyndham. In Nuremberg on the 20th they saw Imma Doernberg; Nazi hostility was making her position precarious and, in December, she left Germany. At Munich on the 25th, Sachie experienced a curious mixture of the old and the new Germany with a day of baroque and rococo delights ending in a beer-hall. His diary read: 'Lunch at Bottner's – saw Pinacoteca [*sic*] – Nymphenburg – Amalienburg – Schleissheim – St John [*sic*] Nepomuk church. Nazi party till 4 a.m.'²⁷ Georgia left for Paris to join her parents on the 30th. Sachie and Dick continued a leisurely journey back via Worms, Mainz, Coblenz, Brühl and Cologne to Aix-la-Chapelle to see the Treasury, then from Rheims to Paris where Sachie spent a week with Georgia. By 10 October Sachie was back in London, staying with Berners and lunching with Zita at the Café Royal. 'Talk,' he noted tersely in his diary. He seems to have been pressing her again. On the 17th she wrote him an embarrassed letter, apologising for not having replied to him before: 'I don't really know what to say. You know that I'm very fond of you *both* & depend a great deal on your affection. I should hate you to withdraw it because what would my life be without you – but you mustn't get too out of hand. . . .'[28] At Weston for the week-end the next day, Georgia noted that Zita was bored with her husband – 'more than ever'.

At Weston after eight months' absence, Sachie and Georgia resumed their old life. Sachie was working on his book of short stories, *Far from My Home*, in the intervals of trips up to London and week-end visits from friends. On 29 December Walton and Imma arrived; she was now a more or less penniless refugee and was to spend ten days at Weston, somewhat to Georgia's chagrin. On the following morning, Sister Edith rang up to say that Aunt Florence had died at Long Itchington. Georgia went over to deal with the arrangements, while Sachie remained at Weston, making only a brief visit to take a curious, apprehensive look at his dead aunt. By her death, he did, however, inherit a much needed few thousand pounds, while Osbert was left the black-and-white timbered house at Long Itchington. Georges Duthuit arrived to stay for three slightly strained days in January and Sassoon came later that month from Wilsford bearing armfuls of flowers and Stephen's diaries, 'full of most bizarre and voluptuous stories and phrases'. Sachie left Weston, where he had been spending a week alone with Walton and Sassoon, for London on 31 January to stay, as he now frequently did, with Gerald Berners in his house in West Halkin Street, where Stravinsky came to dine. The next day he left for Paris, taking the Rome express on 4 February with the Westminsters bound for Naples, where they joined the *Cutty Sark*.

During 1931 Sachie and Georgia were constant guests of the Westminsters. On this occasion they were going to Egypt, via Syracuse, where Osbert and Horner came on board for dinner and Horner irritated Georgia by mockingly referring to their Westminster trips as their *'pêche melba* life'. Taking a special train from Alexandria to Cairo on 13 February, they were met by Alastair Graham with a car from the High Commission. Travelling with the Westminsters was like a royal progress. They dined at the High Commission with Sir Percy Loraine, two carriages were reserved for their use on the train upriver and troops lined the route to Aswan in the Duke's honour. They went to Luxor, Karnak and Thebes. Howard Carter, discoverer of Tutankhamen's tomb, came to lunch and told them that he had just sent off Tutankhamen's viscera to the Home Office in London to be analysed to discover whether or not he had been poisoned. Later he showed them Tutankhamen's tomb, empty now but for the sarcophagus and his laboratory, which, according to Georgia, contained 'Tutank's wife's abortive children and skeletons'. They saw the Valley of the Kings and the Valley of the Queens; then from

Aswan they took a boat, the *Ibis*, which had belonged to General Gordon, to Abu Simbel and Wadi Halfa, where they boarded a train ('oh the luxury of these special trains,' Georgia wrote) to cross the desert to Khartoum. There they dined with Sir John and Lady Maffey in their residency 'reeking of Gordon, Kitchener and their taste'. They travelled by river again to Sennar, Sachie fascinated by the sight of solitary Dinkas, seven feet tall, standing on one leg on the river-bank. Returning to Khartoum, they rejoined the yacht at Port Sudan, sailing through the Suez Canal and the Corinth Canal to Corfu and the Adriatic coast of Yugoslavia, and landing at Venice on 21 March. In Paris on the way back, Sachie made a futile attempt to interview an unco-operative Misia Sert for his projected Liszt biography before returning to Weston on 2 April, leaving Georgia in Paris to spend a few days seeing her parents and pursuing her romance with Duthuit. Reresby's birthday, his fourth, was on 15 April, 'the first we have been home for,' Georgia noted.

Sachie's book of short stories, *Far from My Home*, dedicated to Arthur Waley, was published a month later. It was the first and last time he attempted the short story and he did not, as the title suggested, feel at home with it. Despite lavish praise from Osbert (he was 'revelling' in the book . . . the extraordinary quality in the stories . . . a very rare quality of touching the heart . . . beauty and limpidness of the language, often unbearably poignant, for all their wit'), they were on the whole unsuccessful. The *Times Literary Supplement* review, which Osbert branded 'typically idiotic', was more to the point in doubting whether the short story was the best medium for Sachie's talents. Sachie made the mistake of portraying working- and middle-class life and love, something of which he had no experience except as an outside observer, much as a child might look at animals in a zoo. The settings and stories which he had chosen – a middle-class mother trying jealously to prevent her daughter's marrying, the unhappiness of a dead insurance agent's daughter in a bleak northern town – needed a realistic treatment of which he was incapable. Elizabeth Bowen was to choose 'Annual Visit' for her *Faber Book of Modern Stories*, but it was a slight tale of a snobbish spinster's visit to aristocratic relations who despise her and required Henry James's deftness of touch, a gift which Sachie lacked.

Only one story came to life. 'A Game of Red Indians' was drawn from an experience Sachie had had in Constantinople. It focused on the relationship between a rich, lonely, impeccably dressed dwarf whom he had noticed on several occasions and finally seen, hand in hand in the Seraglio, with a child dancer from the Russian cabaret where he had watched her the previous night. The girl, thinking the dwarf was another child, wanted to play but, when he disappointed her, became impatient to get away leaving him in tears. It was a success because the episode had appealed to Sachie's fascination with the strange and the exotic and exercised his talent for description of a place. Few people can attempt an impression of Venice or Istanbul without being banal, but Sachie could generate excitement with his juxtaposition of images and in this short story he was triumphantly successful.

Just over a month later, on 18 June, *Spanish Baroque Art* appeared, dedicated to Gerald Berners. It was a factual introduction and guide to the subject on the lines of *German Baroque Art* with carefully chosen illustrations, and was to be the last book on the subject of the baroque which he was to write for some thirty years.

In June Sachie and Georgia were with the Westminsters again, this time at The Woolsack, Bendor's Cape Colonial-style hunting lodge in Les Landes. There were week-ends at Denham with the Mosleys, at Wilton with the Pembrokes, at Tickerage with Dick Wyndham and with Beaton at Ashcombe, where Sachie met Bridget Parsons again. Bridget, daughter of the Earl of Rosse, was a cool, blonde beauty with an exquisite face and torso but was heavier below the waist (Zita in her letters to Sachie referred to her as 'piano-legs'). She was proud, aloof, sophisticated, witty and difficult, a heart-breaker and *belle dame sans merci* with many admirers and loyal friends. Sachie was to describe her appearance and character in a long passage in *Dance of the Quick and the Dead* four years later. Her eyes were cold, grey-blue, with tiny pupils ringed with black:

> . . . the hard points of her pupils mark the contraction of her ego into an inward-growing independence which will harden and intensify with age. [She had] an inherited tendency to reserve, inhibition and the pursuit of hopeless objects . . . an incapacity for happiness, an over-reliance on external things, on elegance and fashion. Her beauty and her strong will cannot make her happy. It is a temperamental fault which nothing can remedy . . . which will impede every movement she makes towards happiness [sapping] her vitality and throwing its weight on her companions. [She had] a selfishness and defiance which is, at once, her beauty and her ruin. She affects to despise those who admire her and is, therefore, lonely within the shell where she has imprisoned her pride. She is too strong to allow entrance to others and too weak to make her own escape. She will be kind to animals and not to men, will like those who do not like her, and be silent when everything should be said. . . .[29]

At Ashcombe, Sachie found himself strongly attracted to her. In the only personal section in his diary he chronicled the progress of his pursuit of Bridget culminating in final seduction two years later. At Ashcombe, she had come over to lunch with Henry and Daphne Weymouth; they talked and Sachie drew her hand on a wall. On the Monday following the week-end, he met her with Zita and asked them both to lunch on Friday, when Zita, probably annoyed by Sachie's obvious interest in her friend, 'pretended to be tiresome'; Sachie, therefore, did not include her in a subsequent invitation to Bridget to lunch the following week. They saw each other at parties and privately in places where they were unlikely to meet their friends, like the Zoo and Hampstead Heath. Meanwhile, Georgia had been enjoying herself with Georges Duthuit, who was over in London for ten days, and seems not to have noticed Sachie's flirtation with Bridget. The Sitwells and Bridget were together in a large house party given by the Westminsters at Eaton on 26 June. Sachie had one more rendezvous with her before she left London on 1 July. 'Four months till October,' Sachie wrote in his diary.

Financial troubles were looming in the background, as usual, as they prepared for their customary long holiday. On 25 June they spent the night at Long Itchington with the Dobles and Sister Edith. They were briefly at Renishaw on the eve of the fête which Osbert was to give to launch Mosley's New Party on 1 August, before leaving with the Westminsters for Biarritz on the 6th. At Biarritz they dined and went to the casino with the 'entire Winston Churchill family'. Georgia's nose was very much out of joint because Winston Churchill clearly had no time for her, while one of his daughters flirted with Sachie. Winston, she wrote, was 'unpleasant and smug', while the daughter was 'common and bold and tried to get off with Sach'. At lunch on board the next day, her entry read: 'the girl as plain and vampish as last night & the father ruder than ever'.[30]

They embarked on the *Cutty Sark* for a two-week tour of Spain and Portugal, pursued by agitated telegrams from the Dobles and Sitwells about plans for Reresby. Sachie's and Georgia's habit while cruising with the Westminsters had been to despatch Reresby to one or other of his grandparents. They had caused domestic upset at Renishaw the previoius year when, due to muddles they had made, the cook and butler there had been forced to stay on to look after Reresby after the adults had all left. This year it had been arranged that Robins and Susan, instead of having, as Osbert put it, 'a cold, frosty ten days in October' for their holiday, should have the last week in August and part of September.

Reresby had been due to stay with Sister Edith at Long Itchington after Renishaw was closed up, but, having been threatened with eviction by Sir George, she refused to have him. To his considerable annoyance, Osbert then received a telegram from Sachie on the *Cutty Sark* asking if Reresby could stay on at Renishaw from 20 August and part of September. Osbert passed the request on to Robins, who promptly gave notice. Osbert was getting increasingly critical of his sister-in-law both as a wife and mother; he disapproved of her behaviour with Mosley and considered that she was responsible for involving Sachie too much in useless social life. 'One more grumble about Georgia,' he wrote to Christabel, complaining about her carelessness of Reresby. 'The poor little thing's nursery governess (of whom you may remember G. forgot to take any references) is a perfect horror, though I believe a very good dancer and a great one for "smokes", cocktails and gaiety generally.'[31] On their return to London for a few days on 22 September, accompanied by Duthuit who was to travel to Scandinavia with them, Georgia saw Reresby just twice, for a brief walk in the park after which she lunched with Duthuit, and at the Savoy with his Doble grandparents. On the 25th Reresby left for Eaton Hall, where the Westminsters had agreed to have him. He cried at the station saying goodbye; 'heartbreaking,' Georgia commented, before embarking the next day for Stockholm with Dick Wyndham and his wife, Grethe, Sachie and Duthuit.

For the next three weeks they toured Sweden, Denmark and northern Germany, sightseeing and indulging Sachie's passion for louche night-clubs, particularly in Hamburg. There was a certain amount of friction. 'Frightful scene S. G[eorges] and me,' one entry read. Georgia was disgusted by Grethe's habit of eating the heads of trout and partridge and her efforts to save a dying rat. On arrival at Amsterdam on 21 September they received the worrying news that England had gone off the Gold Standard and an atmosphere of deep gloom descended on the party. 'Dick and Sach in awful panic,' Georgia noted. 'Frightened by bad news in English papers.' They returned to England to find that at Polesden Lacey, where Emerald Cunard had driven them down to stay with Mrs Ronnie Greville, the talk was all of the financial crisis. Gerald Berners suggested that Sachie and Georgia should share Faringdon with him, and in October they were installed in his exquisite Berkshire[32] manor house with Reresby and Nannah.

Money difficulties were to keep them away from Weston for almost a year; no names appear in the visitors' book between May 1931 and April 1932. They simply could not, as Ginger repeatedly reminded them, afford to run the house in the style they wanted. The Wall Street crash, the deepening financial depression and the recent abandonment of the Gold Standard, plus a belt-tightening budget, had set Sir George's financial antennae tingling. By the winter of 1931 he was urging them to shut up Weston and move to Long Itchington, which Osbert had offered them rent-free. 'My darling Sachie,' Sir George wrote on 8 December 1931, 'I could not, I am sorry to say, consent to go on finding money for Weston, if you and Georgia remain there.' Sachie, he went on, had failed to grasp the position. According to figures which he had worked out in May 1930, Sachie had, since his marriage, overspent his income by an average £466 a year – 'after deducting £600 for debt before marriage'. Sir George went on to expound the position in hideous detail – average expenditure (excluding trustee's payments at Weston) was £3,066 a year; they needed to reduce expenditure not just by £466 a year but, with £120 interest on debt and payment for life insurance, to a total of £586.

How could Sachie imagine, therefore, he continued inexorably, that he would be '*better off*' due to Aunt Florence's legacy producing £400 net? If they were to stay at Weston another £100 would have to be found, but, as he waspishly reminded Sachie, 'you & Georgia have often pointed out to me, the charge of household etc. is irreducible'. At Long Itchington they would be able to save £100 a year in wages and £250 in food and sundries, but he realised that Sachie did not want to go there because it was less comfortable and convenient than Weston; however, 'A sacrifice of convenience is far better than getting yourself and me far out of our depths with probable disaster [a perennial nightmare for Sir George since the bankruptcy of the previous century] to us both.' The only answer was for Sachie to get out of Weston immediately and live within his income – 'even doing this means that I shall have to find at least £550 this year, and possibly a good deal more'.[33]

Sachie, however, as his father was well aware, was obstinate and impervious to financial reason, as Sir George did not fail to point out to Georgia:

> . . . Sachie had always a charming disposition, but there is really nothing Bismarckian about him. It is not an iron will, but obstinacy about trifles in cases where he might gracefully give way with great advantage to himself. Florence [Sitwell] was like that. So was Charles I. You will remember that the latter, when the Scotch wanted their old prayer-book back, said to Strafford, 'I will rather die than surrender', and eventually managed to do both. . . .[34]

Sachie did not die, nor did he surrender, to his father at least. He did not move to Long Itchington. Somehow he survived, even managing to pay back Sassoon's loan, as he wrote to him just before Christmas 1931 from Gerald Berners's London house: 'Dearest Siegfried, Yesterday I repaid the loan you made me, and I cannot let it pass by without writing to tell you of the difference it made to all the circumstances of my life – and of working.' As Sachie knew that Siegfried was anguished by Stephen Tennant's refusal to see him, he wrote to tell him how devoted he was to him and how much he believed in him: 'I wonder if this is any comfort or encouragement to you – but I should like it to be as much as your action to me.' In confidence he admitted that he was having to loan £1,300 to Edith, 'who, between ourselves does seem to have been rather extravagant. . . . I think Tchelitchew has got most of it. I fancy she has paid fantastic prices for his pictures.'[35]

·Sachie's finances remain something of a mystery. He was not making more than £150–200 from writing, as he constantly complained to Balston at this time. Even *Southern Baroque Art*, his best-known book which had gone into three editions by 1930, had not sold more than a few thousand copies. As Sachie's debts accumulated, the note of complaint in his own correspondence with Balston intensified. Like most authors he felt that he was working too hard for insufficient reward. On New Year's Eve 1929 he complained that he had been hard at work on *The Gothick North* for over two years:

> I've often felt like chucking up the whole thing, as it seems to me I am
> bound never to have a success and that the better I write the smaller the
> circulation will be. I feel really rather like a charwoman and my
> earnings over two years are rather less because I get 30/- a week
> without meals thrown in and charwomen don't work after 3pm while I
> go on, generally, till 7 pm.[36]

In June that year, after a meeting with Balston in London, he had complained that 'incessant discouragement is more than my nerves can stand', and threatened to leave Duckworth.

Balston hastened to acquit himself: 'I'm so well convinced of your vocation as a writer that I have always urged you to write exactly what you want to write, and to trust that some time soon it will hit the taste of a wider public. . . .' Far from rejecting Sachie's ideas, he thought that they had agreed on a programme of no less than six books, including two books of poems, one volume of long stories and one of short, *Spanish Baroque Art* and an unspecified historical work (Sachie had suggested Napoleon as a subject), to be published over the next year. The harassed Balston wrote:

> I believe my trouble has been that in those hurried meetings we have had, I have been too much engaged in considering your financial difficulties & how to get more money for you, and not sufficiently expressed my interest in your work as such. . . . I think you must admit that I've been continually considering how to push your previous books & have always accepted a new MS with alacrity.'[37]

Anxious to keep Sachie, Duckworth agreed to make him immediate advances on at least three of the projected works, including quarterly payments on the historical work (80,000 words by the end of July 1930). Sachie simmered down for the time being and by April 1930 Balston was able to report that *The Gothick North* had made £3,700, not bad considering the last volume, *The Fair-Haired Victory*, had come out only in January.

Duckworth, in fact, was accommodating as far as Sachie was concerned. In October 1930 it had been prepared to advance £100 on the as yet unwritten *Retreat from Moscow*, a book which never materialised, while Balston wrote encouragingly of the first stories which were to make up *Far from My Home*: 'I haven't the slightest doubt that they are very good & lots of people will like them. . . .' By July 1931, however, he was forced to convey the unwelcome news that there was a balance of £65 against Sachie on his royalty account. The company was prepared to advance him another £100 on the *Retreat from Moscow*, but that would mean an adverse balance of £265. Casting desperately round for ideas, Balston pressed him to write a novel as the best way of earning a substantial sum in the 'present depressed state of the book market'.[38] Balston was a loyal friend with Sachie's interests at heart, but it might be doubted whether he was an editor with vision or perception. It should not have been difficult to tell that Sachie's complete lack of narrative power or gifts of characterisation made it extremely unlikely that he would succeed as a novelist.

In any case, Sachie was becoming increasingly disillusioned with Duckworth. When Balston wrote to him on 18 February 1931 pressing him to accept an offer by Dutton's for the US rights of *Far from My Home* plus the option of the next three books for $250, Sachie turned him down. He had no intention of signing up for another three books because he had no idea when he might have three books ready. Sounding the death knell on the *Retreat from Moscow*, he told Balston haughtily that, having got a little more money (presumably Aunt Florence's legacy), there was 'no necessity to keep on turning out these successive failures, one after another'. He was writing a short biography of Mozart for Peter Davies and, after that, he had decided not to write anything except poetry:

> My prose-books have taken years to write, and have not advanced me in any way at all. I am enjoying myself too much, now, to want to shut myself up for half every year in order to earn £15. I enjoy writing poems, but I do it very slowly; perhaps I shall have a small book of them ready in three years' time. Apart from that, I have no plans, nor want to have any; and so I won't sign any contracts for anything.[39]

Balston responded with commendable self-control, writing ironically that he envied Sachie his present state of freedom after all those years of hard work and even sounding an encouraging note: 'I can't accept the view that all these books which thousands have read with pleasure and admiration, are failures; even from a financial point of view they haven't been nearly as unproductive as you suggest. . . .'[40] Sachie, however, was not to be pacified. He had been putting out feelers towards other publishers. Through Edith he had been in touch with Richard de la Mare of Faber & Faber in March 1930 and had offered them the *Retreat from Moscow*. The chairman, Geoffrey Faber's response had been honourably cautious:

> Such a proposal would clearly involve an interference with the existing relation between you and your present publishers. We should not like to do that, of our own initiative. But if you can tell us that we are free to make and you are free to consider any suggestion, that removes any ground of hesitation on our part.[41]

In December 1931 Sachie, and apparently Osbert, approached Michael Sadleir with a view to being published by Constable, but Sadleir's response had been much the same as Faber's. While he welcomed the proposal that Sachie's books should be dealt with by Constable, he did not want to proceed with any negotiations until Sachie had written to Balston, whom Sadleir regarded as a friend, ending their business connection. This, he gathered from Osbert, Sachie was unlikely to do for another three weeks.[42] In fact, Sachie was not able to bring himself to make the final break with Balston for another thirteen months.

By the New Year of 1932 Balston knew what was going on. Opening the divorce settlement with a derisory offer of £400 for a novel, two books of poems and a travel book, he added firmly:

> On the other hand I am only too well aware that you distrust our efficiency in selling your books, & can only repeat what I said to Osbert, that we are willing to release you from any obligations to us on repayment of the £100 advanced for 'The Retreat from Moscow'. This sum would, of course have to be deducted from any advance made by us.[43]

Sachie wriggled. He does not seem to have been prepared either to break finally with Duckworth or to pay the £100 which would enable him to do so. 'A propos of that £100,' he wrote disingenuously, 'the Retreat from Moscow would have been written long ago, but for the discouragements you gave me over it. "Should I not be attacked by the military critics etc.,'' when you surely know me well enough to be certain I should not embark upon the project without being in fullest possible possession of all the facts about it.' Surely Balston did not think that Philip Guedalla, 'a thoroughly bad writer with half my reputation', had only been given £200 for his biography of Wellington; 'then, again, why £300 to Osbert for his book of travels – and only £200 to me'. The truth was that Osbert's prose sold better than Sachie's, or, for that matter, Edith's poetry, although Edith's prose pot-boilers were to become best-sellers.

On the same day, his feelings of bitterness about repaying the £100 rising, Sachie wrote Balston yet another, angrier letter. He supposed that the only solution was for him to repay the £100 and yet:

> The grotesque side of the situation does not seem to have struck your mind in the very slightest degree. After ten or twelve years of unremitting work and being, though I say it myself, one of the better poets and prose-writers of the time, it is, even now, apparently impossible for me to earn more than £200 a year from you.
>
> This tallies very well with the £20 or £30 to be offered to Edith for each volume of her anthology.

The final paragraph was particularly bitter and intended to wound:

> Will you write back to me, and tell me truthfully, what Evelyn Waugh was given for his book of travels. If you reply that his circulation as a novelist is much bigger than mine, that only raises another point as to why his novels are not published by you. I expect the answer to that

question is, once again, lack of enthusiasm and lack of critical appreciation.[44]

Balston's response was tough. He was perfectly aware, he said, that Sachie expected better advances and higher sales from another publisher. His offer had been based not on his estimate of the literary merit of Sachie's work, but on projected sales figures for the first six months. He reminded him that the last two advances for *Far from My Home* and *Spanish Baroque Art* had not yet been covered. He had advanced the £100 to meet Sachie's convenience at the time in return for an undertaking to write *Retreat from Moscow*; now that Sachie, apparently, did not intend to write the book, he found it difficult to understand why he should retain the money.[45] Firmness, for the moment at least, paid off. Sachie seemed prepared to compromise and even tried to bargain. He had been offered £300 for the travel book, which, he pointed out, Duckworth had been willing to pay Osbert, but 'in order to continue publishing with you', he was prepared to accept £250. This was to be for *Touching the Orient*, a hotchpotch of six essays published two years later and dedicated to 'Loelia and her husband', in acknowledgement of their tour of Egypt and the Sudan in 1931.

It was to be one more year before Sachie could finally bring himself to break with Balston and Duckworth. He had found a reasonable excuse – Duckworth had omitted to make any mention of his books in its recent catalogue –but, as the new deal he had made with Faber involved the use of three poems published by Duckworth in *The Cyder Feast*, he needed its agreement. This omission, he told Balston, made him feel more certain than ever that his books were not commercially viable. He had, however, 'just finished' a book of twenty long poems for which another firm of publishers had offered despite their being, he felt, 'less of a paying proposition than ever', an offer which he felt he must accept. In return for Duckworth's complaisance in this publication, he offered 'a long Canto of Doctor Donne and Gargantua which, with preface, comes to 60 pages, or more . . . without prejudice, in order to pay off any indebtedness', plus the opportunity to write a short volume on Neapolitan baroque to complete the series already published. 'I want to dedicate Dr Donne and Gargantua to you,' he added engagingly; 'it's ready now, and can be sent to you whenever you like.'[46] Balston apparently found this an offer he felt well able to refuse. Sachie eventually published the further cantos of *Dr Donne and Gargantua* privately more than forty years later. As part of the character of Gargantua in that poem was based on Bendor Westminster, it was, perhaps, just as well. In response to a sharp demand from Balston for the repayment of the £100, Sachie finally agreed two months later to repay it by the end of July. Adopting a conciliatory tone, he proposed an edition of his collected poems to be published by Duckworth, adding pathetically: 'I know poetry never sells; but, having written such reams of it, I should like to have a last attempt to publish it collectively. I should be happy to make £20 by it. . . .'

Sachie's 'little book on Mozart' was published by Peter Davies on 28 April. It was dedicated to the memory of Samuel Courtauld's wife, 'Lil', who had recently died leaving £500 per annum to Walton, a bequest that relieved the Sitwells of their perennial anxiety about his finances. (Walton's *Belshazzar's Feast*, for which Osbert had produced the libretto and much of which had been written in the stable block at Weston, had had its London première on 25 November 1931.) Sachie had enjoyed writing *Mozart*. He had a passion for music and often said that, if he had not been a poet, he would have liked to have been a musician. *Mozart*, however, involved him in a ferocious controversy with Ernest Newman, the influential music critic of the *Sunday Times*. Newman attacked him as a 'complete amateur' and a 'bad joke' completely lacking in the requisite technical knowledge. The critic was particularly enraged by his dismissal of Wagner. Sachie had denied that Wagner had the right to be considered an artist in comparison with either Rossini or Verdi, concluding that Wagner's 'loud vulgar personality and unpleasant literary associations should have perished long ago'. Osbert threw himself into the fray in Sachie's defence and the controversy occupied columns in the *Sunday Times*. However, Newman had a point, in attacking not only Sachie's airy dismissal of Wagner but also the self-regarding amateurishness of his approach to Mozart's music. Sachie could not, as Newman guessed, read a score. His opinions and interpretations were entirely subjective and not backed up by any solid argument. Undeterred by this critical barrage, however, Sachie went on working off and on on the biography of Liszt which he had had in mind for some time.

Sachie's life had become increasingly peripatetic: Christmas had been spent with Mrs Greville at Polesden Lacey, New Year 1932 with the Westminsters at Saint-Saens in Normandy, and January with Gerald Berners at Faringdon. In February the entire Faringdon household moved to Halkin Street, Sachie and Berners, Walton and Georgia making a frequent foursome at social events. They were now very much a part of Emerald Cunard's circle and through her on the fringes of royalty. On 23 February they dined at her house in Grosvenor Square in a party which included the Prince of Wales, Freda Dudley Ward and Prince George; in April they moved in to stay with her, lunching, dining and going to the opera with her almost every day. Only on 17 April did they move back to Weston – 'First day at home for nearly a year,' Georgia noted – but not for long before leaving early in May for a tour of Provence with the Westminsters. (The rows between the ducal couple were becoming so bitter that Georgia had to resort to French to describe them in her diary.) They were back briefly at Weston later in May and then took a house in London, 12 Southwick Place, from the beginning of June.

Their love life was equally involved as Sachie continued to pursue Bridget and, at intervals, to flirt with Zita, while Georgia continued her relationship with Georges Duthuit and had a new admirer, discreetly identified in her diary by his initials only as 'R.W.'. Sachie's relationship with Bridget had been developing from an intense flirtation in the summer of 1931 towards an affair. In August Bridget, cruising on the yacht, *Sabrina*, in the Adriatic, had written him a distinctly flirtatious letter: 'Well, Sachie, I do hope the beautiful blondes of Norway won't drive the even more dazzling ones of Ireland [herself] from your memory. If only you could see me now as the sun has created of me a positive work of art. My skin is burnished copper and my hair molten gold. . . .'[47] From Faringdon in November he had sent her a request for a lock of hair with a form letter leaving words to fill in; 'My darling dotty Sachie,' was the response, 'I don't love you *very* much but that is no news to you. . . .'[48] In March 1932 she was in a clinic at Windsor, suffering apparently from mumps and teasing Sachie with her pining for 'Ali'; Sachie went down regularly to visit her there. Convalescing afterwards at Birr, the romantic Gothic family castle in Ireland, she still titillated him with references to 'Ali'. 'If only you would write me a poem to stimulate me in my rural fastness, but I do not expect you feel that way any longer. . . .'[49] Sachie evidently obliged, for on 18 May she wrote from her mother's house in Ireland, Abbey Leix, thanking him for his poems which had arrived that morning and 'flooded me with radiance'.

At the same time in the spring of 1932 he seems to have restarted his *amitié amoureuse* with Zita which had come to a halt in October 1931. Zita replied encouragingly from the German Legation in Lisbon, where she was staying on 1 April, how pleased she was to be back in communication with him. She had dreamed, she told him, that she had arrived home without having written to him,, and that when he met her he had been so hurt that it melted her heart. There was a note of competition between herself and Bridget in a further letter of 20 April asking him teasingly which of them he loved.[51]

From the Westminsters' lodge at Mimizan, where he was staying alone after their tour of Provence and working on a new book, which was to be *Dance of the Quick and the Dead*, Sachie was fired (possibly with the aid of Bendor's cellar) into a late-night declaration of love and lust:

My sweet angel Zita,

I have to mention the sound of your name because it excites me so.

I am living in a lovely wooden house, here, all alone. In fact the loneliness is delightful – but I wish you were here too. Even the bathroom has a delicious and inviting sofa in it. I can't see it without thinking of you on it.

Have you fallen an inch nearer me in the last day or two? Why can't you shut your eyes and fall into my arms.

I wish you were here tonight. I am writing this at 2 in the morning and I would give you such proofs of my love that even your stone heart would melt for me. Indeed, someone else has just done so, but I want you as well. What are these solitary houses in the woods meant for – & sofas – and young poets. Even the sternest religion would forgive me for loving you – and will forgive you if you give into me just once. I'd give you the most enchanting child ever seen by mortal eyes – and if it was a girl it would be lovelier than you, and I hope kinder to her lovers.

No more – quite enough has been written.[52]

The letter was never sent. It was still among Sachie's papers when he died. Perhaps he lacked the courage to send it at the time and took it home with him from Mimizan for future use. Zita, too, seems to have been losing her nerve, even about the cautious lengths to which she had recently gone; a letter of 25 May warns him not to show her letters to anyone. 'We all know you repeat everything to Georgia who repeats it to Cimmie and Willie. . . .'

According to Sachie's diary, however, Bridget was in the ascendant in 1932. Zita's name is not mentioned. Bridget came down to stay at Weston on 28 May when Osbert was there, and when the Sitwells moved to Southwick Place shortly afterwards, she and Sachie saw each other every day for one week, according to his diary: '14 June I met Br: at Harley St: & we went to Hampton Court. We talked on the way and she suddenly agreed. Pier Hotel, then the Mitre – afterwards gardens . . . back at 4pm.'

Whatever Bridget may have agreed to do at the Pier and Mitre Hotels, she did not go to bed with him. Sachie had to wait another year before he could note in his diary: 'Successful in 1933.' Georgia seems not to have noticed Sachie's preoccupation with Bridget; they were leading a frenetic social life that summer and Duthuit featured frequently in her diary. They had seen him in Paris in May, when he had introduced them to his father-in-law, Matisse; in June he spent almost a fortnight in London on an unusually trouble-free visit, probably thanks to Sachie's interest in Bridget. He was with them again in an apparently serene *ménage à trois* at the end of August and part of September on a tour ending in Venice via Bruges, Brussels, Aix-la-Chapelle, Brunswick, Dresden, Prague and Innsbruck.

By 1 October, Sachie and Georgia were back at Weston, ignoring Ginger's admonitions against inviting guests to stay. Robert Byron, Osbert, Arthur Waley and Hazel Lavery were there on 20 October and Evelyn Waugh the following week-end with Spike Hughes, the musician. It was too wet to go out and they spent a good deal of time in 'theological discussion with Evelyn emerging from a conversation about marriage and Baby Jungman'. They spent Christmas again at Polesden Lacey – Sachie took Gerald Berners and Robert Byron down with them to lighten the usually sedate atmosphere – and New Year's Eve with Lady Alexandra Metcalfe, younger sister of Cimmie Mosley and wife of 'Fruity', the Prince of Wales's friend and equerry. Brendan Bracken and Zita were also there and, of course, the Mosleys. It was an uncomfortable occasion when Diana Guinness turned up on 30 December. Everybody knew that she was, as Georgia put it, 'Tom's new girl', although they were perhaps not yet aware that she had left her husband. 'Trying evening for some but alright for onlookers,' Georgia commented. 'Tom and Diana G. v. irritating. Tom revealed all to me at lunch.' The New Year of 1933 was to be a tragic one for the Mosleys and their friends. On 16 May Cimmie, who had been heartbroken over the seriousness of Tom's affair with Diana Guinness, died of appendicitis at the age of thirty-four. Sachie wrote an appreciation of her for *The Times* and dedicated his next biography, *Liszt*, to her. The Sitwells' connection with the Mosleys ended with her death.

Other things had changed. In September 1932 Edith had left Pembridge Mansions for Paris to join Helen Rootham and her sister Evelyn Wiel in Evelyn's flat in the Rue Saint-Dominique and to be near her adored Tchelitchew. Osbert was spending more and more time abroad with Horner, who was now paramount in his life, having moved into Carlyle Square in 1931. In November 1933 the two of them would leave for a prolonged stay in Peking. Edith, who also liked to call Horner 'the Chatelaine', was already suspicious of his influence over Osbert. 'The more I see of little D.,' she had told Sachie, 'the more I am certain that he makes the most hellish mischief about us all. . . .'[53] For Sachie, the ties that bound him to his brother and sister were always there, but the leash was growing longer and longer.

Edith remained his poetry adviser, even at a distance. In the winter of 1932 he sent her the final cantos of *Dr Donne and Gargantua* and the 'Giant Torsos' poems which he had been working on since the autumn of 1925. He had now completed twenty long poems to be published by Faber in May 1933 as *Canons of Giant Art*, which contained three poems previously printed in *The Cyder Feast*, 'The Farnese Hercules', 'The Hermes of Praxiteles' and 'The Laocoon of El Greco', all written in the autumn of 1925. The seventeen new poems had been composed in the winters of 1931–32 and 1932–33, most of them inspired by works of art or classical sites seen on his travels during those years. 'Agamemnon's Tomb' was written after his visits to Mycenae. 'St Maurice and the Theban Legion', inspired by the El Greco painting in the Escorial which had so impressed Sachie on his first visit to Spain in 1919, showed Sachie's gift of transmitting the intensity of an aesthetic experience at his best. His description of El Greco's colour and painting technique was a *tour de force*:

> Such light lived only in the sun on snow,
> Such colour lived but in a fiery frost
> Of water turned blue steel, of rainbow icicles,
> All at mountain-height, in the clear of hills
> In an hour where came no shadow . . .
> It was snow on lapis lazuli, on cerulean blue,
> Of full marine blueness, of cuttle-ink on marble . . .
> And the Boreal daylight, the incandescent day,
> Wrapped them in that element, as if on fire.

When not carried away by the waves of his imagery, piling clouds, nymphs and parhelions one upon another in a repetitious baroque frenzy, Sachie could evoke as well as anyone the landscape of the classical world, the

sense of drama, of distant thunder that haunts many classical sites, in lines
such as this:

> There was heat in the distance, and a sullen silence;
> Silence like a vast bell, a void, a firmament,
> An emptiness to pour into, a field for thunder.

'Agamemnon's Tomb' was undoubtedly the finest poem of the
collection. Its intensity is quite unlike anything else in Sachie's poetry,
transmitting his horror at the physical circumstances of death and his
conviction of the void beyond. It began:

> Tomb
> A hollow hateful word
> A bell, a leaden bell the dry lips mock,
> Though the word is as mud or clay in its own sound;
> A hollow noise that echoes its own emptiness,
> Such is this awful thing, this cell to hold the box . . .
> It is breathless, a sink of damp and mould, that's all . . .

He had a particular fear of the moment of dying, convinced that it could
not come without a dreadful physical sensation of the wrenching of life
from the body, like the uprooting of a tree:

> Much comes before this, for the miser hand
> That clutches at an edge of wood, a chair, a table,
> Must have its fingers broken, have its bones cracked back,
> It's the rigor mortis, death struggle out of life . . .

After a dramatic description of the tomb and the plain of Argos below as
he had seen them, first in storm and rain, then in burning heat, he
concludes:

> You are dead, you are dead, and all the dead are nothing to us
> There's nothing, nothing, not a breath beyond:
> O give up every hope of it, we'll wake no more,

We are the world and it will end with us:
The heart is not a clock, it will not wind again,
The dead are but dead, there is no use for them,
They neither care nor care not, they are only dead.

Canons of Giant Art was greeted with ridicule from the new-wave critics. Since the publication of *The Waste Land* and the emergence of the Auden group, Sachie's poetry both in content and style had become deeply unfashionable. The 'pylon school', Evelyn Waugh wrote of the left-wing writers of the 1930s – W.H. Auden, Christopher Isherwood, Stephen Spender and George Orwell – 'ganged up and captured the decade'. Auden and his friends adopted proletarian attitudes; Auden himself wore a worker's cap, dropped his aitches and ate his peas with a knife. F.R. Leavis's *New Bearings in English Poetry*, in which he dismissed the Sitwells as belonging 'to the history of publicity rather than poetry', had been published the previous year, 1932; *Scrutiny*, the vehicle for Leavisite literary criticism, had already been launched. Aestheticism was dead; by the end of the decade Mrs Leavis was denouncing the Actons and Howards and their followers, not entirely without justification but certainly without humour, as 'odious little spoilt boys who develop into inane pretentious young men'. The Sitwells as icons of the 1920s and standard-bearers of the arts were primary targets. Wyndham Lewis had provided the ammunition in *The Apes of God*; the new literary critics controlling the avant-garde periodicals fired it with gusto. Dilettantism was the Sitwells' chief crime (Lewis had represented them as 'dabbling' in the arts); they were upper-class amateurs in a serious, proletarian world.

Geoffrey Grigson, who, a year later, savaged Edith for plagiarism in her *Aspects of Modern Poetry*, was the most vicious of the critics. Reviewing *Canons of Giant Art* in the *Criterion*, he charged Sachie with using 'a dead individual language, full of empty words for bogus images . . . relevant to the not very valuable or extensive experience which it carries . . . of that kind which is always produced by the amateur'.[54] Frank Chapman, writing for F.R. Leavis's *Scrutiny*, had also read Wyndham Lewis. He accused Sachie of being a mere 'uncritical descendant of Tennyson and Browning with none of their technical skill' and a shallow, cultural sham. Sachie's notes to his poems roused him to fury:

They reveal his culture as that of a curiously naïve and uncritical dilettante. . . . The Sitwells, in fact, reflect a society where dilettante art-worship is synonymous with culture, where poetry is supposed to be 'about' certain things, and where it neither has, nor is expected to have, any relation to any form of living activity.

His Parthian shot was 'Mr Sitwell's verse vies with *Hiawatha* for sheer, unrelieved monotony.'[55] Attacking the Sitwells, Grigson reached heights of vituperation worthy of seventeenth- or eighteenth-century pamphleteers: 'bower-birds, shining oddments of culture . . . mimicking, like starlings, the product of more harmonious throats. . . . Best leave these minimal creatures, these contemptible elvers, wriggling away in their dull habitat.' Virginia Woolf thought that, with Grigson, the reviewing of contemporary poetry had set a new, unworthy standard. 'Isn't it inevitable that one should Grigsonise?' she asked Spender. 'I mean get into a groove, and write out the malice of one's miserable heart.'[56] The Sitwells had become the Aunt Sallies of the literary world. 'It's too easy', Evelyn Waugh was to write anxiously on the occasion of Edith's reception into the Catholic Church, 'to make a booby of a Sitwell.'

Hitler had come to power in January 1933. At the beginning of the most politically polarised decade of the century, Sachie appeared to put himself firmly and publicly on the side of the Right by praising Mussolini in the conclusion of his last poem, 'Grande Adagio – The Enchanted Palace'. His note on this poem read:

> In so far as any poem can have a political intention, it is true of this final passage of the whole book. It is in praise of Fascist Italy. All the arts, and, if half the history of the world, certainly the agreeable half of it, have come out of Italy. With this in mind, an increasing number of people would prefer the world to be conducted, in future, on Italian, rather than on Russian or American lines of progression. The whole book of poems ends, therefore, in Italy, where I have spent the happiest years of my life, and wherein, as ever, I believe the future happiness and wisdom of Europe are to be found.

Sachie had never forgotten his picture of d'Annunzio at Fiume, then a romantic nationalist, a poet with a vision of Italy which belonged to the Risorgimento, and not yet the pathetic prisoner of fascism at Il Vittoriale. He was no ideologist; detesting politics, he had greatly disliked even campaigning for Osbert as the Liberal candidate for Scarborough. He later came to loathe Mussolini and everything he stood for, but at this point he, like Waugh, admired him.

Sachie was profoundly wounded by the hostile reception of *Canons of Giant Art*. It was to be eleven years before he could bring himself to write poetry again.

8

Sacred and Profane Love

1933–1939

'Its flames are nothing transient or hurting. They burn through all of youth into the dark and dreadful ends of life, most valued, now, before it is late, while the living flames still strike out from the heart. It is better to speak of them now, while they are burning. . . .'
Sachie on Georgia's physical passions (and his own), *Dance of the Quick and the Dead*

Like the faun with which Edith compared him, Sachie now retreated from the exposed literary uplands roamed by predators like Leavis and Grigson to more sheltered paths. He pursued his passion for music, completing his biography of Liszt (1934), followed by *A Background for Domenico Scarlatti* (1935) and *La Vie Parisienne* (1937), a tribute to Offenbach. He also established his reputation as a connoisseur with two books on *genre* painting, *Conversation Pieces* (1936) and *Narrative Pictures* (1937). Darting from one subject which fascinated him to another, he co-operated with Cyril Beaumont on *The Romantic Ballet* (1938) and with John Farleigh on *Old Fashioned Flowers* (1939). In 1938 he published the first of his travel books, *Roumanian Journey*.

Sexual success compensated for the literary disappointment he had suffered in 1933. In late April he went to Birr with Bridget. It was exceptionally hot; Bridget's skin took on a coppery glow, her fair hair looked as if it had been sand-blown, her strong, muscular legs set off the narrowness of her waist as she bathed in the river. Three months later he entered in his diary:

At last, on Tuesday, 18 July 1933, I had Bridget,
and, again, the next day.
not on Thursday, because of garden party,
again on Friday, & again on Tuesday.

Beside the passage in which he recorded his conquest of Bridget, he wrote the initials 'PA'. This was Pearl Argyle, a beautiful, young dancer, with whom he had recently fallen in love. Born Pearl Wellmann in Johannesburg in November 1910, she had come to England as a child, gone to school in Devonshire and then studied ballet with Marie Rambert. She had made her début with the Ballet Rambert at the age of sixteen in 1926. Frederick Ashton, who frequently worked with her, later wrote that in his estimation she was 'the most beautiful woman of her generation'. Ashton remembered her coming to class at Madame Rambert's in the early days of his career: '. . . simple, dedicated, and unconscious of her great beauty, an exquisite Botticelli angel . . . so shy that she would blush whenever I spoke to her. . . . She was endowed with a reticent though vivid intelligence. . . .'[1] For Sachie she represented a dream of beauty like the dancer in *All Summer in a Day*. She was Cinderella, young, talented and longing to go to the ball. He described her 'affirmative beauty' as the Sugar-Plum Fairy in *Dance of the Quick and the Dead*:

> . . . the green water of her eyes, the curving or gentle tilting of her nose and her nostrils cut like lyres or the leaves of the tulip tree. All made for pleasure; for poetry, or comedy, and not for danger. Her legs seen in perfect length to the joining of the body are a poem in themselves. Her lovely arms, and the smallness of her wrists. . . .[2]

She gave, he said, an impression of good humour and contentment rare in a person of such exceptional beauty, her wide eyes and large mouth a sign of her generous disposition. For him, Pearl was perfection; he found in her a source of inspiration. She was to reappear in his poetry and prose long after her early death in 1947.

They had met just before Sachie went to Birr. Pearl's first letter to 'Dear Mr Sitwell' mentioned his having taken Reresby to the ballet and thanked him for having her and her friend, Andrée Howard, to lunch. By late May, rumours of his infatuation had spread in the ballet world. Lydia Lopokova reported to Maynard Keynes what she had heard from Ashton: 'Sacha [*sic*] Sitwell has fallen violently in love with Pearl, it is all to his credit, I think. When he asks Pearl to go out with him she says, "I have nothing to say to you & I never read your books", great charm lies in such simple words, so much nicer than the smart set he is used to. . . .'[3] In fact, Pearl had a deep admiration for Sachie's poetry, which she read on the underground on her way to ballet class. On 20 May she wrote to thank 'dear Sachie' for sending her *Canons of Giant Art*: 'They refresh and inspire me as do the poems of Shelley and Keats.'[4] To her, he represented not only poetry but civilisation, sophistication and a glamorous social world.

Sachie's bedding of Bridget and infatuation with Pearl seem to have escaped Georgia, embroiled in her own emotional problems in the midst of a hectic social summer. Georges Duthuit turned up in London in June with his wife, Marguerite. He and Georgia had surreptitious meetings and 'furious telephone conversations'. In July there was Edwina Mountbatten's party at Ciro's, a week-end with the Brownlows at Belton, a ball at Londonderry House and Chips Channon's wedding to Honor Guinness. At the end of the month they went to stay with the Duffs at Vaynol, where their fellow guests were Doris Castlerosse, Beaton, Berners, David Herbert and Olga Lynn. During charades after dinner, 'a crazed drunkard of a young man called Heber-Percy' arrived. This was Robert Heber-Percy, known to Berners's friends as 'the Mad Boy'. 'The Gerald-Heber-Percy joke situation is developing,' Georgia noted in her diary. 'H.P. is certainly crazy but nice. . . .' Heber-Percy was to be the love of Gerald Berners's life and his equal in fantastic pranks and jokes. (It was he who was to be responsible for dyeing the doves at Faringdon in all the colours of the rainbow.)

The fun stopped abruptly in August when Sachie and Georgia left Vaynol for Renishaw, where they found the family assembled, only slightly diluted by the presence of David Horner and Walton, who could scarcely be counted as outsiders, and a brief visit from Christabel and her husband. There were, therefore, no restraints on Ginger, who was on the warpath. 'Ginger is after us all like a fox after chickens,' Edith wrote. The principal victims were Sachie and Georgia, as Osbert told Christabel:

> It's quite 20 years since I've known Ginger in his present delightful
> mood, dying one moment from weakness & sorrow, angry as a bull the
> next. Up till Monday last he spent his time in bullying Sachie and
> Georgia in the most beastly, horrible way. . . .[5]

The *casus belli* this time was Sachie's natural desire to make provision for Georgia, something which Sir George absolutely refused to contemplate. According to Edith, he was trying to tie up his fortune in such a way that if Osbert, Sachie and Reresby all predeceased Georgia, she would not get a penny.

Sachie had been having a protracted battle with his father over the past fourteen months. He needed money to pay his debts, while Sir George was determined to force him to give up his rights in the Weston settlement in favour of Reresby. Sachie's lawyer, Philip Frere, battled tenaciously on his behalf, receiving what he described as 'very angry letters' for his pains. One, dated 30 August 1932, set out Sir George's position clearly, giving some inkling of the family distress the quarrel had caused. According to Ginger, Sachie had 'got himself into a state bordering on nervous breakdown', while Georgia, 'who ought to bear him other children', had had 'an early miscarriage due to distress of mind'. Sir George himself, by his own account, had been 'constantly worried and made ill on more than one occasion'. 'My relations with Sachie,' he continued, 'which were ideal until he sought to pay his debts with money which ought to pass eventually to his son, have been brought to the edge of a complete rupture.' He brought up once again the spectre of past disaster which always haunted him – the débâcle of 1848:

> I feel very strongly on the subject of *honesty* in dealing with money which one has inherited owing to the fact that my Grandfather induced my Father to accept liability for his personal debts, amounting to over £100,000. Renishaw was advertised for sale, the furniture and the library which had grown during more than 200 years were actually sold, my Father was almost ruined and his life was shortened by the misery all this caused him. . . .[6]

Sir George, secure in the possession of his comfortable income, took the dynastic view; Sachie, perennially pressed by debt, the short-term one. Bludgeoning his way through with threats of cutting off Sachie's allowance, Sir George, as usual had his way.

Sachie escaped to Venice with Georgia and their friends, Sir Robert and Lady Abdy, in mid-August to stay at the Palazzo Barbaro, where their host was a rich American named William Odom, whose chief attraction was his willingness to provide hospitality for the Abdys' friends. Their fellow guests included Bridget Parsons's brother, Desmond, Robert Byron, the Channons and Cecil Beaton. Emerald Cunard and her lover, Sir Thomas Beecham, came to visit, but for Sachie, the most important was the prearranged arrival in Venice of Pearl, accompanied by her friends, the Branches, with whom she had been staying at Lerici. According to Georgia's diary, Sachie spent all his time with Pearl. He was besotted with her, seeing her in his dreams, even having daylight visions of her. It is difficult to tell from his writing where fantasy ended and reality began. Did he sleep with her in a lodging on the Zattere during a night of

storm as he hinted in *Sacred and Profane Love* and in his later poems like
'Revenant', written after her death?

> The ravishment of the white rose again,
>   lying under me,
> Who was all fire within her
>   and into deeper sleep with no awakening.

On another occasion, dining *al fresco* in a 'poetic trance', the polished table
transformed itself into a well-head and Pearl's image floated up towards
him as if from the water.

In Venice he introduced her to the Abdys, Beaton, Walton and John
Sutro, a great aficionado of the ballet. Later in London he showered her
with presents, flowers and ardent letters. They often lunched together on
Tuesdays, which became his special day for Pearl as it had been formerly
for Zita, and he frequently turned up on Sundays at the Ballet Club in
Ladbroke Road to see her. Once he stood at dawn in the street beneath
her flat in Avery Row, waiting for the earliest hour at which he could
decently call upon her, only to find that she had not been there. He added
a lock of her hair to his collection, carefully annotated and dated '7. xiii.
1933', and just before New Year's Eve he sent her one of his form letters
to fill in as he had to Bridget.

Pearl was not in love with him and he knew it. 'I am v. fond of you, and
love reading your poetry specially when I feel alone and depressed,' she
replied.[7] She poured out her feelings and ambitions to him:

> I'm impatient & proud, interested in my career more than any one
> person and probably pigheaded, all these things make me unhappy. . . .
> You write beautiful letters, being a poet you can't help it. . . . Write
> more lovely poems and books, the beauty of your art is that it lasts for so
> many centuries.[8]

She was flattered by his devotion, admired him for his writing and his
knowledge of the ballet, and perhaps even, as he was ten years older than
she was, saw him as a supportive, almost father figure. According to her
friends, she never mentioned her father; she lived with her mother and
an aunt in a prim suburban background. Sachie worked hard for her,
bringing Emerald Cunard and other influential friends to see her
matinées. Pearl was grateful and at times temptingly flirtatious. 'If I do
this show that Cecil [Beaton] is designing the scenery for that will be due

to you,' she wrote to him on 23 January 1934. 'That's definitely active service. I must have a council meeting about the reward. . . .'

Georgia seems to have been barely aware of Sachie's obsession with Pearl or, if she was, not to have minded about it. The Bridget affair, involving one of their own social circle, was different. Sachie was reasonably discreet about his relationship with Bridget and in the autumn of 1933 Georgia, preoccupied with a busy social life, had not yet noticed it. Venice had been followed by 'baroque-hunting' and visiting churches designed by the Asam brothers in Austria and southern Germany with the Channons, Beaton and Charlie Brocklehurst, an old St David's friend of Sachie's. Beaton recorded his impressions of 'hysterical fantasy, imagination, gold, silver, feathered turbans . . . a joy to be on this expedition with Sachie who is so well informed & who sees more in a jiffy than anyone else would in an hour', but he and Georgia also found it exhausting and often took refuge in a café while Sachie shot into yet another dizzy interior. There was an equally baroque atmosphere at Munich, where they met up with Dick Wyndham, Odom, Berners and 'the Mad Boy'. Beaton was disconcerted by the arrival of Peter Watson, with whom he was hopelessly in love, writing of 'the complications of Munich – Gerald, hysterical, grey, senile, melancholic. . . .'[9] 'Unattractive dramas,' Georgia noted primly.

Georgia herself was to receive emotional shocks towards the end of the year. Her relationship with Duthuit was steadily deteriorating; her diary for December is full of entries: 'Georges left in a rage', 'Georges very gloomy and sour', 'hideous scene'. On 29 December the entry read: 'Very sad, parted for good, I suppose.' On Duthuit's side it had certainly been a serious affair, as an emotional letter which he had written earlier that year testified. For Georgia, it had probably been less so; it is not entirely certain that she was referring to her relationship with Georges when she wrote in her diary for 16 December: '. . . *que d'illusions et espoirs perdues cette fois à Londres*. . . .' She had been trying unsuccessfully to get pregnant, while hopes of a flirtation with Bridget's handsome brother, Desmond, had proved illusory. Two days later she received another shock. A woman friend spilled the beans about Sachie. 'Lunched at Ciro's – extraordinary revelations about *la vie amoureuse de mon marie* [*sic*].' She returned fuming to Weston alone. 'Still rankling with rage about B[ridget] P[arsons],' she recorded on the 21st.

Bridget was perfectly aware of Sachie's passion for Pearl. Early in 1934 she and Desmond sailed for India; in March Desmond wrote to Sachie to report from The Residency, Indore: 'Poor Bridget grows more morose every day at receiving no news from you, and you will have to spend hours and days in calming her unless you have proved unfaithful and switched over to Miss Argyle. . . .'¹⁰ On her return early in April Bridget wrote rather crossly cancelling a week-end at Weston on the excuse that she 'couldn't face driving alone in a slow car in this weather'. Early in May Sachie was at Birr with Georgia after a visit to the Cavendishes at Lismore. Even in Ireland he had not neglected to keep in touch with Pearl. 'The end of your letter sounds rather desperate,' she wrote to him at Birr. 'Did the lovely lady of the castle look askance at you?'

Pearl still looked to him for help and encouragement. In April she was filming a small part in *Chu Chin Chow* with Anna May Wong, but there were disappointments:

> Things are very frustrated for me [she wrote]. Last summer I should have done Shalotte [*sic*] at the Savoy, and I was going to dance with Lifar, and now this. Madam [Marie Rambert] wants to give a two week season at the Ballet Club to get more members, but what's the point? The place is so small and nobody knows where Notting Hill Gate is. I want to grow, & embrace a wider public, & its [*sic*] a shame that those lovely productions are seen by so few people. How I long for a season in the West End. Madam says we would want a backing of £4000 a week. Do you know anyone, the Courtaulds or someone, who would like to back a good cause? . . . Someone suggested I should ask John Sutro, but I expect he had an interest in the Savoy ballets & would rather leave the subject alone.¹¹

By May, however, her career was improving; she was dancing in *Mermaid* and pressing Sachie to bring Beaton to photograph her in the role.

On 26 April 1934 Sachie's biography of Liszt appeared. It was the first life of Liszt written in English and was to be the best-received and most successful of all his books, almost continuously in print over more than fifty years and selling over 20,000 copies in the English-language editions. It was generally acknowledged as a major interpretative biography, presenting Liszt in his context as a leading figure of the Romantic movement, 'on the same footing of importance as Byron', as Sachie claimed. Although Sachie's old adversary, Ernest Newman, pounced on 'some errors on points of fact' in his *Sunday Times* review, *The Times* critic congratulated him on 'a work which will certainly hold the field'. It was a serious approach to the man and his music, with appendices, a catalogue of Liszt's works and a bibliography. Sachie had curbed his tendency to stylistic extravagance to produce a readable and brilliantly presented portrait against the background of a period with which he was completely at home, as in this passage describing Liszt's affair with Madame d'Agoult in his early Romantic period:

> The glitter of chandeliers, the smoothness of lovely shoulders, the strains of distant waltzes, the camellia for flower of the evening, all the amenities of the city alternate with a 'vie de château', a green leaf-hid summer at the end of avenues, with the ripple of the lake and its answering statues seen through the branches.

He moved from this Liszt of the green gloves and Hungarian pelisse slung carelessly over his shoulders to the Liszt of his Roman period, practising genuflexions for three hours, smoking cigars with cardinals, a serene, disillusioned but still Mephistophelean figure in a black silk cassock, transformed finally into a venerable and kind old man. Some of the most vivid passages of the book were devoted to Paganini, who had always held a particular fascination for Sachie as he did for Liszt. He presented him as a daemonic figure, fleshless, extenuated to the long hands and talon-like fingers necessary for his virtuoso violin performances:

> In his portraits . . . we have but the ghost of this strange being, for his music was an inseparable part of him and without it, his is the soundless body of a cricket or a cicada, dead, and with no shrill and vibrant tones, but only the implements of its song. Even the image of his clothes has a little of the horror left in it, more especially about his black bone-shaped trousers. They are the trousers of someone who has slept in them when too ill or too drugged to bother about it and who has spent the whole night gambling. . . .'

Sachie's diary for the year 1934 is extremely cursory. Georgia's details their usual social life in London centring this summer on Emerald Cunard and her circle, Loelia Westminster, the Channons, Beaton, Bridget, Raimund and Alice von Hofmannsthal, and Evelyn Waugh. Georgia was developing a taste for late hours at nightclubs with a string of beaux and the resulting 'frightful rows all morning with Sach'. Sachie's own behaviour with Bridget and Pearl did not in any way inhibit him from making jealous scenes to Georgia, who, admittedly, invited them. She enjoyed a string of flirtations with Henry Weymouth, Serge Obolensky and Peter Thursby, husband of her friend, Poppy. At Laura Corrigan's party on 9 July, she noted: 'danced Henry, Serge, Peter T . . . Ghastly row with Sach.' '10 July: More rows Sach. . . . Joan Guinness's party. Danced

Peter Thursby. Supper Henry. Sach all cross Daphne [Weymouth] working [him] up.' '11 July: Angry wire from Daphne. Almost funny all this jealousy. . . .' Parties at Holland House and at Syrie Maugham's were ruined for her by a jealous Sachie, who shadowed her all evening. Georgia seems almost to have enjoyed the rows as proof that he was still in love with her. Her comment on the summer: 'What fun summer has been but how much more fun if Sach had been nicer. Still it is worth while as long as he really cares.'

August was spent staying with various friends in Austria: with the Munsters at Wasserleonburg; with Jimmie Foster, a rich friend of Bridget's, at Sekirin; with the von Hofmannsthals at Schloss Kammer; and cruising with the Guinnesses in the Adriatic. They were at Weston for most of the autumn and early winter, when the sensation of the season was Walton's affair with Alice Wimborne. It had blossomed that year while Walton had been staying alone at Weston working in the stables on his symphony. Malcolm Sargent had visited him there and insisted on taking him over to the Wimbornes' house, Ashby St Ledgers. Walton's romance with Imma was almost over; when the pair of them came down to Weston early in December after the first performance of his symphony, Imma confided to Georgia in a series of 'fatiguing' talks the problems of their relationship. Five months later the Sitwells were shocked and astounded to discover that Walton and Alice had gone to Spain together. Osbert, according to Georgia, was 'terribly upset'. Alice was considerably older than Walton and married; worse still from Osbert's point of view, she was one of the great ladies whose friendship he cherished. The Sitwells closed ranks against the errant Walton and there was eventually to be a long estrangement.

Sachie had seen relatively little over the past year of Osbert and Edith, both of whom had spent most of the time abroad, but the publication in November 1934 of Edith's *Aspects of Modern Poetry* dragged the Sitwells into the limelight again. In the first chapter, entitled 'Pastors and Masters', Edith laid into her old and new enemies, Wyndham Lewis, F.R. Leavis and Geoffrey Grigson – her biographer has called the essay 'almost scurrilous'. She then went on to discuss the merits of Gerard Manley Hopkins, W.B. Yeats, W.H. Davies, T.S. Eliot, Ezra Pound and Sachie. These chapters were to get her into deep trouble with the critics, but, surprisingly, the first to find fault with the book was Sachie, who apparently wrote Edith an angry letter objecting to the essay which she had written on him. Edith was surprised and 'terribly hurt'. She replied to him from Italy, where she was staying with Helen Rootham at Levanto:

I cannot understand how you can *so* have misunderstood my essay on you. The book was largely written so as to include that essay, I gave infinitely more thought, more care, and more time to it than to any other. . . . I could not *call* you a poet of genius, because you are my brother, and it would have let loose a million little hands at your throat. But I think I have *proved* you to be a poet of genius.

How could Sachie accuse her of preferring Pound's cantos to his and barely mentioning them when she had devoted sixteen pages to *Dr Donne and Gargantua*, she asked. '. . . I think in my essay, I proved where your place is, with Milton, on one side, and with Marvell on the other.'[12] Sachie wrote back retracting the accusations in his previous letter, but Edith's book brought all three Sitwells into the firing line again. Edith was accused of plagiarising Leavis in her remarks on Yeats and Hopkins, Geoffrey Grigson being particularly venomous. Wyndham Lewis dished up the old insults on the lines of *The Apes of God*, insinuating that the Sitwells were hopelessly out of date:

> . . . these incorrigibly 'naughty', delicately shell-shocked, wistfully age-complexed, wartime Peter Pans – dragging out of their old kit-bags for the thousandth time their toy 'great men' . . .; their Aunt Sallies, their aviary of love-birds, toucans and tomtits; their droned-out nursery melodies. . . . A bit sad, a thought dreary, like all circuses that have survived – dominated, this one, by the rusty shriek of the proprietress. . . .[13]

Edith and Osbert both dashed into the fray; Sachie, as usual, remained uncomfortably on the sidelines. 'I think we are in for an era of impertinence,' Osbert wrote to Sachie from Cyprus on 14 January. Edith's book, he thought, had undoubtedly harmed her. Even he had, temporarily, lost heart for the battle and was depressed by the sniping which was coming in at them from all directions, not only from Lewis and Grigson but from John Hayward, T.S. Eliot's friend, writing in the *New York Sun*. He continued:

> I feel very depressed. Your news about Lewis and Grigson has just about finished it. I feel a craving for a purely private life just now, don't you? . . . Today a foully impertinent column arrived from the N. York Sun, full of abuse at Edith, and saying that I was due now to blow up over Fisbo, which I knew was an attack on me. And that it was all very funny. An odious tone of 'being in the know' pervaded the whole article. . . .[14]

The truth was that the Sitwells, once the avant-garde, had become old hat. They no longer seemed like innovators, merely out of date. They still had some literary friends and defenders, Rebecca West, John Sparrow and Evelyn Waugh among them, but these few were heavily outnumbered by their enemies who controlled all the important literary reviews. Edith had not helped Sachie by including him in her book, nor by concentrating on *Dr Donne and Gargantua*, his least successful long poem, and ignoring *Canons of Giant Art*. An article by Osbert and Sachie published in a glossy magazine the previous year, entitled 'We are hopeless gramophonists' and accompanied by a faintly ridiculous photograph showing the brothers posing beside a huge gramophone, underlined the affected, frivolous 1920s' attitudes which the Sitwells were now seen to represent by a more serious-minded age.

Sachie had no intention of raising his own head above the parapet. In November 1934 he had published *Touching the Orient*, a slight collection of travel pieces dedicated to the Westminsters, and six months later, *A Background for Domenico Scarlatti*, a tribute for the composer's two hundred and fiftieth anniversary. He was working on a new 'entertainment of the imagination' and, according to Georgia, being very secretive about it. He was also still in debt and being tortured by Ginger, who refused to let him see the accounts of the Weston estate. 'How sickening about that old beast,' Osbert sympathised. 'I think you will have to have a showdown with him. . . . You will *never* have a moment's peace until you have obtained permission to have an auditor examine the trust accounts and find out what really has happened. Do be firm and do it.'[5]

There was one compensation, Georgia was pregnant at last. Sir George was given the good news in mid-February with eminently satisfactory results: 'letter of congratulations, genuine enthusiasm & large cheque from Ginger,' Georgia noted on 19 February 1935. She had had difficulty conceiving and in July 1934 had consulted her gynaecologist, who gave her the comforting news that she had a '70% chance' of having another baby. She had had a minor gynaecological intervention the same month but several entries in her diary throughout that year registered her hopes of being pregnant often dashed. She was thrilled when, in mid-January 1935, it seemed that she had at last succeeded.

Pregnancy did not interfere with the usual social programme. They spent the early part of February with Emerald Cunard in London, when, after a party at Loelia Westminster's, 'awful Mrs Simpson brought Emerald home'. Evelyn Waugh spent a week-end with them at Weston at the beginning of March and later that month Berners came over from

Faringdon to read them his novel, *The Girls of Radclyffe Hall*, a comic skit on the homosexual intrigues of his circle featuring himself as the headmistress of a girls' school and his friends, Cecil Beaton ('Cecily'), Oliver Messel ('Olive'), Peter Watson, Robert Heber-Percy and David Herbert among the inmates. Walton was also there that month, prior to his sensational escapade in Spain with Alice Wimborne in May. Georgia's sister, Bunny, was also in Spain, having left behind her a broken marriage, a small son, a trail of debts and an unsuccessful romance with Freddie Birkenhead (which had caused a row of truly Sitwellian proportions between Georgia and the Birkenhead family). Reports filtered through to a worried Georgia that Bunny, who supported the Nationalists, was thoroughly enjoying the discomfort, the sherry and the bullfights and was having an affair with Kim Philby.

In mid-July Sachie and Georgia retired to Weston. Sachie had become an enthusiastic gardener, or rather plantsman, since his interest was never practical. The painting by Rex Whistler showing Sachie with a gardening implement over his shoulder featured a rare occasion because gardening work did not appeal to him. He loved flowers for their names and their historical or human connotations, particularly auriculas, cultivated by the Spitalfield weavers who constructed 'auricula theatres' to show them. He loved old-fashioned roses, primulas, pinks and fuchsias and collected old nurserymen's catalogues featuring hyacinths and lilies. Later in life he found a trigger for poetic inspiration in particular flowers, naming a collection of his privately published poetry *Auricula Theatre*. That spring, with the help of Robert Jenkinson, he had carried out a good deal of new planting at Weston. Later, probably prompted, as were the plant collections, by the nineteenth-century colour-plate books which he consulted in the British Museum, he became fascinated by birds, exotic pheasants, bantams and pigeons (these last for their names and their history; in a later book, *The Hunters and the Hunted*, he devoted pages to sonorous roll calls of different species).

He and Georgia had a shared project at Weston that summer, editing a selection of family letters into a book, *Dear Miss Heber*, to be published the following year. Francis Bamford, who was to edit the letters, arrived on 20 July with Gerald Wellesley, who was employing him on his own family archives. They spent a fascinating time in the attics sorting out the contents of three large boxes, three or four smaller boxes and ten tin trunks, some of which contained two large sacks of papers. Hours were passed arranging and, regrettably, destroying letters. Sachie developed a passion for cutting out and collecting old engraved bill-heads from the family papers.

Walton, now barely admitted to Osbert's circle, returned from a ballet week-end at Renishaw, followed by Osbert, who was himself en route for Alice and Ashby. August was spent relatively quietly at Weston since the new baby was expected the following month. Dick Wyndham came down for the night to recount his African adventures and show them pictures of his Sudanese mistress, Rafa. Edith arrived for four days, amusing them with imitations of Christabel's affectations, but left on the 14th to escape Ginger, who caused the usual nervousness in the household but was for once responsive to Sachie's attempts to extract money from him. 'Adores Reresby and will help a bit,' Georgia recorded. Walton turned up with his mother and Auntie Gert in a car bought for him by Alice followed by Lady Ida, who spent the night at Weston before going on with Sachie to the wedding of her Londesborough nephew at Blankney. It was the first time Sachie had been there since his childhood before the First World War.

In September they moved to London for the birth of the baby. Bridget was very much in evidence, visiting them every day, so much so that one night Georgia had a nightmare that Sachie had gone off with her. Their second son was born at the clinic at 27 Welbeck Street on 17 September. Sachie was delighted and wrote Georgia a love letter:

My darling pugs,
    This is meant to take the place of all the letters I have ever written you, and still more of those I haven't! I do love you so much more than you think I do, and I am absolutely and perfectly happy with you. That lovely little baby is the sweetest thing in the world and is really, as they used to say in old-fashioned novels, the 'pledge' of our affection. . . .
    I do hope, my darling angel, that you are happy with me. I can't bear to think we have been married such a long time, can you! However it does not seem a long time, and I suppose that is the best proof that I have been happy. I only wish we could be married all over again! . . .
    You do know how I love you, my darling, don't you! I know my many shortcomings only too well and that I have not much to give you, but I do really love and adore you, and I am so happy with you. . . .[16]

The birth of his second son did not inspire in Sachie the same kind of panic at the prospect of fatherly responsibility and loss of liberty as had the appearance of Reresby eight years earlier. Although he was too self-absorbed to be paternal and was on the whole completely uninterested in children, he welcomed the new baby, who was to have a far easier row to hoe than his elder brother as far as his parents were concerned. They expected far too much of the Sitwell heir, who was alternately cherished and neglected, bandied from grandparent to grandparent. Two years earlier Georgia had recorded six-year-old Reresby as saying pathetically to Sachie, 'Oh Daddy, nothing could make you happy or ever will.' 'So Queer,' she commented.

The new baby remained nameless for two weeks after his birth until Sachie and Georgia, in a further attempt to ingratiate themselves with Ginger, lighted upon Niccolo, 'after an Archioli [*sic*] former owners of Montegufoni,' as Georgia put it. Ginger, however, contrary as ever, did not like the name and the child remained as either 'Baby' or, occasionally, *faute de mieux*, 'Niccolo' until the summer of 1936, when his mother began to refer to him as 'Trajan'. It was as Trajan that he appeared on the dedication of Sachie's next major book, *Dance of the Quick and the Dead*, published in October 1936. Trajan is or was a common name in Roumania; the Sitwell baby's namesake, the Emperor Trajan, was the conqueror of the Dacians from whom the Roumanians are descended. Possibly Sachie already had in mind the idea of a Roumanian journey, which he undertook the following year. However, towards the end of the year the baby was finally called 'Francis', presumably after his great-uncle Londesborough, Trajan being demoted to his second name.

Sachie did not find his new son of all-absorbing interest. While Georgia remained at Weston with Niccolo-Trajan, he went up to Renishaw on 14 October and, four days later, took Bridget down to Newton Ferrers to stay with the Abdys. Georgia, left behind at Weston, was rather cross. 'Letter from London from Sach,' she wrote in her diary on the 19th. 'Not nearly as nice as the one I wrote him. He is so spoilt and unresponsive but suppose I am *exigeante* and he doesn't mean it. He motored down to the Abdys with Bridget. . . .' Back in London to see the Sadler's Wells Ballet perform *Casse-Noisette* and *The Rio Grande*, she reproached him for his tepid letter and for forgetting to telephone her. He left her behind at Weston again, but the result of her earlier objections was a 'very sweet letter . . . to make up for not responding in sufficiently tender vein'. 'This sort of epistle is not his forte,' she added, 'but one can't do these things to order & I can't complain nor do I wish to.' Sachie accompanied Edith to Tchelitchew's exhibition on 24 October, Edith being in a great state about Berners having included a sketch of Tchelitchew in *Radclyffe Hall*. On the 26th he made a brief visit to Weston to see the baby, but his diary entry for the 27th reads: 'Bridget's 28th birthday – 1907–1935'; and, two days later, he took her to Sadler's Wells to see Pearl dance in *Les Sylphides*, *Pas de Trois* and

Façade. 'Supper afterwards with Pearl at Savoy and drive home with her,' he recorded.

Sachie was seeing less of Pearl, whose career had continued to improve. Walton, doubtless at Sachie's suggestion, had written a dance for her in *Façade* and she was beginning a film version of H.G. Wells's *The Shape of Things to Come* with Raymond Massey playing her father. By January 19–36, when she wrote thanking Sachie for a generous cheque for Christmas, it was 'I have seen you so little lately that you are a stranger.' She was by then involved with Kurt Bernhardt, the German film director, whom she married later that year. 'Life begins again this afternoon,' she wrote somewhat insensitively to Sachie. 'These intervals of being without Kurt show me how dull & lacking in life my life has been. . . .'[7] Georgia, rather late in the day, had woken up to the possibility of an affair between Sachie and Pearl. A mysterious entry in her diary for 3 May read: 'Sachie worried about extraordinary things I have found out. Such Blackmail. Mischief about Pearl made by Alice & Willie & v. odd contraceptive discovery of mine. . . .'

Sachie wove the three women with whom he was in love – Bridget, Pearl and Georgia – into a chapter in *Dance of the Quick and the Dead*, which he had finished at the end of March. His involvement with Zita was over. He had become less interested in her since beginning his physical affair with Bridget in the summer of 1933. Only one letter from her exists among his papers for that year, none for 1934. By 1935 they rarely even saw each other socially, for reasons which Zita herself is now unable to elucidate. A sad letter written by her on 21 August 1935 in response to Sachie's condolences on the death of her father read: 'I often regretted during the last year that you had grown to hate me. . . . One of my greatest disillusionments was the retraction of your friendship – Sachie – I can't help thinking of it each time I lose something out of my life. . . .' They were not to see each other again for almost fifty years.

In *Dance of the Quick and the Dead* Sachie visualised the three women as dancers at a masqued ball after fashion plates by Gavarni. He made clear exactly what each of the three represented for him in this and his subsequent *Sacred and Profane Love*, where Bridget, Pearl and Georgia, were to appear again, this time as the Three Graces. Pearl was the romantic ideal of beauty, grace and lightness – 'no danger'. Bridget represented sensuality. The passages in which he evoked images of her were the most truly physical he ever wrote, but he also made it clear that Georgia was the constant in his life, 'the principal and most enduringly important of the three', assured of her supremacy. She, like himself, was a spectator of the masque, 'the only other person alive to their [*sic*] meaning'. She was, he said, the 'embodiment of beauty in benevolence' signalled by her smiling mouth, huge eyes and a Creole softness of her saffron skin. 'The assurance of this figure in a world of doubts and disbeliefs made his heart tremble and the earth shake beneath his feet . . . its impact was of warmth and comfort.' Warmth, poise and certainty had originally attracted him to her, her soft features contrasting with her independence of character and obvious ability to look after herself:

> The depths of this character are so wholly consistent with her exterior that there is no difference between the expression in the eyes and the answer of the heart. Perhaps there is no human soul of which this is so conspicuously true. Neither is there any other being in whom instinct goes hand in hand with understanding, nor another heart which beats in such harmony with the mind.

After that, the passage became extremely obscure, but appeared to refer to Georgia's physical passions and his own:

> It is better to speak of them now, while they are burning. For this is the end of adolescence . . . after this, comes enjoyment and maturity. That battery of the nerves, and its painful and delicious tremblings, are no more. Instead, there is knowledge and the certainty of what was only hazard before. Or so it seems: but where is any certainty except in the heart?

The embers of Sachie's and Georgia's physical passions were to burn well into middle age. Georgia in particular was highly sexed and felt the need to assert herself in the face of the overwhelming Sitwell personality. Sachie's celebrity and his charm meant, as she was honest enough to admit, that people were interested in him rather than in her. She wrote of one young male guest at Weston whom she herself fancied: 'George is charming. Sach likes him frightfully & he, as usual, is now obviously a slave to Sachie's charm rather than mine.' Lover succeeded lover, and there were many admirers and flirtations, always someone who would be referred to enigmatically by his initials, although if Sachie had happened to read her diary he would certainly have been able to identify his rivals. He was jealous, particularly when the man in question was someone who he did not himself find sympathetic, but pursued his own romantic paths. There would always be some adored object in his life. The main problem between Sachie and Georgia in the 1930s was not so much her lovers but her thirst for smart social life and for dancing until the early hours in Ciro's, the Embassy, the 400, or wherever happened to be the *dernier cri* in nightlife. Sachie hated dancing and inane conversation; he detested being bored, and on one occasion had a fierce row with Dick Wyndham who had taken them to the Gargoyle and left him with a man whom Sachie considered a bore. He required a modicum of intelligence and wit. For Georgia, it was enough that someone should be considered 'smart'. He lived for aesthetic experience, the opera, music, the ballet; she pretended to like it, but secretly preferred cocktails with Chips Channon to Edith's intellectual tea parties at the Sesame Club, and dancing till four at the 400 to an evening with Osbert and his friends at Carlyle Square. For both of them, however, their marriage was central to their lives. Neither of them ever contemplated leaving the other for anyone else and their physical relationship continued until old age.

Reresby, aged just nine, was packed off to his first boarding-school, Sandroyd, on 1 May 1936. 'Most harrowing, nearly died of misery,' Georgia wrote after seeing him off from the station, but she had none the less lunched at Emerald's beforehand, not thinking it necessary to stay with him. Sachie's diary entry for that day read: 'May 1 Poor Reresby went to school. His running round the corner of Tite Street after us. Cecil's Ballet [*Apparitions*] & Liszt's music.' Two days later they embarked with Dick Wyndham, Osbert and David Horner for a tour of Portugal.

Sachie's diary is blank for the summer season after their return to England on 25 May; Georgia's crammed with the usual detail. They went to the opera with Emerald and the German Ambassador, Joachim von Ribbentrop, to the Surrealist exhibition and to a lecture on Surrealism in July, at which Salvador Dali appeared wearing a diver's suit. They went their separate ways in August, Georgia to Sekirin and Venice with the customary collection of smart English and Austrian grandees and the apparently ubiquitous King of Spain, Sachie to Renishaw.

At Renishaw with Osbert and Edith, Arthur Waley and L.P. Hartley ('Bore' Hartley, as Georgia described him), Sachie worked to finish his latest book, *Conversation Pieces*, the first of a series dealing with aspects of English connoisseurship, discussing Hogarth, Zoffany, Stubbs, Devis, Gainsborough among others. Five of the paintings illustrated came from the collection of Osbert's friend, Sir Philip Sassoon, to whom Sachie dedicated the book, which he finished on 28 September for November publication. It was a new, less controversial literary departure for him. Reviewers welcomed the book as a considerable addition to the 'meagre and inaccurate' literature on the subject, praising it for its 'persuasive charm'. However, there were factual inaccuracies. Sachie's knowledge was wide rather than deep and he could be careless on scholarly detail. 'When we turn to attributions,' one reviewer wrote, 'it is to find Mr Sitwell disposed to a wide tolerance of the owners' view. . . .' *Conversation Pieces* was to be followed up by a companion volume, *Narrative Pictures*, published the following year.

More important for Sachie was the publication on 1 October of *Dance of the Quick and the Dead*, on which he had been working over the past two years. Humbert Wolfe called it a 'lovely and bewildering book'; it was, like all Sachie's deeply felt 'entertainments of the imagination', entirely original, patchy but brilliant, absolutely personal, a highly charged mixture of autobiographical 'images of the subconscious' and a *tour d'horizon* of the works of art and the artists acting as triggers for his imagination. He used specific works of art to interpret life: *The Triumph of Death* by Pieter Brueghel the Elder, Watteau's pierrot painting, *Le Grand Gilles*, a head of Debureau, the great Pierrot of the Théâtre des Funambules, photographed in 1846, *The Inferno* by Hieronymus Bosch, and prison engravings by Doré. The book was a heady dash through all the subjects that interested him, at times as difficult to follow as his conversation. Acute artistic judgments – Picasso, 'the sole great artist of our time', who 'has affected the surface of visual life to an extent that . . . has never fallen to the lot of any other painter since the Renaissance' – were mixed with at times shallow and irritating generalisations about modern life. Sachie did not think, he felt and experienced; his images of horror were as strong as his perception of beauty. Of Hieronymus Bosch, the artist whose personal vision perhaps most nearly approximated to his own, Sachie wrote:

> . . . he is in no uncertain sense, a mood or mirror into which the minds of men have inclined in order to look upon their souls. This inner doubtfulness, this lack of hope, is a recurrent thing in history; and, whenever it appears, these woods and thickets of the subconscious self become as entangled and as intricately inhabited as in a picture by Bosch.

The horror of prison and the abyss which his mother's trauma of more than twenty years ago had roused in him as an Eton schoolboy inspired horrific descriptions, in a chapter headed 'Purgatorio', of the cruelties of the 'Hood-Beak System' in Victorian prisons and of the convict settlements at Macquarie Island. In 'The Banquet. . .', devoted principally to Elizabeth Siddal, he paid tribute to Edith's creative genius and her influence upon him. 'I am more touched by and more proud of your most *beautiful* reference to me in the chapter on Miss Siddal, than you will ever know. I can scarcely write of it,' Edith told him. 'I should think all the Pipsqueakery are wringing their flippers. As for me, I am *really floored* by it. It just is a great work . . . I get breathless with it. . . .'[18]

Running through the book was the same sense of transience which underlay *All Summer in a Day*. Then it had been the sensations of childhood; now it was the instinct that the individuality and variety of the European (and English) civilisation which he loved was under threat. The *Times Literary Supplement* remarked on the 'sentiment of precariousness' haunting the entire book. Cyril Connolly later described it as 'apprehension of beauty, awareness of loss'. It was Sachie's personal reaction to the ominous years of the later 1930s, an instinctive, artist's response to political and social movements beyond his control.

Dance of the Quick and the Dead showed how far Sachie was from the mainstream of English contemporary literature and the preoccupations of writers like Graham Greene and George Orwell. It also illustrated, perhaps better than any other, his attitude towards life, his inability to engage directly in its emotions without the intervention of some visual agent. He was a spectator, not a player. As he wrote of Pierrot as played by Debureau: '. . . he is forever and always outside life, midway between the audience and the players, belonging to neither. . . .' This was particularly true in his approach to sex and love. He was incapable of the direct sexual charge of a Mosley, a Wyndham, a Quennell or a Walton. In *All Summer in a Day* he had fantasised about taking the dancer he loved but dared not approach to Venice to show her Cleopatra in Veronese's painting. He had seen Zita as a Titian page, and Georgia, Bridget and Pearl as Gavarni's fancy-dress masquers at a ball.

As James Lees-Milne said of him:

Sachie was a sort of leprechaun. He wasn't totally a human being. He was a spirit, really – almost incorporeal. I don't think of Sachie physically at all. . . . What was most fascinating about him was his conversation – he flitted from bough to bough, twig to twig so rapidly you couldn't keep pace with him. It was about exotic birds in the West Indies and then you'd find that he was talking about architecture in Naples then about nunneries in the Balkans . . . flitting from one thing to another. I often found that difficult because being rather slow on the uptake I was dwelling on the last thing and wishing he'd expand a little more on that when he'd gone off into another sphere. And then those short spurts of laughter almost trills. He was very inspiring and being with him was a treat.[19]

Both Lees-Milne and Quennell compared Sachie's courtships to the elaborate, stately dance of mating birds, Quennell citing the Australian bower bird building up its nest of bright, glittering things its eye lights upon. Once when he took Quennell to stay with one of the ladies in whom he was interested – 'a very dull woman' – Quennell noticed on a table one of Sachie's most recent books which he had inscribed to her with a quotation from Baudelaire. Sachie had written: '*la tranquillité donne aux yeux d'une femme le calme des mers tropicales*', which sounded very fine but what Baudelaire had actually said was: '*la stupidité donne aux yeux d'une femme. . . .*' 'He was in love a great deal and would do rather romantic things like walking up and down outside the beloved's window at night. . . .'[20]

Sachie's *Collected Poems* followed just over a month later in November 1936, six years after Edith's collected poems and five years after Osbert's, at probably the most inauspicious time which could possibly have been chosen for its publication. It was dedicated to Edith, 'for whom these were written and in return for "Façade" '. Sachie wrote a nervous, semi-apologetic preface, which was probably intended to avert the attacks of the 'pipsqueakery', all of whom were on the side of the Left. His early poems, he said, were written at the instigation of his brother and sister, while the title of his first book, *The People's Palace*, was 'a proof of his revolutionary sympathies at that time'. He acknowledged his overriding debt to Edith: 'These poems were written to give her pleasure and this must be . . . their excuse and their recommendation.' It was a loyal but rather feeble explanation for writing poetry and certainly not one calculated to appeal to contemporary critics. Edith only made things worse by contributing a long prefatory essay on the lines of the one she had written for *Aspects of Modern Poetry*. 'I have long wished to write at even greater length than was possible in my *Aspects of Modern Poetry* about the poet who is, to my mind, one of the greatest that our race has produced in the last hundred and fifty years,' she wrote defiantly, 'and I see no reason why the fact of our blood relationship should be an obstacle to my doing so. . . .' Many of the points she made were valid ones: 'Mr Sitwell's world, like my own, is a country world, a world of growth, and of "a green thought in a green shade". . . .' She praised him for his technique, his mastery of vowel sounds and liquids, but spoiled the overall effect by defending him from the 'accusations' of 'the Bungalow School' of inhumanity, producing as evidence 'Outskirts', an early poem which showed only too clearly how uninterested Sachie was in the realities of modern life. '... this great poetry', she declared, 'will remain long after the silly little poems about vulgar little personal troubles or pleasures, about bungalows and motor bicycles and sandwich papers and the doctrines of Marx, have sunk into an early grave.' With rather pathetic defiance, Edith was offering her own and her brother's heads to their critics on a plate.

Sachie's collected poems covered more than 500 pages, including, as he put it in his preface, 'all, or nearly all, that he would wish to preserve'. Even had he been, as Edith claimed, one of the greatest poets England had produced over the past 150 years, such a quantity of verse would have made an indigestible collection. In refusing to weed out his work Sachie was being, as usual, inconsiderate of his readers and indulgent of himself. The *Times Literary Supplement*, reviewing *Collected Poems* on the same page and at the same length as Gerard Manley Hopkins's *Note-books and Papers*, conceded that 'the sensuous beauty of Mr Sitwell's poetry is almost as remarkable as his sister asserts' in the 'magic of his vowel technique or the flowing and flowering and variation of his rhythms', but took issue with her claims that in writing poems like 'The Fisherman' Sachie was dealing with the actual world, 'the common things of life'. Sachie's vision of a fisherman concentrated on 'such jewelled things as glittering fish and water or shining pyramids of grapes, while for lack of a basis in or a wider contact with actuality his imagination is continually tempted to bask in delicious worlds of its own devising'. The critic cited as an example a poem from *The Hundred and One Harlequins* entitled 'In the Train', which began 'In crystal chariots drawn by unicorns. ...' There was 'an excess of sensation over thought', a 'monotony inherent in verse in which structure and significance are so continually sacrificed to the cultivation of sounds and repeated images'. 'Yet if Mr Sitwell', the reviewer concluded, 'fails sufficiently to subdue his imagination and brace it by contact with the world of thought and things, no modern poet has created a richer world of his own out of objects of art.' He cited *Canons of Giant Art* as the outstanding example.[21] It was an absolutely fair review, but not good enough for the Sitwells. Sachie's complaints about it were supported by Osbert and Edith; in their present sensitive mood anything less than total praise seemed like hostility. Osbert tried to cheer Sachie by pointing out that it was at least 'an important review', while Edith, idiotically, condemned the reviewer as 'a dear old country clergyman'. There was some comfort for Sachie in having 'Agamemnon's Tomb' included, with six of Edith's poems, in W.B. Yeats's *The Oxford Book of*

Modern Verse published that year, but he took the reception of his collected poems as a rejection of himself as a poet and confirmation of a favourite Sitwell theme, the suffering and persecution of artists by the brutal power of the Philistine.

All other events in December 1936 were eclipsed by the Abdication crisis. As close friends of Emerald Cunard, who was at the heart of the Wallis Simpson/Edward VIII circle, Sachie and Georgia had met both the King and Mrs Simpson but as no more than acquaintances. Neither of them was much interested in royal affairs and, despite their friendship with Emerald, they were as much taken by surprise by the events of December 1936 as anybody else. Sachie had not even bothered to go up from Weston to watch the Proclamation of Edward VIII in January 1936, despite being invited to view it from the Ponsonbys' privileged apartment in St James's Palace. Georgia, staying at 7 Grosvenor Square with Emerald, had been taken the night before by Ernest and Wallis Simpson to the lying-in-state of the late King George V in Westminster Hall. She had arrived in time to see the four Princes standing vigil over their father's coffin. 'So lucky to go when they were there though so ignominious to go with Simpsons' was her ungratefully snobbish comment. Although Baba Metcalfe was down at Weston the day the ex-King left England to give her insider's view of the King's 'mad obsession' with Mrs Simpson, the Sitwells' principal cause for concern was Emerald's distress. Two days later they arrived at 7 Grosvenor Square to find her the target of concentrated anti-Windsor hostility and terribly upset by the King's abdication and the reproaches levelled at her personally by the Archbishop of Canterbury in his post-Abdication broadcast the previous day. She kept them up until 4.30 a.m. talking about it. Four days later Georgia loyally had a tremendous row with Gerald Berners 'about making mischief to Mrs Ronnie [Greville] about Emerald'. Whatever she may have said, it rankled, causing a rupture between Faringdon and Weston which lasted until the outbreak of the war. At Polesden Lacey on 1 January, they found that Osbert had sent Mrs Greville a copy of his anonymous poem, 'Rat Week', savagely satirising the Windsors' former 'Ritz Bar' friends who had toadied to them in their hour of glory and then deserted them. (He spared Emerald, high priestess of the Simpson court, and Diana Cooper, another member of the circle, because he liked them.) Sachie and Georgia were annoyed that Osbert had not sent them a copy, perhaps because all their friends, like Emerald, Chips Channon and the Brownlows, had ended up on the wrong side.

The new reign brought Sachie a minor benefit, a commission to write a long article for serialisation on the traditions behind the coronation. Osbert was now firmly installed in his role of friend of the royal family, having got to know the new King and Queen on their frequent visits to Polesden. He was on particularly friendly terms with the Queen, who had a penchant for smart, amusing, cultivated men, and was rewarded with an invitation to the royal week-end party at Windsor in April, when the King had enjoyed letting him know that he was perfectly aware of his identity as the author of 'Rat Week'.

Sachie's life with Georgia, peaceful and conjugal at Weston, ran its usual troubled course during the London social season. On 5 January 1937 Georgia had closed her diary account of the previous year with a New Year's resolution: 'To continue, & try harder than ever to forget myself & all that implies, & to be satisfied with S. and the children. God knows I ought to be & I am, *most* of the time.' There was drama over Reresby, who was miserable at Sandroyd and threatened to run away. Sachie and Georgia with considerable moral cowardice carried on with their plans to stay with Emerald in London, despatching Gertrude down to the school to report. Fortunately it was not serious. Even the charms of the new baby were beginning to pall for Georgia by the beginning of March – 'shall miss him terribly but long to get away,' she wrote. Her search for 'fun' and admiration was reaching a crescendo in these last pre-war years. Her diary is full of complaints about Sachie's 'purdah attitude' towards her, which made her 'nervy and depressed'. Poor Sachie could do no right. On one occasion he had agreed to go to the 400, but although bored by it had refused to go to bed, thus cramping his wife's style. Returning to London after a Mediterranean cruise on the SS *Champollion*, there were frequent rows over two new admirers, both named George. A truce was restored by Bridget talking Sachie round, which held over the potentially perilous week-end of the Ronald Trees' ball at Ditchley in June. Sachie, who arrived down at Weston separately with Bridget, seems not to have minded Georgia's exploits with one of the Georges at the Spider's Web roadhouse en route. Both of them spent the evening at the ball with their respective partners, 'no crossness as anticipated,' a relieved Georgia wrote. Domestic warfare broke out again over Cecil Beaton's fancy dress *fête champêtre* in July, with Sachie hating the idea and Georgia determined to go. Even the death on 4 July of Desmond Parsons, aged only twenty-six, from Hodgkinson's disease did not deter her. 'Went to Nathan's to order fancy dress for Cecil's party, row about it still going on with Sach but determined to go in hopes of cheering myself up,' she noted.

Sachie was also worried about his mother's health. The Gingers were in London that month, preparatory to travelling to Scarborough for their golden wedding celebrations. Sachie and Georgia found Lady Ida 'not at all well, very changed, weak & dotty' when they visited her at the Gingers' usual hotel, the Washington in Curzon Street, on 5 July. None the less, they were at Hanover Lodge the following evening, where Alice von Hofmannsthal gave a party for Edith, and then at Desmond's funeral the next day. Meanwhile, Lady Ida had been moved to a nursing home, although the doctors told Sachie when he visited her there on the 9th that she was in no danger. They went down to Mottisfont Abbey to stay for Beaton's party, to which Georgia went in a Winterhalter dress. Her diary does not mention Sachie, merely that she drove back from the party with Clive Bell and Derek Hill. It is possible that he refused to go; at any rate she recorded that the next day he would not speak to her 'because of the party', adding, strangely, 'not my fault but he thinks it is'.

They were dining at Mottisfont the following evening when a telephone message came that Lady Ida's condition had suddenly worsened. They hurried up to London to find her doctor, Lord Dawson, of the opinion that she would not live through the night. Sachie remained at the nursing home all night while Georgia went home; his mother died in the early hours of the next morning. Georgia arrived at the home after a 5.30 a.m. call to find Lady Ida looking 'so changed and utterly away from the world'. Sachie was 'shattered' by his mother's death. He wrote to Bridget's brother, Michael Rosse, that

> The last few days have been too awful to think of. Her death was the most pathetic thing. I did, as you say, adore her and any tragedies and unhappinesses brought out all the protective or chivalrous side of one's nature. Also she had such a wonderful appearance!
>
> Now, of course, the smallest thing, such as her 'patience' board and 'patience' cards, is enough to make me hysterical. I don't see how I am ever to feel better. . . .
>
> Oh, how terrible those last hours are. It is so awful never to see her again. I long to see her hands which were most lovely. . . . I miss her in an agonizing way.[22]

Sachie had deliberately wiped the trauma of his mother's imprisonment from his mind; he may, temporarily, have exorcised it in writing the 'Purgatorio' chapter in *Dance of the Quick and the Dead*. He made no mention of it in the formal unsigned obituary he wrote of her, 'Lady Ida Sitwell. A great Lady of Yorkshire', which appeared in *The Times* on

13 July, the day after her death. He emphasised her good works in Scarborough, her beauty and her air of distinction, glossing over in print, as he undoubtedly did in his mind, the later years when she was lumped together with Sir George as the Gingers, a couple to be outwitted and avoided whenever possible, and when the Edwardian beauty had become a pathetic, even comic figure, taking understandable refuge in alcohol from the shortcomings of her marriage. He may not have mentioned the dreadful days of 1915, submerging the experience in his subconscious, but they were always there to surface again and haunt his old age.

One of the reasons for the 'awfulness' of the days following his mother's death was the usual family squabbling. Edith firmly refused to show any hypocritical remorse at not having been to see her mother before she died and, at dinner at Osbert's that night, 'the atmosphere of gloom was exacerbated by disagreements between Sachie and Edith over their mother'. Sir George was 'very weak & sentimental'; 'after 50 years one is not surprised,' Georgia commented. 'I always knew they loved each other in their way in spite of quarrels.' The funeral took place at Weston on 14 July. Edith did not attend, but Sachie cried all through the service. He does not seem to have had much sympathy from Georgia, who was miserable for quite a different reason. 'Feel worse every day', she wrote, 'because Sach's temper is really unbearable, he is not depressed but cross & still brings up Cecil's party to torture me. Also I am *never* away from one or other members of the family.' Practical, down-to-earth and self-absorbed, her chief regret for that summer seems to have been for the fun she had missed. 'Look back on summer as a waste,' she wrote at the beginning of August, 'the [rented London] house was so very attractive and comfortable but the 2nd half there was so sad & boring. No amusement to take one's mind off except ballet & same old ones I'm tired of most. . . .'

August was a family month for Sachie. After visits to Vaynol and to the Angleseys at Plas Newydd to admire Rex Whistler's murals, they spent two nights with the Aberconways at Bodnant, which Georgia found 'unbelievably boring' despite H.G. Wells being a fellow guest. The remainder of the month was to be devoted to keeping the widowed Sir George company, first at Renishaw and then at Scarborough, where they stayed at the Grand Hotel. Osbert, Edith, David Horner and Constant Lambert were at Renishaw when they arrived, joined by L.P. Hartley and John Sparrow, known in the family as 'Spadger', Edith's knight errant in her battles with Grigson. It was a gloomy week for Sachie in Scarborough with his father, his spirits further depressed by a detour to Londesborough to see the Denison family graves – 'pathetic tombs of Aunt Gracie, her husband & son'. Sachie had not been to Scarborough since his near-fatal illness there in 1920–21; it was a poignantly sentimental journey for him. He took Francis for a walk in the gardens of Londesborough Lodge and looked at the outside of Wood End and of the house where he was born. 'Pathetic relics of the past, S being sentimental about them,' Georgia wrote. The weather was cold and the beach and the Spa overcrowded; Scarborough, apart from its architecture, was no longer elegant. Ginger, unable to play the part of sweet, old widower for long, attacked Georgia about the expense of Weston and the size of their overdraft, so that it was a relief to return to Renishaw to enjoy the cooking, which was always delicious when Osbert was in residence. Sachie's friends, the pianist Louis Kentner and his wife, were there, with Frederick Ashton and Robert Helpmann. The Aberconways arrived: 'Harry Aberconway shocked by Freddie and Bobbie,' Georgia noted with amusement, 'but they don't let it cramp their style. . . .' Edith was reading the proofs of her novel, *I Live under a Black Sun*, based loosely on the lives and characters of Swift, Stella and Vanessa, but with strong autobiographical touches. Both her parents haunted the book, Sir George as Sir Henry Rotherham and Lady Ida's unmistakable voice, speaking of her husband, 'Of course, darling, what I would *really* like would be to get him certified and shut up in an asylum.'

At the end of August Sachie and Georgia left Renishaw for Weston en route for Roumania via Paris. Gertrude, acting as lady's maid to Georgia, accompanied them. She was now as indispensable an adjunct of all their travels as Henry Moat had been to Sir George's. Sachie had been planning the trip for some time. In October 1936 he and Georgia had made a new friend, Costa Achillopoulo, an accomplished photographer who often worked for *Vogue*. Costa, green-eyed and prematurely grey-haired, described by Georgia as '*hideous*, charming, amusing, worldly & yet intelligent'; had become a regular partner of hers on late nights at the 400 and consequently a frequent source of diary entries. He shared a house in London with a vivacious, talkative, Roumanian, Princess Anne-Marie Callimachi, who was to act as their hostess in Roumania. At lunch with Costa and Anne-Marie in April earlier that year they had met another Roumanian aristocrat, Princess Helène Cantacuzene, and Patrick Leigh Fermor, who had just returned from a three-year journey on foot through Europe which had included a year living in the Cantacuzenes' charming, tumbledown country house in High Moldavia not far from the Russian border. Sachie was fascinated by Leigh Fermor's impressions of

Roumania; they instantly became friends and were constantly together with Costa, Anne-Marie and the Cantacuzenes in May, the coronation month.

Sachie's party for Roumania included Bridget and Dick Wyndham and Costa Achillopoulo as official photographers for the book to be published by Batsford. Sachie's Batsford editor, Charles Fry, described by John Betjeman as 'a phallus with a business sense', had previously enraged Georgia by getting blind drunk at a dinner to celebrate the book. The trip was financed by the Roumanian Government and organised by the indefatigably energetic Anne-Marie, in whose magnificent house on the Chaussée Kisseleff in Bucharest they were to be based. The resulting book, *Roumanian Journey*, was one of the most enchanting of Sachie's travel books. It was, like all his work, intensely idiosyncratic and as Patrick Leigh Fermor put it in his preface to a subsequent edition, 'little to do with reportage or travel-writing as it is now understood':

> The glance he cast was a collector's; not quite that of his ancestors' on the Grand Tour, crating marbles and canvasses to be shipped home to the Shires, but akin; his quarry, though never precisely defined, was more portable. He pursued all that interested, moved or amused him in the realms of aesthetics, history, literature, poetry and music; the quest included anything that was out of the ordinary, rare, comic, mysterious, haunted or even macabre. It was a flight from the humdrum, an amassing of detail to corroborate the infinite multiplicity of life. He could spot relationships, find parallels, trace sources and identify hybrids and variants in a flash. A brush-stroke in a picture, a phrase in a sonata or on a barrel-organ, a step in a dance, the moulding on a gateway, the flight feathers of a bird, a snatch of dialect, a recondite schism, the taste of a new drink, the behaviour of bracts and sepals – these were his clues and keys, and Rumania was the ideal maze to wander in. . . .[23]

Sachie was, in Leigh Fermor's opinion, the right author in the right place at the right time. He went with no preconceived notions of what he would find, deliberately refraining from reading anything on the subject beforehand so that his impressions would come to him fresh and as a surprise. The result of letting his eye take control was to fix for ever a kaleidoscopic portrait of Roumanian life, soon to be obliterated under a totalitarian avalanche. With unerring instinct he homed in on the essence of Roumania, the extraordinary richness and integrity of its peasant life and art. Roumania, he wrote, was still unspoilt, perhaps the only country in Europe of which that could be said. There were virtually no major works of art or architecture on a European scale (although the Hohenzollern royal family had no less than nine El Grecos of varying quality). 'What is permanent and unforgettable in Roumania', he wrote, 'is the great plain of Transylvania, the woods of Oltenia, the swamps of the Danube Delta . . . the painted [churches of] Sucevita and Voronet, and the wooden houses and gay costumes seen upon its road.'

Where other people saw Bucharest as a second-rate copy of Paris, Sachie was seduced by its oriental atmosphere, the exotic mixture of Turkish and Russian influences. He wrote of the Byzantine suppleness of the upper classes, descendants of the Phanariot Greeks sent to rule from Constantinople, the extraordinary boyar portraits of the nobility, the extreme of the climate between the snow of a Russian winter and the fierce heat of a Levantine summer. He was fascinated by the cabmen, the Skoptzi, hugely tall eunuchs, members of a self-mutilating Russian dissident sect who believe in a sexless Christ who never died but who wanders the earth assuming the form of Peter III, husband of Catherine the Great. He loved the garden restaurants, the *gradina* of Bucharest, and Roumanian food, which he called the 'best native cuisine in Europe' – fish or chicken soups made with sour cream, quail pilaff, beef roasted on a spit, crayfish with saffron. There was the food in country manor houses straight out of Turgenev – tiny fresh trout, fried like sardines and eaten as an hors d'oeuvres, jam made from wild wood raspberries at Sinaia. Roumanian caviar from the Black Sea was almost as good as Russian from the Caspian, but when Sachie visited Valcov, the sturgeon fishermen's town on the Danube delta, he was so shocked by the brutality of the extraction that it – almost – put him off caviar for life. He shared Liszt's critical view of the musical effect of the Pan pipes, or syrinx, which were a feature of some Roumanian music, but found himself haunted by the nostalgic sadness of the popular songs of Bucharest, the Roumanian equivalent of the Portuguese *fado*.

He called for the establishment of a museum of peasant art in Bucharest, which would do for the region from the Bukovina to the Danube what the Nordiska Museum in Stockholm had done for the Baltic area. '. . . this is the richest part of the world in peasant costumes, peasant architecture, folk lore, folk music and folk dancing,' he wrote. 'The time is not, yet, too late. It is still a living art. . . .' His was not a totally unqualified approval, however; the famous peasant costumes of Rucar reminded him too much of the Chelsea Arts Ball. The costumes and the rugs of Oltenia and Bessarabia were, he considered, Roumania's works of art. Its masterpieces, decorative rather than architectural, were the

wooden peasant houses and, above all, the glorious painted churches of
the Bukovina, with exteriors entirely covered with Byzantine frescoes in
lapis and rose, the colours still bright after centuries because the artists
had used the techniques of illumination, grinding lapis lazuli itself to
achieve the colour. The passages describing the painted churches in this
book illustrate Sachie's true genius as a critic of the fine arts, his ability
to see the real and relative importance of an object, to make the vital
connection, to encapsulate in a phrase the spirit of a style or period:

> The first view of the painted church of Sucevita is among the most
> impressive revelations of the whole Byzantine world . . . the revelation of
> something entirely new to experience. The Byzantines, at the height of
> their spiritual adventure, had the faculty of presenting a vision of the
> heavenly state.

The impact of Voronet seen in a snow meadow against a dark forest of fir
trees is an apparition of Paradise equivalent to the Monastery of St John
on Patmos, Phira on Santorin, or the monasteries of Meteora, perched on
dolomitic spires, celestial cities poised between earth and sky.

For Sachie, however, perhaps the principal fascination of Roumania
was its people, the incredible ethnic mixtures of the Dobrudja and the
existence of isolated sects like the Skoptzi, or the Gagaoutzes, recon-
verted from Christianity to Mohammedanism in the fifteenth century and
still speaking their own language, unintelligible to the rest of Roumania.
Most of all he loved the gypsies in whom he had taken a passionate
interest since he first saw their camp sites on Eckington Common when
he was a child at Renishaw. He always visited the camp when the Smith
family came round to Weston, and, rather more exotically, the *gitanos* of
Cordoba and Seville. The Spanish gypsies, however, were too well known
not to seem rather tame, having ceased to be nomads and living
domesticated in the whitewashed caves of the Albaicin. For Sachie, the
wild, essential gypsies were the Laetzi of Roumania, dark, long-haired,
arrogant thieves of misleadingly biblical appearance – 'they are thieves
and liars with the look of ascetics who have fallen from grace'. The Laetzi,
whose trade was horsecoping, were, however, only the most interesting of
a population of 285,000 Romanian gypsies divided into four tribes. The
delightfully named Mr C.J. Popp Serbianu, whom Sachie cites as his
authority on the gypsies, alleged that one section, the Netotsi, who
formerly lived in Roumania, had practised cannibalism. Twenty-one
Netotsi and their chief, Kolomon Jona, had been convicted for this crime
in Prague as recently as May 1929.

One other ethnic group in Roumania interested Sachie – the Jews. He was as regrettably anti-Semitic as many of his age and class in Europe at the time, but he found the Jews fascinating as a race. He noted that in Bucharest there was a rich colony of aristocratic Sephardim, still speaking Castilian after an exile from Spain of over 450 years. In contrast, the impoverished Ashkenazi Jews of Bukovina lived in settlements like Hotin, the dreariest and most depressing town in Europe, consisting of two rows of shanties like old seaside bathing-huts, patched with petrol tins and lit with candles stuck in bottles. Every town in Bukovina and Bessarabia had a Jewish quarter; some, like Cernăuţi, were almost entirely Jewish. The small market towns were given a medieval aspect by Jews wearing long black gowns and wide black hats trimmed with red fox fur which they had worn since the fifteenth century, at first because they were obliged to and later as a badge of pride in their race. Sachie described the Ashkenazi Jews of Roumania as 'the most implacably medieval population in Europe'. Ominously, in the closing pages of the book, he touched on 'the Jewish problem'; population pressures and cultural clashes were building up to tension with incomprehension and dislike on both sides.

Roumanian Journey, like Sachie's other travel books, suffered from a complete lack of personal detail and, more importantly from a practical point of view, of maps, which he seems to have thought unnecessary. He focused on his own aesthetic sensations and the sights or customs which interested him to the exclusion of his travelling companions or everyday experiences. To him they were irrelevant and not a part of the artistic whole. People who travelled with him were surprised that he never seemed to take notes. He had a photographic memory and a wide grasp of the source material he would need to write up the things he had seen when he got back. This lack of any kind of mundane detail could make his travel books at times heavy going for their readers, who were perhaps less exclusively interested than he was in the sights and customs of the country.

More human background as far as their own party at least was concerned can be found in Georgia's diaries or in Gertrude's recollections of the trip. Georgia, while carrying on a flirtation if not an affair with Costa, was keeping a wary, slightly huffy weather eye on Sachie and Bridget. In Budapest, while she and Costa bathed in 'enormous swimming pools', Sachie and Bridget went off 'sightseeing or "what you will"'. At Sighisoara in Transylvania they were met by Anne-Marie and taken on a tour of monasteries, convents and churches; at Rucar in Wallachia, staying with Madame Duca, the widow of the former Prime

Minister, they attended a village wedding, dancing until 5 a.m. They had tea with Queen Marie of Roumania at Sinaia. 'She good-looking and catty – digs at British royal family,' Georgia recorded. Sachie also had a two-hour interview with Queen Marie's son, King Carol. They lunched at Anne-Marie's country estate, Manesti, greeted by a blaring band and hordes of servants, and then went on to her huge house in Bucharest. Gertrude was horrified by the feudal squalor in which the Callimachi servants lived in contrast to the magnificence above stairs. The Princess's maid, she said, was ashamed to show her their living quarters where they slept several of them to one room. She herself was served apart from both servants and guests with the same food as Sachie and the Callimachis. There was always loads of caviar, which she hated and did not eat; in the end the butler by mutual consent secreted it away for himself. They left Romania by train on 19 September, travelling home via Poland, where Costa insisted on taking them down a salt mine. 'Hideously boring & generally very frightening subterranean experience,' Georgia wrote. 'All v. cross with Costa about it.'

Sachie travelled back to London with Bridget, leaving Georgia in Paris. According to Georgia's diary, he made a show of reluctance about going back to England without her – 'Very sweet & reluctant. Dreads being bored & says has no plans.' When, however, she arrived back in London, 'it turned out that B[ridget] & Sachie *had* plans after all & he has had a very gay time. . . .' She had a talk with Bridget, discovering that 'Sach is slyer than ever'. They lunched with Osbert, fresh from staying at Balmoral and full of royal stories: 'King's peppery but amiable. Queen an angel. Children utterly charming. O is mad on the Queen,' Georgia noted.

November was a relatively busy month with the publication of *Narrative Pictures* and *La Vie Parisienne*, a delightful little book on the Paris of the 1860s, one of Sachie's favourite periods. That month, following Osbert and Edith, he delivered two Harmsworth Lectures, the first on Palladian England, the second on Cruikshank and nineteenth-century England, which were later published as *Trio*. He was, according to Georgia, 'terribly nervous' and much put off by Robert Byron's tactlessly describing Cyril Connolly's imitation of Osbert lecturing. There was a curiously assorted party at Weston on the 7th – Somerset Maugham, Emerald Cunard, Ashton and Helpmann. Sachie was disappointed when the 'boys', despite dressing up as Greta Garbo and a 'Hansom lady 1880', were too intimidated by Maugham and Emerald to do their usual 'turns'. His fortieth birthday, 15 November, was spent in deep gloom: '. . . both felt very sad about it. Awful for him & he does so hate getting older.' Even more disconcerting than this milestone was the news from Osbert, just back from Montegufoni, that Ginger was threatening to marry a Mrs Durden-Muller after less than six months as a widower. 'Apprehension about his will,' an alarmed Georgia recorded.

In the end, Ginger did not marry Mrs Durden-Muller, but contented himself with the discovery of the traces of a huge twelfth-century tower and was now engaged in searching for the ancient moat. When not indulging his passion for archaeology, he was writing 'terrifying' letters to Sachie about his overdraft. Sachie himself was working hard to get his Roumanian book ready for publication at the end of April 1938. In an effort to drum up funds, he had obtained commissions for articles on his travels from various publications, but he had far too much to do and at least one of them, 'A Palace in Poland: Lazienki, Warsaw', published in *Country Life* in June 1938, was written by Georgia. At the end of February he made a brief trip to Hanover with Francis Bamford to research a projected book on Hanover and the royal family; in Paris on the way back he lunched with Edith, who, as Osbert had told him, was 'going through every kind of hell'. Helen Rootham, Edith wrote to Victor Gollancz, was 'dying in this flat, inch by inch, of cancer of the spine and hip, liver and kidneys. The flat is very small and the sounds one hears are unbearable.' Against all the odds, the wretched Helen was to last another six months. Back at Weston the artist, John Farleigh, came to stay to begin preliminary illustrations of Sachie's primula collection for their joint book on old-fashioned flowers. In May Sachie was in Paris again, staying with Joan and Aly Khan at Maisons Lafitte to deliver his Cruikshank lecture to an audience of '*le tout Paris*' followed by a banquet, extensively reported in the press with laudatory remarks about '*les Sitwells*'. They dined with the Paul Morands and Edith who looked very shaken and gave them harrowing details of Helen's sufferings; Sachie then went on to join Osbert, briefly, at Arles.

The three Sitwells were together again in London in June, when Edith came over for Tchelitchew's exhibition on the 16th, after which Sachie and Georgia resumed their hectic social life. The rows were worse than ever. 'Sach very overtired & we are getting terribly on each other's nerves,' Georgia reported. He had been working hard, financial problems were pressing and he had taken a particular dislike to one of Georgia's most recent admirers, Julian 'Lizzie' Lezard, a South African social charmer and Davis Cup tennis player. Sachie later came to be amused by Lezard, but at this period he was the *casus belli* of some particularly violent rows, usually after Georgia came home late after dancing till the small hours. Costa, too, was much in evidence; on one occasion when she got back from dancing with him at the 400, she found 'Sach awake & in a terrible rage. Had locked me out'; the next day she wrote: 'Sach in awful rage. Decided not to go to Cecil's for week-end. Quarrelled dreadfully.' Despite the rows, Georgia made no attempt to modify her search for fun: 'I think really truly he is *most* unreasonable and unkind. . . .'

Sachie and Georgia, with Reresby, spent August in Tunisia, staying first with Baba Metcalfe at the house she had rented from the photographer, George Hoyningen-Huene, at Hammamet, then with Edwina and Leo d'Erlanger at their extraordinary property at Sidi-Bou-Said. In his next travel book, *Mauretania*, Sachie later described in detail the houses built by the international colony at Hammamet, where posies of jasmine, made up of closely packed buds each mounted on a long pine needle, were given to the guests each evening. This was still the old North Africa. On the beach he saw a local harem bathing, the women, veiled from head to foot in voluminous white draperies, surrounded by their servants holding up white sheets around them, an odd contrast, he noted, to the bronzed bodies to be seen sunbathing on the beaches of the South of France just across the Mediterranean. Khalid, a dashing Arab neighbour of Baba's, took them on expeditions to Berber villages, to see a Bedouin wedding and to cafés where they smoked hashish (although Sachie did not mention this). At Sidi-Bou-Said, twelve miles from Tunis overlooking the plain of Carthage, they stayed at Nejma Ez Zohra, the magnificent villa and gardens created by Leo d'Erlanger's father. Sachie, of course, was re-reading *Salammbô*. 'It was a wonderful experience to be able to read *Salammbô*, in bed, near to a window that looked out on Carthage,' he wrote. 'In the terrific August heat all Flaubert's images struck true. Nothing was exaggerated. Such were the real colours. . . .'[24]

Back in England in September, Sachie went alone to Birr to stay with Bridget and her family. He was there when the Munich crisis erupted and curtailed his holiday to retrieve Reresby from Sandroyd and retreat to Weston, where they found the village poised for an invasion by 250 refugees from London.

Sachie was back in North Africa researching for *Mauretania* only five months later with an attendant harem of Georgia, Baba Metcalfe, who was to take the photographs, and Gertrude. It was a carefully planned expedition, the object of which was not so much to visit northern Morocco, with which Sachie was already familiar, but to see the Sud Marocain, the country south of the Atlas which had only been 'pacified' by French military action as recently as 1934. Sachie and his companions were probably the first English people to visit the area since then. Their tour was subsidised by the Moroccan railways and organised with the co-operation of the French civil and military authorities. It was an ambitious operation; the whole of the Sud Marocain – the Sous, the Dra, the Dades, the Todra and the Tafilalet – was practically unknown to foreigners, having been too dangerous to visit. Sachie was particularly interested in the Berber kasbahs of the south and the oases of the Sahara and planned to extend their trip through the desert to Libya.

It was a curious expedition, very much in the grand manner. Sachie, dressed as usual in a Savile Row suit and accompanied by his train of beautiful women, travelled with a guide in two chauffeur-driven cars loaded with luggage. Baba Metcalfe's fame as Lord Curzon's youngest daughter and a friend of the Windsors had preceded her and at Rabat a Reuter's man interviewed and photographed them. 'He was more interested in Baba than us,' Georgia noted indignantly. As a result, Georgia became rebellious and stood on her dignity: 'S. hysterical with annoyance with me as I insist on having a room of my own & on being counselled about plans & resent being treated as Baba's lady-in-waiting by all & sundry. . . .' At Marrakech the Pasha, El Glaoui, who had entertained the Sitwells in 1928, was 'tremendously interested' to hear that Baba was Curzon's daughter and invited them to a delicious ten-course dinner with an orchestra and dancing girls. Sachie wrote an interesting description of El Glaoui's cuisine, which he thought probably the best to be found anywhere, possibly due to the Pasha's collection of old Persian and Egyptian manuscripts on cookery:

A typical dinner will begin with soup, followed by pastilla, an Arab dish composed of pastry made after the fashion of mille feuilles, and containing eggs, aubergine, and chicken. It comes on a round dish of immense size, divided into four or five portions, and dusted in the centre with fine white sugar with which you should touch your handful before eating. . . . After this come pigeons, stuffed with maize, to which a faint flavour of attar of roses has been given. Next, another and more delicate pastilla. Then chickens with almonds and pistachios. Every time a new dish comes in, it is rushed in, as if to sacrifice, by servitors, the immense wicker hood to the basket in which it is carried serving to keep it piping hot until the last moment. After chicken comes the mechaoui, the famous Arab way of cooking lamb . . . roasted whole, almost as though it were suckling pig . . . followed by other and more subtle things. There are young carrots, of a tenderness which cannot be believed, and after them, a dish of cardoons . . . retaining to a marvellous degree the different quality of their stems and roots in the contrast of that warm, root or heartlike consistency, to the crunching of the stems. Now comes couscous and, eventually, the tenth course, a choice of two sugared sweets, of fritter form, but coiled into snakelike convolutions . . . upon another, previous occasion there were ices made of wood strawberries. . . .

Sachie's description of the huge main square of Marrakech, the Djemaa el Fna, at sunset is one of his most famous pieces of travel-writing:

At five o'clock, over most of the town, if you listen for it, there is a confused murmuring. It is mysterious, like a stirring of the waters, or like something glittering out of a cloud of dust. . . . It never stops. It is gathering and insistent. . . . At every corner the noise comes louder. Now it is a beating and a stamping of many feet: the roar of an enormous multitude. . . . A huge square with, in the middle, as it were a circus ring. A crowd of thousands moves round it, while its inner side, towards the centre, has circle after circle watching, moving on. Over all, hangs a haze of dust. The noise is such you cannot hear a person speak. In a moment you are lost in it. This is the Djemaa el Fna, and there is nothing like it in the world. . . .

There followed sixteen pages describing the swarming crowds in the square, the beggars who could have been created by Bosch, the hereditary snake-charmers, the teenage male Chleuh dancers, the acrobats, the witch-doctors with their pharmacopoeia:

. . . a tray of disgusting objects, concoctions of bat or frog . . . the carcass of a raven looking like a body which had been dragged through a town at the horse's tail, a body in black armour from some Gothic tragedy, half-negroid, half-Macbeth . . . there are dead adders, dead vipers, an owl's wing . . . matted, horrid fragments, the disjecta of the owl's nest, of the vulture's lair, things spurned by bat or spider. . . .

There were the hereditary water-sellers, with their horrible goatskins,

headless and limbless, boned, as it were, but with the stumps blown out and distended, coated with pitch as was done in the amputations of a hundred years ago upon the battlefield, but with the trunk still furred, its black locks reduced by cold within and heat without to a matted and horrible, a greasy or gory, consistency.

Last of all, there were the veiled prostitutes, young, black and extremely pretty, sitting in rows with baked bread loaves in front of them, their pimps or lovers behind. 'No living sight that I have ever seen', Sachie wrote, 'can evoke to such a degree the Arab world of the Caliphate . . . from their white dresses and the thin lawn of their veils comes all the illusion of a thousand years ago. . . .' At Fez, the dyers' quarter evoked images of a recurrent dream he had, of bellowing bull-headed men in a valley attacked by armoured figures.

> It is a peculiar sensation, like a tauromachic dream, to look down into a backyard that could be the cloister of a primitive temple and to see upon the floor two or three bulls' heads with glassy eyes and lolling tongues that lick the dust, their crown of horns toppling and beaten to the ground. . . .

Their first view of a Moroccan kasbah was the fortress of El Glaoui's son at Telouet, then, further to the south, Taroudant with its medieval aspect. Sachie described the 'ghostly insubstantiality' of the Berber kasbahs: 'The walls may be fifty to sixty feet in height; but there is something shadowy and unsubstantial even in their strength. The Kasbahs are, in simile, like a dark face seen upon a dark night. They fade into the air, like the image of Berber Africa that they truly are. . . .' At the oasis of Skoura, he was fascinated by Aiso, the so-called 'ape-Man', discovered some years previously by a Danish doctor and proclaimed as 'the missing link', but subsequently diagnosed as the microcephalic product of hereditary syphilis. Sachie devoted no less than five pages to Aiso, who was equally fascinated by Sachie. A photograph shows Aiso, naked but for a ragged cloth slung over his shoulders, incongruously posed with Sachie, tall, impeccably dressed, bespectacled and now a little chubby-faced, unmistakably English.

Abandoning the French railways representative who had acted as their guide, the two cars and the heavy luggage, they drove on in a large Buick chauffeured by a massive Sicilian, through Algeria to the frontier town of Colomb Bechar, where the 'Compagnie de Discipline' of the Foreign Legion was stationed, 'an assembly of every wild or criminal type in the whole corps'. At the hotel a young panther brought down from the Atlas and chained in the courtyard attacked Baba as she was photographing it, breaking its chain and pushing her to the ground. The panther rated a mention, but not Baba's experience: '. . . in the pretty garden of the hotel, the Sudan was foreshadowed by a young leopard [*sic*] tied up to a tree, which broke its chain,' was all Sachie had to say about the incident. From Colomb Bechar they drove south through the Sahara, towing a luggage carrier with an immense barrel of petrol, long planks and spades to dig them out of the sand should they get stuck, and goatskins of water slung across the bonnet. A feature of this part of the trip were the endless picnics which Sachie hated. He had a phobia about seeing food prepared by Georgia or his friends; even the sight of her making fudge with Reresby's French mademoiselle repelled him. In the desert the women would have to wait until he had disappeared to relieve himself behind a rock before hastily opening the inevitable tin of sardines. Sachie did not enjoy this part of the journey:

> Mile after mile was of a dullness beyond description. There was not even a thorn tree. . . . An incessant wind had arisen too. During luncheon, for which it was impossible to find a scrap of shelter, grains of sand blew into the eternal sardine tins and one's mouth was filled with grit. I used to be fond of sardines but found myself . . . beginning to be given the creeps by their skins and backbones and by their truncated necks. I had descended to eating them with the blade of my pocket-knife and would think, while doing so, of Johannes Brahms, who, according to his biographer, would eat a whole tin of sardines with his fingers and then lift the empty tin to his lips and drink down the oil, this, perhaps, while composing the beautiful Liesbeslieder Waltzer. . . .

None the less, there was the compensation of seeing in the Saharan town of Ghardaia, the Ouled Nail, women from a hill tribe who came down to the towns to earn money as dancers and prostitutes and returned home to marry on the proceeds. They were big, strong and good-looking, with a gypsy insolence, fine eyes and smooth, tawny skin. Sachie saw two beautiful sisters, aged about fourteen or fifteen and recently arrived from the mountains; walking with the others in the street were children of seven or eight, sent as apprentices to learn the trade. 'It is now', Sachie commented, 'a shameful exploitation, from both points of view. The genuine Ouled Nail are few in number and are, at least, most interesting to look at. In the bigger Algerian towns, the worst dancers of Montmartre or Marseille affect to call themselves the Ouled Nail.' From Gabes on the coast, they entered Libya, armed with a letter of introduction to Marshal Italo Balbo, Governor-General of Tripoli, given to Baba by Dino Grandi, the Italian Ambassador in London.

Sachie had by now outgrown his earlier admiration of Mussolini and deeply disapproved of the 'Italianisation' of this Arab African country by the Fascists. At the frontier post he noted with distaste the ugly photographs of Il Duce with jutting 'acromegalic chin, wearing the ugliest of steel helmets' to be seen everywhere and that there was not a word written in Arabic, nor a mention of the native population in the whole place. 'An impression was given that they had been removed wholesale, swept away as bores and as the anachronism of the scene. It was New Rome, New Naples, New Milan, no more dark Africa.' In contrast, en route for Tripoli, they saw at twilight more beautiful reminders of an earlier Italian colonisation, the ruins of Sabratha:

> Pillars of honey-coloured marble stood out against a foam-flecked sea. The coolness and purity of the vision took the breath away. They rose up, in the semi-darkness, out of what appeared to be the rocks of the seashore, only a foot or two above the waves, like a sea architecture borne in upon the coast.

At Tripoli, Marshal Balbo arrived hours late for their meeting and talked until half-past three in the morning. Nevertheless, he charmed Sachie by recognising him; they had met before, it turned out, in Fiume in 1920. He was a man of exuberant vitality, but talked a good deal of Fascist nonsense. The British were decadent: 'The population are not trained, like Italians and Germans, to mechanical warfare. They prefer an easy, unpatriotic life and four big meals a day.' He had evidence of low morale brought him by his secret agents, who told him of the grumbling of the British troops stationed near the Egyptian frontier. 'It was not easy to explain to the Marshal', Sachie wrote, 'that this grumbling is both symptom and prerogative of our race. Where British troops do not grumble the position must be ominous indeed. . . .' Outside the Marshal's offices in the Castello, they were amused by an equestrian statue of Il Duce as protector of Islam, wielding the sword of the Prophet and riding without stirrups, wearing what the sculptor must have imagined to be a farmer's costume in ancient Rome – 'easily the most absurd of modern sculptures,' Sachie commented. In the museum a horrific mosaic pavement from a villa at Zliten depicted gladiatorial combats and the punishment of Christians in the most precise and grisly detail. 'There can be few persons who, after closely looking at this mosaic, will not be given a nightmare,' Sachie wrote.

They travelled to Leptis Magna, the ruined city built by Septimus Severus, splendid in its remoteness. But unpleasant undertones kept creeping in. On the road to Leptis they passed huge labour gangs working on the construction of 'positively enormous' new barracks. Sachie described the extermination by the Italians in 1930–1931 of the Senussi at Cufra, an oasis 600 miles from Tobruk. Not more than a quarter of the population had survived. Village headmen and local sheikhs were taken up in aeroplanes and thrown out, their remains spattering the village square. This 'liquidation' of the Senussi, Sachie wrote, was the first appearance of that picturesque phrase in history: ' "Liquidation" has spread rapidly, to Germany, to Russia, and to Spain; now, at the time of writing (1939), it is being applied to Poland. Like all ugly phrases, which invariably "come back" to their inventors, it may recoil, one day, upon the Italians. . . .' He disliked the less brutal but no less systematic 'Italianisation' of Libya: 'Tripoli and Cyrenaica are only considered as Italy overseas. The natives are neither cared for, nor wanted. Their lands have been taken, and they have been driven into the interior, which the Italians would seem to wish to reduce into a vastly enlarged version of the Aldershot plain. . . .'

It was perhaps with a sense of relief that Sachie and Georgia left Tripoli on 28 March by boat for Palermo destined for Montegufoni. Baba joined them there later to be shown all over the castle by Sir George. 'It is more gloomy, uncomfortable and dilapidated than ever & yet he is working harder than ever at elaborate, expensive restorations,' Georgia noted acidly. Baba was impressed by the deliberate medievalism of the furnishings, which included burnished bronze used as mirrors instead of looking-glass, but all three of them were 'astounded' when at luncheon napkin-rings were on the table, an irredeemably middle-class habit.[25] 'It would have killed Ida,' Georgia commented. On 1 April Reresby and Francis arrived at Montegufoni for Easter. Mussolini invaded Albania causing a state of near panic in the English colony at Florence. Mr Acton and the ex-British Consul, Mr Maclean, caused considerable agitation by advising the Sitwells to leave soon because of the British Government's reaction to the attack on Albania. There was further consternation after lunch at L'Ombrellino, where Violet Trefusis announced that she had had wires from England saying 'Come back at once'. Sleepers were booked for an early return; only Sir George remained calm. 'Ginger thinks us very silly to go & also thinks the disintegration of the British Empire would be a good thing,' Georgia reported. None the less, the Sitwells left by train on 18 April with Bridget, who had arrived from Rome to stay five days previously. On the train they met the Queen of Spain and her daughter, who told them that they had been staying at L'Ombrellino and thought that Mrs Keppel had been bored with their visit and had invented the war scare in order to get rid of them.

Back in England Sachie and Georgia spent the last summer before the war in their usual manner: May at Weston, June and July in London for the Season, staying with friends or in a rented house, going to parties and having rows over Georgia's insatiable passion for nightlife and the continuing presence of Lezard. 'Lizzie' departed for Africa in July, which lightened the conjugal atmosphere. After a night out *à deux* with Edward 'Ed' Stanley at the 400, Georgia's diary read: 'Sachie was cross, as usual when I go out alone at night although I seldom do [!] & although he is always taking people out to lunch. However, his nerves and temper have been much better the last fortnight.' The Sitwells' house party at Weston for the Blenheim ball on 7 July, the last grand occasion of the pre-war Season, was glamorous but unexceptionable – the Aly Khans, Chips Channon and Peter Coats. To many people war by then seemed almost inevitable, lending a poignancy to the spectacle of Vanbrugh's great palace as they drove away at dawn, the floodlights dimmed by the red glow of sunrise.

One thing, however, remained the same, as Georgia was to write in her diary summing up the year 1939: 'Money worries get worse and worse but that Sach & I have always had & always will have whatever happens to the rest of the world.' Seemingly immutable too was Ginger with his financial acumen and obsession with their overdraft. 'Horrible Ginger infestation,' Georgia wrote when Sir George arrived in London at the end of July bringing Reresby with him. Sachie took him to Chips Channon's house in Belgrave Square to see the famous blue-and-silver rococo dining room copied from the Amalienburg by a famous and fabulously expensive decorator. Ginger was 'interested but disapproving', no doubt when told how much it had cost. Channon, who had had the room specially lit with candles for his inspection, was fascinated by 'Sachie's eccentric Renaissance father, who really is a cinquecento character. . . . He arrived looking like Barbarossa or Malatesta and today seemed mild, good-mannered and cheerful but I felt his thin lips and tapping fingers could say and do cruel things. . . .'[26]

On 1 August Ginger came down to Weston. He now insisted on having all his meals in bed, but his brain and his capacity to torment his children had in no way softened. It rained outside while long tedious talks about money took place in the library. 'His attitude is more intolerable than ever,' Georgia reported. 'Also he says that he does not mind lying awake at night as he has no unpleasant thoughts & nothing to reproach himself with when he thinks of the past. That is his character & point of view in a nutshell. . . .' 'Ginger trying to make our lives as disagreeable as possible'

was her entry for the next day, and, two days later, 'Ginger worked Sach &
me up to a point of real frenzy about finances, whether to give up this
house or not etc. Felt desperate.' He departed after a six-day stay leaving
them both 'shattered by [his] visit which has brought home to us all
financial and other difficulties of our lives'. Sachie's next published book,
Old Fashioned Flowers, which was to come out in October, bore a filial
dedication, 'to My Father, in admiration for his essay "On the Making of
Gardens" in 1909'. He had even tried, without success, to interest
Balston in a reissue of Sir George's book. As an attempt, if such it was, to
mollify the old tyrant, it was a failure.

Sachie remained at Weston working on *Mauretania*, while Georgia,
taking the children with her, left for Deauville, to stay, as she thought,
with the Aly Khans. It was a disastrous visit; Georgia, apparently, had
invited herself. When she arrived, she found the Villa Gorizia crowded
out with a 'bewildering and noisy crowd' intent on spending as much time
as possible in the casino. Feeling out of it all, she and the children, with
Francis's nanny, Eileen, retreated to sleep at the Hôtel Normandie next
door. The political news grew worse and worse, her intended flirtation
did not materialise and she lost 300 francs. Nervous and depressed, she
decided to flee back to England, taking Reresby with her but inexplicably
leaving behind the four-year-old Francis and Eileen. Sachie met Georgia
and Reresby at Waterloo on 24 August and told her that Edith was
evacuating that day to Renishaw, but neither he nor Georgia seemed
much concerned about the situation or about Francis still on the other
side of the Channel. Instead of returning home, they went down to stay
with Loelia Westminster at Binfield. No one seemed to know how or
when Francis would be returning. 'Georgia has managed to lose
Francis. . . . Last seen at Deauville,' Osbert wrote exasperatedly to
Christabel on the 30th.[27] Bernard Stevenson, the Sitwells' butler-
chauffeur who had married Gertrude in 1933, telephoned from Weston
to retail a message from Eileen saying that they would be back on
Wednesday, but, just after Sachie left for London to meet them, a wire
arrived at Binfield from Aly Khan announcing that they would be coming
on the *Ile de France* instead. Finally, on the 31st, the news broadcast that all
children would be evacuated from London the following day made Sachie
and Georgia decide to leave for home. They arrived just before midnight
to find that Gertrude and Bernard had begun the black-out and that there
was still no sign of Francis. 'News worse & worse,' Georgia wrote as the
saddle room was prepared as a first-aid station. She telephoned the
manager of an hotel at Southampton for information to be told that the *Ile*

de France had not left Le Havre. It was impossible to telephone France and it was not until the morning of 3 September, the day Britain declared war on Germany, that they received a wire from Eileen confirming that she and Francis were on the *Ile de France* and that it had sailed.

9

Gleams of a Remoter World

1939–1945

'One had to live on one's imagination when there was little to feed it but a diet of horrors. . . .'

Sacheverell Sitwell, 1975

To Sachie, living in suspense under unseasonably blue September skies in the autumn of 1939, at the beginning of almost nine months of 'phoney war', the nightmare of 1914 seemed to have returned. It was not, this time, a question of life or death; he did not have to lie awake listening to the passing of the train carrying an idolised brother to the front as he had at Renishaw in August 1914. Osbert was approaching forty-seven, Sachie forty-two; neither of them was likely to be called upon to fight. Indeed, Sachie had been relieved that summer to hear Jack Aird, Colonel of Grenadiers, assure him that he would not be calling on him to rejoin the regiment and suggest the Ministry of Information as the only reasonable alternative.

Georgia's diary depicts their life at Weston in the early months of the war as tranquil, even idyllic. They had vegetables from the garden and the home farm; Sachie's prized breeds of chickens and bantams produced fresh eggs. They hunted for mushrooms, picked plums and redcurrants in the kitchen garden and wild apples in the fields. In October they harvested and stored apples and pears from the orchard. In mid-September, when something went wrong with the plumbing and there was a water shortage at Weston, they retreated to Renishaw, taking Gertrude with them to visit her family at Eckington. There they found the gardens 'looking lovelier than ever' and Osbert, Edith and David Horner, comfortable but edgy. Horner, according to Georgia, was amiable to them, 'but so pampered lives in lap of luxury'. Edith, whose first experience this was of living in the ménage à trois in which she was to spend a good deal of the rest of her life, confessed to Georgia that she was 'not at all happy' and that Osbert had not been kind to her. At Weston they still had servants; although Bernard was to be called up when the real war started in May 1940, Gertrude performed heroic feats as housekeeper and became an excellent cook. There was a daily help and, for most of the war years, a housemaid, a gardener and, for some of the time, a land-girl to look after Sachie's chickens and pheasants. They had petrol, thanks to Georgia's war work for the county constabulary, and occasional bounty from Renishaw in the form of potatoes or loads of coal.

People who stayed at Weston during the war recorded the magical atmosphere the Sitwells created. For Patrick Leigh Fermor it was an oasis of comfort and amusement. Returning on the outbreak of war from High Moldavia, where he had been writing a book, he had applied to the Irish Guards headquarters in Birdcage Walk only to be informed that they could not take him on for several months. He settled in at the Cavendish Hotel, where Rosa Lewis told him that he could pay whenever he got some money as he was broke and living on the remains of a small legacy from his grandfather. Someone reported his plight to Sachie and Georgia; they immediately wrote inviting him to stay at Weston until the Irish Guards could take him. He spent the last week-end in October and the best part of November there:

It's hard to think of a more marvellous haven [he wrote], especially in such a horrible winter. I used to go for long walks in the rain – toughening up for the Guards Depot, I thought – returning again to blazing fires, drinks, feasting and talk. Days started out with breakfast in a cheery dining room with a handsome portrait of an early nineteenth-century relation, Colonel Hely-Hutchinson, and a picture of Renishaw by Dick Wyndham. Sachie wrote all morning in a room at the top of the house; Georgia was doing some war work, driving somebody's car in a very smart uniform. I reading and scribbling and finishing a translation I had been working on in Rumania.

The house was full of books and pictures and a great charm floated in the air, enhanced by the logs and sometimes a liquid heated in a spoon in the hearth, which gave off a delicious aromatic smell. . . .
Unconventional pictures and books and objects were scattered among the inherited stuff of a country house. Georgia was usually doing some needlework in the evening, stitching away at expanses of canvas. There were chests of beautiful eighteenth-century clothes, miraculously intact and carefully looked after, laid away by Sachie's Heber relations. . . .
Sachie was very fond of a whole row of exotic pheasants in the garden, of which a magnificent Amherst was the simplest. Francis used to entertain us by reciting Edith's 'Madame Mouse-trots', and other

poems. One was summoned to luncheon or dinner by an old musical box in the hall. Delicious food and always lashings to drink. . . .

After dinner there was usually some music in a room upstairs, Sachie in a claret-coloured smoking-jacket. The first I remember hearing were Saint-Saëns and Delibes or Chabrier – he was listening to the latter for some esoteric literary reasons – and, *à propos* of our talks about Transylvania, records of the Hungarian and Rumanian music collected by Bartók and Kodály. The last time I stayed there he was listening to Chopin and other Polish composers, I think impelled by reading Mickiewicz's long poem, 'Pan Tadeusz', in translation, which he passed on to me: marvellous descriptions of Polish and Lithuanian country life, feasting, balls, festivals, mazurkas and crakoviaks. . . . He could become totally – and infectiously – involved in abstruse musical and literary byways. Now and then, knowing that I had a passion for Noël Coward's songs, he, in spite of the general bad blood between Noël Coward and the Sitwells, would ask me to sing some of them, listening, as though it were to some secret and illicit enjoyment, occasionally closing his eyes and tut-tutting at all this anathema, but very intrigued too. I don't think the feelings were as strong as Osbert's and Edith's: but solidarity remained inflexible. I think these heretical songs gave him a sense of sin. . . .

Sachie loved getting people to do their stunts or imitate people he knew. There was an elderly cavalry officer with a walrus moustache called Colonel van der Byl whom he would go over to see just in order to make him give an exhibition of javelin and assegai-throwing on the lawn and say things in Afrikaans and Swahili. He adored strange languages. When I got back from the Caribbean two or three years after the War, he insisted on listening to my fragments spoken or sung of Creole *patois*, the slaves' *lingua franca* in Martinique, Guadeloupe and Haiti, and, above all, the strange Dutch Antillean hybrid jargon from Curaçao, Aruba and Bonaire, called Papiamento. . . . Anything to do with Voodoo incantations and fits of possession were the kind of thing he had a passion for. A lot of his conversation consisted of questioning, darting at high speed from theme to theme, often coming back to earlier ones for further elucidation. But one was repaid by his own reminiscences, always fast, glancing and anecdotal, punctuated by his laugh, his mouth turning up at the corners like a crescent.[1]

Charles Ritchie, a young Canadian diplomat, who first came to stay at Weston in December 1940 and often returned there, wrote that Weston was his favourite house and that he was 'happier with them than with anybody': 'Sachie is sensitive, lovable and very funny – an ageless creature. . . . Georgia sparks all talk with her wit and warmth and looks a young beauty. There is a magic about the place that must be distilled in some mysterious way by Sachie.'[2]

Leigh Fermor was also there for Christmas that year with Gerald Berners, now once again an intimate after his ridiculous quarrel with Georgia early in 1937. He had had a nervous breakdown and left Faringdon for rooms in Wadham College, Oxford. The reconciliation was the result of a meeting between Sachie and Berners after he lunched with Paul Nash and Georgia with Maurice Bowra there in mid-November, 'all gloomy & economizing madly because of war,' Georgia noted. 'Absurdly unnecessary for Gerald.' As Osbert reported to Christabel:

> Gerald really seems to be nuts. Sachie saw him yesterday . . . offered him a cigar, & Gerald refused, saying he 'could not afford it now'. They were sitting on a park bench in Oxford. S. said Gerald's refusal was like a starving man refusing bread & brought tears to the eyes. . . . Finally, after abusing *Georgia* all round the town for 2 years, he asked if he might come & stay for Xmas as a paying guest. . . .[3]

Berners arrived on 23 December, 'depressed but amiable', according to Georgia, bringing armfuls of orchids and a 'gloomily-bound' book by Herbert Spencer entitled *Education, Intellectual, Moral and Physical*, with a sepia photograph of the author on the frontispiece. He spent a good deal of his first morning at Weston skilfully retouching this portrait, adding 'the trace of a glint in the eye, a knowing lift of the eyebrow, the hint of a missing tooth and a leer, till the smug, sanctimonious eminent Victorian became a mask of crookedness and louche connivance with a subtle overall air of tipsiness'.[4] Retouching photographs was one of Berners's favourite stunts – he had had great fun with Cecil Beaton's *Book of Beauty* adding curious features to Beaton's idealised portraits of Society women. John Sparrow arrived for the night on Boxing Day, while Osbert and L.P. Hartley dropped in for the night of the 29th. 'Gerald there, all frowns,' Osbert reported to Christabel, 'but better than he was. He lives in one room at Wadham & does his own cooking; as he says he is so poor. It costs, Sachie says, about 7/– a week.'

On Sachie's birthday in November Georgia had written in her diary: 'Both dread going to London . . . so peaceful here & one can feel one is leading a good & useful life. . . . ' Looking back on 1939 in her diary, she summed up: 'It is strange to think that I have felt far more peace of mind, been less nervy inside & happier, since war began. . . . I feel, however, that it is almost selfish not to be more affected by the war than one is *so far*.'

London had lost much of its attraction for her, as she complained on 30 January 1940: 'No one thinks of anything but war, weather & income tax. . . . My women friends stay in bed or do war work alternately & all the men are in the army.' They had lunched with Emerald for the last time at Grosvenor Square; she was giving up the house that week. They had also had a difficult time with Edith, who had made a tremendous scene about a photograph of them at Weston which had recently been published in the *Sketch*. Taken by Costa at Christmas 1938, it showed Sachie and Georgia, with Loelia Westminster, posed before a blazing fire in the drawing room at Weston: 'Mr and Mrs Sacheverell Sitwell enjoying Christmas with the Duchess of Westminster at their home, Weston Hall.' Costa had, apparently, submitted the photograph to the *Sketch* without telling the Sitwells. It was harmless routine material in the context of 1930s' Society pages, but explosive in a period of black-out and suffering all over Europe. Edith, skilful propagandist as she was, had immediately seen its possible implications.

Her instinct was correct. The *Daily Worker* seized on the *Sketch* photograph as a weapon in the class war; worse still, on 6 February 1940, William Joyce, 'Lord Haw-Haw', picked up the report and made a vitriolic attack on Sachie and Georgia in his nightly propaganda broadcast, pointing them out as an example of how the English leisured classes spent their time while the workers starved or fought on their behalf. There was further annoyance for the Sitwells from the press early in February. A young critic, Hamilton Fyfe, reviewing Edith's recently published *Anthology* for the left-wing Sunday, *Reynolds News*, dismissed them as has-beens. 'Among the literary curiosities of the nineteen-twenties will be the vogue of the Sitwells . . . whose energy and self-assurance pushed them into a position which their merits could not have won,' the young man incautiously wrote. 'Now oblivion has claimed them, and they are remembered with a kindly, if slightly cynical smile.' Edith and Osbert pounced immediately on this slur to their reputation. Philip Frere was telephoned and ordered to consult counsel as to whether or not the passage was libellous; counsel replied that it was. Edith passed this on to Sachie and pressed him to write immediately to Frere telling him that he would join Osbert and Edith in taking action. 'O and I think, & know you will agree, that it is about time that people *paid money* for indulging in malicious lies with the intention of injuring us,' she told him. 'They want a lesson, & money is the only thing that teaches them.'[5] *Reynolds* responded with a paltry offer of settlement – £150 each – which the Sitwells rejected and the case was put down for the High Court in February 1941.

What the Sitwells and their friends called 'the Bore War' came to an abrupt end with Hitler's *blitzkrieg* in the second week of May 1940, catching by surprise, among others, Osbert, who had set out to lecture at the British Council in Florence, got as far as Milan and had to retreat hastily home via Monte Carlo. Bunny Lindsay-Hogg, whom Loelia Westminster had reported at the beginning of the month as happy and 'living like a *ménage*' in Paris with Philby, was, like her parents, trapped in France and made her way with them across the Pyrenees to Lisbon. Reresby was in his first half at Eton and complaining bitterly about it, to Georgia's annoyance. Edith came down to the safety of Weston, where she was to live as a paying guest until August.

The fact that Britain and Germany were at war had made not the least difference to Sir George's plans. He had spent October and part of November 1939 in Venice; by the last week of the month he was back at Montegufoni, penning in his neat spidery hand bulletins about his health and unwelcome financial inquisitions. 'I am sorry to hear you suffer from the cold. Can't you shut up half the house? In the Colonel's [Hely-Hutchinson's] time there were five children in it,' he had written to Georgia on 26 November 1939.[6] His one genuine affection was for his grandchildren; he willingly, but not without careful queries, paid for Reresby's doctor's or dentist's bills, and sent little presents to Francis, most recently an album of Venetian views, which seems a curious present for a child of five but was no doubt intended to awaken in him the family passion for Italian architecture. He spent the depth of winter at the Blue Nuns' nursing home in Fiesole, a favourite retreat, and planned to be back in Montegufoni in mid-April, where Osbert had intended to join him. Hitler did, however, succeed in interrupting the steady flow of Sir George's correspondence, allowing his children a respite.

War seemed now to be closing in even on Weston. At the beginning of June, amid invasion rumours after the evacuation of Dunkirk by the British Expeditionary Force, Sachie found himself attending shooting lessons at Wappenham in the company of the local village boys. He had been dreading the possibility of being forced to take a 'war job' since February, when an officious lady had invited herself to Weston and suggested that she might be able to get him one through a brother in the Foreign Office. He wanted to be left alone to get on with his work; he saw quite clearly the futility of employing him in any military post and was terrified at the thought that he might be uprooted from Weston and deposited in some soulless Ministry. 'That woman will get us out of here in the end,' he told Georgia furiously. When he found himself

manoeuvred into a job as adjutant to the general commanding the local
Home Guard, then called the Local Defence Volunteers, he was
absolutely horrified. 'It brought back to me the sensation of my
inadequacies as a soldier the first time round,' he wrote. He detested the
whole thing: the graceless, scratchy uniform (Gertrude was always
deployed to put on his gaiters before he went Home Guarding), the
weekly training sessions, the discomfort of sleepless nights spent lying in
wet ditches on pointless manœuvres at week-ends, and, almost most of
all, the sham military talk and the socialising. At Home Guard dances
he would stand there looking 'utterly miserable'. The Sitwell tradition,
handed down from the First World War, was the reverse of jingoistic.

On 14 June Gerald Berners telephoned, 'as he always does when the
news is really bad,' Georgia noted, to tell them that Paris was in the hands
of the Germans. Sachie attended his first meeting of the Local Defence
Volunteers. Berners came over the next day to advise the immediate
evacuation of the children to Canada; on the 17th the news that France
was to make peace with Germany decided Georgia to send Francis to be
looked after by her aunt in Canada and, on the 25th, she saw him off at
Liverpool with Eileen. Despite the urgings of the Canadian aunt, they
decided 'from the "feudal" point of view', as Georgia put it, not to send
Reresby, the Sitwell heir, as 'it would look like running away'. Bernard left
to join the army – 'v. strange without Bernard but think we shall manage
with electric hot-plate plus Gertie's wonderful energy & good temper,'
Georgia commented – and in July a replacement named Benet arrived.
War or no war, Edith ordered a special dinner of smoked salmon and duck
for Georgia's thirty-fifth birthday on 8 July, while Sachie provided pink
champagne. A new fan of Edith's, Alec Guinness, described by Georgia
as 'a young Shakespearean actor', came to stay – 'he and Edith read poetry
together and talk about it all the time'. On 6 August Edith departed for
Renishaw, having arranged a gala dinner to celebrate her last night – 'so
generous and unpractical,' Georgia remarked.

As the Battle of Britain raged, the Home Guard took up more of
Sachie's time, to his utter disgust. He was bounced into an official post by
a Captain Meredith, who 'wheeled Sach off to see General Allison [who]
announced that Sach was to become his adjutant in command of the local
battalion. Sach was too surprised to refuse,' Georgia reported. Dick
Wyndham, whom they had not seen for a long time, arrived in uniform; he
was now a major and second-in-command in his area. Patrick Leigh
Fermor also came to stay, having obtained his commission but still
wearing a cadet's uniform. Despite these military examples on the part of

his friends, Sachie's wails about the Home Guard grew louder. 'Sachie in despair about Home Guard,' Georgia noted on 21 August. Leigh Fermor and Georgia drove him to Brackley for his first day's work with General Allison and sat waiting for him in a pub, drinking sherry and reading the newspapers. When Sachie turned up, he was 'wild with irritation about HG'. After some Home Guard manoeuvres in October 1940 he told Osbert, 'Yesterday (from a military point of view) was the worst horror I have known since I was 21. One day I shall murder some superior officer in uniform.'[7]

For Sachie, the true horror of war was not the fighting, or even the dying (although, among his close friends, Robert Byron and Rex Whistler were to die on active service),[8] but the destruction of European cities, works of art and ways of life which had evolved over the centuries since the fall of the Roman Empire. He told Charles Ritchie in December that he thought it was 'all up with Europe, its culture and vitality exhausted'. Cut off from Europe and isolated in his Northamptonshire village, he returned to his original primary sources, his imagination and the British Museum. The war years, uninterrupted by travel or by prolonged visits to London for the Season, were his most productive in what he considered to be his major works. Travel books were out of the question; with the increasing paper shortage he was no longer besieged by periodicals with requests for articles. He concentrated on subjects which particularly interested him, which could be worked up by reading in the British Museum or the London Library.

The first of these was *Poltergeists*, published in July 1940, for which he had been gathering material over the last two years. It was the result of delighted burrowings in the British Museum, where Angus Wilson, once a desk assistant, observed that Sachie always took out the most interesting books. It was a highly suitable subject for a Sitwell with first-hand experience of the malevolence of the spirit world; the book began with his Aunt Florence's account of a haunting at Weston and included a poem on a poltergeist manifestation by Edith, 'The Drum'. No Renishaw ghosts were mentioned. *Poltergeists* was not a book of ghost stories but a compilation of reputable evidence of manifestations over the centuries. Sachie's view was that the phenomena were due to human trickery, conscious or unconscious, linked with sexual hysteria and in some cases with witchcraft, involving as it did auto-suggestion and hallucinatory drugs. According to him, the composition of witches' flying ointment with which they rubbed themselves before mounting their broomsticks was now known to have included drugs which would give a sleeping person the sensation of flying. He instanced strange, pagan folk survivals, the remains of pre-Christian fertility worship, such as the Haxeyhood from the Isle of Axholme in Lincolnshire. He had a real talent for flesh-creeping Gothic horror in such introductory passages as this:

> This is the strata from which such emanations rise. They come from the underworld, from caverns or cesspools covered up or hidden. These things creep underground; they are blind like the mole, sightless and pale from their imprisonment, with long rodent fingers, cold and as a dead man's hand. Yet all these monsters live within ourselves. Faiths and religions fall out of the skies and keep, grave deep, in shallows of the sands. They were never more than the motes and chains that float before the eyes. The true underworld, the miasma of the mind and soul is the heaven or hell where nothing ever dies. Every religion, and all superstition, serve one another and are sealed in compact. . . .
>
> All fanaticism, all magic formula [sic], are but a part, small beyond infinity, of the subterranean world. Wherever there is mystery we have made excuses, and, since all is mysterious, the underworld is all legend and no facts. But, as well, there is a meaning. The little details have a theme, or pattern. The abracadabra spells into real words. They are in memory of something and have been worn into their jargon. And those who used them have, on purpose, made it worse. Such are the hands that make a haunted place more frightening. This is the renegade soul, armed against itself. . . .

Sachie chose accounts of manifestations like 'The Epworth Phenomena', recorded by John Wesley and his family; 'The Drummer of Tedworth', reprinted from *Saducismus Triumphatus* (1682), written by the Rev. Joseph Glanvil; and 'Report on the Enniscorthy, Derrygonnelly, and other Poltergeist cases' by Sir William Barrett, FRS (the latter containing one of Sachie's favourites, 'Jeff', the talking mongoose of Cashen's Gap, Isle of Man). Sachie himself was frightened of the dark; hardly surprising in a child brought up at Renishaw. Even at Weston, haunted only occasionally by the rustling silk skirts and tapping high heels of the eighteenth-century Miss Heber, he would not sleep alone in the house at night, insisting, if Georgia was away, on either Gertrude or Bernard sleeping in the next-door room. It was not difficult for him to conjure up the dark fanaticism of seventeenth-century Salem or the loneliness of a haunted mill in which a particularly horrible Victorian murder had occurred.

George Orwell reviewed *Poltergeists* favourably in the September 1940 issue of *Horizon*. Like Sachie he took the subject seriously: 'Ghosts are completely uninteresting but the aberrations of the human mind are not . . . the poltergeist, so long accepted as a real ghost or laughed at as an old wives' story . . . is probably neither, but a rare and interesting form of insanity.' He even wrote to Sachie (whom he had never met) to tell him how intrigued he had been by the book, which had reminded him of an experience he himself had had. While out walking at Walberswick in Suffolk, he had found under a gorse bush a cardboard box containing a miniature room with furniture and 'tiny female garments, including underclothes':

> I have often puzzled over the incident since, and always with the feeling that there was something vaguely unwholesome in the appearance of the little room and the clothes. Then in your book you linked up the doll-dressing impulse in girls with definite mental aberration, and it struck me that this affair had a sort of bearing on the subject.[9]

To Sachie, the war made the pursuit of his cultural pilgrimage in search of all that was beautiful and curious in the world, his 'entertainments of the imagination', even more important to him, as he explained in the 'Preludio' to *Sacred and Profane Love* which he had begun in 1937 and published in November 1940:

> This is written in the dark days, when there is evil in the air. No one knows which way to turn, or what to work for. . . . The mental and spiritual horizon has come as near to our eyes as on an evening of thick fog or mist. . . . Nothing can last, or is secure from destruction. Only the head and heart, the brain and the bloodstream can survive in this tempest. . . . It is the human head and the human heart that are exiled now, and must build for themselves pavilions . . . in the new world of tomorrow. For knowledge can be taught, while feeling is bred in the heart and does not die with death. Both things are immortal. War or tyranny but force them into flower.

Sachie's response was to set out a dazzling panorama of human experience, turning out a cornucopia of his wide-ranging knowledge and interests: gypsies, monks and nuns, convent kitchens and pharmacies and their curious and delicious products, the *fondouks* of Atlantic Africa, the horrific backyard bullfights and *mataderos* of Buenos Aires, the hideous punishment of a slave in Surinam or the unique technique of Jacques Callot's woodcuts. He had long planned, he wrote, a history and handbook of beggars, tracing their line of learned arrogance and insolent idleness from Diogenes's response to Alexander when he stood before the philosopher's tub and asked him if there was anything in the world he could do to please him – 'Get out of my sunlight' – and the 'tramp/beggar physiognomy' from Socrates and the Centaurs down to Verlaine and, curiously, to the snub-nosed Pavlovsk Guards 'instituted by the insane Czar Paul I, and confined to men with snub noses like their master, which portion of the old Russian Imperial Guard continued, with that restriction, until 1917'. His pages on Venice, which he, in the era before mass tourism, saw at its most essential, oriental and ethereal on a hot August morning, are some of the most evocative and perceptive ever written about the city.

Sacred and Profane Love is one of Sachie's most fascinating and revealing books, recapping his literary and sexual career over the past twenty-five years. It is dedicated to Osbert in a specifically limited frame of time: 'To my brother, greatest of spiritual companions 1916–1919'. But Book IV, headed 'Autobiographia Literaria', begins with a profound homage to Edith, 'the strong presence or personality who urged me into creation'. 'Perhaps there can never have been,' he added, 'among women, a more instinctive understanding for poetry, or a physical genius for its creation more compound of poetry itself, or more transcendent in the degree of its selection and separation from the dross of living. It was under the influence of this extraordinary being that I first knew the intoxication of poetry. . . .' He then went on to his own career:

> Before long, I was fairly living in the world of my own discovering. . . .
> My affinity, because of my youth of poetry, is more with architecture or
> with music than with . . . the world of fiction. . . . The creation of a
> personal world of choice has engrossed all my efforts since I was old
> enough to know my own direction . . . my creation has grown with me. It
> is now a world of living persons. . . . One is a living being and must be
> allowed those personal obsessions that work more strongly upon the
> heart than any feat of learning. . . .

He reverted, again, to the three women who obsessed him, first to a sensuous evocation of Bridget, with her provocative, full lower lip, hazel eyes, fair hair and smoky vellum skin, and her 'body of a savage', a combination of male and female proportions – the 'long stem of her neck, with the unreal attenuation of her waist swelling into her lyrelike hips, her masculine shoulders, her long feline back, her thighs, and her legs that had the muscles of a male dancer'. 'It was her temperament to be taken in a storm,' he wrote, 'or lazy and sulky, pretending not to care, in revenge, perhaps, for some failure with another. Her slow and casual fire, in its results ... was of a strength that had no precedent.' Then there was Georgia, with her New World vitality and refinement of bone, her wide-spaced, hazel-green eyes and Creole skin, 'generous, unselfish, accom-modating'. Last of all there was Pearl and her physical perfection, haunting him still although she was now married and living on the other side of the world.

Georgia's comment on reading the proofs of *Sacred and Profane Love* was simply 'beautiful but difficult for me to concentrate on'. Nowadays she often helped with the proofreading; her reactions in her diary were, however, limited to her hopes for the sales of a book or the number of mistakes in the galleys. The large sections of both *Dance of the Quick and the Dead* and *Sacred and Profane Love* dealing with Bridget, Pearl and herself, seem to have provoked no reaction in her.

Bridget was still Sachie's 'other woman'. During the last pre-war years, as Georgia's frenetic social excitement reached its rather unhappy climax, she and Sachie had continued to see each other, usually in London. In the late summer of 1938, when Bridget was staying with Maxine Elliott at the Château de l'Horizon in the South of France, there had been endless complications about plans. On 6 September she had written to Sachie telling him that, typically, she had failed to get a place on the train so that she would not be in London until Saturday evening:

It would be heavenly to find you in London but week-ends there are so grim at this time of yr. that if you have anything else to do & don't come up till Monday I shall more than understand. If, however, you are intending to be there, do let's go to the Ballet Club that night, & of course Monday, Tuesday, & Wednesday too. ... Longing to see you again.[10]

In February 1939, when Sachie was on his Mauretanian tour, she wrote to him at Biskra in Algeria: 'I am not at all resigned to not being with you. ... I do hope that you do realise more and more what a poor substitute the Lady Baba is for me. ...'[11] Like 'the Lady Baba', she too planned to be in Rome at Easter when Sachie was to be at Montegufoni. On 3 April she had written from her stepfather's Shropshire estate, Monk Hopton, near Bridgnorth, to Sachie care of the Sitwell *poste restante* in Florence, the Agenzia Edgidi, suggesting that he should come down to Rome and motor up to Tuscany with her, a romantic but, for him, inconvenient idea. 'You always complain that I never suggest any delectable plans,' she wrote. 'I consider that this one is superior to anything that you have ever suggested & it only remains for you to find it impossible. . . . Do try & arrange that we meet somewhere. . . .' At midsummer, she was making plans to go away with Sachie while Georgia was occupied with Ascot parties with the Aly Khans. Writing from her mother's house, Abbey Leix, in the south of Ireland, she told him that she would be in London on Sunday night and would meet him for lunch or in the afternoon on Monday – 'During the week we might go to Suffolk or Cambridge or both, as I imagine Georgia will be gracing Ascot.'

Gradually, however, Sachie, totally absorbed in his work at Weston, became less and less assiduous; Bridget, always contrary, consequently became all the keener. On 15 March 1940 she wrote from the Langham Hotel in London, afraid that after all they would miss seeing each other and angry that during the three weeks she had been there he had neither bothered to come up to see her nor even telephoned. She stayed at Weston only twice that year, in January and in May. In October she wrote to him from Monk Hopton, where she was working in a canteen, suggesting a meeting in London – 'If we stayed at the same Hotel we would both have company for the long, noisy evenings [the Blitz was still on].'[12] Sachie, however, did not appear, for on the 26th she wrote saying how disappointed she had been not to see him. By November, however, she was really angry with him:

Dearest Sachie

I am feeling somewhat discouraged that you don't think me comprehending enough to be told that you don't think it worthwhile to come to London for a few hours on the chances of seeing me, and that anyhow your train would probably be so late that we wouldn't meet, and it would all be pointless. This would most likely be the result, and I only make the suggestion on the chance that you might be coming up on your own and we could make a vague plan. Instead you take refuge behind a smokescreen of financial stringency and this excuse becomes remarkably transparent when in the same letter you mention week-ends at Dychley [sic] and Cambridge. I should have thought your tips would have been as much as a day ticket to London. . . . Incidentally now that I am being governessy I wish to say that when I visit you on my way to London it costs me double as I have to use another railway and can only take a return ticket from here [Bridgnorth] to Banbury. However, money is no object to me, but just at present I can't be away for more than a couple of days. I would very much like to see you again but hope that before I do your line in excuses will have been improved by contact with the glamorous Mrs Tree [at Ditchley] and the animated Lady Beit [a guest at Weston]. Anyhow in this case there was no point at all in spinning me a yarn when the truth would have filled the bill so nicely and it is very irritating to be treated in such an artificial way. So please stop it. . . . [13]

The war, however, was a great divider for those who did not live and work in London. While Sachie was at Weston, Bridget was pinned down in various parts of the country, either at Bridgnorth or at Bletchley, doing war work; in June 1942 Sachie told her brother, Michael Rosse, that he had not seen her for a year (this was not quite true as Georgia registered in her diary for 19 November 1941 that Sachie had been out with Bridget in London), and it seems not to have been until 1945, when Bridget had a flat in Mount Street and was permanently based in London, that they managed to restart their relationship.

August 1940 was spent at Weston, with Georgia driving Sachie in to Brackley, their local town, for his Home Guard duties every day. At the end of the month they went to Renishaw. It was peaceful despite air-raid warnings and at night noises of bombing raids on Sheffield nearby. Only Osbert and Edith were there, David Horner having joined the RAF. They went for walks in Eckington Woods with Osbert and in the evening Edith read them extracts from her new poems. Even at Weston, when they returned early in September, the war was encroaching more and more. There was a parachute alarm at Weston and Sachie was deputed to escort a one-eyed major in the Home Guard, a veteran of the last war, to give a lecture on house-to-house fighting in Brackley. The Blitz began in London and, at the end of the month, Anne-Marie Callimachi came down; she was to be there on and off as a paying guest for the next six months. 'We sheltered here,' Georgia wrote later in her summing up of 1940, 'listening to the distant Blitz which sometimes seemed to come very near & the echoes of which were always horrifying.' On 14 November, the day before Sachie's birthday, news came from Roumania of the destruction of Anne-Marie's property, and that night they lay awake listening to the noise of aeroplanes, the windows shaking from distant explosions – it was the night of the great German bombing of Coventry.

There were the usual worries about money, exacerbated by the war. The fact that Ginger was now in enemy territory meant that there was no money in the estate account or for Reresby's school fees. Georgia, too, was having problems with the payment of her allowance from her parents, who were now back in Canada. It had been a relief to hear via Osbert in

September that a letterr from Sir George had arrived at Coutts Bank instructing them to continue payments to Sachie. The problem of Sachie's debt mountain, however, remained and on 23 October Philip Frere came down for a business talk. He succeeded in reducing Sachie's debt by the simple, if dangerous, expedient of borrowing from Coutts, as Georgia reported on 15 December:

> Sach has now paid nearly all debts with money borrowed from Coutts who have insisted on this being the last penny lent & have taken almost all capital & forced payment of our huge overdraft so now we are reduced to a fixed sum per month & not allowed to spend a penny more. Sach's total income apart from earnings on books is now down to £900 pa. . . . God knows what will happen if I don't get my allowance. Money situation is very worrying but at last we know where we are & don't owe anything – first time in our lives.

In the midst of all this there was a slight dust-up with Osbert over Long Itchington, always a bone of contention. On this occasion, according to Georgia, 'Osbert rang up and wanted to stampede us into consent to immediate lease of Long Itchington with our furniture. He gets 250 pa and offers us only 20. Mean and tiresome.' Sachie wrote Osbert a hurt letter:

> I wish, darling, you wouldn't stampede me quite so much over Long Itchington. Do remember that being in midst of a terrible financial crisis, neither of us able to draw cheques, having lost (or overspent) all our capital etc: etc: the value of this furniture, even if only £300, is very important to us – just as the rent of £250 is very important to you.
>
> You know well that I would *always* do as you want, and you ought to appreciate this more than you do. You must not become utterly hard and ruthless and stampede without allowing a moment's mercy to anyone else. Surely Father should be an example to us both *not* to do this.
>
> I had rather a boring experience of Long Itch: only 2 years ago, when stampeded in the other direction *out* of the house at about 12 hours' notice, and the whole thing, after all, was a fiasco. And only six weeks ago I found you perfectly good tenants who would have paid you £250 for the war, only to be told that you were moving your furniture there and wanted the house for yourself.

He ended, with a little dig: 'I am wondering now whether, after all, the furniture is as valuable as Aunt Floss's diary?'[14]

Osbert replied by return taking a Sitwellian high tone:

Your letter has just reached me and I return it to you directly, as I am sure on reflection you will regret having sent it.

I won't enter into the charges you make (unless you really want me to do so) except to say that several leases were lost in earlier days because of your wish to keep the furniture in Long Itch, and that I have paid the whole upkeep the whole time. I really *did* mean to live there . . . but various *reasons* (threats of billeting bombed children . . . & military [here]) made me change my mind. I *am* moving my [London] furniture there. It arrives tomorrow.

I was afraid you would make that remark about Floss's diary. But, incidentally, with the papers you have at Weston, you could make a great deal of money – only *without* Francis Bamford. You want them edited in a different way, and I could certainly show you how to do it.

I know only too well how financial worries affect us all: only don't insult and quarrell [*sic*] with people who love you very dearly. . . .[15]

In response, however, to a 'dear letter' from Sachie in reply, Osbert climbed down, claiming busyness, forgetfulness and worries about keeping Renishaw out of the hands of the billeting officers, which he had so far managed to do by housing eleven children and two mothers in one of the cottages. Most of the problems between them over this, he attributed, probably correctly, to the difficulty of getting through on the telephone in wartime. The row simmered down as quickly as it had boiled up, but the potential for trouble was always there with the autocratic instincts of Osbert, elder brother and lord of Renishaw, on the one hand, and the resentments, sensibilities and perennial financial worries of Sachie on the other.

Worrying news about their father came from the continent early in November via Bernard Woog, a Swiss bank manager married to Olga Chandos-Pole, daughter of Derbyshire neighbours of the Sitwells. In November Woog cabled that Sir George was dying at Fiesole. He had had two blood transfusions but his condition had not improved and the haemorrhaging was continuing. Sachie's reactions are unrecorded; Georgia reported it without comment in her diary; but Osbert, despite the years of hostility towards his father, felt moved enough to write what turned out to be a premature obituary of the Baronet, listing Sir George's achievements – 'outside his children' – as: 'the revival of formal gardening, the new understanding of Heraldry, as an *art* & as a science. And, thirdly, his revival of *modern* printing founded on late 17th century models. (He had his own printing press for 40 years.) For all these he is revered in the technical world to which these belong. . . .'[16] By the end of the month, however, Sir George was better, as Osbert wrote to Sachie in a letter full of praise of *Sacred and Profane Love*, and complaints about the jingoistic talk about 'morale': 'I suppose when Winston says we will go on fighting, even if every house in Gt. Britain is flat with the ground, he really means it.' He had had another cable from 'the egregious Woog, our foster-brother, saying "Father out of danger but still nervous about [him]" '.[17]

The three Sitwells were publicly united again in February 1941 in their libel case against *Reynolds News*. Called as witnesses to their own literary reputations, they were supported by the evidence of Arthur Waley, Charles Morgan and Hugh Walpole among others. After a certain amount of disagreeable questioning by defending counsel, whom Edith described variously as 'an insect' and a 'bison', they were awarded £350 each with costs. Sachie, despite his financial troubles, went straight out and spent the money on a celebratory lunch at the Ritz and a peridot ring for Georgia.

That month Sachie, who, on the retirement of General Allison, had succeeded in resigning as adjutant, was, to his dismay, made a second lieutenant in charge of a local platoon at Wappenham. At a Home Guard review later that year, taken by Lord Bridgeman, he was obliged to march past and salute with his men, his expression of misery such that Georgia did not know whether to laugh or cry – 'poor darling, he does so hate this sort of thing'. The formation of the Authors' National Committee had agitated both Osbert and Sachie, since its object was 'to urge on the Government the fuller use of authors in connexion with the war effort'. Denys Kilham Roberts, a member of the committee, wrote to Osbert in February 1941 reassuring him as to the scope of the plans of the Minister of Labour, Ernest Bevin:

> I don't think that there are any real grounds for apprehension that Bevin's scheme will be operated with so little discretion that authors of your brother's eminence will have their pens snatched from them so that they can be used as unskilled labourers in the fields, factories or pits. . . . I do think, however, that Bevin has probably no intention of letting intellectuals off altogether, and that while they are likely to be spared such jobs as those mentioned, some of them may get landed with something almost as uncongenial, and on the whole . . . it might not be a bad idea for your brother to establish provisional contact with any people he happens to know who are at present officials at the Ministry

of Information or at one of the other Ministries which has a use for authors as authors.[18]

In the event, those responsible at the Ministry of Information must have realised that Sachie's style was singularly ill-suited to the writing of propaganda and, in the end, his only war contacts were to be with the Admiralty, where his knowledge of Mauretania was apparently considered useful in the planning of North African operations. In February the following year, he was given some experience of escorting a convoy. After a lavish farewell lunch in his honour given by Bendor Westminster, who now, according to Georgia, 'dotes on him these days more than ever', he left for Portsmouth, reappearing again to join Georgia at Claridge's on 8 February 1942, 'having had very exciting and interesting time. Adored the naval officers & men, never sick although it was wildly rough. Plenty of good food & drink. Little sleep, did not take off clothes or Mae West.' Despite this, Sachie had, apparently, decided against completing the return journey aboard a merchant ship. 'Couldn't face boredom or lack of clean clothes on merchant ships which the return journey would have involved,' Georgia reported of the reluctant warrior.

Sachie took refuge from the war in his work and in correspondence on subjects which interested him. He particularly enjoyed his correspondence with the Rev. Montague Summers, an expert on poltergeists and Satanism, whose work he had used in his own book and who had pointed out to him a story about 'the Fire Insurance Poltergeist'. Principally, however, he and Summers wrote to each other about pre-war delights. In the dark days of 1942 Sachie liked to recall the baroque churches of Naples, Tiepolo's ceiling at the Madonna del Rosario, which had 'enraptured' him aged twenty, the happy days spent with Osbert in Toledo and the huge excitement of coming upon uncatalogued El Grecos. Summers wrote to him with queries about a painter who introduced mother of pearl into his canvases; Sachie remembered seeing something of the kind in Carlos IV's *Casita del Principe* in the grounds of the Escorial, where there were 'several perspective pieces, in the best Bibiena style, made of *rice*! grains of rice, and, also, a sort of rice paste, cut into immense arches and vistas; and, absurd as they may sound, they are beautiful and fantastic in their way. . . .'[19] This gave him an excuse to go off on various fascinating tangents. '. . . I liked Pollock's shop more than anything of the sort I have ever seen, except, perhaps, one or two old pharmacies in monasteries in Italy. . . . Forgive this digression,' he continued, 'but it is a relief to write about these things. . . .'

Perhaps his favourite correspondent was Violet Gordon Woodhouse, an old friend of his and Osbert's from Carlyle Square days, whose playing of the harpsichord and the clavichord had revealed to both of them ' a new world of musical beauty'. Sachie was enchanted by her and by her talent; one of his great delights of the war years was listening to her play at her flat in Mount Street or at beautiful Nether Lypiatt Manor in Gloucestershire. In April 1943 Violet invited George Bernard Shaw to hear her play in Mount Street, suggesting that he should come on a day when Sachie would be there. Shaw replied with one of his postcards: 'Sachie and the clavichord would do me nicely.' 'Your playing was too beautiful and poetical for words,' Sachie wrote to her after another occasion later that year. 'I have never known such a sensation, and can think of nothing else. In the middle of the night, when I am awake, I can remember every note of the Scarlatti pieces . . . and only hope I can "fix" it, so as to remember them in the day. . . . I can't get over the beauty of the Dowland also,' he added. 'How wonderful to get away from the piano altogether into another world.'[20] He urged her to learn more Scarlatti pieces so that he could hear her play them. 'Do please do this,' he wrote to her on 25 February 1944. 'It is the only thing I can think of that interests me: everything else is so deadly, now.'

He had enjoyed writing the successor to *La Vie Parisienne, Valse des Fleurs*, a light-hearted fantasy, expressing nostalgia for a world which he had never known and a place which he had in fact never visited. Inspired by a Tchaikovsky waltz, it was an imagined account of a day in St Petersburg in January 1868, followed by a ball at the Winter Palace. He had written it over two months, February and March 1941; it was published, with fortunate timing, in July, a few weeks after Hitler's invasion concentrated everyone's attention on Russia, and quickly went into a second impression. He had also been working on *Primitive Scenes and Festivals*, which he completed in just under a year between September 1940 and August 1941 and published in February 1942. It was a disappointing book, a slapdash, rambling, self-indulgent re-hash of previous themes – primitive kings and queens, sacrifices, burial rituals and so on, inspired by the Mycenean gold cups of Vaphio, which he had already used in *Canons of Giant Art*, and Crimean works of art in the Hermitage (which he had never seen). There was a good deal about pigeons, one of his recent interests. 'The Scotch Pouter fancy, it has been written, was built almost entirely out of the scattered and ruined lofts of the impoverished Spitalfields weavers,' Sachie noted airily. He revelled in their names, colours and peculiarities: 'Almond Tumblers, whole feathered Tumblers, long-faced Tumblers, Rollers, Mad Tumblers, Tipplers, Twizzlers, Baldheads and Beards, Oriental Frills, Scandaroons and Barbs, Pygmy Pouters, Dutch Croppers, Brunner Pouters from Moravia. . . .' The list, covering pages of text, reeled on from a passage about the oracle of Dodona, allegedly founded by a dove.

At Weston, meanwhile, Georgia had found an unlikely romantic interest in her wartime boss, the Chief Constable, Captain R.H.D. Bolton, referred to by the Sitwell circle as 'the Cop' but by Georgia in the privacy of her diary as 'Bertie'. 'The Cop' was completely unlike Georgia's usual men friends from smart society, which may have been his attraction. He was married, with a son near Reresby's age, but otherwise he was the complete opposite of Sachie, who found his company tedious. 'The Cop' came into Georgia's life in November 1941 at a time when she was finding Sachie difficult. 'Sach fussing madly about whether he will be conscripted, whether to take job at Admiralty if it materializes. . . . Felt quite distracted. Back to our old form of years ago which is seldom so harassing now but now & then ——!' On the 29th Captain Bolton came to dinner; Georgia's first reaction was not favourable: 'the C.C. turns out to be a cracking snob & slightly a bounder'. Within a few days, however, she had changed her opinion while he was obviously in love with her. While Sachie went off on week-end Home Guard manoeuvres, the Chief Constable courted her assiduously. 'Capt. Bolton lunched with me. Drove to Wellingborough & Kettering doing 5th column stuff, trying to catch out the police, great fun. . . . I loved my day & think him one of the nicest men I've ever known & I no longer couldn't care less about him.' In London he acted as her chauffeur, taking her to meet his best friend and his sister-in-law at the Army & Navy Club – 'a new world which took me out of myself. Great fun.' He even fetched her from the dentist's. They met again after she had dined with a new friend of the Sitwells, C.W. 'Billy' McCann, introduced to them by Anne-Marie; at 12.45 he took her back to Claridge's, where she was staying, and then rang to say good-night at 2.30. She saw a good deal of him while in London, he telling her about his life and his career in the police. They drove slowly back to Northampton: 'Sad these last strange hectic happy days are over. Home at 7.30. Sach well, very sweet, not very nervy & only "un peu soupçonneux".' There were more trips to London; then he spent New Year's Eve at Weston. Peggy Dunne, a great friend, who owned Chadshunt nearby, was there for the night; Toby Waddington and Tony Rosslyn, who were stationed locally, also came to dinner. They saw the New Year in with rum punch made by Gertrude and afterwards went to the Home Guard dance in the village hall. 'Sach of course refused to go. A *very* nice time was had by all,' Georgia recorded, although she was honest enough to admit, 'I think no one really likes Cop but me & I do more & more.'

'The Cop' loomed large in her summing-up of 1941:

> The Libel Action, successfully fought, the diminishing Blitz & perhaps a
> little too much of Anne-Marie were the opening features of 1941. . . .
> Life here was humdrum for which one was consciously grateful. Then
> in the autumn came Daddy's illness [Georgia had agonised whether to
> go to Canada or not and, in the end, had decided against it] . . . then,
> just when I was feeling too sad and 'désoeuvrée' for words, 'the Cop'
> came into my life and provided a friendship, an agreeable war-job, a
> change & diversion and a strong protecting arm, so far in every way,
> which have made the whole difference to 'la vie quotidienne' and to my
> morale. If it can go on like this I can only say I am very lucky and very
> very grateful to Fate.

Georgia leaned heavily on Bolton's affection when her father died in Canada on 6 January 1942, his supportive attitude contrasting favourably with Sachie's egotistical fussing about the possibility of being called up to the navy – 'awful of him to torture me about it now'. In February she officially became Bolton's driver and they were away all day together and sometimes overnight as well. Georgia felt guilty about leaving Sachie alone: 'Wish I could think of ways to keep Sach amused on the days I am away but he prefers to be alone rather than à deux with anyone but me. It is such a responsibility.' The Sitwells' friends were becoming bored with 'the Cop'; at lunch at the Coq d'Or in London with Bolton and Anne-Marie Callimachi, it was only too obvious that they did not like each other and, while there, Georgia heard gossip about herself which she did not care for: 'what Bridget says about me is very unpleasing'. When Billy McCann came down to Weston, 'Bertie stayed for dinner & was rather tiresome . . . too much Poona and old school tie stuff. Bored Sach and Billy and irritated me.' Worse still Bolton was becoming possessive and jealous and was consequently disagreeable when taking Sachie and McCann on a sightseeing tour next day. 'Alleged green-eyed god trouble.' Sachie himself was beginning to get suspicious and irritated by Bolton's all-too-obvious dog-like devotion to Georgia and was very cross when at the end of October, after a trip to London, they were allegedly held up by fog and had to spend an unscheduled night at Dunstable. 'Sach cross again – backwash of Dunstable. Does not really believe in fog.' It was hardly surprising that at the end of November an unkind person sent Sachie an 'anonymous letter denouncing Bertie & me'. Sachie, however, received it with relative calm, but it was not long before Georgia heard further 'unpleasing' news of local gossip about herself and 'the Cop'.

Things began to go sour for them in 1943. 'Bertie in trouble with Chairman of Standing Committee accused of using too much petrol and spending too many nights away unnecessarily at public expense,' Georgia recorded in March, adding, 'My fault really.' Mrs Bolton arrived to live in the locality and was also treated to an anonymous letter, which she did not receive calmly. When Georgia went to fetch her boss at the marital home, 'Aileen flounced out and gave me a piece of her mind. Very unpleasant.' When told a no doubt doctored account of a further disagreeable encounter with Mrs Bolton, Sachie, however, was 'angelic & sympathetic', and Georgia, '*So* grateful for his understanding and real affection'.

The anonymous letters and Mrs Bolton's jealous scenes were not the only disturbing results of Georgia's affair with 'the Cop'. On 20 April she received an extremely unwelcome visit from an official, who made a 'fearful scene' about her petrol allowance. No less than seven people had written to the Petroleum Office apparently trying to get her into trouble. In May she had a visit from another 'petroleum man', who came to check on her attendance at the police committee and to look at her police log-book. A week later she had a visit from an Inspector of Constabulary about discrepancies in the log-book. 'Poor darling, I am so sorry about the Ogpu,' Edith sympathised. Both Sachie and Georgia worried about public scandal, the humiliating (although in other circumstances welcome) possibility that he might have to resign from the Home Guard and his imminent appointment as a Justice of the Peace and that she might have to give up her job as a result of the 'petrol trouble'. In the event, 'the Cop' got off with a 'mild rebuke' and no more was heard of it. Naturally, 'the Cop' and Georgia had to keep a lower profile, but Georgia was becoming less fond as the unfortunate Bolton, harried by his wife, made frequent scenes. Now he was compared unfavourably with Sachie. In October 1943, after Sachie had been away: 'Sach so sweet, pleased to be home & I to have him back – seems like a year, not just 6 days.' At Loelia's house, Send Grove, for New Year's Eve, Sachie was the life and soul of the party at after-dinner charades: 'Sach entered in for first time ever in 20 years I've known him & acted marvellously. Great success & huge fun. Sach made the evening for us all,' Georgia wrote.

Georgia gradually became more than disillusioned with 'the Cop'. One can only feel sorry for the poor man whose marriage had been virtually wrecked and who genuinely adored her. When Georgia left for Canada in May 1945 to fetch Francis, Bolton wrote her letters of passionate love, signing himself 'Your devoted slave'. 'Certain things have been given to me', he wrote, 'that only a few get on this earth. . . . I feel a far better man than I was before I met you . . . this thing that has happened to me I shall take with me till I die.'[21] Georgia's last three letters had apparently hinted that their relationship could not be the same after the war. '. . . the future can not be like the Past, I know that,' he wrote. 'Also I know that when ordinary times come you will not resist having a good time with your society friends, you will take all opportunities you get, it is your life & I must understand. . . .'[22] The trouble was that he would not be able to accept the cooling of their relationship on Georgia's side after the war. He appeared at Weston once when only Gertrude was there, declaring that he would kill himself, while in another embarrassing scene he tackled Sachie in the street threatening to publish Georgia's letters to him. In her diary Georgia herself later added an envoi to her earlier enthusiastic comments about him: 'I gradually got to be sickeningly bored by my wartime boss. One thing those years 41–44 taught me to appreciate my home & my adored, unique & wonderful Sachie. I now realize that any time spent away from him is a waste & I only regret any hours, even, when we have been separated. . . .' 'The Cop' was to be succeeded by a string of post-war lovers and admirers, including the French Ambassador, René Massigli, but Georgia's feelings for her 'adored, unique and wonderful Sachie' remained the same.

The darkest year of the war for Britain, 1942, had been the beginning of a literary renaissance for the Sitwells. Edith's most recent collection of poems, *Street Songs*, was published in January to great acclaim, going into four editions. A new literary world was emerging in wartime London; influences hostile to the Sitwells had been removed from the scene. The 'Bungalow Boys' had been scattered by the war, Auden and Isherwood having controversially decamped to the United States, and T.S. Eliot's *Criterion* had collapsed. *Life and Letters*, edited by Robert Herring, had been operating from the stables at Renishaw after its London offices had been blitzed. The editors of two of the influential new magazines, Cyril Connolly at *Horizon* (with Peter Watson as patron and co-editor and Stephen Spender as third co-editor) and John Lehmann at *New Writing*, were favourably disposed towards the Sitwells. They were impressed by the new direction of Edith's poetry, foreshadowed in *Gold Coast Customs*, now flowing through *Street Songs*, 'a deep, imaginative, human response to inhuman happenings', as Lehmann put it. Connolly invited Edith to contribute to *Horizon*, while Spender, an admirer of her early poetry, returned to the fold. As Lehmann wrote: 'In Edith . . . the hour and the poet were matched.' Kenneth Clark praised *Street Songs* and her later *Green Song* as 'the greatest poems of the war', and Maurice Bowra her 'perfected technique . . . used to convey experiences of tragic grandeur and intensity'.

At Renishaw, Osbert was working on his masterpiece, the five-volume autobiography, *Left Hand, Right Hand!*, which was to make him an acknowledged Grand Old Man of English Letters. At Weston, Sachie was occupied with his next and most successful 'entertainment of the imagination', *Splendours and Miseries*, which he was to finish in March the following year. He was in close correspondence with Osbert over the autobiography, of which Osbert had sent him Books One and Two for criticism. 'I am loving every page of it,' he told Osbert on 10 April 1942. He was full of suggestions and encouragement: 'Perhaps you could enlarge on Miss Lloyd?' Earlier he had told him how fascinated he was by Osbert's account of the Sargent portrait group. 'I am dying to talk to you about your book,' he wrote. 'I do hope you will go on with it. I particularly want you to do more of the 1906–1907 time: and, more still, 1911–1914, when you first came to London . . . descriptions of parties, and characters. . . .'[23]

Sachie planned a visit to Renishaw on the 23rd, taking Reresby, who had arrived back from Eton with yet another bad report. 'Sach cross all day about it,' Georgia noted. On occasions Reresby's reports infuriated him so much that he chased the boy round the kitchen with a rolled-up newspaper (but not, as one schoolfriend of Reresby's dramatically reported, with a kitchen knife).

'Do you realize that Sunday (12th) "G" is 80 years a baronet!' Sachie had written to Osbert earlier that month. 'He is mentioned in Debrett as "father of the baronetage".' Ginger had not exactly been in the forefront of his children's minds since the news of his operation, presumably for cancer of the bowel, at Fiesole in November 1940. Sachie, Osbert and Edith seem to have made little attempt to get in touch with their father, apart from worrying how the cheques were getting through. In September 1941, almost a year later, Osbert had been enraged to receive what amounted to criticism of their neglect in an 'impertinent' letter from a Frances Crump, addressed from a Lisbon hospital – 'I suppose, an American, do you think a Red X nurse, perhaps?', he wrote, forwarding it to Sachie:

Your Father was staying at San Girolamo Fiesole with the Blue nuns.
He has had a severe operation, but is now better, & being cared for by
an excellent Day nurse . . . he said he had had no news of his children
for a long time, & asked to give you the following message from him:
'Longing for more news of you all. Hope better health under new
conditions.'

Somewhat officiously, 'Lady Crump', as Edith dubbed her, advised the
Sitwells that, while in Italy, the Crumps had been able to hear 'frequently'
from their children in England via Thomas Cook's Lisbon agency, which
forwarded letters to Italy and other enemy countries. 'I have no doubt you
would be able to communicate with your father in this way,' she added.[24]

Edith was deputed to write a hypocritical letter to 'My Darling Father'
for the three of them, assuring him how 'terribly distressed' they were that
their letters had not reached him:

> . . . you are in our thoughts, always. We are dreadfully unhappy that we
> are separated from you, and most unhappy knowing how ill you are. We
> long for the time when we shall all be together again . . . we all beg you
> to believe that a lack of letters from us means no lack of affection or
> thought for you.[25]

Ginger, even from a distance, had continued to fascinate and trouble
his children, especially Osbert. Where he was concerned there was always
an element of 'Grand Guignol' in the air, even in the sanitized ambience
of a Florentine nunnery. On 2 January 1942 Osbert told David Horner:

> Today I've had a letter from Woog, very nice, saying that Ginger is
> growing worse, and is not likely to recover from the next bronchial
> attack. His mind is odd (because of the increasing poison I suppose),
> and the tumour, poor old boy, is worse. He thinks the chef is putting
> ground glass in his spaghetti and is giving away all his money as fast as
> he can get it. Woog says he thinks Otello is dishonest, as well as the
> nurses, but that if they were to go, there wd. be no one to look after
> him. Father is still at Fiesole, and won't go to Switzerland, having been
> persuaded by the nurses to stay on, because they want his money.[26]

By the end of the month, however, the unwelcome – for Osbert –
bulletin was that Ginger, despite the 'internal tumour', was a great deal
better. 'News from Woog, posted 27th ult., says "Ginger" has declared
his intention of living to be a hundred, eats enormously, starting the day
with a tin of sardines at 5 a.m.!' Osbert told Horner.[27] By June Sir George

seemed to be entirely restored to health and comfortably installed in the Villa Fontanelle at Porto Ronco on the Swiss side of Lake Maggiore. Osbert reported having received a telegram ostensibly from him requesting copies of their most recent work and a diet book: 'Am glad to come to this paradise of food and every thing could you try sending me all your latest books of all. Also Dr Hays Way to Health. Sitwell.'[28] Edith later pointed to this telegram as evidence that he was not in his right mind but had been manipulated by Woog, as Sir George would never have referred to anything as a 'paradise of food'.

More ominous revelations were on the way. Three months later Osbert received a disquieting letter from Woog about Sir George's favourite nurse, who had accompanied him from Florence and whom Woog suspected of bleeding her patient of his money:

> . . . I found out that she was a German and not as she said a Swiss subject. Then I was warned that she had the habit of persuading her patients to give her money, and I strongly suspect that all the money Sir George always wanted, and got by selling out capital at 25–30% of the value, was presented to her and *not* to the Red Cross. . . . That nurse looks perfectly after Sir George (of course he gives her a princely salary) . . . [she] lies every moment in the ear of Sir George to make her over some cash or an annuity. A few days ago she asked me to come to Sir George and make out a draft for him to make her over a capital, or an annuity of 50,000 Lire!!!! I talked it over with Sir George, and he was persuaded that it is his 'duty' to help her for all her life!! In vain I told him that she is paid double of what any other sicknurse gets, he has the fix [*sic*] idea that he 'must help' her! My opinion is that Sir George is not quite responsible any more for his actions and he got to the above decision by persuasion or hypnotic suggestion. . . . He wants me to put a clause in the deed that his sons have to go on paying the annuity in case of his death. . . .[29]

Woog had managed to arrange for the removal of the nurse by the simple expedient of persuading the Swiss authorities not to renew her permit to remain in the country so that she would have to leave at the end of the month, but while Woog himself was out of the way the situation took a turn for the worse. 'The latest news is (written on the 19th) that Ginger wants to marry his German nurse (born in 1896), and has given her a pension of 500£ a year and has left her to Sachie, Edith & me to provide for! . . . Edith is furious, Sachie & G. beside themselves. Personally, I'm amused,' Osbert told Horner.[30] Fortunately for Sir George's children,

Woog's tactic of sending the German nurse away and persuading the authorities not to renew her residence permit had the desired effect. In response to anxious enquiries from Osbert, Olga Woog wired: 'Possibilities of marriage very remote owing to difficulties regarding papers. He is quieter apparently not missing her inordinately. . . .'[31]

When Sachie published a selection of his prose that autumn, under the title *The Homing of the Winds*, he benefited from the changed literary climate. 'Englishness' was in vogue during the war years, nourished by patriotism and nostalgia for a way of life under threat. There was a new sense of the need to emphasise human and civilised values and the national identity. Elizabeth Bowen praised Sachie's writings as 'English prose by an Englishman of today . . . not only individual but traditional . . . not only modern but of the past . . . a reminder that the English have, by their visionary use of language, brought into being an empire of the mind.'[32] Sachie, however, was still wary of the literary world and unwilling to take part in the public resurgence of the Sitwell trio which Osbert and Edith were planning early in 1943. He had refused to attend a revival of *Façade* at the Albert Hall in May 1942, which had enjoyed a rapturous reception; now he turned a deaf ear to Edith's pleadings to get him to join in a celebrity poetry reading in aid of the Free French, which was to be held in April 1943 in the presence of the Queen and the two Princesses:

> You, Osbert and I *have* to read poetry for about five minutes each, at a Poets [sic] Reading O and I are arranging, to be held some time in April, to raise money for Lady Crewe's French in Britain Fund – the other readers are Tom Eliot, Walter Turner, Mr de la Mare (we *hope*), Dr Bottomley, we *hope*, Blunden, Siegfried, old Binyon, Sturge Moore, Lady Gerald Wellesley, Mrs Nicolson [Vita Sackville West] (!!!!!)

She had evidently anticipated his recalcitrance: 'Now then, will you be tempted? . . . actually, it isn't a question of temptation it is a question of force majeure. You *must*.'[33]

Sachie, however, remained obdurate. He had no intention of being dragged once again at the chariot wheels of a resurrected Sitwell troika as Edith intended. There was no ostensible reason for refusing to take part. He had finished *Splendours and Miseries* in March and, while he sulked at Weston, Georgia and Reresby went to the Aeolian Hall. 'I was so miserable at your not reading at the Poetry Reading,' Edith told him. '*Everyone* asked why you would not, and Mr de la Mare and dear old Dr

The Sitwells at Renishaw, August 1930, by Cecil Beaton:
(*left to right*) Sachie (*standing*), Sir George, Georgia, Reresby, Lady Ida,
Edith and Osbert

Montegufoni
as it was in 1909
when Sir George
wrote of it:
'The air of
forlorn
grandeur is very
attractive and
this I hope to
keep. . .'

The Sitwell trio:
Osbert, Edith
and Sachie

'We are hopeless
Gramophonists':
Osbert and Sachie
at Carlyle Square,
1933

'Beautiful Adonis'
– a youthful
David Horner

Christabel
McLaren, later
Lady Aberconway:
portrait by
James McEvoy

Georgia and
Beaton on the
Lido, Venice,
September 1933

Sachie and Gertrude with an unidentified group of Romanians
in a Romanian orchard, September 1937

Family group:
Georgia, Francis
and Reresby
in the gardens at
Connaught Square,
c. 1937

Monsieur Rivain, Baba Metcalfe and Sachie,
Rabat, Morocco, February 1939

The unwilling warrior: Sachie in
Home Guard uniform during the
Second World War

Moira Shearer as
The Aristocrat in Massine's
Mlle Angot, 1947

Georgia and 'the Cop', Captain R.H.D. Bolton, on the Cam, April 1942

Reresby and
Penelope Sitwell
in their first
London flat, 1952

Susanna and
Francis Sitwell
with their eldest
son, George, at
his christening,
June 1967

Sir Sacheverell Sitwell in old age: the octogenarian poet
among the orange trees and scented geraniums in his conservatory at Weston

Bottomley were *frightfully* disappointed. . . .' He must have regretted missing the comic sequence of events with which the proceedings ended, centring on the emotional behaviour of Dorothy Wellesley, retailed to him by Edith:

> Lady Peel (Beatrice Lillie) . . . tried to enfold her in a ju-jitsu grip and hold her down on to her seat, Stephen Spender . . . seeing her wander outside, tried to knock her down and sit on her face, Raymond Mortimer . . . induced her to take his arm and go into Bond Street, where she promptly sat down on the pavement, banging her stick and using frightful language about *A* the Queen and *B* Me – (the worst! being about me) . . . she smacked Harold Nicolson. . . . All we needed was Dylan Thomas. . . .[34]

Edith and Osbert enjoyed being literary lions again. The Aeolian Hall had been the venue for the notorious first public performance of *Façade* just under twenty years ago, the difference now being that they themselves had been transformed from outrageous leaders of the avant-garde to Great Figures of English Literature. They had succeeded in bringing together T.S. Eliot and the Queen in the cause of poetry and patriotism. No one else but Osbert, as his biographer noted, could have organised such a grand event for poetry. Edith, whose star was very much in the ascendant, held court when in London at the quaintly named 'Sesame, Lyceum and Imperial Pioneer Club' (always known as the Sesame) in Grosvenor Street, described by John Lehmann as 'the haunt mainly of elderly ladies of impeccable respectability and well-to-do middle-class origins, among whom Edith, though undoubtedly imperial in mien and a famous pioneer at least in the arts, seemed as out of place as a hoopoe in a flock of starlings'.[35]

Sachie kept apart from this renaissance for reasons which are not altogether easy to fathom. Certainly the memories of the scars he had suffered at the hands of the critics had given him an instinctive fear of being exposed to professional literary men. Pride and a dislike of being regarded as just the younger brother of Osbert and Edith may have contributed, together with a subconscious, rankling resentment of their superior celebrity. He had more than a touch of the artist's natural arrogance; he would pursue his own paths whatever people might say, but he was also, unfortunately for himself, too thin-skinned not to care. His refusal to accept his brother's and sister's help and advice, or to do as they wanted him to, annoyed and upset Osbert and Edith as they pursued their increasingly celebrated double-act.

Sachie and Georgia continued their smart social life. After a brief estrangement at the time of the Westminsters' separation in 1935, Sachie was on very friendly terms with Bendor again, often going down by himself to stay with him at his house, The Aviary, near Southall. They remained great friends with Loelia, Emerald Cunard and Chips Channon. On 8 July they were in London staying at Claridge's for a cocktail party to celebrate Georgia's thirty-eighth birthday given by Loelia and a new American friend, Angier 'Angy' Biddle Duke. The following day Georgia sat to Augustus John and then went back for lunch with Laura Corrigan, while Sachie lunched with Bridget. While Georgia was alone at Claridge's, Osbert telephoned with the news that Ginger had died the previous day. 'Drama. Sach back late owing typical Bridget behaviour,' Georgia wrote acidly. That night, kept awake by a noisy party held by Adolphe Menjou, Clark Gable and Bob Hope next door, they sat up late talking about Ginger. They were both of them preoccupied with the possible financial implications of his death; only Reresby, to whom they broke the news next day at Eton, seemed 'distressed about his grand sire'. On 16 July Sachie went up to Renishaw by train, leaving Georgia to cope with Bolton's complaints of his wife's continuing jealous scenes and to follow on with Reresby for Ginger's memorial service at Eckington church the next day.

At Renishaw, Osbert's first sensation had been one of relief and delight. He had been left £10,000 by Mrs Greville on her death in September the previous year; now he would have his father's money and his title. Signing himself 'Yrs. carefree', he wrote to David Horner on 13 July with details of Sir George's English will:

> Sachie gets £10,000; Edith – poor darling 1,000 (I'm afraid she'd counted on 5,000). Sachie would have got another £550 per annum but it was on the minerals, and since they've been taken, it drops into the residue (being bonds, and not minerals now) and goes, with anything else there is, to Reresby. I get the 2 railways (value at present about 500 to 600 per annum the two, with tax to pay out of it) and Ingmanthorpe farm: but these are settled of course, and not mine outright. . . . Father had left my Mother one *hundred* pounds, as a token of his love for the last 50 years (2£ a year!)[36]

His tongue-in-cheek formula response to letters of condolence was 'Those who knew my father best will not find it easy to forget him.' He was, initially, thoroughly enjoying himself: 'I find the BARONETCY a heavenly new toy, still. I think I shall make a gramophone record, which says "Sir O, Sir O, Sir O", and turn it on when I feel depressed . . . even in this weather there's freedom rolling in the air, and a sense of fun undulled.' But, 'I dread the week-end,' he added.[37]

The repercussions of that week-end were to echo down the years and marked the beginning of an estrangement between Renishaw and Weston. From beyond the grave Ginger still manipulated his children's emotions, dividing them in death as he had never succeeded in doing while he was alive. The necessity of pitting their wills and their wits against their father had bound them together in a common cause. His death and its consequences shattered that unity, reactivating old sibling rivalry which hitherto had been subconscious and causing a rift which never healed but deepened over the years. It was to culminate in a bitter, typically Sitwellian tragi-comedy just over a quarter of a century later. The reading of the will provoked anger and some confusion as it seemed to favour Reresby above the three immediate children and both Sachie and Edith's legacies had been reduced with Edith inheriting the paltry sum of £60. There was no money for Osbert, Sir George having cut him out of the settlement on the unlikely grounds that he had joined the Labour Party and was spending all the money he had been given on subscriptions to it. Everyone (except Georgia) considered that Osbert had been badly treated by his father, as Edith wrote to David Horner on the day after the will reading: 'Sir George – (I am going to call him that in future, *not* Father, as I don't see why I am to give him credit for producing me!!!)'; Sachie, she said, 'could not have been more sweet about Osbert, and realised absolutely how outrageously he had been treated. . . . He really showed at his *very* best.'[38] Edith, of course, was understandably enraged at the pittance she had been awarded; while the issue of how much Sachie would actually get in the end was thought to depend on the settlement of the Swiss fund, the Stiftung, news of which was not yet available. Georgia, mother of Sir George's beloved grandchildren, got nothing at all. 'Great annoyance, nerves, temper & depression at prospect of will which Elmhirst [Sir George's solicitor] and Osbert read yesterday after tea,' Georgia commented.

Osbert had rather more to say, as he wrote to Horner on the 19th:

No one will ever know *what* hell last night was! Everything went fairly well till before dinner (cocktails) when G[eorgia] appeared in a maddening mood, and continued for 3 hours to dance heavily on every corn that Edith or I had ever possessed. Corns, as it were, literary, parental, friendly, every sort. She went out of her way to say how

frightful all our relations were. . . . Evidently G. considers she hasn't been
well treated by Ginger, and complains at not being left anything.[39]

One remark Georgia made, however, struck home: 'of course, *my* son is
the heir presumptive,' indicating that eventually she would be in charge
at Renishaw. To Horner Osbert brushed off her behaviour as 'pure
tactlessness, nothing worse', but it rankled. Georgia's lack of tact made
her enemies, some of them powerful in Osbert's circle, like Christabel,
who would not forgive Georgia's gossip about her affair with Sam
Courtauld. From that moment of the memorial service week-end at
Renishaw in July 1943 Osbert turned against Georgia. In his letters to
Horner, who also did not like her, his references to 'Juggins' or 'G.',
which had often been catty, now became positively hostile. 'Georgia
would eat her own mother if she could,' he wrote to Horner ten days
later.[40]

The rumblings of that week-end continued to echo between Renishaw and Weston as the saga of Sir George's bequests took new and
unexpected turns. On 21 July Osbert reported that Elmhirst had
telephoned the day before to say that the English will was so badly drawn
up that he doubted whether it would stand; as an example of this, Francis
was mentioned in it but the lawyer had forgotten to specify the sum to be
bequeathed. On 26 July he received a long letter from Woog describing
Sir George's death: 'He died, after being unconscious for 2 days – or
rather doped with morphia.' 'I expect new will – thrills hourly,' Osbert
added. Two days later the bulletin from Renishaw was:

> . . . that vindictive old man's wills continue to come in, including now
> the Swiss settlement: from which the first claim is for 600 a year for
> Reresby, 300 a year for Francis, and 250 to an American cousin. Then I
> come, with 1200 a year for Montegufoni, if I live there, and never sell a
> piece of furniture. Then 700 to Sachie, 200 to Edith. But as the money
> isn't there. . . .

On 26 July Sachie went up to London to talk to Frere and to Coutts
about the wills and financial settlements; the result, according to Georgia,
was 'very fussing news about Ginger's will'. He was, apparently, to be
getting far less than he bargained for. Without thinking twice Georgia
seized the telephone, 'like a whirlwind', as Osbert put it, disturbing him to
his annoyance during the ritual of the nine o'clock news, and

began about 'What was happening. Was it true that Sachie was ruined. She must sell Weston at once and get into Armada House [the Elizabethan Manor just outside the front gate].' I said I thought it was an excellent idea – but hardly necessary. Even if Father had left little money, they got all there was (except Edith's 60£ a year). . . . 'Well, I *must* know. The household bills will be coming in'. . . . I said 'Well, you must hold on for 6 weeks the household bills can't come to more than £50 a week, and that's 300£ – which, even if you get nothing from Father, Sachie now gets an extra £5000 down from Mother's marriage settlement, won't make much of a hole in it.'

Osbert, however, lent them £500 and was miffed when neither of them wrote thanking him for it. The mischief-making Christabel retailed to him a conversation she had had with Sachie in the British Musuem, when he understandably told her that he 'hated the idea of [Osbert's] having to pay all his bills and for R[eresby's] education'.[41]

Georgia's diary records Sachie as 'fussing dreadfully . . . about our awful financial prospects'. Osbert attempted to calm his fears. There was, after all, they hoped, money from the Swiss fund still to come, but as yet nothing definite had emerged from Sir George's tangled affairs. 'My darling Sachie,' Osbert wrote on 30 August in reply to what was evidently a desperate letter: 'I sympathise with you deeply: but I think things will not, still, be as bad as you think. It is impossible to tell for another month or two, and meanwhile I should remain as steady as the miserable circumstances allow.' He could not, in any case, sell Weston or its contents without the consent of trustees, and, therefore, as a preliminary, he should appoint them. Nor could he give up what he called his 'advantage', i.e. eventual succession to Renishaw, until after his, Osbert's death ('we seem very giddily now to discuss these things'), as until he was dead it could be presumed that he might have heirs of his own. His best chance for providing adequately for Georgia after his death would be to inherit Renishaw 'should it come to you' and then leave her a jointure on it. 'As for Renishaw,' Osbert added, 'unlike Weston, remember that it is a place that produces money, as well as eats it up: moreover it is far from London, and that in a sense is an economy, for one does not get drawn into it unless one wants to.' The bright side of it, he reminded Sachie, was that at least his two children were provided for. 'In any case,' he added, 'the melting pot is at work. . . . No one knows for the moment what he or she has to live on.'[42] Suspicions about Woog's probity were beginning to dawn upon Osbert after receiving letters from Sir George's nurses accusing the former bank manager of theft.

Fortunately for Sachie's piece of mind, he had finished *Splendours and Miseries* before the Ginger trauma began. It was published on 17 December 1943 and was far and away his most successful of the *genre* so far, going into five impressions by April 1946 (although with the paper shortage print runs were small and the total imprint was probably only about 7,000 copies). It was in many ways the wildest and most fantastic of his books. Sachie described its 'nearly desperate fantasy' as brought on by the feeling that normality would never return. It touched a chord in people clamped in their homes by fuel restrictions and the black-out in a cold climate of austerity. In the totalitarian atmosphere of quasi-military discipline, Sachie's strange, at times incantatory prose and often surreal imagery had an enhanced appeal. John Lehmann called *Splendours and Miseries* the masterpiece of Sachie's imaginative prose works, in which '[he] creates a powerful over-all effect, communicating an apocalyptic vision of light and darkness of the spirit, appropriate to the times in which it was written'.[43]

Book One of *Splendours and Miseries* reflected the preoccupation of the time, the Atlantic. Describing the cliffs of the western coasts of Scotland and Ireland, Sachie's writing is poetic, mysterious, yet at times minutely descriptive, as when he deals with the landscape of Ben Arcuil, which he had observed during a ten-day stay in August 1942 at Bendor Westminster's estate, Lochmore. Yet the section begins with a passage which in its tone and imagery could have been written by a later Aldous Huxley on a mescalin trip:

> Theories of the godhead have been revealed in dreams. Such visions . . .
> are as sensible as waking thought, and have a subterranean or
> subconscious wisdom. The countenance of God must be a mystery
> among birds and animals. Why should it be in human shape? Divine
> wisdom could be born of the eggshell. I had a dream of a huge serpent
> head. . . . I believe I saw the countenance of creation. . . .

Book Two was inspired by three photographs of women inmates of nineteenth-century French and Belgian asylums, taken from a book entitled *Mad Humanity* published in 1898. There is something horrifying (Cecil Beaton inexplicably found it made him 'yell with laughter') in Sachie's minute observations of and speculations about them. He had a unique capacity for finding horror – 'Evil Visions,' he called it – where other people saw only an everyday image. The connoisseur Brinsley Ford, for instance, found Sachie's description of a Fuseli drawing, which he owned, utterly unrecognisable. In this book Sachie describes the drawings of Fuseli as the only 'really evil drawings ever done'. Pieter Brueghel and Hieronymus Bosch, artists whose vision of the human condition was perhaps the most suited to a world at war, came into this chapter, interleaved with a page bitterly headed 'Home Guard' drawn from Sachie's own experiences, including the bombing of Nuneaton: 'The eighteen-stone woman who lived next door was lifted a hundred yards out of her bedroom, when the roof came off, and was stuck, flat, high up on the wall of a public house. She is still there. They have not moved her. . . .

Images of dead women were very much on his mind. Photographs of victims of starvation in Athens had been published in *Life* magazine in August 1942. In one, the body of a Greek woman lying in an Athens street, in a black ragged dress, hands clenched in agony, led him to thoughts of his mother and his earliest memory of her when the big, old rocking-horse was carried out into the garden at Renishaw and he was placed upon it to be photographed with her. He had come to terms with his mother's death and he could even bring himself to refer to the case, admitting how deeply it had scarred him:

> . . . while I was still at school and at the most sensitive part of my childhood, [it] did permanent injury to my nerves and made it so hard for me to face up to certain sides of life, besides fixing in my mind the appalling image of the Purgatorio, in the conclusion of my book *Dance of the Quick and the Dead*.

In one person this affectionate portrayal of their mother touched a raw nerve. Edith received the book at Renishaw and read these passages with growing pain and anger. Her rage over her father's will had resulted in her taking to her bed for several weeks, unable to work, as she had told John Lehmann in August, 'owing to the really ghastly . . . worries and disgust from which I have been suffering. My father died a few weeks ago, and I dare not trust myself to speak of what he did before he died.' Sachie's book brought it all back, 'flaying me alive with the hell of my childhood'. She wrote Sachie a passionate letter:

> I cannot, of course, see the last chapter as an outside person would see it, and do not know, therefore, how it will strike them. It is not how I see the situation. My nerves were completely broken and my nervous system ruined before I was ten years old. This was perfectly well known to the doctors who attended me then, and to the doctors who have attended

me since. One doctor (Vernon Jones), after an interview with the then
family lawyer, told Father, in terms that even *he* could not misunderstand,
exactly what he thought of him for allowing it; and told him what would be
the result for them if anything happened to me. My health has never
recovered.

When Osbert was twenty-two, our Mother nearly succeeded in ruining
his life also. . . . I have forgiven Mother a long time ago [she added
somewhat unconvincingly] and it needed some forgiving. Let us please
never refer to this again. I have had just as much, in one way or another,
as I can endure.

The passage about their mother in *Splendours and Miseries* enraged
her not only because of her personal feelings about her childhood, but
because she saw the book as creatively a step in the wrong direction for
Sachie. It was her duty to keep the flame of poetry alive in him. She knew,
she wrote, that he had been discouraged by

the extraordinary wave of idiocy that has swept over the country on the
subject of poetry – all these miserable incompetent little bungalow boys
being treated as if they were Shelley. But don't you realize [she went on]
that this has *always* happened? I honestly think I shall make a Calendar
specially for you – with a thought for every day in the year about what
has happened to other great artists. . . .

He was, she assured him, at the height of his powers and should forge
ahead. Autobiography was not the way (she may also have thought that
this role in the trio should be left to Osbert). Sachie had long ago been cast
as the young poet and he should not backslide. 'Don't take refuge in some
dream of childhood,' she ordered. '. . . Go straight ahead, and leave these
dreams behind. Now is the time to write more poetry, you owe it to us. . . .
And the tide is turning.'[44]

Sachie was surprised and appalled by this outburst. Ignoring her
exhortations about returning to poetry, he wrote immediately assuring
Edith that he had not in any way intended to hurt her. But relations
between the elder Sitwells at Renishaw and the younger household at
Weston had become edgy and fraught with danger. The subject of their
parents was particularly in the forefront of their minds. Suspicions
about Woog had been festering. Edith's Gothic imagination had already
led her to accuse Woog of foul play, as she wrote to Horner at
the end of February: 'Personally, I think that the sulphoral played its
part in gathering the old gentleman to his forefathers – not self-

administered. . . .' 'There are', she wrote to Horner in March, 'horrible passages in Woog's letters about George's "terrible agitations", and about how, on one occasion, he succeeded in getting into the garden. What was he trying to escape from?'[45] Osbert, at Edith's insistence, even sent his secretary, Lorna Andrade, to consult a medium, armed with letters written by Sir George and Woog. According to Miss Andrale, the medium, Mrs Nell St John Montagu, seemed to think that Sir George had certainly been in danger when he wrote the letters, that Woog had been intent on stealing his money and that the nurse referred to in one of the letters had been hand-in-glove with him.[46]

In April Osbert received a memorandum from the British Consul-General in Zurich, which seemed to confirm his worst fears:

The late Sir George Sitwell created on 3rd December 1928 a trust fund called the Sitwell Stiftung, domiciled at Altdorf, Canton Uri [*sic*, actually Zug], Switzerland. The beneficiary of this fund was Sir George Sitwell, formerly of Renishaw Hall, at the time of Castle Montegufoni, Val di Pesa. . . . By amendment of the 7th July 1941 Herr Bernard M. Woog-Chandos-Pole of Villa Nimet, St Moritz, Engadine, Switzerland, was nominated sole beneficiary. The Banque Populaire of Zurich administers the fund.

It is understood that Herr Woog is a citizen of Zurich and used to be a cashier of the Banque Populaire. Some time before the War he had a motor-car accident in Munich and lost his memory. He retired from the bank and, as he was not entitled to any pension, was given a gratuity. He has apparently recovered his memory since. It appears that he has no employment and no regular income or personal means, but that he does some business from time to time, particularly with foreigners.

A visitor to the late Sir George Sitwell [the local British Vice-Consul apparently summoned by Sir George when Woog was away] . . . received the impression that Sir George was worrying about his trust in Mr Woog. This visitor suggests that the fact that Mr Woog was made sole beneficiary of the Trust and the mental condition of Sir George lead one to think that there is something doubtful about the whole matter.[47]

The Consul's letter seemed to Osbert and Edith to provide circumstantial evidence for their suspicions. The Consul's visit, they surmised, must have frightened the Woogs into thinking that their depredations would be discovered with the result that they had despatched the old man.

'This letter of the Consul's has quite finished me temporarily,' Osbert wrote to Sachie on 13 April 1944:

Both Edith and I feel horribly ill. As you know, the old boy was the plague and worry of my life: but this is really *too* much. One hates to think of what he must have gone through, from fright, and saying to himself the whole time, I must be imagining it. . . . What an end and to what a life! To the cocksureness, and refusal to understand people; to attribute always the worst motives to agreeable and nice people or vice-versa. It is [a] most appalling sequel.[48]

Ten days later Osbert received a report which threw further light on the financial situation. As he wrote to Sachie on 24 April:

Airey [Sir George's accountant in England] came to see me yesterday. We can now know what *Ginger* got through. In 1939 the Stiftung investments were worth between seventy-one and seventy-four thousand pounds – today there is only left between ten and twelve thousand: the income of which has been bequeathed to Woog or Olga for life. . . .
. . . With regard to his possible murder, the 3 nurses *may* have been in it, and the letters from one of them *may* have been due to remorse. . . . Certainly I think he wanted to marry the German nurse because she had protected him. . . . He *may* have been murdered – he certainly was coerced. . . . All through Woog's letters, there is a curious harping on and (according to the nurse) lying about, food: from the opening telegram, purporting to be from father when he arrived in Switzerland 'Happy to be in this paradise of food and drink' . . . Do you think they withheld food from him, in order to get their way?[49]

Although Edith and Osbert, at least, remained convinced that they had Woog 'on toast', there was never any proof that Sir George had been murdered. According to Woog's brother-in-law, Major J.W. Chandos-Pole, Woog was an intelligent and cultivated man not remotely likely to commit murder, while Olga always told him how fond she had been of Sir George. The old Baronet's chief complaint while in Switzerland had been, in fact, constipation, 'which with the wartime shortage of castor oil had become quite a problem'. The possibility of financial malpractice was, however, a different matter. In July 1944 the Banque Populaire Suisse admitted chief responsibility for the disappearance of the money from the Sitwell Stiftung; no finger was directly pointed at any one person. Woog died in 1948 in continued enjoyment of his legacy from Sir George.

The real victim of Ginger's death and its tangled financial aftermath was the relationship between Sachie and Osbert. Osbert began to replace Ginger as the financial ogre on Sachie's and Georgia's horizon. In June

1944, after a visit by Osbert to Weston, Georgia noted resentfully in her diary: 'O in very good and sweet mood but *not* giving any assurances of our financial security which I think most unkind as poor darling S is so worried about it. It is awful to be in bondage for ever to *anyone* and we now are to Osbert more than ever we were to Ginger. Talked alone to him but got nowhere. . . .' Osbert's private thoughts about Georgia, expressed in his letters to David Horner, were becoming increasingly unkind. On arrival at Renishaw after his Weston visit he wrote: 'Sachie was absolutely charming; Georgia fairly bloody – she looks so spoilt & selfish now, & never stops nagging. The naggers here [Edith] are in good form too.' In July he wrote nastily: 'All the usual worries here. . . . I think Georgia is having "changes". . . . I suppose the last five years will be the worst.' In another letter earlier that year he reported: 'I think Sachie seems so *sad* now (Juggins [i.e. Georgia] fault). . . . He certainly has a great capacity for depression, poor darling; though so amusing as a companion & as a character.'[50]

Literary jealousy also played a part. Edith's and Osbert's stars seemed ever in the ascendant in 1944. Edith's second important wartime collection of poems, *Green Song*, came out in August and that summer both she and Osbert became Fellows of the Royal Society of Literature. Sachie did take part with Osbert and Edith in a celebrated poetry reading at the Churchill Club on 25 October 1944, having the previous day attended one of Edith's Sesame Club tea parties which included, among others, T.S. Eliot. According to Lehmann, the Churchill Club reading had drawn the whole of the smarter artistic and literary world. E.M. Forster, who was there, called it 'that immortal evening'. Edith stole the show when, just as she began her poem about the air-raids of 1940, 'Still Falls the Rain', the warning whistle sounded and the rattle of a doodle-bug could be heard approaching. Edith simply lifted her eyes to the ceiling for a moment, then, raising her voice to counter the noise, read on. 'She held the whole audience in the grip of her discipline, the morale of her unspoken asseveration that poetry was more important than all the terrors that Hitler could launch against us. Not a soul moved, and, at the end, when the doodle-bug had exploded far away, the applause was deafening.'[51] Georgia's account of the evening was ungenerous: 'Osbert & Edith did their best to put Sach in the shade and succeeded.'

Georgia had her own reasons for feeling hostile towards Edith and Osbert. There had always been an undercurrent of tug-of-war over Sachie between the two elder Sitwells on the one side and Georgia on the other since the early days of their marriage. Underlying it all was the

Sitwells' conviction that she was an unsuitable wife for and a poor influence on Sachie. In the 1930s Osbert had delivered warnings about her behaviour with Mosley and Lezard, but Edith had never criticised her, preferring to keep on the warmest possible terms. Now, however, she was increasingly convinced that Georgia was keeping Sachie away from the people who could help him as a writer and, particularly, as a poet. In their view, her duty was to be a helpmate to a Sitwell genius. The issue now was whether or not Georgia should go to Canada to see her mother and Francis as she planned. At lunch at the Sesame following the Churchill Club reading and a brilliant celebratory party given by the Kenneth Clarks, Georgia found 'Edith & Osbert rather distant with me . . . they cannot understand my being anxious to see Mother or Francis'.

Osbert took a feline pleasure in teasing Georgia, as he wrote to Horner in April 1945:

> . . . I forgot to tell you something that has amused me frightfully. . . . You'll remember that after Georgia had been such a pest with her 'Shall I or shan't I go to Canada', I used to play the same game, advising her to go one moment, and not to, the next. I kept it up for months. . . .
> Then, suddenly, I rang up a week ago, and found everyone distracted. What had happened was that 'the authorities' had decided to play the same game, had telegraphed for her to London and had said 'Either you go to Canada within *24 hours*, or you don't go for two years!' Isn't [it] lovely. She was absolutely nonplussed. ('Mummy' [Mrs Doble], poor thing, has been knocked over by a bus – or the bus by her, I couldn't make out which, in Montreal. . . .)

There was a replay in May, gleefully retailed by Osbert to Horner, when Georgia, having finally planned to leave for Canada on the 24th, received a telegram at Weston telling her to leave the following day:

> Sachie was in bed after the accident [he had been knocked down by a car crossing Piccadilly], all the telephones in the village had gone off, and she [had] to walk 4 miles in the rain to telephone. They then said, no, it was a mistake! . . . They are splendid, I think, they keep the game up so well. I said to Georgia, 'They're playing a game with you. . . .'[52]

It was sad and petty. The snake in the grass seems to have been David Horner, with whom Osbert was still passionately in love, and whose return to Osbert's side as the war ended boded ill for Osbert's relations with his family. Jealous of anyone who came close to Osbert, Horner worked to separate him first from Sachie, then, finally, from Edith. Playing on Osbert's deep-seated jealousy and resentment of Georgia, exacerbated by her own tactlessness, he succeeded in driving a wedge between Weston and Renishaw in the post-war years. He used Sachie's perennial financial troubles as a weapon against him. When Sachie was on a rare visit to Renishaw in February 1945, Horner wrote to Osbert from Carlyle Square: 'I feel so sorry for you and Edith with old misery moping round the house. That perpetual pessimistic grumble. . . .'[53] Early in 1945 when Adrian Stokes asked Osbert what news he had of Sachie, Osbert replied sadly:

> Alas, I hardly know more than you do. I never see him and he never answers a letter. I don't even know what he is working at. And he has invented a system by which all the faults are mine. And when I do see him he first of all lays down an intensive barrage of small grumbles (for half an hour); then opens up an hour-long bombardment of questions without listening to my answers. This absolutely exhausts me and protects him from any real contact with me. It makes me horribly sad. . . .[54]

More and more Sachie was coming to depend on Georgia for protection, love and support. When she finally left for Canada to see her mother and Francis late in May 1945, he was desolate. As he wrote in his first letter to her after their separation:

> The solitude is aching. . . . I do so love you, my own darling, and you have been my love and my life ever since we first met, truthfully, almost for every moment; except, perhaps, for half a minute when you blow your nose too loudly . . . you know I love you more than anything on earth or in heaven. I love you more than I did when I first saw you; and then there are so many other bonds of companionship and friendship, except that there is no word for it. . . . I adore you, my round-faced angel . . . and I think of you every minute and all day and night.[55]

'I really had never realized how much you love me until I read them,' Georgia told him. 'They are the most beautiful love letters any woman ever received.'[56] They had been married almost twenty years.

10

Embarkations for Cythera

1945–1959

'The career of a writer of my sort . . . could be called a
perpetual exploration of the rose-hung island.'

Sacheverell Sitwell, *Cupid and the Jacaranda*

As the war drew agonisingly slowly towards its close, Sachie began to feel
restless. The V-2 rockets meant that it was almost impossible to get up to
London. 'The "Island Fortress" is getting fearfully on my nerves. . . . A
sort of claustrophobia,' he told Violet Gordon Woodhouse in May 1944.
Worse was to come with the bombing of the European cities he knew
and loved. 'The paper reads, today, like a paper printed by lunatics in an
asylum,' he wrote on 17 February 1945. 'Another town has been what
they called "Dresdened", and the *Express* says all Japan from Tokyo to
Yokohama is on fire.' The final ending of the world conflict, involving
as it did the dropping of the atom bombs on Japan and endless official
celebrations, did not bring him pleasure. 'What a week it has been', he
wrote on 12 August 1945, 'with those two awful bombs – and the two
idiotic VE days, or whatever they are going to be called, hanging ahead.'[1]
He longed to escape to the sun after meeting an American who
described his sister's house in San Miguel:

. . . the terraces of orange trees . . . with orchids growing among the
orange blossom; and of how the Indians make little coffin-like boxes out
of sections of a special tree trunk, fill them with mosses, and sell them
for about 4d full of gardenias and camellias, and orchids too. I have been
reading Berlioz's life and can sympathize when he says all he wants is to
go down to the Mediterranean and fall asleep lying on a bank of violets
. . . how beautiful life *could* be! And instead, as you say, it is nearly
unendurable.[2]

The woman to whom this letter was addressed, Winifred Ellerman, always known as 'Bryher', was, as Georgia put it, Sachie's 'clandestine fairy godmother'. She was already helping him financially, as she did Edith also, and was to provide a good deal of the wherewithal for his post-war escapes from austerity Britain. Bryher was the daughter of the shipping magnate, Sir John Ellerman, to whom she had refused to speak since he had thrown a chair at her when she was a child. A rebellious, romantic tomboy who hated her English childhood and school and, indeed, most of her family, she had escaped to Paris in the 1920s, married the poet, Robert McAlmon, and become a friend of Gertrude Stein, Alice B. Toklas and Sylvia Beach. She divorced McAlmon and married Kenneth MacPherson, the Scottish writer, later separating from him, although they remained on friendly terms. Sachie had met her briefly in Venice in the early 1920s when she was still part of the expatriate artistic Paris circle; he had met her again through Edith when Bryher had returned to live in wartime London, sharing her life with the poet, Hilda Doolittle ('H.D.'), ex-wife of Richard Aldington, in a flat in Lowndes Square. Despite her rejection of her *haut bourgeois* family background, which she had symbolised by dropping the name Ellerman for Bryher, the name of an island in the Scillies where she had spent childhood holidays, Bryher had inherited her father's financial shrewdness and remained extremely rich. Small, stocky, inevitably dressed in a plain mackintosh and blue beret, Bryher was completely uninterested in material things, apart from rare books. She was totally committed to the cause of literature and had become a passionate admirer of Edith, who to her represented the essence of poetry. She had come to know Edith and Osbert when Robert Herring, editor of *Life and Letters Today*, for which she provided financial backing, moved his bombed-out offices to the stables at Renishaw in 1940. Bryher had provided Edith with a house in Bath, once lived in by Dr Johnson's Mrs Thrale, and, at the end of the war, a seven-year Deed of Covenant, which provided her with a monthly income. By October 1944 she was also sponsoring Sachie.

Bryher, like Edith, saw it as her principal duty to encourage him, both as a writer and as a poet. Over the years until her death she provided not only encouragement and cheques for birthdays and Christmases and for special things like travel tickets, but also advice on family matters and the increasingly complicated Sitwell relationships. All three Sitwells corresponded regularly with her, taking her into their confidence to an unprecedented degree as if she were a surrogate member of the family. She was entirely generous and devoted with her money and her friendship and, most importantly for Sachie, her belief in him as a writer. '. . . if I have helped you in any way to give you leisure for your work', she told him, 'I am in your debt, never you in mine. I have a profound admiration for what you write. . . .'[3]

Their correspondence began in February 1945. 'Dear Sachie,' Bryher wrote, 'I hope you will not mind being thus addressed because I have known Osbert & Edith so long that it seems silly to be more formal. . . .' Their letters discussed mutual interests, Bryher describing the Shakespeare first folio she had recently bought and sending him bulbs from the Scillies. Sachie was her aesthetic adviser, pointing out to her the delights of hidden London, which he had found when doing research for his new book, *British Architects and Craftsmen*, published in June that year. He told her to go on a tour of Spitalfields, beginning with the old shop in Artillery Lane, which he was to feature in the book: '. . . go in, at the right hand door, upstairs, to the first floor, where you knock at the door of the Jewish school cap maker, and he will politely show you the most exquisite Palladian room. . . .'[4]

British Architects and Craftsmen established Sachie as a connoisseur of English art and architecture, showing him to be, as *Southern Baroque Art* had done in another field, in the vanguard of taste. It was hardly a coincidence that he had been writing it over the period in which Evelyn Waugh had conceived his romantic celebration of grand English country-house life, *Brideshead Revisited*. In the *Evening Standard* Graham Greene praised Sachie for recalling 'so vividly and lovingly with the sense of poetry indispensable to the study of any art, our long and great tradition', while Cyril Connolly later described it as 'one of the books which preserved my sanity'. Once again Sachie had tapped a cultural vein before it came to the surface; the book was, in terms of copies printed, his most successful and eventually went into six editions.

As might also have been expected of Sachie, the book, although riddled with factual errors, was long on insight, idiosyncratic and curiously well-suited to its subject, with none of the reeling flights of prose which had characterised *Southern Baroque Art*. Sachie reined in his exotic imagination to fit the clear lines of Wren and Vanbrugh. It was intensely readable, written with confidence, boldness and pace, demonstrating the breadth of his knowledge and experience. This was Seaton Delaval, designed by Vanbrugh, a house

stranded in extraordinary and unpremeditated circumstances close to the Northumbrian seashore, but in a web of colliery lines, close to a mining village, and set in a landscape of clinker heaps that, by night, are lit up by flares. Everything to do with the house and its history is dramatically romantic and extreme; not least the Delavals themselves, their lives of debauchery and the violence of their ends. The males of the family drank to excess and fell down dead, but never died in bed, while the daughters were renowned for their beauty, among their number being Lady Tyrconnel, who had hair so long and luxuriant that it floated behind her, upon her saddle, when she rode. The entire family, one night, with Garrick's authority, took the boards at Drury Lane. . . . Such was the family of the Delavals, and Vanbrugh devised the appropriate setting for their beauty and folly . . . .

In Sachie's opinion architecture was, after prose and poetry, England's great contribution to European civilisation – 'our architecture and our language', he wrote, 'are the arts of England'. Under this heading he included the craftsmen who had executed and complemented the designs of Wren and Adam, Kent and Wyatt, the peculiar genius of a surviving eighteenth-century shopfront in Spitalfields or a seaside crescent at Brighton. The book was dedicated to Harry Batsford, whom he later described as coming nearest to his ideal of a publisher in that 'he *almost*, but not quite' believed in him. Batsford had a passion for English architecture and topography, having himself written several books on the subject in collaboration with Charles Fry. He had inspired Sachie to write *Conversation Pieces* and *Narrative Pictures* and had published *Roumanian Journey*. Sachie was to write a series of travel books for Batsford during the 1950s, beginning with *The Netherlands* in 1948, followed by *Spain* in 1950, *Portugal and Madeira* in 1954, *Denmark* in 1956 and *Malta* in 1958.

Since Georgia's departure for Canada at the end of May, Sachie had missed her dreadfully. 'I want to write to you all day and night, and tell you just what I am thinking,' he told her in his first letter to her on 30 May. He was totally dependent on women for comfort and happiness; in Georgia's absence there was Gertrude at Weston and his beloved Violet Gordon Woodhouse in London and at Nether Lypiatt. Bridget had come very much into his life again, having taken a flat in Mount Street towards the end of 1944. 'I do long to see you again,' she had written to him in September 1944, telling him she now planned to be in London indefinitely. Sachie however, to her disappointment and aggravation, had chosen the wrong week to be in London. They were together in London for ten days early in June 1945 while Georgia was away, when Sachie also saw old friends including Harold Acton, accompanied by 'a Chinaman',

Nancy Mitford, John Sutro and Lizzie Lezard, with whom he was now on the best of terms, and also, several times, Baby and Zita.

In mid-June he returned to Weston and Bridget to Monk Hopton. She had evidently been going through some sort of crisis of health or nerves; on the 15th she wrote to thank Sachie for his 'enchanting' letter:

> ... thank you ever so many times for all the exquisite things you say about me. I believe them to be true and consequently to constitute the greatest incentive I have to help battling against disintegration. In fact I don't think the break-up is imminent. I feel ever so much better already and forgive me for being overwrought in London and insisting on my own troubles which are so much less real than yours. With me it is merely '*angoisse de ville*' trouble and thank you very much for being so entirely sweet to me. You probably don't believe how essential you are to me, and it is wonderful to know that I am also important to you. . . .[5]

Sachie continued to write her 'heavenly', comforting letters. 'I assure you that I deeply appreciate them,' she told him:

> My life is so pointless in so many ways that I fear such a glorious build-up may strain my equilibrium to the verge of considering myself perfectly splendid. After all even if it is entirely your imagination that is responsible, it is at any rate an achievement to have been able to start it off. . . .I am returning to London Sunday and will expect and look forward naturally to dining with you Saturday. We will then have days of pleasure in front of us. . . .[6]

In London that June he had also, as he told Georgia, seen a lot of Osbert and Edith, 'The latter, absolutely charming: the former, grumpy as usual.' Edith, whatever the coolness in the general atmosphere between Renishaw and Weston, remained staunchly Sachie's friend and muse, cheering and encouraging him whenever she could. 'My darling,' she had written to him in January after they had seen each other in London.

> I *do know* what a wretched year it has been. It is dreadful that you can't even have one day's innocent enjoyment without these [financial] worries being at the back of your mind. But do try to remember that *A* at least all is safe, financially, for 2 or even 3 years, and that by that time *surely* the Swiss business will be settled. Also that Reresby's education is nearly accomplished. I know it is very easy to say this, but at least it is

someone speaking who has been dragged down – or *might* have been dragged down – by financial worries for years. . . .

Osbert, she assured him, was working '*without ceasing* to sort out the muddles left by that wicked old man'. She was loud in her praise of *British Architects and Craftsmen* – 'what a *wonderful* work . . . completely enthralling . . . it is opening a completely new world to me' – but it was not really her sort of book. '*When are you going to write some new poems?*' she asked. 'I think of this night and day. You *have* to do so. . . .'[7]

While Georgia was out of the way Edith was determined to further Sachie's career by introducing him to more literary circles than those in which he normally moved. The key figure was to be Maurice Bowra, now Professor of Poetry at Oxford and, in Edith's view, 'a sort of Warwick, the king-maker as far as poetry is concerned . . . he got Yeats his doctorate at Oxford'. He was also, she told Sachie, 'one of your enormous admirers'. She was giving a large lunch party in London on 6 September at which Bowra was to be present and after which she would arrange for him to have a long talk with Sachie. 'He and I have a plot and plan about your poems . . . to try to have a Volume of "*Selected Poems*" of yours brought out, which will be boomed.'[8]

'What's this mania of Edith's for Maurice Bowra imply?' Georgia asked suspiciously.[9] 'Edith is giving various parties, and she is most urgent that I should meet various literary people she is asking,' Sachie replied on 1 September, 'and I think she is right about this, as I never meet them, and am never mentioned in consequence. So I think it's a good thing, don't you?' Edith was thrilled when he agreed to be there on the 6th when Bowra would speak to him about the 'absolute *necessity* for you bringing out this book of poems'. She would get her suggestions for the selections ready and would he please do the same; she also thought that he should write two or three more poems, as she had for her collection, and that it should therefore be called 'Poems Old & New'. Meeting Bowra was one thing, but Sachie recoiled at the thought of exposing his poetry once again to public scrutiny and even more of writing new ones. But, Edith told him,

you are quite wrong about the poems, and about what would happen. And, incidentally, what do you mean about those great and wonderful poems being 'old-fashioned'?. . . The fact that you haven't written any poems for 6 or 7 years, or, as you say, looked at them, doesn't point to anything. I didn't write poems for 10 years, but came back to poetry more fresh than ever. *Now is our time* [she urged him] – the tide has turned, we have many and powerful adherents. . . .You speak of not

being able to bear them being torn to pieces. I can assure you that . . . you
have got one most *powerful* ally in Dr Bowra, who . . . would insist on that
book being properly treated. . . . *I know what we are. And I'm damned if I am
going to watch you throwing yourself away.*[10]

Sachie, however, did not respond, nor did he take part in a poetry reading
given by Osbert and Edith at the Royal Pavilion, Brighton, in September.
It was to be a year before he began writing poetry again after a fallow
period of eleven years; *Selected Poems* was to be published in the autumn of
1948. He did not even mention the project in his letters to Georgia. His
news to her was never literary, always social or domestic; there were bats
in all the bedrooms at Weston and the gardener had three sons and all
their wives, children and girlfriends staying in his cottage; as a result, the
garden was neglected and so were the bantams, all but four chicks out of
thirty or forty having died, while the household had to buy vegetables to
supplement those devoured by the gardener's hangers-on. Worst of all
there was a crisis in the Stevenson family and Gertrude might have to
leave Weston. In return Georgia sent him a letter full of wifely instruction,
certain sensitive parts relating to the Stevensons being in French 'because
you will forget to burn it'. 'Please write Reresby a cross letter. He can
quite well find enough time to write you once a week. . . .' As for the
gardener, 'really darling, surely you can exercise *some* control over him &
get him to do some work, get rid of his married sons & their families, and
pay for the vegetables the latter have eaten. . . .' Sachie must advertise for
a gardener to replace him.

> Please get the Rat exterminator over from Towcester. He will tell you if
> there *are* many rats. Of course the orchard soil is terribly overworked
> and 'tired'. *I* would give up *all* chickens but the very best for a year or
> so, at least. Gertrude must have book shelves put up in the Tartan attic
> to accommodate Francis's books. Don't forget to comment on all this
> [*sic*] questions.

Sachie spent the late summer with Violet at Nether Lypiatt, with
Bridget and her family at Monk Hopton for August Bank Holiday, and
with Bendor at Bourdon House at the end of August. Bendor had been
down to Chartwell and reported that Churchill, recently defeated in the
general election, was 'very depressed and at one moment in tears –
absolutely surprised and overwhelmed, and saying that the one thing he
could not understand or forgive is that his defeat was chiefly at the hands
of the three services'. One place Sachie had not visited that year, however,

was Renishaw. He had thought of going in August, but, on discovering that David Horner was to be demobbed on the 18th, decided not to; no one, he told Georgia, had pressed him to go, 'which is sad, isn't it?'

Much time was spent privately worrying over the result of Philip Frere's visit to Switzerland in search of the money missing from the Sitwell Stiftung. On 20 August Sachie reported to Georgia that Frere had returned very disappointed, £77,000 had disappeared from the Stiftung, in compensation for which the Swiss bank responsible had offered £20,000:

> It means £57,000 has gone . . . But a lot had gone already owing to G's idiocy. Philip told the Bank that we considered Woog was a rogue and had reason to think he may have murdered G. We cannot get the money back from Woog. He would be made bankrupt and go to prison, perhaps, but one would not get the money.

Osbert was to have the disposal of the money and might make it all over to Reresby and Francis, but there would be nothing for him or Edith.

> You mustn't be disappointed. I am not. I never expected a penny. It may not be so bad. We have been very happy, my darling. You must rely on me. I can only quote you from a letter written to his wife by Mozart: 'you must be glad to have *me* back and not think of money'. That is what I am saying to myself about you. . . . As I say, we have been completely happy in ourselves, haven't we?

It might be doubted whether the comparison with Mozart was any comfort to Georgia or even her husband's touching final remark: 'Don't worry. It will be as it has always been and that's more than good enough for me. . . .' It was, however, more than a little galling for Sachie to be told by Osbert, in response to Sachie's query as to whether he thought his and Georgia's lives would be bleak in consequence, that 'he didn't see why they should be any bleaker than his'. 'I felt inclined to say', Sachie told Georgia, 'well, only that you have six times my income.'

Georgia replied loyally on 31 August:

> As for the money question I am *not* fussing. I believe in our lucky star & have always felt money to be a secondary consideration. As long as we have each other nothing else really matters. And so long as you love me as you do I shall consider myself unbelievably lucky. Knowing how luxury-loving and extravagant I am I think you will appreciate this tribute, my darling. . . .

Edith wrote to Georgia about the 'Swiss business' to tell her how upset Osbert was over Sachie getting nothing and how he was 'determined not to have a penny of what is left for himself'; she herself offered to give up her share to Sachie. At the beginning of September it appeared that everything might in the end go to Sachie and that Osbert would have to sell Montegufoni, but Sachie was kept in the dark by Osbert over the details. He spent a week in London while Osbert and Edith were there early in September, when, as Sachie reported to Georgia, he had 'luncheon four or five times with darling Edith, and one dinner only with Osbert, who seems to me to take little or no trouble over seeing me. . . .' When they did meet, Osbert, although 'very nice', hardly mentioned business at all. Frere did not talk the situation over with Sachie, nor was Sachie shown his report. In the end Osbert decided to keep the castle, which had been nominally his since he was seventeen, and to use the money for its upkeep. He retained the entire Stiftung for his own use, leaving Sachie and Edith in the dark as to what was rightfully theirs since the £20,000 compensation had been offered to the three of them. It might have been that when he visited Montegufoni with David Horner in May and June the following year, ancestral feelings and Ginger, like *folies de grandeur*, operated in favour of keeping it; almost certainly Horner would have encouraged him to do so at the expense of his siblings. He found Montegufoni 'just the same', he told Christabel; 'at one point the Uffizi pictures were in the ground floor rooms and there were 1,000 people sheltering in the cellars underneath – a folk memory of its strength. . . . No news much,' he added, 'Georgia in a tiresome mood (is that news?) Sachie rather ditto.'[11]

Georgia arrived back in England on 7 November 1945 bringing with her Francis, aged ten, whom Sachie had not seen for five years; the Weston family was now complete. Reresby, whose relaxed attitude towards work while at Eton had been a source of anxiety to his parents, had surprised everyone by winning a scholarship to King's College, Cambridge. He had left Eton at the end of March just before his eighteenth birthday and, before taking up his place at Cambridge, had joined the army. Sachie was naturally pleased about the scholarship, but for practical reasons. Perhaps as a result of his own Oxford experience he took a dim view of the usefulness of universities, an opinion, apparently, shared by Bryher, to whom he wrote:

The one good thing is that Reresby has won a scholarship at King's. Of course, this doesn't prevent his having to go into the army next month;

but I do think it may make it much easier for him to get *out* of the army. I share your views about universities and hate them, and think them an entire waste of time, but I do think this is his best chance of getting released, after, perhaps, a year. He need only stay a term or two at Cambridge. . . .[12]

Reresby was, therefore, now usually away from home, first at Esher, then at the Guards depot at Pirbright, later as a cadet at Mons Barracks, Aldershot, followed by Sandhurst. He was to be commissioned into the Grenadier Guards in February 1946 and then served two years with the 2nd Battalion in occupied West Germany.

The two brothers were by now virtual strangers and altogether it must have been a curious homecoming for Francis. During the general panic over the success of the Labour Party in the general election in July, Bryher had even gone so far as to advise Sachie to keep Francis in Canada, but this he refused to contemplate:

> . . . we must have Francis back. It would be too awful for me not to see him. I feel he may be going to be a remarkable and interesting child and that it would be terrible for him never to see us, or be able to learn anything from me. I am sure I can make something wonderful of him, if I have the chance. . . .[13]

Francis, it was thought, might be destined to be the poet of the next generation, examples of his juvenile verse having been sent to Edith and Osbert and received enthusiastic comments. Sachie's parental dedication was not long-lived. Within six months of his return, Francis was despatched to a preparatory boarding-school.

In the spring of 1946, at the age of forty-eight, Sachie fell wildly, romantically in love with another beautiful young ballerina. Moira Shearer was just twenty, even younger than Pearl Argyle had been when he had first met her and barely a year older than Reresby. Born Moira King in Dunfermline on 17 January 1926, she had lived in northern Rhodesia until she was ten years old, when she had come to London to study at a succession of ballet schools, including Legat (where Pearl's picture hung on the walls) and Sadler's Wells. She had made her debut with the International Ballet in 1941, joined the Sadler's Wells Ballet the following year and, in 1944, made her first appearance as a soloist. In 1946 she was to make her name with a wide public when she made her début at Covent Garden in Frederick Ashton's revival of *The Sleeping Beauty*, first as one of the sisters of Prince Florestan, later dancing the principal role of Princess Aurora, following Margot Fonteyn. Sachie saw her second matinée performance on a Saturday afternoon and was stunned by the grace and beauty of the young red-haired dancer. Afterwards, on 11 March, he wrote her a fan letter, inviting her to lunch when he returned to London three weeks later:

Your performance as Princess Aurora . . . was so perfectly beautiful and I have been so haunted by it ever since . . . I thought *The Awakening* romantic and poetical beyond words, and I say this because as a poet and as one artist to another I know that poetry is born of performances such as yours. . . .[14]

To Sachie, the appearance of Moira in his life seemed, like the Copley portrait in his childhood, a beacon of hope, 'a sign of things being better', amid the advancing gloom (mainly, as usual, financial). 'My whole existence altered from the moment I saw you,' he later wrote to her. They lunched the following month at the Maison Basque in Dover Street. Sachie was totally enchanted. Moira, however, was no 'Cinderella'. As a well-brought-up girl living at home with her parents in Kensington, she was less accessible to Sachie than Pearl had been, but he adored her, showering her with presents of his books, letters, and champagne. Moira depended on Sachie's great knowledge and appreciation of the ballet. 'I miss you very much and feel sure you would like the performances and be able to give suggestions,' she wrote to him from Newcastle where she was touring in *Swan Lake* in August 1946. In July she had sent him the regulation lock of hair he required from all his loves, but the passion was all on his side. He poured out to her not only his love but his troubles, she inspired his poetry. Moira, an intelligent, down-to-earth Scot with literary leanings, was often irritated by his refusal to talk about his work or about other writers and by his idealisation of her as a goddess of beauty irrespective of her brains.[15] 'I adore my bird of paradise though always surprised that you can talk,' he wrote to her in 1951 and, four years later, 'As you know, I am still astonished to see you eating and smoking. . . .' She was also annoyed by his insistence that her fine-boned looks and natural grace indicated aristocratic ancestry – 'strawberry leaves somewhere,' he would say. Their friendship was to last, with obsession on his side, fond, sometimes exasperated loyalty on hers, until his death more than thirty years later.

In May, while Osbert, with Horner, was enjoying his first visit to Montegufoni as 'il Barone', Sachie loyally attended what even Edith called 'That ridiculous Poets' Reading' at the Wigmore Hall. The Queen and the two Princesses were there again and the readers were John Masefield (the Poet Laureate), Cecil Day Lewis, Walter de la Mare, T.S. Eliot, Edith and her former protégé, Dylan Thomas, who was noticeably drunk. Afterwards Sachie was present at an 'awful' dinner party given by Edith at the Sesame, which included Eliot, John Hayward, Dylan Thomas, now drunker than before, and his wife Caitlin, who sat next to Sachie. Dylan attacked Eliot, while Caitlin, having spilt ice cream on her arm, ordered Hayward, who was on her other side, to lick it off; when he refused, she called him a 'great pansy' and had to be led out of the room.

Sachie's first 'escape' from England was to the Netherlands, which he visited in July 1946 in the company and at the expense of Harry Batsford. Writing to Georgia from Amsterdam, Sachie told her of the 'curious sensation' of dining in restaurants where the food was 'plentiful' after London's austerity. It was expensive – dinner was never less than £3 a head – 'but Mr Batsford pays', and all the restaurants had 'such funny Roumanian gypsy bands. But they have left home much too long to be much good any more.' Nightclubs, another of Sachie's particular interests, were 'very amusing, however'.[16] The result was *The Netherlands*, one of the most delightful of his travel books, in which he conjured up images of light, grace and colour quite different from most people's rather limited view of a country of Rembrandt and polders, bulb beds and clogs.

'Trying to see Holland through eyes of our own,' he wrote in his introduction, 'and not following necessarily in the footsteps of our predecessors, we have been led into directions that may appear unorthodox only because they are not familiar.' 'Their national genius', he wrote of the Dutch, 'would seem to consist of a mingling of poetry with prosaic fact'; he was thinking of the Dutch painters with their pure interiors, scenes of everyday life, sea-scapes, still lives and flower paintings. For Sachie, perhaps the 'greatest discovery' of his visit to Holland was the magnificent series of town houses at The Hague with rococo interiors by Daniel Marot (1650–1718), the Huguenot artist, architect and designer of genius, patronised by William III, who had accompanied William to England, where he designed objects as varied as the Speaker's state coach and blue-and-white Delft pyramids eight feet high for the display of flowers at Hampton Court. Sachie wrote of the Dutch gardens of the past, such as the Orangery at Enghien with its 108 orange trees in tubs, some of them 200 years old, with straight stems of six and eight feet and 'globular heads, from which protruding shoots and blossoms are pinched off as soon as they appear, for culinary and perfumery purposes'. He described bedsteps painted with parrots, the dog carts of Walcheren and tilted carts of Zeeland, Frisian costumes and hats the size of coffee tables, the ancestry of the Frisians and their relationship with the fishermen of Leith.

On his return from Holland he completed his fifth 'entertainment of the imagination', *The Hunters and the Hunted*, dedicating it to Bryher. He had been writing it since the spring of 1943 and, in the interim, working on several other subjects which caught his fancy. The result was a disjointed hotchpotch of a book beginning with an exciting description of a French royal hunt as the title might have led one to expect, then leapfrogging to Byzantium and following that with no less than seventy-five pages of uninspired description of exotic birds, which, in the opinion of his bibliographer, Neil Ritchie, would have been much better included in an ornithological treatise. In fact, Sachie later used it as a base for his text in *Tropical Birds* and *Fine Bird Books*. It did not really deserve Bryher's enthusiastic reception when he sent it to her on publication in March 1947. 'What I like so much', she wrote, 'is that the painting, the event, or the landscape is but a cloak or suggestion for a country of your own . . . now that you have written this you must get away again, away from England. I feel with every line that you ought to be out in some tropic country untouched by the wars. . . .'[17] As further encouragement she retailed to him the opinion of a distinguished American critic that Sachie represented 'the best in English prose today' with the 'quality of imagination which distinguished English poetry in the past' and that no living writer had been able to write about Blake as well as he had in *The Hunters and the Hunted*.

Just over a year after Moira Shearer had come into his life, Pearl Argyle departed it with dramatic suddenness. On 29 January 1947 she died of a cerebral haemorrhage at the age of thirty-six in New York, where she had gone on holiday shortly after the birth of her second son. Sachie had not seen her since before the war. In 1939 she had moved with her husband and son, Sachie's godchild, to Los Angeles, but they had corresponded at least once a year. She had given up dancing to become a housewife while her husband was a reasonably successful film director; her former ballet colleague, Maud Lloyd, thought that she had been lonely in Los Angeles. When Sachie sent her *Sacred and Profane Love* in 1941 she wrote to him, somewhat wistfully: 'How right you are, even to me "Cinderella" is a dream of the past. It sometimes seems strange to me that I was ever a dancer. . . .'[18] Pearl remained a source of inspiration to Sachie in poetry and in prose. He often dreamed of her and once he thought he saw her ghost in the garden at Weston:

I saw someone by the white syringa,
I saw someone under the white syringa tree
But it comes to this. That there is no one left
That if I think I saw someone, it was imagination,
For what I never expected to happen, has happened,
And you are dead . . .[19]

After Georgia died, he shocked Gertrude and many of his friends by bringing out a photograph of Pearl and putting it in a prominent position in the drawing room. When Zita and Baby visited him again in the last years of his life, they were struck by the photograph of 'a ballerina'. Pearl remained for Sachie a vision of Cinderella to the end of his life.

In May 1947 Sachie finally made his escape to the south for which he had longed. He and Georgia, taking Francis with them, left Weston on 9 April for a month in Spain arranged by his friend Fernando Berckemeyer, Peruvian Ambassador in London, and Luis Bolin, another old friend of Sachie's whom he had first met in 1917, now Director-General of Tourism. It was the first of three visits to Spain, which resulted in the publication by Batsford of *Spain* in 1950. The list of acknowledgements reeled with the names of Spanish grandees who had helped him. In Madrid the Duke of Alba showed him his picture gallery with the Titian portrait of his famous ancestor, his Goyas and his Dürer etchings, and in Seville, where he and Georgia went with the Berckemeyers for the feria, he was a guest of the Duke at his palace of Las Duenas, 'with its courts of oranges and myrtles, its arum lilies, fountains and Moorish ceilings', and drove with him in his mule carriage round the feria. A roll call of aristocrats showed him their family palaces and their Goyas; in Barcelona the Marques de Villanueva y Geltru[20] introduced him to the Gaudi buildings and the slums of the Parallelo, the Montmartre of Barcelona, which later inspired one of his poems, took him to the abbeys of Poblet and Santa Cruz and invited him to stay on his country estate. The 'genial and perennial doyen of Barcelona nightlife', the Visconde Eusebio Guell, showed him louche and amusing nightclubs and perhaps also the dildo manufactories of which Barcelona was the centre. It was typical of Sachie to be less enthusiastic than anyone else about the Alhambra at Granada:

Why is it that the Alhambra, with so many beauties, is a little boring;
that the first sight of its interior is better than the second or the tenth;
and that, in the end, the red walls and towers become more beautiful
than the memory of those honeycombs and stalactites? Not only that, but
there comes a time when sooner than stand again in the Hall of the

Abencerrages or the Hall of the Two Sisters, we find ourselves admiring
the unfinished palace of Charles V nearby. . . .[21]

Stopping at Cordoba en route for Seville they found the court of the
great mosque full of orange trees in flower – 'It was so lovely that one
wanted to weep after all these awful years!', he told Bryher.[22] The
memory of orange trees and snow in Andalusia was to be crystallised in a
new poem, 'The Mezquita', which he wrote the following month.

> Coming out of the snow,
> I found the court of the mosque
> Full of orange trees in blossom;
> So about the time there was a death [of Pearl]
> There was a birth.
>
> It is the Man God of two wars
> That has lost its scent and lost its wisdom.

The southern experience relived seemed to have broken up his writer's block
after an interval of eleven years. 'It is such a pleasure and an intoxication to
me that I am able to write poems again,' he told Bryher, 'but my hand is so out
of practise [sic], that I cannot tell, yet, if they are good or not. I am going to
show them to Edith.'[23] Edith had never ceased to press him to return to
poetry, insisting that the Sitwells' hour had come round again: 'Don't you
see, darling, that a new generation has risen since Auden (who denigrated
us). Now is the time. . . . We have the new generation *with us*. . . .' Dylan
Thomas had quite eclipsed Auden, she told Sachie, 'and, tiresomely as he is
behaving at present, *he thinks you are a wonder. He told me you can write
everyone off the world; and he is right.*'[24]

The reaction of Edith and Osbert to the news that Sachie would
publish a volume of selected verse, and even more that he had begun to
write poetry again, was ecstatic. Osbert wrote of his joy at receiving the
new poems and of knowing that

> one will once again have poetry to read for the pleasures of sound and of
> the great sweep of your wings. . . . To my mind there is no poet who
> touches you in the sort of antique magnificence you conjure
> up. . . . Edith and I are quite mad over your

> > 'it rained
> > upon the tall windows'

almost the loveliest passage in a most lovely poem.[25]

The poem to which Osbert referred, 'The Lime Avenue', was one of a group of five written by Sachie late that summer and which showed in their pure simplicity and technical skill that he had not lost his touch. 'The Lime Avenue', which so pleased his brother and sister, evoked a rainy morning of his Renishaw childhood; 'Outside Dunsandle' and 'The Sick Man', two haunting poems of the Irish West, were inspired by a grand tour of southern Ireland which he, Georgia and Francis had made that August, staying with Bendor in Co. Waterford, with the Rosses, Bridget and Oliver Messel at Birr, with the Aly Khans in Co. Kildare and the Beits at Russborough.

'What excitement!' Edith wrote. 'Now we can look forward to a long reign of those great poems we have missed so terribly & that nobody else can write – everything from the grandeurs of the First Canto of "Fugal Siege" and the very different grandeurs of Agememnon's Tomb to the heavenly Cherry Tree and "The Red Gold Rain" and the sad magic of these new poems. . . .' She, too, liked 'The Lime Avenue': 'I can't think of any poem about rain that can touch it. It has the sound, the touch, the *space* of rain. . . .'[26] She and Osbert made the final selection of the poems, excluding, on the grounds of length, one of his personal favourites, *Dr Donne and Gargantua*. 'I am so happy that you like the selection, and O's preface,' Edith wrote, adding, soothingly, in response to a protest from Sachie, 'Yes, we were miserable, too, about Dr Donne and Gargantua. But it couldn't be cut *and* give the idea of the *import*. I tried and tried. . . .' She shared Sachie's enthusiasm for the '[Battles of the] Centaurs', 'Actor Rehearsing' and 'Chamber Idyll', his favourites among the long pieces. 'But oh, the short ones – "Fisherman" and "Cherry Tree" are absolute miracles. . . .' 'Why does it make you feel sad?' she asked. 'I suppose because (as it did to me) it made one feel terribly young again.'[27] 'It made me sad reading so much of what I wrote when I was nineteen or twenty,' Sachie told Bryher, '. . . life has not turned out quite how I imagined, then, it could be. . . .[28]

Since December 1947 it had been clear that Violet Gordon Wood-house was dying. 'It makes me miserable to think of it,' he told Bryher. 'I think, apart from Edith, [she is] the most wonderful woman I have ever known. . . .' Early in January 1948 Violet died; 'it will leave a blank in your heart and life that can never be filled,' Bridget wrote to Sachie. In an obituary notice for *The Times* he wrote of his gratitude for a friendship of thirty years 'since the writer was a boy', recalling that one afternoon only two years earlier she had played for him for two and a half hours all the Scarlatti she knew from memory, more than forty sonatas. She was, he said, 'a musical genius ... unique in that she excelled upon both harpsichord and clavichord ... her personality was as magical as her music.'²⁹ There were further losses of close friends that year with the death in May of Dick Wyndham, shot by a sniper in Jerusalem during the Arab-Israeli war, and in July of Emerald Cunard, who bequeathed to Sachie some of her most precious possessions, the letters written to her by George Moore. He wrote in *The Times* recalling being taken to her box at the opera when he was a schoolboy during the First World War, and that less than two months earlier he had been to the revival of *Boris Godunov* with her. Opera, he wrote, 'was what she loved most and perhaps it took the place, for her, of religion'.³⁰

Selected Poems was published on 28 October 1948 and dedicated to Bryher. The inscription in the copy which Sachie presented to Edith acknowledged his great debt to his sister: 'For my darling Edith, with best love from Sachie, who wrote the greater number of these poems to please you.' Osbert had contributed what Sachie's bibliographer called 'an unnecessarily pugnacious preface', written in his worst style, florid and bombastic. Like similar remarks of Edith's on Sachie's poetry, it probably raised more than a few unnecessary hackles. Sachie, he claimed, had 'a prodigious vigour of thought, of imagery and rhythm, a temperamental fire, and an ability to produce a sense of prodigality and profusion in a dingy screwpenny age of pinched and withered talents'. He defended him against the charge by 'certain austere persons' of 'deliberate exoticism', for concentrating on the Battle of the Centaurs rather than the Spanish Civil War, 'that most dreary and dunder-headed beano for international left-wing journalistic busybodies'. Osbert, one might think, would have done better to have left well alone and let his brother's poetry speak for itself.

Selected Poems had been carefully chosen by Osbert and Edith as a showcase for Sachie's talent, with just under 200 pages and a selection of all his best work in a far more easily digestible form than the unwieldy *Collected Poems*. It ended with five of his most recent poems, 'White Rose' (the lament for Pearl Argyle), 'The Lime Avenue', 'Outside Dunsandle', 'The Sick Man' and 'The Mezquita'. It was very favourably reviewed by the *Times Literary Supplement*, which expressed the hope that this selected edition would reach a wider public and 'serve finally to consolidate him as a poet of major significance. From the work in this volume alone there can be little doubt that posterity will find a place for him.'

Having begun to write poetry again, Sachie did not stop, finding in Moira and the lock of hair she had given him ('the feather of the firebird') a source of inspiration. Her engagement in 1949 to Ludovic Kennedy, whom fortunately he liked, was none the less a shock. 'My breath was quite taken away by your news,' he told her on 15 June. At the end of September Moira flew to New York for an American ballet tour. Sachie wrote to her every week. Despite 'worse money worries than ever. I think we may have to sell this house as we can't afford to live here,' he was managing to write poetry. 'It is owing to your friendship that this wonderful thing has happened to me. . . . I wrote a lovely poem about your flight to America,' he told her. This was 'Nimrod', which he sent to her, dated 3 October 1949: 'Blue hyacinth/Smelling like the evening sky/. . .'. When he published it years later he omitted 'M. . .S. . .', which would have identified her. He also sent her 'Nymphs were mentioned', woven round Pearl and Moira. '. . . it started when Edith told me, in September, to read a lovely passage about nymphs in one of Ezra Pound's poems. So I wrote this. . . . It is meant to be in cold impersonal accents like someone speaking who is dead.' One line recalled a dream he had had of Pearl when he had been staying in Tunisia:

> I heard Pearl's voice from the bottom of a well of water and was waiting for her to come up out of the water like a fountain. (She was already married, and in America.) This reminded me of Peele's poem – and it is the most beautiful dream I have ever had . . . it was like *living* in a lovely poem. . . .

It was dated 11 September 1949. The next day he wrote a poem to Moira herself, 'Belle Isis: Ballad of a Rose'. He sent three of them to Edith, including 'Belle Isis' and 'Brother and Sister: A Ballad of the Parallelo', a long, anguished poem inspired by his visits to the Parallelo, which he imagined at the time of Picasso's blue period. ' "Brother and Sister" is one of the few great poems of our time,' Edith told him. 'What *do* you mean by saying you now hate them all?'[31]

The trammels of life were closing in upon Sachie. 'My own worries are worse, I am afraid, and nothing but awful conferences of lawyers,' he wrote to Moira on 26 October. 'Edith is here at the moment (for the first time since 1940!). I have been having a very sad time lately and my nerves have been fearful,' he wrote to Bryher on 21 November 1949. 'At the moment I don't feel as if I shall ever be able to write again. Edith has been so good and wonderful to me. I will not worry you with my troubles. . . . I

think one arrives at nasty moments in one's life. It has been one lately. . . .'
The 'nasty moment' was the revelation of the huge extent of his
indebtedness, some £20,000. Edith, supportive as ever, had written to
him on 30 October that she was 'cut to the quick' by his financial worries,
'*just* when you are writing such wonderful poetry'. She blamed it, as
always, on Ginger: 'It is all that wicked old beast's fault – part of his
attempt to undermine and disorganise everybody's life.' At the end of
November she wrote again about his money worries and 'the *dreadful*
week' he had been going through; anxious, as always, to smoothe things
between her brothers, she assured him: 'I can only say that Osbert,
throughout, has spoken with the deepest affection & love. He *hated* your
going through it – & was very worried.'[32] Osbert, despite intense worries
about his health and the first signs of Parkinson's disease – 'I have
developed a palsy in my left arm – terrifying,' he had told Christabel in
August – had nobly come to Sachie's rescue. With the money gained
from compensation paid by the Coal Board for the mineral rights at
Renishaw after the nationalisation of the coal industry, he bought Weston
for the Renishaw estate, leasing the house back to Sachie for fifty years at
a peppercorn rent.

Osbert still loved Sachie deeply and felt responsible towards him. He
could not steel his heart and let him take his punishment as Ginger would
have done or, as Philip Frere unkindly remarked, 'By rights Sachie and
Georgia should sell the house and move into a flat in London and Georgia
should do the cooking.' Instead, Sachie and Georgia continued to live as they
always had, relying on the services of Gertrude and Bernard, keeping a
butler and other staff. There was a good deal of Lady Ida in Sachie; he hated
to be bored, and almost enjoyed the sense of drama provided by the
Damoclean sword of his overdraft hanging over him. 'I miss my overdraft,'
he told Reresby. He was only half-joking. It was not, however, pleasant to live
at the financial mercy of an elder brother upon whom showers of gold
seemed constantly to fall. Osbert had inherited Renishaw and Montegufoni,
he had the Stiftung, Mrs Greville had left him £10,000 and now the
nationalisation of coal was to prove the salvation of the Renishaw estate and,
in the long run, make Osbert a millionaire when he bought the neighbouring
Barlborough estate with money from the mineral rights. As if all this were
not enough, Osbert was a best-selling author; his autobiography earned him
another small fortune. In November 1949 he told Bryher that he had made
£10,000 that year. The settlement over Weston gave rise to a bitter feud
between Osbert and Georgia, exploited to the hilt by David Horner, with
whom Osbert was as much in love as ever.

Osbert's own feelings about it were expressed in a letter to Bryher, who, devoted as ever, had instantly offered her help. He replied to her on 15 November:

> ... there is nothing to be done ... it is just like throwing money down a well at present. Only, I've always adored Sachie, and feel the whole thing very much. I am buying the estate from him out of settled funds, and Philip is trying to induce order in his mind. But she (Georgia) I am sure fills Sachie with the idea that I wallow in luxury while she and he have no enjoyment (which is not the case): and Reresby (who of course is bound to stick up for their conduct) told me when I saw him, that my duty was to earn as much as I could and give the proceeds to S! ...
>   I'd much rather find money for Edith, who never expects anything. ...

Sachie, he wrote in a sentence that could have been penned by Ginger, 'won't settle down to work as I do, and is always rushing up to London. And the ambience of his wife makes it difficult for me to see them. ...'

Jealousy of Georgia where Sachie was concerned ran deep in Osbert. He thought her a bad influence on him with her love of Society, her affairs and, despite all her efforts to improve herself, her lack of intellectual qualities. He also thought her responsible for Sachie's extravagance. 'The most mysterious thing', he told Bryher, 'is that Sachie used to be so careful and understanding about money.'[33] How Osbert could ever, having lived at close quarters with Sachie, have come to such a conclusion is mysterious. Sachie could, in times of panic, be mean about small things. Once, when Reresby, while at Eton, admitted that he had two toothbrushes, this was held up in true Ginger fashion as an example of feckless extravagance: '*Did* you hear that, Georgia? *Two toothbrushes*!' But his meannesses were those of a financial illiterate; no one who had seen Sachie's reckless over-spending while still at Eton on books, gramophone records, Japanese prints and works of art could possibly consider him 'careful and understanding about money'. It was simply a question of points of view; having two toothbrushes showed a careless disregard for the value of money while spending it on rare plants and books, Chinese pheasants, exotic soap and curious liqueurs did not.

There were, inevitably, hard feelings over the settlement; Georgia seems to have felt that Osbert was behaving meanly towards them, putting the lowest possible valuation on Weston. As was her wont, she went in feet first, accusing Osbert of changing his attitude towards her: 'I seem to have been living in a Fool's paradise all these years and the realisation is a terrible shock and sadness,' she wrote to him on 5 February 1950 from the liner *Ile de France*, en route once again for New York and Canada. '. . . I think you will agree that it would have been better if the worst had been kept from me.' She added, with heavy sarcasm, 'Anyway our love for Sachie must be our greatest link, though mine for him grows every year.'[34] On arrival in Montreal she wrote to Sachie on 22 February instructing him: 'I know how you feel about Renishaw but you *must not* quarrel with Osbert. I long to know what he thinks of the letter I wrote him from the ship,' she concluded, 'in which I expressed very hurt but humble feelings. . . .' Osbert reacted with a viperish reply in which he returned her letter:

> . . . in the midst of the present appalling financial crisis, it is not suitable, I don't understand it.
>
> Misunderstandings accumulate. I have been horribly worried and made quite ill by the financial plight. No one likes to have to stump up £20,000 even when it is easy. I love Sachie; but he doesn't like facing facts. And there must have been extravagance of some silly sort to land you both in this particular difficulty. And the whole time I am having to bully the trust lawyers in order to obtain the help necessary. The valuation at so high a rate is the last straw from their point of view . . . they hold a letter . . . valuing the property at £10,000 less.
>
> I asked Sachie here next week but he has refused to come.

He went on to list his grievances against her: that she had considered Sachie badly treated because Osbert would not take him on their forthcoming American lecture tour; three would be too many, he argued reasonably, and, since he had to underwrite the financial cost of the tour, he could not do so for three. 'I was also angry, as head of the family, at not being told that Reresby had left Cambridge and taken a job: especially as I find his allowance. . . . I admire greatly your devotion to Sachie and the children,' he added, 'and hope now, when this is over, he will settle down and *work*. And that you will also settle down and manage his affairs for him. . . .' There was an added sting in the tail with a postscript: 'I am sure *loyalty* is the thing to be cultivated.'[35]

Georgia described this missive as 'really filthy' to Sachie. 'I am now estranged,' she declared. Couldn't they go it alone, she asked, selling Weston on the open market, keeping the house and selling the land to the highest bidder?

> I do not think we can accept Osbert's very grudging charity. . . . I really

think he would even like to contaminate our love. . . . Poor Osbert, he is warped and tortured . . . & cannot bear to see others happy – though poor! . . . He writes like a caricature of his own version of your father's fulminations. Spite, condescension, recrimination, *threats*. . . .[36]

Sachie reacted surprisingly calmly. 'Try *not* to worry too much about Osbert,' he told Georgia. 'He told me he thought it was better to have it out with you. And his letters are probably crosser than he is really himself. So keep calm.' Otherwise, his reports of his social life, had Osbert seen them, would have brought out all Osbert's most Gingerish feelings. While the lawyers squabbled over the Weston settlement, he seemed determined to enjoy himself as much as possible making repeated trips to London, staying with Tony Gandarillas, seeing Moira for the last time before her wedding to Ludovic Kennedy, going to Lord Camrose's election night party, spending a week-end with the de Traffords at Ascot and with Peggy Dunne at Chadshunt, where Peter Quennell was also staying, meeting Professors Zuckerman and Ayer, and travelling to The Hague with Robert Coe, where he had a very grand time, being introduced to the Master of the Horse, the Mistress of the Robes and the Grand Master of Ceremonies. He went to Covent Garden to see Margot Fonteyn with a new friend and ballet enthusiast, Michael Wood. He was making plans for himself and Georgia to go to Rome with the Herberts in May and in July they were to be guests of Bendor at Fort William in Co. Waterford and again at the end of August at Mimizan.

In the meantime, the settlement between Osbert and Sachie dragged on with endless delays, jealousies and suspicions between the lawyers and problems over valuations of the Weston estate. In March Osbert wrote that the Sheffield lawyer, Elmhirst, and Philip Frere were at loggerheads and offered to pay off Sachie's £5,000 portion of the Renishaw estate if that would help. 'I sit here and tremble, and do no work. I've done nothing this winter,' he added pathetically.[37] In May he was at Montegufoni. Elmhirst was holding things up: 'He is a dear, kind old man, but he cannot bring himself to pay as much as I have told him to' for Weston. By May it was over. The land, chattels and investments were disentailed, the investments and chattels remaining in trust while the land was bought by Osbert. Sachie was to be tenant at a peppercorn rent and, as his part of the bargain, gave up his claim to Renishaw as next male heir. On the 22nd Osbert wrote to Sachie from Montegufoni thanking him for his letter, 'under which I detect the usual strong and warming affection which means so much to me'. He had been hurt by Sachie's note of bitterness and self-pity: '. . . don't say you oughtn't to have married and had two sons. I don't deserve that (nor really did Father, who payed [*sic*] for Reresby's education, in some cases more than once).' There was a distinctly huffy feeling on his side that, after all he had done for them, it was not appreciated. 'Thank Heaven, the whole thing is now over – except that in consequence of my action and of writing frankly to Georgia . . . she and I appear not to be on terms.'[38] Sachie, he told Bryher, blamed David Horner's influence.

On 2 August 1950 Sachie received a frantic note from Edith, express delivery, marked in purple biro 'Burn this'. He later annotated the letter for his files with the date he received it, marking it simply '*Osbert*'. The letter contained the opinion of Sir Henry Cohen as to Osbert's condition, the secrecy dictated by fear that Osbert might read it. In July Osbert had written to Sachie, who had suggested that he should consult Sir Henry: '. . . alas, there is no doubt that I have suffered a physical disaster. It is with the greatest difficulty now that I write. . . .On a fine warm day, there are moments – until I try to work – when I forget my disability. . . .'[39] The Sheffield doctor had diagnosed gout; it was, in fact, Parkinson's disease. Sir Henry appears to have made misleadingly comforting remarks. 'It is the *condition* not the disease,' Edith wrote. 'There is no reason why it should get any worse. Sir Henry thinks it will go on the same for 10 or 15 years.' Sir Henry attributed Osbert's developing the condition to undiagnosed encephalitis from which he had suffered at Montegufoni just after the First World War. For poor Osbert, it was the beginning of a long drawn-out nightmare, the sinister consequences of which, for Edith and Sachie, were to be his increasing and pathetic dependence on the capricious and untrustworthy Horner.

Horner was again with Osbert and Edith when they sailed for New York in September 1950, leaving an apparently resentful Sachie in their wake. On 20 September Edith wrote to him from the *Queen Elizabeth*:

> My darling, I am full of grief at your letter. I cannot bear for you to be unhappy. I love you *most* dearly . . . you have got all this *wrong*.
>
> . . . I can see you think this is harming you, our coming first, our coming two and two. I *assure* you that it is *not*. Everyone in America is expecting you to come, and Colston Leigh [her and Osbert's agent for their US lecture tours] is all set and prepared to make a contract for you. *Nobody* thinks for a fraction of a second that you are being ignored or not regarded as you should be.
>
> I wish [she continued meaningfully] you saw more writers – I mean writers of your own position. Because they would assure you of that.

Nobody, however well they know the world, understands the literary position unless they are writers and mix with other writers. By that I mean that your friends who aren't writers can no more be expected to understand literary ins and outs than I could be expected to understand bishops' affairs. . . .Don't, my darling, I beg of you, let people who are no doubt well meaning, but who can't resist jabbing nerves, and giving pain, put silly and *most wrong* ideas into your dear and wonderful head. We have quite enough to bear with poor O's illness, and with all the dreadful worries there have been. . . .[40]

Sachie was sensitive about his siblings' success and his own lack of it, feelings which were not helped by Georgia's quite unfounded suspicions that Osbert and Edith were deliberately excluding Sachie from public literary occasions or trying to outshine him when the three of them did take part. She seems to have remained oblivious to the fact that Sachie's shyness and fear of confrontation made him refuse to appear at most of these occasions which he detested. Osbert's and particularly Edith's efforts to advance his literary career were unceasing; it was not their fault if he refused to come down into the arena. Edith had a point when she reproached him for never mixing with writers; the only literary figures he saw were people like Peter Quennell and Patrick Leigh Fermor, who were part of his social world anyway.

Georgia, however, had taken Osbert's admonition to 'settle down and manage Sachie's affairs' to heart. She had always seen herself as the guardian of his muse; now she took over from Osbert and Edith the role of his literary adviser. In Canada in the spring of 1950, stinging from the effects of Osbert's 'filthy' letter, she had busied herself promoting Sachie's works:

Everyone is clamouring for your books – all of them – & not one is obtainable. Unless you tell me soon that you have been to Harold Macmillan [Macmillan & Co. had published several of Sachie's books since *Trio*, with Osbert and Edith, in 1938] to go into this properly I am going to write to him myself so please get on with it. I am in touch with the booksellers & am trying to arrange direct orders from McM's & Batsford. I don't think they [the booksellers] are satisfied with having to buy from the U.S. It is fantastic that you should have the possibility of really big sales here & yet the publishers just seem to ignore the Canadian market. . . .

In the autumn of 1950 Sachie secured a coup which seemed to offer a measure of financial security. H.V. Hodson, always known as 'Harry', recently appointed editor of the *Sunday Times*, offered him the 'Atticus' column in succession to the retiring Robert Bruce-Lockhart, at a salary of £2,000 a year. The choice of Sachie was Hodson's; he had met him and admired his work. 'To my generation,' Hodson recalled, 'ten years younger than Sachie, the Sitwells represented something very special, a literary flowering of a particular kind, aristocratic, recherché, very superior. Sachie was a poet in prose.' The idea behind the 'Atticus' column was personal, not political, comment; it was not a gossip column. Hodson thought that Sachie's contacts, his wide knowledge and his travels made him ideally suited for the job, his brief being to write the column round people or events which had come up during the week. Moreover, it had been a *Sunday Times* tradition always to have the best writers on the payroll.[41]

Hodson's initiative was, however, received with caution by his colleagues, some of whom thought Sachie's style too different from that of Bruce-Lockhart, who had been an outstanding success as 'Atticus', and from the generally down-to-earth content of the *Sunday Times*. Their main preoccupation was to raise the paper's circulation despite paper rationing being still in force, against their principal rival, the *Observer*. There were understandable fears that Sachie's contributions might be above the readers' heads. 'Sacheverell Sitwell . . . was then contributing an unsigned column to one of the Sunday papers,' Anthony Powell recalled, 'in which he wrote of anything that had caught his attention, no intellectual or aesthetic holds barred, resulting in a panorama of esoteric items altogether unfamiliar to most newspaper readers. . . .'[42] Another old friend of Sachie's, Constant Lambert, who was in the habit of ringing up Powell on Sunday evenings after the column came out, invariably began his conversations with the words: 'I say, *have* you read Sachie this Sunday?'

Sachie enjoyed writing his weekly column, making the most unlikely connections and idiosyncratic comments, diving deep into his extraordinary memory and coming up with rare *objets trouvés*. Field Marshal Montgomery, he thought, resembled 'Louis XI, one of the cleverest brains of the Middle Ages, who wore on his head a kind of tank beret with lead medals of the saints upon it'. One item, headed 'A Passing Mystery; read:

> A number of Greek bishops came over to London for the Conference at Lambeth and attracted much attention owing to their impressive and venerable appearance. They were taken to Lambeth Palace every

morning in a bus . . . from which all posters had been removed excepting one which advertised a farce called 'Cuckoos! What a Lark!' The superscription may have puzzled onlookers when the bus whirled past, both decks crowded with those black-garbed figures, in their curious top hats, their hair done in a 'bun' behind their heads. . . .

Other pieces might feature rare bulbs, old soaps, European chocolate shops or the dervish who ran backwards all the way from Constantinople to Belgrade. When Sachie later published a collection of them in 1953, the title which he chose was, appropriately, *Truffle Hunt*. He took almost as much pleasure in the variety of correspondence he received as a result of his column, engaged a secretary and replied meticulously to all of them, savouring the range of human eccentricity which his writing had trawled up.

Unfortunately for him, however, not all the correspondence received by his employers was favourable. The dread figure of the Philistine, ancient enemy of all Sitwells, began to rear its head, taking the unlikely form of Ian Fleming, head of Kemsley Newspapers's foreign service, who was influential with the proprietor, Lord Kemsley. At editorial conferences Hodson began to find himself increasingly isolated on the subject of Sachie, against Fleming, the literary editor, Leonard Russell, who had 'a rather prosaïc streak', and the deputy editor, Valentine Hayward, a professional journalist and no intellectual. After six months he found that he had absolutely no support for continuing with Sachie as 'Atticus'. Kemsley himself knew and liked the Sitwells, but was easily persuaded that Sachie's contributions were too fanciful and above the heads of his readers. By the summer of 1951 Hodson could no longer hold out against the majority and, at the end of July, he had to tell Sachie that his services would not be required beyond the end of September. Sachie had just returned home to Weston, happy from a visit to Moira and Ludovic, when the blow fell. 'Darling Moira,' he wrote on 29 July, '. . . on Wednesday, just when I thought I was out of my main troubles, the most appalling crisis broke upon me. It is shattering and I don't know what to do. I have, now, to go abroad . . . and when I come back cannot see my way further than October. . . . It will lose me two-thirds of my income.'[43]

In mid-August 1951 Sachie and Georgia, with Francis, went to stay with the Marques de Villanueva and his family at their estate near Tarragona. From there, he poured out his troubles to Moira:

I have had too *much* and more than my fair share of troubles. And I have tried so far, and done such a lot of work. I think you have been sent into the world to help others, and make them forget their worries and troubles; and all I want, when I think of you, is to write poetry. I had taken the chance, when I got those articles, to do this – as I know I shall never be able to do it again, financially. I have written a number of very good poems. . . .

He felt that he had reached a crisis in his life. He was fifty-three and still financially insecure. He had suffered from a recurrent ulcer and Georgia, too, was unwell, in pain from fibrositis in her hip. Perhaps worst of all was his failure to have a real literary success of the kind that Osbert and Edith now enjoyed. He did not know how to shape his literary future, thinking at first, in desperation, that he would write a novel. Then one evening at sunset, walking by fields of scarlet castor-oil plants, he determined to write a major book, its subject to be 'the problems and mysteries of life and death'. He envisaged it as a two-volume work. The first volume would take him seven years to complete before being published in 1959 as *Journey to the Ends of Time.*

Sachie began work on the book as soon as he returned home, but, with the last of his 'Atticus' pieces appearing on 23 September, the financial outlook took on its customarily bleak tone. Meanwhile, unknown to him, David Horner was working behind the scenes to make his financial future even more uncertain. Horner's malevolence towards both Sachie and Georgia is only too evident in a letter he wrote to Christabel Aberconway in October 1951: 'Sachie and Georgia are, alas, up to their old tricks. He has got the sack from the *Sunday Times* and she is flying to N.Y. to spend 6 weeks with Momma in Montreal. And this means a new financial crisis just after Osbert has forked out £25,000 for them. They are a very tiresome couple.'[44] Christabel had chosen to remain a friend of Osbert's by being a friend of David's. In a letter to Georgia, Sachie had angrily accused Christabel of 'sucking up' to Horner, and on one envelope of this date he had written: 'I HATE CHRISTABEL.'

Unwisely, Sachie chose to quarrel also with Christabel. The row stemmed from an occasion when Christabel apparently told Sachie, after a visit to Osbert, that she thought Osbert's Parkinson's disease had been caused by 'certain worries', which Sachie took to imply that the prolonged negotiations caused by his financial situation had been a factor in the onset of the illness. Since then Sachie had cut her at the theatre – 'Had I been Noël Coward, you could not have turned from me with greater loathing,' Christabel wrote – and refused her invitation to luncheon. In response to her letter asking for an explanation, Sachie wrote a bitter and distressed letter in return: 'I do not think you can realise what a wicked and monstrous load you are fastening on to me. I cannot possibly see or speak to you again. . . . It is, of course, *as always* that fatal and horrible David Horner (who has been such a disastrous influence in Osbert's life) whom I have to thank for this. He was a wicked, evil creature long before he came into poor Osbert's life. . . .[45] Christabel reported all this to Osbert. Unhappily, Osbert replied:

> I was saddened by what from your letter to him I see Sachie has done. He unites great strength of feeling, with a very bad temper, and an absolute resolution not to face anything unpleasant, like having to say one is sorry. Poor Sachie (I should say poor Christabel to have to write the letter): it is sad that he loses his real friends and those who love him. . . .[46]

Sachie was, however, absolutely correct in his instinct that principally David Horner and, secondly, Christabel intrigued against him and made trouble for him with Osbert. Neither he nor Edith had ever really liked Christabel or her influence over Osbert. She, in return, had been jealous of them and made common cause with Horner. According to an emotional pencil note which she made two years later on the eve of going into hospital, she had kept Sachie's 'dreadful' reply with copies of her letters to him for Osbert's possible future use: 'I can't bring myself to destroy Sachie's letter in case, one day, it *helps you*. . . .' A final sheet following her second, apologetic letter to Sachie implies that she sent with it a drawing of Weston by Rex Whistler, her friend and protégé, in expiation – 'no answer came to this letter – But the little picture by Rex Whistler was gratefully accepted.'[47] In April 1952 Horner wrote Christabel an ingratiatingly conspiratorial letter describing how Sachie had cut him in the St James's Club, where he had gone to lunch with a friend. Seeing Sachie there lunching alone,

> I manœuvred to a table close and opposite to him and received a direct cut . . . very soon, as I made it quite clear that I was enjoying the situation, he left. . . . Well, now we know where we are, and, as I have said to Osbert, Sachie has nothing to gain and quite a lot to lose. . . .[48]

Documents dating from that year show Osbert arranging for money which might otherwise have come to Sachie to go to Horner and persuading Edith to do likewise. A fragment draft in Osbert's hand for a will by Edith proposed to leave to my brother Osbert, or to David Stuart Horner, if my brother should no longer be living, and, in any case, with remainder to D.S.H. after my brother's death, the sum of £3,000 at present put aside to buy a house, or, if the house had been bought, I leave that house instead of the £3,000 in the same way. The contents of this house should be offered at a fair valuation to either O.S. or D.H., whichever is the owner, should he desire to buy it.

I also leave to D.S.H. absolutely the sum of £400 or so in my account with. . . .[49]

This will almost certainly dates from 1952, since it was attached to correspondence between Osbert and his Swiss and English lawyers dated 11 November 1952 and 23 March 1953. It does seem strange that, so recently after Sachie had got into such financial difficulties that he had had to give up his right to Weston, Edith should have contemplated leaving her property to Horner. Even more so as Edith's biographer states that the £3,000 in question had been given to Edith by Bryher, who would certainly not have been pleased to see it go either to Osbert, who did not need it, or still less to Horner. Had Sachie known of this, he would have regarded it as a great betrayal, but as there is no mention of it anywhere in his papers, it seems that he did not.

Osbert was, moreover, preparing a second betrayal. It is clear from a letter dated 11 November 1952, addressed to Osbert at the St Regis in New York, by Dr Hans Berger, Osbert's Zurich-based lawyer who dealt with the affairs of the Stiftung, that Osbert was intending to leave Montegufoni and the farms which provided the income to support the house to Horner. Montegufoni was Osbert's property absolutely; the farms, however, were the property of the Sitwell Stiftung, in which both Edith and Sachie had a legal share. Osbert, Berger pointed out, should make one will leaving the castle of Montegufoni to Horner and in another express his wish that the Italian farms in the name of the Stiftung should be transferred to Mr Horner; Berger added that, if the other beneficiaries (by which he principally meant Sachie) should not agree to this transfer, the legal validity of the Stiftung should be questioned and, if it were found to be invalid, Osbert's whole share of it should be bequeathed to Horner. Incidentally, Berger's letter confirms that Edith had made Horner her heir: 'If your Sister has already appointed Mr Horner as her successor by her Will,' he wrote, 'it could happen that Mr Horner would get finally 2/3 of the Stiftung which is, as I understand, not your intention. . . .'[50]

Just as Sachie was despairing of his financial prospects after his last article appeared in the *Sunday Times* on 23 September 1951, once again something seemed to have turned up. In November 1951, while Georgia was in Canada, Sachie signed a contract with Alexander Korda to write a preliminary script for a film of *The Sleeping Beauty* with costumes and designs by Oliver Messel, for which he was to be paid £100 a week. Georgia, who was in New York, again took it upon herself to act as his literary adviser. As a result of her conversation with the impresario, Gilbert Miller, she sent Sachie a peremptory sounding birthday telegram on 15 November: 'Many Happy Returns ... Miller considers film contract absurd & does not trust Dane [Pollinger]. Only expedient change agent.' She followed it up with a letter expressing her disappointment and trampling with her accustomed zeal on literary etiquette:

> I know how you feel about Pearn, P[ollinger] & H[igham][51] but really you must agree this is too much. I knew Korda would not give more if *they* acted for you ... tell Pollinger you are very sorry but you will have to get someone else to act for you, who really knows the film world, & then find a new & more suitable agent.

Sachie had had an enjoyable birthday dining at Bridget's with Beaton and Greta Garbo, Beaton's guest for two months. 'Beautiful, but stupid, and not really very interesting', was Sachie's verdict on the star. 'But charming,' he added. He paid no attention to Georgia's transatlantic instructions, ignoring her advice about a change of agent. Impressed by what Messel and others had told him could be earned from script writing, he had pressed Pollinger to raise the asking price, but to no avail. Korda told Pollinger firmly that he could not give Sachie more as he had never written a script before. His contract was for £100 a week for a minimum of six weeks, but it was envisaged to take longer with a further period in the following autumn when shooting began.

Sachie owed this windfall to Messel, who had already been working with Robert Helpmann on a script and had suggested Sachie when Helpmann had fallen out. Sachie, therefore, found a project half-completed, Messel already having done drawings in accordance with Helpmann's script. There were ominous signs, as Sachie told Moira, who was in the United States: 'endless, endless complications. They haven't even appointed a director or producer yet! Everyone is rather hysterical.'[52] Sachie, however, was feeling confident: 'More and worse worries than ever! But never mind! I am determined *not* to be done in. . . .' He spent the weekdays in London working with Messel every afternoon. ' "The Sleeping Beauty" seems to be slowly taking shape,' he wrote to her, 'but *so* slowly, and difficult to attempt anything else while it is going on. . . . However, I am exhausted with writing long books and rather pleased to be doing something else – I only hope it will lead to something more. . . .' In the meantime, he enjoyed observing the intrigues of the homosexual ballet world centred on Covent Garden and retailing them to Moira:

> So far, thank heavens, very little to do with Freddy [Ashton] who, I think, is trickier than ever. Oliver [Messel] is the nicest, and least tricky of the lot. But they are all the same and you cannot trust them.
> Tomorrow night I go to see 'Billy Budd', and do have good reports of it. The mere fact of Britten having Lord Harewood, Eddy Sackville-West and Desmond Shawe-Taylor after him in a pack is a very bad augury. . . .There, again, I hear Mr [David] Webster says with pride that it is the first time 'this thing' has been put on any operatic stage – but I do not believe any audience will stand it for more than a few performances. They were all in tears on the first night, and of course Mr W[ebster] has found a most 'beautiful-looking' young man in New York to play 'Billy Budd', and it is all too silly for words. They are all so busy conspiring too – and I believe Freddy, even, would like to oust [Ninette] de Valois from Covent Garden, which is mad from his point of view. . . .[53]

A month later he had catty things to say of the recently appointed John and Myfanwy Piper: '. . . the new ballets will be sillier and sillier. Fancy having someone who likes drawing Methodist Chapels as arbiter of taste at Covent Garden. . . .'

Sachie had high hopes of the project, but, like the 'Atticus' job, he was doomed to disappointment. On Christmas Eve he reported that work on *The Sleeping Beauty* had stopped and he was unsure whether they would want him again. It was later postponed until 1953, then finally scrapped. 'So little money that I feel almost cheerful,' he wrote to Moira on 12 January 1952, 'and I think it keeps me cheerful. . . .' 'I am so far from the £10,000 p.a. of Osbert, which, at least, he was able to make out of his own writing,' he told Georgia wistfully. Their income, carefully doled out by Mr Charles Musk, of Coutts in the Strand, was now less than it had been 'in the old days', £105 a month, or £1,260 a year as against £1,430, of which, he said, 'wages and telephone' took up almost three-quarters. Among Sachie's ephemeral projects at this time was a new ballet review, *Foyer*, which he launched in partnership with Michael Wood; only two numbers appeared.

In May 1952 Macmillan published Sachie's *Cupid and the Jacaranda*, the last of his 'entertainments of the imagination' to appear for seven years. He had been working on the book since 1946 and had finished it in 1951. It was one of the most intensely autobiographical of his books and a perfect example of his surrealist technique of dislocation and juxtaposition which tended to make his 'entertainments of the imagination' a demanding read. In it he attempted to describe his creative process, drawing deep on the wells of his imagination in the long hours he spent in his room (now over more than twenty years). For Sachie, his 'interior life is more fully peopled than the world of every day, and with scenes and persons that may have a deeper reality'. The inhabitants of this interior world appeared again and again in his books: himself, his experiences, dreams and nightmares (one of which featured a horrible leering creature with iron feet and hands, the grand master of all evil; characteristically, it was a baronet). Then there were his literary heroes, Baudelaire, Rimbaud, Flaubert and the ghost of his dead love, Pearl. Things seen or experienced would well up in his consciousness years later. When he visited a country to write a travel book or to see a work of art, he never kept a diary or took notes. The sensations he then experienced would stamp themselves into his consciousness adding to the impressions he had already had from books, paintings, objects and photographs. His other principal sources were the notebooks he had made in years of mornings spent in the Reading Room of the British Museum; his collection of old florists' catalogues and coloured plates of old-fashioned flowers; and his notebooks on books of birds, particularly Gould's *Trochilidae* or *Humming Birds*, Bowdler Sharpe's *Birds of Paradise* and the parrots in Gould's *Birds of Australia*. Sometimes the images of these birds or flowers would be transmuted into poetry; at others, and less successfully, they would be used as a roll call of names as in the bird chapter of *The Hunters and the Hunted*. Sachie never disciplined his imagination, which he saw as the source of his strength, an almost divine inspiration. The results could be tedious, over-elaborate, or, at his best, magical.

Sachie had begun to write *Cupid and the Jacaranda* in his fiftieth year. It was natural that he should look back over his first half century, tracing his life experiences and his creative career back to his adolescent passion for a painting by Watteau, *L'Embarcation pour la Cythère*. Watteau's picture of lovers embarking for the island of Venus in search of beauty and pleasure he took as a symbol for his own aesthetic journeys. 'The career of a writer of my sort . . . could be called a perpetual exploration of the rose-hung island. And, indeed, during three decades I have searched it through and through,' – he wrote. He looked back on his travels, on significant moments – 'August 1915' or objects; seeing, in a moment of deep depression in the Musée Carnavalet in Paris, a female harlequin's costume, he had experienced an aesthetic charge of such force that it was 'like falling in love . . . the old dress . . . saved me'. He wove into the text memories of people who had been or were close to him. At Villa Lante, the most beautiful garden in the world, he felt the ghost of his father haunting its shades; he dreamed of 'two sisters', Zita and Baby, and of the two ballerinas, Pearl and Moira, whom he loved. A deep vein of depression ran through the book, the recurrent sense of loss of the world which he had known, with, at the end, a note of optimism:

> Why do I write, or rather why do I go on writing, except for love of this world and the wonders in it, which are enough for all the hours of every lifetime since the first human footprints upon the tawny sands? . . . I have lived to see what I was born to see. I cannot go down in unhappiness after that. It is not a 'poor earth' after all. It has splendours as well as miseries to recommend it.

That for him was his religion. There was a note of defiance to his critics: 'Here, in this book, I write to please myself; and I am my own best audience. I have watched myself ever since I began to write; and I know that I write best when I write to please myself. . . .' For people less interested than Sachie was in his tours round himself, *Cupid and the Jacaranda* seemed repetitious and self-indulgent.

There was too, perhaps, a note of regret that he would not be able to write just what pleased him because he had to try and supplement his income. There now began for Sachie a period of twenty years of ceaseless activity, relentless productivity and bewildering diversification when he seemed incapable of saying 'No' to any project suggested by a persuasive publisher. He was driven partly by a sense of financial necessity, partly by the need for distraction. He travelled not only in order to fulfil his ambition to see every major work of art in the world before he died, but also to escape the underlying melancholy and sense of failure which dogged him when he had time to reflect. In addition he worked, in collaboration, on *Fine Bird Books* (1953) with Handasyde Buchanan and James Fisher, on *Old Garden Roses* (1955) with James Russell and on *Great Flower Books* (1956) with Wilfrid Blunt; he contributed a foreword to a book on Fabergé and arranged an exhibition of the goldsmith's works in 1949; he wrote numerous articles for periodicals and newpapers, and did book reviews and radio talks on subjects or people which interested him. Sachie also travelled unceasingly over the decade, going further and further afield, writing a travel book almost every year.

On 25 February 1952 he had apologised to Moira for not having written to her for three weeks and giving her a picture of the pressure of his life:

> I have been so busy. . . I had to rush through the book on birds – and I managed to finish it in just over six weeks – and then I have had to write 4 articles for 'Picture Post', all of immense length, about the King's reign. This was so uninteresting that the only plan was to sit up practically night and day for 8 or 9 days to get them down. . . .

He had immensely enjoyed writing the bird book, but the articles on the King's reign had left him so bored with the subject that he could not 'contemplate a photograph of any member of the Royal Family without a shudder'. As for *The Sleeping Beauty*, 'At the moment I have an absolute nausea for it, having loved it so in the past. . . ' It was, therefore, almost a relief that it had been postponed.

While relations between Sachie and his brother had become distinctly uneasy over the past decade, new trouble was brewing in the younger generation. Reresby, although charming, good-looking and intelligent, had proved something of a disappointment to the excessively high hopes which his parents, and his mother in particular, had had of him. Georgia, for instance, had been devastated when Reresby had not been elected to 'Pop', the smart Eton society. In view of both Osbert's and Sachie's records at Eton there was no high standard for him to follow, and he had, after all, won a scholarship in medieval history to King's, Cambridge, thus far outshining the elder Sitwells academically. His Cambridge career had not been a success; going up to King's after two years as a Guards officer had seemed to Reresby 'like going back to school'. He found it difficult to take academic life seriously, particularly since, instead of reading history as he had been destined to do, his parents decided that he should do something 'useful'. On the advice of one of Sachie's few friends in business, Rudolph de Trafford, he was to read economics, but in characteristic Sitwell fashion found his tutor so physically repulsive that after three months he changed, at Sachie's suggestion, to modern languages. This again proved a failure and he switched to English literature, his tutor being George 'Dadie' Rylands, the noted Bloomsbury figure. Even this failed to grip Reresby, who, after two unhappy love affairs, decided to leave without a degree.

In 1951 Reresby had met and fallen in love with Penelope Forbes, daughter of Colonel the Hon. Donald Forbes, a member of a prominent Anglo-Irish family. Penelope's father had been killed in a motor accident when she was twelve; despite the grandeur of her father's relations, his brother being the 8th Earl of Granard, Master of the Horse to Edward VII and George V, she and her mother and sister were not left well off. Penelope took various jobs, modelling, working for the Foreign Office and in the antiques trade. It was while working in the Antiques Department at Fortnum & Mason, a traditional source of temporary employment for the children of the upper classes, that she met Reresby, who 'had started in saucepans and moved to antiques'. It was love at first sight on Reresby's side; he was dazzled by her and immediately asked her out.

All went well until Reresby took Penelope down to lunch at Weston to meet his parents, when Sachie, for reasons that have never been satisfactorily explained, took a dislike to her and refused to speak to anyone the entire time. After this bad beginning things went even further downhill as it became apparent that Reresby wanted to marry her. Both Sachie and Georgia violently opposed the idea of their marriage, Georgia's behaviour being particularly outrageous, even to the extent of her making anonymous telephone calls to the unfortunate Mrs Forbes in her distinctive deep-throated voice, which was, of course, instantly recognisable, and sending her local lawyer from Towcester to point out the impossibility of the marriage. Even their Northamptonshire neighbour, 'Freddie' Lord Hesketh, was dragged in and deputed to reason with Reresby. The Hesketh *démarche* proved an utter failure. Reresby was forty-five minutes late arriving for dinner with Hesketh at his club, by which time his Lordship was in a rage and had taken more than a little wine; the result was a violent row with Reresby storming out of the room.

On the other side, Reresby and Mrs Forbes appealed to Edith for help. On 26 August 1952 an agitated and irritated Edith wrote to Osbert that Reresby had rung up to tell her that he '*had to speak* to me about something "very worrying"', followed up by a telephone call from Mrs Forbes, who spoke for twenty-five minutes, with the result that Edith, who was staying at Durrants Hotel, got no lunch at all.

> Apparently R. is wanting to marry the girl at once, and when he went to Weston on Saturday, G. made such scenes that he returned from there in what Mrs Forbes called an awful state – G. having made him promise he wouldn't marry the girl until S. & G. return from America.

G. said they were trying to kidnap R. and that *she didn't know who Mrs Forbes is* – and a lot more of the same kind. Mrs F. said, 'She knows who my nephew Arthur Granard is.' I said, 'Oh nonsense, Mrs Forbes. Of course everybody knows who you are. I never heard such a thing.' Apparently G. has been *insolent*, and it has evidently been repeated. . . . Mrs F then said would I tell S. and G. she isn't an adventuress!! 'Not the awful creature they think me.'

Reresby is coming to see me tomorrow night, & then I am landed with seeing S. & G. on Saturday. *What* a bore these constant hysterical scenes are. . . .

According to Mrs F, "people are beginning to talk" as R. has spent his whole free time in her house since Xmas. This is her theme song.

Oh how tired one is of non-existent people with non-existent emotions, their self-deception, their grabbing greed, their monstrous selfishness, their worked-up 'Design for Living' dramas! (I don't mean poor R. is this. . . .) I don't think *Sachie* is involved in any of this.

My own theory is that it would be best for R. to announce the engagement, & say it will be a long one, as the marriage will only take place on his parents' return from America. By *that* time, if it *isn't* serious, they will be bored with each other. If they *are* serious, there is nothing to be done.

She added a postscript: 'I've just had a letter from Mrs Forbes. It is G. who is kicking up the fuss.'[54]

Georgia's violent reaction to Reresby's proposed marriage has never been explained, even by her friends. Part of it must have been natural jealousy at finding herself supplanted in her son's affections. There may have been an element of personal dislike, but to oppose the marriage on snobbish grounds was, in her case, ridiculous. After all, she herself came from a not particularly distinguished background. The Dobles were neither aristocrats nor millionaires. Penelope had very little money, but her bloodlines were better than Georgia's. She was four years older than Reresby, which was hardly good grounds for objecting, and, being a woman of strong personality, was precisely the character he needed to provide the support which had not always been forthcoming from his mother. Georgia, in fact, had become more Sitwellian than any Sitwell to the extent that she thought nobody good enough for the Sitwell heir. Beauty and character alone would not suffice; there must be a great name and a great fortune to go with it. In Sachie's case his objection seems to have been on a personal level. He was extremely susceptible to women, but Penelope failed to charm him: perhaps she did not try. In any case he was undoubtedly prejudiced against her (probably by Georgia) before he met her; when he did, he decided that she was not his type.

Georgia's behaviour had resulted in a complete rift with Reresby. On 12 September, three days before their departure for a four-month lecture tour of Canada and the United States, Sachie wrote to Moira bemoaning the situation on Georgia's behalf rather than his own. Most of his letter concerned his relationship with Moira, his delight at having been asked to be godfather to her first child and his own feelings at being separated from her for so long: '. . . although I see you so little, I cannot bear to part from you. I feel awful, having been thrown into a sort of ecstasy of sadness by your letter, and can hardly move in my room. . . . Your image has always helped and comforted me. . . .' Almost as an afterthought he wrote: 'Still fearful worries about R. and Georgia has been worrying herself almost silly. She is even fonder of him than she had thought: and now he makes no effort to see, or even '*phone* her, before leaving, which hurts her terribly, poor thing.' After this brief bulletin, he resumed: 'Darling Moira, I am already thinking of when I see you again. . . .'

The blow fell just as they arrived in Chicago on 31 October. That day Reresby and Penelope were married from her aunt, Lady Granard's house, at the *mairie* of the seventh *arrondissement* in Paris. Reresby's promise not to marry until his parents returned, exacted by Georgia under duress, had not prevailed against Penelope's ultimatum. Understandably insulted by the Sitwells' behaviour, she determined to end an impossible situation. She went to Spain to stay with her cousins, leaving Reresby with a choice. He chose his own future, avoiding what would undoubtedly have been protracted guerrilla warfare but precipitating all-out war. The newly married couple sent Sachie and Georgia a telegram announcing their marriage. Georgia denied ever having received it. Sachie's letter about the event to Moira simply says:

> We were both knocked out entirely in Chicago by that news of Reresby
> – whom I am afraid has been so deceitful with us. . . . Poor G. was in
> tears for 48 hours, the blasted girl he has married [he could not bring
> himself to mention her name] is so uninteresting & 30 years old. . . . It
> has been a terrible blow – and a grim prospect being landed with
> someone so boring. I rather liked Chicago – that apart. . . .[55]

There was to be no reconciliation when Sachie and Georgia returned from America early in the following year. Georgia informed all their friends that Reresby and Penelope were neither to be given wedding presents nor to be invited to their houses. She was ruthless. Sachie, accustomed as he was to family feuds, took her side. Just as she had in July 1943 at Renishaw, she had set the fuse of a time-bomb which was to explode in her – and Sachie's – faces years later.

Sachie's American lecture tour was the result of triumphantly successful tours of America by Osbert and Edith. On their first visit in October 1948 they had been lionised wherever they went. Evelyn Waugh, who was in New York at the same time, reported that 'the Sitwells were rampaging about New York cutting a terrific splash' and that 'Every magazine has six pages of photographs of them headed "The Fabulous Sitwells. . .".'[56] *Life* dedicated a huge illustrated feature to celebrating their tour, calling them 'the senior members of England's most celebrated literary family' and claiming that they had given the 'New York literary set its biggest thrill in years'. After a second tour in the winter of 1950–1951, when Hollywood turned out in force to greet Edith for her reading of *Macbeth*, the two elder Sitwells were established as celebrities in the United States.

The success of Edith's and Osbert's tours had prompted Georgia to think that a US tour by Sachie might help to establish him too with the American public. He had never sold well in the States as Farrar Strauss had written to his agent, David Higham, rejecting *The Hunters and the Hunted* in November 1946: 'He is an extraordinary guy and an amazing writer. I wish you would tell me it would be possible to sell him. . . .'[57] The initiative was certainly Georgia's; as she told Higham in a long letter of 31 December 1951 discussing the tour, 'Sachie's reasons against it are just vague inhibitions connected with Osbert & Edith's tours. . . .'[58] While in New York herself she had been in touch with two different US publishing firms trying to get them to offer for Sachie's books. Higham reported Georgia's activities with some exasperation to Sachie's American representative, Helen Strauss of the William Morris Agency, while forwarding her proofs of *Cupid and the Jacaranda*. Georgia had also, he said, received direct from Colston Leigh a proposal for a lecture tour by Sachie. 'I'm not at all sure whether Sachie will agree to go,' he warned. Sachie, however, was warming to the idea; since *The Sleeping Beauty* had been postponed, he had the time available and there was the bait of a mid-tour holiday in Mexico, which he had always longed to visit. After considerable haggling about a minimum guarantee to Sachie by Colston Leigh, the tour was agreed.

Sachie was certainly nervous about his reception in the United States and possible comparisons with Osbert and Edith. He had even poured cold water on Edith's suggestion that there should be an American edition of his poems published that autumn to coincide with the tour. In any case there was little enthusiasm and even less time for autumn publication among the publishers whom Edith contacted. When Higham spoke to him, Sachie was noncommittal about Edith's proposal that copies of the English edition of *Selected Poems* should be sent over for his arrival. 'For your private information', Higham warned Virginia Hamnett of the William Morris Agency, 'the key to Sachie is handling Georgia, his wife, who is difficult (Canadian). Over to you, sister!'[59] '. . . any meeting with any of the Sitwells leaves me a bit awe-stricken,' Hamnett replied. 'Their affairs seem quite complicated even without a Canadian wife named Georgia!'[60]

Complications there certainly were. Higham was, perhaps, not entirely surprised, on receiving a confidential memo from 'Mike' of Ann Watkins Inc., to hear that the Sitwells were flirting with another US agency apart from William Morris:

> He [Sachie] called me up this morning so I went up and had a very pleasant hour with him and with Georgia.
>
> He seems to want us to represent him in this country. He feels that he has never been satisfactorily presented to the American public, that as the author of between thirty and forty books only a few have been made available and those on a limited import basis. . . . He would like me to think of establishing an American book publishing commitment, and to consider him as a writer for such quality magazines as Harper's Bazaar, Atlantic Harper's and Town & Country. . . .

The concluding paragraph was a masterpiece of delicacy, implying that if Higham did not want to break his relationship with the William Morris Agency, then Sachie might look elsewhere for a British representative. His personal view of Sachie as a client was clearly that he considered him to be a prestigious loss-leader:

> To my mind Sachie is in the category of writers who are not immediately profitable and are beyond the point of promising future profit. Yet I don't want to contribute to a possible decision of Sachie to leave you because he is unhappy with your present American associates. I am not sure that he is thinking in this direction, but if he is, I want you to know that we are entirely willing to act for him, so that he can be kept, as it were, in your family. . . .[61]

Higham replied carefully:

> Your letter is a surprise in that Sachie knows that Morris are working
> for him, and isn't so far as I know dissatisfied, though Georgia's views
> might possibly be different. . . . I might be quite stupid, but I should be
> very surprised if Sachie did want to leave us here, especially since in the
> last two years we have been really extremely successful for him and he
> has made a great deal of money . . . if he definitely asks you to represent
> him in America you should use your own discretion. But many thanks
> for the tip-off. . . .[62]

In the meantime, he sent cautious, worried enquiries to Helen Strauss as
to whether or not they had seen Sachie. 'All is well, and you are acting for
him?' In the event, Ann Watkins Inc. backed off, sending Higham a curt
memorandum implying that there had certainly been an approach by the
Sitwells: 'We decided we should not represent him in the future and I
have so told his friend Lawrence Audrain.'[63]

The name Audrain indicates that Georgia was the prime mover in this
playing off of one agent against another, a game which she had already
played with New York publishers Bobbs Merrill and Simon & Schuster.
Audrain, formerly public relations officer at the Canadian High Commission in London, was her lover, their affair continuing over several years
during the periods that Georgia spent in Canada until the death of her
mother. Left to himself, it is extremely unlikely that Sachie would have
indulged in any such negotiations. The William Morris Agency was,
therefore, left in triumphant possession of its author (and perhaps
unaware of any threat from Ann Watkins Inc.), but it was not an unmixed
pleasure, as a memo from Helen Strauss to Higham indicated: 'We've
really been up to our ears in Sitwells, particularly Mrs Sitwell. She seems
to want to run the offices from her hotel suite, and has a rather demanding
way of thinking we should all drop everything the moment she calls.' It
was not long before there were predictable misunderstandings about
money with Colston Leigh. On 2 December Virginia Hamnett sent
Higham a desperate memo:

> We're having a great deal of difficulty with Mr Sitwell. Colston Leigh's
> office is beside themselves because of a misunderstanding concerning
> payments.
>   When he first arrived, they agreed to pay him $250 a week for
> unusual expenses, but of course they cannot continue to do that since
> the money must last till the end of January. As it is, they're losing about

$100 on the whole deal. Does he usually act this way? Is there any way we can smooth over the situation?. . .Perhaps you could let us know if there's a secret to the handling. . . .

Higham preferred to keep out of it. 'I am sorry if you are finding it difficult with Sachie and Georgia,' he replied. 'I don't know what help I can give you on the general point of dealing with them. Georgia is exactly the kind of person you think she is: but Sachie, who has a great deal of charm, is often extremely difficult to bring to the point, and also to convince about anything.' Higham in any case had little sympathy with Colston Leigh, who had, after all, made the original agreement. It was a situation which regularly occurred in this kind of author-agent transaction for lecture or publicity tours.

I don't see how I can take a hand direct with him on this particular matter. I have looked at the agreement again, and I see that it provides for his share of the fees to be paid semi-monthly or monthly as requested. If he has persuaded Leigh to let him have so much a month on account, it is, I suppose, Leigh's funeral if at the end of the time he is down on his guarantee. . . .[64]

Apparently impervious to the strain which he had imposed on his American agents, Sachie returned home to Weston in the first week of February revivified. He had enjoyed himself. The tour which had taken in fifteen states and included a few days in Mexico – 'as beautiful as I used to think it must be when I was twenty' – had been, he thought, 'very successful'. He had liked Helen Strauss and had a high opinion of her 'quickness and intelligence'. He had even liked Colston Leigh, despite thinking him 'rather an old rascal', and had asked Helen Strauss to get in touch with him about the possibilities of another US tour.[65] There had been agreements with Caedmon for recordings and with Bobbs Merrill for a US edition of his *Selected Works*; immediately on reaching home, he had written to his American publisher, Hiram Haydn, with his selection for the contents and was going ahead with a foreword and illustrations. Most important of all, he had decided to write 'a major novel' and, on 14 February, had written to Clarence Paget of Cassell's setting out his plans for it. It was a long, curious letter, part apologia, part blurb, in which Sachie first set out Osbert's and Edith's claims to fame and then his own, as if the comparions were constantly in his mind:

But, as well, there is another brother, myself – a fact which is sometimes overlooked, because the public swallows two members of the same family with difficulty, and has, now and again, hardly appetite for a third. And, now, I have to talk of myself for a moment. I began writing at an earlier age than they did, being ten years younger than my sister and five years younger than my brother. Her first book of poems was published in 1915 – and I was writing, and having poems printed, a year later, in 1916. I believe my first prose book *Southern Baroque Art* . . . broke new ground . . .

I believe I have reached the age when I have seen, heard, or experienced nearly all the works of art, and the sensations, or effects of art, in the world and I am appealing to you to be allowed and encouraged to write a book which will sum up and set a seal on everything upon which I have thought, or which I have seen, or heard.

The book would examine the principles of good and evil in man, nature and art and decide what is and what is not beautiful. Religion would not be touched on – 'I am no Christian myself but a pagan' – but Christ and anti-Christ would appear at the end, a scheme taken from Berlioz in which a mock Day of Judgement conducted by anti-Christ would be interrupted by the real one, with an emphasis on the 'cries of terror of the damned' rather than 'the joy of the blessed'. Sachie wrote:

> It is my belief that from that single sentence about Berlioz a work upon
> a huge scale can be built up that will be of significance to our own, and
> to future generations that are to come. . . . I want to bring all my
> resources to bear, and bring out the meaning of works of art in terms
> not more difficult to understand than spoken dialogue. . . . It will be
> lyrical, humorous, and dramatic, and I will put into it the best writing of
> which I am capable, as it is my bid for immortality . . .[66]

This was Sachie in apocalyptic mood. He appears to have convinced Paget of the viability of the project; Cassell's commissioned what Higham always referred to in future as 'the Great Work' for the not inconsiderable sum of £1,250, payable in five tranches of £250 each. Higham's reaction was also enthusiastic when Sachie sent him a copy of the letter to Paget. It was, perhaps, a welcome change to find Sachie in so positive and optimistic a frame of mind. He forwarded it to Helen Strauss with the comment: 'He seems to have most intelligently charted for himself a major area in the literary sea, which is in substantial contrast to those which Edith and Osbert have found for themselves. . . .'[67] Strauss reported a favourable reaction from Hiram Haydn who claimed partial responsibility for Sachie's new project. 'During our conversations here . . . I urged on him several times that it was certainly his interest to stop turning out so many "special" commission books and to turn his hand to an imaginative effort commensurate with his full ability.'[68]

The original plan was for publication in two volumes, which would take two and a half years to write, the first to be ready in the summer of 1954. Sachie received his initial payment of £250 on 2 April 1953, but 'the Great Work' was not to be published until June 1959. The delay was due to Sachie's inability to resist the lure of travelling the world in search of new aesthetic experiences, his perennial need for cash in hand and the temptations offered by magazine editors and 'special' commissions for coffee-table books on birds, books, flowers, gardens, country houses, porcelain figures or any other of his myriad interests. Within a month of his arrival back in England he had dashed off an article on the new Queen and her forthcoming coronation and was negotiating for an article on Philip Johnson's 'Glass House' in Connecticut for an Ideal Home Book. He was committed to do a series of flower books for Rainbird and another travel book for Batsford, an expanded collection of his *Sunday Times* pieces, *Truffle Hunt*, for Robert Hale, an article on Margot Fonteyn and, later, the possibility of a new ballet for Ninette de Valois at Covent Garden. By the end of July he had written 100 pages of 'the Great Work' but on 6 August he set off for a five-week tour of Portugal and Madeira to research for the book he had promised Batsford.

Sachie was, therefore, very much in demand. David Higham was perhaps too responsive to his pleas of poverty and had beavered away to get him as many commissions and reprints as he could, so that his income from writing in the early 1950s averaged between £500 and £1,000 a year, a considerable improvement. Higham had been Sachie's agent since 1935, introduced to him by Osbert. Higham seems to have had a special affection for Sachie and for his writing, working tirelessly on his behalf despite the fact that Sachie, although a distinguished client, was neither a very profitable nor a very easy one. Sachie had a built-in reaction to business of any kind, or 'Biz-Boz' as Lady Ida had called it, which he had undoubtedly inherited from her. He recoiled from business correspondence, paying bills, opening bank statements, even cashing cheques. Contracts for books would remain unsigned for months and were frequently lost in the meantime in the sea of papers strewn across the floor of Sachie's study. The following letter from Sachie to Higham is typical:

The cheque arrived . . . just a few days before I left for Portugal, and I do remember having one or two cheques to pay into the Bank, at that time and finding myself with less money than I thought I should have. I am afraid it has been very careless of me, but I am apt, out of superstition, not to look at the cheques until it is time to send them in. I think this cheque must have been mislaid by me, and, probably, thrown away. . . .[69]

Morbidly sensitive to criticism, he shrank from any kind of publicity which might bring it in its wake. In September 1952 Edith arranged a luncheon with Leonard Clark with a view to Clark doing a biographical study of Sachie which she hoped would help to promote him. Sachie was at first receptive and encouraging, then drew back:

I am not altogether keen that any article on me should be published. I think such a thing is very difficult unless the writer is on most intimate terms with his subject, & if this is not so, then I think it is better to let the matter rest until long after he is dead. This sounds gloomy, I know, but I know myself so little that I am sure no one else can form a true opinion of me. . . .[70]

Clark persisted, but Sachie, thanking him for his 'most kind & indeed touching' letter, was adamant. Not only did he not want anything written about him 'at this time', but he did not want any honours of any kind, even honorary doctorates:

For instance, I have thought it one of my greatest honours that I was never asked to write anything for 'Horizon', even when it had run to a hundred numbers. I think it is much better for me to keep myself off things of that description, & try & get on with my writing. . . .[71]

No wonder Edith sometimes despaired in her efforts to promote her sensitive brother. It is hard not to detect an element of 'sour grapes' in the remarks about honorary doctorates (he had not been offered one, while Osbert had been made D. Litt by Sheffield University and Edith had been given three, including the prestigious University of Oxford the previous year). Both Edith and Osbert had been invited to contribute to *Horizon*, which prided itself on featuring the best contemporary writers. He was indeed, as he told Clark, in a 'negative mood' about publicity, having only the previous month firmly declined to be included in a book written by Max Wykes-Joyce entitled *Triad of Genius*. Volume I, therefore, featured only Osbert and Edith; volume II, which was supposed to be about Sachie, never appeared.

Sachie hated being too closely identified with Edith and Osbert, but, perversely, resented being ignored and told Edith so. Edith reassured him that there had been 'a general misunderstanding' about the Wykes-Joyce book: 'I didn't know *anything* about your not appearing in the book until it was too late.' She tried to bolster his confidence with extravagant praise of his poetic abilities. He would win in the end because he was a *very great* poet, 'one of the greatest living', and she was preparing a 2,000-page anthology of modern poems, 'the greatest anthology in the language, and you will be seen in your proper perspective'.[72] On the eve of a second trip to Hollywood that year to work on the film script of *Fanfare for Elizabeth*, she raved about his recently issued *Selected Works*: 'If, seeing this *magnificent* selection of your very finest prose works, people do not realise the transcendental writer you are, I absolutely despair of them. . . .'[73] Her next letter announced the tragedies and scenes surrounding the death of Dylan Thomas, whom she had sincerely loved. '*We are going to say he died of diabetes. Don't forget,*' she ordered Sachie.[74]

Meanwhile, Sachie had been working on his travel book, *Portugal and Madeira*, after his five-week tour of the country accompanied by an old friend, Tony Ruggeroni, owner of the Aviz Hotel in Lisbon, and his wife, Anne, a beautiful American from Atlanta. Sachie already knew Portugal well, having made four previous visits there since 1926. His great achievement in this book was to make the Portuguese themselves view the architecture of their country in a different light. In Fascist Portugal, the 'nationalist' view of their history had focused on their 'heroic' periods, the twelfth-century founding of the kingdom as part of the Christian reconquest of Iberia from the Moors, whose relics were Romanesque churches and castles horribly restored by the authorities with crenellations like false teeth, and the Age of the Discoveries with its extraordinary overwrought Manueline style. Sachie highlighted the baroque and the rococo in Portuguese architecture and craftsmanship, the wonderful golden carved interiors like Santa Clara in Oporto, the delicate rococo churches in the Minho and Tras-os Montes designed by António Francisco Lisboa, called 'O Aleijadinho', and the work of Niccolò Nasoni in Oporto, where the bat-like pediments over the windows reminded Sachie instantly of the Uffizi. The success in Portugal of Sachie's book brought official recognition of a kind, an invitation from the British Council to represent the Government at the centenary celebrations in December 1954 of the Portuguese poet and dramatist, Almeida Garrett, of whom he had barely heard and, previously, certainly never read. 'I believe he was a good poet,' he told Moira.

That year, 1954, Sachie had been appointed to his first directorship by his friend and occasional publisher, George Rainbird, of his then company, the Wyndham Press. Rainbird was practically the inventor of the coffee-table book, but he also specialised in the production of high-quality illustrated editions for bibliophiles. Sachie had collaborated with Rainbird on *Fine Books* and had written a long essay on 'Old Roses' for *Old Garden Roses Part I*, which he co-authored with James Russell. He was also working on a long essay for *Great Flower Books* in partnership with Wilfrid Blunt. One of the Rainbird projects for 1954 was a book of drawings by Augustus John, whom Sachie had known as the leonine, gypsy figure of his Café Royal days, and at the suggestion of Brinsley Ford, he had commissioned John to do drawings of Georgia and Reresby in 1941. In mid-July Sachie drove down with Rainbird to discuss the idea with John. 'I had a satisfactory visit on Saturday to see Augustus John', Sachie reported to Higham, 'and think the book will go ahead as he seems anxious to have it done. . . .'[75] However, by September he was backing out of personal involvement with the project. '. . . he doesn't really want to cope further,' Higham reported, adding that Sachie had suggested that Brinsley Ford should take his place. Sachie's antennae for a difficult situation were amply borne out by Brinsley Ford's subsequent experiences. The first session of talks went well; the second, following on a long lunch at the local pub in Fordingbridge, did not:

> We came back – I suppose rather intoxicated. . . . John tottered up to the sideboard and found a drawing of a heifer which was covered in beer or port stains and said, 'I want one of my animal drawings to go into this book'. . . . I should have remained silent but like an ass I spoke up and said, 'I don't think Augustus, that it will reproduce very well only the spots will come out.' John roared, 'I don't care what you think, that drawing's going in.' 'Well,' Ford replied, 'if that drawing's going in, I'm going out.'

Brinsley Ford followed Sachie out of the project; when the book appeared the beer-stained drawing did not feature, but, at John's insistence, some of his late 'perfectly awful' ones did.[76]

Portugal and Madeira was followed by *Denmark*, a last-minute decision. As late as 21 July 1954 Sachie had written to Higham: 'Doing Denmark after all. . . .' He and Georgia toured Denmark by car in August that year and the book was written a year later in only three weeks. At the same time he was contemplating a book on Brazil for Robert Hale and on Russia for Batsford. He does not seem to have cared much where he went as long as it interested him. 'If *Russia* doesn't come off', Higham minuted after a talk with Sachie on 29 May, 'then interested in Holy Land and Syria. . . .'

Later that year Persia was substituted for Brazil, a project that Sachie was to be offered at various times over the next decade but which never really appealed to him as he felt, after the research he had done on Portugal, that he had already visited it in his mind. His long-term objective was to go to Japan, something which he had longed to do since he was a schoolboy at Eton and had first learned for himself about Japanese art. An interview with a Japanese newspaper magnate in July that year from whom he hoped for a subsidy came to nothing, but four years later, with the help of Bryher and an advance from his publisher, he would succeed.

The major family event of 1955 was Edith's conversion to Catholicism. She was received into the Church on 4 August by Father Caraman S.J. in a quiet ceremony attended only by Evelyn Waugh, acting as her godfather, Helen Rootham's sister, Evelyn Wiel, Alec Guinness, the young Portuguese poet, Alberto de Lacerda, and a 'blond youth [the poet, Quentin Stevenson] who looked American but claimed to be English'. Afterwards they lunched at the Sesame; Waugh described it as a banquet – 'cold consomme, lobster Newburg, steak, strawberry flan and great quantities of wine'. Neither Osbert nor Sachie was there. Sachie was actually in London that day and lunched with a family party consisting of his mother-in-law, Georgia and Francis. Georgia's diary records no mention of Edith's great day. Nor did Sachie and Georgia attend Edith's confirmation two months later on 4 October at Farm Street in front of a 'large invited audience, the cream of Catholic London', which included one of their closest and dearest friends, Lady (Christian) Hesketh, standing as godmother to Edith. Again, Georgia made no mention of this in her diary. No comment about his sister's great step appears in any of Sachie's correspondence. Since he was himself a pagan and disliked organised religion of any kind, he can hardly have approved of Edith's conversion and regarded it to a certain extent as letting the side down. 'He didn't take it terribly seriously,' Francis recalled. 'His view was that if it made her any happier then it was a good idea.' Despite his dislike of religion, he liked the two Jesuits responsible for Edith's conversion, Fathers D'Arcy and Caraman, and knew Edith to be dreadfully unhappy and in need of peace of mind. After her first meeting with her confessor, Father Caraman, Edith had written to the priest that it had given her 'a sense of happiness, safety and peace such as I have not had for years'.

The 1950s had been increasingly triumphal for Edith in public, commensurately difficult in private. She had become a transatlantic celebrity, her Gothic features, Byzantine clothes and medieval-looking jewellery familiar to a far wider audience than those who read her books.

Following on her other honours, she had been made a Dame Commander of the British Empire in 1954. Physically and mentally, however, she had reached a low point in her life. The principal reason for her unhappiness was David Horner, who had become an obsession with her. Edith's life with Osbert and Horner was now, as she had told a friend in 1955, 'one long hell', becoming increasingly so over the decade. The trouble had begun with the American tours on which she, Osbert and Horner had regularly embarked each winter. Edith had discovered the joys of alcohol and Horner American homosexuals. The dry Martini had been her downfall; she found that she liked its effects as both a stimulant and an anaesthetic. She was sadly conscious of her failing creative powers; by the mid 1950s she wrote very little poetry and by the end of the decade her inspiration had dried up altogether. Alcohol provided solace for her self-doubt and frustration. It also, unfortunately, increased her tendency towards paranoia, a relic of her persecuted childhood. It was also physically dangerous for her, particularly as she had never liked or taken exercise; when staying at Weston she would rarely take more than a few steps in the garden and never more than 100 yards from the house. Like Ginger, she was prone to take to her bed where she would lie, looking, with her wonderful profile and turban concealing her skimpy hair, like some medieval effigy. The result was that she was extremely weak in her legs and, now heavy in the body, prone to falls, which, in houses with stairs like Renishaw and, more particularly, Montegufoni, could easily prove fatal.

She now hated Horner for his treatment of Osbert. For years they had been on perfectly civil terms; Edith had accepted Osbert's need for Horner and had treated him accordingly, but her attitude towards him had changed as a result of Horner's behaviour in America, where both he and Osbert were naturally in touch with the homosexual underground. In Osbert's case this was largely confined to his cultivated New York friends; it is clear from Horner's correspondence that his network stretched across America from New York to San Francisco, with one particular affair in the unlikely surroundings of Kansas City. ('He is on the police list in Kansas City and dare not return there,' Sachie told Bryher.) When the Sitwell entourage touched down in America, Horner took flight. It is hard to blame him. At fifty, he was exceedingly well-preserved, slim, blond, elegant and amusing as ever. Osbert was fifty-eight, incurably ill, shaky, immobile and in need of constant attention. Edith, however, did blame him. She could not bear to see the suffering inflicted on her beloved brother by the absence and obvious infidelity of Horner. None the less,

Osbert remained totally emotionally dependent upon him and, anxious to keep him whatever the cost, wanted no angry scenes or recriminations. Edith tried to control herself, but in January 1955 she burst out in a letter to Sachie from New York, headed '*Private and Confidential Destroy Let Silence be the Watchword*':

> Dear little Lord Fauntleroy has not been in New York during the whole of our stay, but has been staying with a friend in the country. . . . *Nor* has he gone with O to Florida. O has gone with a very nice young man, a friend of Lincoln's [Kirstein] who was a naval nurse during the war. I am afraid I really let myself go to O on the subject of the little Lord's behaviour, and this has not made me popular. . . . I did not tell you until I could control myself, because it is dangerous for us if we fall into rages over it, because he will come back when there is something to be got out of it. . . .
>
> *Do not mention this on any account to O.* . . . You see, the creature is coming back to England with us, and will infest the house again. O says we have to behave the same, otherwise our domestic life will be hell – because we shall have him there, just the same, but hating us. O says we must show nothing.[77]

On a subsequent trip two years later, it was the same, if not worse. Edith, impotent and raging, exploded in a letter to Sachie from New York:

> As soon as we got on to the boat, Osbert came to my cabin and told me that animal was going off *again* (for the duration) with the same animal as before. . . . I must not refuse to speak to the second animal, as if I did, the other would 'make a scene!' The impudence! The blackmail! The sickening, horrible, creature! And they simply aren't house-trained! If you could have seen them on the dock![78]

She hoped to arrange for their American friend, Minnie Cushing, to speak to Osbert about it and prevent 'the creature' from returning to England. Naturally her plan failed. 'Little Jackal Horner is returning with us,' she told Georgia on 2 May. 'O says he won't kick him out because he was once a good friend to him. If he went of his own accord it would be different. He says it is because his illness bores Little Jackal that he goes off as he does – which is a credit to him. . . .'[79]

Sachie was concerned for Edith, trapped in an impossible situation. Bryher shared his concern; she, too, had received a 'very distressed' letter from Edith in March. 'Personally', she told Sachie, 'I think E. ought not to be with O. when D. is with him. It is far too much of a strain for her. I think it is deplorable but with O. as ill as he is, one has to let him choose his life. I feel very strongly that E. ought not to be involved in it.'[80] But involved she was, as the curious trio moved between Renishaw and Montegufoni, with brief respites in London when Osbert and Horner inhabited Carlyle Square and Edith took refuge with her 'old bores' at the Sesame Club. They were at Montegufoni as usual for the winter months, from whence Edith wrote to Georgia just before Christmas: '. . . that abominable creature that infests this house, insulted me so terribly, and with a face of such unutterable evil, that I was ill, and had to remain in bed for three days and a half. . . .'[81] Sachie retailed the news of the 'nasty scene' with Horner to Bryher: 'It is very unpleasant for her.' There was little he could do; Edith clung to Osbert and Osbert to Horner. Sachie rarely saw them. Edith occasionally came to stay at Weston, although she was now, she confessed to Father Caraman, nervous that her doing so might lead to trouble with Osbert.

None the less, Sachie still relied on Edith to be his muse. She was at Weston again for a week early in June 1958. '. . . thanks to her coming to stay with us', he told Bryher, 'I was able to have a wonderful time of writing poems. . . . What an inspiring force she is.' He had begun to write one of his most beautiful poems, 'Serenade to a Sister', a long, moving act of homage in which he acknowledged his debt to her and which he only completed after her death. 'The Serenade is so *wonderfully* beautiful,' Edith wrote to him. '*Of course* a part of it made me sad – but then I am permanently sad, alas. . . .' She pressed him to allow her to include it in her selection for her anthology of poetry since 1942, *Poems of our Time*, but he was reluctant to let her publish any of his poems and, in the end, only two of his recent poems were among the three which Edith included, 'Belle Isis' and 'O Rose with Two Hearts'.

'When I finish this book, if ever, then I feel I should like to do nothing else except try to write poetry, as I have now written too many books of facts,' he told Bryher in May 1955. '. . . I so much feel that what I am best at is poetry, and I think so strongly that as I am getting older there is much more reason why I should turn to this, and stop writing books of information.' His major task was, however, still 'the Great Work'. By the end of June he had written over 400 pages of volume I, which he delivered to Cassell's, and in July on this evidence of work completed he received a second payment from them. Feeling exhausted, he gratefully accepted a contribution from Bryher and sailed via Venice to Istanbul in September. Another reason for the trip was Georgia's health – 'she never seems well now and I have been worried about her for months,' he informed Bryher.

In fact, he had been 'terribly fussed' about her for at least a year. She seems to have been suffering from menopausal problems, as he told Moira that her 'nerves were frightful, and I felt she was on the verge of a breakdown. . . . I have been told often what an unfeeling, sadistic monster I am – inhuman, cold as ice, cruel etc. which makes me unhappy. But the poor thing can't help it.'[82] The trouble passed. Georgia's diaries for the following years are full of loving references to 'sweet Sach'.

After Istanbul, Sachie's mind was already on further trips to the Middle East. From March to May 1956 he and Georgia visited Iran, Lebanon, Syria, Jordan and Jerusalem, subsidised by Bryher and by Batsford, for whom he was to write *Arabesque and Honeycomb*. Arriving on 22 March in Beirut, where their hosts were M. and Mme Roche of the French Embassy at the 'Residence des Pins', they were instantly plunged into local life. Eddie Gathorne-Hardy, an old friend ('not as raffish as of old but still very amusing, libidinous, witty'), invited them round to see his collection of pornographic literature. After dinner at the Roches' house, there were charades in French with *tableaux vivants*, during which Sachie had a great success as Sardanapalus lounging on the floor among heaps of cushions. There was a lavish party at Madame Linda Sursocks – 'she smokes a hubble-bubble & is a real oriental,' Georgia noted. They were taken on a day trip to Byblos – 'too ruined and heterogenous [*sic*] for Sach' – but he was much taken with a Maronite church. On the 29th they flew to Tehran, staying with Tim and Anna Marten in the British Embassy compound, and were joined there five days later by Baba Metcalfe, who was to tour Persia with them and take photographs for the book. This was her first visit to Persia in the footsteps of her father, Lord Curzon, who had travelled through the country in 1889 and written a celebrated book about it. Curzon's book and Robert Byron's were to be their guides for the trip.

At six in the morning they took a flight for the holy city of Meshed, only forty miles from the Soviet frontier. There was no hotel and they stayed with the American Consul. Sachie, being male though an infidel, was taken up the minaret of a mosque to look down on the centre of the 'Sacred City', the ninth-century shrine built by the son of Haroun-al-Raschid, plated in gold by Shah Abbas in the seventeenth century, and the sixteenth-century mosque surrounding it, with turquoise dome and minaret, built by Tamerlane's daughter-in-law. He was 'thrilled'. Georgia and Baba, who were not allowed nearer than a glimpse from the roof of a turquoise-dealer's shop, were less so. Baba found photography almost impossible, snatching the odd surreptitious snap 'as the milling

crowd may turn nasty'. Meshed was decorated for the forthcoming visit of
the Shah, the main square featuring a stuffed lion with an electric bulb on
its mouth and another on its tail, and a golden crown from which sprang
plumes of dirty white ostrich feathers. Baba recorded that

> Sachie has found two dog kennels in which live two ghastly old hags. He
> is riveted by them, and we have to go back continually and have a peep.
> They are in a back street, and sit crouched up inside with a little door
> propped open. One had a companion inside gossiping. The other was
> draped in a yashmak drinking tea and looked as if once in the bygone
> days she might have been a good-looking houri. . . .[83]

Back in Tehran, Hannibal, the curator of the ethnological museum,
intrigued Sachie by claiming descent from Pushkin and, therefore, from
Peter the Great's Ethiopian slave and embarrassed Baba by weeping with
emotion and bowing to the ground when he discovered that she was Lord
Curzon's daughter. They were shown the Gulistan Palace: '. . . the same
as Daddy's description,' she wrote, 'a mixture of vulgarity, cheapness
and magnificence. Ghastly junk beside Sèvres and Meissen . . . and the
Peacock Throne.' The next day they set off for Isfahan via Qum in a
car lent by the Martens. Marten had kindly provided 'heaps of gin and
whisky', but had forgotten the picnic and the water. At Qum Baba started
to take photographs of the mosque when 'an odious gesticulating
policeman' arrived. 'Taken to Police Station. Sach detained within,'
Georgia reported. After an hour's questioning and thumbing of passports, they were free to leave 'odious Qum'. On the long, dreary road to
Isfahan the car broke a back spring crossing a ford when they were still
100 miles from their destination. After hasty repairs by a local blacksmith,
they crawled on again, not daring to go more than forty-five miles an hour,
but in the midst of a deserted plain in the dark, it broke down irreparably.
Eventually a raffish-looking lorry with three extremely dirty men in the
cab stopped and offered help. Baba and Georgia squeezed into the front
with two of the toughs, while Sachie, 'still clutching his tortoiseshell
walking stick', climbed into the back where he sat on a spare tyre, wrapped
in a blanket, brown Homburg hat firmly on his head, with the third as
his companion. The beauties of Isfahan, however, made up for it all,
including the eleventh-century 'Friday' Mosque, 'which poor Robert
Byron raved about'.

On 11 April they drove to Persepolis, having flown from Isfahan to
Shiraz. Lord Curzon had been there in 1889 and ridden his horse up the

shallow double staircase in the Audience Hall. Sachie was obviously unable to equal this feat, but he did climb up to the tombs of Artaxerxes II and III cut into the steep mountainside above, despite a dramatic thunderstorm. At Shiraz Sachie wangled his way into a closed garden by brandishing a heavily crested Embassy place-card at the custodian, but the famous gardens of Shiraz were a disappointment. 'Perhaps in May when the roses are out they might be better,' Baba commented, 'but now the only flowers are pretty but ordinary English annuals planted drearily in beds, the rest totally unkempt. The Persian garden is a sad dis-illusionment, except for the fact that any green patch is an event in this country. . . .' Back in Tehran, the Prime Minister gave a reception at the Gulistan Palace for the statesmen assembled for the Baghdad Pact conference to which the Sitwells were invited. Afterwards they went on to an opium-smoking party. 'The PM had just made a speech saying it was a crime punishable by death, but at the party was the Deputy PM, the Head of the Senate, and the Lord Chamberlain, all cross-legged on the floor puffing away.' Georgia and Baba joined in, but Sachie refused to try it.

The Sitwells and Baba parted in Tehran to go their various ways, Sachie and Georgia bound for Damascus and Palmyra. Afterwards Baba wrote:

> Georgia and Sachie are wonderful travelling companions. Sachie has his peculiarities which almost drive one mad, never knowing the value of money or what to tip, can't do anything alone, wants only to talk, as he *never* reads or writes while travelling. Has every kind of travel fever and fear, but one must rise above these oddities because they both have a wonderful sense of humour, get the most fun out of anything, and are thrilled and enthusiastic and 'on' for anything.

Sachie and Georgia visited Petra, riding ponies through the gorges, accompanied by screaming American schoolchildren. Despite the children and the other tourists, Petra was not a disappointment – 'the wonder of the first rock carvings as enchanting as we hoped'. They spent an uncomfortable night in a tent for two with a communal Elsan 200 yards away, but 'the beauty of Petra and the sense of adventure made it all worthwhile.' After Petra, they went via Amman and Jerusalem to Aleppo to see Krak des Chevaliers and, on 7 May, left Beirut for home.

The resulting book, *Arabesque and Honeycomb*, published in October 1957, was perhaps Sachie's least successful. It was curiously pedestrian and overstuffed with information, giving the impression that he was grasping at straws to fill his pages and that his imagination, for once, had not been engaged. Perhaps he felt Lord Curzon and Robert Byron looking over his shoulder as he wrote, but the book gave the impression, as one reviewer put it, of 'a hasty journey through places where haste obscures so much'. Sachie's US publishers, Bobbs Merrill, had already turned it down: 'the author's semi-precious verbosity really got out of hand on this one'.

Following a now set pattern, Sachie and Georgia went to Malta in August 1957 accompanied by Antony Armstrong-Jones, who took the photographs for the book, published in October 1958. In August that year Sachie finally achieved his ambition of going to Japan. Having failed to interest the 'Japanese Lord Beaverbrook' in sponsoring him, he now had an advance of £1,000 from Weidenfeld & Nicolson, who were to publish the resulting book, while Bryher put up the money for the air tickets. In Tokyo he and Georgia would be saved expense by staying with a cousin, Isla Sitwell, head of Shell in Japan. *Bridge of the Brocade Sash*, published in December 1959, recorded Sachie's delighted encounter with the country. He was to spend an entire month in Kyoto, 'a city that seemed little less beautiful than Rome or Venice', devoting a third of the book to descriptions of its temples and its gardens, above all the garden of the Zen temple of Ryûanji. He had written about this garden in 1945, inspired, perhaps, by the 'terrible rain' that had fallen on Japan that August and thinking that he would never see it. To him, this garden intended for contemplation, composed in 1500 of rocks and sand, was 'one of the most original works of art in the world . . . [or] conceptions of the human intellect'. *Bridge of the Brocade Sash*, more than any of his other travel books, radiated a childlike enjoyment of everything – sushi bars, department stores, sumo, Kabuki, the art of the kimono, even matchbox covers and the sight of hundreds of Japanese workers swarming in and out of Tokyo immaculate in their short-sleeved white shirts. 'Having enjoyed Japan too much,' he concluded, 'one could perhaps never enjoy anything so much again. . . .' Raymond Mortimer, an expert on the subject, headed his review of the book, 'In Love with Japan and its many Marvels', and called it 'remarkable' in that Sachie, 'with his gift for unearthing whatever is curious and beautiful', had, in only five weeks, succeeded in seeing what most people had missed. William Plomer called it 'enchanting' and 'enriching', essential reading for anyone wanting to see the 'exquisitely various survivals of ancient and cherished refinement, often fragile' before they disappeared under the pressures of Western culture and industrialisation.

Sachie's travel books were the fruit of an intuitive eye, unerring taste and an individual, fresh way of seeing things backed by wide reading. His nonchalance towards factual accuracy brought him brickbats from his English readers, who, having read a detailed description by him of some monument, found, on actually visiting the site, that the building did not exist and had not done so for some 200 years. Peter Quennell, visiting Viana do Castelo in northern Portugal in 1932, had sent Sachie a cross postcard complaining that he had made a complete muddle of the churches there. Thirty years later Quentin Crewe, who had been living in Japan in 1958 when Sachie and Georgia arrived there for Sachie's research on *Bridge of the Brocade Sash*, was asked to review the book. Crewe, who had just written his own book on Japan, combed it for errors. 'It had all the flourish of his famous books of travel,' he later recalled, 'but it was almost a work of fiction. He described seeing from the window of a train the castle of Himeji, standing proud above the town. It had actually been bombed flat during the war. He wrote of the long red-lacquer bridge in the Heian Shrine, whereas it was of plain wood. I counted 208 errors of fact.' When they next met at a party in London, Sachie, in a purely Sitwellian act of revenge, managed, while saying amiably, 'My dear fellow, so nice to see you again', to shake Crewe's wrist so vigorously as to spill his glass of whisky all over him.[84]

The year 1958 had in many ways been a year of achievement. On the family side there had been a rapprochement with the Reresby Sitwells. Reresby and Penelope had spent Christmas 1957 at Weston, when, Sachie told Bryher, she had been 'much nicer than ever before'. Three months later, in March 1958, Reresby's and Penelope's daughter, Alexandra, Sachie's first grandchild, was born. Sachie and Georgia went to London for the birth, which delighted them both and it seemed that, superficially at least, the rift between the Sitwells was healed. By May, Sachie had finally completed volume I of 'the Great Work'. He showed it first to Edith when she came to stay at Weston in the first week in June. Edith's visit and the completion of the long book sparked off another bout of poetry writing for Sachie. 'What an inspiring force she is,' he told Bryher. 'Thanks to her coming to stay with us, I was able to have a wonderful time of writing poems just before we left for Japan.'

Among the poems which Sachie wrote as a result of Edith's visit was 'Serenade to a Sister':

> You, my sister, have just gone away,
> For whom, and whom only, I wrote poetry.
> When young I was to net the Leonids,

> But the world is not as I would have it be,
> Nor you, nor I . . .
>
> My sister,
> And abbess of the nightingales,
> Who wound the clockwork in my mortal frame . . .
> It has sung in me, and sung not,
> Now it sings again . . .

'How can I *ever* thank you for this – one of the most wonderful and moving poems you have ever written!' Edith wrote. 'It arrived a couple of hours ago, and it did, literally, make me cry. I don't know when anything has moved me so much, and I certainly don't know when *anything* has meant so much to me.'[85] Sachie was to add to this long poem over the years until he completed it after Edith's death. 'I think you are now at the very top of your powers,' Edith told him; this long, intensely personal, deeply felt poem was one of his best. One verse referred to the misery of Edith's personal situation:

> How bitter a dichotomy haunts you,
> My sister,
> Divides and haunts you,
> Feeding on poetry from the earth's rough maws,
> With hands like a lily but a lion's paws,
> Compendium of rage and pity;
> Of this world, but not of this world,
> Refuged, and yet still in prison,
> With no escape,
> And that other, we both loved, in the prison with you,
> The one a prisoner of the soul,
> And the other imprisoned in and by his body,
> Without hope of heart or mind to break his fetters,
> Which are your manacles,
> Just as though chained to the wall,
> Though your dungeon alters from country house to castle,
> But you keep indoors at both, and never go out into the
>   garden . . .

Later, in August, before he left for Japan, he sent her another batch of poems, including one which referred to what he saw as his own exile from Renishaw:

Why
        cannot I walk into the wood
We called the wilderness,
Beyond the statues of the warrior and the amazon?
Why
        cannot I walk into the wood
Through the wooden gate
        where I was often frightened as a child,
And look down to the lake between the trees? . . .

' "Nevermore" is enough to make one weep,' Edith wrote on 6 August. Sachie was to rewrite and complete this poem also after her death. He sent her some of his flower poems, the series of *Variations upon old Names of Hyacinths* – 'all of which are of astonishing beauty,' Edith commented, 'and the wonderful *Rose* poems'.

Edith was putting together the Modern Supplement to *Poems of our Time* to be published in an Everyman edition the following year. In vain she pleaded with Sachie to let her include 'Serenade to a Sister':

I think, darling, you are wrong not to let me have it amongst your new poems for the Everyman edition. Everyone who knows anything about poetry *must* know what a great poet you are. What do the rest matter? To hell with them!

If people do not see your poetry, or my poetry, they cannot be blessed for ignorance. I have been so treated that I swore at one moment, I'd never let the English have any poem of mine again. But how long do you suppose the ghastly little pipsqueaks who take themselves seriously as poets and giggle in a frightened manner at the great poets, are going to be remembered?

When you think of that ass Kingsley Amis insulting Keats in the Spectator, and saying he had no technique!! . . .[86]

Sachie, however, was adamant. 'Serenade' was too personal to be exposed to the critical observation of the 'pipsqueaks'.

Edith's anxiety for Sachie's literary success redoubled as the date for the publication of 'the Great Work', June 1959, approached. In March she gave a select drinks party at the Sesame Club for literary editors and critics to meet Sachie and Georgia:

Pamela and Charles Snow who admire Sachie very much, & she is a very important reviewer (mainly of novels, still . . .) and I am asking Joe Ackerley, who, as you know, is the Literary Editor of the Listener, *and* I am asking Mr and Mrs J.W. Lambert of the Sunday Times. . . . Be *aux grands soins* with all these!⁸⁷

She need not have worried. When *Journey to the Ends of Time* came out on 11 June, the major reviewers were enthusiastic. 'Mr [Cyril] Connolly's is absolutely a dream review, and so is Pamela's [Hansford-Johnson], I think, believe and hope that we are all turning the corner. . . . Even the *Telegraph* [the usually hostile Kenneth Young] behaved itself for once.' 'Don't worry about that nasty little highwayman [Duval Smith in the *Observer*],' she adjured him, '[his] blunderbus [*sic*] has missed fire. . . .'⁸⁸

Sachie, however, was so wounded by a hostile review by Simon Raven in the *Spectator* that he threatened to cancel the Foyle's lunch in his honour. Edith rushed to staunch his wounds and save him from disaster. The *Spectator* was her *bête noire*, the principal platform for the Movement, younger poets and writers who included Kingsley Amis, Philip Larkin, Thom Gunn, Elizabeth Jennings, D.J. Enright, Robert Conquest, John Wain and Donald Davie. The Movement poets disliked Sitwellian romanticism, preciosity, elitism and international cultural trappings, and were, in Evelyn Waugh's phrase, always ready 'to make a booby of a Sitwell'. There was not only a generation gap but a cultural gulf between them and the Sitwells (they were also anti-Dylan Thomas and even, surprisingly, T.S. Eliot). Their England was not the Sitwells' England. Neither Osbert, Edith nor Sachie had ever set foot in a pub. This was not necessarily mere snobbishness; Sachie disliked the bar of White's Club for the same reasons he would have hated a pub. Moreover, he thought it pretentious, telling Charles Johnston: 'I don't know why they have this great thing about being the last of the Regency bucks when really they're all stockbrokers.' Raven's review, entitled 'Guide Noir', was metaphorically written from the club/public bar:

By the time Mr Sitwell's 'soul' has got its second wind . . . one is beginning to wish that his earthly personality had been a good deal less assiduous. Here are some brilliant passages . . . but here also are some cod-like slabs of repetitious and relentless appreciation of seemingly every scene in the whole of Baedeker. Now, one may accept Mr Sitwell's sickly proof that the soul survives; one may find his theme, devoid as it is of religious prejudice and insisting on earthly values, to be unexceptionable and even refreshing; what one cannot endure is the feeling that Mr Sitwell has made of his promising afterworld a nightmarish and illimitable museum, that his volume (at 35s) is a rather expensive catalogue, and that above all one will never, never get out.[89]

The mere mention of the *Spectator* was enough to touch a raw nerve with Edith, already in an overwrought state for other reasons. Her reaction was that of a tigress defending her cub from a particularly persistent enemy. In response to Sachie's letter she launched out before even reading the review (which was signed):

> I'll set John Lehmann on to giving the reviewer hell in the London Magazine. If the reviewer is Thom Gunn (as I suspect) I'll insist on John giving him *personal* hell (as T.G. is on the committee of the London Magazine) and if it is Conquest . . . I'll make him look such a fool he'll wish he had never been born.

She was horrified by Sachie's petulant suggestion about the Foyle's luncheon: '*It would be absolutely fatal for you to cancel the luncheon at Foyle* [*sic*]. It would make you look supremely ridiculous. You can't cancel a luncheon given in your honour because someone has been impertinent. You would have the *whole* of the *literary underworld* of London giggling with delight. . . .' He must show more friendship to 'those who are your literary friends' – Maurice Bowra and the C.P Snows. Georgia might not like Jane Clark, but Kenneth was an '*enormous*' admirer of Sachie's and, 'if you could both overcome any small irritations you may feel, you would do well to be friends with him'.

She became positively libellous on discovering that the *Spectator* reviewer was Simon Raven, who, she said, had been ordered out of the editor's office of the *Listener* by J.R. Ackerley for identifying her as a 'lesbian Doctor of Letters who looks like Dante in Angus Wilson's *For Whom the Clock Tolls*'. 'Slime-on Raven', she told Sachie, was a 'man of very bad character'.[90] Sachie, however, took the two adverse reviews very much to heart. 'You *cannot* let creatures like this prevent you from writing the sequel to that great book. What *can* you be thinking about even to contemplate giving way to them like that?'[91] He and Georgia were to come to a large luncheon party she was giving at the Sesame, with television people who could be of the greatest use to him: Hugh Burnett, producer of *Face to Face*, John Freeman, who had interviewed her, and Peter Forster, who happened to be television critic of the *Spectator*, although, she hastened to add, utterly guiltless of the offending review. She was so anxious for Sachie to shine that she gave sisterly warnings against appearing despondent or adopting the darting Sitwellian mode of conversation when talking to these media persons:

The Watchword for the luncheon party is *High Spirits*, and *no interruption* of long conversations. By this I mean: the Television people like rather long *consecutive* conversations, and simply hate being interrupted. So we must not change the subject in one of their conversations. This is very important, as we stand to gain a very great deal. . . .[92]

Sachie's sensitivity about hostile criticism of *Journey to the Ends of Time* was understandable. It was his 'bid for immortalilty'; he had poured all of himself into it over the past seven or so years. It was certainly his most impressive work in prose, principally because it engaged the subjects which really interested him, the meaning of life, time, reality and, above all, death. The same immediacy of feeling which had come through every line of 'Agamemnon's Tomb' inspired *Journey to the Ends of Time*. 'There are moments', Cyril Connolly wrote, 'in this strange and beautiful word-pageant when we completely believe that the author has died or rather descended into the shades . . . and returned to guide us. . . .' 'The power of this strange book', Kenneth Young claimed, 'is that it wrenches us into reality and uses death to put life into perspective.' Sachie approached 'the problems and mysteries of life and death' from his own, pagan viewpoint. '. . . I am not at all religious . . . Christian neither by instinct nor inclination. I do not believe in an after-life; and most decidedly I have no belief in the pains and punishments of hell.' He was obsessed by two ideas: firstly, the absolute physical death of the body, and secondly, that at the moment of death something goes out of it which is the soul. Being Sachie, and speculative rather than philosophical, he was not precise about its nature, hinting rather at a Jungian idea of the survival of thought, or a spark of genius: 'the immortal soul must continue in its humanities . . . the secret of immortality is thought made substantive'. Connolly called this 'a pagan aesthete's blueprint of purgatory'.

Through it all ran a vein of agonised autobiography. Volume I was significantly subtitled *Lost in the Dark Wood*. Sachie, at the age of sixty-two, looked back over his career with bitterness and despair:

I am trudging and stumbling in the furrowed lunar plain, the open fields of Passchendaele, or other fearful scene in driving rain. . . . In Brueghel's painting of *Le Berger fuyant le Loup* at least the shepherd is running over the furrowed plain, running with heavy, lumbering peasant run, and he is no stranger in the land. He knows where to run. But I could be walking in the wet fields in bedroom slippers, which I did all my lifetime, so it seems to me, being hopelessly useless and ineffectual at so many things. Not even making a success with the only thing I was good for, muddling that, too, by trying to do too many things at once and failing in them all. Now becalmed in midst of the whirlwind, a prey to feverish thoughts and notions. With no scrap of faith or religious feeling left in me, not that I ever had any, and looking always for the worst to happen. . . .

He believed in the power of the imagination and, supremely, in poetry:

I believe that poetry and as much of poetry as enter into all the other arts at their highest level of the imagination, should be an aim in itself over and above all other considerations whatever, a religion of its own with its own rewards and punishments. . . . It is the beauty or the poetry in the creations of the human spirit that is more important than the faith, however strongly and to whatever degree that was the motive. Their greatness as works of art is judged by that.

It was his personal credo, the stimulus which for him made life worth living and gave meaning to the world.

'To be, once more a poet, and not to be driven to write prose. Poetry that comes to one when young, and one hopes once more when one is old, but not yet, though I think I may feel it coming. . . .' Something, he felt, was there, if he could only reach it: '. . . I am like someone waiting outside a house to get in, but it is late and pours with rain, and no one will throw down the key.'

11

For Want of the Golden City

1959–1973

'So in the end, the "Golden City" means no more than
somewhere one has been happy.'

Sacheverell Sitwell, *For Want of the Golden City*

Early in August 1959 Sachie and Georgia were invited to Renishaw for the first time for sixteen years, Sachie having last been there in 1943. It was an odd, painful experience, he told Bryher. He felt the estate workers and servants staring at him as if he were the Prodigal Son returned. Memories of the past contrasted sadly with present realities. 'Oh! the depression of seeing the poor things,' he wrote. '[Osbert and Edith] so infirm and with horrid David H. there. Edith and he are so much on each other's nerves.'[1]

Sachie was by now deeply and increasingly concerned about Edith. Over the past year her health and nerves had taken a sharp downward turn, so much so that in December he informed Bryher that he feared she had reached a 'difficult and final phase of her career'. He had accompanied her to Londonderry House the previous month, when she had received the Guinness prize for poetry, and been horrified at her feebleness. He had had to manhandle her up the great staircase and through the long galleries and afterwards had persuaded her to see a doctor. 'I think her nerves are quite exhausted – and that she has become strained and exaggerated as a result,' he wrote. Edith's temperamental troubles and her hatred of Horner were exacerbated by drink. She liked the effects of alcohol and, Sachie thought, drank because she was bored.

The doctor reassured him that there was nothing organically wrong with her and that all she needed was rest, a little peace, 'and to be left alone and not worried by jouranlists and others.' But the day after seeing the doctor, she had a bad fall in her room at the Sesame, which she blamed on her bed collapsing as it was, she said, propped up on a pile of books. It had precipitated her against the ironwork of the other bed in the room (which does not say much for the furnishings of the Sesame Club's bedrooms), badly bruising her face and leaving her thoroughly shaken. Bryher, who went to see her after the accident, wrote to Sachie that she was sworn to secrecy (it had been given out to the press that Dame Edith was suffering from 'flu) but that she had been dreadfully distressed by Edith's condition, which seemed to her like the beginnings of arteriosclerosis; also she did not quite see how the bed could have broken in such a way as to cause the injuries.[2]

Edith did not improve at Montegufoni that winter. Within days of arriving there on the annual transmigration with Osbert and Horner, she had two bad falls and, on the second occasion, was found lying helpless on the floor, where she had been since four o'clock in the morning. Osbert had insisted on her staying in bed, as her legs were so weak, the stairs like 'ladders of stone', while Edith's 'incompetence with things like electric light' hardly helped. 'I don't think she is having any brandy,' he told Sachie, 'and Luigi [the majordomo] is beginning to water the wine again, but she eats nothing and one litre of wine a day as well as glasses of vermouth are quite enough. . . .'[3] By the end of the month she had been in bed for five weeks, refusing to get up, but his suggestion that she would be better off with the Blue Nuns at Fiesole was being 'very ill received'. Sachie transmuted his concern for Edith into poetry, working his fear that she might be hospitalised for the remainder of her life into stanzas of 'Serenade for a Sister', visualising her at Montegufoni:

> You love, I know,
> The pergola of blue wisteria,
> Below the lily-tower
> And the little room
> Where I am painted as a harlequin,
> The hanging garden and the blue paulownia tree;
> But you will not walk there,
> 'a cloister awaits me' . . .

Early in January 1960 Sachie left for New York to join Georgia, who had been with her mother in Montreal, on the first leg of a prolonged journey to Peru, taking in Bolivia, Ecuador, Colombia, Guatemala, the Yucatan and Cuba, and returning home four months later. The trip had been planned with a book in view and had the advantage of providing an escape from Weston, where the roof was being renewed, the electric light rewired and a 'fiendish woodworm campaign' was under way. Osbert, Sachie told Bryher, was paying for nearly all of it. Bryher herself had put up the money for the Sitwells' transatlantic tickets, while the Peruvian Government had been persuaded by Sachie's friend, Fernando Berckemeyer, their Ambassador in Washington, to finance the air fares between Washington and Lima. The rest of the expenses, Sachie hoped, would be backed by his publishers, Weidenfeld & Nicolson, who provided £750 of an £1,000 advance before his departure.

Miami, the starting-point for their South American journey, fascinated Sachie. He noted that there seemed to be more funeral parlours than seafood joints or chicken and burger bars, one whole street being lined with them. At Lima, where, he told Bryher, they received a tremendous reception and stayed with the British Ambassador, Sir Berkeley Gage, he was given his first and for a long time only honour, the Freedom of the City. Sachie was disappointed by the architecture of Lima – 'but little left of Lima except wooden balconies,' he noted – and horrified by the slums of the Barrieras, which he visited on a tour arranged by the mayor of Lima, describing them as 'appalling . . . utterly degrading'. 'The hideous and aching monotony' of life in the Barrieras was such that, for once, he was not moved to any comparisons with Dante's *Inferno*. In a fever of apprehension about altitude sickness, he flew to Cuzco and took the train to Machu Picchu. They spent ten days on the Altiplano, where the thinness of the air discouraged even Sachie and Georgia from smoking. Sachie felt breathless and averaged only two hours of sleep a night, but he enjoyed Cuzco and the adventure of being there so much that he did not mind. Even there he could not escape sadness at the conditions and life expectancy of the indigenous population. 'Going out to buy *Time* at the street corner a small Indian boy . . . looked up at me wheezing and coughing, and drawing his pathetic *poncho* a little tighter round his chest,' he wrote. 'How long would he survive, and what treats had life in store for him? . . . four fifths of the Indian children fail to reach sexual maturity. . . .'[4]

In Havana, Cuba, he found only two things really interesting, the music and the hotels. 'Considering that Havana is one of the oldest and most important Spanish cities in Latin America there is not much to show for it. . . . Its nightmare hotels are of incomparable size and ugliness. . .' Apart from a handful of gamblers with Mafia connections, Americans were too frightened of the Castro Government to visit Havana, although not yet forbidden to do so. 'It was an extraordinary and revealing sight to visit the empty caravanserais in the absence of their occupants, and an insight into

the mentality of mid-twentieth century holidays. . . .' Otherwise, in South
America it was not the traces of the baroque that interested him as much
as the Indians and their ancestors, the Incas, and in the Yucatan, the Maya
and Toltecs. He was fascinated by the bas-reliefs and carved stelae.
'Visually, the Mayan must have been one of the oddest of all human
cultures,' he wrote. 'If one is to think of it in terms of aesthetics one cannot
but prefer it to the stereotyped Egyptian. . . .'

The quality of Sachie's travel books was in direct proportion to his
aesthetic response to his experiences and the depth of his understanding
and knowledge of what he saw. *Bridge of the Brocade Sash* had triumphantly passed this test. *Arabesque and Honeycomb* had not. *Golden Wall and
Mirador*, his account of his Latin American travels, and his subsequent
book on the Far East, *The Red Chapels of Banteai Srei*, were, if anything,
worse. All three of them bore the unmistakable traces of the potboiler,
although their object was not to earn more money but to finance his travels
and winter escapes from Weston. As one reviewer wrote:

> It is sad to have to record that . . . Mr Sitwell . . . is now capable of
> grossly careless writing, and on some occasions of positively
> ungrammatical sentences. . . .One of his worst sins is that of the
> 'hanging participle', as in a sentence like this: 'Coming out of our hotel
> a thunderstorm broke' . . . Can thunderstorms come out of hotels?[5]

At times his style was not just ungrammatical but simply bad, as this
passage from *The Red Chapels* illustrates:

> The naked babies [seen in Bangkok], to return to them, form the instant
> chinoiserie of Thailand and Cambodia (and of Angkor, therefore) in just
> the sense in which we speak of instant coffee. Inferring that it makes
> coffee, then and there, on the spot, and in a second.

The inescapable impression was that these books were written perfunc-
torily and in haste. Sachie's editors seem to have been equally willing to
rush the books through or, to be charitable, they may have been too
intimidated by his reputation to do their job.

Golden Wall and Mirador came over patchily and, in some passages, as
breathless as Sachie had been on the Altiplano. 'Mr Sitwell has been to
the Andes, in a hurry,' Geoffrey Grigson wrote in the *Spectator*. He was
understandably irritated by Sachie's constant, often forced and irrelevant
comparisons:

He writes of churches, sculptures, flowers and so on, by a self-contained process of aesthetic thrill according to which something encountered must be evaluated by something previously encountered somewhere else: a llama by a yak, Cuzco by Lhasa, Machu Picchu by Petra, a Peruvian drink by a French one, Peruvian megalithic walls by the Amsterdam bricks in the paintings of Jan van der Heyden. It is too bad if you have never seen a van der Heyden, have never drunk that French drink, have never been to Petra, or Lhasa, and never watched a yak. . . .[6]

Sachie was also deeply offended by a review by Alan Pryce-Jones, which he took to imply that his research on the ground had been superficial.

Even in South America he had been preoccupied by Edith's state, receiving communiqués from Osbert about her. In January Osbert reported that, after two months in bed, she had at last consented to come downstairs, although she was still spending most of her time in bed writing cross letters to the newspapers.[7] From Lima in February Sachie wrote to Bryher to tell her that he had heard again from Osbert that, although she came down to luncheon every day, 'her mental & nervous state is what worries him – and it's what worries me – She is so exaggerated.' When Sachie arrived back in England towards the end of April, he found Edith much better and installed in the Sesame Club, 'but is in bed every evening – and I feel always will be now!' After lunching with Osbert in June, he told Bryher that he was dreadfully depressed by Osbert's and Edith's decrepitude. 'It is very sad for me how they both have to be hauled and dragged out of their chairs – or out of a motor. . . . I cannot bear them both to be decrepit like that.'

Worse was to come. On 20 July Georgia received a letter from Horner, written at Osbert's request, describing Edith's condition in lurid and repellent detail, her drinking ('Yesterday . . . she polished off *half a bottle* of brandy and a whole bottle of white wine apart from anything else'), incontinence and paranoia. 'She never moves from her bed as she can't walk; her legs & arms are like sticks but she is very fat otherwise so her legs will not support the weight. . . . Her mental state is far worse.' Osbert was embarrassed by one of the stories which she repeated to his secretary, Lorna Andrade, and to the local doctor, that she had wanted to marry several young men but Osbert had prevented her on the grounds that they had not sufficient quarterings. 'This is a perfect example of persecution mania and paranoia with frustrated sex thrown in,' Horner added nastily. The domestic staff could not cope and the doctor thought that she should be sent to a 'private mental home. It seems to me the only solution . . . .This is to give you an idea of what is going on. . . .'[8] Malevolence towards Edith was in every line and continued even after her death. When John Pearson sent him a copy of his Sitwell biography, *Façades*, passages describing Edith's fall at Montegufoni were scored with the comment 'Drunk as usual'; his copy of Elizabeth Salter's life of Edith was similarly marked.[9]

Sachie suspected that Horner was deliberately exaggerating her condition in order to get rid of her. 'Of course David Horner had to write both of us the gloomiest possible letter about her, and I am sure his plan is to get her out of Montegufoni and prevent her going back there this autumn,' he told Bryher on 4 August, reporting that Edith was now in a Sheffield nursing home and, according to Osbert, 'seems happy, and looks much better and marvellously young'. He and Georgia went up to Renishaw on 5 August to see Edith and were not encouraged by what they found. 'Edith *looked* well & seemed 95% alright. But she is not, I am afraid,' he wrote to Bryher on the 10th. 'She has had a really bad breakdown – and I believe very wandering in her mind.' He had to agree with Horner that, with the nursing she needed, she could not go back to Montegufoni and hardly even to Renishaw. Osbert, he said, had been dreadfully worried about her, but 'Someone else is, of course, only too pleased to get rid of her.'

By mid-September things seemed to be getting back to normal. Edith was installed at the Sesame, although unable to walk unaided, and that month her *Swinburne: A Selection* was published. Sachie told Bryher that he thought her introduction 'one of the best things in the way of analysing poetry that she has ever done', despite being written in June and July when at the beginning of her crisis. She was still, however, in a '*very overstrung, over-excited* state'. The doctors in Sheffield had diagnosed 'senile paranoia', but Sachie wrote to Bryher that he had never seen any sign of senility in her. One must remember, he said, that the doctors did not understand her – 'what would they have made of many other artists: J. MN [*sic*] Whistler, for example?' Sachie feared that a 'disastrous side-effect' of Edith's no longer being able to go to Montegufoni would be that Osbert was now completely dependent on Horner, who 'is, of course, delighted to get her out of the house, and poor O. is now entirely in his power'. Her dislike of Horner had been one of the things upsetting her.[10]

Meanwhile, Sachie had been planning a new departure, this time to the Far East, Angkor, Thailand and possibly Nepal. He was very excited about the prospect, telling Higham, 'I think I might do something fairly sensational on this. . . .' He had been due to do a book on Brazil for Weidenfeld, but, not really wanting to do it, told Higham that Bryher, 'my guide and mentor', thought that he should go to the Far East now before the political situation there worsened. In the end, Sachie and George Weidenfeld agreed the new project together on the basis that the publisher should advance the royalties beforehand to help with expenses. Bryher loyally produced another cheque, and Sachie and Georgia left for the Far East on 25 February 1961. For Sachie, Angkor and Bangkok were among the great travel experiences in his life, second only to Japan. He would have liked to have seen more of Cambodia and Indonesia, but it was too late. Reresby, unexpectedly, joined them in Delhi on their way back. 'It is the first time we have been alone with him for 10 years,' Sachie wrote to Bryher from Jaipur, 'and it's a very important thing in our lives, as you may imagine. It has been lovely having him with us. . . .' He enjoyed Nepal and the beautiful clothes he saw in Jaipur. 'The Gypsies are supposed to have come originally from Rajputana – and the villagers look like, and walk like, the Spanish Gypsies,' he told Bryher. They then went south to Bombay to see the caves of Ajanta and Eleora and on to Ceylon, but India, and the Indians, did not attract Sachie, who found the Far East more to his taste.

Even in Jaipur, Osbert and, particularly, Edith, were on his mind. 'Osbert has been seeing Edith', he wrote to Byrher, 'and we are to have a long talk about her when I am back and he has returned from the U.S.A. . . . I cannot get the poor thing [Edith] out of my mind. . . .' She had been worse again in February before he left London, so much so that the secretary of the Sesame had telephoned to say that a night nurse must be got for her or she must go to a nursing home. Her regular doctor, Armando Child, had been on holiday and the present doctor's line, Sachie reported to Osbert, had been ' "Why shouldn't she drink if she wants to – so many old ladies do – I hope she won't put up with any nonsense from the Club etc." ' Sachie, however, managed to discover just how much she was drinking: 'She has now a double-brandy for breakfast – about 1 bottle of brandy in all every day; 2 bottles of wine, and several martinis!!!'[11] 'I think she is quite alright,' he told Osbert, 'or more or less so, if she stops drinking – but it is now on the scale of Constant Lambert . . . she must be spending £30 a week on drink. . . . But she is too old, poor thing, to be expected to do a cure – so what can we do about it?' Dr Child, on his return, had found nothing much to worry about, managing to soothe Sachie's fussing by declaring her organically perfectly healthy and mentally 'clear as a bell'.

He touched on the drink problem, and is going into it in a big way tomorrow. He says we are to remember that people who drink, *do drink* a very great deal, and often more than one imagines to be possible . . . apart from the bedwetting . . . there is absolutely no sign of mental wandering, or senility, or paranoia, such as that silly young doctor at Sheffield complained of. . . .[12]

Within a few days of his arrival back in England in mid-April, however, Sachie had his own health to worry about. On the 26th Georgia wrote to Higham to tell him that Sachie had had a prostate operation in Northampton General Hospital: '. . . the pain he suffered seemed almost intolerable though he was, as usual, incredibly brave. He fusses over trivialities but is a hero in a crisis. . . .'[13] By early June he was beginning to feel better, but Georgia had had to go yet again to Montreal where Mrs Doble, now aged eighty-six, was to have a hip operation. Sachie himself, despite some 'perfectly foul reviews' for the recently published *Golden Wall and Mirador*, was 'trying to write poems again . . . and more cheerful than this letter sounds'.[14]

He found plenty to depress him later that month when he went to Renishaw to find Osbert in good spirits but bent double, bumping into everything and unable to get up without help:

Oh Bryher! It is so pathetic to have to lift him by both hands when he wants to get up. . . . I used to be so proud of his appearance. . . . He can't even get up in the middle of the night to go to the bathroom without help and is making such a fight against it all. It really is heartrending – the walk is terrible and the clattering of spoon and fork at meals. . . . And then Edith! really the infirmity of both of them is perfectly terrible.

The gloom was such, he told Georgia, still in Canada, that he would almost have preferred to have had 'Fauntleroy' there to relieve it. 'The house is full of ghosts for me,' he wrote to Bryher on 29 June. 'I don't mean spooks – but memories of so many people dead and living. I hadn't slept in that bedroom for more than thirty-five years. . . .'

Sachie's relationship with Osbert was becoming closer again as Horner's star appeared to be in the descendant. Osbert's attitude towards him was no longer as adoring as it had been. On 1 June Sachie had reported to Georgia that Horner had told him on the telephone that 'Osbert's character has altered very much – that he is no longer so considerate or kind. What does this mean, I wonder?' he added. Osbert's selfishness, always marked, was increased by his concentration on fighting for his life. Sachie was still hurt at Osbert's exclusion of him both from Renishaw and Montegufoni over the past years. '. . . for reasons I have never yet discovered,' he complained to Bryher, 'I was never asked to Renishaw for *sixteen* years – 1943–1959 – and never yet to Montegufoni. . . .'[15] Both Sachie and Georgia were at Renishaw with Osbert at the end of August, finding him far worse. He had now agreed to go into hospital on 25 September to have a neurological operation on his brain in an attempt to relieve the symptoms of his disease, and was due to convalesce afterwards at Weston in October. Georgia was in Canada pacifying her mother, who had taken to writing 'violently abusive' letters once or even twice a day for most of the time Osbert was at Weston. Sachie had been nervous of possible friction, but since she returned on 3 November they were together for only four days. All went well, as Osbert testified in notes from Montegufoni thanking them both for their affection: 'I feel so grateful to my dearest brother for looking after me so well. . . .'[16]

Edith was now installed in a Hampstead flat, 42 Greenhill, looked after by her Australian secretary, Elizabeth Salter, and an Irish nurse, and surrounded by her old possessions from Pembridge Mansions. Sachie and Georgia had visited her there in September and found her, as usual, in bed and, Sachie thought, looking very old, with her head sunk on her chest and rather wandering in her speech. Sachie had brought with him a bound typescript of all his recent poems and some old favourites which effected an almost instant transformation. '. . . what an extraordinary person [she is]!!' he told Bryher. '*Yesterday*, an extremely sensible letter arrives from her, discussing the poems. I suppose poetry will interest her to her last breath!' Edith's letter was, as always, full of praise; the collection was a 'masterpiece' which she could not avoid comparing favourably with 'the pipsqueak rubbish . . . poured out by The Movement'.

Despite Edith's encouragement, Sachie had been depressed by the reception of *Golden Wall and Mirador* that summer and was not comforted when C.P. Snow told him that he was 'getting the backwash from critics who can't stand Edith's work'.[17] To Higham he wrote that 'the universally bad and horrid' reviews had 'quite broken' his nerve, so that he did not intend to write anything further after finishing the Far East book. 'I shall either have to repay George [Weidenfeld] his advance, or will very slowly write this last book for him. I had wanted to do these travels in order to attempt the world History of Art, but it is quite hopeless. . . .'[18] Higham rushed to offer him a comforting lunch at the Etoile, but the roots of depression were not only a sense of literary failure but, as he told Bryher, the world political situation and the general decrepitude: 'Krushchev, Osbert, Edith and Mrs Doble', the latter now having taken to writing up to four letters a day. Despite what he constantly referred to as his 'disillusionment' with his literary career, he was writing poetry again and, as he told Higham on 20 February, he had begun 'a new long book, *not* the sequel to the one I wrote with Cassell's [*Journey to the Ends of Time*]', and wanted to find a publisher for it.

News of Osbert at Montegufoni was encouraging. He seemed to be greatly improved as a result of his operation. Nothing in the Sitwells' lives, however, could continue on an even keel for very long. Danger lurked beneath the surface and Gothic horror, never far away, was always liable to spring the unexpected. Early in March 1962 David Horner was found at seven o'clock in the morning with a fractured skull in a pool of blood at the foot of one of the notorious stone stairs at Montegufoni; he had been lying there since about 11.30 p.m. the previous night. Sachie heard the news late the following night, when a reporter from the *Yorkshire Post* rang up for further information saying, 'they had nothing on their files about a Mr David Horner'. Horner was taken to the Ospedale Ortopedico in Florence, where he lay in primitive conditions before being transferred to the Blue Nuns at Fiesole. He had had a clot on the brain, which had induced a type of stroke; his right arm was smashed, he was paralysed down one side and barely capable of speech.

The scene might have been staged by Ginger for one of his dinner parties so suited was it to the grim, haunted castle of the Dukes of Athens. Immediately the rumours started. The local peasants pointed the finger at the Sardinian manservant, who was on bad terms with Horner and who they said had the evil eye. Christabel Aberconway, who was given to dramatisation and also by that time to copious draughts of drink, said that he had made a pass at a handsome young airman connected with one of the servants and been given a push. Other people said that it was the cook. Certainly Horner was in a part of the castle in which he would not normally have been, since his own room was near the *salone* while the stairs he fell down were near the kitchens at the back of the house. Horner himself told John Pearson:

> I just don't know what happened then – or *why* it happened. I knew the house so well, and I wasn't drunk – certainly not drunk enough to tumble down a flight of steps. I still believe somebody – or something – made me fall, and I had a definite sensation of being pushed. I'd always known the house was haunted, and as I fell forward in the dark I had the definite sensation of something pushing firmly from behind.[19]

Sir George's vengeful ghost, perhaps, determined that his beloved Montegufoni should not go to this outsider?

Horner slowly recovered, as Sachie informed Bryher on 7 April, less than a month after the accident. To Bryher he did not bother to conceal his detestation of Horner:

> I was sorry for the poor creature when he was so ill – but he is the most spoilt, and one of the most evil persons I have ever come across. A kind of male Madame de Pompadour, but in fact male is not the suitable word. He has never done a day's work in his life, and is utterly worthless, and has had a very bad effect on poor O. . . .

Lorna Andrade had told him that Osbert seemed less worried about Horner's condition than most other people. The love of more than thirty years was waning and the stage being set for the final divorce. Osbert and Horner returned, separately, to London at the end of June, two pathetic invalids sharing a house full of memories at Carlyle Square. Horner would require almost daily outpatient treatment for the next two years, making it, as Sachie told Bryher, impossible for him to get to either Renishaw or Montegufoni. 'What a strange denouement after he had got Edith out of his way!'[20]

Edith herself was enjoying a triumphant apotheosis in the public eye. At the end of August her last prose best-seller, *The Queens and the Hive*, came out; *Fanfare for Elizabeth* was reissued and a volume of her last poems published to coincide with her seventy-fifth birthday on 7 September 1962. Her nephew Francis, who was now working for Shell, organised a celebratory concert at the Royal Festival Hall on 9 October, at which Edith, seated in a wheelchair dressed in red velvet, resplendent in her extraordinary jewellery and Plantagenet hat, read a selection of her most recent poems, Peter Pears sang Benjamin Britten's setting of 'Still Falls the Rain', and Walton himself conducted his music for *Façade*, first heard in the Carlyle Square drawing room forty years before. A few weeks later she made her last television appearance – on *This Is Your Life* – and was a guest with the Queen Mother at a luncheon given by Cecil Beaton.

Sachie took part in his sister's public celebrations, but privately he could not help torturing himself with comparisons as to their relative success. 'There is so much adulation of poor Edith going on', he complained to Higham, 'and nothing to encourage her younger brother, now at my best as a writer, and completely neglected by all and sundry. . . .'[21] Higham hastened to reassure him: 'Don't be depressed.

The fanfare for Edith is something by way of reward for a personality, apart from anything else.' Like most writers with a career apparently in the doldrums he was becoming dissatisfied with his publisher, George Weidenfeld. Weidenfeld, having initially bombarded Sachie with ideas, now appeared to him to be neglecting him. Sachie was disappointed in the quality if not the quantity of his publisher's projects, complaining to Higham in February that Weidenfeld had 'all sorts of schemes – most of them for big "library" books with many illustrations and a text that no one will ever read. . . .' By September he had become 'very dissatisfied with George', having sent him a synopsis for a book on 'Monks and Nuns' on 28 March and heard no more about it. By 29 September it had become 'I still feel in my bones I should leave George and I rather suspect he feels the same about me. . . .' But, as winter came on and Georgia, who always had sinus trouble, now suffered from bronchitis while he was attacked by sciatica, Sachie's desire to travel to a warmer climate became irresistible, even to the point of taking on the Brazil book which he had repeatedly postponed. 'I do want to complete my survey travels with the book on Brazil,' he told Higham. To Bryher, who would again help with expenses, he was quite frank. Weidenfeld had agreed to come up with the customary £1,000 to be paid in advance of the trip. 'I think we had better go to Brazil. . . . At least in Brazil there are the tropical flowers and birds,' he wrote on 15 October.

They were not, however, destined to see Brazil in 1963. Snowed in at Weston in January, Sachie was racked by sciatica, which caused him sleepless nights, while Georgia's sinus problems now necessitated a major operation. Weidenfeld's American publishers were in financial difficulties and the Brazil book project was postponed. The only good news he had to retail to Bryher was about Edith, who was 'very cheerful and like she used to be. Isn't it wonderful?' In February he was astonished to get a telephone call from Edith announcing that she was 'going round the world'. When he asked where exactly she was going, she called to the nurse, 'Sister Farquhar, which ocean is it we are going to see?' 'Sister F. replied "the Pacific". You know how ignorant Edith is of geography.'[22] By coincidence, Sachie and Georgia were booked on the same ship as Edith and Miss Salter, accompanying her as far as Gibraltar. They were going on to Seville and Lisbon, while Edith was bound for two weeks in Sydney before continuing her circumnavigation.

The voyage was not a success for any of them. Francis had been to see them off and committed the unforgivable sin of giving both his parents 'flu, which spoiled their Iberian holiday, while Edith's trip was even more unfortunate. Unlike her brothers, she was no traveller and disliked the ship. At Miami she developed a haemorrhage while being seasick and was taken off the ship at Bermuda and flown home. Sachie attributed her illness to Miss Salter's getting on her nerves – 'the three women had been alone together too long and Edith *does* do this. It happened for instance with Beryl de Zoete,' he told Bryher on 25 May. Osbert went to see her and was disconcerted by her mental state; she did not know the difference between Evelyn Wiel (Helen Rootham's sister) and Evelyn Waugh. In July she developed pneumonia and was taken to hospital, but by the end of the month had made a remarkable recovery and was home again. In late August Sachie and Georgia went to Renishaw; Osbert and Horner were also to be there. 'I think (and know) that Osbert is finding him exceedingly difficult,' Sachie told Bryher, 'but I could have told him that as far back as 1925! I think they have even thought of living seperately [*sic*]! He gives notice to any servant poor Osbert gets which is more or less what he did to me when I was kept away all those years. . . .' Both Horner and Osbert were now hopeless invalids, having to have their food cut up for them at meals, while Horner was subject to fits due to his brain injuries. That winter Osbert went to Montegufoni without him for the first time.

The year 1963 had been a disappointing one for Sachie. That spring Cassell's had finally intimated that they did not want to publish a second volume of *Journey to the Ends of Time*. He was still possessed by a sense of failure. 'It is awful to be 66 – and I am afraid still unsuccessful,' he wrote to Bryher, thanking her for her birthday cheque in November. His only consolation was that he now felt 'better able than ever to write poetry'. He had nearly 450 pages of poems, but was afraid to have them published because 'they would only be torn to pieces and thrown in poor Edith's face'. Higham took him to task for his illogical attitude: 'Surely the way to ensure an awareness of your poetry is to have it published, whereas you tell me you have 500 pages of unpublished poetry, which may satisfy you but can hardly give pleasure to anybody else. . . .'[23] He was working on a book for Weidenfeld, which was to be *Monks, Nuns and Monasteries*, an enjoyable return to old stamping grounds, and Higham had placed the Brazil book with Robert Hale.

The Brazil trip was, therefore, on again for February 1964. Sachie and Georgia travelled there by ship early in February, but Sachie, just as he had feared, did not find it very interesting.

Brazilia is a strange kind of Chirico-Pompeii ruin – all built (and of course unfinished) in the course of four years. The old architecture

hardly exists – and we saw *one* magnificent blue butterfly in a garden near
Rio, but no humming birds or parrots. I suppose after the Far East nothing
is quite the same again. . . .[24]

Not surprisingly, he found the commissioned book difficult to write. 'I am
still worried and distressed about Brazil,' he told Higham. 'I would find it
painful and a task and a burden to write – particularly as at the moment I
want to write poetry. . . . I'm afraid Brazil is really impossible – it's so big
and so dull and so hopeless compared with so many other wonderful and
inspiring themes.' Hale accommodatingly changed the contract to cover
'an autobiographical work', but he felt he could not contemplate this
either, particularly after the publication in 1965 of Edith's *Taken Care Of*,
and paid back the £1,000 advance he had been given for Brazil in April
1965.

On other fronts, however, there was good news. In July the newly
founded Humanities Research Center at the University of Texas agreed
to pay £20,000 for Sachie's manuscript notebooks and correspondence,
and in the same month Sachie's collection of four portrait drawings by
Ingres were sold at Sotheby's for £24,000. 'Can you imagine!' Sachie
wrote triumphantly to Bryher. 'This means the cessation of some at least
of the incessant worries we've had for years – because it has been very
difficult living here on a family income fixed in 1926 – . . . Of course
like Edith, I have a very large overdraft to pay off. . .' Edith, whose
extravagance in many ways equalled Sachie's, had been meanly treated by
Osbert, who had never paid her the £5,000 due to her from her father's
estate, nor given her her share of the Sitwell Stiftung. She, too, had
managed to pay off her debts by the sale of her Tchelitchew paintings and
her own manuscripts at Sotheby's.[25]

She was now comfortably installed with her beloved cats and loyal
Australians, Elizabeth Salter and Sister Doris Farquhar, in a Queen
Anne cottage in Keats Grove, Hampstead, which she named Bryher
House. Sachie had seen the house in June and thought it charming, but,
after visiting Edith there on 26 July, sent a gloomy report on her health to
Bryher. She was living on brandy and milk and smoked salmon snacks.
'She is deteriorating . . . it upset me terribly – and I cannot think it will
go on much longer.' In August he and Georgia were at Renishaw. He
reported that

Osbert was mostly in bed from 2 falls but not too bad. David was
perfectly impossible and we had an extraordinary evening with him on

Sunday, culminating in hearing what *did* seem to be the family ghost.
Georgia and I went to bed at 10.30 – leaving him downstairs – and we heard
him go along the passage past our room at 11.15 – and then we both heard
someone go past again at 12.15. Very odd. I do not, as you know, believe in
such things, but it was very peculiar.

Edith had had the house exorcised after her conversion, clearing it of
some of the more outrageous phantoms, but at least one particularly
persistent ghost remained. One cannot help feeling that Ginger may have
despatched it on a mission to finish off the job botched at Montegufoni. 'If
there isn't a ghost at Renishaw now, there will be one when, if ever, David
H. departs!!!' Sachie commented.[26]

Horner was not, however, at Montegufoni when Sachie and Georgia
went there in September for the first time for twenty-five years. Sachie
had not been there since 1939. 'The old peasant was in tears – I have
known *him* since 1910! . . . And what is it all about? The answer is David
Horner, –' he wrote to Bryher on 5 October. But Horner's long reign was
virtually over. 'I think I shall have to try and disentangle [Osbert] from
David H. who is odious and awful to him.' As the only physically active
member of the family, he was taking charge of his elder brother and sister,
negotiating Osbert's 'divorce' from Horner and sending his Hungarian
doctor, Dr Csato, to deal with Edith:

> [He] is the first doctor who has been brave enough to tell her what is the
> matter with her [he told Bryher]. Isn't it shocking how cowardly the
> others are! But I suppose it is rather like having to speak in such a way
> to the Archbishop of Canterbury! Anyway she took it very well, has kept
> to what he told her, and is incomparably better and, thank God, lucid
> again. It really is a little naughty of her!

Sachie, involved that autumn and winter in the Osbert-Horner
problem, did not seem much concerned about Edith's health when he
wrote to Osbert on 8 December, principally about Horner. Osbert was in
Naples; Sachie wrote nostalgically to him there: 'The Hotel Santa Lucia
where we used to stay is now held in esteem as a kind of Nouveau Art
masterpiece. Don't forget to have lunch on the terrace of the Hotel
Vesuvio. . . . I wish I were in Naples with you.' He also gave the latest
doctor's bulletin on Edith: 'Dr Csato is trying to get rid of the hospital
infection which is what has poisoned Edith's finger, and also thinks she
has a small stone in her bladder which he thinks he can get rid of. . . .'

That evening Edith finished reading the bound proofs of her short,
bitter autobiography, *Taken Care Of*, shutting the book in a 'very decisive

and strange way as though to signify she had finished something', Sachie later told Osbert. At 9.30 p.m. she began an attack of nausea, followed by a haemorrhage, and in the morning, after a night of pain and sickness, was taken to St Thomas's Hospital. Sachie was telephoned by the hospital and told that she was not seriously ill and that they hoped she would be home in a few days. Then at lunchtime there was an urgent call summoning them to London at once. Francis was already there, but, as Sachie told Osbert, 'We got to London at 4, and to the hospital at 4.30, but too late. We could not see her, and she died at 5.30. She had had two or 3 more severe haemorrhages, and could not take the blood transfusions. . . .'[27] Sachie telephoned Osbert in Naples to give him the news; when he returned to Montegufoni he found a letter from her written on the eve of his birthday five days before her death.

The last line of Edith's autobiography read: 'Then all will be over, bar the shouting and the worms. . . .' The shouting started almost immediately. Sachie and Osbert blamed a recent critical article by Julian Symons in Alan Ross's *London Magazine* for causing her death. The charge was ludicrously unfair. The article was hostile and mocking, but no more so than many that Edith had endured before; what is more, no mention of this arose in any of Sachie's correspondence before Edith's death. He felt, however, a need to lash out in defence of his sister and, on 17 December, he wrote a very bitter letter to Alan Ross:

> Sir,
> I have been waiting for you to send me a word of regret on the death of my sister. . . . In my opinion, and in that of others who were near to her, the horrible article by Julian Symonds [sic] was very largely responsible for her death.
> I know that on your instructions he was preparing this quite disgraceful attack on her since last spring. . . . I know, also, that you told someone that you would finish her once and for all. . . .[28]

A requiem mass was held for her at Farm Street at which, somewhat to Sachie's disgust, David Horner appeared, outwardly apparently unconcerned by the ultimatum he had received from Osbert, via Philip Frere, intimating that their life together was over. Some months later, on being told by Sachie that Osbert had at last succeeded in shedding Horner, Father Caraman, who had 'long been imploring me to achieve this, said to me, quite seriously, "Perhaps it is Edith's first work in heaven." Aren't the Catholics unbeatable!'[29] Edith was buried later that day in a simple plot belonging to Lois Weedon churchyard near Weston looking over the rolling Northamptonshire fields, where Lady Ida too was buried; she was nearer to her mother in death than she had ever been in life. Even then the note of tragi-comedy which underlay the Sitwells' lives could not be avoided. Christabel Aberconway in an emotional condition was seen literally to dance on her grave, which the undertakers had put in the wrong place and later had to move.

Sachie had been comforted when Father Caraman told him that he had given Edith absolution when she returned from her world cruise and he had thought that she was dying. She had not been frightened by the thought of death and had talked to him and even made jokes about it. But nothing could console Sachie for her death. 'I feel absolutely shattered,' he told Bryher. 'We will never see anyone like her again. I've been writing poems for months and months, really for her to see, though I knew she was beyond reading more than a page or two of them. Now I feel quite lost. . . .' 'She was always my friend and mentor from the first days I remember wanting to write – and in fact long before that,' he told a mutual friend.[30] But her death inspired him to complete 'Serenade to a Sister' and some of his finest later poems, in which he wrote of her death and evoked their childhood together and their youth of poetry. He later published these ten poems in a collection entitled simply *To E.S.* In 'Epithyte Lily', he wrote:

> Just now,
>   a day or two ago,
> A lion heart and lily soul
> Have left earth and gone into air
> Gone where
>   where where?

and in 'His Blood Colours My Cheek', he described her lying dead, his own doubts about the afterlife and her conviction, 'So she was not dismayed. . . .' He completed it with 'The Octogenarian' written in 1977. In 'Schlaflos (Sleepless)' he evoked the trio as they had been in childhood and now were:

> It so upsets me that you should be back there in your sleep
>   in that primal darkness.
> How pitiful it is!
> While that other?
>   It would have broken my heart when I was twelve years old
> To see him sitting in the corner of his bedroom,

as he sat here after his operation,
As he always sits now.

What else is there for him to do?
It is difficult to hear him when he speaks.
    He is half into that dark, too.
But clutching at the light,
The darkness at back and the dark in front of him,
    And of us all;
The two darks nodding, nodding to each other,
    And drawing nearer.
Ah! what can I say about it all!
What sad, strange memories!

Osbert, vulnerable, ageing, helplessly crouched in his chair, was very much on Sachie's mind after Edith's death. He struggled valiantly and with unwonted energy to help his brother disentangle himself from Horner, even acting at times in tandem with Christabel. By the autumn of 1964 it had not been difficult to persuade Osbert that it was time for them to part. For the last four years or so their relationship had been deteriorating; the fact that Horner was also an invalid and an encumbrance rather than a help was certainly a factor in Osbert's diminishing feeling for him. The feelings were mutual; in 1965 Horner told Sachie that they had been getting on each other's nerves since 1961. Moreover, Osbert was now increasingly dependent on his Maltese valet/nurse, Frank Magro, who had come into his service in January 1963 and of whom Horner was deeply jealous.

At some point Horner gave Osbert an ultimatum: 'Either the Maltese goes or I do.' It was not, by now, a difficult choice for Osbert. Extinct passion and former friendship counted less than present need. He was physically completely dependent upon Magro while Horner had become less agreeable since his accident. He bullied Osbert, who was more physically helpless than he was, even to the extent of forcing him out of the bathroom when he himself needed it. Matters seem to have come to a head in September 1964 at Renishaw, when Osbert had written wearily to Christabel that the garden was looking lovely but 'only man is vile', a letter annotated by Christabel: 'I fear this refers to DH who since his accident is a changed, *grumbling* character. . . .'[31] Horner himself had written to Christabel four days later saying that Sachie and Georgia had been horrified while at Renishaw to see the way 'the Maltese' had treated Osbert. Christabel forwarded his letter to Sachie, asking him if he agreed. He did not:

What an absolute curse and nuisance he [Horner] is! And such a
dangerous one too. . . .I am not sure that it would not be a good idea for
me to ask O. outright if he would not like David H. to be asked to
leave. This could be done when O. is alone at Montegufoni this
winter. . . . I fear that David is getting better & regaining his health &
will be worse and more bullying than ever. It is an obsession with him
about the Maltese, and having lived on Osbert like an incubus for 40
years he resents any other influence. . . .[32]

Two days later he wrote:

The thought of poor O. and that creature [Horner] at Renishaw since
20 July is a horrible thought, isn't it? Having been kept out of Osbert's
life so long by him, I resent it very much. . . . I think a lawyer's letter
when O. is at Montegufoni is the only chance, but unfortunately legal
seperations [*sic*] are not possible in these macabre situations.

'What a comfort that we see eye to eye over all this!' Sachie wrote to
Christabel on 13 October. At lunch at Christabel's on 22 October, he and
Christabel persuaded Osbert to instruct Frere to ask Horner to leave the
flat which he and Osbert now shared in York House, Kensington Church
Street, to which they had moved after the lease ran out on Carlyle Square.
Sachie then saw Osbert's doctor, with whom he had frequently discussed
the subject before, and obtained a letter from him saying that they must
both separate in the interests of their health, which he then took to Frere.
Frere was to write to Horner, enclosing the doctor's letter, and timing the
bombshell to arrive on 9 November, four days after Osbert's departure
for Italy on the 5th. Horner's first, disconcerting reaction was to act as if
nothing had happened. Then, some three weeks later, when pressed for a
response by Frere, he refused to leave the flat, on the grounds that his
own doctor had advised him not to move 'for his health's sake'. Osbert's
response was to order Frere to move all his own possessions out of the flat
and have them taken to Renishaw. Horner then countered with a claim
that before the war Osbert had made a deed of gift of all the contents of
Carlyle Square in his favour and, therefore, the contents of the present
flat were all his. 'What a nuisance he is!' Sachie wrote to Christabel.
'And how dangerous! I remember a Cambridge don whose name I have
forgotten saying about him to me how "charming but dangerous" he was,
in 1923 or 4 before he had finally got his tentacles onto poor Osbert.'[33]
Sachie had no sympathy whatsoever with Horner, whom he described
to Bryher as 'behaving like a kind of highly paid courtesan', but he was

also forced to admit that 'poor Osbert' had behaved far from well. In the days of his passion Osbert had certainly intended to leave Montegufoni and everything he could to Horner, including much of the contents of Renishaw which he had collected, but not the house itself or the heirlooms in which he had only a life interest. The deed of gift was never found, but it seems that it had existed and Sachie informed Osbert that the lawyer's opinion was that if Horner brought a lawsuit against him, he might well win it. At the end of the month, however, Horner appeared to capitulate, telling Christabel that he intended to find a service flat. The one thing he resented was that Osbert had not had the courage to send him a personal letter saying they must part, but had communicated through lawyers. 'I shall never speak to Osbert again.' On Frere's advice, Osbert ordered his furniture and, indeed, most of the furnishings in the York House flat to be moved to Renishaw on 1 February. On the 2nd Horner made a suicide attempt as a gesture of protest. It failed to move Osbert, who told Christabel that he had first tried it in Amalfi in 1928 'and threatened it almost every year since', but Frere's wife, Vera, wrote to Osbert denouncing him, 'You unspeakable swine Osbert – only the most unutterable cad will hit a man who is broken in mind and body – and that is what you have done to David whom you called your dearest friend', and calling down 'God's curse' upon him.[34] Osbert shrugged it off, telling Christabel that Vera had been in love with Horner for years but had been rejected by him, adding nastily, 'She now sees her chance of acquiring the man who has for years spurned her. . . .'

It was an unpleasant way to end a long relationship. Horner had known Osbert since 1922 and they had lived together since 1929. In that time Horner had deliberately alienated Osbert from his brother and sister (above all his sister-in-law) and friends like Willie Walton and caused endless domestic trouble, making himself universally loathed by Osbert's old servants like Robins. But he had also, as he had put it to Christabel in 1929, been 'nurse, scribe, bully, comforter' as well as lover to Osbert, and with the exception of much of the war years and the American escapades been his constant companion, living, as he claimed with some exaggeration to McCann, 'a very secluded life at Renishaw and Montegufoni'. He had helped Osbert out financially in difficult times during the war from the money he had inherited from de Hendecourt which was held in a Swiss bank and he had not, as the family claimed, simply 'lived off' Osbert. He had been promised, as he thought, the contents of Carlyle Square; he had certainly until recently been set to inherit Montegufoni and, he told McCann, in about 1962 Osbert had told him 'that he had left all his personal fortune' to him. 'I think he [Osbert] has been very unkind to his oldest friend, and very forgetful of all that I have done for him, and really very dog in the manger.'[35]

Sachie might have been forgiven in thinking that, with Horner out of the way, his relations with Osbert might return to what they once had been. Edith was dead, there were only the two of them left and he seemed now to be taking a more active role in Osbert's life. He and Georgia spent three days with him at the Grand Hotel in Florence at the end of January 1965, when Sachie discovered that Osbert had changed his will leaving Montegufoni to him after all. He did not initially seem enchanted at the prospect, telling Bryher: 'it's so huge and dilapidated that I don't know what could eventually be done with it'. He also saw Dr Berger, the Swiss lawyer, en route and 'this seemed to go well'. Now that he was, temporarily, more secure financially, his feelings for Osbert were of affection and pity. Osbert's feelings towards Sachie were more complicated, principally by his dislike, jealousy and resentment of Georgia and his own increasingly indulged selfishness.

Edith's death was, however, a liberating factor for Sachie in that although he had lost a mentor, he had also lost a competitor; now that she was dead, he need no longer fear either invidious comparison or that his poems would be 'torn to pieces and thrown in her face'. No one, however, could replace Edith for him. 'I feel lost in a desert,' he had told Bryher on 23 December, but he had at least found someone to provide encouragement for him as a poet. 'The only good thing is that we have had such a charming and intelligent young man, called Alasdair Clayre to stay – he is a poet and a Fellow of All Souls. And he has been reading through my poems – the only person who has seen them except Edith. He has been a great help to me.' Sachie had invited Clayre to read a selection from Edith's poetry at her funeral and had sent him batches of his own most recent verse. Clayre had replied with a long, detailed critique:

> It has always seemed to me that your very best lines were the long
> unrhymed lines from which *Canons of Giant Art* is made . . . what you
> can do, that nobody else can do, is to write in long lines which go on
> flowering unexpectedly into new images from beginning to end . . . this
> is a unique and marvellous gift. . . . Often your lines are most beautiful
> when dealing with the least beautiful things (as in 'Agamemnon's
> Tomb', or the 'bony hand' of these recent poems). . . .[36]

Sachie continued to send him poems, apparently with a view to getting them privately printed; Clayre was always encouraging, taking up Edith's baton with criticism and praise:

> I think the forms where your intuitive rhythms have free play that your poetry is best – a recurrent generally unrhymed line over a tight formal or narrative structure. This is the hardest of all poetry to write well and I don't think anybody now writing, except you, can do it, and you have been able to from the start. . . .[37]

Clayre wrote to him in January 1965 suggesting that his new poems should be published first as pamphlets and circulated either publicly or privately as Sachie preferred; they might then later be printed in hardcover by a London firm. Nothing came immediately of Clayre's suggestion, but it took root in Sachie's mind. Although he himself never doubted the quality of his own poetry, the encouragement of a younger poet, like Clayre, made him think that perhaps he might after all publish them.

Sachie called 1965 'Abdication Year.' That autumn Osbert finally gave in to his lawyer's advice and, in order to avoid crippling death duties on the Renishaw estate, retired to Montegufoni, leaving Reresby in possession, Sachie having already 'abdicated' his title to the property. Osbert had spent a miserable summer at Renishaw suffering continual domestic upheavals principally caused by the servants' resentment of Frank Magro, about whom one of them went so far as to write Sachie an eleven-page letter of denunciation. 'There has been one of those awful internecine wars at Renishaw', Sachie told Bryher, 'because Osbert made Frank his secretary – and the other servants refused to wait on him and walked out.'[38] 'It has been hell here,' Osbert had written to Georgia on 4 August. 'I am longing to leave here which I never thought would happen. . . .'[39] On 9 August he left Renishaw for the last time and moved to the Metropole Hotel at Brighton preparatory to departing for a cruise to Australia. Sachie found Osbert's 'de-domiciling or whatever it is called' 'deeply nostalgic and upsetting. I can't help it,' he told Osbert. 'I suppose it is in my blood – and I used to, and still do, love Renishaw.' To him it seemed, and was, the end of an era, particularly coming as it did within a year of Edith's death. The days of 'Peregrine and Dagobert and I' were well and truly over.

'Sachie was awfully disappointed over Renishaw,' a friend said. 'They felt they were not very welcome there which was possibly their own fault. . . .'[40] Since their happy time with Reresby in India and Nepal, Sachie's relations with him had been once again upset by yet another interminable legal complication of a kind which seemed endemic in the Sitwells, this time over the breaking and division of the Weston trust. There were hurt feelings on both sides. Sachie felt that Reresby had been so much more fortunate than he had been himself. Reresby had been deeply upset by his parents' behaviour over his marriage. He felt to some extent rejected by them in favour of Francis, with whom their relations were so much easier. Strains are evident in a superficially amiable letter which Sachie had written to Reresby on the eve of meeting him in London for Edith's birthday celebration:

> We haven't been in London except for 1 day since July – and *always* let you know, but you generally forget, or else ring up on the last day saying how sorry you are. I'm afraid I remember doing just the same thing with my father, who was, you know, *rather* difficult and perhaps less nice than I am. However, I will be drawing my old age pension in November, so it won't be long now.[41]

Penelope Sitwell had found the treatment she received from Sachie and Georgia difficult to forgive and had not responded to overtures made – too late – by Georgia.

Now the younger generation were in charge at Renishaw and Sachie felt himself once more exiled from his family home. A sense of loss and exile from Renishaw runs through many of the poems he wrote after Edith's death. He felt that it had happened twice over, first because of David Horner, now because of his own 'abdication' and the family troubles. The last verse of 'Serenade to a Sister' is poignant:

> . . . I remember even the shape of the trees
> In the lost paradise,
> But they do not remember me;
> A mist of the spirit hides him who stood between us,
> There has been a spoiling and a tainting of the honeyladen air,
> For it was such while all three of us were young
> And despite our troubles there was eternal spring;
> Now it grows late,
> And the black cloud makes darker still.

On 23 September 1965 Weidenfeld brought out *Monks, Nuns and Monasteries*. Sachie had delivered the manuscript the previous October, having worked on it for a year. It was a compendium of past sightseeing experiences and various books linked by a main theme, the architecture of convents and monasteries in England, Italy, France, Iberia and the territories of the Greek Orthodox Church. The monasteries and convents of Italian and Spanish baroque, and the churches and palaces of German rococo, were old passions revisited; only in middle age had Sachie become interested in English ecclesiastical architecture. In *The Gothick North* he had dismissed cathedrals as being as much of an anachronism as rusting industrial machinery, but in this book he recognised that 'the great works of art are not all Italian or even French', referring particularly to the cathedrals of Ely, Lincoln, York and Durham. The section on England had not appeared before; Sachie had had it in mind since an abortive History of English Churches for Batsford several years earlier about which he had been enthusiastic and had described at the time as 'a very great idea'. It had foundered on a quarrel over financing. Batsford had insisted on offering Sachie a very low advance of £500, arguing that the other £500 should go to an expert cartographer to prepare detailed maps. Since most of the interesting English churches were off the beaten track and difficult to find, Batsford rightly considered accurate, specially commissioned maps to be almost as essential as the text. Sachie, characteristically, had refused to see the point of this, arguing airily that 'anyone in the office' could be employed to fulfil this function. Maps, even inadequate ones, were conspicuously lacking in all his travel books.

Sachie's interest in monastic life was entirely profane and visual. It began, he recalled in the introduction to this book, with the sight of a 'fanatical, wild-looking figure in a white monk's robe' seen in a street in Genoa when he was ten years old. Sachie, brought up in monk-free Yorkshire and Derbyshire, was fascinated by the man, who, he was told, was 'a hermit from the hills'. In his sixties he could still picture that moment's glimpse of a 'fury and wildness' of black hair, eagle nose and fanatical stare, an image which spurred a lifelong interest in 'every kind of Gypsy or "traveller" on the roads . . . every kind of ascetic from the tramp-monks in Magnasco's paintings to the trident-bearing *saddhus* of Ganges. . . . Of such is a personal mythology made up, and it lasts and never fades,' he wrote. *Monks, Nuns and Monasteries* was the first of a trilogy of past aesthetic experience, principally architectural, which he was to write for Weidenfeld during the 1960s. It was followed by *Southern Baroque Revisited* in 1967 and *Gothic Europe* in 1968.

Sachie and Georgia celebrated their fortieth wedding anniversary on 12 October 1965. Despite Georgia's many affairs and Sachie's 'goddesses', they remained devoted and in love with each other. During Georgia's absences with her mother in Canada they continued to write each other love letters. 'My own darling,' Georgia had written to Sachie in October 1959 while she was in London having cosmetic surgery:

> This is just to put into words, however inadequate, how much I miss you & how indescribably I love you. I really feel that the time here has been wasted (being away from you) unless it improves my appearance for *your* sake, which I really think it will. You used to be so proud of me & always pretend to be still. . . .

Francis and Reresby gave a cocktail party in London in their honour, which, Sachie told Bryher, was somewhat spoiled by a misunderstanding with Frank Magro:

> Frank is already causing trouble. He made Osbert write to that tiresome Lady Aberconway to say he couldn't come to Francis's party because Frank had not been invited. Naturally, as it's physically impossible for Osbert to come without him, we assumed Frank would be coming with him. After all this cruising etc. Frank will be utterly impossible![42]

Magro had by now replaced Horner, although to a lesser extent, as an object of suspicion over his influence with Osbert, who was, Sachie said, 'entirely in Frank's hands'. Magro was totally devoted to Osbert, whom he hero-worshipped and called 'The Master'. Intelligent and self-educated, he had read *Left Hand, Right Hand!* while serving with the RAF in Singapore. He considered it a privilege to look after Osbert and dedicated himself entirely to his entertainment and care, nursing him, reading to him and acting as his secretary. Although Horner wrote poisonous letters accusing Magro of using his position to get money out of Osbert, this was quite unfair. As Sachie's lawyer remarked, Magro was certainly in a position to feather his nest had he wanted to, but proved to be singularly ungrasping. With Magro wheeling him in his chair Osbert travelled again, taking cruises, staying in the best hotels, even revisiting Venice. Magro was sensitive, anxious to be accepted as a friend by 'The Master's' family and friends. Christabel Aberconway and the Reresby Sitwells went out of their way to do so, but Sachie, and Georgia in particular, did not conceal their dislike of him, resenting the fact that, as he wrote all Osbert's letters, he was privy to all their financial secrets. Magro's resentment at Georgia's treatment of him was plain in his letters to Christabel. In 1966 Osbert made Magro his literary executor, much to Sachie's disappointment. He had hoped that Osbert would have appointed Francis, as Edith had.

Francis had remained close to his parents, dutifully fulfilling family obligations. He had been a regular visitor to Edith in her declining years in London and had organised her seventy-fifth birthday festivities. It had been his task to bring back (at Reresby's suggestion) Ginger's ashes from Switzerland, handed to him by the Sitwells' Swiss lawyer in a brief, unceremonious meeting at Zurich airport, carrying them with him to London in a plastic airline bag, an undignified and unaesthetic container which would not have met with his grandfather's approval. The remains of Sir George rested on the mantelpiece of Francis's basement flat in London before being taken to Renishaw to be deposited with his ancestors in Eckington parish church. In 1966, after ten years with Shell Petroleum in London and East Africa, Francis was working in London in public relations. In June that year, to his parents' delight, he married Susanna Cross, daughter of the Rt Hon. Sir Ronald Cross, who had had a distinguished career in politics before and after the Second World War, as British High Commissioner in Australia during the war and Governor of Tasmania from 1951 to 1958. Perhaps because of her behaviour over Reresby's marriage, Georgia over-compensated with her new daughter-in-law, particularly after she produced the Sitwell male heir, George, the following year, another son, William, in 1969 and a daughter, Henrietta, in 1973. Susanna, with means of her own and an independent outlook, resisted her mother-in-law's attempts to make her 'the daughter she never had'.

The Red Chapels of Banteai Srei had been Sachie's last travel book. From now on the annual journeys to the sun were simply pleasure trips to escape the cold of Weston in late winter. In February 1966 they went to Mexico, staying with friends at Cuernavaca and with the Brownlows at Roaring River in Jamaica. In September they went to Santiago de Compostela for an article Sachie was writing on the Pilgrims' Way, and afterwards to the Brenners' Park Hotel at Baden-Baden for Georgia to have treatment for her sinus problems. The Baden-Baden sojourns were to become an annual routine, financed by Osbert, who had the grace, perhaps, to feel slightly guilty over his appropriation of the entire Swiss funds. Shortly after his return from Baden-Baden in October Sachie was taken ill and rushed into Northampton General Hospital for surgery on what turned out to be a benign polyp on the colon. It had not been a good year. He had had two attacks of jaundice over the past twelve months and, just as he was recovering at home in November after his operation, he came down with shingles.

He had, however, managed to do some work that year, writing the second of his trilogy, *Southern Baroque Revisited*. The project which interested him most was, however, the possibility of publication of his poems in the *Poetry Review*. The idea had first been put to him by the then editor, John Smith, in the summer of 1962, when his response had been negative. He had, he told Smith, some 300 pages of unpublished poems, among them 'about twenty ballads which I think are the best things. They include a long Serenade which is an attempt at a portrait of my sister.' He had kept to the idea of a 'Hortus Conclusus', which he had had at the time of the publication of *Canons of Giant Art*, and had written 'a lot of flower poems'. He listed them as *Fourteen Variations upon Old Names of Hyacinths*, *Ruralia* – 'Eighteen poems on wild flowers and country themes', *Rosario d'Arabeschi* – 'Twenty-two rose poems and rose portraits, and *Thirteen Poems on Tropical Flowers and Flowering Trees*. 'In all,' he wrote, 'but including poems written earlier, I have 140 poems for a Hortus Conclusus, the typewritten book is 277 pages. Lately (this summer) I have written three long poems on *Indian subjects* – and am at this moment writing more for *Rosario d'Arabeschi*. . . . I do not', he told Smith firmly, 'want any of them ever to be printed or published, or even shown to anyone. . . .'[43] 'Oh dear, how you whet my appetite. . . . What can I do to change your mind?' Smith replied.[44] Sachie, however, remained adamant until three years later he was approached by Smith's successor, Derek Parker (who was then editing Edith's letters with John Lehmann), with the proposal that the 1967 summer issue of the *Poetry Review* should be devoted to the publication of Sachie's post-war poems. Now, after Edith's death and his correspondence with Alasdair Clayre, Sachie's answer was an enthusiastic affirmative. 'I think, at the moment, and if not over-whelmed again with hermetic longings – that I would very much like and feel honoured, to do as you suggest.'[45]

Derek Parker went down to Weston on 19 October 1966 to make a selection of forty-eight poems from over 500 pages in five large, bound volumes. Parker noted, beneath the fascinating flow of Sachie's conversation, 'a hypertension which always seemed to set him on the edge of some dark precipice, the dark side was very deep indeed'.[46] Most people never noticed this since he discussed his work with very few of his friends, but the literary side of his life seemed to cause him anguish when brought into the public domain. Sachie toyed, or pretended to, with the idea of not, after all, letting them see the light of public day. 'I must warn you', he wrote to Derek Parker after their meeting, 'that I may easily be nauseated again by them and want to destroy them all which I have intended to do before and may well do in the end. . . .' All went well until February, when, three days after lunch with Sachie and Georgia at Loelia

Westminster's Grosvenor Square apartment, Parker received another letter from Sachie:

> I am afraid that after all – after all the trouble I have caused you! I have to make up my mind that it is impossible for me to have those poems published. I am already feeling too ill in too many ways because of it – and you cannot remember that I do *not want* readers for them. If you ever not [*sic*] published anything of the kind for more than thirty years I daresay you would agree with me. . . .

The issue was already being printed and had to be stopped, but eventually Sachie was persuaded to let it go ahead and it appeared 'in almost entire silence', according to Parker.

Early that summer Sachie and Georgia were at Montegufoni, spending a few days with Osbert after staying at La Pietra with Harold Acton. On 10 May Sachie sent Bryher a sad report of Osbert's condition, which he had found much worse than when he had last seen him eighteen months earlier in October 1965 before Osbert left England:

> He sits all huddled up with his head on his chest, and it is nearly impossible to hear what he says. This is made worse because the poor thing likes to be talked to for hours on end. He cannot walk at all or stand up – and is gradually losing his sight. Already he can barely read. . . . It is, as you may imagine, terribly sad and depressing.

Later he wrote: 'On getting to Montegufoni I had a terrible flood of nostalgia during the nights there, thinking it was 29 years since I had last slept there, and that we were all young once. . . .'[47] He had found Magro 'terribly tiresome', he told Bryher.

They were suceeded at Montegufoni by Reresby and Penelope, whom Magro described as 'perfect guests and absolutely delightful'. Reresby and Penelope were there again in September when Osbert suffered an attack of prostate trouble and they were, Magro told Christabel, '½ a dozen towers of strength divided in two delightful people'. To safeguard Magro's future, a grateful Osbert gave him a permanent flat at Montegufoni; Reresby and Penelope received the news agreeably, but Magro had his doubts about the reaction at Weston. There was trouble a month later when Georgia complained that Magro was not reporting to them frequently enough on Osbert's condition. In fact, Osbert had forbidden Magro to telephone Weston every week or so as Georgia had requested. As Magro told Christabel:

He is terrified that she and not Mr Sachie will decide on matters of life – & death. Mr Sachie hates speaking on the telephone, so I can only talk to his 'soul-mate' [Osbert's new name for Georgia] which I find anything but satisfactory. If only the duty of deciding on what course to take about Sir Osbert could be delegated to Mr Reresby who is young, intelligent and not hysterical. . . .[48]

Sachie sensed that once again he was being estranged from Osbert and wrote angrily to Magro pointing out that, as Osbert's brother, he, and not Reresby, should be the first to be informed about his health. He was in any case depressed and had developed jaundice the day before the dedication of the Henry Moore memorial to Edith in November. The monument, which had caused some controversy in the family on the grounds of expense and suitability, finally took the form of two bronze hands (not Edith's, but of an unidentified woman and a child, Moore's daughter, which Georgia had chosen in the sculptor's studio) on a simple granite stone carved by Moore on which were lines chosen by Bryher from Edith's poem, 'The Wind of Early Spring'. Sachie had been, apart from the jaundice, in intensely nostalgic mood that year. The appearance of his poems in the *Poetry Review* reminded him of the publication of his first poem in November 1917. Sleeping at Montegufoni had brought back memories of golden pre-war days and the dedication of the Henry Moore memorial to Edith was yet another occasion for reflection on the past. *Southern Baroque Revisited*, which came out on 12 October 1967, could not but remind him of his first success with *Southern Baroque Art* in the spring of 1924. 'It is an odd experience, and one which does not fall to the lot of every author', he wrote in 'Preludio', the first chapter, 'to be writing finally and for the last time upon a subject which first interested him more than forty years ago.' The book was a relaxed ramble through past experiences abroad, from journeys with his father and Henry Moat in Italy to more recent visits to Mexico and Brazil. It was the usual compendium of his knowledge and interests, in art, architecture and music, including biographical essays on Francesco Borromini and the effect of his celibate and reclusive temperament on the High Baroque of seventeenth-century Rome, and a tribute to Violet Gordon Woodhouse leading into a piece on Scarlatti. Unlike the two previous travel books this was Sachie in authentic vein, taking his readers with him on an aesthetic tour in his imagination, as if they were in conversation in the drawing room at Weston.

Sachie's hepatitis attack forced him to cancel plans to spend Christmas with Osbert at Montegufoni. Perhaps it was just as well, since his mood as far as Osbert was concerned was dark. He brooded on his past treatment by his brother: '. . . when I have been so fond of him how could he turn his back on me, as he did, for such long years!' he wrote to Bryher on 19 November. The hepatitis appeared to have recurred in February 1968, but was diagnosed as gall-bladder trouble. An operation in March left him with two fingers temporarily paralysed by anaesthetic which made writing difficult and he had lost two stone. Although he complained, the loss of weight suited him, giving him his mother's lean air of distinction.

His illness meant that he did not visit Montegufoni until November that year, by which time considerable bad blood had accumulated. Meanwhile, there had been a thoroughly Sitwellian row over John Lehmann's biography of the trio, *A Nest of Tigers*, which Osbert had encouraged and of which Sachie thoroughly disapproved. The book itself was flattering rather than otherwise, but Sachie, egged on, Osbert suspected, probably unfairly, by Georgia, was enraged by it. Calling it 'idiotic' and Lehmann 'wooden-headed and humourless', he raged to Bryher: 'I always thought it would be silly from the start – having been irritated from the start by the title, never having felt like a tiger myself.'[49] Among other things he resented the fact that Lehmann had not sent him a proof copy although Francis, as Edith's literary executor, had had one. Had he had the chance, he told Osbert, he would certainly have raised an objection to passages illustrating what he called 'these horror-comic fantasies of Edith's' like her pawning Sir George's false teeth[50]. Worse still from his point of view, it had brought all the Sitwells' literary enemies out of the woodwork again. He complained to Bryher: 'It has let loose floods and floods of abuse, worse than I've ever known, as it lays all three of us together in a bundle to be kicked about. . . .'[51] Sachie bombarded Osbert with angry letters about it and Georgia unwisely joined in the fray, writing Osbert an 'idiotic' letter which Magro forwarded to Christabel.

Reresby, however, was at Montegufoni in July to keep Osbert company while Magro took a much-needed holiday at Abano. Sachie was at last beginning to grasp, however dimly, the truth about his unequal relationship with Osbert, to whom he wrote sadly in August 1968: 'At the moment I feel I have always been more devoted to you than you have been to me: and I am only afraid my visits tire and irritate you. For so many years I could never see you. Do not let's think why!'[52] The contrast between Sachie's gloomy correspondence from a distance and Reresby's cheerful presence must already have prejudiced Osbert in his nephew's favour.

When Sachie and Georgia finally did visit Montegufoni again in November 1968, it was a disaster from all points of view.

Osbert had had double pneumonia while staying in Venice in September, while Sachie and Georgia were at Baden-Baden, and, after a spell in hospital, had returned to Montegufoni in an ambulance. He was clearly failing; his memory was going and his speech and train of thought chaotic. Sachie and Georgia went out to stay at Montegufoni on 24 November, arriving to find Osbert in a 'pitiable condition' and suffering from double vision. The atmosphere in the grim house was tense; Sachie and Georgia were beginning to suspect a conspiracy against them. Reports of Osbert's mental state, and the fact that Magro typed all Osbert's letters using phraseology that was patently not his employer's, led Sachie to fear that history might be repeating itself on the lines of Woog and Sir George. Georgia, apparently, at one point even thought of hiring a helicopter and getting a local priest to exorcise Magro out of Montegufoni. On arrival at the castle, Sachie and Georgia, finding Magro, as he told Bryher, 'so impossibly possessive and mischief-making', had a fierce row with him in the drawing room one evening after Osbert had gone to bed. When Sachie complained to Osbert about Magro, Osbert, according to Magro, described the Sitwells' treatment of him as 'shocking'. The atmosphere was poisonous. Georgia was her usual tactless self, putting Magro in his place whenever she could and making remarks loaded with meaning intended for him to hear. Magro complained to Christabel of how much he had suffered from them; they tried to be nice to him towards the end of their stay but by then it was too late.

Upsetting Magro was one thing; upsetting Osbert quite another. Just as she had in July 1943 after Sir George's memorial service at Renishaw, Georgia mortally offended Osbert by making it plain that she considered herself practically mistress of the house, even to the extent of ordering new curtains. Osbert was still furious about her behaviour two months later when he wrote to Christabel:

> . . . my temper went seriously to pieces when Georgia was here. She insisted that everything in the house should be changed. It reminded me of the occasion when Mrs Doble was found on all fours [at Renishaw] looking at a piece of furniture which she thought might eventually come her way or at any rate Georgia's. Henry came in and said: 'My word, Sir, she'll miss it if it goes.'[53]

He took his revenge. In April, after a more congenial house party comprising the Reresby Sitwells, their daughter Alexandra and Christabel, he decided to change his will and leave Montegufoni not to Sachie, as he had promised, but to Reresby. It seems likely that at the time both Christabel and Magro encouraged Osbert to carry out what he already had in mind. Sachie had no intimation of what was happening, despite having received, as he told Bryher in the middle of April, 'a really horrid letter . . . the only nasty letter ever written me by Osbert practically telling me I was never wanted at Montegufoni again!'[54] Osbert had written on 1 March: 'About your visit to Florence in October, I think it would be better for you if you stayed in an hotel in town', adding, with a swipe at Georgia:

> You will probably won't [sic] agree with me, Sachie, but, unlike you, I am used to running my house my own way, and it naturally upsets me to have someone telling me that things would be better another way, when I am very happy as they are. Such things put me out. I realize that such observations could be made with the best will in the world . . . but I think peace of mind is more important.[55]

Osbert spelled it out for Sachie in a subsequent letter: '. . . although you will not accept this, my quarrel is not with you personally, but with Georgia . . . *you* could never outstay your welcome here. And no one regrets more than I the way that things have turned out between us. . . .'[56]

It was Osbert's final act of revenge on Sachie for his great betrayal in abandoning him for Georgia in 1925. He contemplated going even further, for he summoned his English lawyer, Hugo Southern, out to Florence early in May, no doubt with the intention of making changes to his will. On his way out to Florence, Southern had a meeting with Dr Berger in Zurich at which the Swiss lawyer showed him a puzzling letter he had received from Osbert which appeared to indicate that he meant to cut Sachie out of almost everything.

Whatever Osbert may have intended, he did not have time to carry out. On the evening of 1 May Magro read aloud to him from his Scarborough novel, *Before the Bombardment*. The next morning he had a heart attack and lapsed into a coma. Sachie and Georgia arrived in Florence on the evening of the 3rd and went straight out to Montegufoni to find Reresby, Francis and Hugo Southern already there and Osbert unconscious. Penelope arrived the following day. That evening, 4 May, at 7.30 Osbert died.

The scenario which followed would have appealed to Sir George's malicious sense of humour and his fondness for punishing his descendants through his wills. At the funeral at the Anglican church of St Mark's in Florence, only four people in the congregation knew the truth about Osbert's Italian will – Reresby, Penelope, Magro and, now, Southern. Sachie had naturally inherited the title of baronet from Osbert; he had equally assumed, because he had been told so in 1965, that Montegufoni would go to him plus Osbert's and the family's funds. Reresby had to pluck up courage after the funeral to tell his father that this was no longer the case. Sachie could not bring himself to tell Georgia the truth until two weeks later, and even then he insisted on Gertrude being there as support. Georgia had set her heart on becoming chatelaine of Montegufoni as the 'Baronessa Sitwell'; she had even left clothes there and had already invited guests to stay. When she learned the truth, she retired to the London Clinic for a week, sick with disappointment and humiliation.

For Sachie, losing Montegufoni was 'poor Osbert's betrayal'. Osbert, he told Bryher, had changed his will in Reresby's favour 'because Reresby got on better with his Maltese valet-secretary'. With his temperamental refusal to face unpleasant facts, he would not then admit to himself or to anyone else that the root cause had been Osbert's antipathy towards Georgia and, in consequence, towards himself for abandoning Osbert and cleaving to his 'soul-mate'. Loyally, he never blamed Georgia's tactless behaviour, which had certainly been a contributory factor. The full extent of Osbert's monumental selfishness and his cruel treatment of his brother and sister became clear to Sachie later when, after conferences with the Swiss and English lawyers, he realised that he was a rich man. 'The family turns out to have so much money, though none of it *ever* came Edith's way and not very much in mine either,' he told Bryher. 'For forty-five years my income has been about £2000. . . . It makes me sad and angry to think about Edith, and of course till now we have always had money worries. . . .'[57] Osbert had, if anything, out-Gingered Ginger. Sachie did not so much mind the loss of Montegufoni itself, which under the terms of Osbert's will became, as Sachie told Bryher and as Reresby soon found out, a 'white elephant'. Osbert's action had been a betrayal of love and a lifetime's relationship. The huge Tuscan castle, which had really been a symbol of a Sitwellian *folie de grandeur*, became for him a personal allegory of a lost dream of happiness which he embodied in the title of his next long book, *For Want of the Golden City*. 'There are things', he wrote, 'one never thought to happen and that do happen; and it is the same with long loyalties and affections which do not stand the stress of time.'

In true Sitwell fashion, the complications after Osbert's death almost
rivalled those after Sir George's. At first it appeared that the castle was to
be Reresby's, the contents and a good deal of the money to go to Sachie.
Perhaps fortunately for Sachie, Osbert had died before he could make
his final settlement. The bad blood between the older and younger
generation of Sitwells dating from the time of Reresby's marriage ensured
that there would not be an amicable solution over Montegufoni. Reresby
now turned to international lawyers 'to protect his interests' and the issue
of who was to get what was not finally resolved until well over a year later.

Sachie and Georgia made a last visit to Montegufoni in late September.
It was their intention to live a few months of the year there, if they could
buy the house from Reresby; it had, after all, belonged to the family for
sixty years and, contrary to their expectations, would not need vast sums
spending on it. A year later, complications continued. '. . . we really have
not had a week's peace since Osbert died, a year ago,' Sachie told Bryher.
Reresby and Penelope refused to sell him the house and were making
further claims on the contents and the funds so that nothing could be
settled. Georgia, he said, was still 'terribly sad' about Montegufoni and
would have loved to live there, 'but I think it would have used up most, or
all of the income. Comparative affluence has *not*, so far, brought us much
happiness. . . .'[58]

In October 1969 Sachie had returned, he wrote, 'sad home' to Weston
after their final visit to Montegufoni. It had been a splendid Tuscan
autumn during the vintage. '. . . I must try only to remember the cypress
trees, the headless and broken statues, and the slow tread of the pairs of
white oxen pulling the tumbrils of ripe grapes to the wine press. And
forget the rest. . . .' The loss of Montegufoni inspired some bitter
reflections in the last 'entertainment of the imagination' on which he had
been working since before Osbert died, and which he eventually called,
significantly, *For Want of the Golden City*. As he wrote in the first paragraph
of the chapter entitled 'I came sad home: Disintegration of places,
persons and things':

> The mere repetition of the five syllables of which the name of the house
> is composed bring [sic] back pitiful memories of persons dead and gone,
> and of the changes that can or do occur in them during long illness when
> a lifetime, or what one had thought to be a lifetime of affection and long
> loyalties, can succumb under pressure of failing faculties and infirmity to
> other and alien influences.

He was haunted by a feeling of dispossession, first of Renishaw then of Montegufoni, personal tragedies for which, for once, he was able to realise he could not absolve himself entirely of blame. '. . . I have cheated myself, and been cheated, of my birthright, not once but twice over. I have suffered enough from it, myself . . . to know the weakness and inherent wrongness of hereditary possessions because of the misery they bring. . . .'

The final dissolution of the Sitwell trio inspired a bitter chapter headed 'Persona Perturbata'. 'The legend of devoted families in the context of brothers and sisters is disproved,' he wrote. He was possessed by the feeling that both Osbert and, to a lesser extent, Edith had betrayed him, a charge that could certainly be levelled against Osbert but most unfairly against Edith, always his most loyal supporter. This feeling about Edith derived, apparently most unjustifiably, from Edith's last letter to Osbert to which Georgia had taken great exception. Osbert had sent them a copy (which Georgia indignantly annotated 'Typed by Frank!') in February 1965, with the comment that it showed how 'full of life' she was right until the end. 'My darling,' Edith had written:

I do hope my (and the cats') birthday telegram will have arrived in time for tomorrow. I should have written before, but it wasn't neglect or not thinking of you all the time that prevented me from doing so. Dr Sharto [Csato] (if that is how he spells his name) was having a furious fight with the universal germ I got in that infernal hospital, and on top of it I had acute inflammation of the sheath of my leg tendons. The pain was awful.

A very happy birthday to you, my darling, and I hope with all my heart that you will have less non-stop worries and wretchedness in this coming year. These have been merciless this past year. Everybody seems to think we were simply born for their convenience.

One must never be vaguely polite to 3rd rate writers. Philip Caraman has just sent me his latest enormous book about a Jesuit who was, or was not, mixed up in the Gunpowder Plot.

You are very well out of the incessant quarrels, accusations, jealousy etc., here. How much I hate women. I can't tell you what they have been like! All those by whom I am surrounded are suffering from our old pal C[hange] of L[ife], and are hellish bores about it. All women ought to have been born deaf-mutes, and born only for the sake of producing male children. The quarrels here are quite incessant. Gordon Watson [Australian pianist friend of Edith] seems to be at the root of a lot of it, I should like to wring his neck!

I am so worried about poor Harold [Acton]. Incidentally, he is so kind and thoughtful as to have written a furious letter to the London Magazine about their attack.

Forgive this badly written letter. Two cats are sitting on me, one on the paper, and the fourth is guiding my pen.

I miss you so much.

Very best love.

Ever your loving
                Edith
and all good wishes to Frank. . . .[59]

In Osbert's opinion it was simply 'a very nice letter, full of humour and personality'. Georgia, however, unaccountably described it, in a dated note attached to it, as 'Edith's last letter to Osbert which upset Sachie &, *especially* me, very much – such flattery for Osbert and mendacity'.[60] It is hard to see how Sachie could have been upset by any of this letter – the 'non-stop worries' mentioned by Edith can only have referred to the troubles with David Horner. There had been no difficulties between him and Osbert, or even between Georgia and Osbert, at the time. Georgia must, however, have decided that among the women 'suffering from our old pal C of L' Edith had included her.

One of the saddest and most bitter of Sachie's later poems referred to his disillusionment with his family of both generations. The first line of 'Rosa officinalis: Red Rose of Lancaster' alluded to his descent from John of Gaunt and Katharine Swynford through his Beaufort grandmother, whose family crest was a portcullis, the following lines to the physical dissolution of Osbert and Edith and to what he saw as their betrayal of his affection, and to his disappointment at his failure to 'pollinate', i.e. to pass on the family genius for poetry to his sons.

> Red rose of the portcullis
>   from whom I have a drop of that rose-blood in my veins,
> Or am at least brother to that pretendant,
>   Now fading, falling as we all must
>
> I have not yet felt the drag or weight
>   but for how much longer can that be,
> Who have still your pollen
>   though I cannot pollinate?
>
> Blackspot and rust are all around to see
>   the wrecks of two persons are all that now remains,
> Whom I loved more than they loved me

> But the beauty and poetry
> I learned from her
> Are antidotes to all self-pity.

Sachie sent a copy of the poem to Reresby on his return to England after Osbert's death. Reresby replied, 'immediately on receipt', on 14 May:

> I am very touched by your letter and your strange, sad, bitter poem . . . you must have become unconsciously aware that I am in my 'middle years' no longer impervious to poetry. . . . I have been reading 'Hortus Conclusus' these last sad days. Surely your little poem on Kingcups . . . is one of the loveliest in the English language.
>
> We are going up to Renishaw this evening and I intend to go for a long walk through the Eckington Woods . . . and in my sadness about all the misunderstandings, the bitterness and the wasted talents, the squandered assets and sheer follies that have sundered us all, I will be trampling through the bluebells at the height of their transient glory and will dream about the Venus of Bolsover. Please also think of me.
>
> In deepest admiration and affection. . . .[61]

Gothic Europe, Sachie's last major book on art and architecture, and his last for Weidenfeld, was published on 17 July 1969. Sachie had finished it in August the previous year and dedicated it to Susanna and his first grandson George. He had enjoyed writing it and his pleasure came through in his flowing, vivid prose so different from the stilted clumsiness of his last three travel books. His delight in the beautiful things he was describing was evident on every page. As he explained in his preface, after having written of English domestic architecture in its prime from 1660 to 1830 in *British Architects and Craftsmen*, and contributed the introduction to Katherine Esdaile's *English Church Monuments, 1510–1840*, he had long wanted to write about the earlier period. The book was intended to be 'pure enjoyment'; despite his own fondness for medieval tombs, he had left them out as 'too depressing'. It was a celebration not of religion but of 'the world of human beings' and the 'therapeutic and life-enhancing qualities' of the medieval art and architecture to be found even in remote churches. Sachie saw the hope of any cultural revival in Britain as lying in a recognition of its peculiar past – 'our own past, not that of someone, or anyone else's past. We have to look in the glass and face ourselves, and not the selected, if hypothetical, ancestors of no blood affinity at all. We must be ourselves. . . .' First of all, he warned perspicaciously, 'man will have to control the combustion engine'.

He began with an anthology of towers and spires from all over England, 'the early miracle of sending up a needle to pierce the clouds, and as near a feeling as medieval men would ever know of flying'. He then turned to cloisters and chapterhouses, timber roofs and chantry chapels, flushwork (facing buildings with knapped flints and brick or freestone) and the *Opus Anglicanum*, the exquisite English embroidery which was one of the glories of medieval Europe. There were also some wonderful descriptions of clothes, a subject which had always interested him. Richard II, for instance, wore a costume of white satin embroidered with leeches, water and rocks, hung with fifteen silver-gilt whelks, fifteen silver-gilt mussels, and fifteen cockles of white silver, and doublet embroidered with gold orange-trees on which were set 100 silver-gilt oranges. 'How curious the art-loving Plantagenet must have looked standing there!' Sachie remarked. 'Noisily too. . . .' The second part of the book dealt, more summarily, with French, German, Spanish and Italian Gothic, the Manueline style in Portugal, a chapter on tapestries, and two characteristically entitled 'Fantasia on the Gothic', with emphasis on gargoyles, and 'Charivari of the Gothic', the latter an excuse to bring in Arab architecture and decoration, southern Indian temples, even Angkor and the Shwe Dagon in Rangoon. The book was particularly well illustrated with 160 carefully chosen plates.

Gothic Europe was generally well reviewed as 'the harvest of a long lifetime's looking'. John Betjeman, to whom he had sent a copy, thought it 'one of the best things you have ever done'. 'You probably don't realise', Betjeman wrote, 'what a relief you are after the fearful pedantry & dull art history which kills enjoyment & just gets scholarships for people & breeds more dullards. You are a life-enhancer. For years I've read you. Gothic Europe is so good that the prose is even better than the pictures. . . .'[62] Kenneth Clark told him how much he had enjoyed it: 'You write about such beautiful things – often things hardly anyone else has appreciated & every page has a dozen sentences that make me stop to say "That's just right". . . .' Another old friend, Stephen Tennant, now deluged Sachie with letters in brilliant blue, green and sometimes shocking-pink ink. Sachie delighted in them and also the fact that Osbert had told him that the Queen Mother was also the recipient of wild pink missives. 'Sachie dear,' Stephen wrote in his unconventional hand,

I'm so pleased you're *Writing New Poems*, Glorious News. R. Southey writes to C. Bronte
     'Write poetry for its own *Sake*!!!'

a glorious truth Sachie. . . . I'm Dedicating some Poems to you both –
in my *new tome* (2 vols). . . .[63]

Sachie had enjoyed the sensation of seeing his poetry in print again in
the *Poetry Review*. Since 1968 he had been trying to find a publisher for
another volume of selected poems. The response was discouraging. 'So
far 7 London publishers have rejected the poems,' he told Bryher on 22
November 1970; 'in the end I'll get them out in 2 years' time (for my
jubilee birthday) and pay for them myself.' Within a year he had acquired
a new admirer, the twenty-one-year-old Geoffrey Elborn, who was
instrumental in getting his first new collection of poems, *Tropicalia*
(inspired by his tropical travels), printed in the 'jubilee year' 1972, followed by a reissue of *Agamemnon's Tomb* and *To Henry Woodward*, 'lines
addressed to Garrick's friend who played Harlequin', by the Covent
Garden Press.

The omens were not good, either, for *For Want of the Golden City*, on
which he had been concentrating since the August following Osbert's
death. After Cassell's had indicated that they would not be taking up their
option on the sequel to *Journey to the Ends of Time*, Weidenfeld had not
been interested and, in February 1972, Higham told him regretfully that
Macmillan also had rejected the book. Sachie's original title for it had
been *Soup of the Day*, but he was fortunately persuaded of its lack of appeal
by Michael Raeburn of Thames & Hudson, who eventually published the
book in June 1973.

Sachie thought of this last 'entertainment of the imagination' as his
literary testament and, in the sense that he never wrote another or indeed
any more serious prose, it was. In it, to an even greater degree than *Journey
to the Ends of Time*, he packed all his life experience, both aesthetic and
personal, his opinions and beliefs, his atheism, paganism and his
preoccupation with death. The book opened with a chapter entitled
'Death of a Flie', a minute description of the gyrations of a dying fly on
his bedside table one autumn, 'to show', he explained in his introductory
note, 'how important the moment of death must be to even the humblest
being that has ever been alive'. It is a huge book, 450 closely printed
pages, and, but for the tactful editing of Raeburn, would have been even
more voluminous. For the biographer or addict of his autobiographical
work, it is a rewarding labyrinth of clues to his persona, a kaleidoscopic
monologue by the author. Taken slowly, it is full of wonderfully rewarding
passages, but the overall impression is an over-rich experience, rather
like a sugared, spiced concoction, full of unexpected and curious fruit,

contrived by a Renaissance kitchen, or one of those elaborate multi-course banquets given by El Glaoui which Sachie so much enjoyed.

The book was dedicated to Georgia, his refuge from a hostile world. He recognised at last the effect which his marriage had had on the relationships between the original trio – 'which lasting happiness of our own may have broken, or snapped, or strained the strings of family attachment. But it gave me my liberty, it made my own life, and let me work in peace.' 'It will be obvious to the reader', he wrote in his Note of Explanation to the chapter 'Persona Perturbata', 'that the author has had difficulties which thwarted and impeded him, spread out over most of the two years that the greater part of this present work has taken in the writing . . . a family picture which has been distorted takes on its truer colours. . . .'

The apathetic reception of *For Want of the Golden City*, his life experience in prose, wounded him perhaps almost as much as the hostility which had greeted *Canons of Giant Art*, his greatest poetic achievement. He was haunted by a sense of failure, not because he thought his work was bad, but because of a lack of public recognition. The young genius who had 'thought to net the Leonids' had become the ageing writer whom the world passed by. In 1926 he had written of Harlequin in old age:

> His fate is a tragedy greater still. Always merry, radiating the spirit of wit and comedy and in his movements gay and capricious as a butterfly, he has worn his years lightly. A stranger to sorrow, he feels with added bitterness the neglect that has befallen him in his old age. . . . His career resembles that of an ornament passed out of fashion, first set in triumph in the centre of the drawing-room mantelpiece, then moved from room to room as its attraction grows less and less until it is lodged in the attic to await one further final phase. . . .[64]

12

Journey to the Ends of Time

1973–1988

> 'One must keep young and not have an old person's feelings.
> There is enough of interest to fill a hundred lifetimes. . . .One
> must live for each morning which is a recurring miracle and
> wonder.'
>
> Sacheverell Sitwell, *For Want of the Golden City*

Sachie felt that, like the elderly Harlequin, he had been forgotten. But he remained, like Harlequin, as full of the 'spirit of wit and comedy' and as fascinated by the world as he had always been. The dark streak which underlay much of his writing was not evident in his daily life, which was full of jokes, laughter and contact with a wide circle of friends. He had always been good company and old age did not make him less so. The financial worries which had dogged him all his life ceased with Osbert's death. He and Georgia were now able to travel in the style to which they had become accustomed but never been able to afford, staying in the best hotels. In Rome at Easter it would be the Hassler, in Venice in September the Cipriani, followed by the Brenners' Park in Baden-Baden. Sometimes, in the luxury of these hotels, he would feel a twinge of guilt when he recalled how he and Osbert used deliberately to book their parents into the worst rooms on the rare occasions they travelled together.

At Weston they lived in some style, with Gertrude as cook-housekeeper, Bernard as gardener, and a butler, the most noteworthy being Mr Boneham, who was with them for some fifteen years until his death in 1971, a man of exquisite manners whose talents included shining Sachie's shoes like glass. To Derek Parker, who visited Weston in 1966, Boneham appeared to be 'the important figure in the household'. Sachie seemed to spend quite a lot of time worrying about him and on one occasion leapt from his chair to answer the telephone, saying, ' "This is the hour at which Boneham likes to listen to his wireless!" ' Even when there were only three of them, Sachie and Georgia dressed for dinner, Sachie in his traditional velvet smoking-jacket, Georgia in a long dress. Parker was amused when Boneham appeared after dinner bearing on a salver a silver hot-water jug and a tin of Nescafé, which he presented to Georgia to prepare.[1]

Sachie's daily routine remained unalterable: down for cooked breakfast at nine, then half an hour's gossip with Georgia in her room, then in trousers, shirt and dressing-gown to work in his first-floor study, sitting bolt upright at the small wooden table in front of the window, the floor strewn with correspondence which no one was allowed to touch. He would stay there until twelve, when he shaved, and at twelve-thirty went downstairs for a glass of sherry with Georgia in the drawing room; he had lunch punctually at one, then a walk round the garden or in the surrounding lanes, and back to work from five until seven, when he bathed and went downstairs for drinks. Dinner would be at seven forty-five and afterwards they would go to the drawing room, where Sachie would play records and Georgia would do her embroidery. He worked seven days a week, making a particular point of working on Sundays or other 'holy days'.

The visitors' book at Weston showed a stream of friends staying during the 1970s, the most regular name being that of Peter Quennell, who had stayed there the first Christmas at Weston in 1928, although the names of his wives had changed five times over the intervening years. There were old friends like Baba Metcalfe, Diana Cooper, Loelia Westminster (now Lady Lindsay), the Anthony Powells, Costa Achillopoulo, Peter Coats, Mary Pembroke, Elizabeth von Hofmannsthal and Robert Heber-Percy. Charles Ritchie, now Canadian High Commissioner in London, came frequently with his wife, as did Charles and Natasha Johnston, whom they had met in Madrid in 1948, James and Alvilde Lees-Milne, the Gladwyn Jebbs, and Philippe de Rothschild, with whom they often spent New Year's Eve at Mouton.

Sachie was attracting new, younger friends. Among them was Susan Hill, born like him in Scarborough but forty-five years later. When she went to interview him for a projected BBC programme in 1971, they struck up an instant rapport. He sent her his *Collected Poems*, 'written before I was born, it seems now', pointing out to her the two that referred specifically to Scarborough, 'Mrs H . . . or a Lady from Babel' and 'Upon an Image from Dante'.[2] 'I am decidedly interested in Scarborough and cannot help it and always will be,' he had written to her before they met. Susan Hill was already a Sitwell fan; as a child she had stood in front of

Wood End reciting 'Osbert, Edith and Sacheverell' under her breath, and the name Sacheverell had appealed to her so much that she had named one of her dolls after him. The 'legendary Sacheverell' and Georgia became to her 'dear and generous friends'. 'Having a conversation with Sachie', she recalled, 'is rather like dipping into a treasure trove – you simply never know what will come up, but it's always something marvellous.'[3] Barry Humphries, an admirer of Sachie's poetry since his schooldays, wrote telling him how important his *Collected Poems* had been to him since he first read them at his Melbourne boarding-school. The connoisseur, Gervase Jackson-Stops, having been greatly influenced by Sachie's earlier books on architecture, regarded him as 'my cultural grandfather'. Later, when engaged on the restoration of Canons Ashby nearby, he often dropped in to listen to Sachie's conversation sometimes on the most sinister subjects when Sachie's v-shaped smile would suddenly crinkle up his face, even his nose, dispelling the gloom.

'Poetry', Sachie had written in *Journey to the Ends of Time*, '. . . comes to one when young, and, one hopes, once more when old. . . .I think I may feel it coming. . . .' He now no longer cared, or maintained that he did not, whether his poetry was published. He could afford to write it for his own pleasure and have it privately printed for circulation to his friends. The beauty of this, he told Bryher, was that no review copies would be sent out, inviting hostile criticism. 'I think I must be getting like my father [who] used to amuse Osbert and I, years ago, by saying that he must ask anyone who came to stay at Renishaw who contradicted him to leave the house at once as it interfered with his digestion and kept him awake at night!'[4]

His poetic inspiration had been flowing intermittently since 1946 and latterly most strongly since Edith's death. Sitting at his window in Northamptonshire he continued to live through his poetry the world of memory and imagination that he had created for himself. His own books were his source material, particularly his travel books. The tables at Weston held piles of the best recent books, but later in life he rarely read them, preferring to furrow through dog-eared copies of his own books, mining them for material for his poems. The result of this trawling through memory was a prodigious output and a stream of booklets of poems sent to his friends. As Patrick Leigh Fermor wrote:

Every few months a new slim volume would find its way to Greece, inscribed in his clear and decorative hand. Birds, flowers, music and architecture were some of the predominating themes – flame trees, white ibises, parrots, cockatoos; every kind of rose – especially old-fashioned ones, Bibiena scenery, operatic arias, cactuses, mushrooms and fungi, stitchwort, foxglove, the cembalom and the syrinx, the ruins of Segesta, Mayan temples, the *Commedia dell'Arte*, Watteau, strange tribes from Benin . . . Vierzehnheiligen . . . Chichen Itza. . . .[5]

Flowers from his garden or even their names in a catalogue set off a train of thought, sometimes mixed in with a recently received image as in 'L[ilium] Tigrinum splendens': 'Cyclic change and metamorphosis/of a crimson and white lily/into an entire pack of hounds/All with protruding tongues dripping saliva. . . .' The hunting simile came from reading Trollope, a new interest. Although he himself detested hunting and refused to have anything to do with the local hunt, he particularly enjoyed the fox-hunting scenes in *The Duke's Children*, finding in them a technical perfection and exhilaration that made them irresistible. Some of the poems were intensely autobiographical. 'Ah! Everyone was born once' recalled the first images of death and sex received at Renishaw; others contained coded references to the women he loved, Pearl Argyle over and over again, and Moira Shearer. Among his best were the series dedicated to Edith, with their deeply felt nostalgia and sense of loss. Sachie was, as Peter Quennell pointed out, a very personal poet.

The two years following Osbert's death had been a low point. Charles Johnston, visiting Weston in 1975, found Sachie still bitter about Osbert's 'betrayal', but the publication of his poems had provided a continuing therapy. He had found the encouragement he needed from a neighbour, Diana Cooke, formerly Diana Witherby, a poet herself, who had previously worked with Cyril Connolly on *Horizon*. Now married to a judge, Sir Samuel Cooke, she had come into Sachie's life through a mutual friend, Celia Paget (now Goodman). She was one of the very few people with whom Sachie discussed his work and, in June 1971, he had given her his five manuscript volumes of recent poems to read for her opinion. In August, thanking her for 'all the help you have given me', he sent her the almost completed manuscript of *For Want of the Golden City*. Later that month he told her: 'I can never thank you enough for your help and kindness [about the poems]. I have been, all along, and am still, on the point of destroying them, as I see no future, *really*, for anything . . .' A year later, he sent her the first booklets: '*I can never forget* how kind and helpful you have been, when I was in great need of it owing to isolation and lack of interest.'[6]

In October 1971 Sachie had been interviewed at Weston by Roy Plomley for *Desert Island Discs*. He chose Bach's *Goldberg Variations* played by Landowska, the slow movement of Mozart's *Piano Concerto no. 15 in C Major* with Daniel Barenboim as soloist, Schumann's *Warum* played by Paderewski, and his *Frühlingsnacht* in an arrangement by Liszt, performed by Josef Lhevinne, a chorus from Act III of *Carmen*, recorded by Thomas Beecham, the end of Act I of Verdi's *Ballo in Maschera* conducted by Toscanini, *Benediction à Dieu dans la Solitude*, by Liszt, played by Aldo Cicciolini, and Liszt's arrangement of *Valse Infernale* by Meyerbeer, played by Earl Wilde. His choice of literature was unremarkable – 'a kind of omnibus version of *War and Peace* and *Anna Karenina*'. 'Bound together?' Plomley queried dubiously. 'Bound together,' Sachie replied firmly. 'And one luxury to take with you to the island?' 'Well, I was going to say a hot water bottle, but it's a desert island, isn't it? – A refrigerator . . . and something to put in it too . . . .'

Desert Island Discs apart, Sachie was still wary of publicity, particularly where it concerned his family. In November 1973 the *Sunday Times* approached Sachie on behalf of John Pearson, whom they had commissioned to write a book on the Sitwells. 'I answered that it made me too sad to be interviewed and asked questions about it', he told Bryher, '– and that it makes me feel as though a full stop were being put to my life as well as theirs . . .' Somehow, however, he was persuaded at least to see Pearson and an initial meeting took place later that month on relatively neutral ground at Claridge's. 'Strange to be meeting him at last,' Pearson noted. 'I realised that I had been regarding him as dead – a piece of history along with the other two.' He also noted Sachie's comment about Osbert and Edith – 'they were so overwhelming' – and suspected a degree of resentment against the dominant Osbert. 'Is the worm turning after a lifetime in the stronger brother's shadow?' Pearson asked himself. Sachie's ploy, he correctly estimated, would be to reverse Osbert's line and to emphasise his father's formative influence on the family genius – 'to re-instate Sir George'. Sachie seemed helpful and offered to link Pearson's research with the work which Denys Sutton, editor of *Apollo*, was doing on his life. Pearson struggled to remain objective: 'I must avoid being nobbled by the old charmer. . . .'[8]

At Weston in mid-February 1975 Pearson came up against Georgia, the wary tigress defending her cub. Sachie he found charming and vague, giving the (misleading) impression that he did not really care about the past, his brother and his sister. Georgia, in contrast, was very much on the alert:

His wife, the gravel-voiced and bright-eyed Lady Georgia [*sic*] is the

one who cares. Passionately, I should think. For she's the one who's had the
real battles to fight, the snubs to bear. And I should think she really runs
him. She was a tough one. Carborundum-tipped and rather frightening.
Admirable I suppose for him. He must have needed a tough woman and the
house is beautifully run, the background quite impeccable. But oh, what a
feeling one got of her husband, the aristocratic man of letters, being her life
work – him and his lovely house. . . .

Despite his resolution, Pearson found himself drawn by Sachie's
vulnerable charm, describing him as 'so hurt and vague and so afraid of
getting old and dying', and not realising that any discussion of his family
and their literary past put Sachie on a knife edge. Comparing the real man
with the recently completed portrait by Graham Sutherland which hung
in the hall, he thought Sutherland had got the likeness but, unlike the
Wyndham Lewis drawing of the youthful poet, 'none of the magic which
is still curiously there'.[9]

The Sutherland portrait had a comic history. When Georgia went up to
look at it, the gallery assistant had by mistake shown her a portrait of the
German Chancellor, Konrad Adenauer. While not being particularly
pleased by Sutherland's portrayal of Sachie, she had not realised that it
was not him at all until the gallery telephoned to apologise for its error.
Later, travelling through Europe with the Egremonts, they were surprised
by the ceremony with which they had been treated by a casino in Germany
and the stares of the guests, only to find that the management had identified Sachie as Adenauer.

Sachie's hurt feelings over the lack of interest shown in *For Want of the
Golden City* when it came out in 1973 were somewhat assuaged when he
learned in May 1974 that Derek Parker was preparing a *festschrift* of
pieces by his friends to be printed by Bertram Rota for publication the
following year. The contributors included Cyril Connolly, C.P. Snow,
Raymond Mortimer, Kenneth Clark, Humphrey Searle, John Piper,
Susan Hill, Hugh MacDiarmid, Diana Cooper, Georgia and Christian
Hesketh. It was a disappointingly slim volume. Many of the contributors
when approached by Parker had replied that they 'really knew Osbert
better', an indication of how much Sachie had withdrawn from the literary
world. Fortunately Sachie was unaware of this and was thrilled with it
when it came out in May 1975. 'Even now, I have only been able to read
about half of it', he wrote to Parker, 'as I cannot read it before going to
sleep as it would make me too excited. . . .'[10]

Cyril Connolly, in an essay titled '*Foi d'Esthète*', praised Sachie's
devotion to the pursuit of beauty over fifty years of unrewarded and

scarcely acknowledged work since the publication of *Southern Baroque Art*, which he called 'a milestone in the development of our modern sensibility'. Connolly quoted as an illustration of Sachie's personal faith a passage from *British Architects and Craftsmen* describing his favourite painting, the *Banquet of Antony and Cleopatra* at the Palazzo Labia: 'Never, never shall I forget, for it is my belief and faith, the only religion I ever had, the negro in green velvet holding a flask of wine. . . .' C.P. Snow supported Pamela Hansford-Johnson's thesis (in an article, 'On Being the Wrong Size') that Sachie was too non-conformist and in various dimensions too large to suit the scaling-down predilections of our time:

> He is alone in his blend of cultivated civility and macabre imaginative insight . . . the expression of a unique tension between one side of his artistic persona, excessively civilised, a man of taste in the eighteenth-century fashion, world traveller, connoisseur of the visual arts . . . and the hidden side, more profound, deeply suspicious of all men's depravity and his own. . . . His ultimate imagination is much more like Dickens at his darkest. . . . His sense of human experience has its own outward shape of the baroque, with wild and whirling decorations. Underneath that, there is the feeling for the romantic agony. Underneath that again his gaze is steady, and what he sees is jet-black.

Raymond Mortimer called Sachie 'the latest of our romantic poets', while Kenneth Clark recalled how 'a single volume . . . *Southern Baroque Art* had created a revolution in the history of English taste'. Georgia's short piece was one of the best. Of their fifty years of married life together, she wrote, 'Never a dull moment and with poetry never far from the surface.'

Their golden wedding anniversary, on 12 October 1975, was cele-brated with the presentation of an exquisite tulip painting by Christian Hesketh's brother, Rory McEwen, and a party for all the village and the neighbours. Everyone was touched to see their mutual devotion after fifty years. Both of them were still exceptionally well-preserved for their age, tall, slim and elegant. Philip Purser, television critic of the *Sunday Telegraph*, who had recently moved into the village, described them:

> They are charmers in the true sense of the word: hospitable, considerate, amusing, saved from saintliness by a nice acerbity if the conversation should shift to certain mutual acquaintances – as it almost certainly will, because conversation with them never stays on the same subject for more than half a minute. . . .[11]

Both of them played their traditional roles in local life as the squire and his lady. Georgia, with her exceptional flair for organisation, ran the Women's Institute, while Sachie had sat on the local bench as Justice of the Peace for years. However, he was a most unusual squire; he neither rode, nor shot, nor fished. He detested hunting, never inviting the local hunt to meet at the house and refusing to allow them to retrieve a fox which had taken refuge in the culvert in the grounds. He hated hunt balls, the gatherings of 'the Golden Horde' of his youth, and if Georgia wanted to go she had to go alone. He never went to the pub. 'You'll find Sir Sacheverell Sitwell the perfect gentleman,' the landlord of the Crown Arms in Weston told Jilly Cooper, bound for Weston Hall to interview the Sitwells in 1976. 'But he's never been in here for thirty years', adding, by way of compensation, 'His butler comes in every day. . . .' (Once, in the late 1930s Dick Wyndham and Celia Paget had succeeded in dragging him into a pub. 'What shall I order?' Sachie asked. 'A quarter of a pint?')

He would often be seen in the village, a tall, thin figure in a long overcoat walking the dogs, a King Charles spaniel and a Yorkshire terrier, the smallness and fluffiness of the dogs accentuating his height. He would never go to church and the vicar was one of his bugbears. On one occasion when trapped by the vicar in a narrow lane and realising that he could not turn back because that would be too rude, he avoided speaking to him by bursting into tears. Gervase Jackson-Stops recalled that the only time Sachie had ever been seen to kneel in church was in Santiago de Compostela at Whitsun during the ceremony of the *Portafumero*, when the gigantic incense burner was swung across the aisle from transept to transept by fifteen men hauling on ropes, almost decapitating those in the front row where Sachie's party was sitting. He proclaimed his atheism repeatedly and defiantly. 'There is no outside power or influence to help us,' he had written in *For Want of the Golden City*. 'There never has been and there is not now. Our fate is in our own hands.'

Despite the gaiety on the surface at Weston social occasions, there was the sense of the shades closing in. Sachie enjoyed exaggerating this, mendaciously telling Jilly Cooper: 'We hardly see anyone these days. We sit and worry terribly about death; neither of us believes in an afterlife. Rose Macaulay had the right attitude to death. She just wrote me a letter saying "I'm thinking of pushing off this summer. . . ." ' He was by now in his eightieth year. In August 1977 he wrote a long poem, 'The Octogenarian', recalling his sister's poem in *Façade*: 'The octogenarian/leaned from his window,/To the valerian . . .', and Edith writing poems in bed at Pembridge Mansions in the early morning, or a hot June evening there when they would throw a coin down to the man playing the barrel-organ in the street:

> And the barrel-organ moves on
>   into receding time
>
> while the octogenarian,
>   myself,
> Is still at my window
> thinking of her and hearing that haunting fanfare
> Till no one remembers . . .
>
> *A quoi bon?* Who cares?
> Not I,
> Who am here remembering,
> While the days rush by
> And the long night is looming
>
> Thinking just now
> What an exciting world it was
> When the three of us were young together:–
> Even in trouble for being young
>
>   and having talent:–
> Well! It is over and finished now,
>   long ago,
> And will never be again . . .

As Sachie had approached his eightieth birthday in 1977 concerted efforts were made to obtain for him an honour which would signal public acknowledgement of his long, prolific career. Christian Hesketh and Sir Edward Ford, both friends and Northamptonshire neighbours, began a movement to press Downing Street on Sachie's behalf. Sir Edward, formerly Assistant Private Secretary to the Queen, masterminded the campaign from December 1976, when he and Raymond Mortimer drafted a letter pointing out that, while Osbert had received a CBE in 1956 and the CH in 1958 and Edith the DBE in 1954, Sachie, the only survivor of the trio, had received no national recognition. Their letter, signed by Kenneth Clark and Hugh Casson among others, received a negative response from Downing Street. Sachie was not, perhaps, the candidate most likely to succeed under a Labour Government, but the responsibility for his rejection most probably lay with the membership of the secret Maecenas Committee, who advised on honours in the Arts. It could be conjectured that certain members on that committee were of a generation most strongly opposed to the Sitwells and that in this case Sachie, as always, reaped the whirlwind sown by Osbert and Edith. Approaches were also made to the universities of London, Leeds and Oxford, through their Chancellors, the Queen Mother, Edward Boyle and Harold Macmillan. A game of 'pass the parcel' was the only result. Queen Elizabeth had been an old friend of Osbert's and had once invited Sachie and Georgia down to the Royal Lodge. She wrote that she was surprised that Sachie had not been honoured in any way and was willing to help, but thought that Oxford under Macmillan's Chancellorship might be more suitable. Macmillan put Sachie's name forward but covered himself by stressing that he had no influence over the selection committee, who subsequently rejected it. One influential philosophy don described Sachie's work as 'unreadable'. When Sachie's sponsors appealed again to Macmillan to put his cause to Downing Street, Macmillan answered, probably correctly, that any recommendation of his would be 'counter-productive'. Edward Boyle merely replied dismissively that the selection of honorands had already been made. Only Sheffield University gladly obliged by giving him an honorary doctorate as a 'favourite son' in 1979.

Sachie had never been a member of any literary or Establishment clique. Living in what he liked to describe as 'permanent interior exile' at Weston, he was completely out of the public eye. It is significant that even a well-informed journalist like John Pearson should have assumed that he was dead. The image presented by the Sitwell name would, as far as the incumbents of No. 10 Downing Street were concerned, have been of a vaguely élitist group of 1920s' aesthetes of a type that was hardly to be encouraged. Mrs Thatcher, when again approached by Sir Edward Ford through Sir Robert Armstrong, turned the idea down flat. Only in 1984, when the Earl of Gowrie was Minister of Arts, did Sachie's friends finally succeed. Gowrie, a poet and a former fine arts dealer, put forward a strong personal recommendation that Sachie should and must be honoured for his original and influential contributions to connoisseurship. Mrs Thatcher agreed and Sachie was made a Companian of Honour in the New Year's Honours List for 1984. He was by then eighty-six and, like Disraeli on finally making it to the 'top of the greasy pole' as Prime Minister after a long, hard struggle, might well have said that it came too late.

Meanwhile Georgia, although much younger, had begun perceptibly to fail. A heavy smoker, which partly accounted for her deep 'bullfrog' voice, she had chronic bronchial trouble and a touch of emphysema. At times her fine ankles seemed incapable of supporting her. In Venice in 1975 when they were staying as usual at Cipriani's on the Giudecca, she could not accompany Sachie when he went sightseeing with Celia Goodman and her daughter, her legs being too weak to manage the steps on the mainland. She began to lose her spirit and her zest for life. Perhaps the burden of out-Sitwelling the Sitwells, and the responsibility of separating Sachie from his siblings and protecting him from the world, had been too much for her. She had struggled so long to keep up the glamorous façade on a relative shoestring among friends like the Westminsters and the Aly Khans who were vastly richer than she was. The money and the title had come too late for her and, in some ways, had turned to ashes in her mouth.

The loss of Montegufoni had come as a more severe blow to her than it had to Sachie, who, when he came to his senses, realised that it would have been the white elephant which it turned out to be for Reresby. He far preferred to travel as he liked and not to worry about money, being, like Edith, less attached to material possessions than Georgia and other members of his family. Georgia, however, always less socially secure than Sachie and with her direct North American sense of what really counted in Society, minded a good deal about the status conferred by real estate. She had dreamed of living at Renishaw after Osbert's death, but that too had been taken from her. Even Weston now belonged to Reresby's daughter as a result of Sachie's and her own extravagance. She resented the fact that both her daughters-in-law had houses in London, something which she and Sachie had never managed to afford. She took her bitterness out on her sons, telling them what a disappointment they had been to herself and Sachie. Having been a beauty, she minded losing her looks. 'You think I look like a frog, don't you?' she once said sharply to her daughter-in-law, Susanna. With her looks she lost her life-enhancing vitality, which had been one of her greatest charms. Charles Johnston, visiting Weston in the summer of 1979, found Sachie bent but 'otherwise remarkably spry', while Georgia was 'stuck in her armchair looking like death and knowing it. When asked how she was she answered, "Not as well as I look. . . ."'[12]

Sometimes she drank more than was good for her and snarled at people she considered her social inferiors like Sotheby's experts, invited down by Sachie. Sachie affected not to notice, remaining unperturbed on occasions such as those when she would suddenly demand in a loud voice in the middle of luncheon, 'When are these people going to go?' In the last months of her life she ceased to care about her appearance, a danger sign in a woman who had been so chic. She became incontinent, a terrible humiliation for her. In her bitterness and despair she would ask

Gertrude, 'Why did it happen to me?' She and Gertrude had a curious relationship, more like siblings than employer and employee. They would have fierce rows when, like Sir George and Henry Moat, Georgia would threaten to sack Gertrude and Gertrude would riposte by resigning. As Georgia's personal maid since 1928, Gertrude knew all the family secrets and, indeed, thought of herself as part of the family. Sachie was central to both their lives. Now Georgia was physically dependent on Gertrude and on Sachie, who was 'wonderfully patient' with her. Every night he and Gertrude would more or less carry her upstairs to the bed which they still shared, despite everything. Sachie was sleeping beside her when he was woken at 2 a.m. by a noise and saw Georgia's eyes open and roll back. She had had a massive cerebral haemorrhage and lay in a coma for two hours. At 4 a.m. she died, watched by Sachie and Gertrude. It was 21 October 1980, nine days after their fifty-fifth wedding anniversary.

It was a terrible moment for Sachie, after more than half a lifetime's total dependence. At Georgia's funeral five days later he somehow kept up a dignified front while shaking with emotion, as Sir Edward Ford, giving the address, underlined Georgia's 'complete and utter devotion' to her husband, her beauty, her gift for friendship and her direct character, 'her integrity, which prompted her to speak with utter honesty and frankness – often laced with a rapier wit. With Georgia, you always knew where you were. . . .' Among the mourners was Moira Kennedy, who had driven overnight down from her home in Roxburghshire to give Sachie her support. In his letter thanking Sir Edward for the address, Sachie could not bring himself to refer explicitly to Georgia's death, 'the awful thing that has happened. I don't think I will ever get over it.' He told his lawyer, Hugo Southern, that he could not bear to wake up and not see her head upon the pillow. 'If I thought that I would see her again, I'd take an overdose tonight,' he said to Philip Purser.

Letters and tributes to Georgia poured in. Peter Quennell wrote of her that she was an 'exceptional and exceptionally endearing' woman, mercifully unlike 'that often rather grim personage, the dedicated "writer's wife" '. Diana Cooper sent Sachie a loving letter: 'I saw you in yr. new uniform off to the 1st War – I was in a nursing home – Osbert brought "the kid brother". You charmed me & have done so ever since. . . .' 'Darling Diana,' Sachie replied on 7 November,[13] 'I feel utterly and entirely miserable, and do not know how to bear it. The loneliness is awful. . . .Oh! *the idea of you does comfort me*, and to think how beautiful you are and have always been . . . your broken and miserable

Sachie.'[14] 'Kisty' Hesketh, half Sachie's age but a widow herself, wrote to tell him how much his and Georgia's friendship had meant to her:

> It seems such a long time ago since I came to Weston for the first time with Freddy [Hesketh] and felt instantly at home. . . .And in the years since on a hundred happy occasions, I have warmed my hands and heart at your hospitable fire . . . and cherished the loving friendship I have had from you and dear Georgia ever since. . . .[15]

Sachie wrote his own tribute, one of only two poems which he had addressed to Georgia. It was called 'La Reine Claude', the name of the small yellow plum or 'greengage' which had been one of his pet names for her, and subtitled 'In memory of my darling Georgia':

> . . . Ah! my companion and my love
>   through many difficulties,
> If we could but sleep the winter
>   through all the centuries;
>   But it changes everything,
>   till there is nothing left
> Where we lived happily,
>   Time is like that:
> It had no pity and no sympathy
>
> And yet,
>   my greengage,
> My pledge of love and my security,
> You would not have it otherwise
> Than that it is ours alone
>   for all eternity;
> I'll lend the harlequin your soft cheek to kiss,
>   my shadow and my ghost,
> And Time has no pity
>   takes another meaning and new emphasis

Sachie immediately took out his favourite photograph of Pearl Argyle and put it on the table beside the armchair he always sat in in the drawing room. He set a picture of his mother on his dressing-table. He was eighty-three and the tide of recollection which had begun fifty-five years earlier in *All Summer in a Day* flowed more strongly than ever. Of the women he had loved, Georgia, Pearl and Bridget (who had died in 1972) were all dead. Bridget's affair with Sachie had long been over; she had never married, become hugely fat and taken to drink. 'Poor Bridget,' Sachie had remarked unkindly, 'she looks now like the sort of woman you'd ask to take your children to school.' One of her friends said of her that she was the unhappiest woman she had ever known, but her long affair with Sachie had been a happy and satisfactory one. Zita, however, was very much alive. In November 1982 she and Baby came over to Weston for tea, having been brought together with Sachie by their mutual friend, Peggy Willis, 'after 35 years separation'. The news of Zita's visit prompted Walton to write, no doubt tongue-in-cheek, to ask if there were any truth in the rumour that he was going to marry Zita. Moira was living in Scotland. Sachie still adored her, but his passion had cooled a little with the years and his fantasy was fixed on another 'goddess', Pamela Egremont, wife of John Wyndham, Macmillan's private secretary and owner of Petworth. Sachie's passion for Pamela, which, as in Moira's case, was absolutely unrequited, had begun in the mid-1950s. He and Georgia had often stayed at Petworth, where Pamela's presence and her possessions inspired him to poetry. 'A look at Sowerby's English Mushrooms and Fungi' took its title from a volume in the library, and 'Strawberry Feast' from the strawberry beds at Petworth and a silver dish by Paul de Lamerie.

Now that Georgia was dead, Gertrude had her beloved 'Mr Sachie', as she still always called him, to herself. She was closer to him than any of his own family, sharing their Derbyshire roots and a life experience of almost sixty years. She cooked for him and kept him company, talking for hours about Renishaw. As he grew older his mother's tragedy seemed to weigh ever more heavily on his mind. He would repeat over and over again to Gertrude: 'My poor darling mother . . . how she must have suffered. . . .' Friends rallied round, summoned by Gertrude to cheer up 'Mr Sachie'. Before a series of accidents reduced his mobility, he still travelled or went up to London to ee exhibitions, disconcerting his friends by the lightning rapidity with which he would be in and out of a church and on to the next one. Philip Purser took him to the mammoth Japanese Exhibition at the Royal Academy. 'He was round it in 12½ minutes. . . .' One result of Georgia's death was the healing of the rift between Sachie and the Reresby Sitwells. They went on holiday together to Vienna and Sachie now often stayed at Renishaw. He adored his granddaughter Alexandra, an extremely pretty girl in her early twenties, and enjoyed the company of her friends. 'Tell me, do you take opium?' he would ask them. Georgia's forceful personality had stood between him and his grandchildren. 'The children only really became close to Sachie after Georgia died,' Susanna said. 'Before, she kept them away from him, insisting how difficult and eccentric he was. They adored him and he was sweet to them.' In October 1983 Francis and his family moved into a wing of Weston to take some of the strain of keeping Sachie company off Gertrude. Later, as Sachie's health deteriorated, Susanna took over the running of the house and organised the professional nursing he required.

Despite being the most unathletic of men, Sachie had a strong constitution and an abundance of energy, recovering quickly from a series of major operations. In 1965 he had had a partial colectomy to remove a polyp and in May 1982, at the age of eighty-four, he had further major surgery resulting in his being left with only half his colon. Guy Lewis, a local practitioner and Sachie's doctor for thirty-five years, was astounded by his physical resilience, the fuss he made over small things and conversely his philosophical stoicism when something was seriously wrong. In July 1985 he fell and fractured his left shoulder and was incapacitated for six months. As he lay in pain on the floor, Sachie told Bernard: 'Bernard, if you go on trying to pick me up, I shall have to hit you!' The following year, another fall left him with a fractured left hip requiring major surgery and a hip replacement. His memory and concentration failed him, although 'the old charmer' was skilful in concealing it from strangers who came to interview him.

In June 1982 Macmillan's had brought out *An Indian Summer*, a selection of one hundred of the best of Sachie's recent poems with a preface by Peter Quennell. *An Indian Summer* was the end of Sachie's long voyage round himself. 'An Old Snapshot' recorded the octogenarian's reflections on a photograph of himself taken in The Crescent as a child:

> A round world,
>   or it comes round in a circle,
> As you can see or it comes round in a circle
> As round as the 'round O' of the wooden playhouse,
>   and all of life played in it,
> Or foretold there . . .

Perhaps saddest of all was the concluding poem of the selection, 'The Climacteric':

> The climacteric,
>   a climacteric, no less,
> With another birthday only a week ahead

and nearly a lifetime of failure
If not wholly unsuccess:
   so little of time left
And the summing-up still hot on the printing press:–

Oh! stay with me, my Muse,
   and do not leave me
With my family skeletons around me:–
   a father and a mother
My sister and my brother.

Soon, however, his muse did leave him. In May 1985 he wrote his last prose, the preface to *Sacheverell Sitwell's England*, to be published the following year. It was an anthology of his prose, a palimpsest of the book which he always should have written. Having begun with *British Architects and Craftsmen*, he should have followed up with the projected English Churches if he had not refused to share Batsford's advance with a cartographer. The chapters on England in *Monks, Nuns and Monasteries* had been in a sense the sequel. Michael Raeburn made the selection, arranging the excerpts from various books geographically to give them coherence. He concluded with a fine nostalgic passage from *All Summer in a Day*, in which Sachie is once again with 'Brockie' on the Scarborough cliff-top:

A bright stab of sunlight, that kind which comes out of the void of
winter to live for a few moments only and remind you of its summer
potency came down through the windows and we were taken back again
. . . till we stood once more by a bed of yellow flowers . . . at the edge of
an asphalt path that wound away like a molten river through the grass.
That cropped lawn seemed to run straight into the sky just a few feet in
front of us, but no sooner did we walk out upon it than the horizon took
a vast leap away from us beyond a huge surging bay, a kind of immense
amphitheatre. . . .

In his memory Sachie escaped to run down the cliff to watch the pierrots: 'as I best remember them, in a waning afternoon when the tide upon the sands put an end to their performance'.

For Sachie, television was the modern equivalent of the pierrot show. He particularly liked *Fawlty Towers*, but also *Porridge* and *The Two Ronnies*. Wrestling was another of his passions and the local news bulletins which provided the minutiae of human life which so interested him.

Duncan Fallowell visited Sachie on four separate occasions over the twelve months before he died. His skilfully edited tapes of his visits provide the best written record of Sachie's conversational style, full of wit, anecdote and a delight in the human comedy: Queen Victoria's sense of humour, a shop in Ootacamund called Spencer's which sold Dundee cake and Cheddar cheese, Max Beerbohm on Mussolini – 'There goes the Black Bottom' – the lavatory attendant at the Café Royal who was called Sigismondo Pandolfo Malatesta and really was descended from the tyrants of Rimini, and the ten-year-old knickerbocker-clad Waugh's response to Edmund Gosse's patronising 'Where are these little knees going to carry you?' 'Wherever I damn well like.'

Meeting Sachie for the first time in the hall where the Sutherland portrait hung, Fallowell was struck by the contrast between the apprehensive but twinkling Sachie and the tight-lipped figure in the painting. 'He is generally ill-at-ease, alive, sensitive, and in the drawing room says, "Would you like sherry or somefing [pronouncing th as f or v]? Those are jolly nice shoes. . . ." ' Liking treats, he was delighted with the white Belgian chocolates Fallowell brought him. He was still interested in food and drink, the English dishes Gertrude made for him: Bakewell tarts, a Derbyshire speciality, crown of lamb, chocolate pudding, mulberry fool. When Patrick Leigh Fermor and Pamela Egremont had lunched there recently, he had pressed them to try *Beaume de Venise*, then almost unknown as a dessert wine, and he still loved champagne. 'I'm certainly fearfully greedy,' he told Fallowell. (Like Evelyn Waugh's, Sachie's selfish greed had impressed his children unfavourably in the period of austerity after the Second World War. Where Waugh had devoured rare bananas and cream in front of them, Sachie used to appropriate Francis's cheese ration.)

Sachie reminisced, comparing his recent visit to the inside of Buckingham Palace to receive the CH with an earlier experience on the outside:

> I do remember when I was in the Grenadiers, we had to go on guard
> there, and the band was playing and we saw an absolutely furious face at
> the window. It was King George V. The band had got it into their heads
> to play the March from *Prince Igor*, and he was on to it like that
> [snapping his fingers]. He sent down a message saying, 'Stop it now,
> and never again!' So the poor fings had to stop it in the middle and they
> were rather offended by that too. . . .
>   'What didn't he like about it, that it was Russian [i.e. an
> uncomfortable reminder of the recent murder of his cousin Tsar
> Nicholas II]?

That it was Russian. And he wanted the Maidens' Chorus from *The Maid of the Mountains* or somefing of that sort.

His muse had not quite yet deserted him. He told Fallowell that he had been writing a poem that morning. 'Poetry is much less trouble than writing prose. You can write poems beside the fire, for example. You can sit very comfortably in a chair and meditate, and that sort of fing. . . .' Later, Fallowell asked him if he had any vices:

'Well, obviously, selfishness. Jealousy is a big one . . . jealousy of people who've had an undue amount of success.'
'You've not had success?'
'Not nearly the success I deserve.'
'What is the success you deserve?'
'Well . . . I think I ought to be known as a really first-rate poet. . . . And a damn good prose writer too.'
'What is your most treasured possession?'
'Er, well . . . I was going to say *myself*. . . .'[16]

'It's wonderful to be alive,' Sachie had told Fallowell, an unusual sentiment for a man of ninety-one. He enjoyed life all the more because of his constant awareness of death. 'Ah! Until something happens,' he had written in *For Want of the Golden City*. 'Nothing can go on for ever, except entire negation and nothingness itself, which has no beginning and no end, and therefore no existence and no being. But it is there, yet, and all the time, although you can neither see nor hear it.' He was convinced that dying would be a physically painful experience, a wrenching and severing as the mind and soul were torn from the body and from life. In the early summer of 1988 he retreated to his bed, lying there, listening to music, always with Gertrude or one of his family or close friends talking to him. His grandson, William, taped a brief interview with him in June. Sachie was already far away, but there was a brief spark when William mentioned Peter Quennell. 'Peter Quennell?' 'He's eighty-three. . . .' 'Well,' Sachie almost chuckled, 'that ought to keep him quiet.' When Quennell came to see him, he seemed content. 'We've both had interesting lives, haven't we Peter,' he said.

In the last week of September it became obvious that he was dying, curled up for three days in a foetal position and refusing food. On the morning of Friday 30 September, he became lucid again, asking Francis, when he came in to see him, where he was going. On being told that he was off shopping in Towcester, he said, 'Don't be too long. . . .' Kisty

Hesketh came in to see him; he was still aware enough of beauty and colour to tell her how lovely she looked in her bright pink coat. Towards evening he seemed to become aware of the approaching night and became restless, fighting to hold on to life. After a family conference with the doctor he was given valium to ease his passage towards the inevitable end. He died, 'of old age' as the certificate registered, at 1.15 in the morning of 1 October 1988. He had long ago written his own epitaph: 'To have been alive and sentient is the grand experience. . . .'

Source Notes

Note on Manuscript Sources

The three principal manuscript collections of source material for this book are the private family papers in the possession of Sacheverell Sitwell's sons, Sir Reresby Sitwell, Bt, and Mr Francis Sitwell, referred to respectively as the 'Renishaw Papers' and the 'Weston Papers', and the Sitwell Collection at the Harry Ransom Humanities Research Center, University of Texas, at Austin, referred to below as HRC. Neither the Renishaw nor the Weston Papers have been catalogued; therefore no file reference numbers can be given beyond Box numbers for the Renishaw Papers.

In the United Kingdom the British Library holds the Aberconway Papers, some of which are still reserved from public consultation, the McCann and the Schiff Papers. Cecil Beaton's Papers are at St John's College, Cambridge, David Horner's in the School Library at Eton College. Many friends of Sachie have given me access to their correspondence with him or papers relating to him, notably Richard Buckle, Zita James, Lady Alexandra Metcalfe, Celia Goodman, Lady Cooke and Roland Pym. Jessica Douglas-Home has provided me with copies of his letters to Violet Gordon Woodhouse. Neil Ritchie has shown me manuscripts from his private collection and Hugo Vickers has guided me towards relevant parts of the Cecil Beaton diaries and correspondence and the diaries of Sir Charles Johnston.

Otherwise the major collections are to be found in the United States: the Sitwell Papers at the University of Texas at Austin, referred to above; the Bryher Papers and other Sitwelliana in the Beinecke Rare Book and Manuscript Library at Yale University; Sitwell Collections at the Mugar Memorial Library at Boston University and the McFarlin Library at the University of Tulsa; and Sacheverell Sitwell's correspondence at Cornell University, the University of New York at Buffalo, Washington State University at Pullman, the Berg Collection at the New York Public Library and the Houghton Library at Harvard University.

1 Physical Landscapes – Scarborough and Renishaw, 1897–1900

1. 'Finale' in *Dodecameron*
2. *For Want of the Golden City*, p. 70
3. Susan Hill in Derek Parker (ed.), *Sacheverell Sitwell: A Symposium*, p. 78
4. *For Want of the Golden City*, p. 298
5. *Some Scarborough Faces. . .* , Scarborough, 1901, p. 18
6. 'Souvenir Publication of the *Scarborough Mercury*', centenary publication, Scarborough, 1955
7. Osbert Sitwell, *Left Hand, Right Hand!*, p. 4
8. Osbert liked to believe in his great-grandfather's royal descent. It has never been officially established.
9. Edith Sitwell, 'Readers and Writers', *The New Age*, July 1922
10. 'Serenade to a Sister'
11. Duncan Fallowell, *To Noto*, p. 7
12. *See* Osbert Sitwell, *Great Morning!*, Appendix A
13. Osbert Sitwell, *Left Hand, Right Hand!*, pp. 99–100
14. Ibid., pp. 97–9
15. Osbert Sitwell, *Tales My Father Taught Me*, p. 34
16. *All Summer in a Day*, pp. 40 and 60
17. *Ibid.*, pp. 56–7
18. *Ibid.*, pp. 60–1
19. *Ibid.*, p. 118.
20. *For Want of the Golden City*, p. 185
21. *Ibid.*, p. 186
22. 'Japonica, or Cydonia' in *Pomona*
23. *All Summer in a Day*, pp. 26, 14–15, 26
24. *Ibid.*, pp. 76–7
25. *Ibid.*, pp. 18, 19–20, 31
26. Edith Sitwell, *Troy Park*

2 Family Portrait, 1900–1915

1. Cited in John Lehmann, *A Nest of Tigers*, p. 61
2. Osbert Sitwell, *Left Hand, Right Hand!*, p. 6
3. *Splendours and Miseries*, pp. 241–2
4. Osbert Sitwell, *Left Hand, Right Hand!*, p. 104
5. *For Want of the Golden City*, p. 288
6. Weston Papers, as are the following letters from Sir George Sitwell to Lady Ida
7. Weston Papers: A. Closson to SS, *12. 3. 1985*
8. Neil Ritchie Collection: undated fragment MS, c. 1975

9. *Splendours and Miseries*, p. 245
10. *For Want of the Golden City*, p. 126
11. *The Gothick North: The Visit of the Gypsies*, pp. 33 and 23
12. *See* Clayre Percy and Jane Ridley (eds.), *The Letters of Edwin Lutyens to His Wife Emily*
13. Osbert Sitwell, *Tales My Father Taught Me*, p. 1
14. Richard Buckle Collection: SS to Richard Buckle, *15 June 1977*
15. *Splendours and Miseries*, p. 246
16. 'Mulberry, or Morus' in *An Indian Summer*
17. Ritchie Collection, *loc. cit.*
18. Renishaw Papers, Box 80
19. Renishaw Papers, Box 79
20. *Loc. cit.*
21. *Loc. cit.*
22. Weston Papers
23. *Loc. cit.: n. d. [c. 1912]*
24. Renishaw Papers, Box 65
25. *All Summer in a Day*
26. Weston Papers: *25. 6. 11*
27. Renishaw papers, Box 65
28. Weston Papers: *n. d. 'Saturday'*
29. John Pearson, *Façades*, p. 65
30. Weston Papers
31. HRC, Sitwell Family Letters: Sitwell, Osbert. Recip. Sitwell, Sacheverell: *26. xii. 12*
32. Weston Papers: *31. xii. 12*
33. *Loc. cit.: 20 Feb. 1913*
34. *Loc. cit.: Eton, 17. 3. 13*
35. *Loc. cit.: 2. viii. 13*
36. *Loc. cit.*
37. *Loc. cit: 9. 6. 13*
38. *The Times*, 16 October 1913
39. Weston Papers: *20 Oct. 1913*
40. Renishaw Papers, Box 79
41. Weston Papers: *31. 12. 1912*
42. *Loc. cit.: n. d. [October/November 1913]*
43. *Loc. cit.*
44. *Loc. cit.: n. d. [November 1913]*
45. Renishaw Papers, Box 79: *n. d. [late November/early December 1913]*
46. Weston Papers: *n. d. [December 1913]*
47. HRC, *loc. cit: 23. xii. 13*
48. *Loc. cit.*
49. *Loc. cit.: 24. xii. 13*

50. Osbert Sitwell, *Great Morning!*, p. 286
51. Weston Papers: *18. 8. 14*
52. *Loc. cit.*
53. *Loc. cit: 21. 8. 14*
54. *Loc. cit: 24. 7. 14*
55. *Loc. cit: Park House, Harrogate, n. d. [late August/early September 1914]*
56. *Loc. cit.*
57. *Loc. cit.: n. d. [September 1914]*
58. *Loc. cit.: 12. 9. 14*
59. *Loc. cit.: 17. 9. 14*
60. *Loc. cit.*
61. Renishaw Papers, Box 65: A. B. Brockwell to SS, *31 December 1914*
62. Renishaw Papers, *Box 80*
63. *Loc. cit.: 12 Hans Road, 26. 1. 15*
64. *The Times*, 9 March 1915
65. *Loc. cit.*, 12 March 1915
66. Renishaw Papers, Box 80: *n. d. [postmarked '12 March 1915']*
67. Renishaw Papers, Box 79
68. Weston Papers: *n. d. [March 1915]*
69. Renishaw Papers, Box 80: *n. d. [c. 16 March 1915]*
70. Renishaw Papers, Box 79
71. Weston Papers: *Brantwood, Bournemouth, 25. 4. 15*
72. *Loc. cit.: 19. 5. 15*
73. Renishaw Papers, Box 79
74. Renishaw Papers, Box 80: *n. d. [27 June 1915]*
75. *For Want of the Golden City*, p. 292

3 The Education of an Aesthete, 1915–1918

1. Peter Hunt, writer and broadcaster
2. Renishaw Papers, Boxes 25, 26, 27, 31, 34
3. Cited in Marianne W. Martin, *Futurist Art and Theory 1909–1915* p. 40
4. Eton College Library, A. A. Somerville's House Debating Society Record
5. *Cupid and the Jacaranda*, p. 140
6. In *Credo, or an Affirmation*
7. Renishaw Papers, Box 65: *16 March 1916*
8. Anthony Powell, *To Keep the Ball Rolling, vol. iv: The Strangers are all Gone*, p. 150
9. Renishaw Papers, Box 65
10. *Loc. cit.*
11. *For Want of the Golden City*, p. 275
12. *Ibid.*, p. 276

13. *Ibid.*, p. 292
14. *Ibid.*, p. 276
15. Renishaw Papers, Box 65: *28 October 1915*
16. Renishaw Papers, Box 79: *6, 9 and 18 October 1915*
17. Eton School Library: *23. xi. 1971*
18. Renishaw Papers, Box 80: *19 February 1916*
19. Renishaw Papers, Box 79: *n. d. [postmarked '30 March 16']*
20. Renishaw Papers, Box 80: *n. d. [?June/July 1916]*
21. *Loc. cit.: n. d. [postmarked '12 July 1916']*
22. Renishaw Papers, Box 79: *28 July [1916]*
23. *Loc. cit.: 31 July 1916*
24. Renishaw Papers, Box 65: *18. 12. 13*
25. Cited in Victoria Glendinning, *Edith Sitwell: A Unicorn among Lions*, p. 77
26. *For Want of the Golden City*, p. 291
27. 'Serenade to a Sister'
28. Marie-Jacqueline Lancaster, *Brian Howard: Portrait of a Failure*, p. 90
29. Renishaw Papers, Box 65: *22 December 1915*
30. Cited in Edith Sitwell (ed.), *Wheels 'An Anthology of Verse'*, second edition, March 1917
31. Renishaw Papers, Box 65
32. Renishaw Papers, Box 79: *1 October 1916*
33. Renishaw Papers, Box 65: *5 October 1915*
34. Grover Smith (ed.), *Letters of Aldous Huxley*, 3 August 1917
35. Valerie Eliot (ed.), *The Letters of T. S. Eliot*, vol. I: 1898–1922
36. Smith (ed.) *op. cit.*, 13 December [1917]
37. Eliot (ed.), *op. cit.*, 7 November 1918
38. Cited in Edith Sitwell (ed.), *Wheels, Fourth Cycle*
39. Cornell University, Lewis Collection: SS to Wyndham Lewis, *11. 1. 18*
40. *Loc. cit.*: SS to Wyndham Lewis, *19 August 1918*
41. Weston Papers: *12/8/18*
42. Prologue in Arnold Haskell, Mark Bonham-Carter and Michael Wood (eds.), *Gala Performance*, p. 17
43. Osbert Sitwell, *Laughter in the Next Room*, pp. 17–22

4 Looking for the Gods of Light, 1919–1924

1. University of Tulsa, Special Collections, McFarlin Library, Sitwell Collection, IV: John Pearson interviews with SS
2. Susana Walton, *William Walton: Behind the Façade*, p, 48
3. Osbert Sitwell, *Noble Essences*, pp. 68–88
4. *For Want of the Golden City*, p. 392

5. Cornell, Lewis Collection: SS to Wyndham Lewis, *misdated '10. 6. 19' but presumably 18. 4. 19*

6. *Loc. cit:* SS to Wyndham Lewis, *17. 5. 19*

7. Renishaw Papers, Box 80: *27. 4. 19*

8. Courtesy of Mrs Valerie Eliot: SS to T. S. Eliot, *4. 3. 19*

9. *For Want of the Golden City*, p. 110

10. Weston Papers: *16. 4. 19*

11. Haskell, Bonham-Carter and Wood (eds.), *op. cit.*, p. 24. The frescoes were eventually executed by Gino Severini in 1921–1922

12. *See* Osbert Sitwell, *Laughter in the Next Room*, Appendix A

13. *Ibid.*, p. 158

14. Weston Papers: *20. x. 19*

15. Powell, *op. cit.*, vol. II: *Messengers of Day*, pp. 37–8

16. Norman Flower (ed.), *The Journals of Arnold Bennett, 1911–1921*

17. Nigel Nicolson (ed.), *The Question of Things Happening: The Letters of Virginia Woolf*, vol. II: 1921–1922, Virginia Woolf to Lytton Strachey, 12 October [1918]

18. Richard Aldington, *Life for Life's Sake*, p. 203–4

19. British Library Add. MS 52922, Papers of Sydney and Violet Schiff: OS to Schiff, *17. 10. 19*

20. *Loc. cit.*: OS to Schiff, *19. 10. 19*

21. Eliot (ed.), *op. cit.*, 26 March 1920

22. *Ibid.*, 22 February 1920

23. Neil Tierney, *William Walton: His Life and Music*, p. 29

24. Edith Sitwell, *Taken Care Of*, p. 127

25. *The Gothick North: These Sad Ruins*, p. 63

26. *The Adelphi*, August 1923

27. *Southern Baroque Revisited*, pp. 3–5

28. Osbert Sitwell, *Discursions, on Travel, Art and Life* p. 237–8

29. *Cupid and the Jacaranda*, p. 36

30. Harvard University, Houghton Library, bMS Am 1432 (135): SS to T. S. Eliot, *18. 2. 21*

31. Rupert Hart-Davis (ed.), *Siegfried Sassoon, Diaries 1920–1922*, 24 to 27 August 1921

32. *Ibid.*, 11 February 1921

33. Renishaw Papers, Box 79: *n. d. [November/December 1921]*

34. Cornell, Lewis Collection: SS to Wyndham Lewis, *7. x. 21*

35. New York Public Library, Berg Collection: SS to Richard Aldington, *26. xi. 22*

36. Renishaw Papers, Box 79, *see* note 33

37. Haskell, Bonham-Carter and Wood (eds.), *op. cit.*, pp. 17–18

38. Cornell, Lewis Collection: SS to Wyndham Lewis: *7. x. 21*

39. 'Serenade to a Sister'

40. Edith Sitwell, *Taken Care Of*, p. 123

41. Nicolson (ed.), *op. cit.*, Virginia Woolf to Vanessa Bell, 20 February 1922
42. Lancaster, Brian Howard: *A Portrait of Failure.*, p. 54
43. *Eton Candle*, 1922
44. Harold Acton, *Memoirs of an Aesthete*, vol. I, p. 99
45. *Times Literary Supplement*, 5 October 1922
46. Powell, *op. cit.*, vol. II: *Messengers of Day*, p. 89
47. Weston Papers: *12. 3. 22*
48. Hart-Davis (ed.), *op. cit.*, 17 May 1922
49. Renishaw Papers, Box 79: *n. d. [November/December 1921]*
50. Yale University, Beinecke Library, YCAL MSS 34, Dial Scofield Thayer Papers, Series I, Office Correspondence #228: Sitwell, Sacheverell, *18. 1. 23*
51. NYPL, Berg Collection: SS to Aldington, *27. 2. 23*
52. State University of New York at Buffalo, the Poetry/Rare Books Collection, NYBR-A538: SS to Harold Monro, *20. 3. 23*
53. *Loc. cit.: 1. 6. 23*
54. Acton, *op. cit.*, pp. 205–6
55. Tierney, *op. cit.*, p. 41
56. Walton, *op. cit.*, p. 59
57. Anne Olivier Bell (ed.), *The Diary of Virginia Woolf*, vol. III: 1925–1930, 20 May 1925
58. Powell, *op. cit.*, vol. II: *Messengers of Day*, p. 35
59. Review of *Left Hand, Right Hand!*
60. *The Adelphi*, August 1923
61. Powell, *op. cit.*, vol. II: *Messengers of Day*
62. Acton, *op. cit.*, p. 207
63. Sybille Bedford, *Aldous Huxley: A Biography*, vol. I: 1894–1939, p. 119
64. *Cupid and the Jacaranda*, p. 39
65. *Southern Baroque Art*, p. 133
66. In Parker (ed.), *op. cit.*, p. 16
67. *Ibid.*, p. 109
68. Preface in *An Indian Summer*, p. ix
69. Renishaw Papers, Box 65: *'Oct. 27' [1924]*
70. *Times Literary Supplement*, 6 November 1924
71. From then on Walton was often referred to by the Sitwells as 'the late' William Walton.

5 Harlequin and Columbine, 1924–1925

1. *See* 'The Weeping Boy of Teruel' in *Dodecameron*
2. *All Summer in a Day*, p. 115
3. *Ibid.*, p. 283

4. In Parker (ed.), *op. cit.*, pp. 4–5
5. The Sachie/Georgia correspondence quoted in this and subsequent chapters comes from two sources: Sachie's letters to Georgia in the Weston Papers and Georgia's letters to him in the Renishaw Papers, Box 80, unless otherwise stated.
6. In Parker (ed.), *op. cit.*, pp. 1–2
7. Cited in Lehmann, *op. cit.*, p. 82
8. *Sacred and Profane Love*, p. 227
9. Supplementary Aberconway Papers, 70831, Sitwell Letters, vol. I: *[14 July 1924]*
10. *17. 8. 24*
11. *20. 8. 24*
12. *4. 10. 24*
13. *Hotel Regina, Venice, Oct. 8th [1924]*
14. *8. x. 24, 9. x. 24 and another of the same date*
15. *18. x. 24*
16. *24. x. 24*
17. *29. x. 24*
18. *4 November [1924]*
19. *10. xi. 24*
20. *12. xi. 24*
21. *13. xi. 24*
22. *16. xi. 24*
23. *20. xi. 24*
24. *22 November 1924*
25. *25 November 1924*
26. *28. xi. 24*
27. *30 November 1924*
28. *1. xii. 24*
29. *7. xii. 24*
30. *10. xii. 24*
31. *26. 1. 25*
32. *December 12th 1924*
33. *13. xii. 24*
34. *21. xii. 24*
35. *17. xii. 24*
36. *23 Jan. 1925*
37. *24 February 1925*
38. *11 March 1925*
39. *12. 3. 25*
40. *27. 3. 25*
41. *11. 4. 25*
42. Cited in Pearson, *op. cit.*, p. 188

43. Cited in Martin Green, *Children of the Sun*, p. 213
44. *n. d. [postmarked '7 April 1925']*
45. *23. 4. 25*
46. *n. d. [April 1925]*
47. *23. 4. 25*
48. BL, Aberconway Papers, 70837, vol. VII: *n. d. [postmarked '23 September 1925']*
49. *21. 6. 25*
50. *30. 6. 25*
51. Powell, *op. cit.*, vol. II: *Messengers of Day*, p. 162
52. Peter Quennell, *The Marble Foot: An Autobiography 1905–1938*, p. 157
53. *Ibid.*, p. 132
54. Powell, *op. cit.*, vol. I: *Infants of the Spring*, p. 160
55. Quennell, *op. cit.*, p. 131
56. Powell, *op. cit.*, vol. II: *Messengers of Day*, p. 165
57. *9. 8. 25*
58. BL, Schiff Papers, vol. VII: *23. 5. 25*
59. *10. 8. 25*
60. *21 August [1925]*
61. BL, Aberconway Papers, 70831, vol. I: *August 1925*
62. BL, Aberconway Papers, 70832, vol. II: *n. d. [May 1935]*
63. *16. 8. 25*
64. HRC: Sitwell, Sacheverell. Recip. Sitwell, Edith. Folder 1925–1930
65. HRC: Sitwell, Sacheverell. Recip. Sitwell, Osbert. Folder 1925–1926
66. *Loc. cit.: 20 October [1925]*
67. *Loc. cit.: n. d. [October 1925]*
68. Weston Papers: *22. 9. 25*
69. *For Want of the Golden City*, p. 417

6 Sitwelldom, 1925–1929

From this date onwards Georgia's unpublished manuscript diary is the principal source for the social and intimate record of their lives unless otherwise stated.

1. Renishaw Papers, Box 80: *29 October 1925*
2. *Loc. cit.: 9 November 1925*
3. *Loc. cit.: 26 November 1925*
4. St. John's College, Cambridge Cecil Beaton MS diaries, *November 1940*
5. Quennell, *op. cit.*, pp. 141–3
6. Renishaw Papers, Box 64: *n. d. [14 January 1926]*
7. Interview with Peter Quennell, 13 February 1990

8. HRC: Sitwell, Sacheverell. Misc. Sitwell, Edith. Letters to Georgia: *n. d.*
   [16 December 1925]
9. *Loc. cit.*: *n. d. [4 January 1926]*
10. Acton, *op. cit.*, p. 161
11. Richard Buckle Collection: SS to Richard Buckle, *18 January 1976*
12. Weston Papers: *18 October 1926*
13. *Times Literary Supplement*, 28 October 1926
14. HRC: Sitwell, Sacheverell. Recip. Sitwell, Edith: *4 January 1926*
15. *Loc. cit.*: *[16 September 1926]*
16. *Times Literary Supplement*, 7 October 1926
17. Berg Collection: Arthur Bannerman to Humbert Wolfe, *22. 11. 26*
18. Weston Papers: *15 August 1926*
19. Richard Buckle Collection: SS to Richard Buckle, *27. 1. 76*
20. Cecil Beaton MS diaries, *3 December 1926*
21. Weston Papers: *15 October 1926*
22. HRC: Sitwell, Sacheverell, Misc. Sitwell, Osbert. Letters to Georgia: *15
    April [1927]*
23. HRC: Sitwell, Sacheverell. Misc. Sitwell, Osbert: *n. d. [4. 5. 27]*
24. HRC: Sitwell, Sacheverell. Misc. Sitwell, George. Letters to Georgia.
    Folder 1: *1 March 1927*
25. Weston Papers: *22 November 1926*
26. *The Cyder Feast*, p. 90
27. Cecil Beaton MS diaries, *15 November 1926*, part cited in Hugo Vickers,
    Cecil Beaton, p. 81
28. Cecil Beaton MS diaries, *10 November 1926*
29. Interview with Zita James, 27 February 1990
30. Washington State University Libraries, Manuscripts, Archives and
    Special Collections, Cage 165, Siegfried Sassoon Papers, Folder 15,
    Letters from Sacheverell Sitwell to Siegfried Sassoon, 1925–1931: *29
    September 1927*
31. Zita James MS diary, vol. October-December 1927: *19 October 1927*
32. *Ibid.*
33. Zita James Collection: SS to Zita Jungman, *25 October 1927*
34. Philip Hoare, *Serious Pleasures: The Life of Stephen Tennant*, p. 96
35. HRC, *loc. cit*: *8 March 1928*
36. Weston Papers: Georgia Sitwell MS diary, *16 March 1928*
37. HRC: Sitwell, Sacheverell. Recip. Sitwell, Osbert. Folder 1927–1928: *n.
    d. [c. Christmas to New Year 1927]*
38. *8 February [1928]*
39. BL, Aberconway Papers, 70831, vol. I: *n. d. and 18 February 1928*
40. Zita James MS diary, vol. January to June 1928: *27 March 1928*
41. Interview with Zita James, 27 February 1990
42. Georgia Sitwell MS diary

43. Zita James MS diary, *16 April 1928*
44. Nicholas Mosley, *Rules of the Game*
45. Weston Papers: unpublished autograph MS poem
46. Percy and Ridley (eds.), *op. cit.*
47. Penelope Middleboe (ed.), *Edith Olivier from Her Journals 1924–1948*, 25 and 27 August 1928
48. Edith's explanation for this phrase: 'Pansies grow in herbaceous borders.'
49. BL, Aberconway Papers, 70831, vol. I: *15 November 1928*
50. HRC, *loc. cit.*: *n. d. 'Wed'*
51. BL, Aberconway Papers, *loc. cit.*: *n. d. [postmarked '24. 11. 28' and '6. 12. 28']*
52. Zita James Collection: unpublished poem
53. Washington, Sassoon Papers, *loc. cit.*: *4. 1. 29*
54. BL, Aberconway Papers, *loc. cit.*: *26. 2. 29*
55. *Ibid.*

7 *The End of the Harlequinade, 1929–1933*

1. Martin Stannard, *Evelyn Waugh: The Early Years, 1903–1939*, p. 130
2. *Ibid.*, *see* p. 223*n* where Stannard, despite this quote, insists that the Waughs 'dined' at the Embassy
3. *The Gothick North: These Sad Ruins*, pp. 86–7
4. *Ibid.*, pp. 87–8
5. *Ibid.*, pp. 87–133
6. BL, Aberconway Papers, 70837, vol. VII/5, Letters of David Horner: *18 September 1929*
7. Eton School Library, David Horner Papers
8. BL, Aberconway Papers, 70832, vol. II: William Walton to OS, *25. 8. 1929*
9. BL, Aberconway Papers, 70837, vol. VII/5: *1 September 1929*
10. Richard Buckle Collection: SS to Richard Buckle, *18 January 1976*
11. Renishaw Papers, Box 80: Zita James to SS, *26 November 1929*
12. *Loc. cit*: *29 December 1929*
13. Washington, Siegfried Sassoon Papers, *loc. cit.*: *27. 2. 1930*
14. Loelia, Duchess of Westminster, *Grace and Favour*, p. 190
15. *Ibid.*, p. 232
16. Renishaw Papers, Box 65: *2 February 1933*
17. Weston Papers: SS to Hugo Southern, *6 April 1978*
18. HRC: Sitwell, Sacheverell, Recip. Sitwell, Osbert: *n. d. [?31 January 1930]*
19. Osbert Sitwell, *Tales My Father Taught Me*, p. 65
20. BL, Aberconway Papers, 70832, vol. II: *2. v. 1930*

21. HRC: Sitwell, Osbert. Letters to David Horner 1926–1935. Folder 2: *19 and 21 May 1930*

22. Printed as Appendix B by Osbert in *Laughter in the Next Room*. The original typescript with autograph emendations by Waugh and initialled EW is in the Weston Papers.

23. Michael Davie (ed.), *The Diaries of Evelyn Waugh*

24. BL, Aberconway Papers, *loc. cit.*: *17 September 1930*

25. Beaton Papers: ES to Cecil Beaton, *n. d. [September 1930]*

26. Tulsa, Sitwell Collection, I/A, Edith Sitwell 1:3 'Family Portrait'

27. Boston University, Mugar Memorial Library, Sacheverell Sitwell Collection, Box 14/1, MS diary notebook

28. Renishaw Papers, Box 80: *17 October 1930*

29. *Dance of the Quick and the Dead*, pp. 169 and 165

30. Diary, *8 and 9 August 1931*

31. BL, Aberconway Papers, 70832, vol. II: *n. d. [17 June 1931]*

32. Faringdon is now in Oxfordshire since the boundary changes.

33. Boston, Sitwell Collection. Sitwell, Osbert, George and family. #606B, Box 1, Folder 7: *8 December 1931*

34. HRC: Sitwell, Sacheverell. Misc. Sitwell, George. Letters to Georgia. Folder 1: *17 March 1930*

35. Washington, Sassoon Papers: *23. xii. 31*

36. Washington, Cage 9, Balston, Thomas. Sitwell Papers, 1924–1960. 10: SS to Thomas Balston, *31. 1. 29*

37. Renishaw Papers, Box 64: *17 June 1919*

38. Renishaw Papers, Box 65: *21 July 1931*

39. Washington, Sitwell Papers: *9. xi. 31*

40. Renishaw Papers, Box 65: *12 November 1931*

41. Weston Papers: Geoffrey Faber to SS, *6 March 1930*

42. Renishaw Papers, Box 65: Michael Sadleir to SS, *5 December 1931*

43. *Loc. cit*: *5 January 1932*

44. Washington, Sitwell Papers: *6. 1. 32*

45. Renishaw Papers, Box 65: *12 January 1932*

46. Washington, Sitwell Papers: *27. 2. 1933*

47. Renishaw Papers, Box 79: *10. viii. 31*

48. *Loc. cit.*: *24 November 1931*

49. *Loc. cit.*: *n. d. [4 ?May 1932]*

50. Renishaw Papers, Box 80: *1 April 1932*

51. *Loc. cit.*: *10 May 1932*

52. Renishaw Papers, Box 65: SS to Zita James, *n. d. [?May 1932]*

53. HRC: Sitwell, Sacheverell, Recip. Sitwell, Edith: *14 December 1931*

54. *Criterion*, October 1933

55. *Scrutiny*, vol. 2, pp. 201–2

56. Virginia Woolf to Stephen Spender, in Nicolson (ed.), *op. cit.*, vol. V

8 Sacred and Profane Love, 1933–1939

1. Frederick Ashton, 'Pearl Argyle: A Tribute', *Ballet Today*, April–May 1947
2. *Dance of the Quick and the Dead*, p. 294
3. King's College Cambridge, MS Sources, Keynes-Lopokova Letters: *21 May 1933*
4. Renishaw Papers, Box 79
5. BL, Aberconway Papers, 70833, vol. III: *18 August 1933*
6. Weston Papers: Sir George Sitwell to Philip Frere, *30 August 1932*
7. Renishaw Papers, Box 79: *28 December 1933*
8. *Loc. cit.*: *27 October 1933*
9. Cecil Beaton MS diaries, *15 September 1933*
10. Renishaw Papers, Box 65: Desmond Parsons to SS, *13 March 1934*
11. Renishaw Papers, Box 79: *n. d. [postmarked '9 April 1934']*
12. HRC: Sitwell, Sacheverell, Recip. Sitwell, Edith: *n. d. [26 September 1934]*
13. *Time and Tide*, 15 December 1934
14. HRC: Sitwell, Sacheverell, Recip. Sitwell, Osbert: *n. d. [23 February 1935]*
15. *Ibid.*
16. *29 September 1935*
17. Renishaw Papers, Box 79: *3 April 1936*
18. HRC, *loc. cit*: *n. d. [?September 1936]*
19. Interview with James Lees-Milne, 1 March 1990
20. Interview with Peter Quennell, 13 February 1990
21. *Times Literary Supplement*, 23 January 1937
22. Earl of Rosse Collection, Birr Papers T/144: *14. 7. 1937*
23. Foreword to Preface to OUP paperback edition of *Roumanian Journey* (1992) from a typescript kindly sent to the author pre-publication by Patrick Leigh Fermor
24. *Mauretania*, p. 229
25. Interview with Lady Alexandra Metcalfe, 7 February 1990
26. Robert Rhodes James (ed.), *Chips: The Diaries of Sir Henry Channon*, 26 July 1939
27. BL, Aberconway Papers, 70835, vol. V

9 Gleams of a Remoter World, 1939–1945

1. Unpublished MS 'Notes on Sachie' written for the author by Patrick Leigh Fermor, dated 'Kardamyli' *27. 3. 1991*
2. Charles Ritchie, *The Siren Years*, 28 December 1941

3. BL, Aberconway Papers, *loc. cit.*: *n. d. [?November 1939]*
4. Leigh Fermor, 'Notes'
5. HRC: *3 March 1940*
6. HRC, *loc. cit.*
7. Renishaw Papers: *28. xi. 1940*
8. Rex Whistler dined at Weston en route in his tank to take part in the invasion of Normandy in June 1944. Sachie recorded Rex's conviction that he would not survive the war. He was killed a month later. Robert Byron had been drowned on active service in February 1941.
9. Daniel J. Leab Collection: George Orwell to SS, *6. 7. 1940*. Dan Leab kindly brought this letter to my attention.
10. Renishaw Papers, Box 79: *6. ix. 38*
11. *Loc. cit.*: *23 February 1939*
12. *Loc. cit.*: *13 October 1940*
13. *Loc. cit.*: *n. d. [?5 November 1940]*
14. Renishaw Papers, Box 80: *28. x. 1940*. Osbert published Florence Sitwell's diary in *Two Generations* (24 September 1940).
15. Renishaw Papers, *loc. cit.*: *29. x. 40*
16. BL, Aberconway Papers, *loc. cit.*: *n. d. [November 1940]*
17. HRC, *loc. cit.*: *25. 11. 40*
18. HRC: Sitwell, Sacheverell. Misc./Unidentified – Z: Denys Kilham Roberts to OS, *27 February 1941*
19. Yale, Beinecke Library, Osborn Files, Sitwell: SS to Rev. Montague Summers, *9 May 1942*
20. Jessica Douglas-Home Collection: SS to Violet Gordon Woodhouse, *29 November 1943*
21. Weston Papers: Captain R. D. Bolton to GS, *n. d. [May 1945]*
22. *Loc. cit.*: *19. 7. 45*
23. HRC: Sitwell, Osbert. Recip. Sitwell, Sacheverell: *6 April 1942*
24. HRC: Frances Ashbrooke Crump enclosed with letter from OS to SS, *6 September 1941*
25. HRC: ES to Sir George, *22 November 1941*, cited in Pearson, *op. cit.*, p. 353
26. HRC: Sitwell, Osbert. Letters to David Horner, 1942. Folder 1: *n. d. [2 January 1942]*
27. *Loc. cit.*: *n. d. [February 1942]*
28. *Loc. cit.*: text in letter from OS to David Horner, *22 June 1942*
29. Eton School Library, David Horner Papers: Bernard Woog to OS, *4 September 1942*
30. HRC, *loc. cit.*: *n. d. [30 September 1942]*
31. *Loc. cit.*: *n. d. [9 October 1942]*
32. *Tatler*, 21 October 1942
33. HRC, *loc. cit.*: *n. d. [1943]*

34. *Loc. cit.*: *n. d. [April 1943] and letter to GS of the same month*
35. Lehmann, *op. cit.*, p. 205
36. HRC, *loc. cit.*, Folder 2: *n. d. [13 July 1943]*
37. *Loc. cit.*: *n. d. [15 July 1943]*
38. Cited in Pearson, *op. cit.*, p. 362
39. HRC, *loc. cit.*: *n. d. [19 July 1943]*
40. *Loc. cit.*: *n. d. [28 July 1943]*
41. *Ibid.*
42. *Loc. cit.*: *30 August 1943*
43. Lehmann, *op. cit.*, p. 185
44. HRC, *loc. cit.*: *4 January 1944*
45. Cited in Pearson, *op. cit.*, p. 367
46. *See ibid.*, pp. 368–9
47. HRC, Letters to David Horner: typed memorandum enclosed with letter from OS to David Horner, *11 April 1944*
48. *Loc. cit.*
49. *Loc. cit.*: *24 April 1944*
50. *Loc. cit.* Folder 4: *'Tuesday June 27' [1944]*
51. Lehmann, *op. cit.*, p. 199
52. HRC, *loc. cit.* Folder 3: *n. d. [April/May 1945]*
53. Weston Papers: *5 February 1945*
54. Cited in Pearson, *op. cit*, pp. 379–80
55. *29 May 1945*
56. *12 June 1945*

10 *Embarkations for Cythera,* 1945–1959

1. SS's letters of 17 February and 12 August 1945 are part of his voluminous correspondence (1945–1974) with his patroness, Winifred Bryher (*née* Ellerman), in the Beinecke Library at Yale: Yale, Gen. MSS 97, Bryher Papers. Most of Bryher's letters to Sachie are in the Renishaw Papers, Box 78, although a certain number are in the Weston Papers.
2. *22 February 1945*
3. Renishaw Papers: *23 December 1947*
4. *22 February 1945*
5. Renishaw Papers, Box 79
6. *Loc. cit.*: *28 June 1945*
7. HRC, *loc. cit.*: *?20 May 1945*
8. *Loc. cit.*: *10 August 1945*
9. *31 August 1945*
10. HRC, *loc. cit.*: *n. d. [August/September 1945]*
11. BL, Aberconway Papers, 70835, vol. V: *16 June 1946*

12. *4 April 1945*
13. *21 August 1945*
14. This and the following letters from SS to Moira Shearer are in the collection of Mrs Ludovic Kennedy. Her letters to SS are in the Renishaw Papers, Box 79.
15. Interview with Moira Kennedy, 3 February 1992
16. *5 July 1946*
17. Renishaw Papers: *30 March 1947*
18. Renishaw Papers, Box 79: *3 December 1941*
19. 'Ballad: White Rose' in *Lyra Varia* (c. 1972)
20. Villanueva, later also known by his Mexican title as Salvador, Marques de Marianao, became a lifelong friend of Sachie and Georgia, who often stayed with him in Paris.
21. *Spain*, p. 30
22. *27 June 1947*
23. *28 October and 25 September 1947*
24. HRC, *loc. cit.*: *n. d. [?22 May 1946]*
25. HRC, *loc. cit.*: *n. d. [?27 September/October 1947]*
26. *Loc. cit.*: *n. d. [24 July 1947]*
27. *Loc. cit.*: *n. d. [?27 October 1947]*
28. *24 May 1948*
29. *The Times*, 15 January 1948
30. *Loc. cit.* 17 July 1948
31. HRC: *17 September 1949*
32. *Loc. cit.*: *29 November 1949*
33. Yale, Gen. MSS 97, I/60/2205
34. HRC: Sitwell, Edith. Works 181. Fair copy in Edith's hand
35. *Loc. cit.*
36. *22 February 1950*
37. HRC, *loc. cit.*: *n. d. [16 March 1950]*
38. *Loc. cit.*: *22 May 1950*
39. HRC: *30. vii. 50*
40. HRC: Sitwell, Sacheverell. Misc. Horner, David to Georgia Sitwell: *20 July 1960*
41. Interview with H. V. Hodson, 23 January 1992
42. Powell, *op. cit.*, vol. III: *Faces in My Time*, p. 222
43. *20 August 1951*
44. BL, Aberconway Papers, 70837, vol. VII/4: *31 October 1951*
45. BL, C. W. McCann Papers: SS to Christabel Aberconway, *16. xii. 1951*
46. BL, Aberconway Papers, 70836, vol. VI: *27 December 1951*
47. BL, McCann Papers
48. *Loc. cit.*: David Horner to Christabel Aberconway, *6 April 1952*
49. Renishaw Papers, Box 80: *n. d. [?1952]*

50. *Loc. cit.*
51. Pearn, Pollinger and Higham were Sachie's literary agents.
52. *17 November 1951*
53. *9 December 1951*
54. Weston Papers
55. *19 November 1952*
56. Mark Amory (ed.), *The Letters of Evelyn Waugh*, pp. 290–1
57. HRC, David Higham Archive: *6 November 1946*
58. *Loc. cit.*
59. *Loc. cit.*: *12 August 1952*
60. Loc. cit.: *27 August 1952*
61. *Loc. cit.*: *25 September 1952*
62. *Loc. cit.*: *29 September 1952*
63. *Loc. cit.*: *28 October 1952*
64. *Loc. cit.*: *9 December 1952*
65. *Loc. cit.*: SS to David Higham, *9 February 1953*
66. Neil Ritchie Collection, 14 February 1953
67. HRC, David Higham Archive: *6 March 1953*
68. *Loc. cit.*: *14. 5. 53*
69. *Loc. cit.*: *20 April 1954*
70. NYPL, Berg Collection: SS to Leonard Clark, *20 June 1953*
71. *Loc. cit.*: *24 June 1953*
72. HRC, *loc. cit.*: *19 August 1953*
73. *Loc. cit.*: *n. d. [?1 November 1953]*
74. *Loc. cit.*: *10 December 1953*
75. HRC, David Higham Archive: *15 July 1954*
76. Interview with Sir Brinsley Ford, 8 February 1990
77. HRC, *loc. cit.*: *17 January 1955*
78. *Loc. cit.*: *26 February 1957*
79. HRC: Sitwell, Sacheverell. Misc. Sitwell, Edith. Letters to Georgia: *2 May 1957*
80. Renishaw Papers, Box 78: *14 March 1957*
81. HRC, *loc. cit.*: *21. 12. 1957*
82. *4 July 1954*
83. Lady Alexandra Metcalfe's unpublished diary
84. Quentin Crewe, *Well, I Forget the Rest*, extract published in *Sunday Telegraph*, 18 August 1991
85. HRC, *loc. cit.*: *24 July [1958]*
86. *Loc. cit.*: *n. d. [?mid-August 1958]*
87. *Loc. cit.*: *27 February 1959*
88. *Loc. cit.*: *n. d. [June 1959]*
89. *Spectator*, 19 June 1959
90. HRC, *loc. cit.*: *n. d. [June 1959]*

91. *Loc. cit.*: *25 June 1959*
92. Loc. cit.: *29 June 1959*

II For Want of the Golden City, 1959–1973

1. *7 August 1959*
2. Renishaw Papers, Box 78: *12 December 1959*
3. HRC, *loc. cit.*: *4 December 1959*
4. *Golden Wall and Mirador*, p. 123
5. Denis Rhodes in *The Literary Half-yearly*, vol. 4, no. 2, July 1963
6. *Spectator*, 30 June 1961
7. HRC, *loc. cit.*: *19 January 1960*
8. *Loc. cit.*: Sitwell, Sacheverell. Misc. David Horner Letters to Georgia Sitwell
9. Eton School Library, David Horner Papers
10. *19 October 1960*
11. Renishaw Papers, Private Collection: SS to OS, *17 February 1961*
12. *Loc. cit.*: same to same, *21 February 1961*
13. HRC, David Higham Archive
14. SS to Bryher, *9 June 1961*
15. *11 August 1961*
16. HRC, *loc. cit.*: *13 and 16 November 1961*
17. SS to Bryher, *24. ix. 61*
18. HRC, David Higham Archive: *18 September 1961*
19. Pearson, *op. cit.*, p. 475
20. *7 August 1962*
21. HRC, David Higham Archive: *13. ix. 62*
22. *17 February 1963*
23. HRC, David Higham Archive: David Higham to SS, *29 July 1963*
24. SS to Bryher, *12 April 1964*
25. Kenneth Clark had generously bought her paintings at the sale and returned them to her.
26. SS to Bryher, *20. viii. 1964*
27. Harvard, Houghton Library, bMS Eng 1293: *15. xii. 1964*
28. Renishaw Papers, Box 80. According to Sachie, Harold Acton, out of loyalty to Edith, managed to get a proposed lecture by Symons to the British Institute in Florence cancelled.
29. SS to Bryher, *5 February 1965*
30. McCann Papers: SS to C. W. McCann, *15. xii. 1964*
31. BL, Aberconway Papers, 70838, vol. VIII: *22. 9. 64*
32. *Loc. cit.*: *25 September 1964*
33. *Loc. cit.*: *31. xii. 64*

34. *Loc. cit.*: *16 February 1965*
35. BL, McCann Papers: David Horner to C. W. McCann, *2 November 1965*
36. Weston Papers: Alasdair Clayre to SS, *n. d. [1964]*
37. *Loc. cit.*: *n. d. [postmarked 'II Nov 1964']*
38. *7 October 1965*
39. Weston Papers: *4 August 1965*
40. Interview with Viscountess Camrose, 27 March 1990
41. Renishaw Papers, Private Collection: SS to Reresby, *1. x. 1965*
42. *12 October 1965*
43. Boston, Sitwell Collection. Sitwell, Sacheverell. #606C: *3 August 1962*
44. HRC: Sitwell, Sacheverell. Recip. [The Poetry Review]: *n. d. [September 1963]*
45. Derek Parker Collection, *3 September 1966*
46. Derek Parker's recollections in a note written for the author.
47. *10 June 1967*
48. BL, Aberconway Papers, 70838, vol. VIII, Res. MS 135 Pt I: Frank Magro to Christabel Aberconway, *1 October 1967*
49. *22 June 1968*. Sachie's remarks about Lehmann were made in a letter to Osbert in Renishaw Papers, Box 80, *20 August 1968*.
50. Renishaw Papers, Box 80: *20 August 1968*.
51. *22 June 1968*
52. Renishaw Papers, *loc. cit.*, *20 August 1968*
53. BL, Aberconway Papers, 70838, vol. VIII, Res. MS 135, Pt I: *14 February 1969*
54. *15. iv. 1969*
55. Weston Papers: *1 March 1969*
56. *Loc. cit.*: *13 April 1969*
57. *10 August 1969*
58. *31 May 1970*
59. Renishaw Papers, Box 79: *5 December 1964*
60. *Loc. cit.*: *'February 9th 1969'*
61. Weston Papers: *14 May 1969*
62. *Loc. cit.*: John Betjeman to SS, *II. 7. 69*
63. *Loc. cit.*: Stephen Tennant to SS, *'1965'*
64. Preface to C. W. Beaumont, *The History of Harlequin*

12 Journey to the Ends of Time, 1973–1988

1. Derek Parker note to author
2. Eton School Library: SS to Susan Hill, *12 January 1971*
3. In Parker (ed.), *op. cit.*, p. 80
4. *19 January 1973*

5. Leigh Fermor, 'Notes'
6. Lady Cooke Collection: *25. 5. 72*
7. *5 November 1973*
8. Tulsa, Sitwell Collection IV, 9:5–6: Pearson's transcript of notes of interviews with SS
9. *Ibid.*
10. Derek Parker Collection: SS to Derek Parker, *3 May 1975*
11. Philip Purser, in *Sunday Telegraph*, 13 November 1977
12. Sir Charles Johnston, unpublished diaries, 3 July 1979
13. Weston Papers
14. Eton School Library: SS to Lady Diana Cooper, *7 November 1980*
15. Weston Papers: Christian, Lady Hesketh to SS, *28 October 1980*
16. Duncan Fallowell, 'Sir Sacheverell Sitwell at Weston Hall', *Encounter*, May 1988

Select Bibliography

For Sacheverell Sitwell's major works see pages 467–70. The definitive bibliography is by Neil Ritchie (see below). Works by Osbert and Edith used as sources for the text are listed below; for further information see Richard Fifoot's bibliography (see below).

Ackroyd, Peter, *T. S. Eliot*, 1984
Acton, Harold, *Memoirs of an Aesthete*, vol. I, 1970
Aldington, Richard, *Life for Life's Sake*, 1968
Amory, Mark (ed.), *The Letters of Evelyn Waugh*, 1980
Beaumont, C. W., *The History of Harlequin*, 1926
Bedford, Sybille, *Aldous Huxley: A Biography*, vol. I: 1894–1939, 1973
Bell, Anne Olivier (ed.), *The Diary of Virginia Woolf*, vol. III: 1925–1930, 1980
Buckle, Richard, *Diaghilev*, 1979
Callimachi, Anne-Marie, *Yesterday was Mine*, 1952
Connolly, Cyril, *The Evening Colonnade*, 1973
Cooper, Jilly, *Super Jilly*, 1977
Davie, Michael (ed.), *The Diaries of Evelyn Waugh*, 1976
Eliot, Valerie (ed.), *The Letters of T. S. Eliot*, vol. I: 1898–1922, 1988
Fallowell, Duncan, *To Noto*, 1988
Fielding, Daphne, *Emerald and Nancy*, 1968
Fifoot, Richard, *A Bibliography of Edith, Osbert and Sacheverell Sitwell*, second
    revised edition, 1971
Flower, Newman (ed.), *The Journals of Arnold Bennett, 1911–1921*, 1932
Glendinning, Victoria, *Edith Sitwell: A Unicorn among Lions*, 1981
Green, Martin, *Children of the Sun: A Narrative of 'Decadence' in England after
    1918*, 1977
Hart-Davis, Rupert (ed.), *Siegfried Sassoon, Diaries 1915–1918, 1920–1922*,
    1981; *1923–1925*, 1988
Haskell, Arnold, Bonham-Carter, Mark, and Wood, Michael (eds.), *Gala
    Performance*, 1955
Hoare, Philip, *Serious Pleasures: The Life of Stephen Tennant*, 1990
Hooker, Denise, *Nina Hamnett, Queen of Bohemia*, 1986
Lancaster, Marie-Jacqueline, *Brian Howard: Portrait of a Failure*, 1968

Lehmann, John, *A Nest of Tigers*, 1968

Lewis, Wyndham, *The Apes of God*, 1930

Luke, Michael, *David Tennant and the Gargoyle Years*, 1991

Martin, Marianne W., *Futurist Art and Theory 1909–1915*, 1968

Meyers, Jeffrey, *The Enemy: a Biography of Wyndham Lewis*, 1980

Middleboe, Penelope (ed.), *Edith Olivier from Her Journals 1924–1948*, 1989

Mosley, Nicholas, *Rules of the Game*, 1982

Motion, Andrew, *The Lamberts: George, Constant and Kit*, 1986

Nicolson, Nigel (ed.), *The Question of Things Happening: The Letters of Virginia Woolf*, vol. II: 1921–1922, 1976

Parker, Derek (ed.), *Sacheverell Sitwell: A Symposium*, 1975

Pearson, John, *Façades: Edith, Osbert and Sacheverell Sitwell*, 1978

Percy, Clayre, and Ridley, Jane (eds.), *The Letters of Edwin Lutyens to His Wife Emily*, 1985

Powell, Anthony, *To Keep the Ball Rolling*, vol. I: *Infants of the Spring*, 1976; vol. II: *Messengers of Day*, 1978; vol. III: *Faces in My Time*, 1980; vol. IV: *The Strangers are all gone*, 1982

Quennell, Peter, *The Marble Foot: An Autobiography 1905–1938*, 1976

Quennell, Peter, *The Wanton Chase*, 1980

Rhodes James, Robert (ed.) *Chips: The Diaries of Sir Henry Channon*, 1967

Ritchie, Charles, *The Siren Years*, 1974

Ritchie, Neil, *Sacheverell Sitwell: An Annotated and Descriptive Bibliography 1916–1986*, 1987

Rose, W. K. (ed.), *The Letters of Wyndham Lewis*, 1963

Sitwell, Constance, *Bright Morning*, 1942

Sitwell, Constance, *Bounteous Days*, 1976

Sitwell, Edith, *Façade*, 1922

Sitwell, Edith, *Troy Park*, 1925

Sitwell, Edith, *Taken Care Of*, 1965

Sitwell, Edith (ed.), *Wheels (First Cycle)*, 1916; *Wheels, Second Cycle*, 1917; *Wheels, Third Cycle*, 1919; *Wheels, Fourth Cycle*, 1919; *Wheels, Fifth Cycle*, 1920; *Wheels, Sixth Cycle*, 1921

Sitwell, Francis, *Weston Hall*, Privately Printed, n. d.

Sitwell, Sir George R., *On the Making of Gardens*, 1909

Sitwell, Osbert, *Discursions on Travel, Art and Life*, 1925

Sitwell, Osbert, *Before the Bombardment*, 1926

Sitwell, Osbert, *Left Hand, Right Hand!*, Boston, 1944; London 1945

Sitwell, Osbert, *The Scarlet Tree*, 1946

Sitwell, Osbert, *Great Morning!*, 1947

Sitwell, Osbert, *Laughter in the Next Room*, 1948

Sitwell, Osbert, *Noble Essences*, 1950

Sitwell, Osbert, *Tales My Father Taught Me*, 1962

Sitwell, Reresby, *Renishaw Hall and the Sitwells*, Privately Printed, n. d.

Smith, Grover (ed.), *Letters of Aldous Huxley,* 1969
Stannard, Martin, *Evelyn Waugh: The Early Years 1903–1939,* 1986
Sutton, Denys, *The World of Sacheverell Sitwell,* published by *Apollo Magazine,*
    1980
Tierney, Neil, *William Walton: His Life and Music,* 1984
Vickers, Hugo, *Cecil Beaton,* 1985
Walton, Susana, *William Walton: Behind the Façade,* 1988
Westminster, Loelia, Duchess of, *Grace and Favour,* 1961
Whistler, Laurence, *The Laughter and the Urn: The Life of Rex Whistler,* 1985
Wyndham, Violet, *The Sphinx and Her Circle,* 1963

Books by Sacheverell Sitwell

The following list includes the principal works. It does not include contributions
to books or periodicals. For further information, Neil Ritchie's *Sacheverell
Sitwell: An Annotated and Descriptive Bibliography 1916–1986,* Giardo Press, 1987,
is the definitive source.

The People's Palace, Blackwell, Oxford, 1918
Dr Donne and Gargantua, First Canto, Favil Press, London, 1918
The Hundred and One Harlequins, Mayflower Press, Plymouth, 1922; Boni &
    Liverlight, New York, 1923
Dr Donne and Gargantua, Canto the Second, Favil Press, London, 1923
Southern Baroque Art, Grant Richards, London, 1924; Alfred A. Knopf, New
    York, 1924
The Thirteenth Caesar, Grant Richards, London, 1924; George H. Doran,
    New York, 1925
Poor Young People, Curwen Press, London, 1925
Exalt the Eglantine, The Fleuron, London, 1926
All Summer in a Day, Duckworth, London, 1926; George H. Doran, New
    York, 1926
Dr Donne and Gargantua, Canto the Third, Shakespeare Head Press, 1926
The Cyder Feast, Duckworth, London, 1927
German Baroque Art, Duckworth, 1927
All at Sea, Duckworth, London, 1927; Doubleday, Doran, 1928
A Book of Towers, engravings by Richard Wyndham with introduction by
    Sacheverell Sitwell, Frederick Etchells and Hugh Macdonald, London,
    1928
The Augustan Books of English Poetry. Second Series, No. 29, Ernest Benn,
    London, 1928
The Gothick North: A Study of Medieval Life, Art and Thought, Duckworth,
    London, 1929–1930

The Gothick North: The Visit of the Gypsies, 1929
The Gothick North: These Sad Ruins, 1929
The Gothick North: The Fair-Haired Victory, 1930
Two Poems, Ten Songs, Duckworth, London, 1929
Dr Donne and Gargantua, The First Six Cantos, Duckworth, London, 1930;
    Houghton Mifflin, 1930
Beckford and Beckfordism, An Essay, Duckworth, London, 1930
Far from My Home, Stories: Long & Short, Duckworth, London, 1931
Spanish Baroque Art, Duckworth, London, 1931
Mozart, Peter Davies, Edinburgh, 1932; D. Appleton, New York, 1932
Canons of Giant Art, Faber and Faber, London, 1933
Liszt, Faber and Faber, London, 1934; Houghton Mifflin, 1934
Touching the Orient, Duckworth, London, 1934
A Background for Domenico Scarlatti, Faber and Faber, London, 1935
Dance of the Quick and the Dead: An Entertainment of the Imagination, Faber and
    Faber, London, 1936; Houghton Mifflin, New York, 1937
Collected Poems, Duckworth, London, 1936
Conversation Pieces: A Survey of English Domestic Portraits and their Painters,
    B. T. Batsford, London, 1936; Charles Scribner's Sons, New York, 1937
Narrative Pictures, B. T. Batsford, London, 1937; Charles Scribner's Sons,
    New York, 1938
La Vie Parisienne, Faber and Faber, London, 1937; Houghton Mifflin, New
    York, 1938
Roumanian Journey, B. T. Batsford, London, 1938; Charles Scribner's Sons,
    New York, 1938
Edinburgh (with Francis Bamford), Faber and Faber, London, 1938;
    Houghton Mifflin, New York, 1938
German Baroque Sculpture (with descriptive notes by Nikolaus Pevsner),
    Duckworth, London, 1938
*Trio, Dissertations on some aspects of National Genius by Osbert, Edith and
    Sacheverell Sitwell, delivered as the Northcliffe Lectures*, Macmillan & Co.,
    London, 1938
The Romantic Ballet in Lithographs of the Time (with Cyril Beaumont), Faber
    and Faber, London, 1930
Old Fashioned Flowers, Curwen Press, London, 1939; Charles Scribner's Sons,
    New York, 1939
Mauretania: Warrior, Man and Woman, Duckworth, London, 1940
Poltergeists: An Introduction and Examination followed by Chosen Instances, Faber
    and Faber, London, 1940; University Books, New York, 1959
Sacred and Profane Love, Faber and Faber, London, 1940
Valse des Fleurs: A Day in St Petersburg and a Ball at the Winter Palace, Faber
    and Faber, London, 1941
Primitive Scenes and Festivals, Faber and Faber, London, 1942

The Homing of the Winds and other Passages in Prose, Faber and Faber, London, 1942

Splendours and Miseries, Faber and Faber, London, 1943

British Architects and Craftsmen: A Survey of Taste, Design and Style during Three Centuries 1600 to 1830, B. T. Batsford, London, 1945; Charles Scribner's Sons, New York, 1946

The Hunters and the Hunted, Macmillan & Co., London, 1947; Macmillan, New York, 1948

The Netherlands: A Study of some Aspects of Art, Costume and Social Life, B. T. Batsford, London, 1948; Hastings House, New York, 1974

Selected Poems, Duckworth, London, 1948; Macmillan, New York, 1949

Morning, Noon and Night in London, Macmillan & Co., London, 1948

Theatrical Figures in Porcelain, The Curtain Press, London, 1949

Spain, B. T. Batsford, London, 1950; Hastings House, New York, 1975

Cupid and the Jacaranda, Macmillan & Co., London, 1952

Truffle Hunt, Robert Hale, London, 1953

Fine Bird Books 1700–1900 (with Handasyde Buchanan and James Fisher), Collins & Van Nostrand, London, 1953; New York, 1953

Selected Works, The Bobbs-Merrill Company Inc., Indianapolis, New York, 1953

Portugal and Madeira, B. T. Batsford, London, 1954

Old Garden Roses, Part I (with James Russell), Collins, London, 1955

Selected Works, Robert Hale, London, 1955

Denmark, B. T. Batsford, London, 1956; Hastings House, New York, 1956

Great Flower Books: a Bibliographical Record of Two Centuries of Finely-Illustrated Flower Books (with Wilfrid Blunt), Collins, London, 1956

Arabesque and Honeycomb, Robert Hale, London, 1957; Random House, New York, 1958

Malta (with Tony Armstrong-Jones), B. T. Batsford, London, 1958

Austria (with Toni Schneiders), Thames and Hudson, London, 1959; Viking Press, New York, 1959

Journey to the Ends of Time, vol. One: *Lost in the Dark Wood*, Cassell, London, 1959; Random House, New York, 1959

Bridge of the Brocade Sash: Travels and Observations in Japan, Weidenfeld and Nicolson, London, 1959; World Publishing, New York, 1960

Golden Wall and Mirador: From England to Peru, Weidenfeld and Nicolson, London, 1961; World Publishing, New York, 1961

The Red Chapels of Banteai Srei, and Temples in Cambodia, India, Siam and Nepal, Weidenfeld and Nicolson, London, 1962; Ivan Obolensky, New York, 1963

Monks, Nuns and Monasteries, Weidenfeld and Nicolson, London, 1965; Holt, Rinehart & Winston, New York, 1965

Southern Baroque Revisited, Weidenfeld and Nicolson, London, 1967; G. P. Putnam's Sons, New York, 1967

Gothic Europe, Weidenfeld and Nicolson, London, 1969; Holt, Rinehart &
     Winston, New York, 1969
For Want of the Golden City, Thames and Hudson, London, 1973; John Day, New
     York, 1973
An Indian Summer, 100 Recent Poems, Macmillan, 1982
Sacheverell Sitwell's England, edited by Michael Raeburn, Orbis, 1986

Privately printed pamphlets, printed at Brackley, Northamptonshire, and known
as the 'Brackley booklets':

The Archipelago of Daffodils (1972); *Auricula Theatre* (1972); *A Charivari of Parrots*
     (1972); *Flowering Cactus* (1972); *The House of the Presbyter* (1972); *Lily Poems*
     (1972); *Lyra Varia* (1972); *Nigritian* (1972); *Rosario d'Arabeschi* (1972);
     Ruralia (1972); *The Strawberry Feast* (1972); *A Triptych of Poems* (1972);
     Variations upon Old Hyacinths (1972); *Tropicalia* (1972); *Agamemnon's Tomb*
     (1972); *To Henry Woodward* (Covent Garden Press, 1972); *Baraka and
     Dionysia* (1973); *Battles of the Centaurs* (1973); *Pastoral and Landscape with the
     Giant Orion* (1973); *To E. S.* (1973); *Les Troyens* (1973); *Twelve Summer Poems*
     (1973); *Two Poems* (1973); *Badinerie* (1974); *Dr Donne and Gargantua, Cantos
     Seven and Eight* (1974); *An Indian Summer* (1974); *A Look at Sowerby's
     Mushrooms and Fungi* (1974); *L'Amour au Théâtre Italien* (1975); *Temple of
     Segesta* (1975); *Notebook on Twenty Canons of Giant Art* (1975); *Nymphis et
     Fontibus and Nymphaeum* (1975); *A Note for Bibliophiles* (1975); *A Pair of Entra'
     Actes for August Evenings* (1975); *Credo, or an Affirmation* (1976); *Placebo*
     (1976); *Serenade to a Sister* (1976); *Two Themes* (1976); *J. S. Bach, Liszt,
     Domenico Scarlatti* (1976); *Fugue* (1976); *A Second Triptych of Poems* (1976); *To
     Henry Woodward, the Harlequin* (1976); *Brother and Sister, a Ballad of the
     Parallelo* (1977); *Tropicalia* (1977); *Diptycha Musica* (1977); *Dodecameron*
     (1977); *Nine Ballads: Four More Lilies* (1977); *The Octogenarian* (1977); *Little
     Italy in London* (1977); *Looking for the Gods of Light* (1978); *The Rose-Pink
     Chapel* (1978); *Scherzo di Capricio* (1978); *The Rose Pink Chapel* (1978);
     Sherzo di Capricio (1978); *Scherzo di Fantasia* (1978); *A Retrospect of Poems*
     (1979); *Op. Cit. Et Cetera* (1979); *Catalysts in Collusion* (1979); *Pomona
     Lactodorum* (1980); *Nocturnae Silvani Potenti* (1980); *Allotment or Assignment?*
     (1980); *Prende la mia Chitarra* (1981)

Index